UNITED NATIONS CONFERENCE ON TRADE AND DEVELOPMENT
Geneva

THE LEAST DEVELOPED COUNTRIES
REPORT 2004

Prepared by the UNCTAD secretariat

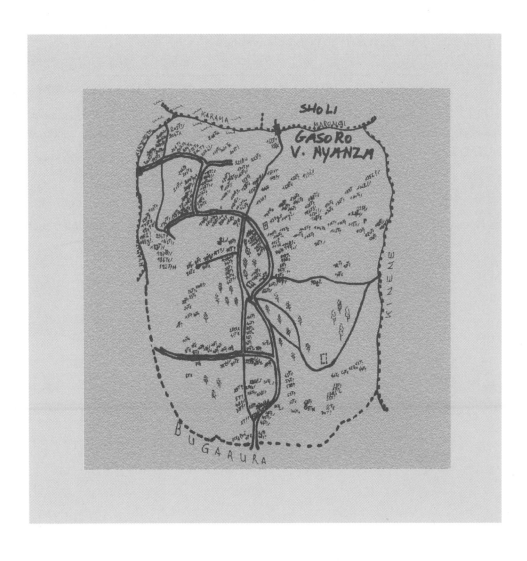

UNITED NATIONS
New York and Geneva, 2004

Note

Symbols of United Nations documents are composed of capital letters with figures. Mention of such a symbol indicates a reference to a United Nations document.

The designations employed and the presentation of the material in this publication do not imply the expression of any opinion whatsoever on the part of the Secretariat of the United Nations concerning the legal status of any country, territory, city or area, or of its authorities, or concerning the delimitation of its frontiers or boundaries.

Material in this publication may be freely quoted or reprinted, but full acknowledgement is requested. A copy of the publication containing the quotation or reprint should be sent to the UNCTAD secretariat at: Palais des Nations, CH-1211 Geneva 10, Switzerland.

The Overview from this Report can also be found on the Internet, in both English and French, at the following address:

http://www.unctad.org

UNCTAD/LDC/2004

UNITED NATIONS PUBLICATION

Sales No. E.04.II.D.27

ISBN 92-1-112581-2

ISSN 0257-7550

The Front Cover

The front cover shows detail from a social map of Sholi Cellule in Nyanza District, Butare Province, Rwanda. The map is part of the Rwanda Poverty Reduction Strategy Paper published in 2002. The map is the result of a participatory process of project planning and implementation at the cellule level through which the community seeks to identify its most important development problems. As part of the process, the cellule members collectively draw a social map that indicates details of every household's location, their social category, type of shelter, all social and economic infrastructure and landmarks in the cellule. The map is first drawn on the ground using local materials and later copied onto a piece of cloth for the community to keep as a tool for future planning.

The community itself defines how they categorise the people in their community. In Sholi Cellule, they identified four social categories which are marked on the map as follows:

Category of poor	Map Symbol	Number of households	Characteristics
Umutindi/Umukene Nyakujya	!	43	They have to beg and have nothing; no clothes, no food, no shelter. Their children cannot go to school, they cannot afford medical care and have no farmland.
Umutindi/Umukene	?	114	They do not have sufficient food but can work for others to survive, they dress poorly, have insufficient farmland and can hardly get medical care. They have shelter but no livestock and are always suffering.
Umutindi/Umukene wifashije	x	60	They have small and poor shelter, and a minimal harvest, their children can go to primary school, they can clothe themselves but with difficulty, they can hardly access medical care, but manage to have sufficient to eat and they have small ruminants.
Umukungu	u	13	They have excess harvest to sell and livestock, they can afford medical care, and have a little money. Their children can go to secondary school. They eat well, are neat, have a good house and a bicycle, and can engage others as labour.

The map is reproduced with permission.

Symbols on the Map

Symbol	Meaning	Symbol	Meaning
!	umukene/umutindi nyakujya	s	house being built, already with roof
?	umukene	d	house being built not yet with roof
x	umukene wifashije	r	a water point
u	umukungu	(tree symbol)	a tree
/	household with a small landholding	(church symbol)	a church (Adventist in this case)
(.)	household with no land	(road symbol)	a road
•	household with no shelter	(path symbol)	a path
T	house with tiles	(river symbol)	a river
B	house with iron sheeting	#	a bridge
i	house with thatch	(memorial symbol)	a genocide memorial site
g	destroyed house (still visible)	(cemetery symbol)	a cemetery
t	destroyed house (no longer visible)	(wetland symbol)	wetland

Acknowledgements

The Least Developed Countries Report 2004 was prepared by a team consisting of Charles Gore (team leader), Lisa Borgatti, Marquise David, Michael Herrmann, Ivanka Hoppenbrouwer-Rodriguez (from 23 February 2004), Zeljka Kozul-Wright, Madasamyraja Rajalingam and Utumporn Reungsuwan. Juliana Gonsalves also worked with the team between 21 May 2003 and 21 November 2003 on secondment from the Economic Commission for Africa. Massoud Karshenas acted as principal consultant to the Report. Detailed comments were received from Mussie Delelegn, Samuel Gayi, Lev Komlev, Joerg Mayer, Marcel Namfua and Taffere Tesfachew. Specific inputs and advice were also received from Céline Bacrot, Pierre Encontre, Gunter Fischer, Massi Malmberg and Jean-Claude Mporamazina. The work was carried out under the overall supervision of Habib Ouane, Head, Special Programme for Least Developed, Landlocked and Island Developing Countries within UNCTAD.

As part of the preparations for the Report an ad hoc expert meeting on "New Trade and Development Strategies in Least Developed Countries" was held in Geneva on 10 and 11 June, 2003. The participants in this meeting were: Elsa Assidon, Jean-Claude Berthélemey, Mario Cimoli, Mulat Demeke, Ajit Ghose, Massoud Karshenas, Jonathan Kydd, Guy Mhone, Kenichi Ohno, Gustav Ranis, Ignacy Sachs, Amelia Santos-Paulino and Marc Wuyts. Background papers or specific inputs for the Report were commissioned from Peter Gibbon, Massoud Karshenas, Amelia Santos-Paulino, Ignacy Sachs and Marc Wuyts. Gerry Helleiner also provided comments on an early version of part 2, chapter 1.

The staff of the Division on International Trade and Commodities within UNCTAD fully supported the work. Alberto Gabriele and David Vanzetti, and Michiko Hayashi and Victor Ognivtsev, prepared background papers and notes. Advice and comments were also received from Mehmet Arda, Aki Kuwahara, Sam Laird, Bonapas Onguglo, Olle Ostensson, Ralf Peters and Lakshmi Puri, as well as from Masataka Fujita of the Division on Investment, Technology and Enterprise Development. The staff of the Central Statistics Branch of the Division on Globalization and Development Strategies within UNCTAD also fully supported the work on the Report, particularly Henri Laurencin, Nelly Berthault, Arunas Butkevicius, Yumiko Mochizuki and Laurence Schlosser. Makameh Bahrami also provided statistical advice.

The Report also benefited from background inputs or advice from: Sonali Wickrema of the World Food Programme (WFP); Friedrich von Kirchbach, Fabrice Leclercq, Mondher Mimouni, Roberto Smith-Gillespie and Wayne Wittig of the International Trade Centre (ITC); Rudolphe Petras and Frans Lammersen (OECD); David Stewart and Claes Johansson of the UNDP Human Development Office; and Harmon Thomas (FAO).

Information on the trade regimes of the LDCs was collected through the good offices and very helpful support of the national trade ministries and the missions to the UN and WTO of the Governments of Benin, Burundi, Cape Verde, Ethiopia, the Gambia, Haiti, Madagascar, Mali, Mauritania, Nepal, Senegal, Sudan, Togo, Uganda, the United Republic of Tanzania and Zambia. We are also grateful to the Ministry of Finance and Planning of Rwanda for providing permission for publication of the map of Sholi Cellule on the front cover.

Secretarial support in the final production of the Report was provided by Corazon Alvarez, Sylvie Guy, Regina Ogunyinka, Sivanla Sikounnavong and Stephanie West. Diego Oyarzun-Reyes designed the cover, and the text was edited by Graham Grayston and Praveen Bhalla (mostly chapter 5).

The overall layout, graphics and desktop publishing were done by Madasamyraja Rajalingam.

Contents

Part One
RECENT TRENDS

Part Two

LINKING INTERNATIONAL TRADE WITH POVERTY REDUCTION

List of Boxes

List of Charts

Annex Chart

Box Charts

List of Tables

Annex Tables

Box Tables

Explanatory Notes

The term "dollars" ($) refers to United States dollars unless otherwise stated. The term "billion" signifies 1,000 million.

Annual rates of growth and changes refer to compound rates. Exports are valued f.o.b. (free on board) and imports c.i.f. (cost, insurance, freight) unless otherwise specified.

Use of a dash (–) between dates representing years, e.g. 1981–1990, signifies the full period involved, including the initial and final years. An oblique stroke (/) between two years, e.g. 1991/92, signifies a fiscal or crop year.

The term "least developed country" (LDC) refers, throughout this report, to a country included in the United Nations list of least developed countries.

In the tables:

Two dots (..) indicate that the data are not available, or are not separately reported.
One dot (.) indicates that the data are not applicable.
A hyphen (-) indicates that the amount is nil or negligible.
Details and percentages do not necessarily add up to totals, because of rounding.

WHAT ARE THE LEAST DEVELOPED COUNTRIES?

Fifty countries are currently designated by the United Nations as "least developed countries" (LDCs): Afghanistan, Angola, Bangladesh, Benin, Bhutan, Burkina Faso, Burundi, Cambodia, Cape Verde, Central African Republic, Chad, Comoros, Democratic Republic of the Congo, Djibouti, Equatorial Guinea, Eritrea, Ethiopia, Gambia, Guinea, Guinea-Bissau, Haiti, Kiribati, Lao People's Democratic Republic, Lesotho, Liberia, Madagascar, Malawi, Maldives, Mali, Mauritania, Mozambique, Myanmar, Nepal, Niger, Rwanda, Samoa, Sao Tome and Principe, Senegal, Sierra Leone, Solomon Islands, Somalia, Sudan, Timor-Leste, Togo, Tuvalu, Uganda, United Republic of Tanzania, Vanuatu, Yemen, Zambia. The list of LDCs is reviewed every three years by the Economic and Social Council of the United Nations, in the light of recommendations by the Committee for Development Policy.

The criteria underlying the current list of LDCs are:

(a)   A low-income criterion, as measured by the *gross national income (GNI) per capita*;

(b)   A weak human assets criterion, as measured by a composite index (the *Human Assets Index*) based on indicators of: (i) nutrition (per capita calorie intake as a percentage of the relevant requirement); (ii) health (child mortality rate); (iii) school enrolment (secondary school enrolment ratio); and (iv) literacy (adult literacy rate); and

(c)   An economic vulnerability criterion, as measured by a composite index (the *Economic Vulnerability Index*) based on indicators of: (i) instability in agricultural production; (ii) instability in exports of goods and services; (iii) the economic importance of non-traditional activities (share of manufacturing and modern services in GDP); (iv) economic concentration (UNCTAD's merchandise export concentration index); and (v) economic smallness (population in logarithm).[1]

Different thresholds are used for addition to, and graduation from, the list of LDCs. A country qualifies to be added to the list if it meets inclusion thresholds on all three criteria, and if its population does not exceed 75 million. A country qualifies for graduation from LDC status if it meets graduation thresholds under at least two of the three criteria in at least two consecutive triennial reviews of the list.

At the time of the 2003 review of the list of LDCs, the low-income threshold for addition to the list was a GNI per capita of $750, and the counterpart threshold for graduation was $900.

---

[1]   As a supplement to data on the instability of agricultural production, the percentage of population displaced by natural disasters has been added to these five components, thereby creating a modified Economic Vulnerability Index.

Note on Timor-Leste

On 4 December 2003, the United Nations General Assembly endorsed the Economic and Social Council's recommendation that Timor-Leste be added to the list of the least developed countries.

Much of the work for this Report was prepared during 2003. In the light of this, the analysis in the Report refers to the 49 countries that were included in the list of least developed countries before Timor-Leste was added. The majority of the tables in the Statistical Annex to this Report also refer to these 49 countries. However, table 34 in the Statistical Annex shows some basic economic and social indicators for Timor-Leste.

Abbreviations

ACP	African, Caribbean and Pacific
ADLI	agricultural-development-led industrialization
AGOA	African Growth and Opportunity Act
AIDS	acquired immune deficiency syndrome
ATC	Agreement on Textiles and Clothing
CDP	Committee for Development Policy
CGE	computable general equilibrium
CUTS	Consumer Unity and Trust Society
DAC	Development Assistance Committee
DFID	Department for International Development, UK
DRAF	domestic resources available for finance
DTIS	Diagnostic Trade Integration Study
EBA	Everything But Arms
ECOSOC	Economic and Social Council
EITI	Extractives Industry Transparency Initiative
EPRP	Export-led Poverty Reduction Programme (ITC)
EPZ	export processing zone
ESAF	Enhanced Structural Adjustment Facility
ETB	environment-related trade barriers
EVI	Economic Vulnerability Index
FAO	Food and Agriculture Organization of the United Nations
FDI	foreign direct investment
GATS	General Agreement on Trade in Services
GATT	General Agreement on Tariffs and Trade
GDP	gross domestic product
GNI	gross national income
GSP	Generalized System of Preferences
GSTP	Generalized System of Trade Preferences
GTAP	Global Trade Analysis Project
HAI	Human Assets Index
HIPC	heavily indebted poor country
HIV	human immunodeficiency virus
HS	Harmonized Commodity Description and Coding System
IDA	International Development Association
IF	Integrated Framework for Trade-Related Technical Assistance
IFI	international financial institutions
IFSC	Integrated Framework Steering Committee
IFWG	Integrated Framework Working Group
IFPRI	International Food Policy Research Institute
ILO	International Labour Organization
IMF	International Monetary Fund
ITC	International Trade Centre UNCTAD/WTO
JITAP	Joint Integrated Technical Assistance Programme to Selected Least Developed and Other African Countries
LDC	least developed country

MDG	Millennium Development Goal
MFA	Multifibre Arrangement
MFN	most favoured nation
NEPAD	New Partnership for Africa's Development
NGO	non-governmental organization
NTB	non-tariff barrier
ODA	official development assistance
ODC	other developing countries
OECD	Organisation for Economic Co-operation and Development
POA	Programme of Action for the LDCs for the Decade 2001–2010
PPP	purchasing power parity
PRGF	Poverty Reduction and Growth Facility
PRSC	Poverty Reduction Support Credit
PRSP	Poverty Reduction Strategy Paper
PRIO	International Peace Research Institute
RCA	revealed comparative advantage
RTAs	regional trade agreements
SAF	Structural Adjustment Facility
SARS	Severe Acute Respiratory Syndrome
SDT	special and differential treatment
SITC	Standard International Trade Classification
SMEs	small and medium-sized enterprises
SPS	sanitary and phytosanitary measures
STABEX	Stabilization of Exports
SYSMIN	System for the Stabilization of Export Earnings from Mining
TBT	technical barriers to trade
TNC	transnational corporation
TRI	trade restrictiveness indicator
TRIMs	Trade-related Investment Measures
TRIPS	Trade-related Aspects of Intellectual Property Rights
UNAIDS	United Nations Joint Programme on HIV/AIDS
UN COMTRADE	United Nations Commodity Trade Statistics Database
UNCTAD	United Nations Conference on Trade and Development
UNDP	United Nations Development Programme
UNECA	United Nations Economic Commission for Africa
UNFPA	United Nations Population Fund
UNIDO	United Nations Industrial Development Organization
VAT	value-added tax
WHO	World Health Organization
WTO	World Trade Organization

Overview

THE CHALLENGE OF POVERTY REDUCTION IN THE LEAST DEVELOPED COUNTRIES

International trade is vital for poverty reduction in all developing countries. But the links between trade expansion and poverty reduction are neither simple nor automatic. The purpose of this Report is to clarify the links and to contribute thereby to a better understanding of the national and international policies that can make international trade an effective mechanism for poverty reduction in the least developed countries (LDCs).

On the front cover of this Report, to put the problem in perspective, is a map of poverty. This map, reproduced from the Rwanda Poverty Reduction Strategy Paper, is the result of a participatory process in which a community — Sholi in Nyanza District, Rwanda — sought to identify its most important development problems. The map shows every household's location, its type of shelter, and also, most crucially, the community members' own assessment of their social category. There are 230 households and they were classified as follows:

- Umutindi/Umukene Nyakujya (43 households). They have to beg, for they have nothing — no clothes, no food, no shelter. Their children cannot go to school, they cannot afford medical care and they have no farmland.
- Umutindi/Umukene (114 households). They do not have sufficient food but can work for others to survive; they dress poorly, have insufficient farmland and can hardly get medical care. They have shelter but no livestock and are always suffering.
- Umutindi/Umukene wifashije (60 households). They have shelter, but it is small and poor. They have a minimal harvest; their children can go to primary school; they can clothe themselves but with difficulty; they can scarcely access medical care, but manage to have sufficient to eat and they have small ruminants.
- Umukunga (13 households). They have excess harvest to sell and livestock; they can afford medical care, and have a little money. Their children can go to secondary school. They eat well, are neat, have a good house and a bicycle, and can engage others as labour.

The situation in Sholi in Rwanda illustrates the nature of poverty in the LDCs. Poverty in these countries is not a phenomenon that affects a small proportion of the total population. Rather, it affects the majority. Moreover, this is a situation in which the majority of the population are living at or below income levels which are sufficient to meet their basic needs. In these societies, the available resources, even when equally distributed, are barely sufficient to cater for the basic needs of the population on a sustainable basis.

Conditions of life such as those in Sholi are an ethical affront to a civilized world. But they are not rare in the LDCs. Both World Bank and UNCTAD poverty estimates suggest that 49–50 per cent of the population in the LDCs were living on less than $1/day at the end of the 1990s. Although the LDCs had a much better economic performance in the late 1990s, the overall incidence of extreme poverty for the group as a whole did not decline during that decade. If these trends persist, it may be estimated that the number of people living in extreme poverty in the LDCs will increase from 334 million people in 2000 to 471 million in 2015. By that time, and assuming that the current progress in China and India continues, the LDCs will be the major locus for global poverty in 2015.

Living conditions such as those in Sholi exist in other developing countries. But dealing with these conditions in the LDCs is especially challenging because extreme poverty is so pervasive throughout society. In this situation, mass poverty reinforces the tendency towards economic stagnation, and vice versa. Amongst the domestic vicious circles the following may be noted:

- There are few surplus financial resources available for investment and for funding vital public services, including education, health, administration, and law and order. Low income leads to low savings; low savings lead to low investment; low investment leads to low productivity and low incomes.
- To reduce risks in conditions of extreme scarcity, people pursue economic activities with low but certain returns, including production for their own subsistence and survival through multiple activities.
- The lack of effective domestic demand associated with all-pervasive poverty reduces profitable investment opportunities.
- There is a dearth of domestically available skilled personnel, and the lack of domestic opportunities encourages skilled people to seek work outside the country.

- Pervasive poverty leads to environmental degradation as people have to eat into the environmental capital stock simply to survive, but this in turn undermines the productivity of key assets on which livelihood depends.
- There is a high risk of civil conflict in countries where low per capita income is associated with economic stagnation or regress.

Three facts illustrate the situation most clearly. First, in the second half of the 1990s the average per capita income in the LDCs when measured in terms of current prices and official exchange rates was $0.72 a day and the average per capita consumption was $0.57 a day. This implies that on average there was only $0.15 a day per person to spend on private capital formation, public investment in infrastructure and the running of vital public services, including health, education, administration, and law and order. Second, in 2001, 34 per cent of the population aged between 15 and 24 were illiterate in the LDCs. Third, 60 per cent of the LDCs experienced in the period 1990–2001 civil conflict of varying intensity and duration that, in most cases, erupted after a period of economic stagnation and regression. In Rwanda, for example, average private consumption per capita fell by over 12 per cent between 1980 and 1993, the year before the genocide occurred. Average private consumption per capita is somewhat higher now than it was in 1993.

The challenge of poverty reduction in the LDCs is how to reduce poverty given this starting point. The households in Sholi have a good idea of what to do. They see increasing their assets and the productivity of those assets to be the key element. The priority is quite simply to get goats that will provide all kinds of by-products, including manure to increase and maintain the productivity of their fields. But does this mean that international trade is irrelevant for poverty reduction? What has international trade got to do with poverty reduction in such circumstances?

This Report is about the relationship between trade and poverty in the LDCs. The central questions that it seeks to answer are:
- What is the potential role of international trade in poverty reduction in the LDCs?
- How does the relationship between international trade and poverty work in practice in the LDCs?
- What are the national and international policies that can make international trade a more effective mechanism for poverty reduction in the LDCs?

WHY INTERNATIONAL TRADE MATTERS FOR POVERTY REDUCTION IN THE LDCS

This Report argues that in conditions of mass poverty such as those found in the LDCs, poverty reduction requires sustained economic growth of a type that substantially increases average household incomes and consumption. Sustained poverty reduction cannot be achieved through welfare transfers, although these may be used, at any moment in time, to alleviate instances of the most extreme misery. Rather, it requires the efficient development and utilization of productive capacities in a way in which the working-age population becomes more and more fully and productively employed.

International trade can play a powerful role in poverty reduction in the LDCs. It is important because exports and imports facilitate a process of sustained economic growth, the development of productive capacities and expansion of employment opportunities and sustainable livelihoods. For most LDCs, the primary sector, particularly agriculture, dominates production and employment in the economy, and productive capacities are weakly developed. In this situation, exports enable the acquisition, through importation, of goods which are necessary for economic growth and poverty reduction, but which are not produced domestically. These include food, manufactured consumer goods, fuel and raw materials, machinery and equipment and means of transport, and intermediate inputs and spare parts. Through exports it is possible to transform underutilized natural resources and surplus labour into imports which support economic growth. Exports must grow fast enough, and in a sufficiently stable way, to meet growing import demand. If they do not, the sustainability of economic growth will be threatened by the build-up of an unsustainable external debt.

International trade is particularly important for poverty reduction in the LDCs because, contrary to popular impressions, their "openness", measured by the level of trade integration with the rest of the world, is high. During 1999–2001, exports and imports of goods and services constituted on average 51 per cent of the gross domestic product (GDP) of the LDCs. This ratio is somewhat smaller than that for low- and middle-income countries. But the average level of trade integration of the LDCs was actually higher than that of high-income OECD countries, which stood at 43 per cent in those years. In only 10 of the LDCs for which data are available was the trade/GDP ratio lower than that in the high-income OECD countries.

In addition, international trade matters for poverty reduction because the LDC economies are highly "import-sensitive". The higher the proportion of imports that are essential to the continuation of ongoing economic activities and their development, the higher the import sensitivity of an economy. In LDCs, import bottlenecks hamper the full utilization of domestic productive capacities. In addition, the import content of investment processes is high owing to the absence of a domestic capital goods industry and engineering capabilities. Lastly, for a few LDCs, food security is highly dependent on food imports.

But the relationship between international trade and poverty reduction is neither automatic nor straightforward. There are at least three reasons for this.

First, in poor predominantly natural-resource-based or agrarian economies such as most LDCs, economic growth depends on the development of a range of new capabilities, institutions and services. New agricultural technologies need to be adapted, or developed from scratch, in conformity with the countries'agro-climatic and soil conditions. Schools, universities, hospitals, technical training centres, and research and development institutions need to be strengthened or set up. Roads need to be built and extension services need to be established to bring the majority of the agricultural population into the orbit of the modern economy. The rule of law needs to be enforced, and the monopolistic activities of particular interests need to be curtailed. In short, there is a need for investment of all kinds of physical, human, social and institutional capital, and innovation and technological progress adapted to the conditions of the countries. Capital accumulation and technological progress are the engine of growth, and international trade is the fuel for the engine. If the fuel dries up, the engine will not run.

Thus sustained economic growth requires not simply export expansion but also a strong investment–export nexus through which imported equipment, raw materials and production inputs are put to good use and lead to continuous improvements in labour productivity in the economy as a whole. Meeting this condition is particularly difficult in the LDCs given the paucity of surplus financial resources available for financing investment and also the weak development of domestic entrepreneurial capacities. Many of the central capital accumulation and budgetary processes in the LDCs are highly dependent on international financial assistance, and thus the link between international trade and poverty reduction also depends on the efficiency and effectiveness of the delivery of international assistance.

Secondly, the positive role of exports in expanding import capacity in the LDCs needs to be seen in the context of the nature of their balance-of-payments constraint. An important feature of LDC economies is that they almost all have persistent and high trade deficits. In the period 1999–2001, the trade deficit was over 10 per cent of GDP in 25 out of 44 LDCs for which data are available, and over 20 per cent of GDP in 8 of them. Excluding oil exporters, which tend to have trade surpluses, export earnings financed only 65 per cent of the LDCs' imports in those years. For the LDCs whose major exports are agricultural commodities, export earnings covered a mere 54 per cent of total imports. These trade deficits are mainly financed by aid inflows, but workers' remittances are becoming increasingly important.

In these circumstances, it is possible for the positive role of exports in increasing import capacity to be neutralized by declining capital inflows or increased debt service obligations. A major aim of all LDCs should be to reduce their aid dependence and external indebtedness. But in the short run, the link between trade expansion and poverty reduction can be broken if increased trade is seen as an opportunity for reduced aid. If improvements in export performance are associated with decreases in international assistance and increases in debt service obligations, there is a danger of leaving a country running on the same spot despite a major effort to finance its own development.

There is a third reason why the relationship between international trade and poverty reduction in the LDCs is complicated. Although the national economies of most LDCs are highly integrated with the rest of the world through trade, the lives and livelihoods of most people in most LDCs are not directly linked to the international economy. It is difficult to get precise data on this. It is notable, however, that agriculture constitutes over 60 per cent of the labour force in all except 11 LDCs, but the ratio of agricultural exports to agricultural value-added is generally low. Although there are some exceptions, agricultural exports are equivalent to less than 10 per cent of agricultural value-added in more than half the LDCs for which data are available. In the urban centres, wage employment constitutes a very small fraction of total employment in most LDCs. Very little informal-sector activity is export-oriented and although some of it is potentially import-competing, in practice poverty segments the market, creating a niche for domestic producers of goods. Another telling indicator is that for over half of the LDCs, food imports constitute less than 10 per cent of total food consumption.

Against this background, there is no guarantee that export expansion will lead to a form of economic growth that is inclusive. Indeed, there is a strong likelihood that export-led growth will actually turn out to be "enclave-led growth". This is a form of economic growth that is concentrated in a small part of the economy, both geographically and sectorally. It is exemplified by the pattern of development in the colonial period in African LDCs, where a relatively rich commodity-exporting sector, well connected to roads and ports and supported by ancillary services, existed side by side with large undeveloped hinterlands where the majority of the population lived. But it can also occur with the expansion of labour-intensive manufactures exports confined to an export processing zone based on assembly of imported inputs, or tourism enclaves which are supplied through imports, or capital-intensive extractive industries concentrated in a few localities within a country.

An inclusive form of economic growth requires not simply export expansion but also an economy-wide expansion of income-earning opportunities, encompassing exports and import-competing activities, and non-tradables as well as tradables, which occurs at a rate that exceeds the rate at which the working-age population is growing. What is required is not simply a process of export expansion, but also the promotion of developmental linkages between growing export activities and the rest of the economy. For an inclusive process of economic growth, it is particularly important that the development complementarities between agriculture and non-agricultural activities be strengthened.

How the trade–poverty relationship works in practice

Although international trade can play a powerful role in poverty reduction in the LDCs, this Report finds that in practice the positive role of trade in poverty reduction is actually being realized in very few LDCs.

The first and obvious reason for this is that there has been a lack of export dynamism in many LDCs. This is closely related to export structure, and in particular commodity dependence. As discussed in detail in *The Least Developed Countries Report 2002*, many non-oil commodity-exporting LDCs have been caught in an international poverty trap in which external trade and financial relations are reinforcing, rather than serving to break, the domestic vicious circles that perpetuate poverty. The non-oil commodity-exporting LDCs generally depend on a narrow range of low-productivity, low-value-added and weakly competitive primary commodities serving declining or sluggish international markets. A weak export performance has been associated with the build-up of external debt and the emergence of an aid/debt service system in which aid disbursements have increasingly been allocated, either implicitly or explicitly, to ensure that official debts are serviced. These countries have been increasingly marginalized in world trade. In 2001, the share of world exports of goods and services supplied by the LDCs that export predominantly agricultural commodities was just 56 per cent of its level in 1980, and the share supplied by LDC mineral exporters was just 16 per cent of that former level.

International trade cannot work for poverty reduction if export performance is weak. But even when the LDCs have increased their overall export growth rate — as many (including non-oil commodity-exporting LDCs) did in the 1990s — better export performance rarely translates into sustained and substantial poverty reduction. *The relationship between trade and poverty is thus asymmetrical. Although LDCs with declining exports are almost certain to have a rising incidence of poverty, increasing exports do not necessarily lead to poverty reduction.*

The frequency of export expansion without poverty reduction

The basic evidence that the Report uses to show this phenomenon is derived from examination of the trends in real exports and average private consumption per capita (in 1985 purchasing power parity dollars). Within the LDC context, there is a close long-term relationship between average private consumption per capita and the incidence of $1/day and $2/day poverty. This enables the identification of three types of trade–poverty relationship:

- A virtuous trade effect, where average private consumption per capita is rising along with export growth;
- An immiserizing trade effect, where average private consumption per capita is falling along with export growth;

- An ambiguous trade effect, where there is no clear trend in average private consumption per capita along with export growth.

This classification is likely to provide the best possible view of the trade–poverty relationship. It is almost certain that the incidence of poverty is increasing in situations where average private consumption is falling. But it may be that, in the short term, increases in average private consumption per capita are concentrated in the richest sections of the population and are not associated with poverty reduction. Deviations from the long run typical relationship between private consumption and the incidence of poverty can arise, but they are unlikely to be sustainable in the long run.

If one focuses on trends in those LDCs for which there are data for 1990–1995 and/or 1995–2000, some positive signs can be seen. Out of the 66 observations (one country in one period), exports grew in 51 of them. If the countries are simply divided into those in which average private consumption per capita is increasing and those in which it is falling, export expansion can be said to be occurring along with rising private consumption per capita in 59 per cent of cases (30 out of 51). Moreover, export expansion with increasing average private consumption per capita was more common in the period 1995–2000 than in 1990–1995. But using a very conservative threshold growth rate of average private consumption per capita (+1 per cent per annum and –1 per cent per annum) to distinguish between situations where there is a virtuous trade effect, an ambiguous trade effect or an immiserizing trade effect, it is clear that the potential role of trade in poverty reduction is not working as expected. To be precise:

- The immiserizing trade effect is present in 18 of the 51 cases.
- The ambiguous trade effect and the immiserizing trade effect, which together account for 29 of the 51 cases, occur more frequently than the virtuous trade effect.
- The virtuous trade effect is present in only 22 of the 51 cases.

Some may wish to see this as a glass half full rather than a glass half empty. However, the fact that there is no statistically significant relationship between export growth and changes in private consumption per capita in either period should be a matter of concern. Moreover, there are only three LDCs — Bangladesh, Guinea and Uganda — in which the virtuous trade effect is observed during both 1990–1995 and 1995–2000. Poverty reduction in the LDC context can be expected to occur only if there is a sustained and substantial increase in average private consumption per capita. There have been significant export take-offs in a large number of LDCs since the late 1980s. But export growth is simply not having a strong and sustained virtuous poverty-reduction effect in most of the LDCs.

The trade–growth relationship

One of the reasons why export expansion does not often lead to poverty reduction is the nature of the trade–growth relationship. Generally, there is a positive association between export growth and output growth in the LDCs as in other developing countries. However, the relationship is slightly weaker in the LDCs than in the other developing countries in terms of the closeness of the association between the two variables. Moreover, at any level of export growth, a given export growth rate is associated with a slightly lower output growth rate in the LDCs than in the other developing countries. This turns out to be quite significant because a necessary minimum condition for poverty reduction is that the rate of economic growth is fast enough for GDP per capita to increase. Population growth rates tend to be higher in the LDCs, and in these circumstances, despite the positive relationship between export growth and output growth, export growth is not generating a sufficiently high output growth rate to ensure increasing GDP per capita in a number of LDCs. Indeed, during the 1990s, positive export growth was associated with declining GDP per capita in about a third of the LDCs.

What seems to be important is not simply export growth but a real export growth rate that exceeds 5 per cent per annum. Below that threshold, there is a greater probability that export growth will be associated with declining GDP per capita than with increasing GDP per capita.

The reason why the trade–growth relationship is somewhat weaker in the LDCs than in other developing countries is an issue which requires further investigation. There was actually a very strong relationship between import growth and investment growth in the LDCs in the 1990s. This suggests the possibility of a strong investment–export nexus through increased exports enabling increased imports, increased imports enabling increased investment in the domestic economy, and increased investment leading to higher economic growth. However, the evidence suggests two major missing links in the relationship between exports, imports, investment and economic growth. First, the growth in import capacity in the 1990s was much slower than export growth. This is likely to reflect decreased aid inflows and changes in contractual debt service obligations. Second, increased investment is not as strongly associated with increased economic growth in the LDCs as in other developing countries.

International trade cannot work to reduce poverty in countries where the level and efficiency of investment are not adequate to support sustained economic growth. On the basis of analysis in *The Least Developed Countries Report 2000*, major reasons for the breakdown of the investment–growth relationship are the following: constraints on domestic resource mobilization and the weakness of the domestic entrepreneurial class; aid ineffectiveness; and the multiple negative effects of external indebtedness. Basic conditions for ensuring a better trade–poverty relationship in the LDCs are the emergence of a domestic entrepreneurial class oriented towards productive activities, increasing and effective international financial and technical assistance to build production and trade capacities, and a durable exit from the debt problem.

Trade expansion and the inclusiveness of the economic growth process

The trade–poverty relationship is also breaking down because export expansion is not associated with an inclusive form of economic growth that is poverty-reducing. The limited amount of data makes it difficult to draw general conclusions on the inclusiveness of economic growth. Indeed, there is an urgent need for country case studies on employment and trade in order to have a better indication of what is actually happening. But this Report finds that immiserizing trade tends to occur more often in LDCs with high levels of income inequality. Moreover, indications from the Diagnostic Trade Integration Studies (DTIS) prepared within the context of the Integrated Framework for Trade-related Technical Assistance for the LDCs (IF) provide important evidence of export-led growth that is not inclusive.

Madagascar can be taken as an exemplar. Its Diagnostic Trade Integration Study includes a simulation which assumes that garments exports will grow at 20 per cent per annum from 2000 to 2003, and then at 10 per cent per annum from 2003 to 2009, and that tourism will grow at 10 per cent per annum throughout the period. But if agricultural production grows at 1.5 per cent per annum, as it did in the 1990s, and domestic industry outside the export processing zone (EPZ) grows at 2 per cent per annum, the projection indicates that the proportion of the population living below the poverty line will rise from 71 per cent in 1999 to 72 per cent in 2009. In effect, export growth rates as high as the best-performing LDCs can expect will be associated with no decline in the incidence of poverty and, given population growth, with an increase in the number of people living below the poverty line of almost 3.8 million in 10 years.

The Report identifies two important factors which affect the chances of achieving an inclusive form of economic growth based on export expansion. The first is the extent to which export expansion, import substitution and domestic demand expansion each contribute to economic growth. The evidence shows that the least favourable trade–poverty relationships in the LDCs in the 1990s tend to be found in countries in which export expansion is the most important demand-side component of economic growth and in countries in which import substitution is the major demand-side component of economic growth. Virtuous trade effects are most likely to occur if there is a balanced pattern of economic growth, in which domestic demand expansion is the major component of economic growth, but export expansion also makes a significant contribution to the overall process.

The second factor is the intensity of the domestic resource mobilization effort. It is a striking fact that two thirds of cases of an immiserizing trade effect or ambiguous trade effect in the LDCs in the periods 1990–1995 and 1995–2000 are related to an increasing domestic resource mobilization effort and a falling share of private consumption in GDP. The domestic resource mobilization effort supporting export expansion is positive from the perspective of growth sustainability to the extent that it is associated with efficient investment. But it is very difficult for such "belt tightening" to occur in very poor countries, where the average consumption of the population as a whole is equivalent to just $1 a day, without a rising incidence of poverty. Moreover, if the "belt tightening" associated with export expansion becomes too much, it may be that the whole growth process cannot be sustained.

The trade-off between increased domestic resource mobilization, which can help to strengthen export growth, and reduced poverty is a major dilemma in poor countries. It becomes less acute to the extent that average private consumption per capita is not at basic subsistence levels. Moreover, the trade-off between the two desirable goals is loosened if the trade–growth relationship is stronger. But if export growth is associated with slow increases in GDP per capita, as it is in many LDCs, the trade-off is likely to be particularly pronounced. In these circumstances, ensuring that export expansion, increased domestic resource mobilization and poverty reduction all occur together depends critically on the availability of external resources to diminish the trade-off between domestic resource mobilization and poverty reduction.

Civil conflict and the trade–poverty relationship

A further factor contributing to the weak trade–poverty relationship in the LDCs is civil conflict. This is an increasingly important issue in the LDCs. Databases disagree on the precise pattern. But the widely used Uppsala/PRIO database indicates that during the period 1978–1989, 40 per cent of the current LDCs experienced civil conflict of varying intensity and duration, whilst during the period 1990–2001, this proportion increased to 60 per cent.

The causes of this trend are very complex. The analysis in this Report suggests that an export specialization in some products, notably diamonds, oil, timber and narcotic crops, is associated with higher conflict risk. But it is much too simple to suggest that trade opportunism rooted in greed is the key determinant of civil conflict in the primary commodity dependent LDCs. However, the Report has some important findings in terms of the consequences of civil conflict.

Depending on the level of intensity of the conflict and also on whether or not a country has had a previous experience of conflict, it is clear that civil conflicts do not always result in a collapse in trade or even lower levels of exports than in the period immediately preceding the conflict episodes. The absorption components of GDP (domestic consumption and investment) generally decline during conflict. However, there is a tendency for exports to be positive during conflict episodes, and sometimes even higher than in the period preceding the conflict. This is particularly evident in cases of conflict recurrence. It reflects partly the fact that some economic actors increasingly just get on with their business regardless of, and even adjusting to, an environment of repeated conflict.

Overall, civil conflict is clearly a major cause of poverty. But because exports can also expand during civil conflicts, there is a strong tendency for conflict episodes to be characterized by immiserizing trade effects. Civil peace is a necessary condition for a virtuous trade–poverty relationship. Good governance, including good management of the revenues from natural resources, is essential for civil peace.

IS IT POSSIBLE TO IMPROVE THE TRADE–POVERTY RELATIONSHIP THROUGH UNILATERAL TRADE LIBERALIZATION?

The major policy challenge now is to bridge the gap between the powerful role which international trade can play in poverty reduction in the LDCs on the one hand, and the ambiguous or immiserizing trade effects which are occurring in too many LDCs on the other hand. One possible policy solution which could be suggested to improve the situation is to undertake unilateral trade liberalization and thereby increase the "openness" of LDCs' national economies. But there are two caveats which must be entered with regard to the role this can play. First, there has actually been an extensive process of trade liberalization in the LDCs since the late 1980s. In many LDCs there is not much of a trade liberalization agenda left to implement. Second, the emerging post-liberal trends, although they have both positive and negative aspects, do not indicate that substantial and sustained poverty reduction will occur. On balance, future poverty reduction prospects seem to have worsened.

The depth and extent of trade liberalization

The depth and extent of trade liberalization in the LDCs can be gauged by using the IMF index of trade restrictiveness, which classifies countries according to their average tariff rate and also the extent of non-tariff barriers. From these data it is apparent that very few LDCs have restrictive trade regimes now. In 2002, on the basis of this evidence:

- The average tariff rate of 42 out of 46 LDCs for which data are available was less than 25 per cent.
- The average tariff rate of 36 of these 46 LDCs was less than 20 per cent.

- The average tariff rate of 23 of these 46 LDCs was less than 15 per cent.
- In 29 of these 46 LDCs, non-tariff barriers were absent or minor in the sense that less than 1 per cent of production and trade is subject to non-tariff barriers.
- Twenty-eight of these 46 LDCs had no or minor non-tariff barriers coupled with average tariff rates of below 25 per cent.

The extent and the depth of trade liberalization reflect the wide and long involvement of most LDCs with structural adjustment programmes. As a result, most of the LDCs now have more open trade regimes than other developing countries and as open trade regimes as high-income OECD countries. The whole process has also been undertaken very rapidly in quite a number of LDCs. In some cases, they liberalized faster than Chile did in the 1970s and 1980s. In the case of Rwanda, a recent consultant report recommended that it should declare itself an economy-wide free-trade zone. This was considered to be a practical proposition because its trade policy regime, the report stated with only a little exaggeration, was "not far removed" from that of Hong Kong (China) and Singapore.

Trade liberalization and short-term poverty trends

The usual view of the relationship between trade liberalization and poverty is that trade liberalization is likely to have adverse effects in the short run, particularly as social groups which formerly benefited from a protectionist tariff regime are exposed to international competition, but that in the long run the effects will be favourable because trade liberalization will increase the growth potential of the economy. The findings of this Report are the opposite, however. Poverty trends during and immediately after trade liberalization in the LDCs are very mixed, and not invariably negative as some claim. But there are many grounds for concern about the long-term effects in terms of both the sustainability of economic growth and its inclusiveness.

The short-term effects of the process of trade liberalization on poverty vary considerably between the LDCs. The few studies which seek to isolate the impact of policy change econometrically show limited positive effects in some countries and limited negative effects in others, with some groups benefiting and others losing in each case. If one focuses on growth rates of exports and average private consumption per capita, it is clear that the trade–poverty relationship improved between the first half of the 1990s and the second half of the 1990s in countries which were "open", "moderately open" or "restricted", according to the IMF classification, in 2000. But the greatest improvement came in those that opened moderately during the decade rather than those that opened most. Together with results of the analysis in *The Least Developed Countries Report 2002*, the evidence suggests that there has been a tendency for the countries that have opened more gradually and less deeply to have a better trade–poverty relationship than those that have opened furthest fastest on the one hand, and those that have remained most restrictive on the other hand. This pattern, it should be noted, is related to export specialization as much as to trade liberalization, and also to differences in the speed of trade liberalization in Asian and African LDCs. African LDCs have undertaken deeper and faster trade liberalization than Asian LDCs. But it is the latter that have generally had a better performance in terms of poverty reduction and also have been more successful in developing more market-dynamic manufactures exports, partly through regional trade and investment linkages.

Trade liberalization and future poverty reduction prospects

Whatever the short-term trends, the central issue now is whether the new policy environment is likely to facilitate substantial and sustained poverty reduction in the long run. In this regard, there are some positive elements and some negative elements. For the LDCs which have undertaken deep trade liberalization, comparisons of economic trends before and after trade liberalization indicate that GDP growth rates, export growth rates and investment growth rates are all higher in the post-liberal economic environment. But, given high population growth rates, the rates of economic growth that are being achieved are in many cases not sufficient to yield GDP per capita growth rates that will make a major dent in poverty.

Moreover, there are reasons to believe that the sustainability of the positive growth, export and investment trends is still not assured. First, the rate of domestic savings remains very low and thus the post-liberal countries remain highly dependent on foreign savings, particularly aid. Secondly, there is evidence of post-liberalization aid fatigue, in the sense that aid inflows tapered off after trade liberalization. The Monterrey Consensus may have reversed this for a number of LDCs. Third, although there are higher export growth rates, the composition of exports is not yet shifting towards a more favourable one with greater specialization in dynamic products and increased competitiveness. Certainly, new export products are emerging, and this, together with a trend towards decreasing export concentration, is a positive sign. But in the post-liberal cases examined in this Report, the effect of the emergence of new products is as yet so limited that overall export performance has not improved sufficiently to reverse marginalization in the world economy. In general, the process of trade liberalization in the LDCs has reinforced specialization in commodity exports rather than promoted a shift to manufactures exports.

Analysis of the impact of trade liberalization on the balance of payments in the LDCs shows that the process has increased both exports and imports, the latter more than the former. In comparison with the situation in other developing countries, the process of trade liberalization in the LDCs has had a more limited effect on both exports and imports. For exports, this is likely to reflect lower export supply responsiveness. For imports, the shift to a liberal trading regime is associated with a fall in aid in the LDCs which in turn has reduced import growth, whilst in other developing countries trade liberalization has been associated with higher private capital inflows after liberalization. Trade liberalization has worsened the trade balance of LDCs. The effect is more limited in the LDCs than in developing countries as a whole because the effect of liberalization on import growth is less. However, given the continuing marginalization of LDCs in global private capital flows, the effect on the trade balance implies that the process of trade liberalization has exacerbated aid dependence. Moreover, to the extent that aid is not provided in grants and is not building up trade capacity, it may have increased the likelihood of a renewed debt crisis in the future.

The inclusiveness of the post-liberal growth process also gives cause for concern. Information in the DTIS makes it clear that a form of economic growth in which expansion is localized within a small geographical and sectoral enclave is becoming a problem in some LDCs whose major exports are manufactures and mining. With this form of economic growth, there are weak links between the rapidly growing export enclave and the agricultural sector where the majority of the population and the majority of the poor have their livelihoods. In these circumstances, it is possible to have very high rates of export growth but no change in the incidence of poverty.

A further factor that diminishes the inclusiveness of the post-liberal growth process arises because deep trade liberalization at the national border has been undertaken in countries with very weak internal transport and communications infrastructure, weak levels of domestic market integration and a high level of subsistence orientation. In these circumstances, many poor people and poor regions are being left out. Moreover, the liberalization process itself cannot break the vicious circles which reduce the market involvement of rural households and render a large proportion of local output only locally tradable. This is exacerbating the problem of enclave-led growth in countries exporting manufactures, minerals and oil, and it is also particularly evident in agriculture-exporting LDCs with a low population density.

Finally, in agriculture-exporting LDCs with a high population density, such as Rwanda, a different problem is emerging. This problem is increasing population pressure on land, environmental degradation and impoverishment, as farm sizes and yields are too low to support households. The development of non-agricultural employment is necessary in order to relieve the pressure on land. But in the LDCs for which trends are reported in the DTIS, rapid and deep liberalization has been associated with de-industrialization as import-substitution industries collapse when they are exposed to international competition without any prior preparation, and as the processing of primary products before export is cut back. It has proved difficult for the agriculture-exporting LDCs with high population density to develop manufactures or service exports sufficiently as an alternative source of non-agricultural employment, and thus the increasing pressure on land resources continues to intensify.

MAKING INTERNATIONAL TRADE A MORE EFFECTIVE MECHANISM OF POVERTY REDUCTION

The central policy issue facing the LDCs and their development partners now is how to promote development and poverty reduction in a very open subsistence-level national economy situated in a very asymmetrically liberalized international economy. The central recommendation of the Report is that *making international trade a more effective mechanism of poverty reduction in the LDCs requires a development approach in which three pillars work together coherently and synergistically.*

The three pillars of this approach are:
- Better national development strategies which integrate trade objectives as a central component;
- Improvements in the international trade regime, including issues which go beyond the scope of the WTO, to reduce international constraints on development in the LDCs;
- Increased and effective international financial and technical assistance for developing production and trade capacities.

PILLAR ONE:
BETTER NATIONAL DEVELOPMENT STRATEGIES

Mainstreaming trade in poverty reduction strategies

The first key to making international trade a more effective mechanism of poverty reduction in the LDCs is the design of better national development strategies. For most LDCs, this is a question of the formulation and implementation of Poverty Reduction Strategy Papers (PRSPs).

The PRSPs have been criticized because they are said to pay insufficient attention to trade issues. This was true of the first generation of PRSPs that essentially sought to integrate pro-poor public expenditure patterns with deeper and broader structural reforms and the macroeconomic policies adopted in earlier structural adjustment programmes. But the recent PRSPs in the LDCs have been much more growth-oriented. Trade issues are central to these PRSPs. Targets for export growth and import growth appear in all of them as part of the macroeconomic framework. Moreover, although few of the PRSPs have a separate section on trade, they invariably include a range of trade objectives, among which are: increasing openness, increasing competitiveness and diversification; reducing export instability; developing new exports, including high-value agricultural exports, manufactures and tourism; and developing regional trade links. In general, trade development is closely linked in the PRSPs to the issue of private sector development and an improved investment climate. But in general, there are weak links between the overall strategic goals and the priority public actions. Moreover, the trade targets that form part of the macroeconomic framework — which usually assume faster export growth than in the recent past and a low income elasticity of demand for imports — float freely, disconnected from the rest of the content of the PRSP.

The Report proposes a methodology for mainstreaming trade in poverty reduction strategies. The methodology focuses on the balance-of-payments constraint and the changes in the income elasticity of imports and exports which are necessary in order to achieve sustainable growth at rates sufficient for meeting poverty reduction targets. It includes examination of export demand prospects of traditional exports and also the criteria for identifying promising tradable sectors that can help in achieving trade development goals. On this basis, alternative trade policy measures can be explored. This would be most effective within the context of a strong national trade policy process in which a wide range of stakeholders, and particularly the private sector, are involved.

This approach can help to integrate trade into poverty reduction strategies. But as argued in *The Least Developed Countries Report 2002*, the critical challenge is not simply to mainstream trade into poverty reduction strategies, but also to move more closely to development-oriented poverty reduction strategies that are anchored in a national development strategy. From this perspective, the task of integrating trade into PRSPs is best seen as a two-way mainstreaming of both trade and development within poverty reduction strategies.

Post-liberal development strategies

A critical challenge facing the LDCs at the moment is how to promote development and poverty reduction in a newly liberalized open economy. Key issues which require innovative thinking are: What is the nature of a post-liberal development strategy? What kinds of public action can facilitate development and poverty reduction in an economy without barriers to international trade? These issues are urgent. As a Permanent Representative to the UN and WTO from an LDC — a person who comes from a country which liberalized the furthest and fastest in the 1990s but still faces pressing problems in raising living standards, ensuring fuller employment and reducing poverty — recently put it in a statement at the WTO, "the majority of us [LDCs] are galloping in the darkness".

As emerges from the analysis in this Report, it is unlikely that an export-led growth strategy will of itself lead to a virtuous trade–poverty relationship in the LDCs. In the LDCs, where there is mass poverty with most people living at or below income levels sufficient to meet their basic needs, export-led growth is generally synonymous with an exclusionary growth trajectory with benefits concentrated in an enclave. However, an important argument of this Report is that export-led growth is not the only promising open development strategy that can be pursued after trade liberalization. *There are a number of alternative open development strategies in which trade is an element of growth rather than the major source of growth, and which can be implemented in an open-economy trade regime in which incentives are biased in favour neither of exports nor of imports and in which there is no discrimination between agriculture and manufacturing sectors.* Such development strategies are defined here as post-liberal development strategies.

Possible post-liberal development strategies include but are not limited to:
- An export-led growth strategy with a human face, including increased linkages to diffuse benefits, and also a basic needs strategy;
- A balanced growth strategy based on agricultural productivity growth and export-accelerated industrialization;
- An agricultural-development-led industrialization (ADLI) strategy — which includes infrastructure investment and technological progress in agriculture together with forward linkages into processing activities — with an export component;
- Development and diversification through management of mineral revenues;
- Development of natural-resource-based production clusters;
- A triadic development strategy that includes the promotion of competitive tradables, employment-intensive non-tradables and technological change in subsistence-oriented activities to reduce constraints on household labour time.

Export growth is an important component of all these development strategies. But whereas in the first one exports are the major demand-side component of economic growth, the others are open development strategies which seek to achieve adequate export growth rather than export-led growth. In the strategies that seek adequate export growth, domestic demand expansion is an important demand-side component of economic growth. There is thus more balance between domestic demand and export expansion in the process of growth.

At the present time what seems to be emerging in some LDCs, implicitly rather than deliberately, is the first hybrid strategy which combines export-led growth with a basic needs strategy. Within this new, frankly experimental, synthesis, the export-led growth leg of the strategy is founded on trade liberalization, together with "behind-the-border" measures to reduce internal constraints on external trade (such as high transaction costs associated with weak trade facilitation and port infrastructure) and measures to foster linkages so that the effects of export growth reach poorer groups and poorer regions. At the same time, the basic-needs leg of the strategy is increasingly taken up by the LDCs' development partners, who are allocating development assistance increasingly to meet basic needs.

This strategy is certainly likely to result in a more positive trade–poverty relationship than in a pure export-led growth strategy. However, it remains to be seen whether it will be sustainable. As limited international assistance becomes absorbed more and more in basic needs provision, it is less available for developing the production sectors and for private sector development. The great danger of this strategy is that countries will end with a deepening debt problem.

It is in this context that the relevance of the alternative post-liberal development strategies described in this Report needs to be more broadly debated and explored.

Policies for promoting development

Whatever strategy is followed, new types of policies will be required in order to promote development in the new open trading environment. A key insight which must be grasped here is that, as Jagdish Bhagwati argues, free trade is not the same as laissez-faire. Domestic policies are required to correct domestic distortions, market failures and coordination failures, which are all manifold in very poor countries. Such policies should seek to complement rather than supplant market mechanisms.

In implementing post-liberal development strategies, public policies in LDCs should use market-supporting mechanisms aimed at market creation, market development and market acceleration. These policies must not simply provide the right price incentives, but also create the right institutions and the infrastructure necessary for a modern market economy to function properly. The provision of public goods that address the current gaps and shortages in the productive sectors of LDCs is vital. New investment should also be directed towards increasing the absorption capacity of imported technologies and new techniques of production throughout the economies of the LDCs. Private sector development should be a priority. A major effort must be made to develop a domestic enterprise sector oriented towards production rather than simply exchange. Particular emphasis must be placed on small and medium-sized enterprises, and also new market-oriented approaches to agricultural development need to be devised to fill the vacuum left by the dismantling of old commodity marketing boards.

PILLAR TWO:
IMPROVING THE INTERNATIONAL TRADE REGIME

Without improvements in the international trade regime to reduce international constraints on development in the LDCs, the positive effects of better national development strategies will not be realized.

This requires not simply attention to WTO rules but also multilateral norms, rules and practices which go beyond WTO issues. It is necessary to define the international trade regime in these broad terms because in practice, many of the key international problems facing LDCs in terms of the international trade environment are actually outside the WTO agenda. They relate, for example, to the working of the international commodity economy, part of which is affected by WTO issues and part of which is not. Another important issue is the nature of agreements on preferential market access between developed countries and LDCs and between developing countries and LDCs, and also the nature of regional trade agreements. The transparency of mineral rents and revenues is another key issue, and the process of the untying of aid, which is very important for import competition, is being monitored through the OECD Development Assistance Committee (DAC). Against this background, limiting the discussion to WTO issues would considerably foreclose proper analysis of how it is possible to link international trade to poverty reduction in the LDCs through improvements in the international trade regime.

The Report argues that improvements to the international trade regime should encompass (i) measures at a global level that are generally applicable to all developing countries, (ii) special international support measures targeted at the LDCs, and (iii) enhanced South–South cooperation in the fields of trade and investment.

Generally applicable measures

The Report argues that the LDCs cannot be expected to gain much from the current round of multilateral trade liberalization unless improvements are made in their productive capacities to enable them to benefit from any subsequent global growth. Amongst the issues currently under discussion, the phasing-out of agricultural support measures in OECD countries is particularly important for the development prospects of the LDCs. Although these measures may help countries import cheap foods and meet food security needs in the short term, they have a depressing effect on agricultural production in the LDCs, breaking the potential complementarities between agricultural and non-agricultural development that are central to the development process. The Report identifies rice, sugar, maize, sorghum, wheat, potatoes, cotton, beans and beef and veal as some of the key products that receive support in the developed countries and are also of great importance to production in least developed countries. Even though food imports are a small proportion of total food consumption in many LDCs, the OECD agricultural support measures serve to discourage domestic agricultural production, increasing future dependence on food imports.

However, there are also a number of generally applicable measures, beyond multilateral trade liberalization, which can play a very important role in making international trade a more effective mechanism for poverty reduction in the LDCs. The major sin of omission in the current international approach to poverty reduction is the failure to tackle the link between commodity dependence and extreme poverty. Any measures in relation to commodities are likely to have a high poverty-reduction intensity in the LDCs. Priority areas include general measures to reduce vulnerability to commodity price shocks (for example, linking debt repayment schedules to world prices) and initiatives to ensure international transparency in the revenues derived from oil and mineral exploitation. System-wide measures with regard to the mineral economies, which are off the radar screen in current analyses of the effects of multilateral trade liberalization (which focus on agriculture and manufactures), are likely to be particularly important as extreme poverty has been increasing in most mineral-dependent LDCs.

Special international support measures for LDCs

Against the background of the potential gains which LDCs are likely to derive from multilateral trade liberalization, special international support measures have an important role to play in making international trade a more effective mechanism for poverty reduction in the LDCs. Current special measures, including both market access preferences and special and differential treatment for the LDCs written into WTO provisions, have various limitations which reduce their effectiveness. There is considerable room for strengthening these measures. For preferential market access, improvements can come through the following: changes in the rules of origin; helping countries to meet sanitary and phytosanitary standards (SPS) and technical barriers to trade (TBT) requirements; wider product coverage; and more stability and predictability, which may be achieved through the binding of market access preferences in a WTO context. Special and differential treatment for LDCs within WTO provisions can be improved through better targeting to countries and problems; a shift from best-endeavour provisions to binding provisions; and closer attention to provisions which help build production and supply capacities, notably the encouragement to WTO members given in the Trade-Related Aspects of Intellectual Property Rights (TRIPS) Agreement to transfer technology to the LDCs. It is also important that acceding LDCs automatically receive the same special and differential treatment as LDCs that are already WTO members.

As multilateral trade liberalization deepens, market access preferences for LDCs will gradually erode and the major market-based approach to supporting the LDCs will be undermined. As this happens it is important to consider complementary international support measures for the LDCs. One possible course of action is to introduce new supply-side preferences, encourage foreign direct investment (FDI), technology transfer and cheaper finance. These could usefully complement preferential market access as a market-based approach to supporting LDCs.

South–South cooperation

Finally, international trade can be made a more effective mechanism for poverty reduction in the LDCs through increasing South–South cooperation in the field of trade. This has become increasingly important as South–South trade has grown. Other developing countries supplied only 32 per cent of total LDC imports in 1989, but by 2001 this had increased to 56 per cent. However, there is a danger that LDCs may become marginalized in South–South trade as they are in North–South trade. The proportion of total exports of LDCs going to other developing countries only rose from 15 per cent to 34 per cent between 1989 and 2001. The LDCs have a deficit in their international trade with other developing countries which increased from $5.5 billion in 1990 to $15.6 billion in 2002.

Measures to reverse the marginalization of LDCs in South–South trade include further use of the Global System of Trade Preferences (GSTP), encouragement of regional FDI from more advanced developing countries directed to the LDCs and of triangular relationships with developed countries, as well as special provisions within regional agreements. In the end, a major obstacle to increased South–South cooperation is the difficulties which the more advanced developing countries face in the global economy. As these difficulties are removed growth in those countries could play a key role in enabling the LDCs to benefit from global growth rather than face persistent marginalization.

PILLAR THREE:
IMPROVED INTERNATIONAL ASSISTANCE FOR
DEVELOPING PRODUCTION AND TRADE CAPACITIES

The final element of the three-pillar approach is increased and effective international assistance for developing production and trade capacities in the LDCs. Building productive and supply capacities at the national level will contribute to both trade expansion and poverty reduction and play a central role in improving the trade–poverty relationship in the LDCs. There is a need for massive investment in enhancing the supply capacities of the LDCs and improving their competitiveness. In the approach being advocated here, trade capacity building is central to that process. But it is difficult to separate this activity from assistance to private sector development, and also assistance to the development of production capacities more generally.

The need for international financial and technical assistance arises because of the limited domestic resources available for doing this, the short-term trade-off between domestic resource mobilization and poverty reduction, and also limits to the potential of private capital inflows to meet many of the investment needs. With regard to the latter, there are indeed some encouraging signs in terms of private capital inflows for infrastructure in the LDCs. But these inflows tend to be highly concentrated in a few countries, and also focus on a few localities and sectors, notably telecommunications.

The scale of international assistance

Improving international assistance for the development of production capacities and trade capacities involves both increasing assistance and improving the effectiveness of assistance. With regard to the scale of international assistance, as aid inflows declined in the 1990s there was a compositional shift away from economic infrastructure and services (particularly transport and communications, and energy) and production sectors (agriculture, industry, trade and tourism) towards social infrastructure. In the early 1980s, the share of total bilateral aid commitments by DAC member countries to LDCs that went to economic infrastructure, production sectors and multi-sectoral and cross-cutting issues was 45 per cent. But in 2000–2002 this had fallen to 23 per cent. In real terms, external assistance to agriculture in the LDCs in the 1990s was half the level it was in the 1980s. It is vital that the upturn in international assistance following the Monterrey Consensus be also associated with a shift in the composition of aid back towards building production capabilities and not simply meeting basic needs and providing social infrastructure.

Aid for trade has been particularly neglected. It is difficult to estimate past trends owing to the way in which aid for trade has been defined in the OECD Creditor Reporting System. But over the period 1990-2001, according to this data base, total bilateral and multilateral aid commitments to trade policy and administration to all the LDCs was on average $13.8 million per year, which was equivalent to 0.1 per cent of total aid commitments. In 7 of those 12 years aid commitments for trade policy and administration were less than $6 million for all the LDCs. The recently established WTO/OECD database on aid for trade-related technical assistance and capacity-building gives a fuller picture, suggesting higher levels of aid for trade. In 2002, according to the latter database the LDCs received $75 million for trade policy and regulations, with the key priority being negotiations of Economic Partnership Agreements (post-Cotonou), and $249 million for trade development, with business support services and market analysis and development being priorities. But to put these in perspective, aid commitments for trade policy and regulation and for trade development were only 0.5 per cent and 1.5 per cent, respectively, of total aid commitments in that year.

A particular priority in terms of financial assistance for trade capacity building is trade-related infrastructure. This should be part of a major effort to meet the quantitative targets included in the United Nations Programme of Action for the Least Developed Countries for the Decade 2001–2010. The lack of any clear definition of trade-related infrastructure means that estimates of the current scale of assistance will vary with the definition. According to the WTO/OECD database, which includes all aid commitments in the areas of transport and storage, communications and energy, the LDCs received $1.4 billion in 2002, 9 per cent of total aid commitments in that year. Aid commitments for trade-related infrastructure, defined more narrowly as transport, storage and communications, declined by 43 per cent in real per capita terms from 1990 to 2001.

The effectiveness of international assistance

Finally, it is necessary that improvements be made in the effectiveness of assistance. There are three particular problems for the development partners of the LDCs which need to be addressed here. The first of these is that the development objectives of developed countries in their role as donors overlap with their commercial interests in their role as trading powers. It is important that this does not bias assistance for trade development. The untying of aid to LDCs provides a major opportunity for a culture shift in this regard. Second, there is an urgent need to strengthen donors' own trade-related capacities. Mainstreaming trade in aid programmes is as important and urgent as mainstreaming trade in PRSPs. Third, donors need to elaborate innovative approaches to private sector development in the LDCs. Post-liberal aid policies need to complement post-liberal development strategies.

The major initiative to improve the effectiveness of assistance for trade capacity building is the Integrated Framework for Trade-related Technical Assistance for the LDCs (IF). The diagnostic studies produced through this initiative provide much useful information on trade and poverty in the LDCs, but they have focused more on identifying unfinished trade policy reforms and on trade facilitation and export constraints in particular sectors, and less on how to reduce poverty through trade and development. However, the key feature of the IF is that it has as yet had limited concrete trade capacity-building outcomes.

THE NEED FOR POLICY COHERENCE WITHOUT DEVELOPMENT PESSIMISM

The need for policy coherence

Each of these three pillars is important for success. Improvements in the international trade regime are a necessary condition for success since that regime provides the framework for linking trade more effectively with poverty reduction in the LDCs. However, whether or not the increased opportunity for poverty reduction which can come from such improvements will be translated into reality depends on whether the opportunity is grasped at the national level. The fundamental priority here is that Governments formulate and implement national development strategies that integrate trade within them in a way that effectively supports poverty reduction. This is pivotal because it is the area where the LDCs themselves potentially have the most leverage to make trade work for poverty reduction. But the development partners of the LDCs also need to support these efforts through international financial and technical assistance to build both public and private trade capacities. Policy incoherence between international assistance policies and national trade objectives, insufficient and biased financial and technical assistance for trade, and the failure to facilitate and nurture national ownership of trade and development policies can all undermine national efforts to grasp opportunities which changes in the international trade regime provide.

This three-pillar strategy to make trade a more effective mechanism of poverty reduction in the LDCs also needs to be embedded within a broad approach to international development policy which encompasses increased trade opportunities, more effective international financial and technical assistance, deeper debt relief, the promotion of private capital flows, and international assistance for technology transfer and acquisition. The challenge of development in the LDCs is so great that it will be counter-productive to see trade as a substitute for aid, or to imagine that private capital flows can substitute for official capital flows in these countries. The goal of the LDCs themselves must be to promote a progressive transition in which sustained economic growth is increasingly founded on domestic resource mobilization, the attraction of developmental FDI and the tapping of international financial markets, and imports are increasingly paid for by exports rather than covered by aid inflows. This is likely to be best achieved if, during this transition, international assistance, debt relief, trade preferences and measures to facilitate FDI and technology transfer all work together to promote development.

What is encouraging at the present time is that there is a wide consensus on better national policies, a better international trade regime and better international assistance for trade capacity building as three key pillars of a broad strategy for making international trade a more effective mechanism of poverty reduction in the LDCs. However to be effective, these three pillars need to be articulated and implemented in the way that is most appropriate at the present time. This requires shaking off the grip of development pessimism.

Loosening the grip of development pessimism

In the past, development strategies and international policy recommendations were influenced by both export pessimism and agricultural pessimism. At the present time, development pessimism constitutes one of the greatest obstacles to global poverty reduction.

Development pessimism is apparent in the belief that past development efforts have failed, or that the deliberate, purposeful acceleration of development through policy does not work, or that if it worked in the past it will not work now in the new globalized economic environment. Development pessimism is shared by those who would argue that the State should play a minimal role in guiding economic activity in developing countries, and also those who argue that it should play an important role but cannot do so because international rules reduce "policy space" and thus prevent countries from doing what they need to do. Within an LDC context, weak State capabilities are added as a further ingredient reinforcing the view that development promotion simply cannot be done.

Development pessimism has led to the view that the best way to reduce poverty in the LDCs and other developing countries is not through development but rather through closer integration with the world economy. Global integration certainly must be central to any effective development and poverty reduction strategy in the LDCs. International economic relations can play a key role in helping LDCs to break out of the domestic vicious circles which cause generalized poverty to persist:

- Access to foreign savings can play a catalytic role in helping poor countries to break out of the cycle of low incomes, low savings, low investment, low productivity and low incomes.
- Exporting to international markets enables land and labour resources, hitherto underutilized owing to the weak effective demand associated with mass poverty, to be productively mobilized.
- Increased access to available modern technologies enables latecomers to achieve significant productivity increases without continually having to reinvent.
- Increased FDI can increase investment and provide technology and managerial skills.
- Increased international migration enables poor people in poor countries to find employment abroad even if opportunities are limited in their own country.

However, it is an illusion to think that persistent mass poverty in the LDCs is the result of a lack of integration and insufficient trade liberalization rather than the consequence of underdevelopment.

The policy problem for the LDCs is not the level of integration with the world economy but rather the form of integration. The current form of integration is not supporting sustained economic growth and poverty reduction. The process of trade liberalization has created a new environment for poverty reduction in the LDCs. The central issue now is how the LDCs, supported by their development partners and enabled through a facilitating international trade regime, can promote development and poverty reduction in this new environment.

There should be no grounds for development pessimism. One of the most important achievements of the second half of the twentieth century was the lifting of millions of people out of poverty through the promotion of development. Moreover, these achievements are now being continued in China and India. The question is how to make this happen in the LDCs as well.

* * *

To conclude, I would like to emphasize that this Report is part of a wider programme of work which UNCTAD envisages in the area of trade and poverty. There has been intense interest in this subject in the last five years. But so far, the major focus has been on trade liberalization and poverty rather than on looking at trade and poverty from a development perspective. This Report is a contribution to the latter task, providing not simply an analysis of the LDCs but also a possible conceptual framework for a development approach.

The subject of trade and poverty is of immense importance. This is not simply because of the ethical dimension which it brings to the international policy debate but also because it extends trade policy analysis from questions of the quantity of trade to questions of the quality of trade. This notion needs to be elaborated in the same way as the notion of the "quality of growth" and the "quality of employment", and practical strategies to link trade, development and poverty reduction have to be worked out to meet the needs of developing countries at all levels of development.

There is much to be done.

Rubens Ricupero
Secretary-General of UNCTAD

Part One

Recent Trends

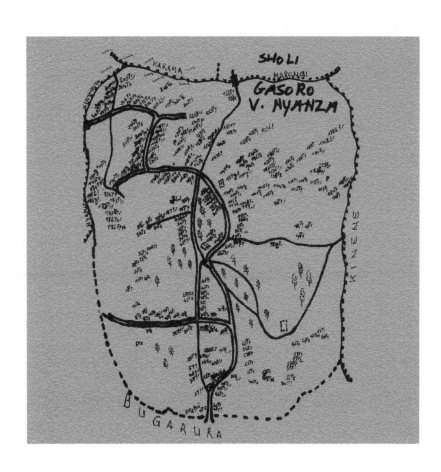

Recent Economic Trends

A. Overall economic growth trends

During the period 2000–2002, the latest years for which data are available, the economic performance of the LDCs as a group continued to improve. Indeed, the average annual real GDP growth rate exceeded that of other developing countries during this period. But there are significant differences amongst the LDCs, with some doing very well and some doing very badly. Moreover, the types of LDCs that did best are those which, during the 1990s, experienced the highest levels of growth instability.

The real GDP of the LDCs as a group grew faster in the late 1990s than in the early 1990s, and during the period 2000–2002 the group grew slightly faster than during the later 1990s. For the 45 LDCs for which data are available, the average growth rate was 4.9 per cent per annum during 2000–2002, that is 0.5 of a percentage point more than in 1998–2000 (see table 1). It is also estimated that the growth rate of the real GDP per capita of the group of LDCs also accelerated — from an annual average of 2.0 per cent in 1998–2000 to 2.6 per cent in 2000–2002.

Bangladesh, whose economy constitutes a quarter of the total GDP of all the LDCs, pulls up the overall growth rate. But the improvement in growth performance is still evident in the rest of the LDCs — the rate of growth of their real GDP per capita increased from 1.4 per cent per annum in 1998–2000 to 2.5 per cent per annum in 2000–2002 (table 1).

During the period 2000–2002, the economic performance of the LDCs as a group continued to improve. But there are significant differences amongst the LDCs.

TABLE 1. REAL GDP AND REAL GDP PER CAPITA GROWTH RATES OF LDCS AND OTHER COUNTRY GROUPINGS, 1998–2000 AND 2000–2002

(Average annual growth rate, percentage)

	Real GDP growth					Real GDP per capita growth				
	1998–2000	*2000*	*2001*	*2002*	*2000–2002*	*1998–2000*	*2000*	*2001*	*2002*	*2000–2002*
Least developed countries	4.4	4.3	4.9	5.0	4.9	2.0	1.9	2.5	2.7	2.6
Of which:										
Bangladesh	5.4	5.9	5.3	4.4	4.8	3.6	4.1	3.5	2.6	3.0
Other LDCs	3.9	3.6	4.7	5.2	5.0	1.4	1.1	2.2	2.7	2.5
African LDCs	3.7	3.2	4.9	5.7	5.3	1.2	0.7	2.4	3.2	2.8
Asian LDCs	5.4	6.0	5.0	4.0	4.5	3.4	3.9	3.0	2.0	2.5
Island LDCs	3.0	2.0	1.4	1.9	1.6	0.5	-0.4	-1.0	-0.5	-0.8
Other developing countries	4.4	5.6	2.7	3.5	3.1	2.9	4.1	1.3	2.2	1.8
Low-income countries	4.4	4.1	4.5	4.1	4.3	2.4	2.2	2.6	2.3	2.5
Middle-income countries	3.8	5.3	2.6	3.2	2.9	2.8	4.3	1.7	2.2	2.0
High-income countries	3.3	3.7	0.7	1.3	1.0	2.6	2.9	0.0	0.8	0.4
World	3.4	3.9	1.1	1.7	1.4	2.1	2.6	-0.1	0.5	0.2

Source: UNCTAD secretariat estimates, based on World Bank, *World Development Indicators,* online data.

Notes: Real GDP is measured in constant 1995 dollars. No data were available for Afghanistan, Myanmar, Somalia or Tuvalu. The group of other developing countries is composed of 78 non-LDC developing countries (excluding Central and Eastern Europe) for which real GDP data were available.
Low-, middle- and high-income countries are country groups defined by the World Bank.
For the classification of LDCs, see the annex to the chapter.

It is notable that this improvement in the economic growth rate within the LDCs occurred as that of other developing countries slowed down — from 2.9 per cent per annum in 1998–2000 to 1.8 per cent per annum in 2000–2002 in real per capita terms. This difference is explained by the fact that the GDP growth of the group of other developing countries decelerated strongly in 2001, with the average per capita GDP growth rate falling from 4.1 per cent in 2000 to 1.3 per cent in 2001, from which point it slowly recovered to 2.2 per cent in 2002. Unlike that of other developing countries, the aggregate GDP growth of LDCs kept pace in 2001. The relative resilience to the global economic downturn in 2001 is also apparent in the group of low-income countries (chart 1).

The improved growth performance in the group of LDCs in 2000–2002 is encouraging as between 1990 and 1997 real growth rates were lower in the LDCs than in other developing countries. However, the higher growth rates in the LDCs have not yet been sufficient to reduce the increasing gap in the level of per capita GDP between the two country groups. In the 45 LDCs for which data are available, the average growth rate of per capita GDP of 2.6 per annum in 2000–2002 translates into an additional $15 per capita per year in real terms, whereas in the group of other developing countries, the per capita growth rate of 1.8 per cent per annum translates into an additional $54 per capita per year.

There is also much divergence amongst the LDCs. GDP growth decelerated between 2000 and 2001 in all seven Asian LDCs for which data are available. Comparatively, only one-third of the African LDCs experienced GDP deceleration between 2000 and 2001. Globally, out of the 45 LDCs for which real GDP data are available, more than half (24 LDCs) displayed either negative or slow per capita growth rate in the period 2000–2002. In contrast, less than one third (14 LDCs) demonstrated a per capita growth performance exceeding 3 per cent per annum. Only seven LDCs, namely Angola, Bhutan, Chad, Eritrea,

The improvement in the economic growth rate within the LDCs occurred as that of other developing countries slowed down.

However, the higher growth rates in the LDCs have not yet been sufficient to reduce the increasing gap in the level of per capita GDP between the two country groups.

CHART 1. REAL GDP GROWTH RATES IN LDCs, LOW-, MIDDLE- AND HIGH-INCOME COUNTRIES AND WORLD IN 2000, 2001 AND 2002

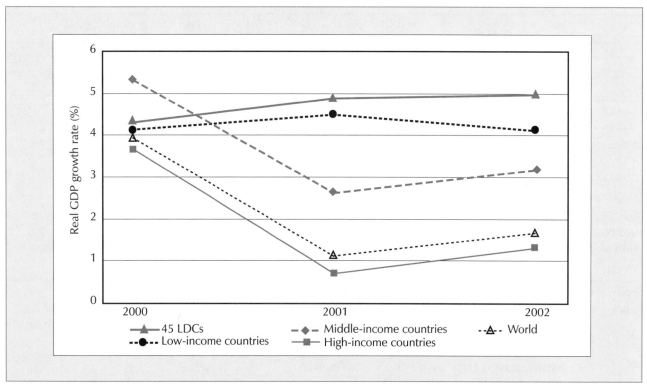

Source and notes: See table 1.

Mozambique, Rwanda and Sudan, achieved the 7 per cent growth target set under the Programme of Action for the Least Developed Countries for the Decade 2001–2010 (United Nations, 2001: para. 6) (see table 2).

TABLE 2. REAL GDP AND REAL GDP PER CAPITA GROWTH RATES OF LDCS, BY COUNTRY, 1998–2000 AND 2000–2002

(Average annual growth rate, percentage)

	Real GDP growth		Real GDP per capita growth	
	1998–2000	*2000–2002*	*1998–2000*	*2000–2002*
High-growth economies				
Mozambique	4.5	11.8	2.3	9.5
Angola	3.2	9.9	0.3	6.8
Eritrea	-5.9	9.5	-8.5	6.7
Chad	0.8	9.7	-1.9	6.6
Sudan	6.3	8.7	4.3	6.5
Rwanda	6.8	8.0	3.8	5.0
Bhutan	7.0	7.3	3.9	4.4
Ethiopia	5.3	6.4	2.7	4.0
Sierra Leone	-2.3	5.8	-4.3	3.8
United Rep. of Tanzania	4.3	5.8	1.9	3.5
Cambodia	6.3	5.4	4.0	3.4
Mali	5.2	5.5	2.8	3.1
Burkina Faso	4.0	5.6	1.5	3.1
Bangladesh	5.4	4.8	3.6	3.0
Moderate-growth economies				
Lao PDR	6.6	5.3	4.1	2.9
Uganda	5.5	5.5	2.7	2.8
Lesotho	2.7	3.9	1.3	2.6
Benin	5.2	5.1	2.5	2.5
Samoa	4.7	3.7	3.8	2.5
Zambia	2.9	4.0	0.7	2.1
Liberia	21.6	4.7	18.3	2.1
Slow-growth economies				
Mauritania	4.6	4.9	1.1	1.8
Guinea	3.0	4.1	0.7	1.8
Niger	-1.0	5.0	-4.3	1.7
Senegal	5.4	4.1	2.6	1.6
Burundi	-0.9	3.4	-2.8	1.5
Central African Republic	2.9	2.8	1.4	1.3
Cape Verde	7.7	3.6	4.9	1.0
Sao Tome and Principe	2.7	3.0	0.5	0.9
Maldives	6.0	2.9	3.5	0.6
Togo	0.2	2.8	-2.8	0.2
Comoros	0.4	2.5	-2.1	0.0
Regressing economies				
Kiribati	0.2	2.2	-2.4	0.0
Yemen	4.3	3.0	1.4	-0.1
Gambia	6.0	2.6	2.7	-0.1
Nepal	5.3	2.0	2.8	-0.3
Djibouti	1.5	1.6	-0.5	-0.3
Equatorial Guinea	28.6	0.8	25.2	-1.8
Malawi	2.9	0.1	0.7	-1.9
Dem. Rep. of the Congo	-5.7	0.5	-8.3	-2.2
Vanuatu	0.1	-1.1	-2.7	-3.2
Haiti	1.7	-1.3	-0.4	-3.3
Guinea-Bissau	7.6	-2.0	5.4	-4.1
Madagascar	4.7	-3.4	1.5	-6.1
Solomon Islands	-7.6	-7.0	-10.0	-9.6

Source: UNCTAD secretariat estimates, based on World Bank, *World Development Indicators,* online data.

Note: Real GDP is measured in constant 1995 dollars. The countries are ranked by average annual growth rate of real GDP per capita, 2000–2002. No data were available for Afghanistan, Myanmar, Somalia or Tuvalu.

During the period 2000–2002, only seven LDCs achieved the 7 per cent growth target set under the Programme of Action for the Least Developed Countries for the Decade 2001–2010.

World Bank data indicate that in terms of both GDP and GDP per capita, and in spite of a higher population growth rate, African LDCs grew faster than Asian and island LDCs during 2000–2002, and also faster than other developing countries. Furthermore, they experienced the highest growth acceleration between 1998–2000 and 2000–2002. In real per capita terms, GDP increased from 1.2 per cent per annum in 1998–2000 to 2.8 per cent per annum in 2000–2002 in African LDCs, whereas it slowed down from 3.4 per cent to 2.5 per cent in Asian LDCs and from 0.5 per cent per annum to -0.8 per cent per annum in island LDCs over the same periods. The contrast between Africa and Asia reflects the fact that the proportion of African LDCs in which GDP contracted between 2000 and 2001 was smaller than that of Asian LDCs. The negative per capita growth rate displayed by small island LDCs in 2000–2002 reflects the great vulnerability of small island States, and particularly that of their tourism sector, to the effects of terrorism on the volume of airline travel. In Asian LDCs and unlike in other LDC groups, real GDP continued to decelerate between 2001 and 2002, which coincided with the outbreak of the Severe Acute Respiratory Syndrome (SARS) in the Asian region.

Improvements in the real GDP growth rate from 1998–2000 to 2000–2002 are evident in LDCs whose exports are agricultural commodities and also minerals. In the former group the annual GDP growth rate increased from 4.2 per cent to 5.5 per cent, whilst in the latter it increased from 0.2 per cent to 3.3 per cent. LDC oil exporters also experienced a strong real GDP annual growth — 7.5 per cent — in 2000–2002, largely because of Angola and Sudan. But economic growth in LDCs whose major exports are manufactures and/or services slowed down from 5.2 per cent per annum in 1998–2000 to 4.2 per cent per annum in 2000–2002 (see table 3).

African LDCs grew faster than Asian and island LDCs during 2000–2002.

The improved performance of non-oil commodity-exporting LDCs in the period 2000–2002 is a notable feature of recent economic trends. However, a critical question is the sustainability of recent trends. Many LDCs have in the past been characterized by growth instability. Moreover, in the 1990s real GDP growth was over five times more unstable in African than in Asian LDCs and between two and three times more unstable in agriculture-dependent LDCs than in manufactures and/or services-exporting LDCs. Growth rates in mineral-exporting LDCs were between three and four times more unstable than those of manufactures and/or service-exporting LDCs, while those of oil-exporting LDCs were about five times more unstable (see table 3).

TABLE 3. REAL GDP GROWTH RATE IN LDCS CLASSIFIED BY EXPORT SPECIALIZATION, 1998–2000 AND 2000–2002, AND STANDARD DEVIATION, 1991–1999

| | Average annual growth rate (%) | | % point difference | Standard deviation[a] |
| | *1998–2000* | *2000–2002* | | *1991–1999* |
	(a)	*(b)*	*(b-a)*	*(% point)*
Non-oil primary-commodity exporters	2.9	4.9	1.9	2.5
Of which:				
Agricultural exporters	4.2	5.5	1.3	2.3
Mineral exporters	0.2	3.3	3.0	3.1
Oil exporters	5.4	7.5	2.1	4.7
Manufactures and/or services exporters	5.2	4.2	-0.9	0.9
Least developed countries	4.4	4.9	0.5	1.9

Source: UNCTAD secretariat estimates, based on World Bank, *World Development Indicators,* online data.

Note: For the classification of LDCs by export specialization, see the annex to the chapter.

  a   As proxy for instability of real average annual GDP growth rate.

In short, the GDP data of LDCs indicate that on average the LDC sub-groups which performed best in 2000–2002 and which contributed most to the LDCs' growth acceleration are those which in the 1990s demonstrated highest GDP growth instability. In this regard, the results in relation to the aggregate GDP performance of LDCs in 2000–2002, although immensely encouraging, should not lead to premature conclusions.

Growth sustainability remains central to the analysis of LDCs' economic performance. In this regard, it is notable that between 2000 and 2002 the ratio of gross capital formation to GDP increased in three quarters of the 28 LDCs for which data on domestic investment and domestic savings are available (table 4). For this group of countries, the ratio of gross capital formation to GDP increased from 20.2 per cent in 2000 (the same level as in 1998) to 23 per cent in 2002. But only seven LDCs (Burkina Faso, Chad, Eritrea, Guinea, Lesotho, Mozambique and Sao Tome and Principe) exceeded the 25 per cent investment target of the Programme of Action for the Least Developed Countries for the Decade 2001–2010 in 2002 (United Nations, 2001: para. 6). Between 2000 and 2002, the average domestic savings rate for the 28 LDCs increased, but only slightly, from 4.4 per cent to 4.8 per cent. The savings rate remains very low in most LDCs, and in seven LDCs it is recorded as being negative in 2002. Thus

The LDCs which performed best in 2000–2002 and which contributed most to the LDCs' growth acceleration are those which in the 1990s demonstrated highest GDP growth instability.

TABLE 4. GROSS CAPITAL FORMATION AND GROSS DOMESTIC SAVINGS IN LDCs, 1998–2002

(As a percentage of GDP)

	Gross capital formation			Gross domestic savings			Resource gap[a]		
	1998	2000	2002	1998	2000	2002	1998	2000	2002
Bangladesh	21.6	23.0	24.0	16.7	17.8	19.4	4.9	5.2	4.7
Benin	17.0	18.9	19.2	6.6	5.9	6.8	10.4	13.0	12.4
Burkina Faso	30.1	25.5	26.0	12.8	7.3	10.8	17.3	18.2	15.2
Burundi	8.8	9.1	7.9	-2.9	-5.7	-4.5	11.6	14.7	12.4
Central African Republic	13.5	10.8	14.4	5.3	7.8	9.9	8.2	3.1	4.5
Chad	17.4	17.0	54.6	4.1	1.5	3.8	13.3	15.5	50.8
Comoros	17.9	13.1	15.7	-4.7	-1.4	-0.3	22.6	14.5	16.0
Dem. Rep. of the Congo	20.0	4.2	7.1	16.9	5.4	4.0	3.1	-1.2	3.1
Eritrea	36.9	35.7	46.7	-31.1	-28.4	-24.2	68.0	64.0	70.8
Ethiopia	17.2	15.3	20.2	7.7	-0.1	1.9	9.4	15.3	18.3
Gambia	18.4	17.0	19.0	2.8	2.7	3.8	15.6	14.3	15.2
Guinea	18.0	21.7	25.6	14.3	16.6	21.3	3.7	5.1	4.3
Lesotho	47.1	39.5	36.1	-27.0	-20.2	-5.8	74.1	59.7	42.0
Madagascar	14.8	15.0	11.8	7.0	7.7	5.9	7.8	7.3	5.8
Malawi	13.5	12.5	9.0	7.5	0.5	-16.0	6.0	12.1	24.9
Mauritania	19.0	31.6	24.7	5.0	17.5	9.0	14.0	14.1	15.7
Mozambique	24.2	36.4	45.7	10.8	14.0	21.6	13.5	22.4	24.0
Nepal	24.8	24.2	24.1	13.8	15.0	13.3	11.1	9.1	10.8
Niger	11.3	10.8	13.3	2.7	3.3	4.1	8.6	7.5	9.2
Rwanda	14.8	17.5	18.8	-2.8	1.4	1.9	17.6	16.1	17.0
Sao Tome and Principe	35.8	43.5	44.0	-7.0	-3.6	-1.4	42.8	47.1	45.4
Senegal	18.6	19.8	20.8	12.9	10.8	13.0	5.7	9.0	7.8
Sierra Leone	5.5	8.0	17.4	-1.7	-8.1	-8.8	7.2	16.1	26.2
Togo	20.8	20.9	21.7	5.5	4.1	4.7	15.3	16.8	17.0
Uganda	16.2	19.8	22.4	4.1	6.9	6.4	12.1	12.9	16.0
United Rep. of Tanzania	13.8	17.6	17.4	-0.8	9.2	9.3	14.7	8.4	8.1
Yemen	32.1	17.6	18.6	11.5	28.3	21.8	20.6	-10.7	-3.2
Zambia	16.4	18.7	18.0	3.9	8.3	2.4	12.5	10.4	15.6
LDCs[b]	**20.2**	**20.2**	**23.0**	**3.3**	**4.4**	**4.8**	**16.9**	**15.7**	**18.2**

Source: UNCTAD secretariat estimates, based on World Bank, *World Development Indicators 2003*, online data.

    a   Measured by gross capital formation % GDP less gross domestic savings % GDP.

    b   Simple average based on the 28 LDCs for which data were available for the 1998–2002 period.

reliance on external finance remains high, and indeed slightly increased between 2000 and 2002.

Finally, it is worth noting that the good or bad economic performance of individual LDCs during 2000–2002 is not associated with civil conflict in the way one usually expects. That is to say, conflict is not always associated with stagnation and regression. According to the Uppsala/PRIO data base on armed conflict, 15 LDCs were affected by civil conflict in 2000 and in 2001, and 12 in 2002.[1] But six of the affected countries (five for all three years) were amongst the 14 "high-growth" LDCs during 2000–2002. Moreover, if one adds the inter-State conflict between Eritrea and Ethiopia, which was still active in 2000, half of the high-growth economies were conflict-affected during this period.

This, of course, does not mean that the destabilizing effects of conflict should be played down. The economies of some of the regressing and slow-growth LDCs during the period, notably Burundi, Central African Republic, the Democratic Republic of the Congo, Guinea, Nepal and Senegal, were adversely affected by civil conflict. Nor does it imply that the incidence of civil conflicts is not an important development issue for the LDCs. In 2002, 12 out of 20 of all civil conflicts in developing countries (i.e. 60 per cent) occurred in the LDCs. However, it does show that the relationship between economic performance and civil conflict is a complex one, particularly in countries that have prior experience of conflict and in which conflict is localized in particular parts of the country. This issue will be examined more closely in relation to trade–poverty links in the second part of the Report.

B. Trends in external trade

The growth rate of merchandise exports of the LDCs as a group slowed down in 2000–2002 after a major surge during 1998–2000. The divergence amongst LDCs in terms of their export performance continued. The LDCs that export manufactures experienced the steadiest growth. The merchandise exports of LDCs that export agricultural commodities also recovered after a decline in 1998–2000. But this increase was founded on the improved performance of a few countries, and the increase for agricultural exporters as a whole in 2000–2002 was not sufficient to offset the decline in 1998–2000. World price instability remained a significant influence on the export performance of all primary-commodity-exporting LDCs.

According to UNCTAD statistics, merchandise exports of the LDCs as a group increased from $26.1 billion in 1998 to a record level of $37.8 billion in 2002 (see table 5). In nominal terms this represents a 44.5 per cent increase. In comparison, merchandise exports increased by 15.3 per cent in other developing countries (without China) between 1998 and 2002.[2]

In interpreting these figures it is important to recognize that a large proportion of the total exports of LDCs come from a few countries and that amongst the LDCs export performance is very mixed. The differences in performance are closely related to what products are exported (see the annex to this chapter for classification by export specialization). For the period from 1998 to 2002, whilst exports for the LDCs as a group increased spectacularly, the merchandise exports decreased by 6 per cent in nominal terms in LDCs exporting agricultural products and by 16.6 per cent in mineral exporters. The merchandise exports of LDCs exporting manufactures and/or services increased by 43 per cent and those of oil exporters by 134.4 per cent.

Merchandise exports of the LDCs as a group increased from $26.1 billion in 1998 to a record level of $37.8 billion in 2002. In nominal terms this represents a 44.5 per cent increase.

There is also a significant contrast between export performance in 1998–2000 and in 2000–2002. LDCs' merchandise exports increased by 36.7 per cent between 1998 and 2000, but then by only 5.7 per cent between 2000 and 2002. The rapid expansion of trade in the late 1990s was driven by oil exporters, whose exports more than doubled in value terms between 1998 and 2000. This rapid increase in oil exports mainly reflected the increase in world oil prices and the start-up of Sudan's oil production. The merchandise exports of LDCs exporting manufactures and/or services increased by 25.5 per cent between the same years, but those of non-oil primary commodity exporters contracted by 19.6 per cent. The impressive export performance of oil- exporting LDCs was followed by a slight contraction in 2000–2002. The merchandise exports of manufacture-/service-exporting LDCs continued to increase but at half the 1998–2000 pace, whilst the exports of non-fuel primary-commodity-exporting LDCs reversed the earlier contraction. The 11.4 per cent increase between 2000 and 2002 was not, however, sufficient to bring exports back to the 1998 level.

With regard to the period 2000–2002, the concentration of exports amongst LDCs is apparent in the fact that during that period 56 per cent of total LDC merchandise exports originated from only five LDCs, namely Angola, Bangladesh, Equatorial Guinea, Sudan and Yemen. Four of these are oil exporters, and Bangladesh is the largest economy in the LDC group.

The differential performance amongst LDCs is evident in the fact that the nominal value of exports declined between 2000 and 2002 in 23 LDCs. Amongst the 20 LDCs whose major exports are agricultural products, total merchandise exports declined in 11 countries. Agricultural exporters that did

During the period 2000–2002, 56 per cent of total LDC merchandise exports originated from only five LDCs.

The differential performance amongst LDCs is evident in the fact that the nominal value of exports declined between 2000 and 2002 in 23 LDCs.

TABLE 5. LDCS' EXPORTS, IMPORTS AND BALANCE IN MERCHANDISE TRADE, 1998–2002

	1998	2000	2001	2002	1998–2002	1998–2000	2000–2002
		($, millions)				(% change)[a]	
Merchandise exports							
LDCs	26 140	35 737	35 755	37 780	44.5	36.7	5.7
Of which:							
Non-oil primary-commodity exporters	9 653	7 763	8 547	8 648	-10.4	-19.6	11.4
Agricultural exporters	5 646	4 714	5 025	5 305	-6.0	-16.5	12.5
Mineral exporters	4 007	3 049	3 522	3 343	-16.6	-23.9	9.6
Oil exporters	6 076	14 904	13 040	14 242	134.4	145.3	-4.4
Manufactures and/or services exporters	10 411	13 070	14 168	14 890	43.0	25.5	13.9
Merchandise imports							
LDCs	38 860	41 504	43 863	43 494	11.9	6.8	4.8
Of which:							
Non-oil primary-commodity exporters	13 977	13 189	14 784	14 281	2.2	-5.6	8.3
Agricultural exporters	10 128	9 600	10 903	10 388	2.6	-5.2	8.2
Mineral exporters	3 849	3 589	3 881	3 893	1.1	-6.8	8.5
Oil exporters	6 488	7 368	7 787	9 316	43.6	13.6	26.4
Manufactures and/or services exporters	18 395	20 947	21 292	19 897	8.2	13.9	-5.0
Trade balance							
LDCs	-12 720	-5 767	-8 108	-5 714	-55.1	-54.7	-0.9
Of which:							
Non-oil primary-commodity exporters	-4 324	-5 426	-6 237	-5 633	30.3	25.5	3.8
Agricultural exporters	-4 482	-4 886	-5 878	-5 083	13.4	9.0	4.0
Mineral exporters	158	-540	-359	-550	-448.1	-441.8	1.9
Oil exporters	-412	7 536	5 253	4 926	-1 295.6	-1 929.1	-34.6
Manufactures and/or services exporters	-7 984	-7 877	-7 124	-5 007	-37.3	-1.3	-36.4

Source: UNCTAD secretariat estimates, based on UNCTAD, *Handbook of Statistics 2003*.

a Percentage change in trade values between initial year and end year.

badly in nominal terms included Burundi, Eritrea, Ethiopia and Guinea-Bissau. Burkina Faso, Kiribati, Malawi, Mali, Togo and the United Republic of Tanzania, in contrast, did well, with exports increasing by at least 6 per cent per year in nominal terms during 2000–2002. Amongst the 18 LDCs whose major exports are some combination of manufactures and/or services, the nominal value of merchandise exports declined between 2000 and 2002 in only seven countries — Bangladesh, Gambia, Haiti, the Lao People's Democratic Republic, Madagascar, Nepal and Vanuatu.

Data on the trade balance indicate that the aggregate LDC trade deficit improved by 55.1 per cent between 1998 and 2002. This improvement mostly took place, however, between 1998 and 2000 and was mainly driven by the spectacular export performance of oil-exporting LDCs. The average trade deficit increased by 30.3 per cent in the non-oil primary-commodity-dependent LDCs between 1998 and 2002 and these countries also displayed the lowest import growth (in nominal terms) between these years. The trade deficit of LDCs exporting manufacture and/or services narrowed by 37.3 per cent between the same years.

Trends and instability in world commodity prices remain important determinants of trade and economic performance in LDCs, and in primary-commodity-dependent LDCs in particular.

Trends and instability in world commodity prices remain important determinants of trade and economic performance in LDCs, and in primary-commodity-dependent LDCs in particular. UNCTAD data on world primary commodity prices of importance to LDCs show price firming for cocoa and fish meal between 2000 and 2002 (see table 6). But world prices declined sharply over the same period for aluminium, coffee, copper, cotton, sugar and tea, and, to a lesser extent, for tobacco. World oil prices continue to be relatively high but volatile.

TABLE 6. PRICE INDICES OF SELECTED PRIMARY COMMODITIES OF IMPORTANCE TO LDCs

(Index, 1997 = 100)

	Price indices				Standard deviation[a]
	1997	*2000*	*2001*	*2002*	*1980–2002*
All food	100	69	69	67	16
Coffee (Arabicas)	100	46	33	33	20
Coffee (Robustas)	100	53	35	38	48
Cocoa	100	55	67	110	29
Tea	100	104	83	75	13
Sugar	100	72	76	61	44
Fish meal	100	68	80	100	16
Agricultural raw materials	100	82	80	74	13
Cotton	100	75	61	58	19
Non-coniferous woods	100	97	95	100	19
Tobacco	100	85	85	78	11
Minerals, ores and metals	100	92	83	81	15
Aluminium	100	97	90	84	21
Iron ore	100	96	100	99	8
Copper, grade A	100	80	69	68	21
Copper, wire bars	100	83	72	71	21
Gold	100	84	82	94	23
Memo item: Crude petroleum	100	147	128	130	35

Source: UNCTAD secretariat estimates, based on UNCTAD *Commodity Price Bulletin,* various issues.
    a   As proxy for instability of price indices.

C. Trends in external finance

1. OVERALL PICTURE

In nominal terms, following a slump in 2000, aggregate net resource flows to LDCs as a group increased significantly in 2001 and 2002. This surge was successively driven by net FDI inflows to LDCs in 2001 and by grants in 2002. As a consequence, aggregate net transfers to LDCs as a group increased by over 43 per cent between 2000 and 2002. But profit remittances are much higher than they were in the second half of the 1990s, and there are signs that the multilateral debt problem, which the HIPC Initiative was meant to resolve, may be starting to build up again.

According to the latest World Bank estimates,[3] aggregate net resource flows to LDCs reached a record level of $16.7 billion in 2002. This was up from $12.4 billion in 2000, which also was a record low since 1990 (table 7). Aggregate net resource flows increased by $3.2 billion between 2000 and 2001, and by an additional $1.1 billion between 2001 and 2002.

In 2001, the driving force of this upsurge in long-term capital inflows to LDCs was a $2 billion increase in FDI inflows, which had previously declined by $2.3 billion between 1999 and 2000. As a result, 63 per cent of the additional long-term capital flows to LDCs in 2001 were attributable to recovery in FDI inflows.

In nominal terms, following a slump in 2000, aggregate net resource flows to LDCs as a group increased significantly in 2001 and 2002...and reached a record level of $16.7 billion in 2002 — up from $12.4 billion in 2000.

TABLE 7. LONG-TERM NET CAPITAL FLOWS TO LDCS, BY TYPE OF FLOW, AND AGGREGATE NET TRANSFERS, 1990–1994, 1995–1999, 2000, 2001 AND 2002

($ millions)

	1990–1994	1995–1999	2000	2001	2002
	Annual average				
Aggregate net resource flows	**14 249.4**	**13 488.3**	**12 368.3**	**15 611.0**	**16 739.0**
Official net resource flows	12 616.7	9 869.8	9 168.9	9 771.3	11 634.5
Grants, excluding technical cooperation	9 005.8	7 413.6	7 331.0	7 235.2	8 811.1
Official debt flows	3 611.1	2 456.2	1 838.1	2 536.4	2 822.8
Bilateral	578.9	-245.5	-589.7	-372.0	-362.1
Bilateral concessional	635.3	-162.2	-485.0	-373.2	-302.8
Multilateral	3 032.2	2 701.7	2 427.8	2 908.4	3 184.9
Multilateral concessional	3 052.2	2 818.1	2 547.4	3 005.7	3 398.1
Private net resource flows	1 632.7	3 618.6	3 199.4	5 839.7	5 104.5
Foreign direct investment	1 262.9	3 525.5	3 564.9	5 608.2	5 160.8
Portfolio equity flows	28.9	-10.7	3.9	-1.7	-
Private debt flows	341.0	103.8	-369.4	233.2	-56.3
Private non-guaranteed	-18.2	-10.9	-49.4	49.2	-51.2
Private, publicly guaranteed	359.2	114.7	-320.0	184.0	-5.1
Aggregate net transfers	**12 090.1**	**10 765.7**	**8 753.0**	**11 867.6**	**12 534.1**
Interest payments on long-term debt	1 071.1	1 170.1	977.0	814.9	1 134.6
Profit remittances on FDI	1 088.3	1 552.6	2 638.2	2 928.7	3 070.4
Memo item:					
IMF, net flows	-137.1	179.0	0.6	240.4	448.1
IMF, concessional net flows	-448.1	-142.8	-57.7	-125.7	-149.1
IMF, non-concessional net flows	311.0	321.8	58.3	366.0	597.2
Debt forgiveness or reduction	-1 370.2	-2 713.3	-916.1	-3 300.0	-3 301.6

Source: UNCTAD secretariat estimates, based on World Bank, *Global Development Finance 2003,* online data.

Note: No data were available for Afghanistan, Kiribati or Tuvalu.

The increase in profit remittances on FDI is a significant development.

Whereas private net resource flows to LDCs increased by 82.5 per cent between 2000 and 2001, official net resource flows increased by only 6.6 per cent, with grants actually declining by 1.3 per cent. But this impressive surge in private net resource flows was not sustained in 2002. This was a result of the fall in FDI flows and also, to a lesser extent, in private debt flows, which for the majority of the LDCs remain either insignificant or negative. In contrast to private flows, official net resource flows increased by 19.1 per cent between 2001 and 2002, owing to a 21.8 per cent increase in grants worth an additional $1.6 billion, and to a 11.3 per cent increase in official debt flows, driven by an increase in multilateral concessional loans.

As a result of these offsetting shifts in the composition of aggregate net resource flows in 2001 and 2002, the structure of long-term capital inflows to LDCs has remained rather stable. Between 1997–1999 and 2000–2002 the share of official capital flows increased slightly from 66 to 69 per cent of aggregate net resource flows, whereas the share of private net resource flows decreased slightly from 34 to 31 per cent. FDI remained the main component of private net resource flows, and portfolio equity flows remained negligible for most LDCs.

In 2000–2002 the sum of interest payments on long-term debt plus profit remittances on FDI represented 50 per cent of grants (excluding technical cooperation) disbursed to LDCs and 23 per cent of grants disbursed to non-oil LDCs.

It is also notable that whereas the share of FDI inflows in aggregate net resource flows to LDCs remained constant between 1997–1999 and 2000–2002 at 32 per cent, the share of profit remittances on FDI within aggregate net transfers increased dramatically from 14.2 per cent in 1997–1999 to over 26.4 per cent in 2000–2002.[4] This is mainly a result of FDI in oil-exporting LDCs. If these LDCs are omitted, the contribution of profit remittances on FDI to aggregate net transfers increased from 5.7 per cent in 1997–1999 to 8.3 per cent in 2000–2002. Over the period 1990–1999, this share was equivalent to about 12 per cent in the group of LDCs as a whole and to 4.8 per cent in non-oil-exporting LDCs. Nevertheless, the increase in profit remittances on FDI is a significant development. In relation to grants, this implies that on average in 2000–2002, 37 per cent of the amount received in the form of grants by the group of LDCs (12 per cent of the amount received by non-oil-exporting LDCs) left the countries through profit remittances on FDI. In the 1990s, this ratio was equivalent to 17 per cent in the group of LDCs (6.9 per cent in the group of non-oil-exporting LDCs). In 2000–2002 the sum of interest payments on long-term debt plus profit remittances on FDI represented 50 per cent of grants (excluding technical cooperation) disbursed to LDCs and 23 per cent of grants disbursed to non-oil LDCs.

Recent trends in aggregate net resource flows imply that LDCs have been receiving increasing shares of aggregate net resource flows to all developing countries (see table 8). The LDC share of long-term capital flows to all

TABLE 8. LDCs' SHARE OF CAPITAL FLOWS TO ALL DEVELOPING COUNTRIES, BY TYPE OF FLOW, 1990–1996, 1997–1999 AND 2000–2002

(Percentage)

	1990–1996	1997–1999	2000–2002	2000	2001	2002
		Period average				
Aggregate net resource flows	7.5	4.7	7.4	5.7	7.5	9.5
Official net resource flows	24.2	21.8	34.0	27.4	27.7	54.9
Grants, excluding technical cooperation	29.2	26.0	26.6	25.5	25.9	28.2
Private net resource flows	1.3	1.9	2.8	1.8	3.4	3.3
Foreign direct investment, net inflows	2.1	2.6	2.9	2.2	3.2	3.5

Source and note: See table 7.

developing countries increased from 4.8 per cent in 1997–1999 to 7.6 per cent in 2000–2002. There was a particularly marked increase in the share of LDCs in multilateral debt flows to all developing countries, which increased from 13.5 per cent in 1997–1999 to 31.1 per cent in 2000–2002. In comparison, the share of LDCs in grants disbursed to all developing countries increased only slightly — from 26 per cent in 1997–1999 to 26.6 per cent in 2000–2002. At the level of private flows, the share of LDCs increased from 1.9 per cent in 1997–1999 to 2.8 per cent in 2000–2002.

The increase in the LDC share of multilateral debt flows reflects a sharp decline in such flows to other developing countries (by $14.7 billion) between 2001 and 2002. The increase in the LDC share of private capital flows is mostly attributable to the surge of FDI inflows into LDCs in 2001 and to the fact that between 2001 and 2002 FDI decreased at a slower pace in LDCs (-8 per cent in nominal terms) than in other developing countries (-15.6 per cent).

There was a particularly marked increase in the share of LDCs in multilateral debt flows to all developing countries. In comparison, the share of LDCs in grants disbursed to all developing countries increased only slightly.

2. TRENDS IN AID FLOWS

A more detailed account of aid flows in LDCs can be obtained from statistics compiled by OECD's Development Assistance Committee (DAC). These data show that in both nominal and real terms net ODA flows into LDCs grew in 2002 for the third consecutive year. In 1999 aid inflows were $19.1 per capita (in current terms), which was the lowest level of the 1990s. In 2002, this had risen to $25.1 per capita (see table 9).

In real terms, aid inflows increased on average by 13.4 per cent per annum during the period 1999–2002. Without Afghanistan, a large recipient of aid in 2002, the increase is still an impressive 11 per cent per annum. In real terms this brings the 2002 level of net ODA inflows to LDCs to a level almost comparable with that of the early 1990s. However, in real per capita terms, net aid inflows to

In real terms, aid inflows increased on average by 13.4 per cent per annum during the period 1999–2002.

TABLE 9. NET ODA INFLOWS INTO LDCs FROM ALL DONORS, 1990–1994, 1995–1999, 2000, 2001 AND 2002

	1990–1994	1995–1999	2000	2001	2002
	Annual average				
Net ODA (current $, millions)					
LDCs	16 578.9	13 878.6	12 449.6	13 633.0	17 282.2
of which:					
Afghanistan	259.6	184.8	140.9	408.2	1 285.0
Other LDCs	16 319.3	13 693.8	12 308.7	13 224.8	15 997.2
Net ODA per capita (current $)					
LDCs	30.5	22.7	18.9	20.2	25.1
of which:					
Afghanistan	13.7	7.8	5.3	15.0	46.0
Other LDCs	31.1	23.3	19.5	20.4	24.2
Net ODA (2001 prices, $ millions)					
LDCs	15 590.9	12 055.3	12 086.8	13 633.0	16 477.6
of which:					
Afghanistan	257.7	158.9	137.8	408.2	1 224.3
Other LDCs	15 333.2	11 896.4	11 949.0	13 224.8	15 253.2
Net ODA per capita (2001 prices, $)					
LDCs	28.7	19.7	18.3	20.2	23.9
of which:					
Afghanistan	13.6	6.7	5.2	15.0	43.8
Other LDCs	29.3	20.2	18.9	20.4	23.1

Source: UNCTAD secretariat estimates, based on OECD/DAC, *International Development Statistics,* online data.

In real per capita terms, net aid inflows to LDCs in 2002 were still 16.7 per cent lower than in the early 1990s.

LDCs in 2002 were still 16.7 per cent lower than in the early 1990s ($23.9 in 2002 versus $28.7 in 1990–1994).

Since 2000, the donor community has increasingly concentrated aid inflows on LDC economies (see chart 2). In 2002 LDCs received 27.9 per cent of total ODA disbursements as compared with 23.4 per cent in 1999. Moreover, within the LDC group aid inflows have also become increasingly concentrated. Aid inflows actually declined in 13 LDCs in the period 1999–2002 (see table 10). In contrast, they increased by at least 20 per cent per annum in 16 LDCs. When

CHART 2. ODA DISBURSEMENTS TO LDCS AS SHARE OF TOTAL ODA DISBURSEMENTS, 1990–2002

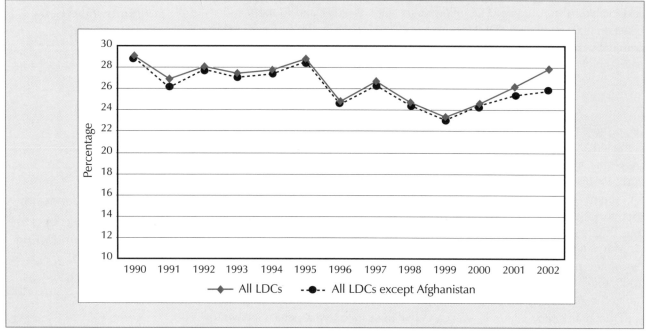

Source: See table 9.

TABLE 10. REAL ODA GROWTH RATE PER ANNUM IN LDCS, BY COUNTRY, 1999–2002

Less than 2.5%		Between 2.5% and 15%		More than 15%	
Liberia	-20.7	Maldives	2.6	Yemen	15.1
Central African Republic	-16.9	Uganda	3.1	Myanmar	18.3
Haiti	-15.9	Angola	3.3	Niger	20.0
Solomon Islands	-12.1	Nepal	3.7	Mauritania	20.9
Togo	-11.9	Benin	4.2	Comoros	21.0
Cape Verde	-11.3	Madagascar	4.5	Eritrea	21.0
Vanuatu	-9.9	Bhutan	7.0	Somalia	22.2
Bangladesh	-7.9	Burkina Faso	8.9	Cambodia	22.3
Zambia	-5.6	Sudan	9.9	Gambia	22.8
Malawi	-4.5	Guinea	10.0	Samoa	26.0
Equatorial Guinea	-4.2	Mali	10.3	Ethiopia	31.3
Senegal	-3.0	United Rep. of Tanzania	10.8	Burundi	34.2
Rwanda	-1.1	Chad	12.5	Tuvalu	34.2
Lao PDR	0.0			Mozambique	34.8
Kiribati	0.1			Lesotho	38.5
Sao Tome and Principe	0.3			Sierra Leone	71.0
Djibouti	1.9			Dem. Rep. of the Congo	81.2
Guinea-Bissau	2.1			Afghanistan	116.7

Source: See table 9.

the latter are omitted, it can be seen that in real per capita terms aid inflows into LDCs increased during the period 1999–2002 by only 1.8 per cent per annum.

Breaking down aid inflows into grant and non-grant disbursements, OECD data show that in real terms grant disbursements to LDCs represented 82 per cent of net aid inflows in 1999–2002. Grants increased by an average annual rate of 10.6 per cent during these years (7.8 per cent without Afghanistan). Loans to LDCs are driven by multilateral concessional loans. These increased by an annual rate of 27.2 per cent during 1999–2002. This needs to be carefully monitored as it implies increasing multilateral debt service obligations.

Since 2000, the donor community has increasingly concentrated aid inflows on LDC economies.

It is possible to have an idea of the sectoral distribution of aid by using OECD/DAC data on ODA commitments. These data clearly indicate that bilateral aid commitments by DAC donors, which were equivalent to about 58 per cent of total ODA commitments to the LDCs in 2000-2002, and multilateral aid commitments are increasingly concentrated on social infrastructure and services. This has, however, been done at the expense of economic infrastructure (see table 11). Between 1994–1996 and 2000–2002, the share of ODA commitments from multilateral institutions to economic infrastructure decreased from 23.3 per cent to 19.6`per cent, whilst the share of commitments going to social infrastructure and services increased from 28.8 per cent to 36 per cent. Bilateral ODA commitments to LDCs' social infrastructure and services increased in real terms by an average 19 per cent per annum in 2000–2002, whereas commitments to the LDCs' economic infrastructure declined by an average 20.3 per cent per annum in the same years. Similarly, the share of ODA commitments to the production sector from all donors decreased from 12.8 per cent in 1994–1996 to 7.5 per cent in 2000–2002. The potential negative implications of the shift away from production sectors for the development potential and prospects of the LDCs, including their ability to reduce their level of aid dependence in the long run, need careful consideration.

During 1999–2002, grants increased by an average annual rate of 10.6 per cent and multilateral loans increased by an annual rate of 27.2 per cent

Emergency assistance continues to be an important element of aid to LDCs, and between 1999 and 2002, total commitments to emergency assistance to those countries more than doubled. This was a sharp increase in an earlier increasing trend. ODA commitments to LDCs in emergency assistance grew annually by 28.2 per cent in 1999–2002, as compared with 15.6 per cent per annum in 1990–1996. From 6.1 per cent of total ODA commitments in LDCs in 1997–1999, the share of emergency assistance reached 10.6 per cent in 2002.

TABLE 11. BILATERAL DAC AND MULTILATERAL ODA COMMITMENTS TO LDCS, BY SECTOR, 1994–1996, 1997–1999 AND 2000–2002

(Annual averages, percentage)

Sector	Bilateral DAC ODA commitments, by sector			Multilateral ODA commitments, by sector		
	1994–1996	*1997–1999*	*2000–2002*	*1994–1996*	*1997–1999*	*2000–2002*
Social infrastructure and services	29.9	34.2	35.1	28.8	28.8	36.0
Economic infrastructure, production sectors and multisector	36.6	28.5	22.6	46.9	49.9	35.4
Commodity aid/ general programme assistance	10.5	9.2	13.9	18.8	13.4	22.8
Action relating to debt	14.3	18.8	15.2	-	-	0.5
Emergency assistance	6.8	7.1	11.5	4.3	4.7	4.2
Other	1.8	2.1	1.7	1.2	3.1	1.1
Total	100.0	100.0	100.0	100.0	100.0	100.0

Source: UNCTAD secretariat estimates, based on OECD/DAC, *International Development Statistics*, online data.

At the level of bilateral ODA commitments to LDCs in 2000–2002, the share of emergency assistance (11.5 per cent) even exceeded that of economic infrastructure (8.6 per cent). During the period 2000–2002, donors committed ODA to emergency assistance in all but three LDCs, namely Samoa, Sao Tome and Principe, and Tuvalu.

Following a sharp increase in 2001, FDI flows into LDCs slightly declined in 2002.

3. TRENDS IN FDI INFLOWS

The UNCTAD FDI/TNC database indicates that following a sharp increase in 2001, FDI flows into LDCs slightly declined in 2002. In nominal terms, FDI inflows were $5.6 billion in 2001 and $5.2 billion in 2002.

FDI inflows remain highly concentrated (see table 12). The four oil-exporting LDCs — Angola, Equatorial Guinea, Sudan and Yemen — absorbed no less than 45.5 per cent of the total FDI inflows in 2002. If Chad (which is now receiving FDI to develop its infrastructure for oil exporting) is added, these five oil-exporting countries received 62.7 per cent of the total FDI inflows to LDCs in 2002. The top 10 FDI recipients (Angola, Chad, Sudan, Mozambique, Equatorial Guinea, Uganda, United Republic of Tanzania, Zambia, Myanmar and Mali) absorbed 87.3 per cent of total FDI inflows into LDCs in 2002. If the top 10 recipient LDCs are excluded, FDI inflows into the 39 remaining LDCs actually decreased from $766.1 million in 2001 to $665.6 million in 2002. Amongst the top 10, FDI inflows also actually declined between 2001 and 2002 in five countries (Angola, Equatorial Guinea, United Republic of Tanzania, Myanmar and Mali).

FDI inflows remain highly concentrated. In 2002, the top 10 FDI recipients absorbed 87.2 per cent of total FDI inflows into LDCs.

At the regional level, the data indicate a decrease in FDI inflows in 2002 in both African and Asian LDCs. In fact, FDI inflows decreased in all Asian LDCs between 2001 and 2002, except in the Lao People's Democratic Republic, where FDI inflows increased by a mere $1.5 millions, and in Bhutan, where the inflows stagnated. In African LDCs, the massive upsurge of FDI inflows into Chad in 2002 (equivalent to $900.7 million) was not sufficient to offset the regional decline. But the rate of decline in FDI inflows was more than twice as great in Asian than in African LDCs. FDI inflows decreased in 2002 by 44.5 per cent in Asian LDCs and (omitting Chad) by 20.6 per cent in African LDCs (see table 13).

TABLE 12. FDI INFLOWS TO LDCS, BY GROUP: 1995–1999, 2000, 2001 AND 2002

	1995–1999 Annual average	2000	2001	2002
In $ millions				
Total LDCs	3 570.3	3 427.3	5 628.5	5 231.8
Top ten recipient LDCs	2 649.4	2 762.7	4 862.4	4 566.2
Rest of LDCs	921.0	664.6	766.1	665.6
Oil-exporting LDCs[a]	1 087.9	1 385.0	3 800.0	2 380.8
In percentage				
Share of top ten recipient LDCs	74.2	80.6	86.4	87.3
Share of rest of LDCs	25.8	19.4	13.6	12.7
Share of oil-exporting LDCs[a]	30.5	40.4	67.5	45.5

Source: UNCTAD secretariat estimates, based on UNCTAD, FDI/TNC database.

a   Excluding Chad, which in 2002 was not classified as an oil-exporting LDC.
Had it been included, the share of oil-exporting LDCs would have reached 62.7 per cent in 2002.

TABLE 13. FDI INFLOWS INTO LDCS, BY REGION, 1995–1999, 2000, 2001 AND 2002

	Annual average 1995–1999	2000	2001	2002	1995–1999ᵃ	2000–2001	2001–2002
	($ millions)				(% change)		
Total LDCs	3 570.3	3 427.3	5 628.5	5 231.8	63.5	64.2	-7.0
Africa	2 742.8	2 703.3	5 004.3	4 876.1	80.8	85.1	-2.6
Of which:							
Chad	33.1	114.8	0.0	900.7	-18.4	..	..
Other African LDCs	2 709.7	2 588.5	5 004.3	3 975.3	83.0	93.3	-20.6
Asia	786.0	689.9	612.1	339.7	7.4	-11.3	-44.5
Pacific and the Caribbean	32.2	20.8	7.7	10.3	-26.8	-63.1	34.2

Source: UNCTAD secretariat estimates, based on UNCTAD FDI/TNC database.

Note: In this table, small island LDCs are not presented as a distinct group and are therefore included in their respective regions.
    a   Percentage change between 1995 and 1999.

D. Trends in external debt

As a result of three years of consecutive decline, external debt stock decreased significantly in the group of LDCs between 1998 and 2001. But almost half of these gains were wiped out in 2002 when the debt stock increased again.

In nominal terms the debt stock of the 46 LDCs for which data are available declined from $154.4 billion to $137.3 billion between end of 1998 and the end of 2001. This decline was mainly the result of debt forgiveness and changes in cross-country valuation. In 2002, however, and despite large amounts of debt forgiveness and a negative change in interest arrears, the total debt stock of the group of LDCs rose to $145 billion. This was mainly due to cross-country valuation effects and an increase in debt stock from multilateral concessional loans. As a consequence, the average debt stock to GDP ratio of LDCs, which had declined from 128.7 per cent in 1999 to 117 per cent in 2001, increased to 119.8 per cent in 2002 (see table 14).

The increase in debt stock was widespread amongst LDCs, occurring in 43 out of 46 countries for which data are available. Out of the 33 LDCs (of which 27 are HIPC-LDCs) in which debt stock declined between 1999 and 2001, only two experienced a further decrease in debt stock in 2002, namely the Democratic Republic of the Congo and Mali. However, data indicate that the ratio of debt to GDP declined in 28 LDCs, including 23 HIPC-LDCs, between 1999 and 2001, and that this improvement was sustained in 2002 in half of the countries, including 12 HIPC-LDCs. It should be stressed that in all but the two HIPC-LDC cases mentioned above, the sustained improvement in the debt to GDP ratio between 2001 and 2002 was attributable to an increase in the countries' current GDP.

In 2002, the total debt service payments of the group of 46 LDCs for which data are available reached a record level of almost $5.1 billion, that is an additional $0.6 billion compared with 2001. This represented 3 per cent of their combined gross national income (GNI). Not enough data on exports of goods and services, income and workers' remittances are available to provide the corresponding ratio in that year.

External debt stock decreased significantly in the group of LDCs between 1998 and 2001. But almost half of these gains were wiped out in 2002 when the debt stock increased again.

The increase in debt stock was widespread amongst LDCs in 2002.

In 2002, the total debt service payments of 46 LDCs reached a record level of almost $5.1 billion, that is an additional $0.6 billion compared with 2001.

TABLE 14. EXTERNAL DEBT BURDEN INDICATORS FOR THE LDCs, 1999–2002[a]

| | Total debt stock | | | | Total debt stock | | | Total debt service | | | Present value of debt |
| | As % of GDP[b] | | | | As % of exports of goods and services, income and workers' remittances[c] | | | | | | |
	1999	2000	2001	2002	1999	2000	2001	1999	2000	2001	2001
Afghanistan	..	..	..	..	..	..	..	..	..	..	..
Angola	169.1	106.2	98.2	89.1	191.9	113.2	142.0	27.8	21.3	27.6	138.3
Bangladesh	36.1	33.2	32.4	36.0	211.7	181.1	166.2	9.2	9.2	7.3	106.1
Benin	70.7	71.0	70.5	68.5	242.5	251.3	264.8	10.1	11.0	7.9	133.6
Bhutan	41.3	42.0	50.3	63.4	141.0	145.5	178.2	5.4	4.7	4.2	164.6
Burkina Faso	62.3	60.9	60.0	55.6	401.2	434.5	465.5	16.4	14.5	11.8	223.7
Burundi	158.4	162.5	155.2	167.5	1 791.9	1 910.9	1 842.7	45.6	37.2	39.8	1 122.1
Cambodia	76.2	78.2	79.3	79.1	225.3	169.2	161.9	2.9	2.0	1.3	137.8
Cape Verde	55.7	58.6	63.9	65.5	154.0	133.9	141.5	9.4	6.6	5.5	91.0
Central African Republic	86.5	90.0	85.0	99.1	896.1	784.6	738.4	18.4	12.9	11.9	481.5
Chad	73.0	79.2	69.0	66.2	388.4	394.0	374.5	11.0	9.3	7.9	213.1
Comoros	102.4	113.4	110.1	105.6	380.2	409.7	382.7	5.2	4.8	3.6	275.6
Dem. Rep. of the Congo	271.7	240.9	222.1	153.0	1 162.2	1 193.1	1 105.0	2.0	2.5	1.7	1 029.1
Djibouti	51.2	47.4	45.6	56.2	112.4	106.9	..	4.1	5.5	..	..
Equatorial Guinea	31.1	18.5	12.9	12.0	19.1	10.5	6.3	0.4	0.2	0.1	5.1
Eritrea	35.9	49.7	60.1	90.6	125.6	101.4	100.2	1.6	1.1	1.7	57.5
Ethiopia	86.0	86.1	91.3	108.9	566.7	520.8	577.5	15.9	13.1	18.5	295.5
Gambia	107.6	114.6	124.7	147.5	186.0	180.8	172.8	8.5	8.0	3.8	93.6
Guinea	101.8	108.9	107.3	107.1	451.9	446.3	381.1	16.4	20.4	12.3	202.8
Guinea-Bissau	416.2	373.3	335.7	324.0	1 608.9	1 135.4	1 177.6	15.7	28.2	41.1	747.1
Haiti	28.5	29.6	33.5	34.8	208.3	219.9	252.0	8.8	7.7	5.2	164.8
Kiribati	..	..	..	..	..	..	..	..	..	..	..
Lao People's Dem. Rep.	174.2	146.2	142.6	158.6	527.8	487.5	516.5	7.7	7.9	9.0	268.1
Lesotho	74.9	74.7	74.6	87.3	125.9	123.7	106.6	10.1	11.4	12.4	73.1
Liberia	470.2	386.6	413.8	412.3	3 230.6	1 513.6	1 361.8	4.0	0.5	0.5	1 320.8
Madagascar	127.9	121.2	90.4	100.1	510.9	388.4	2 678.5	17.1	9.6	43.3	1 316.7
Malawi	152.0	159.1	148.9	154.9	503.0	542.9	518.9	12.6	11.7	7.8	296.3
Maldives	37.1	33.0	37.6	43.8	49.4	44.1	49.9	4.0	4.2	4.6	37.6
Mali	117.5	121.7	110.0	88.6	413.5	408.8	317.1	13.7	12.8	8.8	154.4
Mauritania	264.5	265.8	228.1	234.9	649.5	577.5	552.5	27.1	19.3	22.7	359.2
Mozambique	174.8	191.0	124.7	117.6	1 095.8	917.4	175.2	16.4	11.7	3.4	35.9
Myanmar	..	..	..	..	311.6	252.4	211.6	5.0	3.7	3.1	150.5
Nepal	59.0	51.5	48.4	53.8	201.5	158.3	147.8	7.3	5.6	4.9	85.8
Niger	82.6	93.8	81.7	82.8	477.9	466.2	428.0	9.8	8.1	6.8	282.1
Rwanda	66.9	70.2	75.3	82.7	1 063.8	998.6	787.3	25.9	27.5	11.4	411.1
Samoa	82.9	83.3	83.6	89.7	151.6	251.1	..	5.1	10.8	..	..
Sao Tome and Principe	681.0	677.9	666.5	663.8	2 161.4	2 130.0	1 791.9	29.8	28.4	22.9	573.4
Senegal	80.7	78.2	75.1	79.3	224.0	213.4	215.1	14.3	13.7	13.3	149.6
Sierra Leone	194.0	193.1	172.9	183.4	1 740.5	1 384.3	1 265.4	35.9	52.6	102.0	888.4
Solomon Islands	52.4	53.4	55.3	75.3	72.9	117.9	..	4.8	6.9	..	..
Somalia	..	..	..	..	..	..	..	..	..	..	..
Sudan	151.6	139.9	123.1	121.5	1 044.2	635.5	623.5	3.7	2.5	2.3	591.0
Togo	107.1	117.3	111.7	114.3	301.5	303.3	289.4	8.9	6.3	6.6	205.7
Tuvalu	..	..	..	..	..	..	..	..	..	..	..
Uganda	58.5	59.5	65.9	69.9	450.1	500.5	525.6	16.9	10.7	7.0	162.0
United Rep. of Tanzania	93.4	81.4	71.5	77.2	658.6	551.3	450.9	17.9	14.6	10.3	90.6
Vanuatu	27.6	29.7	29.8	35.7	38.2	36.7	38.2	1.1	1.2	1.0	21.3
Yemen	82.3	54.6	55.9	50.9	135.8	95.3	85.0	3.9	4.5	4.9	61.1
Zambia	187.3	176.9	155.8	162.0	636.0	624.6	512.9	16.1	20.2	11.7	365.1
LDCs (weighted average)	**90.1**	**83.1**	**78.0**	**78.5**	**351.3**	**277.8**	**254.3**	**11.7**	**10.1**	**9.2**	**183.7**
LDCs (simple average)	**128.7**	**123.3**	**117.0**	**119.8**	**616.8**	**526.0**	**530.5**	**12.9**	**12.0**	**12.7**	**323.4**

Source: UNCTAD secretariat estimates, based on World Bank, *Global Development Finance 2003*, online data; and *World Development Indicators 2003*, online data.

Note: This table is based on data as at January 2004. For more recent data, see annex table 31.

a   2002 data were not available for export of goods and services, and income and workers' remittances.

b   The LDC group average has been weighted by GDP and excludes Afghanistan, Kiribati, Myanmar, Somalia and Tuvalu, for which no data were available.

c   The LDC group average has been weighted by exports of goods and services, income and workers' remittances and excludes Afghanistan, Djibouti, Kiribati, Samoa, the Solomon Islands, Somalia and Tuvalu, for which no data for 2001 were available.

In July 2003 the World Bank classified 26 LDCs as severely indebted (this represents over half of the total number of severely indebted countries), 9 LDCs as moderately indebted countries and 13 LDCs as less indebted.[5] Thirty-two of the LDCs are also classified as highly indebted poor countries (HIPCs). As of July 2003, of the 32 HIPC-LDCs, 7 had reached completion point within the enhanced HIPC initiative, 14 had reached decision point, 2 (both of them oil exporters) were identified as potentially sustainable cases and 9 had not yet reached decision point. Six of these nine countries were classified as conflict-affected LDCs.

IMF data on the ratio of debt service to government revenue in the 21 HIPC-LDCs that had reached decision point by July 2003 indicate a decrease in this ratio in all but four LDCs[6] between 1999 and 2002 (see table 15). On average, the ratio of debt service to government revenue declined from 17.4 per cent in 1999 to 10.4 per cent in the seven HIPC-LDCs that had reached completion point. In the LDCs that have reached decision point this ratio declined from 19.9 per cent to 15.3 per cent. In 2002, the ratio of debt service to government revenue still exceeded 15 per cent in 10 out of the 21 HIPC-LDCs which had reached decision point or completion point.

The ratio of debt service to government revenue in the 21 HIPC-LDCs that had reached decision point by July 2003 decreased in all but four LDCs between 1999 and 2002.

TABLE 15. RATIO OF DEBT SERVICE PAID TO GOVERNMENT REVENUE IN SELECTED LDC-HIPCs,[a] 1999–2002

| | Date of approval of | | Debt service paid as % government revenue | | | |
	Decision point	*Completion point*	*1999*	*2000*	*2001*	*2002*
Benin	July 2000	April 2003	17.3	14.6	9.4	7.2
Burkina Faso	July 2000	April 2002	15.8	15.6	10.6	11.3
Mali	September 2000	March 2003	19.6	20.8	12.7	11.9
Mauritania	February 2000	June 2002	30.4	36.1	36.6	19.9
Mozambique	April 2000	September 2001	12.3	4.1	6.7	8.3
United Rep. of Tanzania	March 2000	November 2001	19.8	16.0	8.5	9.9
Uganda	February 2000	May 2000	12.9	13.6	11.7	8.4
Chad	May 2001		24.0	28.7	14.0	18.4
Dem. Rep. of the Congo	July 2003		1.4	..	..	7.4
Ethiopia	November 2001		11.0	9.7	16.4	12.3
Gambia	December 2000		25.5	16.2	26.3	26.5
Guinea	December 2000		35.3	45.5	22.2	22.0
Guinea-Bissau	December 2000		15.5	31.6	1.2	12.0
Madagascar	December 2000		25.0	14.3	9.7	15.4
Malawi	December 2000		20.5	34.5	23.8	14.1
Niger	December 2000		10.6	14.3	19.1	21.4
Rwanda	December 2000		23.0	23.4	6.2	6.4
Sao Tome and Principe	December 2000		21.4	42.4	17.9	15.9
Senegal	June 2000		22.0	20.7	17.0	16.4
Sierra Leone	March 2000		77.4	44.4	88.6	18.4
Zambia	December 2000		22.9	29.6	21.7	20.0

Source: UNCTAD secretariat compilation, based on IMF and IDA (2003).
   a   The list includes all LDC-HIPCs which had reached decision point by the end of July 2003.

E. ODA targets for donor countries

1. QUANTITY OF AID

The Programme of Action for the Least Developed Countries for the Decade 2001–2010 includes commitments by donor countries to increase aid to the LDCs and also to improve its quality, amongst other things, by untying most aid other than food aid and technical cooperation (United Nations, 2001: paras. 83–84). The commitments are formulated with some flexibility. But there are long-standing targets, which are now also being monitored as part of the Millennium Development Goals, namely that 0.20 or 0.15 per cent of each donor's GNI should go to LDCs.

Table 16 shows that six DAC member countries, namely Denmark, Ireland, Luxembourg, Netherlands, Norway and Sweden, surpassed the target of making net ODA disbursements more than 0.20 per cent of their respective GNI in 2002. Between 2001 and 2002 Ireland increased its ODA to GNI ratio from 0.16 to 0.21 per cent. Except for these six countries, all other DAC countries were below the 0.15 per cent target. Moreover, following a $494.2 million fall in net ODA disbursements from the United Kingdom to the LDCs, the ratio of ODA flows to LDCs to GNI of that country fell from 0.12 per cent in 2001 to 0.07 per cent in 2002. In contrast, Italy increased its net ODA disbursements to LDCs by $558.2 million and its ODA to GNI ratio increased from 0.04 to 0.09 per cent. On average, the EU members' contribution, which accounted for 58.6 per cent of total ODA disbursements to LDCs[7] from DAC member countries in 2002, increased only slightly — from 0.09 to 0.10 per cent between 2001 and 2002.

Six DAC member countries, namely Denmark, Ireland, Luxembourg, Netherlands, Norway and Sweden, surpassed the target of making net ODA disbursements more than 0.20 per cent of their respective GNI in 2002.

The United States remains the leading ODA contributor for LDCs in value terms amongst DAC member countries. It accounted for 19.9 per cent of total net ODA disbursements to LDCs in 2002. But its ODA to GNI ratio increased only from 0.02 per cent in 2001 to 0.03 per cent in 2002. Japan, the second largest ODA donor to the LDCs, accounted for 12 per cent of total ODA disbursements from DAC member countries. Its ODA to GNI ratio in 2002 stood at 0.04 per cent.

Overall, aid effort of all DAC member countries as measured by the ODA/GNI ratio increased slightly — from 0.05 per cent in 2001 to 0.06 per cent in 2002. As a result, net ODA disbursements to LDCs increased, but they remain below the UN ODA targets for LDCs.

Overall, aid effort of all DAC member countries as measured by the ODA/GNI ratio increased slightly — from 0.05 per cent in 2001 to 0.06 per cent in 2002.

2. THE UNTYING OF AID

Improving the quality of aid is as important as improving the quantity of aid. In this regard, one of the most important decisions in the Programme of Action is the recommendation that by 1 January 2002 ODA to LDCs be untied in the following areas: balance of payments and structural adjustment support; debt forgiveness; sector and multisector programme assistance; investment project aid; import and commodity support; commercial services contracts; and ODA to NGOs for procurement-related activities. Technical cooperation and food aid, as well as activities with a value of less than SDR 700,000, are excluded from the coverage of the recommendation.

The OECD/DAC is monitoring the implementation of the recommendation. No data are yet available beyond a description of DAC members' initial starting points (see table 16). But it is reported that DAC members' implementation of the recommendation to untie aid has "in general, been rapid and comprehensive" (OECD, 2004: 4). As this progress report goes on,

- "Almost all Members have by now untied all categories of ODA covered by paragraph 7i) of the Recommendation. In the few remaining cases, full implementation of the coverage provisions still awaits the conclusion of the co-ordination process among the various implementing agencies.

- In addition, both prior to and since the Recommendation, numerous Members (e.g. Australia, Finland, France, Germany, Ireland, Japan, the Netherlands, Norway, Sweden, Switzerland, and the United Kingdom) have also untied ODA beyond the requirements of the Recommendation — e.g. commitments below the thresholds, technical co-operation, food aid and or ODA beyond the LDCs group of countries.

- Moreover, the Commission of the European Union, in accordance with its commitments, has introduced new provisions in favour of further untying, and has introduced the necessary elements to allow further

It is reported that DAC members' implementation of the provision to untie aid has "in general, been rapid and comprehensive".

TABLE 16. NET AID DISBURSEMENTS FROM DAC MEMBER COUNTRIES TO LDCs,[a] 2001 and 2002, AND ODA UNTYING RATIO, 1999–2001

	$ millions	% of total DAC	% of donor's total	% of donor's GNI	$ millions	% of total DAC	% of donor's total	% of donor's GNI	ODA untying ratio[b]
		2001				2002			1999–2001
Norway	449	3.7	33	0.27	625	4.1	37	0.33	0.99
Denmark	540	4.5	33	0.34	547	3.6	33	0.32	0.78
Luxembourg	47	0.4	34	0.25	58	0.4	40	0.30	..
Netherlands	995	8.3	31	0.26	1 180	7.8	35	0.29	0.91
Sweden	458	3.8	27	0.21	629	4.2	32	0.26	0.91
Ireland	143	1.2	50	0.16	210	1.4	53	0.21	1.00[c]
Belgium	295	2.5	34	0.13	353	2.3	33	0.14	0.49[c]
Finland	114	1.0	29	0.10	154	1.0	33	0.12	0.69
France	1 083	9.0	26	0.08	1 626	10.7	30	0.11	0.34
Portugal	119	1.0	45	0.11	120	0.8	37	0.10	0.61
Italy	487	4.1	30	0.04	1 045	6.9	45	0.09	0.30
Switzerland	257	2.1	28	0.10	250	1.7	27	0.08	0.89
Austria	106	0.9	20	0.06	170	1.1	33	0.08	0.36
United Kingdom	1 647	13.7	36	0.12	1 153	7.6	23	0.07	0.53
Germany	1 173	9.8	24	0.06	1 332	8.8	25	0.07	0.43
New Zealand	29	0.2	26	0.07	30	0.2	25	0.06	..
Australia	175	1.5	20	0.05	192	1.3	19	0.05	0.49
Canada	231	1.9	15	0.03	349	2.3	17	0.05	0.40
Japan	1 783	14.8	18	0.04	1 813	12.0	20	0.04	0.76
Spain	193	1.6	11	0.03	252	1.7	15	0.04	0.21
United States	1 673	13.9	15	0.02	3 012	19.9	23	0.03	0.01
Greece	22	0.2	11	0.02	37	0.0[d]	13	0.03	..
Total DAC	**12 019**	**100.0**	**23**	**0.05**	**15 137**	**100.0**	**26**	**0.06**	**0.53**
of which:									
EU Members	7 422	61.8	28	0.09	8 867	58.6	30	0.10	..

Source: UNCTAD secretariat estimates, based on OECD/DAC online data and OECD (2004).

  a   Including imputed multilateral flows, i.e. making allowance for contributions through multilateral organizations, calculated using the geographical distribution of multilateral disbursements for the year of reference.
  b   The bilateral LDC ODA untying ratio is: untied bilateral LDC ODA divided by total bilateral LDC ODA (commitments basis).
  c   2000–2001 average.
  d   0.002 per cent.

untying of Community assistance. The United States Congress has recently authorized creation of a new Millennium Challenge Corporation (MCC), the purpose of which is to provide additional foreign assistance in a manner that promotes economic growth and the elimination of extreme poverty while strengthening good governance, economic freedom and investments in people. The U.S. Congress appropriated just under US$ 1 billion for the 2004 Fiscal Year. With no legislative preference expressed as to the tying status of MCC financing these funds are currently untied." (ibid.: 4).

It will be important to monitor the progress of untying at the recipient country level as well as at the OECD/DAC level. Given that about 50 per cent of bilateral aid (excluding technical cooperation and food aid) was tied before the recommendation to untie aid to LDCs, the decision could have significant effects in improving the efficiency of aid. In order to maximize the economic benefits, not only will all donors have to proceed swiftly with untying, and as comprehensively as possible, but also the LDCs will have to make major efforts to improve their government procurement systems. It is only in this way that the full economic benefits of the untying decision in terms of lower import costs will be realized. This issue will be taken up further in part two of this Report.

> *It will be important to monitor the progress of untying at the recipient country level as well as at the OECD/DAC level.*

F. Conclusions

The economic performance of the least developed countries as a group continues to improve. In terms of real GDP growth rates, the late 1990s were better than the early 1990s. Similarly, the period 2000–2002, the latest for which international data are available, was better than 1998–2000. Indeed, with growth decelerating sharply in 2001 in many other developing countries, the annual real average annual GDP growth rate of LDCs exceeded that of other developing countries in the 2000–2002 period.

> *The economic performance of the least developed countries as a group continues to improve...but the tendency for increasing divergence amongst the LDCs also continues.*

The encouraging growth performance of LDCs as a group was underpinned by a significant increase in aggregate net resource flows to the LDCs. These capital inflows increased by 35.3 per cent from 2000 to 2002. The increase was driven by increased FDI inflows in 2001 and by increased ODA inflows in the form of grants in 2002. Net ODA inflows to the LDCs have increased by 38.8 per cent in nominal terms and 36.3 per cent in real terms since 2000. The composition of aid commitments, however, is increasingly oriented away from productive sectors.

For the LDC group as a whole, continued progress has also been made in terms of increasing exports. But this has been much slower than during the period from 1998 to 2000, when merchandise exports surged by 36.7 per cent, mainly owing to increased exports of oil and manufactures.

Within this overall growth performance, the tendency for increasing divergence amongst the LDCs, which has emerged since the early 1990s, continues. Whilst the real GDP per capita growth rate exceeded 3 per cent per annum in 14 LDCs during 2000–2002, it stagnated or declined in 24 LDCs, more than half of those for which data are available. Only seven LDCs achieved the 7 per cent growth target of the Programme of Action for the Least Developed Countries for the Decade 2001–2010. Merchandise exports declined in nominal terms in 23 LDCs. Net ODA inflows increased by over 15 per cent between 1999 and 2002 in 18 LDCs, but declined in 13. The four LDC oil exporters, plus Chad, which is establishing an infrastructure for oil exportation, absorbed 68 per cent of net FDI inflows into LDCs in 2001 and 63 per cent in 2002.

One of the most encouraging aspects of the recent economic performance in the LDCs has been the improved performance in African LDCs, including some of those that have been dependent on non-oil commodity exports. But the fact that the African LDCs' growth rates exceeded those of Asian LDCs for the first time is a reflection of the slowdown in economic growth in the latter countries as much as of an improvement in the African countries.

The sustainability of recent growth improvements remains an important issue for all LDCs. Many of the countries which showed an improved economic growth performance in the period 2000–2002 are also those where the instability of GDP growth was highest in the 1990s. The high level of dependence on external aid inflows, as well as on primary commodity exports with volatile world prices, continues to give cause for concern. Moreover, it is notable that debt stocks in LDCs rose in 2002 for the first time since 1998.

The high level of dependence on external aid inflows, as well as on primary commodity exports with volatile world prices, continues to give cause for concern. Moreover, it is notable that debt stocks in LDCs rose in 2002 for the first time since 1998.

Two recent trends deserve careful monitoring in terms of their potential effect on sustainability: the increase in the level of profit remittances on FDI, and the increase in multilateral debt. In 2000–2002, the sum of interest payments on long-term debt plus remittances on FDI were equivalent to 50 per cent of grants (excluding technical cooperation) disbursed to the LDCs and 23 per cent of grants disbursed to non-oil exporting LDCs. The increasing level of profit remittances is not necessarily a problem in itself. But it will become one if FDI inflows do not significantly contribute to the development of domestic productive capacities and value added.

Finally, the weak growth performance of island LDCs may be noted. This reflects the vulnerability of these countries in spite of their having a level of GNI per capita and human assets that is generally higher than that of most other LDCs.

Annex to Chapter 1

The LDCs which are analyzed in this Report do not include Timor-Leste, which was included as the 50th LDC on 4 December 2003. The 49 LDCs are sub-divided into (i) geographical groups, and (ii) according to their export specialization.

GEOGRAPHICAL CLASSIFICATION

The geographical classification is as follows:

African LDCs (plus Haiti): Angola, Benin, Burkina Faso, Burundi, Central African Republic, Chad, Democratic Republic of the Congo, Djibouti, Equatorial Guinea, Eritrea, Ethiopia, Gambia, Guinea, Guinea-Bissau, Haiti, Lesotho, Liberia, Madagascar, Malawi, Mali, Mauritania, Mozambique, Niger, Rwanda, Senegal, Sierra Leone, Somalia, Sudan, Togo, Uganda, United Republic of Tanzania and Zambia.

Asian LDCs: Afghanistan, Bangladesh, Bhutan, Cambodia, Lao People's Democratic Republic, Myanmar, Nepal and Yemen.

Island LDCs: Cape Verde, Comoros, Kiribati, Maldives, Samoa, Sao Tome and Principe, Solomon Islands, Tuvalu and Vanuatu.

CLASSIFICATION ACCORDING TO EXPORT SPECIALIZATION

Classification according to export specialization is difficult. First, it is necessary to aggregate data on the composition of merchandise exports with data on services exports. Secondly, there can be year-to-year fluctuations in a country's export structure, particularly as commodity prices change.

The classification used here is the same as that used in *The Least Developed Countries Report 2002*, although Sudan is now classified as an oil exporter. It is based on the export structure of the late 1990s. As with all classifications of this type, some arbitrary decisions have to be made. The decisions are set out in the annex chapter 3 of that Report (UNCTAD, 2002: 131–132).

The classification according to export specialization is as follows:

A. Exporters of primary commodities

1. Non-oil commodity exporters:

(i) Agricultural exporters: Afghanistan, Benin, Bhutan, Burkina Faso, Burundi, Chad, Eritrea, Ethiopia, Guinea-Bissau, Kiribati, Malawi, Mali, Mauritania, Rwanda, Sao Tome and Principe, Solomon Islands, Somalia, Togo, Uganda and United Republic of Tanzania.

(ii) Mineral exporters: Central African Republic, Democratic Republic of the Congo, Guinea, Liberia, Niger, Sierra Leone and Zambia.

2. Oil exporters: Angola, Equatorial Guinea, Sudan and Yemen.

B. Exporters of manufactures and/or services

1. Manufactures exporters: Bangladesh, Cambodia, Haiti, Lao People's Democratic Republic, Lesotho, Madagascar, Myanmar and Nepal.

2. Services exporters: Cape Verde, Comoros, Djibouti, Gambia, Maldives, Samoa, Tuvalu and Vanuatu.

3. Mixed manufactures and services exporters: Mozambique[1] and Senegal.

---

[1] As from 2001, Mozambique should be classified as a mineral exporter as a result of the surge in its exports of aluminium.

Notes

1. The dataset is a joint project between the Department of Peace and Conflict Studies, Uppsala University and the Centre for the Study of Civil War at the International Peace Research Institute, Oslo (PRIO). Armed conflict is defined as "a contested incompatibility that concerns government and/or territory where the use of armed force between two parties, of which at least one is the government of a state, results in at least 25 battle-related deaths." (Strand, Wilhelmsen and Gleditsch, 2004: 3).
2. With China, the increase was 25.3 per cent.
3. Data on the value and composition of long-term capital flows to LDCs are available for 46 LDCs from the World Bank's *Global Development Finance* database. No data are available for Afghanistan, Kiribati and Tuvalu. The latest data include new estimates for private capital flows which diverge somewhat from those available at the time of the publication of *The Least Developed Countries Report 2002*.
4. Aggregate net transfers are equal to aggregate net resource flows minus interest payments on long-term debt and profit remittances on FDI. For definition of profit remittances, see World Bank's *Global Development Finance* database.
5. Tuvalu is not listed.
6. These four LDCs, namely the Democratic Republic of the Congo, Ethiopia, Gambia and Niger, were decision point countries.
7. Including imputed multilateral flows.

References

OECD (2004). Implementing the 2001 DAC recommendation on untying official development assistance to the least developed countries, 2004 progress report, DCD/DAC(2005)15, paper submitted for information to the DAC High Level Meeting, 15–16 April 2004.

IMF and IDA (2003). Heavily Indebted Poor Countries (HIPC) Initiative — Status of Implementation, Prepared by the staffs of the IMF and World Bank, September, (http://www.imf.org/external/np/hipc/2003/status/091203.pdf).

Strand, H., Wilhelmsen, L. and Gleditsch, N. (2004). Armed conflict dataset codebook, International Peace Research Institute, Oslo.

UNCTAD (2002). *The Least Developed Countries Report 2002*, United Nations publication, sales no E.02.II.D.13, Geneva.

United Nations (2001). Programme of Action for the Least Developed Countries for the Decade 2001–2010, 8 June, A/CONF.191/11.

Selected Recent Social Trends:

Population Growth, Human Development Goals, the HIV/AIDS Epidemic

A. Population growth, age structure and urbanization

In 2003, the total population of the least developed countries was 718 million people, of whom some 428 million lived in African and Caribbean LDCs, 287.3 million in Asian LDCs and 2.7 million in island LDCs.

In comparison with other developing countries, population growth rates are high in the LDCs. They were actually increasing in the 1980s, and although they are now declining, the decrease is slow. It is estimated that the population growth rate has declined from 2.7 per cent per year in 1990–1995 to 2.4 per cent per year in 2000–2005. Although projections are difficult because of the progress of HIV/AIDS, the total population of the current group of LDCs is expected to reach 1.04 billion by 2020 and to double between 2001 and 2035. Chart 3 and chart 4 show the difference between trends in the LDCs and in other developing countries.

The high rates of population growth are due to the fact that the LDCs are at a much earlier stage of demographic transition than other developing countries.[1] The crude birth rate in 2000–2005 is estimated at 38.9 live births per 1,000 people in the LDCs as compared with 21.3 in other developing countries. The crude death rate in the same period was 15.1 per 1,000 people in the LDCs as compared with 7.8 per 1,000 in other developing countries (table 17).

Although projections are difficult because of the progress of HIV/AIDS, the total population of the current group of LDCs is expected to reach 1.04 billion by 2020 and to double between 2001 and 2035.

CHART 3. ESTIMATED AND PROJECTED POPULATION GROWTH RATES IN THE LDCs AND IN OTHER DEVELOPING COUNTRIES, 1980–2025

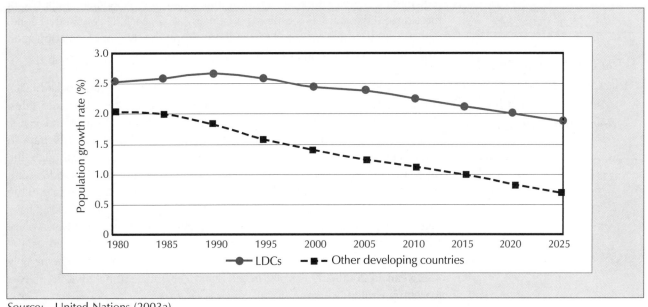

Source: United Nations (2003a).

CHART 4. INDICES OF THE POPULATION SIZE OF THE LDCS
AND OF OTHER DEVELOPING COUNTRIES, 2001–2035
(Index, 2001 = 100)

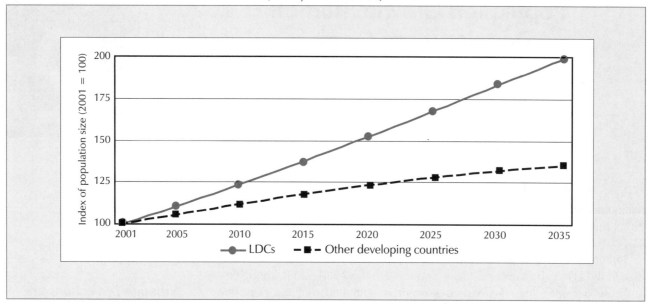

Source: UNCTAD secretariat estimates based on United Nations (2003a).

TABLE 17. CRUDE BIRTH RATE, CRUDE DEATH RATE AND TOTAL FERTILITY IN THE LDCS
AND IN OTHER DEVELOPING COUNTRIES, 1995–2000 AND 2000–2005 AVERAGES

	Crude birth rate (per 1,000 population)		**Crude death rate** (per 1,000 population)		**Total fertility** (children per woman)	
	1995–2000	*2000–2005*	*1995–2000*	*2000–2005*	*1995–2000*	*2000–2005*
Least developed countries	40.7	38.9	15.9	15.1	5.46	5.13
Other developing countries	23.2	21.3	7.8	7.8	2.79	2.60

Source: United Nations (2003a).

The LDCs are at a much earlier stage of demographic transition than other developing countries.

Underlying the high birth rates in LDCs are very high fertility rates. During the period 2000–2005, it is estimated that every woman in the LDCs will give birth to 5.1 children. This is much higher than in other developing countries, where the fertility rate is 2.6. Within the LDC group, the fertility rate is higher in African LDCs (6.0 children per woman in 2000–2005) than in Asian LDCs (4.9). There are 16 LDCs where the fertility rate is over 6 children per woman — Afghanistan, Angola, Burkina Faso, Burundi, Chad, the Democratic Republic of the Congo, Ethiopia, Guinea-Bissau, Liberia, Malawi, Mali, Niger, Sierra Leone, Somalia, Uganda and Yemen. Most of these countries have very high population growth rates, as shown in table 18.

It is worth noting that amongst the LDCs, island LDCs and landlocked LDCs are at opposite ends of the spectrum in terms of birth rates and death rates. During the period 2000–2005, the average crude death rate in island LDCs, which stood at 5.9 per 1,000 population, was much lower than the rate in landlocked LDCs, which stood at 18.8 per 1,000. Similarly, although the difference was somewhat less, the average crude birth rate, which stood at 32.3 per 1,000 in the island LDCs during 2000–2005, was lower than the rate in the landlocked LDCs, which stood at 43 per 1,000. In general, island LDCs have better social indicators than other LDCs, and landlocked LDCs have worse ones. Life expectancy at birth provides an overall indicator that summarizes the pattern. Within the landlocked LDCs life expectancy is estimated as being only 45.9 years in 2000–2005, whilst in the island LDCs it is estimated at 53.6 years (based on United Nations, 2003a).

TABLE 18. POPULATION GROWTH RATES AND AGE STRUCTURE IN THE LDCs, 2000–2010

	Population Average annual growth rate (%)		% of population under 15	% of population under 25	Dependency ratio
	2000–2005	2005–2010	2000	2000	2000
LDCs in which population growth rate is above the 2000–2005 LDC average					
Somalia	4.2	3.7	47.9	67.2	1.01
Liberia	4.1	2.7	46.6	66.6	0.95
Afghanistan	3.9	3.7	43.5	62.8	0.86
Sierra Leone	3.8	1.9	44.2	63.4	0.88
Eritrea	3.7	3.3	43.9	63.2	0.92
Niger	3.6	3.6	49.9	69.3	1.08
Yemen	3.5	3.6	50.1	68.2	1.06
Uganda	3.2	3.6	49.2	69.3	1.10
Angola	3.2	3.0	48.2	67.1	1.00
Burundi	3.1	3.3	47.6	68.0	1.04
Mali	3.0	3.2	46.1	65.8	1.06
Maldives	3.0	2.9	43.6	64.3	0.90
Mauritania	3.0	2.8	44.1	63.8	0.87
Chad	3.0	2.9	46.5	65.6	0.99
Bhutan	3.0	2.5	42.7	62.3	0.89
Burkina Faso	3.0	3.0	48.7	69.5	1.07
Guinea-Bissau	3.0	2.9	43.5	62.1	1.00
Solomon Islands	2.9	2.6	44.7	64.9	0.86
Democratic Republic of the Congo	2.9	2.9	48.8	67.7	0.98
Madagascar	2.8	2.7	44.7	64.0	0.91
Comoros	2.8	2.6	42.9	64.4	0.84
Gambia	2.7	2.3	40.3	58.2	0.81
Equatorial Guinea	2.7	2.5	43.8	62.1	0.91
Benin	2.7	2.6	46.3	66.6	0.96
Sao Tome and Principe	2.5	2.4	41.2	65.0	0.84
Ethiopia	2.5	2.4	45.2	64.3	0.95
Vanuatu	2.4	2.2	42.0	61.3	0.83
LDCs in which population growth rate is below the 2000-2005 LDC average					
Cambodia	2.4	2.3	43.9	62.5	0.86
Senegal	2.4	2.3	44.3	64.3	0.87
Togo	2.3	2.2	44.2	64.5	0.90
Lao People's Democratic Republic	2.3	2.2	42.7	62.1	0.86
Nepal	2.2	2.1	41.0	60.2	0.80
Sudan	2.2	1.8	40.1	59.9	0.77
Rwanda	2.2	2.1	44.3	66.5	0.92
Bangladesh	2.0	1.8	38.7	59.1	0.73
Cape Verde	2.0	1.9	39.3	61.1	0.85
Malawi	2.0	1.9	46.3	66.3	0.96
United Republic of Tanzania	1.9	1.8	45.0	65.6	0.93
Mozambique	1.8	1.5	43.9	63.6	0.90
Guinea	1.6	2.6	44.1	64.2	0.90
Djibouti	1.6	1.4	43.2	62.3	0.86
Haiti	1.3	1.3	40.6	62.2	0.80
Central African Republic	1.3	1.5	43.0	62.8	0.89
Myanmar	1.3	1.0	33.1	53.1	0.61
Zambia	1.2	1.3	46.5	67.3	0.97
Samoa	1.0	1.1	40.6	62.2	0.82
Lesotho	0.1	-0.5	39.3	59.1	0.82
LDCs	**2.4**	**2.3**	**43.2**	**63.2**	**0.86**

Source: UNCTAD secretariat estimates, based on United Nations (2003a).

Note: No data were available for Kiribati and Tuvalu.

63.2 per cent of total LDCs' population were under 25 in 2000.

For LDCs as a group, it is estimated that in 2000 the dependency ratio was 0.862. This compares with 0.582 in other developing countries.

The majority of the population in LDCs, some 74 per cent, are located in rural areas. Urbanization is accelerating, however...The total number of cities with over one million people is projected to increase from 22 in 2000 to 27 in 2015 in LDCs.

An important consequence of the relatively high rate of population growth within LDCs generally is a relatively youthful age structure of the population. It is estimated that in 2000 43.2 per cent of the population were children less than 15 years old, and fully 63.2 per cent of the total population were under 25. The median age of the population in the LDCs, namely the age at which 50 per cent of the population is younger than and 50 per cent of the population is older than that age, was 18.1 years in 2000, compared with 17.5 years in 1980. The median age is projected to be 20.3 years in 2020.

Inevitably, there is a high dependency ratio, which is measured as the ratio of the dependent population (persons aged between 0 and 14 years, and 65 and over) to the working-age population (those aged between 15 and 64 years). For LDCs as a group, it is estimated that in 2000 the dependency ratio was 0.862. This compares with 0.582 in other developing countries. However, there are significant differences amongst the LDCs between the African and the Asian LDCs. In the African LDCs, the number of dependants is almost the same as the number of people of working age. There has been no change in this situation over the last 20 years, with the dependency ratio in 2000 standing at 0.936, the same level as it was in 1980. In Asian LDCs, in contrast, the dependency ratio is lower and has fallen slightly over the same period — from 0.857 to 0.832.[2]

The age structure puts considerable pressure on the provision of social services of all types and also implies that a high rate of employment creation is necessary in order to ensure that the population is fully employed. It is estimated that in 2000, 30.4 per cent of the population was of school age (6–17 years old). This figure is estimated to decrease only slightly — to 29.6 in 2010. ILO projections for the period 2000–2010 suggest that the total population of working age (15–64 years old) in LDCs as a group will increase by 29 per cent between 2000 and 2010. The annual increase in the population of working age will exceed 100,000 in 25 out of 44 LDCs for which data are available (table 19). Generating sustainable livelihoods, with remuneration above poverty lines, is a daunting challenge.

Finally, it is worth emphasizing that the majority of the population in LDCs, some 74 per cent, are located in rural areas. Urbanization is accelerating, however. The urban population share increased from 19 per cent in 1985 to 20.8 per cent in 1990, but it is estimated that in 2005 it will reach 28.4 per cent. A number of major metropolises are emerging. It is estimated that Dhaka in Bangladesh had a population of 12.5 million in 2000, and Kinshasa in the Democratic Republic of the Congo a population of 5 million. There were 17 other LDCs that had a city with a population of over 1 million in 2000. The total number of cities with over one million people is projected to increase from 22 in 2000 to 27 in 2015 in LDCs (based on United Nations, 2002).

B. Progress towards selected human development goals[3]

The LDCs are identified as the poorest countries not just in terms of per capita income but also in terms of their low level of human assets and human development. The current gap between the LDCs as a group and developing countries as a whole and high-income OECD countries may be gauged from the following statistics:

- In 2001, life expectancy at birth in the LDCs was 50.4 years as against 64.4 years in developing countries as a whole and 78.1 years in high-income OECD countries.

TABLE 19. TRENDS IN THE WORKING-AGE POPULATION[a] OF THE LDCs, 1990–2010

	Working-age population (Thousands)			Average yearly change in working-age population[b] (Thousands)				Change[c] (%)
	1990–1995	1996–2000	2001	1990–1995	1996–2000	2000–2001	2000–2010	2000–2010
Afghanistan	10 538	13 197	14 600	458	507	350	421	42.7
Angola	5 192	6 142	6 715	162	183	196	190	32.0
Bangladesh	63 886	73 223	79 585	1 405	1 963	2 319	2 124	27.5
Benin	2 488	2 987	3 306	81	100	113	110	34.9
Bhutan	343	400	438	8	13	12	34	30.4
Burkina Faso	4 548	5 310	5 792	111	164	144	181	29.7
Burundi	2 959	3 320	3 565	55	75	92	154	41.4
Cambodia	5 070	5 963	6 617	104	215	208	242	34.0
Cape Verde	191	218	236	6	4	10	7	35.1
Central African Republic	1 655	1 909	2 048	44	48	40	34	17.3
Chad	3 170	3 508	3 748	93	34	172	134	33.3
Comoros	237	282	310	8	8	11	13	35.3
Dem. Rep. of the Congo	20 186	23 937	26 059	698	668	749	859	37.4
Djibouti	281	325	346	9	7	7	..	..
Equatorial Guinea	200	228	247	4	6	7	6	30.2
Eritrea	1 784	2 036	2 192	45	47	60	84	41.5
Ethiopia	28 297	31 510	33 643	534	630	847	763	24.7
Gambia	568	691	753	23	22	16	19	26.2
Guinea	3 203	3 720	4 018	97	91	111	99	22.0
Guinea-Bissau	542	610	649	13	11	16	15	24.8
Haiti	3 588	4 181	4 564	92	122	131	84	21.5
Kiribati	..	54	55	..	..	1	..	..
Lao People's Dem. Rep.	2 311	2 682	2 921	58	76	83	91	31.0
Lesotho	987	1 101	1 152	23	18	14	5	5.2
Liberia	1 180	1 477	1 692	25	81	45	57	43.9
Madagascar	6 498	7 595	8 322	176	220	274	281	33.2
Malawi	4 464	5 076	5 468	75	143	98	135	22.2
Maldives	115	138	154	3	5	6	5	39.8
Mali	4 558	5 166	5 526	111	110	135	179	29.0
Mauritania	1 110	1 316	1 446	31	43	42	41	31.0
Mozambique	7 931	8 997	9 647	185	203	233	190	17.8
Myanmar	25 197	28 532	30 301	619	596	551	494	17.3
Nepal	10 647	12 130	13 077	245	292	349	320	26.5
Niger	4 034	4 902	5 431	139	176	164	222	39.9
Rwanda	3 388	3 754	4 256	- 45	164	158	113	24.5
Samoa	89	97	103	0	2	1	..	..
Sao Tome and Principe	..	80	82	..	..	2	..	..
Senegal	4 059	4 731	5 152	112	132	150	140	30.2
Sierra Leone	2 270	2 544	2 711	55	45	75	74	40.9
Solomon Islands	177	209	228	6	6	6	9	35.4
Somalia	3 606	4 074	4 504	25	138	145	183	43.9
Sudan	14 553	16 729	18 004	390	401	453	429	31.6
Togo	1 900	2 237	2 447	52	69	67	67	31.4
Uganda	8 715	10 272	11 186	266	299	299	450	35.6
United Rep. of Tanzania	14 135	16 648	18 006	465	450	433	556	27.6
Vanuatu	83	101	113	2	4	3	..	..
Yemen	6 615	8 284	9 201	346	264	371	304	49.6
Zambia	4 286	5 010	5 399	121	141	98	127	25.9
African LDCs	166 333	192 042	207 991	4 270	5 040	5 581	5 980	29.9
Asian LDCs	124 606	144 410	156 741	3 243	3 925	4 244	4 028	27.8
Island LDCs	894	1 179	1 281	25	30	40	34	36.0
LDCs	**291 833**	**337 631**	**366 013**	**7 538**	**8 995**	**9 865**	**10 042**	**29.0**

Source: UNCTAD secretariat estimates, based on World Bank, *World Development Indicators 2003*, CD-ROM; and ILO, LABORSTA database.

Note: No data were available for Tuvalu.
  a   The working-age population is the number of people between the ages of 15 and 64.
  b   The average yearly increase in working-age population was calculated as the average of the year-to-year changes in the given period.
  c   Percentage increase in working-age population between 2000 and 2010.

- During 1998–2000, 38 per cent of the population was undernourished as against 18 per cent in developing countries as a whole.

- In 2001, 33.7 per cent of the 15–24-year-old population was illiterate as against 15.2 per cent in developing countries as a whole.

- In 2001 the infant mortality rate was 101 per 1,000 live births in the LDCs as against 62 in developing countries as a whole and 5 in high-income OECD countries.

- In 2001, 16 out of every 100 children born alive in the LDCs died before their fifth birthday as against 9 out of every 100 in developing countries as a whole and less than 1 in every 100 in high-income OECD countries.

- In 1995–2001 only 31 per cent of births were attended by skilled health personnel in the LDCs as against 56 per cent in developing countries as a whole and 99 per cent in high-income OECD countries.

- In 1995, the maternal mortality rate was 1,000 per 100,000 live births in the LDCs as against 463 per 100,000 in developing countries as a whole and 12 per 100,000 in high-income OECD countries.

- In 2000, only 55 per cent of the rural population had sustainable access to an improved water source in rural areas of LDCs as against 69 per cent in developing countries as a whole (UNDP, 2003).

In 2001 the infant mortality rate was 101 per 1,000 live births in the LDCs as against 62 in developing countries as a whole and 5 in high-income OECD countries.

Progress is, nevertheless, being made in a number of LDCs. Table 20, based on the more detailed information in annex 1 to this chapter, sets out the trends since 1990 regarding a number of human development indicators which are used to measure progress towards achievement of the Millennium Development Goals (MDGs). Those targets are as follows:

(i) Halve, between 1990 and 2015, the proportion of people who suffer from hunger;

(ii) Ensure that, by 2015, children everywhere, boys and girls alike, will be able to complete a full course of primary schooling;

(iii) Eliminate gender disparity in primary and secondary education, preferably by 2005 and at all levels of education no later than 2015;

(iv) Reduce by two thirds, between 1990 and 2015, the under-5 mortality rate;

(v) Halve, by 2015, the proportion of people without sustainable access to safe drinking water.

The lack of data is making it difficult to formulate any generalizations about progress by the LDCs as a group towards achievement of either the Millennium Development Goals or the POA targets.

These targets are also contained in the Programme of Action for the Least Developed Countries for the Decade 2001–2010 (POA), although there are differences between the goals of the POA and the MDGs (see box 1). For example, in the POA, as it was negotiated, the first target is actually more stringent, namely to halve the number of people suffering from hunger rather than the proportion of such people.

From the table and annex a number of points stand out.

First, there is a serious lack of data to monitor progress. Data coverage exceeds two thirds of the LDCs for only two of the five indicators. This problem was emphasized by UNCTAD soon after the POA was agreed (UNCTAD, 2001). There is an urgent need to improve national statistical capacity in the LDCs to monitor progress and provide data for informed policy-making on all fronts, including human development (see also UNDP, 2003: box 2.1). The lack of data is making it difficult to formulate any generalizations about progress by the LDCs

TABLE 20. PROGRESS TOWARDS ACHIEVEMENT OF SELECTED HUMAN DEVELOPMENT TARGETS[a] IN THE LDCs, 1990–2000

	Data availability	Achieved	Achievable by 2015	Low progress	Reversal/stagnation[b]
Hunger	34 LDCs		11 Chad Myanmar Malawi Sudan Benin Haiti Mozambique Guinea Mali Angola Togo	8 Lao People's Dem. Rep. Cambodia Mauritania Niger Central African Republic Uganda Yemen Lesotho	15 Afghanistan Burundi Dem. Rep. of the Congo Liberia Madagascar Rwanda Senegal Sierra Leone Somalia United. Rep. of Tanzania Zambia Bangladesh Burkina Faso Gambia Nepal
Primary education	25 LDCs	7 Cambodia Cape Verde Malawi Maldives Samoa Uganda Vanuatu	5 Rwanda Togo Bangladesh Lao People's Dem. Rep. Benin	10 Gambia Mali Senegal Eritrea Lesotho Mozambique Burkina Faso Niger Burundi Central African Republic	3 Dem. Rep. of the Congo United. Rep. of Tanzania Djibouti
Gender equality in education	29 LDCs	9 Bangladesh Lesotho Madagascar Maldives Rwanda Samoa Sudan Vanuatu Zambia	9 Mauritania Malawi United. Rep. of Tanzania Nepal Djibouti Myanmar Gambia Senegal Dem. Rep. of the Congo	8 Guinea Lao People's Dem. Rep. Niger Sierra Leone Togo Mali Burkina Faso Mozambique	3 Burundi Eritrea Ethiopia
Child mortality	48 LDCs		11 Bangladesh Bhutan Samoa Vanuatu Lao People's Dem. Rep. Nepal Cape Verde Comoros Solomon Islands Maldives Guinea	23 Eritrea Equatorial Guinea Uganda Yemen Malawi Kiribati Madagascar Djibouti Gambia Haiti Sao Tome and Principe Niger Guinea-Bissau Mozambique Myanmar Benin Sudan Ethiopia Lesotho Mali Togo Senegal Burkina Faso	14 Cambodia Rwanda United. Rep. of Tanzania Zambia Afghanistan Angola Burundi Central African Republic Chad Dem. Rep. of the Congo Liberia Mauritania Sierra Leone Somalia
Access to safe water	22 LDCs	7 Bangladesh Comoros Djibouti Maldives Nepal Samoa United. Rep. of Tanzania	6 Central African Republic Burundi Zambia Sudan Mali Senegal	6 Malawi Niger Uganda Togo Guinea Madagascar	3 Ethiopia Haiti Mauritania

Source: UNCTAD secretariat estimates, based on UNDP Human Development Report Office: direct communication. For details, see annex 1, table 1 of this chapter.

a   The quantitative variables used to monitor the targets on hunger, primary education, gender equality in education, child mortality and access to safe water are under-nourished people as percentage of total population, net primary school enrolment ratio, ratio of girls-to-boys in primary and secondary school, under-five child mortality rate (per 1,000 live births) and percentage of people with sustainable access to improved water sources, respectively.

b   Reversal or stagnation concerns cases in which the selected human development indicator either worsened or stagnated between 1990 and 2000.

BOX 1. THE NEED TO RECONCILE THE MDGS AND QUANTIFIABLE TARGETS OF THE PROGRAMME OF ACTION FOR THE LEAST DEVELOPED COUNTRIES FOR THE DECADE 2001–2010.

An important feature of the Programme of Action for the Least Developed Countries for the Decade 2001–2010, which was agreed at the Third United Nations Conference on the Least Developed Countries held in Brussels in May 2001 (United Nations, 2001), was the inclusion of quantifiable development targets. These are similar to the targets associated with the MDGs, but they are not identical.

There are differences regarding the level of improvement that is expected, the indicators that are used and the time frame that is applied. One MDG target, for example, is a 75 per cent reduction of the maternal mortality rate between the base year 1990 and the target year 2015, while the corresponding POA target is a 75 per cent reduction of the maternal mortality rate between the base year 2001 and the target year 2015. Inconsistencies can be observed with respect to development targets on poverty, nutrition, health, education, gender equality and infrastructure.

There are not only overlaps between MDG targets and POA targets, but also several overlaps between different types of POA targets themselves. Furthermore, a good number of development targets in the Programme of Action are formulated in a manner that does not allow for measurement and monitoring of progress. This is because many of the targets have no base years (where necessary), no target years or no indicators associated with them.

In order to promote progress towards the monitoring of international development goals for the least developed countries it is necessary that the different targets be made measurable and the data situation improved, but it is also highly desirable that inconsistencies between different sets of international development goals be resolved. The failure to harmonize the two sets of targets until now has effectively led to a focus on the MDG targets and a widespread neglect of POA targets. This does not matter for those POA targets that are similar to those of the MDGs, but it does for those that are different. In sum, it is essential that the POA and MDG targets be harmonized and that the inconsistencies amongst the POA targets themselves be resolved.

Source: Herrmann (2003).

as a group towards achievement of either the Millennium Development Goals or the POA targets.

Secondly, with regard to the only indicator for which data coverage is more or less complete (under-5 mortality), only 11 out of the 48 LDCs for which data are available are likely to achieve the target. Six of these are island LDCs which start with relatively low levels of under-5 mortality.

Thirdly, for each individual target there are some countries where significant progress has been made. Notable cases include the following:

For each individual target there are some countries where significant progress has been made.

- The proportion of the population that is undernourished has fallen sharply from very high levels during the 1990s in Chad, Haiti, Malawi and Mozambique. In these four countries, the proportion undernourished during 1990–1992 was 58 per cent, 64 per cent, 49 per cent and 69 per cent respectively. During 1998–2000, the proportion had fallen to 32 per cent, 50 per cent, 33 per cent and 55 per cent respectively.

- Net primary school enrolment rates increased substantially from 1990 to 2000 in Bangladesh (from 64 per cent to 89 per cent), Benin (from 49 per cent to 70 per cent), Eritrea (from 24 per cent to 41 per cent), Gambia (from 51 per cent to 69 per cent), the Lao People's Democratic Republic (from 61 per cent to 81 per cent), Malawi (from 50 per cent to 100 per cent), Mali (from 21 per cent to 43 per cent), Rwanda (from 66 per cent to 97 per cent), Senegal (from 48 per cent to 63 per cent) and Togo (from 75 per cent to 92 per cent).

- The ratio of girls to boys in primary and secondary school rose impressively from 1990 to 2000 in Bangladesh (from 72 per cent to 103 per cent), Gambia (from 64 per cent to 85 per cent), Mauritania (from 67 per cent to 93 per cent), Nepal (from 53 per cent to 82 per cent) and Sudan (from 75 per cent to 102 per cent).

- The under-5 mortality rate fell sharply between 1990 and 2001 in Bangladesh (from 144 per 1,000 live births to 77), Bhutan (from 166 to 95), Comoros (from 120 to 79), Guinea (from 240 to 169), the Lao People's Democratic Republic (from 163 to 100), Maldives (from 115 to 77) and Nepal (from 145 to 91).

- The proportion of the population with sustainable access to improved water sources has risen particularly sharply in the United Republic of Tanzania. It is estimated that in 1990 only 38 per cent had such access, while in 2000 the proportion was 68 per cent.

Fourthly, no country is on course to meet all five of these human development targets by 2015. However, three countries — Bangladesh, Maldives and Samoa — are on course to meet four of them.

Fifthly, more progress is being made in human development dimensions that are directly affected by the quantity and quality of public services (primary education, gender equity in education and access to water) than with regard to those that are the outcome of both public services and levels of household income (hunger and child mortality). Progress is most promising in the area of gender equity: 9 out of the 29 LDCs for which data are available have already achieved the target, and a further 9 will achieve it by 2015 if current rates of progress continue.

More progress is being made in human development dimensions that are directly affected by the quantity and quality of public services than with regard to those that are the outcome of both public services and levels of household income.

C. The HIV/AIDS epidemic[4]

1. THE GRAVITY OF THE PROBLEM IN LDCs

The HIV/AIDS epidemic is an important problem for LDCs and in some, particularly in Africa, it is turning into a development crisis which is threatening growth prospects and the achievement of human development goals. The advance of the epidemic in LDCs is a matter of acute concern because of their limited domestic resources to limit the spread of the virus and cope with its effects.

There are major data difficulties in tracking the progress of the epidemic. But according to data in UNAIDS (2002), in 2001, when the LDCs comprised 11 per cent of the global population:

- 25.5 per cent of all men living with HIV in the world lived in LDCs (4.7 million out of 18.6 million);

- 35 per cent of all women living with HIV in the world lived in LDCs (6.5 million out of 18.5 million);

- 46 per cent of all children living with HIV in the world lived in LDCs (1.4 million out of 3 million);

- 37 per cent of all deaths from HIV/AIDS in the world occurred in LDCs (1.1 million out of 3 million);

- almost 50 per cent of all child deaths from HIV/AIDS in the world occurred in LDCs (about 280,000 out of 580,000);

- 48.5 per cent of children orphaned by HIV/AIDS live in LDCs (6.8 million out of 14 million) (UNAIDS, 2002).

The HIV/AIDS epidemic is an important problem for LDCs and in some, particularly in Africa, it is turning into a development crisis which is threatening growth prospects and the achievement of human development goals.

Out of the 54 countries in which infection rates were above 1 per cent of the adult population in 2001, 28 were LDCs (see table 21). Most of these are located in Africa. For LDCs as a whole the adult HIV prevalence rate in 2001 was 4.1 per cent. But it was much higher (6.6 per cent) in African LDCs than in

TABLE 21. HIV PREVALENCE RATES IN ADULTS (AGED BETWEEN 15 AND 49) IN THE LDCs, 2001

Less than 3 per cent		Between 3 and 6 per cent		Between 6 and 13 per cent		Above 13 per cent	
Bangladesh	<0.1	Equatorial Guinea	3.4	Haiti	6.1	Malawi	15.0
Bhutan	<0.1	Benin	3.6	Ethiopia	6.4	Zambia	21.5
Lao People's Dem. Rep	<0.1	Chad	3.6	Burkina Faso	6.5	Lesotho	31.0
Maldives	0.1	Dem. Republic of the Congo	4.9	Sierra Leone	7.0		
Yemen	0.1	Uganda	5.0	United Rep. of Tanzania	7.8		
Madagascar	0.3	Angola	5.5	Burundi	8.3		
Senegal	0.5	Togo	6.0	Rwanda	8.9		
Nepal	0.5			Djibouti[a]	11.8		
Somalia	1.0			Central African Republic	12.9		
Gambia	1.6			Mozambique	13.0		
Mali	1.7						
Myanmar[a]	2.0						
Sudan	2.6						
Cambodia	2.7						
Eritrea	2.8						
Guinea-Bissau	2.8						
Liberia[a]	2.8						

Source: UNCTAD secretariat classification based on UNAIDS (2002).

Note: Data on HIV/AIDS prevalence rate were not available for the following LDCs: Afghanistan, Cape Verde, Comoros, Guinea, Kiribati, Mauritania, Niger, Samoa, Sao Tome and Principe, Solomon Islands, Tuvalu and Vanuatu.
      a   1999 data.

The intensity of HIV/AIDS within LDCs as a group at the present time reflects the current epicentre of the global epidemic in Africa and the weight of African countries within the LDC group.

Asian LDCs (0.2 per cent). There are 15 LDCs in Africa where the adult HIV prevalence rate exceeds 5 per cent. Infection rates are also high in Haiti and, within Asia, it exceeds 2 per cent in Cambodia and Myanmar. Overall deaths due to AIDS in 2001 were 2 per 1,000 persons in LDCs, as compared with 0.5 in the world as a whole.

A very disturbing feature of the epidemic is that the infection rates are high amongst young women. For LDCs as a group, 4.9 per cent of women aged between 15 and 24 live with HIV, as compared with 1.4 per cent for the world as a whole. Within African LDCs, 7.2 per cent of young women live with HIV, and there are at least 5 African LDCs in which one in ten of women aged between 15 and 24 live with HIV.

The intensity of HIV/AIDS within LDCs as a group at the present time reflects the current epicentre of the global epidemic in Africa and the weight of African countries within the LDC group. Within Sub-Saharan Africa, there does not appear to be an overconcentration of people living with and dying from HIV/AIDS in LDCs. Within Sub-Saharan Africa, LDCs constituted over 50 per cent of the population in 2001, and accounted for 39 per cent of the men, 40 per cent of the women and 51 per cent of the children living with HIV/AIDS in the region. Similarly, 47 per cent of the adult and child deaths from HIV/AIDS in Sub-Saharan Africa occurred in LDCs.

There is some evidence that the epidemic has declined in Uganda and Zambia.

Perhaps the only positive feature of the current situation is that there is some evidence that the epidemic has declined in Uganda and Zambia. In Uganda, HIV prevalence rates among pregnant women in Kampala fell, according to UNAIDS (2002: 24), for eight consecutive years — from 29.5 per cent in 1992 to 11.3 per cent in 2001, a fact which suggests that the HIV/AIDS epidemic is being brought under control. More Ugandans are receiving antiretroviral drugs, but the rate of new infections remains high. It is hoped that Zambia is now becoming the second African country to reverse the epidemiological crisis. HIV prevalence, though still high in Zambia, has significantly decreased among 15–29-year-old urban women from 28.3 per cent in 1996 to 24.1 per cent in 1999. For rural women aged between 15 and 24, HIV prevalence rates fell from 16.1 per cent to 12.2 per cent over the same period (UNAIDS, 2002: 26).

2. THE ECONOMIC AND SOCIAL IMPACT OF THE EPIDEMIC

The HIV/AIDS epidemic is having, and will have, major detrimental consequences for economic activity as well as for the achievement of human development goals. This negative impact lags behind the spread of the HIV infection because it takes approximately seven to eight years before HIV-infected people become seriously ill and die.

Increasing evidence suggests that the effects of the HIV/AIDs epidemic are particularly severe in the agricultural sector.

There are various estimates of the macroeconomic impact (see McPherson, 2003). UNDP (2001) estimates that in the 1990s AIDS reduced Africa's per capita annual growth by 0.8 per cent. Other calculations suggest that the rate of economic growth has declined by 2–4 per cent in sub-Saharan Africa as result of AIDS (UNAIDS, 2002). It is also suggested that in the worst affected countries one to two percentage points will be pared off per capita growth in the coming years. If this happens, a number of economies will, after two decades, be about 20–40 per cent smaller than they would have been in the absence of AIDS (UNDP, 2001). According to UNAIDS (2002), for those countries with national HIV/AIDS prevalence rates of 20 per cent, annual GDP growth may fall by an average of 2.6 percentage points. Moreover, there is an adverse fiscal impact. Public revenues could drop by an expected 20 per cent by 2010 — as in Botswana — in AIDS-affected LDCs as a result of the economic impact of the HIV/AIDS epidemic (UNDP, 2002: 3).

Owing to labour bottlenecks, the problems of rural women, and especially female-headed households, can be particularly severe.

Increasing evidence suggests that the effects of the HIV/AIDS epidemic are particularly severe in the agricultural sector. This is going to have important negative consequences in countries such as the LDCs, in which the majority of the population live in rural areas and earn their living from agriculture. The reason for the severity of the impact is that the human resource losses associated with the epidemic are much less easily absorbed given the structure of agriculture, especially smallholder agriculture. The illness of productive members of the household leads to a double loss — the productive individual works less and there is a major demand for care for the sick person. About 20 per cent of rural families in Burkina Faso, for example, have reduced the amount of agricultural work done or abandoned their farms because of HIV/AIDS. In Ethiopia AIDS-affected households spent 11.6 to 16.4 hours per week performing agricultural work as compared with an average of 33.6 hours for non-AIDS-affected households (UNAIDS, 2002: 49). In Malawi, Mozambique and Zambia, there has been a progressive increase in cassava production (less labour-intensive) as a shift from staple-food maize production to compensate for lost labour (De Waal and Tumushabe, 2003). As labour bottlenecks tighten, malnutrition increases and traditional community-level support mechanisms are subjected to strain. The problems of rural women, and especially female-headed households, can be particularly severe. Food security worsens owing to reduced food availability caused by falling production with disruptions of the farming cycle, as well as owing to reduced food access due to declining income for food purchases.

Food security worsens owing to reduced food availability caused by falling production with disruptions of the farming cycle, as well as to reduced food access due to declining income for food purchases.

The HIV/AIDS epidemic is also affecting non-agricultural enterprises. In Zambia, for example, it is estimated that nearly two thirds of deaths among managers are related to AIDS (UNAIDS, 2002: 58). Studies in southern Africa suggest that direct and indirect expenses incurred by firms on account of AIDS could cut profits by 6 to 8 per cent (ibid.: 54).

The public sector has also been suffering the costs of AIDS as service delivery has faltered, with experienced State employees falling sick and dying. This is affecting school teachers and health workers. In the Central African Republic, 85 per cent of teachers who died between 1996 and 1998 were HIV-positive, and they died on average 10 years before they were due to retire. Malawi has reportedly been losing at least one teacher a day (UNFPA, 2002). According to UNAIDS (2002), in Malawi and Zambia there has been a five- or sixfold increase in illness and death rates among health workers. To compensate for this, expenditure on the training of doctors and nurses to replace dying medical personnel would have to increase by 25–40 per cent in southern Africa in 2001–2010.

In sub-Saharan Africa, the annual direct medical costs of AIDS, excluding antiretroviral therapy, have been estimated at $30 per capita, although overall public health spending is less than $10 per capita for most African countries.

The epidemic is also adversely affecting school attendance. Children, especially girls, are removed from school, and kept at home to care for parents and family members, or to do housework to free older women for nursing, thus damaging growth prospects for the next generation. Children may become the household's only breadwinners, as working-age adults start falling victim to AIDS, and with other household members too old or too young to work. Carrying the burden of AIDS, the household may become unable to afford school fees and other expenses, and this could have serious intergenerational implications for future income, savings, productivity and growth, creating a vicious downward spiral. Spending on education is often redirected to the AIDS patient if he or she is a household member. Moreover, AIDS-infected children may not survive through the years of schooling.

Among the LDCs, in the Central African Republic school enrolment is reported to have fallen by 20 to 36 per cent, with girls being most affected (UNAIDS, 2002: 52). It is also notable that orphan school attendance in African LDCs is estimated to be 79 per cent of non-orphan school attendance.

For LDCs as a group child mortality rates in 2015–2020 are expected to be 14 per cent higher with the HIV/AIDS epidemic than they would have been without it.

Finally, the epidemic is overwhelming the capacity of health budgets and systems. In sub-Saharan Africa, the annual direct medical costs of AIDS, excluding antiretroviral therapy, have been estimated at $30 per capita, although overall public health spending is less than $10 per capita for most African countries (UNDP, 2001: 8). It is in this context that access to cheap retroviral drugs is so important. The quality of care is being adversely affected for all diseases owing to the high patient load and the inadequate number of hospital beds in AIDS-affected countries.

Some evidence of the expected social impact of the epidemic in LDCs is shown in table 22. For LDCs as a group child mortality rates in 2015–2020 are expected to be 14 per cent higher with the HIV/AIDS epidemic than they would have been without it. Life expectancy at birth in LDCs in 2010–2015 is expected to be 46.1 years rather than 58.7 years, which would have been attained without the HIV/AIDS epidemic. Life expectancy at birth in the LDCs with the highest rates of adult HIV prevalence now — Lesotho, Malawi and Zambia — is expected to be as low as 32.2, 39.7 and 35.3 years respectively during 2010–2015. Without the HIV/AIDS epidemic they would have been 63, 59.2 and 57.4 years respectively.

TABLE 22. ESTIMATED AND PROJECTED IMPACT OF AIDS ON UNDER-5 MORTALITY RATE AND LIFE EXPECTANCY AT BIRTH IN THE LDCs, GROUPED BY ADULT HIV PREVALENCE RATE RANGES,[a] 1995–2000, 2000–2005, 2015–2020 AND 2010–2015

(Annual average)

	Under-5 mortality rate (per 1,000 live births)						Life expectancy at birth (years)					
	With AIDS	Without AIDS	% diff.	With AIDS	Without AIDS	% diff.	With AIDS	Without AIDS	% diff.	With AIDS	Without AIDS	% diff.
	1995–2000			*2015–2020*			*2000–2005*			*2010–2015*		
Adult HIV prevalence rates above 13%												
Lesotho	159	121	32	132	67	98	35.1	59.0	-68.1	32.2	63.0	-95.7
Malawi	238	207	15	159	132	20	37.5	55.2	-47.2	39.7	59.2	-49.1
Zambia	167	122	38	84	68	24	32.4	53.4	-64.8	35.3	57.4	-62.6
Adult HIV prevalence rates between 6 and 13%												
Burkina Faso	170	153	11	87	82	7	45.7	54.2	-18.6	50.2	58.2	-15.9
Burundi	211	185	14	145	122	19	40.9	51.5	-25.9	44.3	55.4	-25.1
Central African Republic	170	145	17	103	85	20	39.2	53.4	-36.2	41.5	56.4	-35.9
Djibouti	199	178	11	158	116	37	45.7	52.3	-14.4	46.2	56.3	-21.9
Ethiopia	197	177	12	122	100	22	45.5	52.5	-15.4	48.2	56.5	-17.2
Haiti	115	109	5	75	71	5	49.5	59.2	-19.6	53.4	63.3	-18.5
Mozambique	235	210	12	164	141	17	38.1	48.5	-27.3	39.3	52.5	-33.6
Rwanda	220	191	15	134	120	12	39.3	50.7	-29.0	44.7	54.9	-22.8
Sierra Leone	287	281	2	195	190	2	34.2	37.9	-10.8	35.1	41.9	-19.4
United Rep. of Tanzania	129	113	14	72	62	15	43.3	52.1	-20.3	46.5	54.1	-16.3
Adult HIV prevalence rates between 3 and 6%												
Angola	218	213	3	151	144	5	40.1	44.1	-10.0	41.5	48.1	-15.9
Benin	145	140	3	93	83	12	50.6	53.8	-6.3	52.9	57.9	-9.5
Chad	212	207	3	137	133	3	44.7	48.8	-9.2	48.5	52.8	-8.9
Dem. Rep. of the Congo	151	141	7	84	77	9	41.8	48.0	-14.8	45.4	51.0	-12.3
Equatorial Guinea	..	..	..	..	..	..	49.1	52.0	-5.9	50.1	56.0	-11.8
Togo	139	125	11	78	70	13	49.7	57.0	-14.7	52.3	61.0	-16.6
Uganda	186	165	13	107	102	5	46.2	55.5	-20.1	55.0	59.5	-8.2
Adult HIV prevalence rates less than 3%												
Cambodia	119	116	3	58	53	9	57.4	59.9	-4.4	59.2	63.9	-7.9
Eritrea	156	150	4	89	80	12	52.7	55.2	-4.7	54.9	59.3	-8.0
Gambia	214	210	2	144	141	2	54.1	56.5	-4.4	58.1	60.5	-4.1
Guinea	..	..	..	..	..	..	49.1	51.5	-4.9	53.1	55.5	-4.5
Guinea-Bissau	225	220	2	154	150	3	45.3	47.8	-5.5	47.9	51.8	-8.1
Liberia	172	164	5	64	61	7	41.4	46.0	-11.1	42.9	50.0	-16.6
Mali	261	257	2	181	158	14	48.6	50.6	-4.1	52.3	54.4	-4.0
Myanmar	142	139	2	81	79	3	57.3	59.2	-3.3	58.8	63.2	-7.5
Sudan	..	..	..	..	..	..	55.6	57.5	-3.4	57.0	61.5	-7.9
LDCs, average	**186**	**171**	**9**	**117**	**103**	**14**	**44.6**	**54.9**	**-23.1**	**46.1**	**58.7**	**-27.4**
African LDCs, average	**188**	**172**	**10**	**121**	**106**	**14**	**44.1**	**51.7**	**-17.4**	**46.7**	**55.6**	**-18.9**
Memo:												
Africa, average	164	146	12	101	86	17	45.2	52.5	-16.3	47.8	56.4	-18.0
World average	121	114	6	77	69	12	50.6	58.9	-16.2	52.1	62.4	-19.8

Source: UNCTAD secretariat estimates, based on United Nations (2002).

a Refers to the countries' 2001 adult HIV prevalence rates, except for Djibouti, Liberia and Myanmar for which 1999 was the latest year available.

3. THE NEXUS BETWEEN POVERTY AND HIV/AIDS

There is a close, two-way relationship between poverty and HIV/AIDS. As UNFPA (2002: Overview of Chapter 6) has put it, "HIV/AIDS accompanies poverty, is spread by poverty and produces poverty in its turn". Poverty is one of the factors that create situations that cause people to engage in high-risk behaviour that makes them more vulnerable to HIV. For survival in conditions of extreme poverty, people, especially women and young girls, trade sex, often unprotected under the threat of competition, for food, money, school fees or other essentials for themselves or their families, thus exposing themselves to HIV infections. This is contributing to the high incidence of HIV amongst young women noted earlier. Migration, some of which is associated with economic stress and the search for work, is also associated with the spread of the disease.

Extreme income poverty is associated with a lower nutritional status and a poorer general state of health. This can result in a less robust immune system, which lowers resistance to HIV exposure, and makes those already infected more susceptible to related infections. The poor may also have less access to sexual health and HIV education programmes, and less access to public health facilities, including treatment for sexually transmitted infections.

> *"HIV/AIDS accompanies poverty, is spread by poverty and produces poverty in its turn."*

HIV/AIDS also exacerbates poverty. The very limited resources of households are drained as sick wage earners lose their jobs, and household assets are used for medicines and health care for sick family members. Savings and capital, which are so important for recovery and rebuilding, are drawn upon, and available resources are utilized for survival consumption instead of investment. According to one case study on the United Republic of Tanzania cited by UNAIDS (2002: 48), in households where one person was ill because of AIDS, as much as 29 per cent of savings was redirected in order to cope with the illness, with families thus being driven to the brink of economic ruin. The financial burden of funerals is high, for example in the United Republic of Tanzania, where households are reported to spend up to 50 per cent more on funerals than on medical care (UNDP, 2001). The vicious spiral is even more evident when AIDS strikes one family member and the family disposes of its assets, and other family members with bleak prospects for decent work are forced into high-risk activities to help cope with the costs of the disease.

> *In Southern Africa, the negative effects of the combination of food insecurity and AIDS have been further reinforced owing to a weakened capacity for governance following the death from AIDS of key personnel in government institutions.*

The great danger is that this process will reach such a scale that communities break down and economic regress occurs at the national level. It has been argued that parts of Africa, including a number of LDCs, are now facing, or will soon face, a "new variant famine" (De Waal and Tumushabe, 2003). This is a type of famine that is closely associated with the undermining of productive capacities in agriculture and the breakdown of community support systems as an increasing proportion of the local population succumbs to AIDS. The situation in parts of southern Africa in 2002 is said to exemplify this phenomenon. There too the negative effects of the combination of food insecurity and AIDS have been further reinforced owing to a weakened capacity for governance following the death from AIDS of key personnel in government institutions.

To sum up, the nexus between poverty and HIV/AIDS is a particularly vicious link in the various domestic vicious circles that make it so difficult for poor countries and poor people to escape from poverty. It may also lead to economic regress which will intensify poverty and threaten human development achievements. Dealing with this will be a key challenge in the coming years not only for the LDCs where the epidemic is already raging, but also in the Asian LDCs.

D. Conclusions

A defining characteristic of the LDCs is that they have low levels of life expectancy, widespread hunger, disease and illiteracy, and high rates of infant, child and maternal mortality. The data in this chapter show that a few of them made significant progress in the 1990s towards the achievement of some of the human development targets set following the Millennium Declaration and contained in the Programme of Action for the Least Developed Countries for the Decade 2001–2010. These successes suggest what may be possible. But overall the picture is one in which urgent action will be needed in most LDCs to achieve agreed goals. With regard to under-5 mortality, the only indicator where data coverage is almost complete, only 11 out of 48 LDCs can be expected to meet the goal of reducing child mortality by two thirds between 1990 and 2015 if the trends of the 1990s continue.

The task that the LDCs face is difficult because of the very low starting level in relation to most social indicators. But in addition, population growth rates in the LDCs are higher than in other countries and the age structure is much younger. It is estimated that in 2000 30 per cent of the population of LDCs was of school age (6–17 years old) and 43 per cent were under 15 years old. The dependency ratio was 0.862 in that year. Thus, each person aged between 15 and 64 had to support almost one "dependant" (under 15 or 65 years and over). By 2020 the median age of the LDC population, the age at which half the population is younger than and half the population is older than that age, is projected to be 20.3 years, up from 18.1 years in 2000. The pressure on education and health services from the very youthful population is thus going to continue for the next 20 years.

It is expected that the population of the LDCs, some 718 million in 2003, will increase to over 1 billion in 2020. The working-age population will increase by 29 per cent between 2000 and 2010. Reducing poverty will depend on creating remunerative employment for these new entrants to the workforce, as well as on improving the incomes of the existing workforce. The latter task is a major challenge, given that in 2001 34 per cent of the population aged between 15 and 24 in LDCs was illiterate.

The social and human challenges facing LDCs are all the more difficult because in some, particularly in Africa, the HIV/AIDS epidemic has reached a level where it is threatening growth prospects and further reducing the likelihood of achieving human development targets. At the present time the LDCs are disproportionately affected by the epidemic. This is perhaps best exemplified by the fact that whilst the LDCs constituted 11 per cent of the world population in 2001, they were the location for 46 per cent of the children recorded as living with HIV, 50 per cent of recorded child deaths from AIDS and 48.5 per cent of children orphaned by HIV/AIDS.

The HIV/AIDS epidemic threatens to become a particularly vicious link in a cycle of pervasive poverty, economic stagnation and low levels of human development. The seriously affected LDCs have very limited resources to cope with the problem, and urgently need external assistance to reverse current trends. Unless trends improve, as they have done in Uganda, not simply the achievement of the MDG and POA targets for reducing HIV infection rates, but also the achievement of all other poverty and human development targets will be put in jeopardy. Those LDCs that currently have low rates of infection need to ensure that the epidemic does not spread further among the population.

Finally, the need for better, more and more timely information on economic and social trends in the LDCs needs to be reiterated. As noted in the 2002 LDC Report, the data that are internationally available for measuring progress towards achievement of the MDGs and also the POA targets are "woefully inadequate in terms of their coverage of LDCs, their quality and their timeliness" (UNCTAD, 2002: 32). There is an urgent need for increased investment in national statistical systems. Better policies, at the national and international levels, ultimately depend on better information.

The LDC working-age population will increase by 29 per cent between 2000 and 2010. Reducing poverty will depend on creating remunerative employment for these new entrants to the workforce, as well as on improving the incomes of the existing workforce.

The HIV/AIDS epidemic threatens to become a particularly vicious link in a cycle of pervasive poverty, economic stagnation and low levels of human development. The seriously affected LDCs have very limited resources to cope with the problem, and urgently need external assistance to reverse current trends.

Annex 1: Progress towards achievement of selected Millennium Development Goals in LDCs

This annex, based on data provided by the UNDP Human Development Report Office, sets out the trends since 1990 regarding a number of human development indicators which are used to measure progress towards achievement of the Millennium Development Goals. These targets are:

(i) Halve, between 1990 and 2015, the proportion of people who suffer from hunger;

(ii) Ensure that, by 2015, children everywhere, boys and girls alike, will be able to complete a full course of primary schooling;

(iii) Eliminate gender disparity in primary and secondary education, preferably by 2005 and at all levels of education no later than 2015;

(iv) Reduce by two thirds, between 1990 and 2015, the under-5 mortality rate;

(v) Halve, by 2015, the proportion of people without sustainable access to safe drinking water.

ANNEX TABLE 1. PROGRESS TOWARDS SELECTED HUMAN DEVELOPMENT TARGETS IN LDCs

	Target[a]	1990 level	2000 level	2015 target	Required 2000 level	Expected date of achievement[b]
Afghanistan	Hunger	63.0	70.0	31.5	52.5	Reversal
	Primary education	..	..	100.0	..	..
	Gender equality in education	50.0[c]	..	100.0	..	..
	Child mortality	260.0	257.0	86.7	183.7	Stagnation
	Access to safe water	..	13.0	..	..	..
Angola	Hunger	61.0	50.0	30.5	50.8	2015
	Primary education	..	36.9	100.0	..	..
	Gender equality in education	..	84.1[d]	100.0	..	..
	Child mortality	260.0	260.0	86.7	183.7	Stagnation
	Access to safe water	..	38.0	..	..	..
Bangladesh	Hunger	35.0	35.0	17.5	29.2	Stagnation
	Primary education	64.0	88.9	100.0	78.4	2004
	Gender equality in education	72.5	102.8	100.0	Achieved	Achieved
	Child mortality	144.0	77.0	48.0	101.8	2006
	Access to safe water	94.0	97.0	97.0	Achieved	Achieved
Benin	Hunger	19.0	13.0	9.5	15.8	2004
	Primary education	48.8[c]	70.3[d]	100.0	65.2	2010
	Gender equality in education	..	62.2[d]	100.0	..	..
	Child mortality	185.0	158.0	61.7	130.7	2040
	Access to safe water	..	63.0	..	..	..
Bhutan	Hunger	..	..	..	..	..
	Primary education	..	..	100.0	..	..
	Gender equality in education	..	..	100.0	..	..
	Child mortality	166.0	95.0	55.3	117.3	2007
	Access to safe water	..	62.0	..	..	..
Burkina Faso	Hunger	23.0	23.0	11.5	19.2	Stagnation
	Primary education	26.9	35.5	100.0	56.1	After 2040
	Gender equality in education	60.6	69.6	100.0	76.4	2034
	Child mortality	210.0	197.0	70.0	148.4	After 2040
	Access to safe water	..	42.0	..	..	..
Burundi	Hunger	49.0	69.0	24.5	40.8	Reversal
	Primary education	52.0[e]	53.7	100.0	67.4	After 2040
	Gender equality in education	82.0	79.4	100.0	89.2	Reversal
	Child mortality	190.0	190.0	63.3	134.3	Stagnation
	Access to safe water	69.0	78.0	84.5	75.2	2006
Cambodia	Hunger	43.0	36.0	21.5	35.8	2018
	Primary education	..	95.4	100.0	Achieved	Achieved
	Gender equality in education	..	83.2	100.0	..	..
	Child mortality	115.0	138.0	38.3	81.3	Reversal
	Access to safe water	..	30.0	..	..	..
Cape Verde	Hunger	..	..	..	..	..
	Primary education	..	98.8[f]	100.0	Achieved	Achieved
	Gender equality in education	..	..	100.0	..	..
	Child mortality	60.0	38.0	20.0	42.4	2010
	Access to safe water	..	74.0	..	..	..

Annex table 1 (contd.)

	Target[a]	1990 level	2000 level	2015 target	Required 2000 level	Expected date of achievement[b]
Central African Rep.	Hunger	49.0	44.0	24.5	40.8	2034
	Primary education	53.1	54.7	100.0	71.9	After 2040
	Gender equality in education	61.4	..	100.0	..	..
	Child mortality	180.0	180.0	60.0	127.2	Stagnation
	Access to safe water	48.0	70.0	74.0	58.4	2001
Chad	Hunger	58.0	32.0	29.0	48.3	2000
	Primary education	..	58.2	100.0	..	..
	Gender equality in education	..	55.5[d]	100.0	..	..
	Child mortality	203.0	200.0	67.7	143.5	Stagnation
	Access to safe water	..	27.0	..	..	..
Comoros	Hunger	..	..	..	..	..
	Primary education	..	56.2	100.0	..	..
	Gender equality in education	..	83.3[d]	100.0	..	..
	Child mortality	120.0	79.0	40.0	84.8	2011
	Access to safe water	88.0	96.0	94.0	Achieved	Achieved
Dem. Rep. of the Congo	Hunger	32.0	73.0	16.0	26.7	Reversal
	Primary education	54.3	32.6[f]	100.0	68.9	Reversal
	Gender equality in education	69.4[c]	79.8[f]	100.0	78.0	2012
	Child mortality	205.0	205.0	68.3	144.9	Stagnation
	Access to safe water	..	45.0	..	..	..
Djibouti	Hunger	..	..	..	..	..
	Primary education	31.6	32.6	100.0	59.0	Stagnation
	Gender equality in education	70.4[c]	85.3[d]	100.0	79.9	2007
	Child mortality	175.0	143.0	58.3	123.7	2030
	Access to safe water	..	100.0	..	Achieved	Achieved
Equatorial Guinea	Hunger	..	..	..	..	..
	Primary education	..	71.7	100.0	..	..
	Gender equality in education	..	71.5[d]	100.0	..	..
	Child mortality	206.0	153.0	68.7	145.6	2019
	Access to safe water	..	44.0	..	..	..
Eritrea	Hunger	..	58.0	..	..	..
	Primary education	24.1[c]	41.0	100.0	51.5	2032
	Gender equality in education	81.6[e]	76.7	100.0	87.5	Reversal
	Child mortality	155.0	111.0	51.7	109.5	2016
	Access to safe water	..	46.0	..	..	..
Ethiopia	Hunger	..	44.0	..	..	..
	Primary education	..	46.7	100.0	..	..
	Gender equality in education	68.3	68.0	100.0	81.0	Reversal
	Child mortality	193.0	172.0	64.3	136.4	After 2040
	Access to safe water	25.0	24.0	62.5	40.0	Reversal
Gambia	Hunger	21.0	21.0	10.5	17.5	Stagnation
	Primary education	50.9[c]	68.7	100.0	68.5	2016
	Gender equality in education	64.3	84.6	100.0	78.6	2008
	Child mortality	154.0	126.0	51.3	108.8	2030
	Access to safe water	..	62.0	..	..	..
Guinea	Hunger	40.0	32.0	20.0	33.3	2013
	Primary education	..	47.0	100.0	..	..
	Gender equality in education	43.1	57.3[f]	100.0	61.3	2022
	Child mortality	240.0	169.0	80.0	169.6	2015
	Access to safe water	45.0	48.0	72.5	56.0	After 2040
Guinea-Bissau	Hunger	..	..	..	..	..
	Primary education	..	53.5[d]	100.0	..	..
	Gender equality in education	..	64.9[d]	100.0	..	..
	Child mortality	253.0	211.0	84.3	178.8	2034
	Access to safe water	..	56.0	..	..	..
Haiti	Hunger	64.0	50.0	32.0	53.3	2011
	Primary education	22.1	..	100.0	..	..
	Gender equality in education	..	..	100.0	..	..
	Child mortality	150.0	123.0	50.0	106.0	2031
	Access to safe water	53.0	46.0	76.5	62.4	Reversal
Kiribati	Hunger	..	..	..	..	..
	Primary education	..	..	100.0	..	..
	Gender equality in education	97.9	..	100.0	..	..
	Child mortality	88.0	69.0	29.3	62.2	2024
	Access to safe water	..	48.0	..	..	..
Lao People's Dem. Rep.	Hunger	29.0	24.0	14.5	24.2	2016
	Primary education	61.4[c]	81.4	100.0	75.3	2008
	Gender equality in education	74.8[c]	82.0	100.0	83.8	2023
	Child mortality	163.0	100.0	54.3	115.2	2009
	Access to safe water	..	37.0	..	..	..

Annex table 1 (contd.)

	Target[a]	1990 level	2000 level	2015 target	Required 2000 level	Expected date of achievement[b]
Lesotho	Hunger	27.0	26.0	13.5	22.5	2112
	Primary education	72.8	78.4	100.0	83.7	2039
	Gender equality in education	123.8	106.8	100.0	104.6	Achieved
	Child mortality	148.0	132.0	49.3	126.3	After 2040
	Access to safe water	..	78.0	..	..	..
Liberia	Hunger	33.0	39.0	16.5	27.5	Reversal
	Primary education	..	83.4[d]	100.0	..	..
	Gender equality in education	..	69.7[d]	100.0	..	..
	Child mortality	235.0	235.0	78.3	166.1	Stagnation
	Access to safe water	..	..	..	..	..
Madagascar	Hunger	35.0	40.0	17.5	29.2	Reversal
	Primary education	..	67.7	100.0	..	..
	Gender equality in education	..	96.6	100.0[f]	Achieved	Achieved
	Child mortality	168.0	136.0	56.0	118.7	2029
	Access to safe water	44.0	47.0[d]	72.0	55.2	After 2040
Malawi	Hunger	49.0	33.0	24.5	40.8	2004
	Primary education	49.7	100.6	100.0	Achieved	Achieved
	Gender equality in education	78.9	93.9	100.0	87.4	2004
	Child mortality	241.0	183.0	80.3	170.3	2020
	Access to safe water	49.0	57.0	74.5	59.2	2019
Maldives	Hunger	..	..	..	..	..
	Primary education	..	99.0	100.0	Achieved	Achieved
	Gender equality in education	..	101.0	100.0	Achieved	Achieved
	Child mortality	115.0	77.0	38.3	81.3	2012
	Access to safe water	..	100.0	..	Achieved	Achieved
Mali	Hunger	25.0	20.0	12.5	20.8	2013
	Primary education	21.3	43.3[f]	100.0	46.5	2019
	Gender equality in education	57.0	66.3[f]	100.0	70.8	2027
	Child mortality	254.0	231.0	84.7	179.5	After 2040
	Access to safe water	55.0	65.0	77.5	64.0	2010
Mauritania	Hunger	14.0	12.0	7.0	11.7	2022
	Primary education	..	64.0	100.0	..	..
	Gender equality in education	67.5	92.5	100.0	80.5	2003
	Child mortality	183.0	183.0	61.0	129.3	Stagnation
	Access to safe water	37.0	37.0	68.5	49.6	Stagnation
Mozambique	Hunger	69.0	55.0	34.5	57.5	2012
	Primary education	46.8	54.4	100.0	68.1	After 2040
	Gender equality in education	73.4	74.6	100.0	84.1	After 2040
	Child mortality	235.0	197.0	78.3	166.1	2035
	Access to safe water	..	57.0	..	..	..
Myanmar	Hunger	10.0	6.0	5.0	8.3	2001
	Primary education	..	83.2	100.0	..	..
	Gender equality in education	94.7	97.8	100.0	96.8	2007
	Child mortality	130.0	109.0	43.3	91.9	2035
	Access to safe water	..	72.0	..	..	..
Nepal	Hunger	19.0	19.0	9.5	15.8	Stagnation
	Primary education	..	72.4	100.0	..	..
	Gender equality in education	52.8	82.1	100.0	71.7	2006
	Child mortality	145.0	91.0	48.3	102.5	2010
	Access to safe water	67.0	88.0[d]	83.5	Achieved	Achieved
Niger	Hunger	42.0	36.0	21.0	35.0	2022
	Primary education	24.9	30.4	100.0	55.0	After 2040
	Gender equality in education	53.8	67.3	100.0	72.3	2024
	Child mortality	320.0	265.0	106.7	226.1	2033
	Access to safe water	53.0	59.0	76.5	62.4	2025
Rwanda	Hunger	34.0	40.0	17.0	28.3	Reversal
	Primary education	65.9	97.3[d]	100.0	78.2	2000
	Gender equality in education	97.6	97.1[d]	100.0	Achieved	Achieved
	Child mortality	178.0	183.0	59.3	125.8	Reversal
	Access to safe water	..	41.0	..	..	..
Samoa	Hunger	..	..	..	..	..
	Primary education	..	96.9	100.0	Achieved	Achieved
	Gender equality in education	99.7	102.0	100.0	Achieved	Achieved
	Child mortality	42.0	25.0	14.0	29.7	2008
	Access to safe water	..	99.0	..	Achieved	Achieved
Sao Tome and Principe	Hunger	..	..	..	..	..
	Primary education	..	..	100.0	..	..
	Gender equality in education	..	..	100.0	..	..
	Child mortality	90.0	74.0	30.0	63.6	2031
	Access to safe water	..	..	..	..	..

Annex table 1 (concluded)

	Target[a]	1990 level	2000 level	2015 target	Required 2000 level	Expected date of achievement[b]
Senegal	Hunger	23.0	25.0	11.5	19.2	Reversal
	Primary education	48.1[c]	63.1	100.0	66.8	2022
	Gender equality in education	68.7[c]	83.9	100.0	80.0	2010
	Child mortality	148.0	138.0	49.3	104.6	After 2040
	Access to safe water	72.0	78.0	86.0	77.6	2011
Sierra Leone	Hunger	46.0	47.0	23.0	38.3	Reversal
	Primary education	..	..	100.0	..	
	Gender equality in education	67.4	76.5	100.0	80.4	2026
	Child mortality	323.0	316.0	107.7	228.3	Stagnation
	Access to safe water	..	57.0	..	..	..
Solomon Islands	Hunger	..	..	..	..	..
	Primary education	..	..	100.0	..	..
	Gender equality in education	77.1	..	100.0	..	..
	Child mortality	36.0	24.0	12.0	25.4	2012
	Access to safe water	..	71.0	..	..	..
Somalia	Hunger	67.0	71.0	33.5	55.8	Reversal
	Primary education	..	..	100.0	..	..
	Gender equality in education	..	..	100.0	..	..
	Child mortality	225.0	225.0	75.0	159.0	Stagnation
	Access to safe water	..	..	..	..	..
Sudan	Hunger	31.0	21.0	15.5	25.8	2004
	Primary education	..	46.3[d]	100.0	..	..
	Gender equality in education	75.1	102.4[d]	100.0	Achieved	Achieved
	Child mortality	123.0	107.0	41.0	86.9	After 2040
	Access to safe water	67.0	75.0	83.5	73.6	2009
United Rep. of Tanzania	Hunger	36.0	47.0	18.0	30.0	Reversal
	Primary education	51.4	46.7	100.0	70.9	Reversal
	Gender equality in education	96.8	98.9	100.0	98.1	2005
	Child mortality	163.0	165.0	54.3	115.2	Reversal
	Access to safe water	38.0	68.0	69.0	Achieved	Achieved
Togo	Hunger	28.0	23.0	14.0	23.3	2015
	Primary education	74.7	92.3	100.0	84.8	2004
	Gender equality in education	59.2	70.4	100.0	75.5	2027
	Child mortality	152.0	141.0	50.7	107.4	After 2040
	Access to safe water	51.0	54.0	75.5	60.8	After 2040
Tuvalu	Hunger	..	..	..	..	..
	Primary education	..	..	100.0	..	..
	Gender equality in education	..	..	100.0	..	..
	Child mortality	..	..	..	..	..
	Access to safe water	..	..	..	..	..
Uganda	Hunger	23.0	21.0	11.5	19.2	After 2040
	Primary education	..	109.5	100.0	Achieved	Achieved
	Gender equality in education	..	88.9	100.0	..	..
	Child mortality	165.0	124.0	55.0	116.6	2020
	Access to safe water	45.0	52.0	72.5	56.0	2025
Vanuatu	Hunger	..	..	..	..	..
	Primary education	..	95.9	100.0	Achieved	Achieved
	Gender equality in education	85.7[c]	101.9	100.0	Achieved	Achieved
	Child mortality	70.0	42.0	23.3	49.5	2008
	Access to safe water	..	88.0	..	..	..
Yemen	Hunger	36.0	33.0	18.0	30.0	After 2040
	Primary education	..	67.1	100.0	..	..
	Gender equality in education	..	49.9[f]	100.0	..	..
	Child mortality	142.0	107.0	47.3	100.3	2020
	Access to safe water	..	69.0	..	..	..
Zambia	Hunger	45.0	50.0	22.5	37.5	Reversal
	Primary education	..	65.5	100.0	..	..
	Gender equality in education	..	92.4	100.0	Achieved	Achieved
	Child mortality	192.0	202.0	64.0	135.7	Reversal
	Access to safe water	52.0	64.0	76.0	61.6	2008

Source: UNCTAD secretariat compilation, based on UNDP Human Development Report Office: direct communication.

Notes: a The quantitative variables used to monitor the targets on hunger, primary education, gender equality in education, child mortality and access to safe water are under-nourished people as percentage of total population, net primary school enrolment ratio, ratio of girls-to-boys in primary and secondary school, under-five child mortality rate (per 1,000 live births) and percentage of people with sustainable access to improved water sources, respectively.

   b This corresponds to the year in which the selected target will be achieved if the current rate of progress continues.

   c Refers to the 1991 level. d Refers to the 1999 level. e Refers to the 1992 level. f Refers to the 1998 level.

Annex 2: Progress towards graduation from LDC status

An important indicator of economic and social development in the LDCs is progress made towards graduation from the LDC category. Useful information on trends in this respect is provided by the Committee for Development Policy (CDP) of the United Nations Economic and Social Council (ECOSOC). One role of the CDP is to assist in identifying the countries to be included in, or graduated from, the LDC category. Table 1 summarizes data which the CDP has provided in this respect, on the basis of the latest (revised) criteria which it suggested as criteria for identifying LDCs in its latest triennial review of the list of least developed countries conducted in 2003.

Countries are eligible for inclusion in the list of LDCs if they have a population of less than 75 million and meet the following criteria and thresholds: gross national income (GNI) per capita less than $750;[5] Human Assets Index (HAI), based on indicators of nutrition, health and education, less than 55; and Economic Vulnerability Index (EVI), based on indicators of merchandise export concentration, instability of export earnings, instability of agricultural production, share of manufacturing and modern services in GDP and population size, greater than 37. A country must meet all the criteria. Thresholds for graduation from the list are: per capita GNI greater than $900; HAI greater than 61; and EVI greater than 33. A country must meet at least two criteria to be eligible for graduation. The Committee also proposed a modified EVI, which included a sixth component, that is data on population displaced by natural disasters. The threshold for inclusion with the modified EVI is greater than 38 and the threshold for graduation less than 34.

The CDP recalled the importance of a smooth transition for countries graduating from LDC status. Two LDCs — Cape Verde and Maldives — have met the GNI and HAI graduation thresholds in two consecutive reviews and have accordingly been recommended by the CDP for graduation. The decision itself is the responsibility of the ECOSOC and ultimately the General Assembly. Three other small island LDCs — Kiribati, Samoa and Tuvalu — also met the GNI and HAI graduation thresholds under the 2003 review, and the CDP has noted that Samoa might qualify for graduation in the 2006 review if the country continues to meet two of the three graduation criteria.

According to the 2003 review, the only other low-income country eligible for addition to the list was Timor-Leste, which joined the group of LDCs on 4 December 2003.

ANNEX TABLE 2. INDICATORS USED IN DETERMINING ELIGIBILITY FOR LEAST DEVELOPED COUNTRY STATUS: GRADUATION FROM, AND INCLUSION IN, THE LDC LIST

		Population 2002 (millions)	Per capita GNI ($)	HAI[a]	EVI[b]	EVI (modified)[c]
A. Low-income developing countries						
LDC	Afghanistan	23.3	523	11.6	50.1	49.0
LDC	Angola	13.9	447	25.6	48.5	46.8
LDC	Bangladesh	143.4	363	45.3	22.9	29.5
LDC	Benin	6.6	367	40.2	57.0	56.4
LDC	Bhutan	2.2	600	40.4	40.6	41.0
LDC	Burkina Faso	12.2	217	26.5	49.3	47.0
LDC	Burundi	6.7	110	19.7	53.8	49.6
LDC	Cambodia	13.8	263	44.5	49.7	48.1
	Cameroon	15.5	583	43.8	31.9	31.2
LDC	Cape Verde	0.4	**1 323**	**72.0**	55.5	56.7
LDC	Central African Republic	3.8	277	29.9	43.1	42.0
LDC	Chad	8.4	203	26.1	59.2	56.6
LDC	Comoros	0.7	387	38.1	59.1	58.7
	Congo	3.2	610	55.2	50.3	46.8
	Côte d'Ivoire	16.7	687	43.0	25.4	25.9
	Dem. People's Rep. of Korea	22.6	440	62.9	32.8	29.5
LDC	Dem. Rep. of the Congo	54.3	100	34.3	40.8	42.3
LDC	Djibouti	0.7	873	30.2	48.6	49.5
LDC	Equatorial Guinea	0.5	743	47.2	64.4	55.8
LDC	Eritrea	4.0	190	32.8	51.7	50.2
LDC	Ethiopia	66.0	100	25.2	42.0	40.7
LDC	Gambia	1.4	340	34.0	60.8	56.5
	Ghana	20.2	337	57.9	40.9	41.9

Annex Table 2 (contd.)

		Population 2002 (millions)	Per capita GNI ($)	HAI[a]	EVI[b]	EVI (modified)[c]
LDC	Guinea	8.4	447	30.3	42.1	40.0
LDC	Guinea-Bissau	1.3	170	31.2	64.6	60.7
LDC	Haiti	8.4	493	35.3	41.7	43.5
	India	1 041.1	450	55.7	13.5	19.6
	Indonesia	217.5	610	73.6	18.1	21.9
	Kenya	31.9	350	49.3	28.4	29.0
LDC	Kiribati	0.1	**923**	**67.5**	64.8	60.4
LDC	Lao People's Dem. Republic	5.5	297	46.4	43.9	43.4
LDC	Lesotho	2.1	573	45.4	44.2	44.5
LDC	Liberia	3.3	285	38.7	63.1	58.3
LDC	Madagascar	16.9	253	37.9	21.6	27.0
LDC	Malawi	11.8	177	39.0	49.0	49.4
LDC	Maldives	0.3	**1 983**	**65.2**	33.6	37.5
LDC	Mali	12.0	230	19.9	47.5	45.4
LDC	Mauritania	2.8	377	38.2	38.9	37.7
	Mongolia	2.6	393	63.3	50.0	48.9
LDC	Mozambique	19.0	220	20.0	35.6	39.2
LDC	Myanmar	49.0	282	60.0	45.4	45.6
LDC	Nepal	24.2	240	47.1	**29.5**	**31.0**
	Nicaragua	5.3	395	60.8	39.4	42.5
LDC	Niger	11.6	180	14.2	54.1	53.1
	Nigeria	120.0	267	52.3	52.8	51.1
	Pakistan	148.7	437	45.5	20.2	26.1
	Papua New Guinea	5.0	673	46.2	36.1	38.6
LDC	Rwanda	8.1	230	34.1	63.3	59.6
LDC	Samoa	0.2	**1 447**	**88.8**	40.9	50.8
LDC	Sao Tome and Principe	0.1	280	55.8	41.8	37.0
LDC	Senegal	9.9	490	38.1	38.4	38.8
LDC	Sierra Leone	4.8	130	21.7	45.7	43.3
LDC	Solomon Islands	0.5	657	47.3	46.7	49.1
LDC	Somalia	9.6	177	8.5	55.4	53.1
LDC	Sudan	32.6	333	46.4	45.2	46.5
	Timor-Leste	0.8	478	36.4	..	..
LDC	Togo	4.8	293	48.6	41.5	42.8
LDC	Tuvalu	0.01	**1 383**	**63.7**	70.3	67.3
LDC	Uganda	24.8	297	39.8	43.2	41.6
LDC	United Republic of Tanzania	36.8	263	41.1	**28.3**	**30.2**
LDC	Vanuatu	0.2	**1 083**	57.4	44.5	46.4
	Viet Nam	80.2	390	72.7	37.1	39.4
LDC	Yemen	19.9	423	46.8	49.1	49.0
LDC	Zambia	10.9	317	43.4	49.3	47.6
	Zimbabwe	13.1	463	56.5	33.7	30.3
B. Economies in transition						
	Armenia	3.8	523	79.4	30.7	34.0
	Azerbaijan	8.1	607	72.8	38.9	40.6
	Georgia	5.2	647	76.2	47.6	48.2
	Kyrgyzstan	5.0	287	77.6	38.2	39.9
	Republic of Moldova	4.3	397	81.1	39.6	39.1
	Tajikistan	6.2	173	69.5	37.7	39.1
	Turkmenistan	4.9	780	84.5	60.9	53.8
	Ukraine	48.7	723	86.3	23.8	26.1
	Uzbekistan	25.6	607	81.3	40.3	36.3

Source: United Nations (2003b).

Notes: Figures in boldface type indicate a graduation criterion that has been met by a current LDC.

a   The Human Asset Index (HAI) reflects the following: (a) nutrition, measured by the average calorie consumption per capita as a percentage of the minimum requirement; (b) health, measured by the under-5 child mortality rate; and (c) education, measured by: (i) the adult literacy rate and (ii) the gross secondary school enrolment ratio.

b   The Economic Vulnerability Index (EVI) is an average of five indicators: (a) merchandise export concentration; (b) instability of export earnings; (c) instability of agricultural production; (d) share of manufacturing and modern services in GDP; and (e) population size.

c   EVI with a sixth component, i.e. percentage of population displaced by natural disasters, to supplement data on the instability of agricultural production.

Notes

1. The demographic transition is the process of change whereby a country's previously high birth and death rates shift to lower values. In general, the fall in death rates, which occurs with rising living standards, advances in public health and better nutrition, occurs before the fall in birth rates, and thus during the transition period there is a high rate of population growth.
2. All the LDC regional averages in this section are simple, not weighted averages.
3. This section is based on data kindly provided by the UN Human Development Report Office.
4. This section is based on Gonsalves (2003).
5. For countries classified by the World Bank as low-income in at least one year between 1999 and 2001.

References

De Waal, A. and Tumushabe, J. (2003). HIV/AIDS and food security in Africa, Department for International Development, Pretoria, February.

Gonsalves, J. (2003). HIV/AIDS in the least developed countries: Can it become a development catastrophe?, background paper prepared for *The Least Developed Countries Report 2004.*

Herrmann, M. (2003). Millennium development goals and LDC-specific development goals: An assessment of differences and recommendations towards harmonization, mimeo.

McPherson, M.F. (2003). Macroeconomic models of the impact of HIV/AIDS, Harvard University, February.

UNAIDS (2002). *Report on the Global HIV/AIDS Epidemic 2002*, UNAIDS/02.26E, Geneva.

UNCTAD (2001).The development goals of the Programme of Action for the Least Developed Countries for the Decade 2001–2010: Towards a set of indicators to monitor progress, TD/B/48/14, 3 August, Geneva.

UNCTAD (2002). *The Least Developed Countries 2002 Report*, United Nations publication, sales no. E.02.II.D.13, Geneva.

UNDP (2001). HIV/AIDS implications for poverty reduction, background paper prepared for the United Nations Development Programme for the UN General Assembly Special Session on HIV/AIDS, 25–27 June.

UNDP (2002). UNDP Statistical Fact Sheet HIV/AIDS, http://www.undp.org/hiv/docs/Barcelona-statistical-fact-sheet-2July02.doc

UNDP (2003). *Human Development Report 2003,* Oxford University Press, New York.

UNFPA (2002). *State of World Population 2002: People, Poverty and Possibilities,* United Nations Population Fund, New York.

United Nations (2001). Programme of Action for the Least Developed Countries for the Decade 2001–2010, 8 June, A/CONF.191/11.

United Nations (2002). *World Urbanization Prospects: The 2001 Revision,* United Nations Population Division, New York.

United Nations (2003a). *World Population Prospects: The 2002 Revision,* United Nations Population Division, New York.

United Nations (2003b). Local development and global issues, report of the Committee for Development Policy on the fifth session, 7–11 April 2003, Department of Economic and Social Affairs, New York.

Selected Recent Policy Trends: Accession of LDCs to the WTO

A. Introduction

A rule-based multilateral trading system provides transparency, stability and predictability with respect to market access conditions and various other trade-related issues. The provision of these public goods is intended not simply to promote the development of trade relations but also to foster the economic prosperity of trading partners. As the preamble to the Agreement Establishing the World Trade Organization states, "relations in the field of trade and economic endeavours should be conducted with a view to raising standards of living, ensuring full employment and a large and steadily growing volume of real income and effective demand, and expanding the production of and trade in goods and services, while allowing for the optimal use of the world's resources in accordance with the objective of sustainable development, seeking both to protect and preserve the environment and to enhance the means for doing so in a manner consistent with their [i.e. the Parties to the Agreement] respective needs and concerns at different levels of economic development". Like their trading partners, the LDCs view their participation in the multilateral trading system as a means of integrating into the global economy and maximizing their benefits from international trade. However, achieving this depends on supportive terms of accession.

Like their trading partners, the LDCs view their participation in the multilateral trading system as a means of integrating into the global economy and maximizing their benefits from international trade. However, achieving this depends on supportive terms of accession.

This chapter provides a comparative description of the terms of accession of the first three LDCs to have completed accession negotiations since the establishment of the WTO — Cambodia, Nepal and Vanuatu. Of these three countries, only Nepal has so far acceded to the WTO. On 23 April 2004 Nepal became the 147th member State of the WTO and it is so far the only LDC to have joined the WTO since its establishment in 1994.

Comparing these three cases with one another highlights the fact that the commitments made by the LDCs in question are characterized by significant differences, and a comparison of the three cases with countries that are already WTO members shows that the commitments made by these LDCs are often much greater than commitments made by existing WTO members, particularly in the area of market access commitments. It can, for example, be observed that while developing countries that are already WTO members benefit from different types of special and differential treatment, it is not guaranteed that the developing countries which are in the process of acceding to the WTO will automatically be granted the right to special and differential treatment. The outcomes reflect the fact that the current accession practice requires all developing countries, including the least developed ones, to negotiate all provisions on a case-by-case basis.

B. The challenge of accession

All countries acceding to the WTO face substantial difficulties in their efforts to join the multilateral trading system.[1] The accession process itself is long and complicated, requiring the pursuit of negotiations on three different tracks. The first track is the systemic or multilateral track. It provides for examination of the foreign trade regime and economic system of the acceding country and their compatibility with the WTO Agreements. This examination is made on the basis of the Memorandum on the Foreign Trade Regime submitted by the acceding country and subsequent rounds of questions and answers, as well as delivery of the Working Party's report and the Protocol of Accession setting out detailed terms of accession. There are also two bilateral tracks of market access negotiations on goods and services with interested WTO members. Market access in the goods track includes negotiations of concessions in the area of trade in goods (mainly in the form of reductions and bindings of import tariffs). These negotiations are carried out bilaterally with the main trading partners of an acceding country. The list of concessions in a WTO format (a table) forms an integral part of the Protocol of Accession, and the concessions should be extended on an unconditional MFN basis to all other WTO members. Market access in the services track involves negotiations of commitments on trade in services, which are also conducted bilaterally and result in a schedule of specific commitments formatted appropriately (in a table) and annexed to the Protocol of Accession. Finally, there is a "sub-track", which is concerned with plurilateral discussions on agricultural domestic support and export subsidies commitments with interested WTO members.

> *All countries acceding to the WTO face substantial difficulties in their efforts to join the multilateral trading system. The accession process itself is long and complicated, requiring the pursuit of negotiations on three different tracks.*

Difficulties for countries seeking accession arise from:

- Substantive policy issues relating to adjustments in their development strategies and implementing instruments, economic and social goals, and legislative reforms — which are all necessary for compliance with the WTO Agreements;

- Insufficient knowledge, experience, resources, infrastructures and analytical capacities required for accession negotiations;

- Increasing demands by some WTO members that require from acceding countries, in one way or another, a higher level of obligations and commitments than the level of obligations and commitments made by the original WTO members in the Uruguay Round, which thus affect the balance of their WTO rights and obligations. WTO members have not agreed on common approaches to the terms of accession and often express different views on this matter. In this situation, those members that are most active in the accessions succeed in imposing their vision and demands on the acceding countries.

> *Difficulties for countries seeking accession also arise from increasing demands by some WTO members.*

Although these difficulties apply to all developing countries and countries with economies in transition, it should be recognized that the challenges are particularly difficult for the least developed countries, which have extremely weak human and institutional capacities and limited technical know-how and financial resources. These problems were acknowledged by the WTO members in the Doha Ministerial Declaration (WTO, 2001a). Accordingly, they agreed "to work to facilitate and accelerate negotiations with acceding LDCs" and reaffirmed the commitments undertaken in the Programme of Action for the Least Developed Countries for the Decade 2001–2010 agreed at the Third United Nations Conference on the Least Developed Countries, held in Brussels in May 2001 (WTO, 2001a). In the Programme of Action, development partners

> *The challenges are particularly difficult for the least developed countries, which have extremely weak human and institutional capacities and limited technical know-how and financial resources.*

of LDCs agreed to facilitate the accession process of non-members "on the basis of terms that take into account their stage of development and the basic principles of special and differential treatment" and to "support efforts of LDCs seeking to accede" in various ways, including:

"(i) Ensuring that the accession process is more effective and less onerous and tailored to their specific economic conditions, *inter alia* by streamlining WTO procedural requirements;

(ii) Providing for automatic eligibility of all acceding LDCs for all provisions on special and differential treatment in existing WTO agreements;

(iii) In view of LDCs' special economic situation and their development, financial and trade needs, WTO members should exercise restraint, where appropriate, in seeking concessions in the negotiations on market access for goods and services in keeping with the letter and spirit of the provisions of the Ministerial Decision on Measures in Favour of the Least Developed Countries;

(iv) Seeking from LDCs in the accession stage only commitments that are commensurate with their level of development;

(v) Continuing to provide adequate and predictable assistance to LDCs for their accession process, including technical, financial or other forms of assistance;

(vi) Accelerating the accession process for LDCs that are in the process of accession to WTO" (para. 68(o)).

In addition, on 10 December 2002, the WTO General Council, in pursuance of the Doha mandate, and in an attempt to mainstream the Brussels Programme of Action into WTO work and actions adopted a decision on the Accession of LDCs (WTO, 2003b). This is reproduced in box 2. It was expected that the decision (which is also called "guidelines") would substantially facilitate LDC accessions, particularly by exercising restraint on WTO members in seeking concessions and commitments on trade in goods and services from acceding LDCs, and allowing acceding LDCs to benefit from the special and differential treatment provisions under the WTO Agreements. By mid-2003, 10 LDCs were still negotiating WTO accession and were at various stages of the process. However, at the Fifth WTO Ministerial Conference, held at Cancún in September 2003, the terms of accession for Cambodia and Nepal were approved.

This was an important breakthrough. However, as table 23 shows, of the LDCs seeking accession six — Bhutan, Cape Verde, Ethiopia, the Lao People's Democratic Republic, Sudan and Yemen — are still in the initial stage of negotiations, although some of them have been in the negotiating process for six to nine years. One country (Vanuatu) completed accession negotiations in 2001, but the results were suspended by the acceding Government. Another country (Samoa) has reached an advanced stage in negotiations after more than five years. Afghanistan applied for accession in March 2003, but its application has not yet been considered. Eight other LDCs are not members of the WTO and have not yet applied to join.

This chapter describes the accession terms of Cambodia and Nepal, the first LDCs ever to have completed accession negotiations with the WTO under the full negotiating process laid down in Article XII of the Agreement establishing the WTO.[2] The accession terms are also compared with those for Vanuatu.

In September 2003, the terms of accession for Cambodia and Nepal were approved. They were the first LDCs ever to have completed accession negotiations with the WTO under the full negotiating process.

However, of the LDCs seeking accession, six — Bhutan, Cape Verde, Ethiopia, the Lao People's Democratic Republic, Sudan and Yemen — are still in the initial stage of negotiations, although some of them have been in the negotiating process for six to nine years.

Box 2. Accession of Least Developed Countries
Decision of 10 December 2002

[The General Council] Decides that:

Negotiations for the accession of LDCs to the WTO be facilitated and accelerated through simplified and streamlined accession procedures, with a view to concluding these negotiations as quickly as possible, in accordance with the guidelines set out hereunder:

I.   Market Access:

- WTO Members shall exercise restraint in seeking concessions and commitments on trade in goods and services from acceding LDCs, taking into account the levels of concessions and commitments undertaken by existing WTO LDCs' Members;
- acceding LDCs shall offer access through reasonable concessions and commitments on trade in goods and services commensurate with their individual development, financial and trade needs, in line with Article XXXVI.8 of GATT 1994, Article 15 of the Agreement on Agriculture, and Articles IV and XIX of the General Agreement on Trade in Services.

II. WTO Rules:

- Special and Differential Treatment, as set out in the Multilateral Trade Agreements, Ministerial Decisions, and other relevant WTO legal instruments, shall be applicable to all acceding LDCs, from the date of entry into force of their respective Protocols of Accession;
- transitional periods/transitional arrangements foreseen under specific WTO Agreements, to enable acceding LDCs to effectively implement commitments and obligations, shall be granted in accession negotiations taking into account individual development, financial and trade needs;
- transitional periods/arrangements shall be accompanied by Action Plans for compliance with WTO rules. The implementation of the Action Plans shall be supported by Technical Assistance and Capacity Building measures for the acceding LDCs. Upon the request of an acceding LDC, WTO Members may coordinate efforts to guide that LDC through the implementation process;
- commitments to accede to any of the Plurilateral Trade Agreements or to participate in other optional sectoral market access initiatives shall not be a precondition for accession to the Multilateral Trade Agreements of the WTO. As provided in paragraph 5 of Article IX and paragraph 3 of Article XII of the WTO Agreement, decisions on the Plurilateral Trade Agreements shall be adopted by the Members of, and governed by the provisions in, those Agreements. WTO Members may seek to ascertain acceding LDCs' interests in the Plurilateral Trade Agreements.

III. Process:

- The good offices of the Director-General shall be available to assist acceding LDCs and Chairpersons of the LDCs' Accession Working Parties in implementing this decision;
- efforts shall continue to be made, in line with information technology means and developments, including in LDCs themselves, to expedite documentation exchange and streamline accession procedures for LDCs to make them more effective and efficient, and less onerous. The Secretariat will assist in this regard. Such efforts will, *inter-alia*, be based upon the WTO Reference Centres that are already operational in acceding LDCs;
- WTO Members may adopt additional measures in their bilateral negotiations to streamline and facilitate the process, e.g., by holding bilateral negotiations in the acceding LDC if so requested;
- upon request, WTO Members may through coordinated, concentrated and targeted technical assistance from an early stage facilitate the accession of an acceding LDC.

IV. Trade-related Technical Assistance and Capacity Building:

- Targeted and coordinated technical assistance and capacity building, by WTO and other relevant multilateral, regional and bilateral development partners, including *inter alia* under the Integrated Framework (IF), shall be provided, on a priority basis, to assist acceding LDCs. Assistance shall be accorded with the objective of effectively integrating the acceding LDC into the multilateral trading system;
- effective and broad-based technical cooperation and capacity building measures shall be provided, on a priority basis, to cover all stages of the accession process, i.e. from the preparation of documentation to the setting up of the legislative infrastructure and enforcement mechanisms, considering the high costs involved and in order to enable the acceding LDC to benefit from and comply with WTO rights and obligations.

The implementation of these guidelines shall be reviewed regularly in the agenda of the Sub-Committee on LDCs. The results of this review shall be included in the Annual Report of the Committee on Trade and Development to the General Council. In pursuance of their commitments on LDCs' accessions in the Doha Ministerial Declaration, Ministers will take stock of the situation at the Fifth Ministerial Conference and, as appropriate, at subsequent Ministerial Conferences.

TABLE 23. PROCESS OF LDCS' ACCESSION TO WTO (AS OF 1 OCTOBER 2003)

	Bhutan	Cambodia	Cape Verde	Ethiopia	Lao PDR	Nepal	Samoa	Sudan	Vanuatu	Yemen
Application	09/99	12/94	10/99	01/01	07/97	05/89	04/98	11/94	07/95	04/00
WTO Working Party established	10/99	12/94	07/00	02/03	02/98	06/89	07/98	11/94	07/95	07/00
Memorandum on the Foreign Trade Regime submitted	02/03	06/99	07/03		03/01	02/90 08/98	02/00	01/99	11/95	11/02
First meeting of Working Party		05/01				05/00	03/02	07/03	07/96	
Tariff offer and revisions submitted		12/00 07/02 03/03 07/03				07/00 05/02	08/01		11/97 05/98 11/99	
Services offer and revisions submitted		12/00 07/02 03/03 06/03				07/00 05/02 08/03	08/01		11/97 11/99	
Agricultural support data Accession package approved		12/01 07/02 09/03				09/98 07/99 09/03	08/00 06/03	06/03	09/99 10/01	
Length of accession process (as of 1 October 2003)	4 years, 1 month (ongoing)	8 years, 9 months (final)	4 years (ongoing)	9 months (ongoing)	6 years, 2 months (ongoing)	14 years 3 months (final)	5 years, 5 months (ongoing)	8 years, 11 months (ongoing)	8 years, 3 months (ongoing)	3 years (ongoing)

Source: UNCTAD compilation, based on WTO (2003).

C. Three country cases

The accession package for Cambodia, Nepal and Vanuatu consisted, as for any other acceding countries, of three major parts:

(i)   Protocol of Accession and the Report of the WTO Working Party, in which all of the "systemic" commitments and obligations (i.e. those reflecting consistency with the WTO rules) are undertaken with reference to the WTO rules and disciplines;

(ii) Schedule of concessions on market access in goods, namely bound tariffs. This also includes data on domestic support measures and export subsidies in agriculture;

(iii) Schedule of specific commitments in services.

Cambodia undertook 29 systemic commitments in its Protocol of Accession.

1. THE CASE OF CAMBODIA[3]

(a) Systemic commitments

Cambodia undertook 29 systemic commitments in its Protocol of Accession. It was granted four transition periods delaying implementation of:

•   The Agreement on Trade-Related Aspects of Intellectual Property Rights (TRIPS) (excluding pharmaceuticals and agricultural chemicals) until 1 January 2007. Before adoption of the terms of accession, the WTO Ministerial Conference in Cancún (11 September 2003) agreed that "the terms of this accession do not preclude access to the benefits under the

Doha Declaration on the TRIPS Agreement and Public Health to Cambodia as a (least-developed country)";

- The Agreement on Technical Barriers to Trade (TBT) until 1 January 2007;

- The Agreement on Sanitary and Phytosanitary Measures (SPS) until 1 January 2008;

- The Agreement on Customs Valuation until 1 January 2009.

Other main systemic commitments include:

- Non-application of the Agreement on Trade-Related Investment Measures (TRIMs) upon accession (these measures do not exist, and are not foreseen as a policy instrument, in Cambodia);

- *De minimis* levels (up to 10 per cent of the value of agricultural production) for domestic support in agriculture;

- Binding export subsidies in agriculture at zero and committing not to use any such subsidies in the future;

- Cambodia's right to use export subsidies in industrial sectors (allowed for LDCs under the Agreement on Subsidies and Countervailing Measures, although there were strong pressures from several members for that right to be forgone).

Cambodia did not join two plurilateral agreements — those on government procurement and trade in civil aircraft.

(b) Bound tariffs

> *Cambodia bound 100 per cent of tariff lines... On agricultural products, Cambodia's average bound rate is 30 per cent... For industrial products, the average bound rate is 18.2 per cent.*

Cambodia bound 100 per cent of tariff lines. This means that it has effectively set ceilings on the tariff rates of all imported products, which prevents it from increasing tariff rates on imported goods above the tariff rate to which it has committed. On agricultural products, Cambodia's average bound rate is 30 per cent, peak bound rates for the most sensitive products are 50–60 per cent and the lowest bound rates are 5 per cent. For industrial products, the average bound rate is 18.2 per cent, peak bound rates are 50 per cent and minimal rates are 0 per cent. Cambodia did not join any of the optional "tariff initiatives" – "zero-for zero", the Information Technology Agreement and "chemical tariff harmonization".

(c) Services

Services commitments cover the 11 main service sectors under the WTO classification (excluding "other services not included elsewhere")[4], some sectors with full sub-sector commitments, and other sectors with partial commitments and transition periods (for example, up to 1 January 2009 for the telecommunication sector). These commitments are carefully drafted and reflect Cambodia's development policies aimed, in particular, at attracting foreign investment.

2. THE CASE OF NEPAL[5]

(a) Systemic commitments

> *Nepal undertook 25 systemic commitments in its Protocol of Accession.*

Nepal undertook 25 systemic commitments in its Protocol of Accession. It was granted transition periods until 1 January 2007 for implementing four WTO Agreements — TRIPS, the Agreement on Customs Valuation, TBT and SPS.

Other systemic commitments include:

- Non-application of TRIMs upon accession;
- *De minimis* levels (up to 10 per cent of the value of agricultural production) for domestic support in agriculture;
- Right to use export subsidies in industrial sectors (allowed for LDCs under the Agreement on Subsidies and Countervailing Measures).

Nepal did not join two plurilateral agreements — those on government procurement and trade in civil aircraft. Other commitments undertaken are usual for WTO members and reflect obligations under specific WTO Agreements.

Nepal bound 100 per cent of tariff lines. Average bound tariffs on agricultural products are almost 44 per cent, while for industrial products they are 23 per cent.

(b) Bound tariffs

Nepal bound 100 per cent of tariff lines. Average bound tariffs on agricultural products are almost 44 per cent, while for industrial products they are 23 per cent. Tariff peaks on agricultural products include rates of 100 and 200 per cent, and minimal rates are 10 per cent. Peaks on industrial products amount to 130 per cent, and minimal rates are 0 per cent. Nepal did not join any of the optional "tariff initiatives" — "zero-for-zero", the Information Technology Agreement and "chemical tariff harmonization".

(c) Services

Nepal's commitments specify the 11 main sectors, but the actual level of market openings is subject to different conditions in line with Nepal's development goals, for example equity limitations for foreign services providers in individual sectors (WTO, 2003d).

3. THE CASE OF VANUATU[6]

Vanuatu applied for WTO membership in July 1995, and was expected to be the first LDC to accede to the WTO. However, the accession negotiations proved to be difficult for it. The rights that the LDC WTO members are entitled to were largely denied to Vanuatu, and the country was subjected to strong pressure to make sweeping liberalization commitments. In particular, Vanuatu had difficulty in meeting demands by the United States, and by the end of the 1990s accession negotiations has stalled.

Vanuatu applied for WTO membership in July 1995, and was expected to be the first LDC to accede to the WTO. Since 2001 the accession process has been on hold, and no steps have been taken to conclude the accession negotiations.

In 2001, Vanuatu and the United States resumed their negotiations. By then the dynamics between the two negotiating teams had shifted in a more positive direction, owing in part to the compromises the two countries had reached on most of the outstanding issues. Just before the Fourth WTO Ministerial Conference in Doha, the Working Party met for the last time. After the meeting the world's press reported that Vanuatu had completed its accession negotiations and that its membership would be announced in Doha. However, a few days later the Government of Vanuatu asked the WTO secretariat for a "technical delay" in its accession procedure. Since then the accession process has been on hold, and no steps have been taken to conclude the accession negotiations. There has been no official explanation as to why the Government resorted to the "technical delay".

D. Comparative assessment amongst the accession countries

Examination of the commitments made or agreed to by the three countries will indicate the extent to which the decision by the WTO General Council (Guidelines for Accession of LDCs) has been respected.

As will be shown below, the overall assessment indicates that this is not fully the case. With regard to market access commitments both in goods and in services, Cambodia and Nepal made substantially greater commitments than Vanuatu. In terms of transition periods Cambodia and Nepal were able to obtain better conditions than Vanuatu. Furthermore, as indicated below with regard to the textiles regime, the terms which Cambodia and Nepal obtained with respect to trade in textiles and clothing do not reflect the WTO members' agreement to help LDCs increase their exports.

1. IMPLEMENTATION OF AGREEMENTS

(a) Trade-related investment measures

In their Sun City Declaration of 1999 the trade representatives of the LDCs asked for an open-ended transition period for the LDCs with respect to TRIMs, and in their Zanzibar Declaration of 2001 the trade ministers of the LDCs asked for a complete exemption of the LDCs from TRIMs

Vanuatu and Cambodia undertook not to maintain any measure inconsistent with the TRIMs Agreement, while Nepal undertook not to introduce new measures unless they were in conformity with the requirements of the Agreement, which in practice means the same. Thus these three countries went further than the stated objective of the least developed country group in this area. In their Sun City Declaration of 1999 the trade representatives of the LDCs asked for an open-ended transition period for the LDCs with respect to TRIMs, and in their Zanzibar Declaration of 2001, the trade ministers of the LDCs asked for a complete exemption of the LDCs from TRIMs (WTO, 1999, 2001c).

(b) Trade-related aspects of intellectual property rights

These three countries went further than the stated objective of the least developed country group in the area of TRIMs.

In this area, Cambodia and Nepal obtained a three-year transition period, while Vanuatu obtained a two-year period. Cambodia made explicit commitments to comply with obligations concerning Part II, sections 5 and 7 of the TRIPS Agreement, namely patents and protection of undisclosed information, although the Doha Declaration on the TRIPS Agreement and Public Health exempted the LDC members from the obligations of these provisions for pharmaceutical products until 1 January 2016. Subsequently, the Fifth WTO Ministerial Conference assured Cambodia that it is entitled to all the rights of the LDCs.

(c) Anti-dumping, countervailing duties and safeguard regimes

All countries agreed that they would ensure compliance with the relevant rules and regulations of the WTO in this area. This is different from the desire expressed by the trade representatives of the least developed countries, which at their previous meetings had requested that (i) they benefit from an expansion of non-actionable subsidies; (ii) they should not be subjected to safeguard actions or anti-dumping measures; (iii) they should be able to impose safeguard actions without providing compensatory measures; (iv) they should benefit from simplified rules to initiate anti-dumping actions; and (v) they should not be subjected to other contingency measures (WTO, 1999, 2001c, 2003a).

(d) Other agreements

The countries also agreed to make progress in the implementation of the Agreement on Rules of Origin, and to ensure full compliance with the Agreement on Preshipment Inspections. Vanuatu also agreed to implement the provisions of the Agreement on Government Procurement, which ensures equal treatment of foreigners. The three countries also agreed to comply with the usual WTO rules and disciplines upon their accession, including (i) trade registration requirements/trading rights, (ii) fees and charges for services rendered, (iii) export regulations, (iv) publication of information on trade, and (v) notifications.

(e) Transition periods

In terms of transition periods, Cambodia and Nepal were able to negotiate with more flexibility than Vanuatu. Of the three countries, Cambodia obtained the longest transition period — five years for customs valuation, three years for technical barriers to trade, four years for sanitary and phytosanitary measures, and three years for TRIPS. Nepal negotiated a three-year period for customs valuation, TBT and SPS and TRIPS. Vanuatu had only a one-year transition period for customs valuation and a two-year period for TRIPS.

(f) Framework for making and enforcing policies

All countries agreed to put in place the legal and administrative conditions for the making and enforcement of policies related to the different negotiation commitments and the different trade agreements. Cambodia obtained a one-year transition period to establish its tribunal system, while Nepal and Vanuatu committed to establishing it upon accession.

All countries agreed to put in place the legal and administrative conditions for the making and enforcement of policies related to the different negotiation commitments and the different trade agreements.

2. MARKET ACCESS IN AGRICULTURAL AND INDUSTRIAL GOODS

(a) Tariffs

Cambodia and Vanuatu agreed to implement their tariff offers largely upon accession, but Nepal delayed full implementation of its tariff cuts mostly until 2006. Simple-average agricultural bound tariff rates for the three countries were 43 per cent for Vanuatu, 30 per cent for Cambodia and 44 per cent for Nepal. The corresponding figures for industrial tariff rates were 49 per cent for Vanuatu, 18.2 per cent for Cambodia and 23 per cent for Nepal. Tariff peaks and minimal rates for agricultural products were 75 per cent and 0 per cent for Vanuatu, 60 per cent and 5 per cent for Cambodia, and 200 per cent and 10 per cent for Nepal. For industrial products the corresponding rates were 75 per cent and 0 per cent for Vanuatu, 50 per cent and 0 per cent for Cambodia, and 130 per cent and 0 per cent for Nepal.

For optional "tariff initiatives" — namely, the zero-for-zero tariff reduction initiatives, the Information Technology Agreement, and chemical tariff harmonization — Vanuatu committed to providing duty-free access for more than 160 tariff lines in aircraft, aircraft parts and pharmaceutical products by 2005. Cambodia and Nepal did not participate in the tariff initiatives.

(b) Other duties and charges

For other duties and charges, the three countries committed to binding at zero and complying with the relevant WTO provisions (especially Article II:1 (b) of the GATT 1994). Unlike Cambodia and Vanuatu, Nepal obtained a 10-year transition period for full implementation for a wide range of products — that is, the right to apply additional duties other than bound tariffs.

Cambodia obtained a one-year transition period to establish its tribunal system, while Nepal and Vanuatu committed to establishing it upon accession.

Nepal obtained the most flexible commitments in terms of tariff peaks and implementation periods for tariff cuts and zero-binding commitments for other duties and charges. However, simple-average bound tariff rates, especially for industrial goods, for the three countries indicate that Cambodia and Nepal have made significantly greater tariff cut commitments than Vanuatu. With regard to bound tariff reductions, Cambodia made the most significant commitments.

3. MARKET ACCESS IN TEXTILES AND SERVICES

(a) Trade in textiles

Application of the retroactive growth rate under the Agreement on Textiles and Clothing to LDC acceding countries would be in line with the WTO's policy of helping LDCs increase their exports.

For Cambodia and Nepal, it was agreed that the first stage of the growth rate provisions of the Agreement on Textiles and Clothing would be applied. Textile products are very important for these two countries' exports. Both countries should have been granted the growth rate retroactively from the day before the entry into force of the WTO Agreement since they had accepted the obligations of the WTO rules and made substantial market access commitments. Moreover, application of the retroactive growth rate under the Agreement on Textiles and Clothing to LDC acceding countries would be in line with the WTO's policy of helping LDCs increase their exports.

(b) Trade in services

Cambodia and Nepal made substantially greater liberalization commitments than Vanuatu. The coverage of Cambodia's offer was slightly wider than that of Nepal. The number of services included in the three countries' service schedules totalled 21 with Cambodia including 19 categories, and Nepal and Vanuatu 17 and 12 respectively. At the sub-category level, Cambodia, Nepal and Vanuatu included 74, 61 and 46 sub-categories, respectively, in their schedules.

Cambodia, Nepal and Vanuatu made substantial liberalization offers in the areas of financial, professional, distribution, education and environmental services.

With regard to horizontal limitations and commitments, there was no noteworthy difference among the three countries. All of them scheduled Mode 4 (movement of persons) unbound except a few categories such as managers, executives, specialists and intra-corporate transferees. Other limitations scheduled included the obligation to train and promote local staff (Cambodia), and the right to provide subsidies only to domestic services providers (Cambodia and Nepal), the approval requirement for commercial presence (Cambodia and Nepal), and foreign exchange restrictions and fees (Nepal). As additional commitments, Nepal scheduled its offer to make decisions on approval of commercial presence within 30 days and to guarantee entitlement for repatriation.

The three countries made substantial liberalization offers in the areas of financial, professional, distribution, education and environmental services. However, it is interesting to note that for basic telecommunications services for the major liberalization of which the industrialized countries usually press hard, Nepal offered a notably limited market opening. The other two countries, however, made substantial liberalization commitments in this sector. The three countries kept Mode 4 unbound for all the services scheduled, but Mode 1 (cross-border supply) and Mode 2 (consumption abroad) usually had no restrictions. For Mode 3 (commercial presence) restrictions on equity participation were occasionally scheduled.

4. TRADE AND COMPETITION POLICY

(a) Import restrictions, quantitative

The three countries agreed that they would not introduce, reintroduce or apply quantitative restrictions on imports, or other non-tariff measures such as licensing, quotas, prohibitions, bans and other restrictions having equivalent effect that cannot be justified under the provisions of the WTO Agreements.

(b) Import restrictions, tariff rate quota

Although Cambodia has not resorted to tariff rate quotas so far, it reserves the right to implement such quotas while it would respect WTO disciplines on tariff rate quotas. Nepal and Vanuatu made no commitment in this area.

(c) Export subsidies

Cambodia and Vanuatu made a commitment to bind export subsidies in agriculture at zero and not to apply such subsidies in the future, while Nepal did not make such a commitment. For Cambodia and Vanuatu this means that they have effectively forgone the right to use export subsidies for agricultural goods, a right that is granted to other least developed member countries by the Agreement on Agriculture. Cambodia, Nepal and Vanuatu have maintained the right to provide export subsidies for industrial goods, although Cambodia was encouraged to forgo this right in the negotiation process.

(d) Industrial policies

All three countries agreed to bring their industrial policies and export subsidy programmes into line with the Agreement on Subsidies and Countervailing Measures.

(e) Internal taxes

The countries agreed that they would apply internal taxes in a manner that does not discriminate between imported goods and domestically produced products. The taxes would be in compliance with WTO provisions.

(f) Pricing policies

The countries also agreed that price controls would be brought into line with WTO rules and regulations (especially Article III.9 of GATT 1994).

5. PUBLIC SECTOR

(a) State trading entities

Cambodia, Nepal and Vanuatu all agreed to ensure that current or potential State trading entities conformed with the rules and regulations of the WTO, especially Article XVII of the GATT.

(b) State ownership and privatization

Cambodia made commitments to ensure transparency with regard to its privatization programme and to make periodic reports on reforms of its economic and trade regimes, as well as on the progress of the privatization programme. Nepal and Vanuatu made no commitments in this area.

> *Cambodia and Vanuatu made a commitment to bind export subsidies in agriculture at zero and not to apply such subsidies in the future, while Nepal did not make such a commitment.*

> *Cambodia made commitments to ensure transparency with regard to its privatization programme and to make periodic reports on reforms of its economic and trade regimes, as well as on the progress of the privatization programme. Nepal and Vanuatu made no commitments in this area.*

6. Other trade arrangements

(a) Free-trade zones and special economic areas

All three countries made the commitment that the rules and regulations governing free-trade zones would be compatible with the rules and regulations governing international trade, namely the relevant agreements of the World Trade Organization. The countries also agreed to inform the WTO about the establishment of possible free-trade zones in the future.

(b) Regional trade agreements

Cambodia and Vanuatu agreed to provide notifications of regional trade agreements to the WTO under Article XXIV of GATT 1994 and Article V of GATS, although Cambodia's only free-trade agreement (within ASEAN) should be governed by the Enabling Clause as an agreement between developing countries and notified to the WTO Committee on Trade and Development. Nepal's commitment deals with this nuance by inserting a direct reference to the Enabling Clause (i.e. the 1979 GATT Decision on Differential and More Favourable Treatment, Reciprocity and Fuller Participation of Developing Countries).

E. Comparison with current WTO member States

While the comparison of the cases of Cambodia, Nepal and Vanuatu with one another highlights the fact that the different countries reached agreement about accession on very different terms, comparison of the commitments of these three countries with those of current WTO members reveals that the three LDCs made commitments that significantly exceed commitments made by current WTO members.

The multilateral trading system has many provisions of special and differential treatment. The majority of the provisions grant developing countries flexibility with respect to the implementation of trade agreements and some also grant them flexibility with respect to trade policies. In many instances, special and differential treatment provisions are time-bound exemptions from obligations (see chapter 6). It is expected that the time frames provided, which typically differ for least developed countries and other developing countries, will give the different groups of developing countries sufficient time to advance their development and acquire the necessary capacities to comply with international trade rules. But the developed members of the multilateral trading system are also encouraged, although not obliged, to provide both technical and financial assistance to developing countries in order to help them acquire the necessary capacities to comply with those rules.

It is notable that Cambodia, Nepal and Vanuatu accepted a significant reduction of their rights to special and differential treatment compared with other least developed countries that are already members of the WTO. Unlike LDCs that have been WTO members for some time, Cambodia and Vanuatu have, for instance, forgone their rights to use export subsidies in the agricultural sector.

In comparison with other developing countries and with developed countries that are members of the WTO, the least developed countries that have just completed their negotiations for accession to the WTO have also made

All three countries made the commitment that the rules and regulations governing free-trade zones would be compatible with...the relevant agreements of the World Trade Organization.

The comparison of the commitments of Cambodia, Nepal and Vanuatu with those of current WTO members reveals that the three LDCs made commitments that significantly exceed commitments made by current WTO members.

relatively strong commitments with respect to market access. For example, in comparison with current WTO members, the three LDCs in question have committed to comparatively high levels of tariff bindings and low levels of tariff peaks.

By way of comparison, while Cambodia, Nepal and Vanuatu have agreed to bind 100 per cent of their tariff lines, other countries that are already members of the WTO have often bound a much smaller share of their tariff lines. For example, a least developed WTO member, United Republic of Tanzania, has a binding coverage of 13.3 per cent, another developing WTO member country, Cameroon, has a binding coverage of 13.3 per cent and a developed WTO member, Australia, has a binding coverage of 97 per cent. Furthermore, while Cambodia's bound rates are as high as 60 per cent for sensitive agricultural products, and Nepal's bound rates are as high as 200 per cent for selected agricultural goods, least developed WTO members have bound rates on agricultural goods as high as 550 per cent (Myanmar), other developing WTO member countries have bound tariff rates on agricultural goods as high as 3,000 per cent (Egypt), and developed WTO members have bound tariff rates on agricultural goods as high as 350 per cent (United States).[7] It must be noted, however, that the extremely high tariff binding of Egypt (3,000 per cent) is an outlier, the next highest tariff binding being that of the Republic of Korea (887.4 per cent). Finally, while Cambodia has bound tariff rates on non-agricultural goods at a maximum level of 50 per cent, and Nepal has bound tariff rates on non-agricultural goods at a maximum level of 130 per cent, least developed WTO members have bound their tariffs in this product category as high as 550 per cent (Myanmar), and other developing WTO member countries have bound them as high as 220 per cent (Romania), while developed WTO members, which typically have a well developed industrial sector, have bound their tariff rates at a maximum level of 48 per cent (Australia).[8] Amongst the least developed WTO members, Myanmar is followed by Maldives, which has bound tariff rates for agricultural goods as well as tariff rates for non-agricultural goods at 300 per cent. Other least developed countries also have relatively high tariff bindings in the non-agricultural goods sector. Bangladesh, Djibouti, Lesotho and Niger all have peaks in tariff bindings at levels as high as 200 per cent.

A comparison of the commitments made by Cambodia and Nepal on the one hand, and the commitments made by the Quad countries on the other hand, shows these two least developed countries were expected to make some commitments in the accession process that even exceed the commitments that have been made by some of the most advanced countries. The Quad countries, namely Canada, the European Union, Japan and the United States, are the most important importers of products from least developed countries, including Cambodia and Nepal. The binding coverage of both the European Union and the United States is 100 per cent, and Canada and Japan have a binding coverage of over 99 per cent. However, in the agricultural goods sector, all Quad countries have peaks in tariff bindings that exceed those of Cambodia, and both Canada and the United States also have peaks in tariff bindings that exceed those of Nepal. The tariff bindings in this sector are as high as 350 per cent for the United States, followed by 238.4 per cent for Canada, 74.9 per cent for the European Union, and 61.9 per cent for Japan. In the non-agricultural goods sector, however, the peaks in tariff bindings of all Quad countries are lower than those of Cambodia and Nepal, although the peak in tariff bindings of the United States is only 2 per cent lower than that of Cambodia. The tariff bindings in this sector are as high as 48 per cent for the United States, followed by 30 per cent for Japan, 26 per cent for the European Union, and 20 per cent for Canada. The relatively low peaks in tariff bindings in the non-agricultural

In comparison with current WTO members, the three LDCs in question have committed to comparatively high levels of tariff bindings and low levels of tariff peaks.

goods sector by the Quad countries should not come as a surprise, however, since those countries have strong international competitiveness in non-agricultural (i.e. industrial) products.[9]

In short, this comparison shows that the LDCs that have just completed the accession negotiations with the WTO have made more stringent commitments than many of the developing countries and even more stringent commitments than some of the developed countries — including the Quad countries, which are the LDCs' most important export markets. The fact that each tariff line is bound implies that there is no single good in respect of which these countries can raise tariff rates without facing an upper limit, and the fact that many tariff rates are bound at relatively low levels implies that there are only very few goods in respect of which these countries can raise tariff rates to high levels. The combination of these factors effectively limits the ability of those countries to use tariffs in the future as an instrument to promote economic development.

> *LDCs that have just negotiated their WTO accession have accepted limitations with respect to trade policies...They also have forgone many of their rights to benefit from special and differential treatment, from which other developing countries, including least developed countries, benefit.*

However, the LDCs that have just negotiated their WTO accession have accepted limitations not only with respect to trade policies, but also limitations in other areas. These are, for instance, associated with the fact that they have forgone many of their rights to benefit from special and differential treatment, from which other developing countries, including least developed countries, benefit.

F. Conclusions

The terms of accession of Cambodia and Nepal to the WTO clearly reflect the spirit, but not the exact letter, of major decisions and commitments by the international community in the Third Programme of Action for the Least Developed Countries for the Decade 2001–2010 and the Doha Ministerial Declaration, as well as the decision of the WTO General Council on Accession of LDCs. Both LDCs were certainly given flexibilities, particularly in technically complex areas such as TRIPS, customs valuation, TBT and SPS, but normally all other special and differential treatment provisions (except for TRIMs, which applies to neither LDC) would also apply to the two LDCs. However, substantial questions remain about whether WTO members did really exercise restraint in seeking concessions and commitments on trade in goods and services from Cambodia and Nepal. The commitments undertaken by them certainly go well above and beyond the levels of concessions and commitments undertaken by the existing 30 WTO LDC members.

> *There is a continued need for clear and objective rules and disciplines for accession negotiations. These should ensure that the accession process is not excessively costly for the LDCs.*

There is a continued need for clear and objective rules and disciplines for accession negotiations. These should ensure that the accession process is not excessively costly for the LDCs. The lengthy accession process saps the meagre financial and technical resources of the LDCs, and there is much merit in the LDCs' proposal in the WTO that the LDC accession process be completed within a three-year period.

> *It is also necessary that accession terms reflect LDCs' levels of development, and, most importantly, their ability to implement their obligations.*

It is also necessary that accession terms reflect LDCs' levels of development, and, most importantly, their ability to implement their obligations. While weaker States *de jure* have the right to benefit from special and differential treatment, many of them are *de facto* stripped of this right in the accession process. The experience of Cambodia and Nepal shows that, rather than being integrated into the multilateral trading system on terms that are more favourable, weaker countries are integrated into that system on terms that are at best equal to those of other developing countries and at worst less favourable than those of more advanced member States. There is a danger that the current process of accession of weaker countries is effectively overriding the provisions of special and differential treatment for those countries.

It cannot be expected that relatively underdeveloped countries will become the equals of the more advanced members of the multilateral trading system by encouraging them to make the same or even higher commitments. To ensure that such countries become the equals of relatively advanced members of the multilateral trading system, it is desirable that they first be the subject of strong international support measures. Accordingly, the trade ministers of the least developed countries have argued that WTO member States should automatically grant all LDCs the right to benefit from the special and differential treatment provisions contained in the WTO Agreements, and that the more advanced WTO member States should commit themselves to actively helping the LDCs develop the technical and financial capacities to comply with the rules and regulations required by the WTO Agreements (WTO, 1999, 2001c, 2003a).

There is a danger that the current process of accession of weaker countries is effectively overriding the provisions of special and differential treatment for those countries.

Notes

1. For more details, see UNCTAD (2002).
2. Article XII states: "1. Any State or separate customs territory possessing full autonomy in the conduct of its external commercial relations and of the other matters provided for in this Agreement and the Multilateral Trade Agreements may accede to this Agreement, on terms to be agreed between it and the WTO. Such accession shall apply to this Agreement and the Multilateral Trade Agreements annexed thereto.
    2. Decisions on accession shall be taken by the Ministerial Conference. The Ministerial Conference shall approve the agreement on the terms of accession by a two-thirds majority of the Members of the WTO.
    3. Accession to a Plurilateral Trade Agreement shall be governed by the provisions of that Agreement." The Plurilateral Trade Agreements mentioned in paragraph 3 are: the Agreement on Trade in Civil Aircraft and the Agreement on Government Procurement. Accession to these Agreements is not obligatory for WTO members.
3. Based on WTO (2003c).
4. The service offers were made on the basis of the WTO classification of services. There are 12 categories of services. These are: (i) business services, (ii) communication services, (iii) construction and related engineering services, (iv) distribution services, (v) education services, (vi) environmental services, (vii) financial services, (viii) health-related and social services, (ix) tourism and travel-related services, (x) recreational, cultural and sporting services, (xi) transport services, and (xii) other services not included elsewhere. Disaggregation of these categories differs widely from one category to another. For example, business services have three levels of disaggregation, and comprise 46 services, while tourism and travel-related services have two levels of disaggregation, and contain only four services.
5. Based on WTO (2003d).
6. Based on WTO (2001b).
7. While bound tariff rates are typically higher than the tariff rates actually applied, many OECD countries also apply relatively high tariff rates on agriculture imports, and in addition they provide very large subsidies for their domestically produced agricultural goods. This combination implies a relatively high rate of protection in both nominal terms and real terms.
8. The least developed countries that are already members of the WTO have an average tariff binding of 55 per cent, average bound tariff rates for agricultural goods of 79 per cent, and average bound tariff rates for non-agricultural goods of 44 per cent.
9. Information on tariffs is based on data provided by the WTO (2003e).

References

UNCTAD (2002). *WTO Accessions and Development Policies*, UNCTAD/DITC/TNCD/11, October 2002.

WTO (1999). Integrating least developed countries into the global economy: Proposals for a comprehensive new plan of action in the context of the Third WTO Ministerial Conference, Coordinating Workshop for Senior Advisers to Ministers of Trade in LDCs in Preparation for the Third WTO Ministerial Conference, Sun City, South Africa, 21–25 June 1999, WT/GC/W/251, 13 July 1999.

WTO (2001a). Doha Declaration, Ministerial Conference, Fourth Session, 9–14 November 2001, Doha, Qatar, WT/MIN(01)/DEC/1, 20 November 2001.

WTO (2001b). Draft Report of the Working Party on the Accession of Vanuatu, WT/ACC/VUT/13 and Add.1–2, 16 October 2001.

WTO (2001c). Zanzibar Declaration, LDC Trade Ministers Meeting, Zanzibar, United Republic of Tanzania, 22–24 July 2001, WT/L/409, 6 August 2001.

WTO (2003a). Dhaka Declaration, Second LDC Trade Ministers Meeting, Dhaka, Bangladesh, 31 May–2 June 2003, WT/L/521, 26 June 2003.

WTO (2003b). Accession of Least Developed Countries, General Council's decision of 10 December 2002, WT/L/508, 20 January 2003.

WTO (2003c). Report of the Working Party on the Accession of Cambodia, WT/ACC/KHM/21 and Add.1–2, 15 August 2003.

WTO (2003d). Report of the Working Party on the Accession of the Kingdom of Nepal to the WTO, WT/ACC/NPL/16 and Add.1–2, 28 August 2003.

WTO (2003e). *World Trade Report 2003*, online-version (www.wto.org/english/res_e/booksp_e/anrep_e/wtr03_append_IIB1_7._e.xls).

Part Two

LINKING INTERNATIONAL TRADE WITH POVERTY REDUCTION

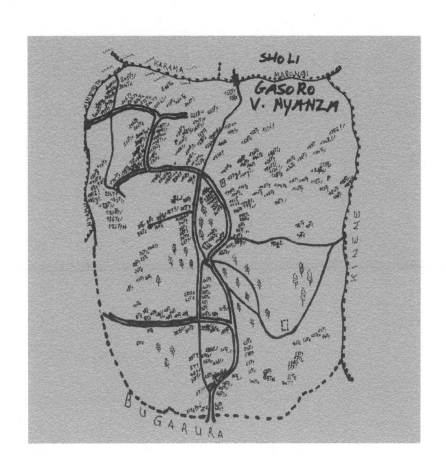

Trade and Poverty from a Development Perspective

Chapter

1

A. Introduction

International trade is vital for poverty reduction in all developing countries. But the links between trade and poverty are in practice neither simple nor automatic. The purpose of this Report is to clarify those links and to contribute to a better understanding of the national and international policies which can make international trade an effective mechanism for poverty reduction in the least developed countries.

The basic argument of the Report is that international trade can play a powerful role in reducing poverty in the least developed countries as well as in other developing countries. But the national and international policies which can facilitate this must be rooted in a development-driven approach to trade rather than a trade-driven approach to development. An exclusive focus on trade, which assumes that poverty is reduced through trade rather than through development, is likely to prove counter-productive. Rather, it is necessary to look at the relationship between trade and poverty from a development perspective.

The Report does three things:

- It defines an approach to analysing trade and poverty from a development perspective.

- It applies the analytical approach to examine the nature of the trade–poverty relationship in the LDCs.

- It sets out the policy implications of the approach for linking international trade more effectively with poverty reduction in the LDCs.

The present chapter sets out the analytical framework. Chapters 2, 3 and 4 apply the approach to examine the links between trade expansion and poverty reduction in the least developed countries. Chapter 5 discusses the relationship between trade liberalization, the major trade policy adopted by most LDCs since the latter half of the 1980s, and poverty reduction. Chapters 6 and 7 examine the policy implications of the analysis and identify some national and international policies which can strengthen the relationship between international trade and poverty reduction in the LDCs.

This chapter begins by describing briefly the current state of the debate on trade and poverty (section B), and identifying the limitations of the current approach (section C). Section D sets out the main elements of the development approach to the trade–poverty relationship, and summarizes the analytical framework which will be used in the present Report. Section E sets out the policy implications of the development approach at both national and international levels. The concluding section summarizes the major points.

International trade can play a powerful role in reducing poverty in the least developed countries as well as in other developing countries.

But the national and international policies which can facilitate this must be rooted in a development-driven approach to trade rather than a trade-driven approach to development.

B. Trade, trade liberalization and poverty: Where do we stand?

The relationship between trade and development has been an important policy issue since the early 1950s. An extensive literature has evolved to help policy makers understand how to ensure that international trade can more effectively support development through national policies and the international trade regime. But it is only recently that the subject of trade and poverty has become a subject of intense interest.

There was important conceptual work on the topic of stabilization, structural adjustment and poverty in the late 1980s (Helleiner, 1987; Kanbur, 1987; Demery and Addison, 1987). The World Bank's *World Development Report 1990* placed the problem of poverty reduction in a global context for the first time (World Bank, 1990). UNCTAD (1996) provided a first estimate of the impact of the international trade regime on poverty in developing countries. But most policy-oriented poverty analysis in the 1990s continued to focus on the role of national factors as causes of poverty, and particularly household characteristics (such as the level of education of household members, their access to land and credit, type of employment, and rural or urban location), and it generally ignored the influence of international economic relations on poverty.

In the last five years, there has been a proliferation of studies on the subject of trade and poverty.

In the last five years all this has changed. There has been a proliferation of studies on the subject of trade and poverty. This has occurred partly because poverty reduction has increasingly become a focal concern of national and international development policies, and partly because the social consequences of globalization have become a major political issue in both developed and developing countries (see DFID, 2000; World Bank, 2002; OXFAM, 2002; UNDP et al., 2003).

The new interest in trade and poverty is most welcome. However, a striking feature of current policy debate on trade and poverty is that it is narrowly framed. Indeed, its central focus is not actually trade and poverty, but rather trade liberalization and poverty.

A striking feature of current policy debate on trade and poverty is that it is narrowly framed. Indeed, its central focus is not actually trade and poverty, but rather trade liberalization and poverty.

This situation is evident in the fact that most current policy analyses relating to trade and poverty focuses on understanding the effects of trade liberalization on poverty. This can be verified through an examination of some recent authoritative reviews or conceptualizations of the field, including Winters (2000), Bannister and Thugge (2001), Bhagwati and Srinivisan (2000), and Berg and Krueger (2003). These are entitled "Trade and poverty: Is there a link?", "International trade and poverty alleviation", "Trade and poverty in the poor countries", and "Trade, growth and poverty: A selective survey", respectively. But despite their titles, they all actually focus on trade liberalization and poverty. This is also the topic of most of the papers in the bibliography on trade and poverty on the World Bank website and of the chapter in the PRSP Sourcebook which is intended to show policy makers how they can integrate trade into their poverty reduction strategies (Hoekmann et al., 2002).

Much useful progress is now being made on the issue of trade liberalization and poverty (see Reimer, 2002, for a review). An analytical framework has been constructed to identify at the national level the various channels through which price changes associated with the removal of border trade barriers are "passed through" the economic system to influence the welfare of richer and poorer households (Winters 2000; McCulloch et al., 2002). Within this analytical framework, trade policy reform is seen as a price shock which has (i) expenditure effects, which arise because of changes in the prices of the goods that are consumed; (ii) income and employment effects, which arise because of changes in the remuneration of factors of production; and (iii) effects on changes in tariff revenues and taxes, which affect transfers and the provision of public goods (see chart 5), as well as affecting the risk and uncertainty that poor households face and giving rise to short-term and medium-term adjustment costs.

Using this general framework, new methodologies have also been proposed to examine the links between trade and poverty (McCulloch, 2003; Nicita et al., 2003). These methodologies are being applied in more advanced developing countries (see Bussolo, Van der Meubrugghe and Lay, 2003, on Brazil and Mexico), but more particularly within some of the least developed countries, where they are being included within the Diagnostic Trade Integration Studies (DTIS) undertaken within the framework of the Integrated Framework for Trade-Related Technical Assistance for the LDCs (IF).

Work at the national level is also now complemented by work at the international level to estimate the global and national welfare effects of multilateral trade liberalization. This research builds on earlier modelling efforts to estimate the effects of multilateral trade liberalization on economic growth using the Global Trade Analysis Project (GTAP) model, extending it to transform growth effects into global and national poverty impacts (see, for example, World Bank, 2004; Cline, 2004). New methodological syntheses are now emerging. One approach attempts to link applications of computable general equilibrium (CGE) models which have sought to assess impacts of trade liberalization on poverty and income distribution at the national and regional levels using social

Work at the national level is now complemented by work at the international level to estimate the global and national welfare effects of multilateral trade liberalization.

CHART 5. ALAN WINTER'S ANALYTICAL FRAMEWORK FOR LINKING TRADE LIBERALIZATION AND POVERTY

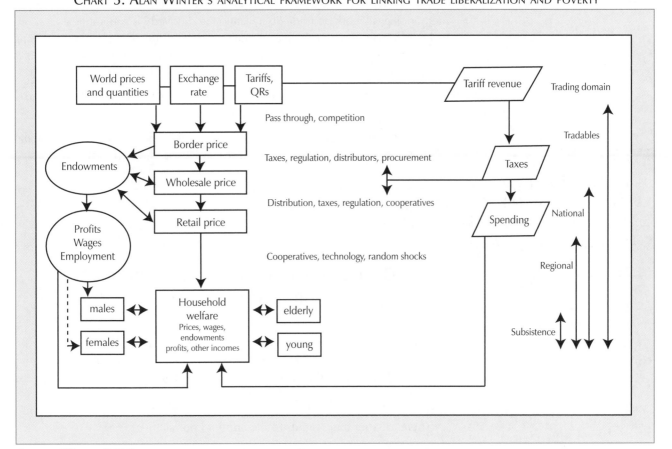

Source: Winters (2000).

accounting matrices (for example, Decaluwe et al., 1998; Decaluwe et al., 1999; Cockburn, 2001; Lofgren et al., 2001; Harris, 2001) with the results from GTAP simulations (see, for example, Evans, 2001; Hertel et al., 2003a). Another approach seeks to use data derived from household surveys on the composition of sources of income of households at different levels within the overall income distribution to obtain a much more socially disaggregated view of the impact of multilateral trade liberalization (Hertel et al., 2003b, 2003c).

A key insight from all of this work at both national and international levels is that the direct impact of trade liberalization on poverty varies widely from country to country depending on internal structures, and that domestic factor markets are critically important to the nature of the relationship. A useful checklist of questions which a Government undertaking trade liberalization should ask when determining the poverty impact of trade liberalization has also been proposed (Winters, 2000). There is also deeper understanding of the relationship between trade liberalization and food security (FAO, 2003). However, the links between trade liberalization and economic growth are not treated as well. There is a very large literature on this subject[1]. But the debate on whether or not "openness" is good for growth and poverty reduction does not die down. There are strong methodological objections to some of the key empirical findings which indicate a positive relationship between openness and growth (see, in particular, Pritchett, 1994; Rodriguez and Rodrik, 2000). But recent objections have prompted further responses (Srinivasan and Bhagwati, 1999; Berg and Kreuger, 2003; WTO, 2003) as well as amendments to the case for openness (Dollar and Kraay, 2002).

The ongoing methodological work on trade liberalization and poverty is generating ever more technically complex, model-based analyses, which are in their turn spawning their own empirical and methodological controversies.

The controversy about the effects of openness has now seesawed between "it is good" and "it is bad" to reach the more nuanced position that "it is good if the right complementary policies are adopted". This common-sense proposition is, unfortunately, tautological and empirically irrefutable. The ongoing methodological work on trade liberalization and poverty is generating ever more technically complex, model-based analyses, which are in their turn spawning their own empirical and methodological controversies. But as this occurs, it is important to stand back and ask:

- Is it right to limit the analysis of trade and poverty to the analysis of the effects of trade liberalization on poverty?

- Will it be possible to identify the most effective policies to link international trade with poverty reduction if the analysis is limited in this way?

Is it right to limit the analysis of trade and poverty to the analysis of the effects of trade liberalization on poverty?

This Report is founded on the view that the answer to these questions is no. A broader approach to policy analysis of the links between trade and poverty is necessary.

C. The limits of the current approach to analysing the trade–poverty relationship

The problem with the current approach is not a question of the value of the work being conducted. Good work is being done on different sides of the openness debate, and that work is yielding policy insights. The problem arises because the current approach is very limited.

There are four major limits to the current approach:

- It puts the cart before the horse in policy analysis.

- It prioritizes trade liberalization over poverty reduction as a policy objective.

- It excessively narrows the field of trade and poverty.

- It cannot address issues of long-term dynamics which are central to sustained poverty reduction.

1. THE CART AND THE HORSE

Analysing the relationship between trade policy and poverty is different from analysing the relationship between trade and poverty. Conclusions about the former should ideally be based on an analysis of the relationship between trade and poverty. To start by focusing on trade policy and poverty before examining the relationship between trade and poverty is to put the cart before the horse. It puts the cart first in a way that is likely to exaggerate the role of trade policy in trade development. This is because trade development depends on macroeconomic policies and non-trade policies as well as trade policies. Particularly important in this regard are policies which promote the development of productive capabilities through capital investment, skills acquisition, organization change and technological modernization. It also puts the cart first in a way which is likely to exaggerate the role of trade liberalization within trade policy. Trade policy, which may be understood as "the overall structure of incentives to produce and consume, and hence import and or export, tradable goods and services" (Helleiner, 1998,: 588), cannot be reduced to trade liberalization.

The current approach is likely to exaggerate the role of trade policy in trade development and to exaggerate the role of trade liberalization within trade policy.

A great danger of the current approach is that "unrealistic expectations will be created regarding what can be accomplished by trade policy alone" (Rodrik, 1992: 103), and in particular unrealistic expectations will be created regarding trade liberalization. As Rodrik (ibid.: 103) puts it: "A reasonable hypothesis is that trade policy plays a rather asymmetric role in development; an abysmal trade regime can perhaps drive a country to economic ruin; but good trade policy cannot make a poor country rich. At its best, trade policy provides an enabling environment for development. It does not guarantee entrepreneurs will take advantage of this environment, nor that private investment will be stimulated...Claims on behalf of liberalization should be modest lest policy-makers become disillusioned again".

2. THE PRIORITIZATION OF TRADE LIBERALIZATION

The importance of macroeconomic and non-trade policies for trade development is widely recognized. But within the current approach to trade liberalization the question being asked is the following: "What are the complementary policies necessary for ensuring the expected positive effects of trade liberalization, in terms of economic growth and poverty reduction?" This is a very different approach to non-trade policies from one that asks: "What trade and non-trade policies are required in order to achieve growth and poverty reduction objectives?" In the former case, the best complementary policies are chosen subject to the constraint that trade liberalization is being, or has been, undertaken. In the latter case, the task is to find the best trade and non-trade policies that are likely to achieve growth and poverty reduction objectives.

What the current approach does is to take trade liberalization as a given and then see how to make poverty reduction goals compatible with it, rather than to make poverty reduction the priority and then ask how trade liberalization might fit into this. The latter approach may well lead to the conclusion that the best policy option is to undertake trade liberalization and then adopt complementary policies. But this cannot be determined empirically if one just focuses on the relationship between trade liberalization and poverty and then gives policy makers advice on how "to develop suitable responses to ensure the poor gain from trade liberalization" (McCulloch et al., 2002: xxvi). It requires one to stand back and examine the relationship between trade and poverty, how trade and non-trade policies affect the relationship between trade and poverty, and the role of trade liberalization in those trade policies.

3. THE NARROW FOCUS

The current focus on trade liberalization and poverty also excessively narrows the subject of trade and poverty. It does this, firstly, by concentrating on a limited part of the overall problematique of trade and poverty, and secondly by limiting the aspect of international trade which is the focus of attention.

The field of trade and poverty should be drawn so that it encompasses all issues which are relevant to a proper understanding of the relationship between trade and poverty.

The field of trade and poverty should be drawn so that it encompasses all issues which are relevant to a proper understanding of the relationship between trade and poverty. What it might encompass has not been a matter of debate given the current focus on trade liberalization and poverty. But chart 6 suggests possible topics which might be included in the field. Within this view, trade liberalization and poverty is a subset of a number of policy issues within the general problematique of trade and poverty. These include the following: (i) the

CHART 6. ISSUES IN TRADE AND POVERTY

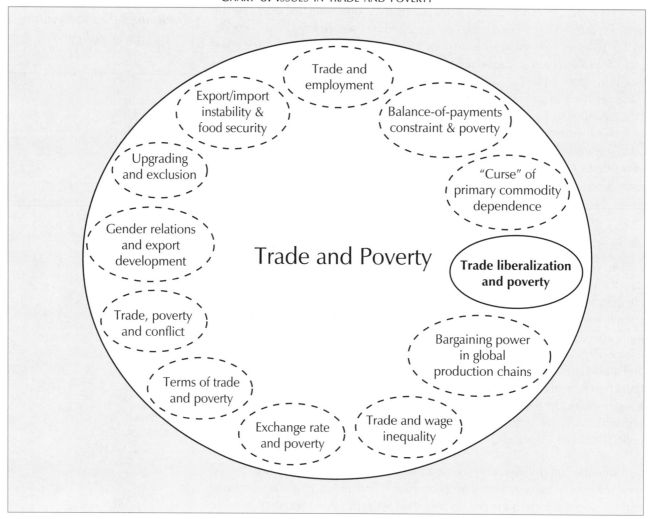

effects of primary commodity dependence; (ii) the balance-of-payments constraint on poverty reduction; (iii) the relationship between export and import instability and vulnerability; (iv) the relationship between upgrading the composition of exports towards higher-quality and higher-skill products and the social exclusion of poorer producers from livelihoods; (v) bargaining power in global production chains and the distribution of gains from trade; (vi) how the development of non-traditional exports affects gender relations; (vii) the effects of trends in, and variability of, the terms of trade on poverty; (viii) the relationships between trade and employment; and (ix) the relationships between trade and inequality.

The field of trade and poverty should also be drawn to encompass all aspects of trade. The focus in the current approach is the "openness" of the economy. This term is the subject of considerable semantic confusion as it is used to refer to both the level of trade integration of the economy (measured by the ratio of imports and exports to GDP) and the level of trade restrictions (tariff and non-tariff barriers). But the point here is that there are many aspects of trade beyond "openness" which are important to poverty reduction. Imports are as important as exports, and a key constraint on economic growth may be import instability. The types of exports and imports, and their growth rate, are also as important as the level of trade integration. The growth effects of international trade are also related to the organization of trade through global production chains and buyer–seller links. Moreover, lifting the balance-of-payments constraint may be the key to faster economic growth and poverty reduction. Table 24 indicates schematically some sources of economic growth and some of the aspects of trade that are associated with them. The relative importance of, and also interrelationships between, these links between trade and growth vary between countries.

The field of trade and poverty should also be drawn to encompass all aspects of trade.

TABLE 24. SELECTED MECHANISMS THROUGH WHICH INTERNATIONAL TRADE CAN HAVE GROWTH EFFECTS

Source of growth	Associated aspect of trade
1. Static and dynamic efficiency gains arising from specialization according to current comparative advantage	• Openness • Exposure to international trade competition
2. Exploitation of a "vent for surplus"	• Export growth, particularly natural-resource-based or tourism-based
3. Increased capacity utilization	• Increased import capacity
4. Increased investment	• Economies of scale through selling to domestic and external markets • Reduced costs of capital goods through imports • Reduced costs of wage goods through imports
5. Increased technology acquisition and learning	• Buyer–seller links • Machinery and equipment imports embodying foreign technology • Exports that have great potential for learning through technology transfer
6. Structural change	• Composition of exports and imports • Product and market diversification
7. Releasing the balance-of-payments constraint on economic growth	• Export growth • Import substitution • Reduced income elasticity of imports • Increased elasticity of export growth with respect to growth of world income • Reduction of non-essential imports

4. WEAKNESSES WITH RESPECT TO LONG-TERM DYNAMICS AND INDIRECT IMPACTS

A further limitation of the current approach is that it cannot adequately address the isues of long-term dynamics which are so important for sustained poverty reduction. What the current approach to the issue of trade and poverty is very good at is understanding the direct impact on poverty of changes associated with trade liberalization, which is conceptualized, as noted above, as a policy shock, and at understanding the short-term dynamics of that change. What it is less good at understanding is the indirect impact on poverty of change in a country's level and pattern of trade, and the long-term dynamics of that change.

The difficulty of the current approach as regards dealing with long-term dynamics has a simple origin. The theoretical core of the analysis of the link between trade liberalization and poverty is the efficiency and welfare gains, that can be achieved in economies that have previously discouraged export production through a shift in the incentive structure away from import-competing activities and non-tradables towards exportables. Trade is also expected to lead to factor price equalization between countries. What this means is that in countries with relative labour abundance, real wages should rise, and thus the process of resource reallocation will not only increase the level of national income, but also, in situations where the major asset of the poor is labour, it will be pro-poor.

The great merit of the current work on trade liberalization and poverty is that it is testing this theory. But the point here is that the efficiency and welfare improvements are one-off gains which occur as resources are reallocated. If the conditions are right, GDP should grow whilst the reallocation occurs. But the sustained growth which is necessary for poverty reduction will not occur unless it positively affects fundamental sources of economic growth. As Cooper (2001: 9) put it, "once resource re-allocation has occurred the 'growth' will cease unless it is sustained by one or more of five factors:

(1) the redistribution of real income raises the national savings rate, leading directly or indirectly (via the capital market) to a higher rate of investment;

(2) the relative price of investment goods is reduced, so that a given level of national savings finances greater investment;

(3) productive foreign investment flows into a country in greater amount on a sustained basis;

(4) the redistribution of income or new competitive pressure leads people to attain higher levels of economically useful skills;

(5) the efficiency of labour and/or capital is continually improved as a result of the imports, which convey useful information from abroad as well as enhanced competitive pressure on domestic producers".

Various "grey area dynamic effects" of trade liberalization have been proposed, including improved economic efficiency through exposure to international trade competition, reduction of rent-seeking (or directly unproductive profit-seeking) activities (Krueger, 1974), and improved quality of national institutions (Dollar and Kraay, 2002). Moreover, using theories of endogenous growth, models have been constructed to show how trade can have dynamic effects and thus increase the rate of growth (Young, 1991; Romer and Rivera-Batiz, 1991). But these models often incorporate assumptions on increasing returns which contradict those required for the static welfare gains

What the current approach to the issue of trade and poverty is very good at is understanding the direct impact on poverty of changes associated with trade liberalization...

...What it is less good at understanding is the indirect impact on poverty of change in a country's level and pattern of trade, and the long-term dynamics of that change.

which are the bedrock of the analysis. In the end, the identification of dynamic effects of trade liberalization rests on empirical investigation, and as stated earlier, the results in this area remain inconclusive. As Winters (2000: 59) puts it, "Overall, the fairest assessment of the evidence is that, despite the clear plausibility of such a link, open trade alone has not yet been unambiguously and universally linked to subsequent economic growth".

In short, the current approach is helpful for understanding the problem of poverty alleviation during liberalization reforms. But the most important effects of trade on poverty are likely to occur through indirect impacts and long-term effects of sustained economic growth and development. The current approach does not take us very far in understanding how to achieve the sustained reduction in the incidence of poverty by half which is the goal of the international community. That depends on sustained economic growth and development.

D. A development approach to the trade–poverty relationship

1. ELEMENTS OF A DEVELOPMENT APPROACH

It is possible to elaborate various approaches to the relationship between trade and poverty which go beyond the question of trade liberalization. This Report adopts a development approach. The essence of a development approach to trade and poverty is that it begins with an analysis of how development occurs, rather than an analysis of how trade occurs, examining the role of trade within processes of development and assessing the effects of trade on poverty from this perspective. The advantage of this approach is that it can build on existing policy analysis and research which examine international trade from a development perspective (see box 3). There is a rich literature in this regard on the development implications of export expansion and export composition, including both commodities and manufactures, as well as some work on the growth effects of imports, import composition and import instability. But the analytical challenge is to extend this work to the relationship between international trade, development and poverty.

This Report adopts a development approach. The essence of a development approach to trade and poverty is that it begins with an analysis of how development occurs, rather than an analysis of how trade occurs, examining the role of trade within processes of development and assessing the effects of trade on poverty from this perspective.

The trade and poverty relationship is of immense importance as it extends the discussion of international trade from questions of the quantity of trade to questions of the quality of trade. Unlike the "quality of growth" and the "quality of employment", about which much has been written, the concept of the "quality of trade" has not been elaborated in the recent debate on trade theory and trade policy analysis. Focusing on trade and poverty entails opening up this question of the quality of trade in terms of the social outcomes of expanded international trade.

The seven basic elements of the development approach adopted in this Report can be summarized as follows:

(1) The issue of trade and poverty cannot be reduced to the issue of trade liberalization and poverty.

(2) Sustained poverty reduction occurs through the efficient development and utilization of productive capacities in a way in which the population of working age becomes more and more fully and productively employed.

BOX 3. LINKING DEVELOPMENT, INTERNATIONAL TRADE AND POVERTY

It is possible to base analysis of the links between development, international trade and poverty on two overlapping sources: theories about how trade occurs and the gains from trade; and theories about how development occurs and how trade fits into this process. These different starting points can lead to different conclusions. Potential conflicts between international trade theory and growth theory in terms of their principles of resource allocation were identified early by Chenery (1961). He noted that, within trade theory, the optimum pattern of production and trade for a country is determined from a comparison of the opportunity cost of producing a commodity with the price at which the commodity can be imported or exported. This approach is particularly concerned with conditions of general equilibrium. Growth theory, in contrast, places more emphasis on sequences of expansion of production and factor use by sector. It shows how endowments that are the basis for comparative advantage are created.

Chenery suggested that five main considerations should be taken into account in applying the principle of comparative advantage from a development perspective.

- Firstly, the possibility of a structural disequilibrium in factor markets, which means that the costs of labour and capita do not reflect their opportunity costs, must be recognized.

- Secondly, the fluctuating nature and the low income and price elasticities of demand for primary products must be allowed for. This implies that the market value of the stream of export earnings should be reduced to reflect the economic effects of instability.

- Thirdly, the possibility of rising efficiency as labour and management acquire increasing experience in actual production needs to be recognized. This implies that changes in comparative advantage need to be accounted for, as well as differences in the potential for cost reduction through learning and accumulation of experience in different sectors.

- Fourthly, there are dynamic external economies in which cost reductions or demand increases in one sector lead to cost reductions in other sectors. If a group of investments is only profitable if undertaken together, the comparative advantage approach must assess different combinations of investment and address the simultaneous determination of the levels of consumption, imports and production in related sectors.

- Finally, the limited ability of policy makers to foresee changes in demand and supply puts a premium on flexibility. Optimum development policy should result in a pattern of resource allocation that allows for unforeseen changes in supply and demand even at the cost of some loss of short-term efficiency.

Both development theory and international trade theory have been transformed since Chenery's insights about the differences between growth theory and trade theory. But the problem of integrating these two bodies of knowledge, focusing on trade on the one hand and development on the other, remains. Since the early 1980s, there has been a strong tendency for ideas from international trade theory to dominate understandings of development processes. This occurred initially through comparisons between the relative success of "outward-oriented" and "inward-oriented" development strategies. When these terms were used precisely they were defined in terms of incentive structures in relation to production for exports or the domestic market (see Bhagwati, 1986). An outward-oriented development strategy was one that had a trade regime in which, on average, incentives are neutral, biased neither for nor against exports.

The domination of the international trade perspective within development thinking was further strengthened in the 1990s through arguments that fast and full integration with the world economy was the key to seizing the opportunities of globalization and minimizing the chance of being left behind. From this perspective, global integration began to substitute for national development as the major policy objective of Governments.

Although the mainstream tendency has been for trade theory perspectives to dominate development thinking in recent years, a number of researchers and policy analysts have continued to start from the development end, rather than the trade end, of the relationship between trade and development. Notable in this regard is the extensive work of Rodrik, including his interpetation of East Asian development success as being due not to changes in the incentive structures and profitability of production for exports or the domestic markets but rather to incentives for investment (Rodrik, 1995), and also the work of Helleiner (see in particular Helleiner, 1994, 2003). The work of UNCTAD on the East Asian development strategies (UNCTAD 1994, 1996), the relationship between globalization, growth and distribution (UNCTAD, 1997), the underlying causes of Africa's weak economic performance and possible policy responses (UNCTAD, 1998), the Latin American experience with economic reform (UNCTAD, 2003) and the international poverty trap facing many least developed countries (UNCTAD, 2002) has also been informed by an approach which starts by examining the sources of growth and development, and then considers how international trade fits into this process. This Report seeks to build on that body of work concerned with international trade from a development perspective, extending it to the issue of trade and poverty.

(3) International trade can facilitiate, hinder or modify this process.

(4) The relationship between trade and poverty varies with the composition of the international trade of a country.

(5) The relationship between trade and poverty varies with the level of development of a country and the structure of its economy.

(6) The relationship between trade and poverty is affected by the interdependence between trade and international financial and investment flows, between trade and debt, and between trade and technology transfer.

(7) Sustained development and poverty reduction expand international trade.

The first element of this approach has been dealt with above. This section continues by elaborating the second and third elements, which constitute the basic analytical framework of the approach, and then goes on to examine the fourth, fifth and sixth elements — which are a major source of variation in the trade–poverty relationship between developing countries — and finally the seventh element.

2. The basic analytical framework

The basic analytical framework, which is set out in chart 7, has three components: (i) international trade; (ii) the development and utilization of productive capacities; and (iii) poverty. The latter is defined in a multidimensional way to include low income and consumption, lack of human development, and vulnerabilities such as food insecurity. For income and consumption poverty, an important issue is the choice of an international poverty line. This Report focuses on the $1/day and $2/day international poverty lines as these are relevant to the LDCs. But there is a debate as to whether these

CHART 7. THE RELATIONSHIP BETWEEN TRADE, THE DEVELOPMENT OF PRODUCTIVE CAPACITIES, EMPLOYMENT AND POVERTY

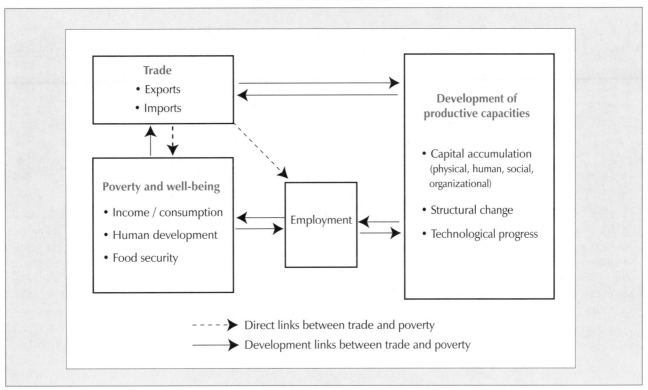

BOX 4. PRITCHETT'S PROPOSAL FOR A THIRD INTERNATIONAL POVERTY LINE BASED ON THE STANDARDS
FOR DEFINING POVERTY IN INDUSTRIALIZED COUNTRIES

The $1/day international poverty line is based on the median of the national poverty lines of the 10 poorest countries for which data is available (World Bank, 2000/2001). For more advanced developing countries as well as transition countries, this low standard is largely irrelevant, and thus a $2/day international poverty line is also increasingly being used in international analyses of poverty. But is there a case for complementing these with a third international poverty line based on the national poverty lines or standards for defining poverty of industrialized countries?

Pritchett (2003) argues that there is a strong case. Most OECD countries, with the exception of USA, do not have an official national poverty line. Using a range of estimates, notably the threshold of less than 50 per cent of median household income (adjusted for household size), which is a common way of defining poverty in OECD countries, and using an estimate based on the minimum wage, he suggests that $15/day (in 2000 purchasing power parity dollars) represents a reasonable approximation of what constitutes a minimally adequate level of income in industrialized countries. He proposes that this can thus serve as a third international poverty line, complementing the $1/day and $2/day standards which he calls "destitution" and "extreme poverty" respectively.

He presents various arguments as to why the adoption of the third international poverty line makes sense. First of all, it is not ethically justifiable to argue that what is considered unacceptable human deprivation in one country is not also unacceptable in another. This, of course, depends on the income poverty line being defined in a way that takes account of differences in what a dollar can purchase in different countries. But the purchasing power parity exchange rates do this. With income defined equivalently in this way, it is difficult people in a rich country to say, "We adopt one standard of living as poverty for our own citizens but for your citizens we think a much lower level of well-being is sufficient". Moreover, it is difficult for developing countries to argue that the poverty reduction to which they are aspiring is the eradication of the level of human deprivation considered unacceptable in the five very poorest countries in the world.

Secondly, even the rich in poor countries are experiencing human deprivation compared to the poor in rich countries. This is important, as a key objection to the adoption of the higher poverty line is its implication that nearly everyone in many poor countries are poor and that people in the upper part of the income distribution in poor countries would be classified as poor by the new common standard, even though they are not "really" poor. Pritchett tests this argument by comparing various physical indicators of well-being between the poor in rich countries and the richest quintile in poor countries. He finds that:

- While the average infant mortality rate among the poor in most OECD countries was 10 per 1000 or less, infant mortality of the richest quintile in all of the [developing] countries examined was much higher than 10 – from substantially higher in Brazil to 4–6 times higher in Côte d'Ivoire, Nepal and Nicaragua, and up to ten times as high in Pakistan. More than 3 in 10 children of the "rich" [richest quintile] in India, Nepal, Nigeria and Pakistan, show signs of chronic malnutrition.

- In industrialized countries completion of basic education is nearly universal, even among the very poor. In contrast, even among the richest quintile in poorer countries, between a quarter and three quarters of children do not complete even 9th grade.

Thirdly, with the adoption of a high poverty line, poverty reduction can be a shared national project. Pritchett argues that poverty reduction is not a politically viable stance for a democratic government if there is a very low poverty line and the poor constitute only a small proportion of the total population.

Fourthly, he argues that if the poverty reduction objective is interpreted strictly, any income gains above the poverty line contribute nothing to the desired results, and thus a whole range of important development activities become more difficult to justify. In this context, with the adoption of the low poverty line, there is the danger that development institutions can become relief and charity institutions.

Pritchett argues that governments and development institutions should focus on poverty reduction. He proposes that a $15/day international poverty line, based on the standards of poverty in the rich countries, should complement the existing $1/day and $2/day standards, which can be considered global standards of "destitution" and "extreme poverty" respectively. Within this new framework more complex anti-poverty goals should be adopted. These should go beyond simply reducing the proportion of the population living below the poverty threshold; instead, they should pay more attention to the distribution of income amongst the poor, attaching different degrees of policy priority to achieve income increases for various more and less impoverished strata amongst the poor.

Source: Pritchett, 2003.

should be complemented with a higher international poverty line in a global analysis of poverty (see box 4).

The framework indicates that there are direct and indirect links between trade and poverty. Trade affects poverty directly through its impact on the cost of living, jobs and wages, and government revenue for public goods such as health and education and for socio-economic security systems. But there are also development links between trade and poverty which occur indirectly through the development and utilization of productive capacities. Whilst the former types of links are important for short-term poverty alleviation, it is the latter types that are most important for sustained poverty reduction in most developing countries.

The importance of the development of productive capacities for poverty reduction can be understood in intuitive terms through the simple wisdom that if you give a hungry person a fish they can eat that day, but if you give them a fishing rod and teach them how to fish and manage fish stocks with others sustainably, they can eat for the rest of their lives. Unless one envisages a world in which millions of people depend on international welfare transfers, the only way to reduce global poverty sustainably is through the development of productive capacities.

The development of productive capacities involves three basic processes: first, accumulation of physical, human and organizational capital; second, structural transformation; and third, technological progress.

Investment in the acquisition of ever-increasing stocks of various forms of capital is the first and most basic component of increasing productive capacity. The process of capital accumulation entails investment in material capital equipment, but it goes beyond this. It involves investment in education, health and human skills as well. The development of human capabilities is an integral part of the development of productive capacities. The development of institutional arrangements to transform natural resources and intellectual property into economic assets (through, for example, changes in property rights regimes), and the expansion of the social and organizational capital underpinning economic activity (for example, through creating business firms), are also important. It also involves maintaining renewable natural capital which is used in the economic process.

Unless one envisages a world in which millions of people depend on international welfare transfers, the only way to reduce global poverty sustainably is through the development of productive capacities.

Along with increasing capital per worker, productive capacities increase through structural transformation. As Adam Smith recognized, this process begins with people specializing in different economic tasks, rather than meeting their subsistence for themselves, and the development of an increasing domestic division of labour. However, sustained poverty reduction has usually involved a process of structural change in which the proportion of the labour force employed in primary activities (agriculture, mining, forestry, fishing) declines and the proportion employed in other sectors of the economy which are not subject to diminishing returns rises. Historically, industrialization has been a potent mechanism of productivity growth through changes in the occupational distribution because of sectoral productivity differences between agriculture and manufacturing.[2]

Finally, productive capacities increase through technological progress. Improvements in agricultural productivity are particularly important in the earliest stages of development. Rapid technological progress can also be achieved in the manufacturing sector in late-industrializing countries owing to the existence of a technological gap between the latter and the more advanced industrial countries and the possibility of acquiring and mastering existing technologies (Grossman and Helpmann, 1990). Opportunities for catch-up growth have been particularly evident in the manufacture of standardized industrial products and of goods at a mature stage in the product cycle.

The development of productive capacities depends critically on the availability of a surplus for investment over basic consumption needs, and on adequate incentives for the private entrepreneurs, whose initiatives animate the development process. Institutions to deal with the multiple coordination failures which can arise in the development process are also important. At any moment in time, the level of development of productive capacities acts as a constraint on what goods and services a country can trade efficiently and also on the scale of trade. But international trade plays an essential role in supporting the efficient development and full utilization of productive capacities.

This occurs through both exports and imports and, as discussed earlier, may involve a variety of channels. Trade can enable more efficient use of a country's resources by enabling imports of goods and services which, if produced domestically, would be more costly. It can enable increased capacity utilization and the realization of a "vent for surplus" if external demand enables the employment of previously idle (or surplus) labour and land resources which were previously not utilized owing to a dearth of effective domestic demand. It can lift a balance-of-payments constraint on sustained economic growth. It can improve the returns on investment by reducing production costs or enabling economies of scale. Exposure to international trade competition can act as a spur to greater efficiency. Exports and imports can also be associated with the acquisition of technology.[3]

It is through these positive effects on the development of productive capacities that international trade works to reduce poverty. Indeed, sustained poverty reduction occurs through the development of productive capacities. However, as chart 7 shows the relationship is mediated by changes in employment opportunities (jobs and livelihoods) and employment conditions that occur along with productive development. But the link between productive development and poverty is complex, involving trade-offs and also social conflict and negotiation. In a capitalist system, profits are the engine of accumulation and innovation, but the higher the profit share, the lower the wage share. Income disparities also act as an incentive. Without access to foreign savings, there will inevitably be a short-term trade-off between the average level of consumption, which is closely associated with poverty in the poorest developing countries, and the level of investment. Productivity growth associated with technological progress also often creates employment losses in the short term. Moreover, industrialization involves major social transformations. Changes in systems of socio-economic security, which are usually inter-related with forms of employment and which assure support or compensation during periodic events which result in income or employment loss, are particularly important. As Amartya Sen (1981) has pointed out, vulnerabilities may be particularly great during the development process in the period after the "moral economy" which guarantees a basic subsistence to members of a rural community breaks down, but before the safety nets associated with widespread wage employment are put in place. The nature of all these links between productive development and poverty is affected by the level and manner of a country's trade integration with the rest of the world.

For the development of productive capacities to be poverty-reducing it must occur in a manner in which productive capacities are not simply developed but must also be fully utilized and developed in an efficient way. The development

At any moment in time, the level of development of productive capacities acts as a constraint on what goods and services a country can trade efficiently and also on the scale of trade. But international trade plays an essential role in supporting the efficient development and full utilization of productive capacities. This occurs through both exports and imports.

of productive capacities must also ensure that natural capital which provides livelihoods for the majority of the population in the early stages of the development process is not excessively depleted before replacement income-earning opportunities are available. Resources allocated for the public provision of health, education, housing, water and sanitation, as well as economic infrastructure, are all part of the process of productive development.

Finally, and most basically, the development of productive capacities must occur in a manner in which the working age population becomes more and more fully and productively employed. How trade affects this process is central to understanding the trade–poverty relationship. Krueger (1983) did important empirical work on the relationship between trade and employment and established an agenda of questions which need answering. Morover, a number of empirical studies have recently been completed on the impact of trade with industrialized countries on manufacturing employment and wages in selected more advanced developing countries (Ghose, 2003). But apart from discussion of wage inequality, the current literature remains particularly thin on the relationship between trade and employment (for reviews see Sen, 2003; Rama, 2004). Better understanding of the links between trade and employment must be a key priority for better understanding of the links between trade and poverty.

For sustained poverty reduction, the development of productive capacities must occur in a manner in which the working age population becomes more and more fully and productively employed. How trade affects this process is central to understanding the trade–poverty relationship.

If poverty reduction occurs, various feedback mechanisms can start to reinforce the process of development of productive capacities. One aspect of this is a falling birth rate, which provides a demographic bonus to the trend in income per capita. As the ratio of the population of working age to the total population increases, a larger fraction of the total population is employed and the gap between output per worker and income per capita declines. But the population also becomes more productive and more skilled, investment in human capital bears more fruit as life expectancy rises and wasted human talent of all kinds, pursuing its own interests, is mobilized to support the development process.

3. Variations amongst developing countries in the trade–poverty relationship

There is much diversity amongst developing countries in the interrelationships between international trade, productive capacities and poverty. International trade can facilitate or hinder the process of productive development and also modify the relationship between productive development and poverty reduction. Three dimensions of this variation are the following: the composition of the trade; the level of development and production structure; and the interdependence between trade and other international economic relations.

(a) The composition of trade

The composition of trade is as important for the nature of the trade–poverty relationship as the level of trade. This applies both to exports and imports. Ignoring the form of a country's integration with the rest of the world through trade can lead to major fallacies (see box 5, and also Sprout and Weaver, 1993).

For exports, there is a particularly sharp distinction between commodities and manufactures. Commodity exports are subject to short-term price and demand fluctuations, as well as having episodes of medium- to long-term terms-of-trade decline. Commodities are also subject to intense price competition, as

BOX 5. GLOBALIZERS, NON-GLOBALIZERS AND COMMODITY DEPENDENCE

One of the most influential recent articles on trade and poverty is by Dollar and Kraay (2001). It seeks to identify developing countries "that have significantly opened up to foreign trade since 1980s" and to compare their experience with that of developing countries "that have remained closed" (p. 7). The two groups, called "globalizers" and "non-globalizers" respectively, are identified on the basis of trade/GDP ratios (in constant prices) and reductions in average tariffs. The globalizers are the top third of 72 developing economies in terms of the increase in their trade/GDP ratio between 1975–1979 and 1995–1997, or the top third of tariff-cutters (on the basis of absolute decline in average tariff rates) between 1985–1989 and 1995–1997. Dollar and Kraay compare trends in growth and income inequality in the two groups of countries and conclude:

"The poor countries that have reduced trade barriers and participated more in international trade over the past twenty years have seen their growth rates accelerate. In the 1990s they grew far more rapidly than the rich countries, and hence reduced the gap between themselves and the developed world. At the same time the developing countries that are not participating in globalization are falling further and further behind. Within the globalizing developing countries there has been no general trend in inequality" (p. 12).

Thus "on average, greater globalization is a force for poverty reduction" (p. 26) and "open trade regimes lead to faster growth and poverty reduction in poor countries" (p. 27).

This work has generated intense discussion, much of which is methodological (for critiques, see Rodrik, 2000b, on an early version, and Nye et al., 2001). But Birdsall and Hamoudi (2002) have also shown that there is a close overlap between "globalizers" and "non-globalizers" on the one hand, and countries classified as "least commodity-dependent" and "most commodity-dependent" economies (on the basis of the share of primary commodities in their total merchandise exports during the period 1980–1984) on the other hand. Only two of the most commodity-dependent countries (Rwanda and Mali) are classified as "globalizers".

Birdsall and Hamoudi show that the comparative evolution of trade/GDP ratios of countries classified as "globalizers" and "non-globalizers" is almost the same as that of "most commodity-dependent" and "least commodity-dependent" countries. The non-globalizers start in the 1960s with much more "open" economies than the globalizers, if openness is measured by the trade/GDP ratio. The increase in the ratio among the non-globalizers is at least equal to if not slightly faster than that of the globalizers until the late 1970s or early 1980s, but then it falls sharply in the early 1980s.Exactly the same pattern is observed for the most and least commodity-dependent economies (see box chart 1A and B).

They decompose the trade/GDP ratio into import/GDP ratio and export/GDP ratio, and show that the increase in the trade/GDP ratio in the late 1970s and the collapse in the early 1980s in the most commodity-dependent economies are associated with the emergence of trade deficits and their rapid closing in the 1980s with the debt crisis.[8] The changes reflect the fact that the most commodity-dependent economies financed large trade deficits in the late 1970s and early 1980s (when prices were high) with expected export revenue. When prices collapsed, their capacity to import fell sharply and they were forced to close their trade deficits in order to balance the current account (see box chart 1C and D). The apparent stagnation in the "openness" of the non-globalizers thus partly reflects the shift in global demand for primary commodities and the structure of world prices beginning around the world at the start of the 1980s.

They go on to consider whether trade liberalization in the 1980s caused both increases in trade/GDP ratios in the "globalizers" and shifts in export content. They test this by dividing the most and least commodity-dependent countries into those that cut tariffs most (the top 33 per cent of tariff-cutters) and those that cut tariffs least. The evidence suggests that the most commodity-dependent countries "were not able to achieve an increase in their trade/GDP ratio, whether they cut tariffs steeply or not. By comparison, the vast majority of the least commodity-dependent countries saw increases in their trade/GDP ratios, regardless of whether they cut tariffs steeply or not" (ibid.: 16).

Finally, they show the comparative growth experience of the most and least commodity-dependent groups of countries in the 1980s and 1990s. The commodity- dependent countries grew more slowly in both decades, and the overwhelming majority of them saw declines in PPP-adjusted per capita incomes during the 1980s.

Birdsall and Hamoudi conclude that "Dollar and Kraay have not isolated the benefits of 'participating in the global trading system' but rather the 'curse' of primary commodity dependence" (ibid.: 5). As they put it most starkly,

"Countries with high natural resources and primary commodity content in their exports are not necessarily 'closed' nor have they necessarily chosen to 'participate' more in the global trading system. For them, reducing tariffs and eliminating non-tariff barriers to trade may not lead to growth. In this context, terms like openness, liberalization and globalization are red herrings" (ibid.: 5–6).

Box 5 (contd.)

This may be going too far in the sense that a key issue for the primary-commodity- dependent economies is the relationship between commodity dependence and liberalization and globalization. But their analysis certainly shows the fallacies and also serious policy errors which can arise from analysis of the links between trade and poverty that does not include an examination of the type of exports.

BOX CHART 1. TRENDS IN EXPORT/GDP, IMPORT/GDP AND TRADE/GDP RATIO IN GLOBALIZERS AND NON-GLOBALIZERS VERSUS MOST AND LEAST PRIMARY-COMMODITY-DEPENDENT COUNTRIES, 1960–1995

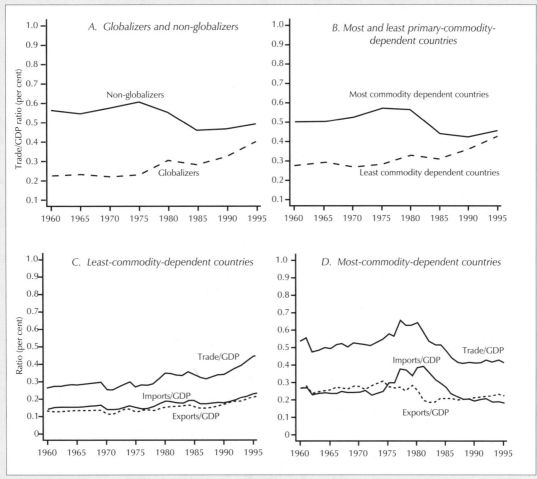

Source: Birdsall and Hamoudi (2002).

a result of which productivity gains are normally passed to the consumers rather than benefiting the producers. Because of the involvement of fixed factors of production, such as land and reserves in mines, they can be also subject to diminishing returns. In contrast, manufacturing is subject to substantial static and dynamic economies of scale. There is often higher income elasticity of demand for manufactures exports than for commodity exports.

The composition of imports also matters. There is less research in this area. But a careful analysis of the way in which imports can act as a channel for technology transfer has found that import-induced technology transfer is more important in sectors with medium productivity growth in high-income countries and that it is of little importance in "traditional" sectors (Choudri and Hakoura, 2000). Moreover, capital goods imports have been found to have specific important growth effects (Lee, 1995; Maurer, 1998; Egwaikhide, 1999).

The composition of trade is as important for the nature of the trade–poverty relationship as the level of trade. This applies both to exports and imports.

In very low-income economies which depend on a narrow range of low-value-added primary commodities and have deep mass poverty, there is a strong tendency for the domestic vicious circles of economic stagnation and persistent poverty to be reinforced by external trade and financial relationships. In this situation trade can be part of an international poverty trap in which low and unstable commodity prices interact with unsustainable external debts and an aid/debt service system (see UNCTAD, 2002).

In contrast, some more advanced countries which have managed to upgrade their commodity exports and diversify into exporting manufactures have been able to use international trade to achieve very high rates of economic growth. This occurs in particular in countries where there is a strong profits-investment and export-investment nexus (see UNCTAD, 1996). In some countries there has been a virtuous circle in which increased manufactures exports lead to faster growth of manufactures output, which, because of the positive effect of the overall level of manufacturing output on labour productivity, induces greater productivity growth.[4] This in turn makes manufactures more competitive and enables increased manufactures exports.

Exports can have a particularly strong poverty-reducing impact in these cases. But not all countries which export manufactures have experienced export-accelerated industrialization. Indeed, the more common recent experience, in which the growth of manufacturing exports is linked to integration into global production chains and assembly of imported inputs, is more likely to be associated with stagnant or even declining manufacturing output (UNCTAD, 2002).

A major research issue within a development approach would be to assess how the trade–poverty relationship varies with the types of exports and types of imports. This would encompass not simply commodity and manufactures exports, but also the development and poverty-reducing potential of service exports and also exports based on the new "knowledge-based" creative industries. It would also entail deeper analysis of how import composition matters.

The relationship between trade and poverty also varies with a country's level of productive development and structure of production and employment. This overlaps with the composition of trade, but it is not quite the same.

(b) The level of development and structure of production and employment

The relationship between trade and poverty also varies with a country's level of productive development and structure of production and employment. This overlaps with the composition of trade, but it is not quite the same.

The fact that the relationship between export growth and output growth varies with the level of development was an important element of initial research on the relative merits of inward-oriented and outward-oriented development strategies. This early research focused on what were then described as "semi-industrial countries" (see Balassa, 1970), and the kind of positive relationship between outward orientation and growth that was identified in the semi-industrial countries was difficult to find in the poorer developing countries (Feder, 1986). Later analysis appears to have forgotten this insight and to apply conclusions derived from countries with more advanced levels of productive development to all countries. Research on the trade–poverty relationship from a development perspective would seek to recover this finding and examine how the relationship applies in the least developed countries as well as in more advanced developing countries.

Variations in the trade–poverty relationship amongst the developing countries owing to their structure of production and employment is also an important issue. In many developing countries, a large proportion of the poor work in agriculture and live in rural areas. This has led to the view that agriculture is the key issue for trade and poverty reduction, particularly in international negotiations. But from a dynamic development perspective poverty reduction does not depend simply on agricultural productivity growth and improved employment prospects in agriculture: productivity growth and employment expansion in non-agricultural sectors are also important. Indeed, historically, most successful cases of sustained poverty reduction have involved a shift in the occupational distribution away from agriculture. In these cases productivity growth has occurred in agriculture and other sectors of the economy in a balanced way such that there is a net addition to income-earning opportunities (jobs and livelihoods) on an economy-wide scale (Bhadhuri, 1993).

International trade can have either positive or negative effects on this process of production and employment change. There are a number of agrarian-labour-surplus economies in East Asia where international trade has facilitated the process of productivity growth and labour reallocation from agriculture to industry (see Fei and Ranis, 1997). In these cases, international trade has built upon and strengthened positive development interlinkages between agriculture and a growing capitalist industrial sector within the domestic economy. However, it is possible for international trade to weaken those links, thus leading to an enclave-based pattern of economic growth. This will be discussed later in this Report in the context of the least developed countries.

*(c) Interdependence between trade and
other international economic relationships*

The relationship between trade and poverty is also influenced by the interdependence between trade and various other international economic relationships. To put it simply, how trade is related to poverty is affected by how trade is related to aid, debt, private capital flows and technology acquisition. For example, trade flows which are associated with FDI building global production chains might have different poverty-reducing effects from trade flows associated with domestic entrepreneurs extending a local industrialization process to external markets. Or imports based on tied aid might have different effects from imports financed out of export revenue.

These interdependencies matter for the trade–poverty relationship. From the point of view of developing countries, the knot through which the relationship between international trade and external finance is drawn together is the balance of payments. This critical constraint on development and sustained poverty reduction is conspicuously absent in the current debate on trade and poverty. Trade performance is also strongly linked to the level and stability of the exchange rate. The management of the exchange rate to achieve external trade and financial objectives is a key and complex issue.

*How trade is related to
poverty is affected by how
trade is related to aid, debt,
private capital flows and
technology acquisition.*

4. The feedback from sustained poverty reduction to international trade

A final element of the development approach to poverty reduction outlined here is that it would examine not only the impact of international trade on poverty trends but also the feedback effects from poverty reduction to international trade. What is important in this regard is that development and sustained poverty reduction are major motors for expanding international trade. On the one hand, the development of productive capacities enables developing countries to expand their exports. But on the other hand, rising income per capita and reduced poverty lead to increased imports.

Development and sustained poverty reduction are major motors for expanding international trade.

Simple evidence of the relative importance of trade liberalization and economic growth for import growth in developing countries is shown in chart 8. This compares the rate of growth of real imports per capita over the period 1997–2001 in developing countries classified according to the openness of their trade regime in 1997 and according to their real GDP growth rate during 1997–2001. If economic growth was closely correlated with the trade regime this exercise would not make much sense. But out of the 108 countries for which data are available, only 10 out of 35 classified as having been "open" have high GDP growth, and only 7 out of 36 countries classified as restrictive have low GDP growth. There are 37 countries which have either high GDP growth with a "restrictive" trade regime or low GDP growth with an "open" trade regime.

Given the mismatch between the trade regime and the growth performance, which reflects the fact that economic growth depends on so many factors in addition to the trade regime, the question that arises is the following: is trade liberalization more important than economic growth in explaining the growth of imports per capita in developing countries? What chart 8 shows is that openness of the trade regime is not in fact a good indicator of the rate of import growth. Real imports per capita grew at a rate that was slightly higher in "open" economies than in moderately restricted economies (2.1 per cent per annum as against 1.9 per cent per annum over the period 1997–2001). But the restrictive economies actually have slightly higher import growth rates — 2.9 per cent per annum. However, there is a very clear distinction between the developing

CHART 8. GROWTH RATE OF REAL IMPORTS PER CAPITA IN DEVELOPING COUNTRIES CLASSIFIED ACCORDING TO THE RESTRICTIVENESS OF THEIR TRADE REGIME AND TO THEIR GDP GROWTH PERFORMANCE, 1997–2001
(Average annual growth rate, percentage)

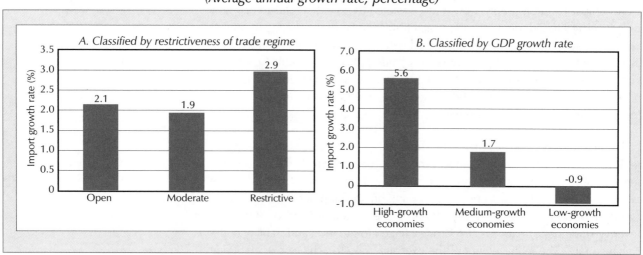

Source: World Bank, *World Development Indicators 2003*, CD-ROM; and IMF, Trade Restrictiveness Indicator.

Note: The imports and GDP figures are expressed in constant local currency terms. The countries' trade regimes were divided into open, moderate and restrictive according to the IMF trade restrictiveness indicator in 1997. A country's trade regime rated between 1 and 4 is considered to be open, while ratings between 5 and 6 are considered to be moderate and ratings above 7 restrictive. Countries were divided into high-, medium- and low-growth depending on their growth performance during the period 1997–2001. The high-growth developing countries are the top third (with a real GDP growth rate higher than 4.2 per cent), the medium-growth developing countries are the middle third (with a real GDP growth rate between 4.2 per cent and 2.08 per cent), and the low-growth developing countries are the remaining third (with a real GDP growth rate lower than 2.08 per cent). The GDP growth averages are calculated using the simple arithmetic average formula. India and China are included in the sample, but the overall average is not significantly affected by their presence.

countries when they are classified according to their GDP growth rates. Imports per capita grew by 5.6 per cent per annum in the high-growth economies, and by 1.7 per cent per annum in the medium-growth economies, while they declined by 0.9 per cent per annum in the low-growth economies.

This is a very simple statistical tabulation over a short period. However, it suggests that in terms of the expansion of global markets, economic growth is much more important than trade liberalization. During the structural adjustment era from 1980 to 2000, extensive trade liberalization was undertaken by developing countries. This resulted in a more import-intensive pattern of economic growth (UNCTAD, 1999). If economic growth and poverty reduction could be stimulated and sustained in developing countries now, there would be a major expansion of their imports per capita and also of world trade, which could benefit the developed countries in particular, as well as the developing countries.

In terms of the expansion of global markets, economic growth is much more important than trade liberalization.

E. Policy implications of the development approach

The development approach advocated here is an approach for analysing the trade–poverty relationship. However, it is worthwhile to outline briefly some of the policy implications of this approach.

1. NATIONAL POLICIES

A major danger which has arisen from an exclusive focus on the question of trade liberalization and poverty is that integration into the global economy has come to be seen as a mechanism of poverty reduction in itself. But it is development, the long-term process in which the incomes, productive capacities and freedoms of people increase, which is in practice the key to poverty reduction. Trade liberalization is certainly part of the development process and a very important policy issue. But it is wrong to assume that trade liberalization, or increasing trade integration as measured by the trade/GDP ratio is, in and of itself, the same thing as development.

A major danger which has arisen from an exclusive focus on the question of trade liberalization and poverty is that integration into the global economy has come to be seen as a mechanism of poverty reduction in itself. But it is development, the long-term process in which the incomes, productive capacities and freedoms of people increase, which is in practice the key to poverty reduction.

The approach adopted here implies that the national policies which best support poverty reduction should not be based on an integration strategy alone but rather on a national development strategy with an integration component.[5] The aim of such a strategy should be:

- To create and sustain a dynamic process of capital accumulation, structural change and technical progress in order to develop productive capacities;

- To manage integration with the global economy, including both external finance and external trade, and technology acquisition;

- To ensure that development is inclusive, incorporating marginal groups, paying attention to gender equity, and ensuring the achievement of certain minimum standards of human well-being, which are expressed in terms of poverty reduction, human development and food security.

Making international trade a more effective mechanism of poverty reduction is a policy problem which is embedded within this triple challenge. It is in this context that the important policy questions of how trade liberalization fits into a development strategy and how integration with the world economy can best support national development and poverty reduction arise. There are no easy answers or quick fixes. However, linking international trade to poverty reduction is best achieved through national development policies that are pragmatic, inclusive and outward-looking.

The hallmark of pragmatic development policies is that they are continuously learning on the basis of past experience. This entails a rejection of economic fundamentalism, of all varieties, and instead an evaluation of what works and what does not work in different contexts. Pragmatic development policies are private-sector-led. However, they recognize that it is not only government failures that are constraints on development and poverty reduction. There are significant market failures as well. Moreover, there are unequal outcomes associated with poverty which arise because markets work as well as because markets fail. This is partly because markets reward those who already have productive assets — financial assets, human capital, access to land and the equipment to work it (Birdsall, 2002). But the response of entrepreneurs to effective demand can also marginalize the needs of the poor. This is most dramatically evident in famine situations when food is shipped out of regions where people are starving because of the lack of a local purchasing power (Sen, 1981).

Linking international trade to poverty reduction is best achieved through national development policies that are pragmatic, inclusive and outward-looking.

Successful poverty reduction also requires inclusive development policies. This is clear when the majority of the population are poor. But it applies even if the poor are only a small proportion of the national population. In this situation, targeting the poor rather than pursuing broad-based development may actually be counter-productive. Firstly, it is clear that within a private-sector-led approach it is actually the behaviour of the rich that has an important impact on social outcomes. This comes partly through demand effects, which were first underlined by Adam Smith. But equally important are the ways in which the business class uses profits — whether for luxury consumption or reinvestment in ways which create more jobs for the majority (see UNCTAD, 1997). Secondly, the narrow focus on the poor rather than on broad-based development may undermine the sense of national community which has often provided the hidden ingredient of successful poverty reduction through development.

Finally, successful poverty reduction requires outward-looking development policies. The term "outward-looking" is used here to refer to policies which are based on "constant attention to" trade, technological and investment opportunities globally (Keesing, 1967: 304). An outward-looking policy is not necessarily the same as a policy of trade and financial liberalization. The latter can be one form of an outward-looking policy. But laissez-faire is not a necessary condition for an outward-looking policy. On the contrary, it is possible to undertake an outward-looking policy with varying degrees of government intervention.[6] Moreover, it is now becoming an important lesson of cumulative experience with economic reforms since the early 1980s that Governments may undertake liberalization without in practice being outward-looking in the active sense in which this term is defined here.

2. International policies

The development approach also has implications for international policies, and in particular for the design of the international trade regime. That trade regime is founded on two visions of global justice (Helleiner, 2003). The first, non-developmental, vision sees the purpose of the rules system as to provide stability and predictability for market participants, and to set certain restrictions on how national Governments may pursue their own diverse purposes. Economic freedom is seen as a good in itself, rather than as a means to development and poverty reduction. The second vision sees the rules system (and trade) as a means to an end rather than an end in itself, something which is instrumentally rather than intrinsically valuable. From this point of view, the purpose of the rules system is to facilitate positive development and poverty reduction outcomes. The critical question for negotiators designing the international trade regime would not be "how do we maximize trade and market access?" but rather "how do we enable countries to grow out of poverty?" (Rodrik, 2001: 10).

The design of the international trade regime seeks to incorporate both visions. Thus the concern to establish stability, predictability, market access and a level playing field for all participants is complemented by the concern, expressed in the first substantive paragraph of the agreement establishing the WTO, that the system be also designed in such a way that it contributes to raising living standards, ensuring full employment and promoting sustainable development. Reconciliation of possible tensions between these two visions of global justice has now become central to the design of the international trade regime. This follows expansion of its membership to include most developing countries, the perception of a "development deficit" in the current round of WTO negotiations, and also an increasing concern to make poverty reduction the "litmus test" of the success of the trading system.[7] It is in this context that a proposal to monitor the working of the international trade regime in terms of development and poverty reduction benchmarks has been made (UNCTAD, 2003).

If poverty reduction is taken as the priority goal, then the development approach to trade and poverty sketched out in this chapter has important implications for the design of the international trade regime.

If poverty reduction is taken as the priority goal, then the development approach to trade and poverty sketched out in this chapter has important implications for the design of the international trade regime. It implies that an international regime which facilitates the expansion of international trade is not sufficient for poverty reduction. Rather, it is necessary to have an international trade regime which does not constrain the national policies of developing countries for developing their productive capacities. To be precise, *the international trade regime should enable rather than constrain the efficient development and utilization of the productive capacities in a way in which the population of working age becomes more and more fully and productively employed.* What this means in practice depends on the relationship between international trade, the development of productive capacities and poverty reduction.

Giving priority to poverty reduction does not mean that it is possible to ignore the value of stability, predictability and economic freedom. But it is important to recognize that freedoms of all kinds, including the freedom of choice which underpins the working of a market economy, are severely curtailed in societies where most people live with barely sufficient income to meet their basic subsistence needs. It is through poverty reduction that personal liberty can be actually rather than formally realized. It is through development and poverty reduction that the two visions of global justice can, in the end, be reconciled.

Finally, the development approach to trade and poverty implies that the international trade regime is not the sole international policy issue which needs to be addressed in order to link international trade more effectively with poverty reduction. Because the way in which trade is related to poverty is affected by how trade is related to aid, debt, private capital flows and technology acquisition, a central international policy issue is the question of coherence between action in the different domains.

The interdependence between these domains implies that a slogan such as "trade not aid" is misleading. The issue is not one or the other. It is rather how to make any existing negative synergies between aid and trade into positive synergies, how to use aid to build productive capacities and thus how, in the long term, to reduce the need for aid. Similarly, it is necessary to link trade with external debt problems. For the poorest countries, the close connection between primary commodity dependence and the build-up of unsustainable debt is clear (UNCTAD, 2002). For middle-income countries, the links between growing trade deficits, excessive reliance on unstable forms of private capital inflows and currency crises are also evident (see UNCTAD 1999, 2002). These systemic links must be taken into account in the design of international policies which make international trade a more effective means of poverty reduction in developing countries.

F. Conclusions

The focus on trade liberalization and poverty is hampering identification of the most effective national and international policies to ensure that international trade supports sustained economic growth, which is the key to substantial poverty reduction on a scale necessary to meet Millennium poverty reduction goals.

This chapter has argued that the current approach to policy analysis and research on trade and poverty is too narrowly focused on the issue of trade liberalization and poverty. Progress is being made in this subject. There is a better understanding of the short-term and direct channels through which border price changes associated with trade policy reforms impact at the household level, and also new methodologies to estimate these impacts and the poverty impacts of multilateral trade liberalization. This is helping policy makers to alleviate poverty during trade liberalization. However, the narrow focus is hampering identification of the most effective national and international policies to ensure that international trade supports sustained economic growth, which is the key to substantial poverty reduction on a scale necessary to meet Millennium poverty reduction goals.

The chapter argues that in order to identify such policies it is necessary to stand back from the subject of trade liberalization and poverty, and focus objectively on the links between trade and poverty. It proposes a development approach to analysing the trade–poverty relationship. After this has been done, it is then possible to see how trade liberalization can fit into a broader development strategy.

It is necessary to stand back from the subject of trade liberalization and poverty, and focus objectively on the links between trade and poverty.

The analytical core of this development approach is the idea that sustained poverty reduction occurs through the efficient development and utilization of productive capacities in a manner in which the working age population becomes more and more fully and productively employed. International trade can facilitate, hinder and modify this process. This approach thus encompasses the long-term and indirect impact of trade on people's lives and livelihoods through the development of productive capacities, as well as the short-term and direct impact which is currently considered in the literature on trade liberalization and poverty. It makes trade and employment a central issue for understanding trade and poverty.

An important aspect of the approach is that it seeks to identify variations amongst developing countries in terms of the trade–poverty relationship. Three key dimensions of diversity are: the composition of trade; the level of development and structure of production; and the nature of the interdependence between trade and financial and investment flows, as well as between trade and debt and trade and technology transfer. Finally, the approach encompasses analysis of the way in which poverty reduction affects trade.

The rest of the Report applies this development approach to understanding the relationship between trade and poverty in the particular situation of the least developed countries. The Report is a first attempt at understanding this complex issue. It cannot answer all the difficult questions which the approach raises. But the outline of ways to link international trade to poverty reduction in LDCs more effectively can be discerned, and a deeper programme of policy analysis and research should be able to extend and refine the findings.

Notes

1. See, for example, Dollar (1992), Edwards (1992), Levine and Renelt (1992), Sachs and Warner (1995), Krueger (1998), Frankel and Romer (1999), Dollar and Kraay (2001), Greenaway, Morgan and Wright (2002), Yanikkaya (2003) and Santos-Paulino and Thirlwall (2004).

2. Recent research has shown that labour reallocation effects away from a Malthusian traditional sector can increase the effective return on physical capital by around 30 per cent in industrializing countries (Landon-Lane and Robertson, 2003). Also, work on research into the sources of economic growth in sub-Saharan Africa shows that reallocation of labour from the agricultural sector to more productive sectors has "contributed significantly to growth in the current and earlier periods" (Berthelemy and Söderling, 2001: 333). Another estimate, for low-income countries from 1960 to 1980, suggests that the shift of labour from agriculture to industry can explain as much as two thirds of growth per capita in those countries during that period, but a much lower amount in more advanced developing countries (Pack 1992, quoted in Fei and Ranis, 1997: 43).

3. These different channels are rooted in different theories on the gains from trade.

4. The relationship between manufacturing output and productivity, which was particularly emphasized by Kaldor, is known as Verdoorn's Law. It has been found in various settings – see Thirlwall (2002: chapter 3) and, for the test of this relationship within Africa, see Thirlwall and Wells (2003).

5. This position is similar to that of Rodrik (2000b), who identifies the shift from a concern with development to a concern with integration as a major weakness in current policy debates. As he puts it, "The trouble with the current discourse on globalization is that it confuses ends with means. A truly development-oriented strategy requires a shift in emphasis. Integration into the world economy has to be viewed as an instrument for achieving economic growth and development, not as an ultimate goal" (p. 28).

6. This point is vital for interpreting the successful East Asian development experience. See, for example, Bradford (1994).

7. On the notion of a development deficit in the current round of negotiations, see Ricupero (2004), and on the importance of poverty reduction as a litmus test of the multilateral trade agreements, see Puri (2003).

8. The emergence of trade deficits is important as they show that the trade/GDP ratio is "a highly idiosyncratic statistic". Changes in the ratio are driven not simply by the value of exports and imports but also by changes in the trade deficit. This is because the ratio is exports plus imports (X+M) divided by GDP, which equals total domestic consumption and investment (both public and private) plus exports and minus imports (+X-M). A country running a trade deficit will be more open by this measure than a country running an identically sized trade surplus even though the sum of their export/GDP ratio and import/GDP ratio is the same.

References

Balassa, B. (1970). Growth strategies in semi-industrial countries, *Quarterly Journal of Economics*, 84: 24-47.

Bannister, G.J. and Thugge. K. (2001). International trade and poverty alleviation, *IMF Working Paper*, WP/01/54.

Berg, A. and Krueger, A. (2003). Trade, growth, and poverty: a selective survey, *IMF Working Paper*, WP/03/30.

Berthélemy, J-C. and Söderling, L. (2001). The role of capital accumulation, adjustment and structural change for economic take-off: empirical evidence from African growth episodes, *World Development*, 29 (2): 323–343.

Bhaduri (1993). Alternative development strategies and the rural sector, in *Economic Crisis and Third World Agriculture*, ed. by Singh A. and Tabatabai, H., Cambridge University Press.

Bhagwati, J. (1986). Rethinking trade strategies. In: Lewis, J.P. (ed.), *Development Strategies Reconsidered*, Overseas Development Council, Washington, D.C.

Bhagwati, J. and Srinivasan, T.N. (2002). Trade and poverty in the poor countries, *American Economic Review*, 92 (2): 180–183.

Birdsall, N. (2002). Asymmetric globalization: global markets require good global politics, Working Paper No. 12, *Center for Global Development*, Washington DC.

Birdsall, N. and Hamoudi, A. (2002). Commodity dependence, trade, and growth: when "openness" is not enough, Working Paper No. 7, *Center for Global Development*, Washington DC.

Bradford, C.I. (1994). From trade-driven growth to growth-driven trade: Reappraising the East Asian development experience, OECD, Paris.

Bussolo, M., Van der Menbrugghe, D. and Lay, J. (2003). A Preliminary Assessment of the Economic and Poverty Impacts of the Doha and the FTAA Agenda for Latin America, paper prepared for the Second Poverty and Economic Policy General Meeting, Hanoi, 4-8 November 2003, (http://132.203.59.36/PEP/Group/meetings&workshops/HANOI/bussolo.pdf).

Chenery, H. (1961). Comparative advantage and development policy, *American Economic Review*, 51 (1): 18-51.

Choudhri, E.U. and Hakura, D.S. (2000). International trade and productivity growth: Exploring the sectoral effects for developing countries, *IMF Staff Papers*, 47 (1), Washington DC.

Cline, W. R. (2004). *Trade Policy and Global Poverty*, Center for Global Development, Washington DC.

Cockburn, J. (2001). Trade Liberalization and Poverty in Nepal. A Computable General Equilibrium Micro Simulation Analysis, Oxford University, mimeo, (http://www.crefa.ecn.ulaval.ca/cahier/0118.pdf)

Cooper, R. N. (2001). Growth and inequality: The role of foreign trade and investment, Working Paper No. 1729, World Bank, Washington DC, (http://www.econ.worldbank.org/files/1729_cooper.pdf).

Decaluwé, B., Patry, A. and Savard, L. (1998). Income distribution, poverty measures and trade shocks: a computable general equilibrium model of an archetype developing country, CREFA Working Paper No. 9812, Université de Laval, Canada.

Decaluwé, B., Patry, A., Savard, L. and Thorbecke, E. (1999). Poverty analysis within a general equilibrium framework, CREFA Working Paper No. 9909, Université de Laval, Canada.

Demery, L. and Addison, T. (1987). Stabilization policy and income distribution in developing countries, *World Development*, 15 (12): 1483–1498.

DFID (2000). *Eliminating World Poverty: Making Globalization Work for the Poor*, HMSO, London.

Dollar, D. (1992). Outward-oriented developing economies really do grow more rapidly: evidence from 95 LDCs, 1976-1985, *Economic Development and Cultural Change*, 40 (3): 523–545.

Dollar, D. and Kraay, A. (2001). Trade, growth and poverty, World Bank Policy Research Department, Working Paper No. 2615, Washington DC.

Dollar, D. and Kraay, A. (2002). Institutions, trade and growth, *Journal of Monetary Economics*, 50: 133–162.

Edwards, S. (1992). The sequencing of structural adjustment and stabilization, *International Center for Economic Growth Publication*, Occasional Paper No. 34, California.

Egwaikhide, F. (1999). Determinants of imports in Nigeria: a dynamic specification, Research Paper No. 91, African Economic Research Consortium, Nairobi, Nigeria.

Evans, D. (2001). Identifying winners and losers in Southern Africa from globalisation: integrating findings from GTAP and poverty case studies on global trade policy reform, Institute for Development Studies Working Paper No. 140, Institute of Development Studies, Brighton.

FAO (2003). *Trade Reforms and Food Security: Conceptualizing the Linkages*, Commodities and Trade Division, Rome, Italy.

Feder, G. (1986). Growth in semi-industrial countries: A statistical analysis. In: Chenery, H., Robinson, S., Syrquin, M. (eds.), *Industrialization and Growth: A Comparative Study*, Oxford University Press, Oxford and New York.

Fei, J. C. and Ranis, G. (1997). *Growth and Development from an Evolutionary Perspective*, Blackwell Publishers, United Kingdom.

Frankel, J. and Romer, D. (1999). Does trade cause growth?, *American Economic Review*, 89 (3): 379–399.

Ghose, A. (2003). *Jobs and Incomes in a Globalizing World*, International Labour Office, Geneva.

Greenaway, D., Morgan, C.W. and Wright, P.W. (2002). Trade liberalization and growth in developing countries, *Journal of Development Economics*, 67: 229–244.

Grossman, G. and Helpman, E. (1990). Trade, innovation, and growth, *American Economic Review*, 80 (2): 86–91.

Harris, R. (2001). A computable general equilibrium analysis of Mexico's agricultural policy reforms, IFPRI Discussion Paper No. 65, International Food Policy Research Institute, Washington DC.

Helleiner, G. (1987). Stabilization, adjustment, and the poor, *World Development*, 15 (12): 1499–1513.

Helleiner, G. (1994). *Trade Policy and Industrialization in Turbulent Times*, Routledge, United Kingdom.

Helleiner, G. (1998). Trade policy: meaning, measurement and instruments. In *Export-Led Versus Balanced Growth in the 1990s,* ed. by Singer, H., Hatti, N., Tandon, R., Delhi, B. R. Publishing Corporation, Delhi.

Helleiner, G. (2003). After Cancun, free trade area of Americas talks show limits of the single undertaking, *Bridges,* European Commission, 7 (8), (http://www.ictsd.org).

Hertel, T.W., Ivanic, M., Preckel, P.V. and Cranfield, J.A.L. (2003a). Multilateral trade liberalization and poverty in Brazil and Chile. *Economie Internationale,* 94–95: 201–234.

Hertel, T.W., Ivanic, M., Preckel, P.V. and Cranfield, J.A.L. (2003b). The earnings effects of multilateral trade liberalization: implications for poverty in developing countries, mimeo.

Hertel, T.W., Ivanic, M., Preckel, P.V. and Cranfield, J.A.L. (2003c). Trade liberalization and the structure of poverty in developing countries, GTAP Working Paper No. 25, University of Purdue, U.S.A., (http://www.gtap.agecon.purdue.edu/resources/res_display.asp?RecordID=1207).

Hoekmann, B, Micalopoulos, C., Schiff, M., Tarr, D. (2002). Trade policy, PRSP Sourcebook, World Bank, Washington DC. (http://www.worldbank.org/poverty/strategies/chapters/trade/trade.htm)

Kanbur, S.M.R. (1987). Structural adjustment, macroeconomic adjustment and poverty: a methodology for analysis, *World Development,* 15 (12): 1515–1526.

Keesing, D.B. (1967). Outward-looking policies and economic development, *Economic Journal,* 77(306): 303–320.

Krueger, A. O. (1974). The political economy of rent-seeking society, *American Economic Review,* 65: 291-303.

Krueger, A. O. (1983). *Trade and Employment in Developing Countries,* University of Chicago Press, Chicago.

Krueger, A. O. (1990). *Perspectives on Trade and Development,* Harvester Wheatsheaf, London.

Krueger, A. O. (1998). Why trade liberalization is good for growth, *The Economic Journal,* 108 (450): 1513–1522.

Landon-Lane, J., Roberston, P. E. (2003). Accumulation and productivity growth in industrializing economies, Paper prepared for the Royal Economic Society Conference. University of Warwick, United Kingdom.

Lee, J.W. (1995). Capital goods imports and long-run growth, *Journal of Development Economics,* 48 (1): 91–110.

Levine, R. and Renelt, R. (1992). A sensititivity analysis of cross-country growth regressions, *American Economic Review,* 82 (4): 942–963.

Lofgren, H., Chulu, O., Sichinga, O., Simtowe, F., Tchale, H., Tseka, R. and Wobst, P. (2001). External shocks and domestic poverty alleviation: Simulations with a CGE model of Malawi, Discussion Paper No. 51, International Food Policy Research Institute, Washington DC.

Maurer, R. (1998). Economic growth and international trade with capital goods, Kiel Institute of World Economics, Kiel, Germany.

McCulloch, N., Winters, L.A. and Cirera, X. (2001). *Trade Liberalization and Poverty: A Handbook,* Centre for Economic Policy Research, London (http://cepr.org/pubs/books/P144.asp).

McCulloch, N. (2003). The impact of structural reforms on poverty, World Bank Working Paper No. 3124, World Bank, Washington DC.

Nicita, A., Olarreaga, M. and Soloaga, I. (2003). A simple methodology to assess the poverty impact of economic policies using household data, Working Paper No. 3124, The World Bank, Washington DC.

Nye, H.L.M., Redding, S.G. and Watkins, K. (2001). *Dollar and Kraay on "Trade, growth, and poverty": A critique,* mimeo. (http://www.maketradefair.com/en/assets/english/finalDKcritique.pdf).

OXFAM (2002). *Rigged Rules and Double Standards: Trade, Globalisation, and the Fight against Poverty,* London (http://www.tradeobservatory.org/library/uploadedfiles/Rigged_Rules_And_Double_StandardsTrade_Globali.pdf).

Pritchett, L. (1994). Measuring outward orientation in developing countries: Can it be done?, World Bank Policy, Research and External Affairs Working Papers. No. 566, Washington D.C.

Pritchett, L. (2003). Who is *not* poor? Proposing a higher international standard for poverty, Working Paper No. 33, Center for Global Development, Washington D.C.

Puri, L. (2003). Statement at the International Conference on Trade, Growth and Poverty, organised by DFID, European Commission, International Monetary Fund, UNDP, held in London, 8-9 December 2003.

Rama, M. (2004), Globalization and workers in developing countries, In *Trade and Labour: Issues, Perspectives and Experiences from developing Asia*, ed. Hasan, R., Mitra, D., NothHolland, Amesterdam.

Redding, S. (1999) Dynamic comparative advantage and the welfare effects of trade, *Oxford Economic Papers* No. 140, 51 (1): 15-39.

Reimer, J. J. (2002). Estimating the poverty impacts of trade liberalization, GTAP Working Paper No. 20. University of Purdue, U.S.A.

Ricupero, R. (2004). Opening statement to the eight session of the Commission on Trade in Goods and Services and Commodities, held in Geneva on 9 February 2004.

Rivera-Batiz, G. and Romer, P. (1991). International trade and endogenous techonological progress, *European Economic Review*. 35 (4): 971–1004.

Rodriguez, F. and Rodrik, D. (2000). Trade policy and economic growth: a skeptic's guide to the cross-national evidence, In Bernanke, B., Rogoff, K. *NBER Macroeconomics Annual 2000*, MIT Press, Cambridge, U.S.A.

Rodrik, D. (1992). The limits of trade policy reform in developing countries, *Journal of Economic Perspectives*, 6 (1): 87–105.

Rodrik, D. (1995). Getting Interventions Right: How South Korea and Taiwan Grew Rich, *Economic Policy*, 20, 53–108.

Rodrik, D. (2000a). *Comments on "Trade, Growth and Poverty" by D. Dollar and A. Kraay*, mimeo, (http://ksghome.harvard.edu/~.drodrik.academic.ksg/)

Rodrik, D. (2000b). Development strategies for the next century, Paper prepared for presentation at the conference on *Developing Economies in the 21st Century*, January 26–27, 2000, Ciba, Japan, (http://ksghome.harvard.edu/~.drodrik.academic.ksg/).

Rodrik, D. (2001). The global governance of trade as if development really mattered, background paper to the UNDP Project on Trade and Sustainable Human Development, (http://ksghome.harvard.edu/~.drodrik.academic.ksg/).

Rodrik, D., Subramanian, A. and Trebbi, F. (2002). Institutions rule: the primacy of institutions over geography and integration in economic development, CEPR Discussion Papers No. 3643, Center of Economic Policy Research, London.

Rutherford, T.F. and Tarr, D.G. (2002). Trade liberalization, product variety and growth in a small open economy: a quantitative assessment, *Journal of International Economics*, 56 (2): 247–272.

Sachs, J. and Warner, A. (1995). Economic reform and the process of global integration, *Brookings Paper of Economic Activity*, 1–118, Washington DC.

Santos-Paulino, A., Thirlwall, A. P. (2004). The impact of trade liberalisation on exports, imports and the balance of payments of developing countries, *The Economic Journal*, 114 (493): 50–72.

Sen, A. (1981). *Poverty and Famines*, Oxford University Press, Oxford.

Sen, K. (2003). Globalisation and labour market outcomes in the South: a critical survey. Discussion Paper No. 1, Project on Globalisation, Production and Poverty, Overseas Development Group, Norwich.

Sprout, R. V. A., and Weaver, J. H. (1993). Exports and economic growth in a simultaneous equations model, *Journal of Developing Areas*, 27: 289–306.

Srinivasan, T.N., and Bhagwati, J. (1999). Outward-orientation and development: are revisionists right?, Economic Growth Center, Center Discussion Paper No. 806, Yale University, U.S.A.

Thirlwall, A.P. (2002). *The Nature of Economic Growth. An Alternative Framework for Understanding the Performance of Nations*, Edward Elgar, Cheltenham, United Kingdom.

Thirlwall, A.P. and Wells, H. (2003). Testing Kaldor's growth laws across the countries of Africa, *Africa Development Review* 15 (2): 89–105.

UNCTAD (1994). *Trade and Development Report, 1994*, United Nations publication, sales no. E.94.II.D.26, Geneva.

UNCTAD (1996). *Trade and Development Report, 1996*. United Nations publication, sales no. E.96.II.D.6, Geneva.

UNCTAD (1997). *Trade and Development Report, 1997 — Globalization, Distribution and Growth*, United Nations publication, sales no. E.97.II.D.8, Geneva.

UNCTAD (1998). *Trade and Development Report, 1998. Growth in Africa*, United Nations publication, sales no. E.98.II.D.6, Geneva.

UNCTAD (1999).*Trade and Development Report, 1999 — Trade, Finance and Growth*, United Nations publication, sales no. E.99.II.D.1, Geneva.

UNCTAD (2002). *The Least Developed Countries Report 2002 — Escaping the Poverty Trap*, United Nations publication, sales no. E.02.II.D.13, Geneva.

UNCTAD (2003). *Trade and Development Report, 2003 — Capital Accumulation, Growth and Structural Change*. United Nations publication, sales No.E.03.II.D.7, Geneva.

UNDP, Heinrich Boll Foundation, Rockefeller Brothers Fund, The Rockefeller Foundation 1913 and Wallace Global Fund (2003). *Making Global Trade Work for the Poor*, Earthscan, London.

Winters, L.A. (2000) Trade, trade policy, and poverty: what are the links?, CEPR Research Paper No. 2382, Center of Economic Policy Research, London.

World Bank (1990). *World Development Report,* Washington DC.

World Bank (2000/2001) *World Development Report, Attacking Poverty*, Washington D.C.

World Bank (2002). *Globalization, Growth and Poverty: Building an Inclusive World Economy,* A World Bank Policy Research Report, World Bank and Oxford University Press.

World Bank (2004). *Global Economic Prospects. Realizing the Development Promise of the Doha Agenda.* Washington D.C.

WTO (2003). *World Trade Report 2003, The Role of Trade and Trade Policy in the Development Process,* section A, part II Trade and Development.

Yanikkaya, H. (2003). Trade openness and economic growth: a cross-country empirical investigation, *Journal of Development Economics*, 72: 57–89.

Young, A. (1991). Learning by doing and the dynamic effects of international trade, *Quarterly Journal of Economics,* 106 (2): 369–405.

The Potential Role of International Trade in Poverty Reduction in the LDCs

Chapter 2

A. Introduction

This chapter and the next two apply the development approach outlined in the previous chapter to consider the relationship between trade and poverty in the least developed countries. The present chapter examines the role that international trade could play in poverty reduction in the LDCs, and identifies some of the key conditions for the realization of this role. The next two chapters consider how the trade–poverty relationship works in practice.

The chapter is organized into three sections. Section B examines the relationship between sustained economic growth and poverty reduction in the LDCs. Section C discusses the relationship between exports and economic growth in LDCs and identifies some of the conditions through which exports can lead to sustained economic growth. Section D identifies some of the conditions that must be fulfilled if exports are to lead to a form of economic growth which is poverty-reducing. The concluding section summarizes the main points of the argument.

The chapter builds on the empirical analysis in *The Least Developed Countries Report 2002*. A more detailed description of the nature of poverty in the LDCs and of the methodological issues are available there. Box 6 summarizes the approach of this Report to defining and measuring poverty.

B. The importance of sustained economic growth for poverty reduction in the LDCs

1. THE NATURE OF POVERTY IN THE LDCs

The relationship between economic growth and poverty critically depends on the nature of poverty, the definition of the poverty line and the level of per capita income in a country. Using the $1/day and $2/day international poverty lines to identify the proportion of the population which are poor, it is clear that the key feature of poverty in the LDCs is that there is a generalized or mass poverty. The majority of the population lives at or below income levels which are sufficient to meet their basic needs. The available resources in the economy, even when equally distributed, are barely sufficient to cater for the basic needs of the population on a sustainable basis.

Table 25 shows our estimates of the incidence and depth of poverty during 1995–1999 in 39 LDCs for which data were available. At that time, 81 per cent of the population of the LDCs lived on less than $2/day and 50 per cent on less than $1/day (table 25). The average daily consumption of the $2/day poor was only $1.03, whilst the average daily consumption of the $1/day poor was $0.64

The majority of the population lives at or below income levels sufficient to meet their basic needs...

... and the available resources in the economy, even when equally distributed, are barely sufficient to cater for the basic needs of the population on a sustainable basis.

BOX 6. THE MEANING AND MEASUREMENT OF POVERTY IN THIS REPORT

This Report follows the approach to defining and measuring poverty that was adopted in *The Least Developed Countries Report 2002*. The major, though not exclusive, focus is on poverty defined as the inability to attain a minimally adequate level of private consumption. The incidence of poverty and the depth of poverty are measured by the specification of a poverty line that represents, in monetary terms, the level of consumption that is regarded as minimally adequate. It includes both purchased goods and the imputed value of consumption from a household's own production. The incidence of poverty is calculated as the proportion of the total population living below the poverty line, i.e. on less than a minimally adequate amount. The depth of poverty is calculated by estimating, in monetary terms, the average level of income of the poor, namely those people living below the poverty line.

Within this consumption-based and money-metric approach, the choice of the poverty line is an important issue. The Report utilizes the $1/day and S2/day international poverty lines using purchasing power parity (PPP) exchange rates, which enable comparisons in levels of private consumption between countries. The $1/day poverty line is a standard of extreme poverty that has become a focal concern for the international community through the Millennium Development Goals. The $2/day standard is increasingly being used in international poverty comparisons because the $1/day is most relevant for the poorest countries. The adoption of the $1/day and $2/day poverty lines in this Report does not imply that higher international poverty lines should be excluded in analysis of the trade–poverty relationship, particularly in more advanced developing countries.

One advantage of a focus on consumption poverty is that it is possible to build on past insights that link trade, economic growth and poverty. However, even with this relatively simple definition of poverty, a number of difficult issues arise in making precise poverty estimates. Critical methodological issues are: the specification of the purchasing power parity exchange rates which are used to make national consumption estimates internationally comparable; and discrepancies in estimates of average private consumption per capita derived from household surveys and national accounts.

The current state of global poverty monitoring can best be described as one of statistical turmoil. Firstly, the purchasing power parity exchange rates in the latest revision of the Penn World Tables (version 6.1) differ considerably from the PPP exchange rates that provided the basis for the original specification of the $1/day international poverty line and from those used by the World Bank in its more recent global poverty estimates (Karshenas, 2004). Secondly, national-accounts estimates of the average level of private consumption per person differ from estimates of the average level of private consumption per person in household expenditure surveys. Poverty estimates which incorporate the national-accounts estimates suggest that global $1/day poverty is lower in total than purely household-survey-based poverty estimates (see, for example, Bhalla, 2002). *The Least Developed Countries Report 2002* also found that the global distribution of poverty was different, with the current purely household-survey-based estimates underestimating the incidence and depth of poverty in the poorest countries, and particularly in Africa (UNCTAD, 2002).

Against this background of statistical turmoil, the present Report has not made any new poverty estimates for the LDCs. The estimates of the incidence and depth of poverty quoted in this Report are thus derived from the same database as that used for *The Least Developed Countries Report 2002*. These are national-accounts-based poverty estimates, which are calculated on the basis of average private consumption per capita as reported in the national accounts, and the distribution of private consumption as reported in household surveys. As this chapter indicates, there is a close relationship between average private consumption per capita and the incidence of $1/day and $2/day poverty in lower-income Asian and African countries. Thus chapter 3 also uses trends in private consumption per capita from the national accounts data as a proxy measure of trends in poverty (see box 8).

Some would argue that combining unadjusted national accounts estimates of average private consumption per capita with survey-based estimates of distribution "will certainly give poor measures of poverty" (Deaton, 2004: 38; see also Ravallion, 2003). However, this Report retains the view that both national-accounts-based and household-survey-based statistics are flawed (see UNCTAD, 2002: 45–49) and that the national-accounts-based methodology used here provides "as plausible poverty estimates as purely household-survey-based estimates" (p. 47). This is partly for the arguments outlined therein, particularly in relation to the fact that household-survey methodology is less standardized internationally than national-accounts methodology. But in addition, it is clear that the biases in the household surveys are not simply a question of errors in the distribution of consumption, but more importantly they also relate to the level of consumption and questions of survey design and recall period.

The view that only household surveys would allow us to measure poverty renders analysis of the relationship between globalization, development and poverty in the LDCs impractical. In these circumstances, it is necessary to develop statistically sound methods to fill the data gaps.

Box 6 (contd.)

What is necessary now is that the international community agree on a common set of best-practice protocols for household surveys, in order to increase the international comparability of these data (Deaton, 2004); and an effort is made to reconcile discrepancies between household surveys and national accounts estimates of private consumption (Pyatt, 2003). In the mean time more effort needs to be devoted to obtain poverty estimates which make full use of the information contained in both national accounts and household surveys (see Karshenas, 2004, for an attempt to create a unified framework). In the next LDC Report, this will be done.

Finally, it should be noted that consumption-based and money-metric approach to defining and measuring poverty adopted here is regarded as being complementary to, rather than superior or inferior to, other approaches that may be adopted within a general multidimensional view of poverty. Thus broader views of poverty, encompassing in particular access to health and education services and the question of food security, enter the discussion in this chapter.

(in 1985 purchasing power parity dollars). The incidence of poverty was particularly high in the African LDCs, where 65 per cent of the population was living on less than $1/day in the second half of the 1990s. Even if total private consumption expenditure had been distributed equally amongst all the population in the African LDCs, the average daily consumption would still only have been $1.01 per day. In the Asian LDCs, the situation was better. However, 68 per cent of the population was living on less than $2/day in those countries during 1995–1999. If the total private consumption expenditure had been equally distributed amongst all the population in the Asian LDCs, their average private consumption would have been $2.21 per day.

Associated with low levels of income and consumption there are human deprivations of all kinds. Daily existence is marked by hunger, seeing one's children die before they reach the age of five, long hours of drudgery, high levels of risk and uncertainty, a constant struggle for existence, little freedom of choice and, in the end, a short life.

TABLE 25. AVERAGE INCOME, PRIVATE CONSUMPTION AND THE INCIDENCE AND DEPTH OF POVERTY IN AFRICAN AND ASIAN LDCS AND SELECTED OECD COUNTRIES, 1995–1999

	GDP per capita per day		Per capita private consumption per day								Percentage share of population living on less than:	
			Total population		Poor (living below $1 a day)		Poor (living below $2 a day)					
	Current $	1985 PPP $	Current $	1985 PPP $	Current $	1985 PPP $	Current $	1985 PPP $			$1 a day	$2 a day
Weighted averages												
LDCs[a]	0.72	2.50	0.57	1.39	0.29	0.64	0.44	1.03			50.1	80.7
African LDCs	0.65	1.51	0.52	1.01	0.30	0.59	0.44	0.86			64.9	87.5
Asian LDCs	0.88	4.59	0.69	2.21	0.28	0.90	0.45	1.42			23.0	68.2
Selected OECD countries[b]					*Poorest 10%*		*Poorest 20%*					
United States	90.1	57.9	58.2	41.4	10.5	7.5	15.1	10.8			..	..
Switzerland	99.3	44.6	61.9	28.2	16.1	7.3	21.4	9.7			..	..
Sweden	73.8	43.7	37.3	23.5	13.8	8.3	17.9	10.8			..	..
Japan	94.1	43.4	50.5	24.2	24.2	11.6	26.7	12.8			..	..
France	66.9	41.9	36.7	25.4	10.3	7.0	13.2	9.0			..	..
United Kingdom	66.4	41.6	43.7	29.9	11.4	7.4	14.4	9.4			..	..

Source: UNCTAD (2002: 52, table 18).

    a   Thirty-nine countries, including 4 island LDCs. For an exhaustive country list, see UNCTAD (2002: 57, table 19).
    b   Data on individual OECD countries refer to 1998. The share of the bottom deciles in OECD countries is calculated by applying per capita consumption averages to decile income distribution.

In the majority of the LDCs, poverty is not only all-pervasive throughout society, but it has also been quite persistent. For the LDCs as a group, the proportion of the population living on less than $1/day was about the same at the end of the 1990s as it was at the start of the decade (see UNCTAD, 2002: chapter 1).

2. THE RELATIONSHIP BETWEEN PRIVATE CONSUMPTION GROWTH AND POVERTY

In conditions of generalized poverty, there is a close relationship between the level of average private consumption expenditure per capita and the incidence of poverty...

In conditions of generalized poverty, there is a close relationship between the level of average private consumption expenditure per capita and the incidence of poverty. This is shown by the poverty curves in chart 9, which trace the incidence of $1/day and $2/day poverty in relation to average private consumption per capita. Those curves are based on 32 low-income and lower-middle-income countries in Africa and Asia and include available observations, from LDCs and other developing countries, over three decades.[1] The poverty curves are analogous to the inverted U-shaped curve of Simon Kuznets that suggests that income inequality will increase in the early stages of development and then decrease. But instead of specifying the inequality–development relationship, they show the poverty–development relationship in African and Asian developing countries. They indicate the normal path of poverty reduction that should occur during the development process as average private consumption per capita rises in countries characterized by mass poverty.

The poverty curves are gentle at the top, steep in the middle and gentle again at the bottom. The $1-a-day poverty curve is steeper than the $2-a-day poverty

CHART 9. $1/DAY AND $2/DAY POVERTY CURVES

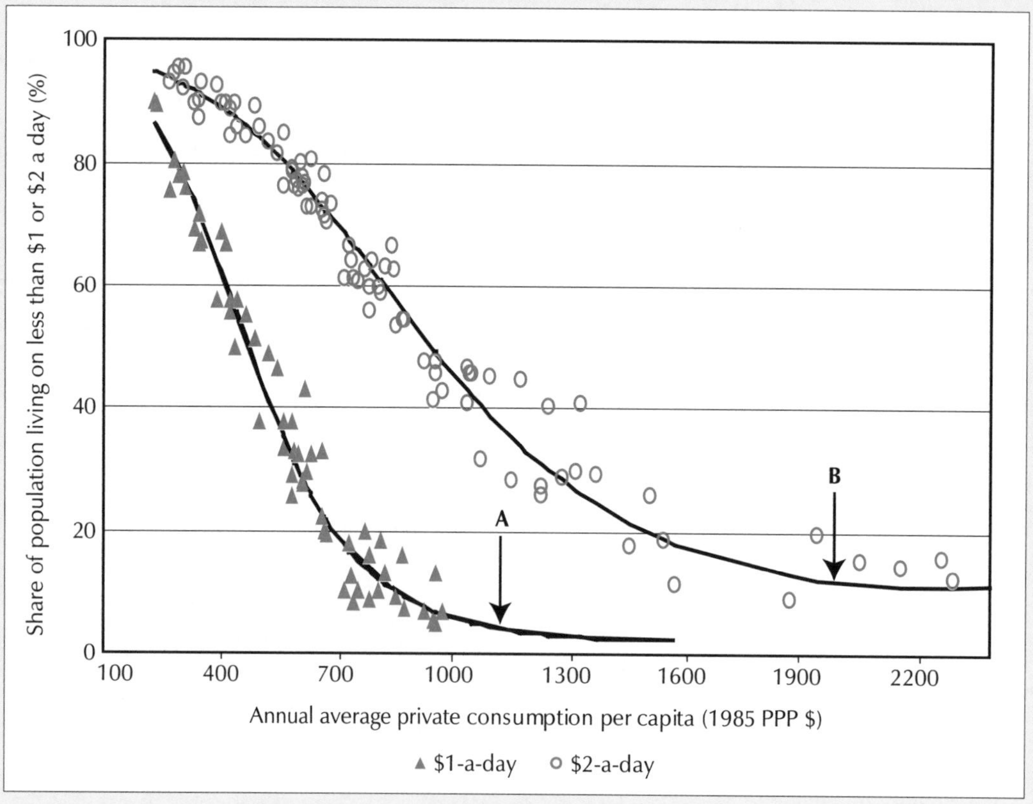

Source: UNCTAD (2002: 72, chart 13).
Note: For significance of points A and B, see text.

curve, which means that a given amount of consumption growth will reduce the $1-a-day poverty rate faster. Thus, for example, if average private consumption per capita doubles from $400 to $800 a year, the proportion of the population living on less than a dollar a day is expected to fall from around 65 per cent to less than 20 per cent. However, the shape of the curves is also such that once a country passes a certain threshold of average private consumption per capita, the impact of economic growth on reducing poverty becomes considerably smaller. This point is reached first for $1/day poverty (at average annual private consumption per capita of about $1,100, in 1985 PPP $) and then for $2/day (at average annual private consumption per capita of about $2,000). The poverty curves suggest that for $1/day and $2/day poverty, the growth–poverty relationship becomes weak after those points (represented by point A and point B in chart 9), and reducing poverty must then rely more on special measures targeted at the poor.

The normal paths of poverty reduction depicted by the curves result from a combination of consumption growth and the typical patterns of change in the distribution of consumption that accompany such growth during the development process. The scatter of individual observations around the poverty curve indicates that poverty in each country may be higher or lower than expected owing to the deviation of the consumption distribution in individual countries from the typical distribution at different levels of consumption that underlies the poverty curves. The tightness of the fit of the observation points indicates that in low-income countries with generalized poverty, the average level of private consumption expenditure is most important in explaining the incidence of $1/day and $2/day poverty. Research to reproduce these curves in middle-income countries with higher levels of private consumption per capita, and including Latin American countries, shows a much less close relationship between the incidence of poverty and average private consumption per capita (Karshenas, 2004). Beyond a certain level of private consumption per capita, where one leaves the realm of generalized poverty, the close relationship between average consumption per capita and poverty is lost and variations in the incidence of poverty between countries is explained more by differences in the distribution of consumption expenditure between countries than by differences in the level of consumption expenditure.

...as well as a close relationship between the average level of private consumption and the depth of poverty.

At low levels of development and in conditions of mass poverty, when the average level of private consumption per capita is very low, there is not only a close relationship between the level of average private consumption per capita and the incidence of poverty, but also a close relationship between the average level of private consumption and the depth of poverty. This is shown in chart 10 which depicts the relationship between the average consumption of the poor and per capita consumption expenditure for the $1-a-day and $2-a-day international poverty lines. The curves fitted to the observations in chart 10 show that the relationship between the average level of private consumption per capita and the depth of poverty is as close as the relationship between the average level of private consumption per capita and with the incidence of poverty. This is significant because although the incidence of poverty is totally independent of the distribution of consumption expenditure amongst the poor, the average level of consumption of the poor depends on such distribution. However, the power of economic growth to raise the level of consumption of the poor diminishes at much lower levels of average private consumption per capita than its power to reduce the proportion of the population living in poverty. The form of the curves is such that the effect of economic growth on the average private consumption per capita of the poor weakens once the average private consumption for the country as a whole is about $800 per capita (in 1985 PPP $) for the $1/day poverty line and about $1,400 per capita (in 1985 PPP$) for the $2/day poverty line. These are represented by points A and B in chart 10.

The poverty curves indicate that in very poor countries, which are characterized by generalized or mass poverty, sustained economic growth is a precondition for a significant reduction in poverty. But it will be sufficient only if growth is of an appropriate form. Only that form of economic growth which leads to a commensurate increase in per capita consumption on a sustainable basis will lead to poverty reduction. For this to take place, economic growth should be inclusive. If inequalities become too large and are linked to a sense of exclusion on the basis of social identity, it is possible that a legitimacy crisis will emerge and the whole growth process may then be threatened. But if a country focuses on policies to reduce poverty by purely redistributional devices, to the neglect of economic growth, this is likely to be unsustainable in the long run. If redistribution is attempted in situations of mass poverty, poverty may be falling for a specific section of the population benefiting from redistribution policies, but the cost may be an even higher poverty increase in other parts of the economy.

In the end, sustained and substantial poverty reduction requires sustained economic growth of a form that leads to creation of productive employment for the working-age population that is sufficient for there to be growth in households' real per capita income and consumption. Rising output per capita that is not associated with a net increase in income-earning opportunities (jobs and livelihoods) will not be enough.

> *The poverty curves indicate that in very poor countries, which are characterized by generalized or mass poverty, sustained economic growth is a precondition for a significant reduction in poverty. But it will be sufficient only if growth is of an appropriate form.*

3. ECONOMIC GROWTH AND THE PROVISION OF PUBLIC SERVICES

Income or consumption poverty, no matter how it is measured, does not fully reflect the consumption of goods and services by the poor. An important part, which is normally missing from the household budget surveys on the basis of which income poverty is measured, is access to important public services such as sanitation, health and educational services. To the extent that such services are procured through market transactions they are reflected in the income or consumption poverty measures. A large part of such services, however, are

CHART 10. RELATIONSHIP BETWEEN AVERAGE PRIVATE CONSUMPTION PER CAPITA AND AVERAGE PRIVATE CONSUMPTION OF THE POOR

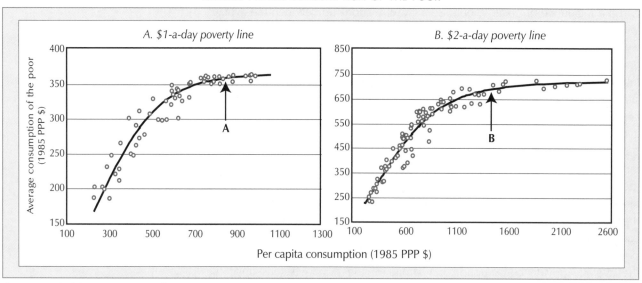

Source: UNCTAD (2002: 49, chart 9).
Note: For significance of points A and B, see text.

normally provided either free of charge or at highly subsidized levels by the public sector. This can be particularly important for poor households, and can substantially increase their access to vital services which would otherwise be difficult for them to procure. A more complete picture of the nature of poverty in the LDCs, therefore, would require coverage of their access to such public services. The total value of public sector expenditure on those services, the distribution of that expenditure and the quality of service provision decide the final impact on poverty.

In conditions of generalized poverty sources of government revenue are limited and hence total public sector expenditures on social services are relatively low. The example of per capita public health expenditure in the LDCs compared with other developing countries, shown in chart 11A, highlights this point. The Asian and African LDCs on average spend $4.6 a year per head on public health expenditure, in contrast to an average of $73 in other low-income and middle-income developing countries. The per capita public health expenditure of $4.6 in the LDCs shows the stark realities of generalized poverty in an even more glaring light when compared with per capita public health expenditure of $1,456, and per capita total health expenditure of $2,391, in the high-income OECD countries. The low per capita health expenditure in the LDCs is not because health services are neglected in those countries as compared with other items of public sector expenditure. As can be seen from chart 12, the share of general government expenditure on health in the LDCs is not significantly different from other that of developing countries. The low per capita expenditure on health in the LDCs is rather a reflection of the condition of generalized poverty. This also applies to education and other public social services in countries subject to generalized poverty.

The Asian and African LDCs on average spend $4.6 a year per head on public health expenditure, in contrast to an average of $73 in other low-income and middle-income developing countries.

It is sometimes argued that the inability of public social services to substantially contribute to the alleviation of poverty in the developing countries, including the LDCs, is to a large extent due to the distribution of such services being skewed in favour of the rich (see for example World Bank, 2003). This argument breaks down in the case of countries suffering from generalized poverty, even though it may be true that in some countries the rich may benefit to a greater extent than the poor from public services. The reason is that where there is generalized poverty, even if one distributes the entire public health expenditure amongst the poor, the increase in per capita expenditure allocated to the latter will be relatively small. This can be seen from chart 11B, where the distribution of the entire health budget to the poor in the Asian and African LDCs has increased the average per capita health expenditure from $4.6 to only $5.3 a year, which is still less than a tenth of the average public health expenditure in other developing countries. This is not of course to deny that the distribution of public social services amongst the poor in the LDCs can be improved, but rather to point out that in conditions of generalized poverty such redistribution will improve poverty on only a limited scale.

Even if one distributes the entire public health expenditure amongst the poor in the LDCs, the increase in per capita expenditure allocated to the latter will be relatively small.

Similar remarks may be made about the extent to which improving the efficiency of public services in the LDCs can improve the lot of the poor in conditions of generalized poverty. To put it simply, $4.6 per capita public health expenditure needs to be stretched a long way by efficiency improvements to come anywhere close to providing the $73 average per capita expenditure in other developing countries.

The question of the efficiency and effectiveness of public services is, of course, not irrelevant. But in conditions where there is mass poverty, the efficiency and effectiveness of public services are not independent of the level of

CHART 11. PER CAPITA ANNUAL PUBLIC HEALTH EXPENDITURE IN ASIAN AND AFRICAN LDCS, 1990–2000
($, annual average)

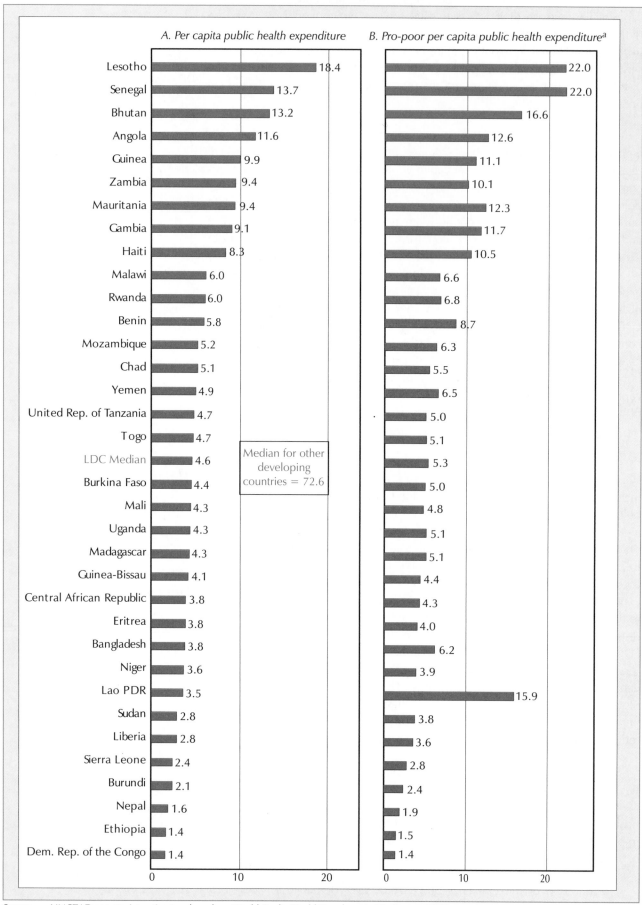

A. Per capita public health expenditure

B. Pro-poor per capita public health expenditure[a]

Country	A	B
Lesotho	18.4	22.0
Senegal	13.7	22.0
Bhutan	13.2	16.6
Angola	11.6	12.6
Guinea	9.9	11.1
Zambia	9.4	10.1
Mauritania	9.4	12.3
Gambia	9.1	11.7
Haiti	8.3	10.5
Malawi	6.0	6.6
Rwanda	6.0	6.8
Benin	5.8	8.7
Mozambique	5.2	6.3
Chad	5.1	5.5
Yemen	4.9	6.5
United Rep. of Tanzania	4.7	5.0
Togo	4.7	5.1
LDC Median	4.6	5.3
Burkina Faso	4.4	5.0
Mali	4.3	4.8
Uganda	4.3	5.1
Madagascar	4.3	5.1
Guinea-Bissau	4.1	4.4
Central African Republic	3.8	4.3
Eritrea	3.8	4.0
Bangladesh	3.8	6.2
Niger	3.6	3.9
Lao PDR	3.5	15.9
Sudan	2.8	3.8
Liberia	2.8	3.6
Sierra Leone	2.4	2.8
Burundi	2.1	2.4
Nepal	1.6	1.9
Ethiopia	1.4	1.5
Dem. Rep. of the Congo	1.4	1.4

Median for other developing countries = 72.6

Source: UNCTAD secretariat estimates, based on World Bank, World Development Indicators 2003.

Notes: LDC median refers to the countries listed in the Chart. Other developing countries refers to the 78 low- and middle-income countries (World Bank definition) excluding the LDCs and high-income oil-exporting countries.

a   Pro-poor public health expenditure assumes that all spending goes to the poor.

CHART 12. SHARE OF PUBLIC HEALTH EXPENDITURE IN GENERAL GOVERNMENT EXPENDITURE
IN THE LDCS AND OTHER DEVELOPING COUNTRIES, 1990–2000

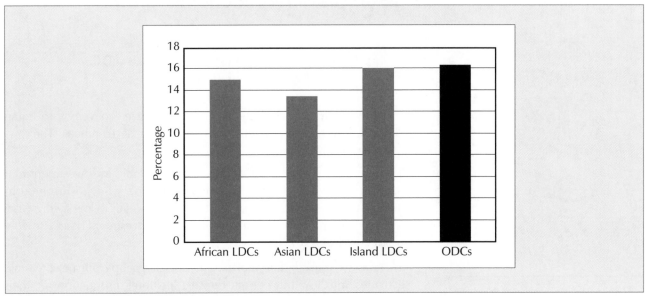

Source: Same as for chart 11.

per capita GDP or the level of economic development in general. For example, household diet and nutrition, which are highly correlated with per capita income, affect the susceptibility of children and adults to disease. Poverty can hinder the children of poor households from benefiting from education services, even if adequate provision is made on the supply side. There are also important externalities between different public services that can make the effectiveness of each category increase with the total government expenditure on public services, which in turn normally rises with the level of per capita GDP. For example, education together with better water and sanitation can make health services more effective by helping to prevent disease. An adequate public transport infrastructure also can improve the effectiveness of all the other services. It is plausible to assume that these interdependences are particularly important for countries with mass poverty, and are likely to become less significant after countries pass a certain per capita income threshold where a basic minimum set of social and economic infrastructures has been put in place.

In conditions where there is mass poverty, the efficiency and effectiveness of public services are not independent of the level of per capita GDP or the level of economic development in general.

The above has important implications for the design of development policy in general and public expenditure policy in particular, in the case of countries in which the majority of the population are living at or around basic subsistence levels. The first implication is that in countries facing such mass poverty, there is a need for substantial increases in public expenditure in a concerted manner on a host of social services if the policy is to make a noticeable dent in poverty. Such expenditure increases are normally beyond the financing capacities of countries facing generalized poverty and need to be financed by foreign aid. The second important implication is that, the focus on social services such as health and education should not lead to the neglect of economic growth. To a large extent, measures to improve health and education in the LDCs are also growth–enhancing, particularly in the long term, if they are combined with other appropriate measures to enhance economic growth. However, if policy makers become preoccupied with attempts at poverty alleviation by focusing solely on income redistribution or social expenditures and neglect economic growth, in the conditions of generalized poverty the desired outcomes cannot be achieved.[2]

C. The importance of trade expansion for sustained economic growth

1. HOW INTERNATIONAL TRADE CAN HELP LDCS TO ESCAPE THE POVERTY TRAP

The LDCs which are characterized by generalized poverty are often enmeshed in a low-income trap of poverty and underdevelopment. The low-income trap has various elements:

- There are few surplus financial resources available for investment and for funding vital public services, including education, health, administration, and law and order. Low income leads to low savings; low savings lead to low investment; and low investment leads to low productivity and low incomes.

- To reduce risks in conditions of extreme scarcity, people pursue economic activities with low but certain returns, including production for their own subsistence and survival through multiple activities.

- The lack of effective domestic demand associated with all-pervasive poverty reduces profitable investment opportunities.

- There is a dearth of domestically available skilled personnel, and the lack of domestic opportunities encourages skilled people to seek work outside the country.

- Pervasive poverty leads to environmental degradation as people have to eat into the environmental capital stock simply to survive, and this in turn undermines the productivity of key assets on which livelihoods depend.

- There is a high risk of civil conflict in countries where low per capita income is associated with economic stagnation and regress (see chapter 4).

Escaping this poverty trap is not impossible. However, it is highly unlikely without integration into a wider international economy or, more particularly, without a form of integration which supports sustained economic growth and poverty reduction. The lack of surplus resources for financing investment implies that external finance usually plays a critical role in generating the big push which is necessary in order for LDCs to move to a virtuous circle of economic growth and poverty reduction. But international trade is equally vital.

International trade is particularly important for poverty reduction in the LDCs because, contrary to popular impressions, their "openness", measured by the level of integration with the rest of the world, is high.

International trade is particularly important for poverty reduction in the LDCs because, contrary to popular impressions, their "openness", measured by the level of integration with the rest of the world, is high. During 1999–2001, exports and imports of goods and services constituted on average 51 per cent of the GDP of the LDCs (chart 13). This is somewhat lower than the average trade/ GDP ratios of low-income and low- and middle-income countries. But the average level of trade integration of the LDCs was actually higher than that of high-income OECD countries, which stood at 43 per cent in those years. In only 10 of the LDCs for which data are available was the trade/GDP ratio lower than that in the high-income OECD countries (table 26).

The high level of trade integration implies that international trade is of major significance for the economies of the LDCs. But it is notable that exports of goods and services constitute a lower proportion of GDP than imports of goods and services. Exports of goods and services constituted 20 per cent of GDP in

CHART 13. THE ECONOMIC IMPORTANCE OF TRADE IN LDCS AND OTHER COUNTRY GROUPS, 1999–2001[a]

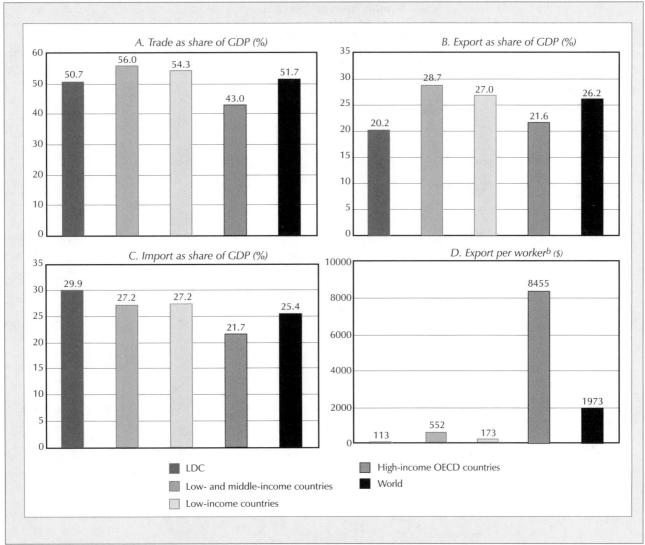

Source: UNCTAD secretariat estimates, based on World Bank, *World Development Indicators 2003,* CD-ROM.

Note: The country classification follows the one used by the World Bank. The data based on its national accounts.

a The figures for high income OECD countries refer to the period 1999–2000.

b The working population is equated with the economically active population between 15 and 64 years old.

the LDCs during 1999–2001. This level is below the average level of low-income countries (29 per cent) and low- and middle-income countries (27 per cent), though it is not far below the level of high income OECD countries (22 per cent). One may expect that the share of exports in GDP would vary systematically between countries according to their income per capita levels and size of population. But even so, the relatively low export/GDP ratios in the LDCs are indicative of weak export capacities.

As outlined in the last chapter, export growth can play a number of different roles in supporting economic growth. These include: (a) static efficiency gains which arise through specialization according to current comparative advantage; (b) increased capacity utilization which arises if external demand enables the employment of previously idle (or surplus) labour and land resources which previously were not utilized owing to a dearth of effective domestic demand or if trade reduces the costs of wage goods; (c) increased physical and human capital investment owing to improved returns to investment which can arise either through the identification of new opportunities associated with external demand or through the improved profitability of investment following the cheapening of the production costs; (d) productivity growth which can arise

Export growth can play a number of different roles in supporting economic growth.

TABLE 26. THE IMPORTANCE OF TRADE IN LDCS BY COUNTRY, RANKED BY "OPENNESS",[a] 1999–2001

(Annual average, percentage)

	Trade as share in GDP	Exports as share in GDP	Imports as share in GDP	Trade balance as share in GDP	Exports as share in imports	Exports per capita	Imports per capita
Above average "openness"							
Equatorial Guinea	299.2	187.3	111.8	75.5	167.5	5 545.3	3 310.4
Maldives	169.9	77.5	76.8	0.7	121.2	1 982.1	1 635.2
Angola	155.1	84.0	71.0	13.0	118.6	521.4	439.7
Vanuatu	134.0	65.7	68.4	-2.7	96.0	738.5	768.9
Solomon Islands	124.2	61.3	62.9	-1.5	97.5	411.7	422.1
Sao Tome and Principe	120.5	36.0	84.3	-48.3	42.9	114.5	266.5
Lesotho	114.6	30.3	87.2	-57.0	31.3	116.7	372.4
Gambia	113.8	63.1	64.6	-1.4	76.3	156.9	205.6
Djibouti	105.5	40.7	60.8	-20.1	73.6	393.0	533.7
Cambodia	104.3	43.2	57.0	-13.7	83.1	128.4	154.6
Samoa	102.6	32.9	69.6	-36.7	47.4	462.9	976.9
Eritrea	95.6	15.4	80.2	-64.8	19.2	25.3	131.7
Guinea-Bissau	89.7	28.2	57.6	-29.4	55.8	57.0	102.3
Mauritania	89.1	37.8	50.7	-12.9	75.7	141.3	186.7
Bhutan	83.0	30.8	55.2	-24.4	50.5	168.2	332.9
Cape Verde	81.6	26.6	58.8	-32.2	38.8	303.5	781.6
Togo	79.7	33.8	47.3	-13.4	68.5	93.1	135.9
Yemen	76.3	42.8	37.0	5.8	106.3	193.8	182.4
Senegal	68.5	30.1	38.3	-8.2	78.7	145.5	185.0
Malawi	66.3	29.0	39.7	-10.7	67.1	45.4	67.6
Mali	64.9	27.3	38.0	-10.7	71.0	64.7	91.1
Lao PDR	64.4	29.5	34.9	-5.4	84.5	91.6	108.4
Liberia	62.0	23.1	38.9	-15.8	59.4	36.7	61.8
Madagascar	61.8	18.4	33.9	-15.4	82.6	73.3	88.7
Zambia	60.2	28.0	36.6	-8.6	64.7	78.3	121.1
Below average "openness"							
Mozambique	55.0	31.3	40.5	-9.2	35.8	31.2	87.1
Nepal	54.3	25.3	31.4	-6.2	72.6	53.1	73.1
Chad	54.1	18.8	38.7	-19.9	39.8	30.4	76.6
Guinea	52.8	24.4	28.4	-4.0	86.1	104.5	121.3
Sierra Leone	46.4	12.2	30.4	-18.1	52.9	21.9	41.3
Comoros	45.4	14.6	30.8	-16.2	47.4	56.6	119.3
Ethiopia	45.4	15.0	30.4	-15.4	49.4	14.8	30.0
Haiti	44.6	12.7	32.1	-19.4	38.9	61.9	159.1
Benin	43.6	24.0	28.2	-4.2	54.6	57.3	105.1
Niger	40.9	16.7	24.1	-7.5	69.4	29.8	42.9
Dem. Rep. of the Congo	40.3	20.7	20.3	0.4	98.2	18.9	19.3
United Rep. of Tanzania	39.1	14.2	24.4	-10.2	60.1	39.3	65.4
Burkina Faso	38.2	11.6	27.7	-16.1	38.2	22.9	60.0
Uganda	36.4	11.7	24.7	-13.0	47.6	30.9	64.9
Bangladesh	34.3	14.2	20.1	-5.9	70.8	50.6	71.4
Rwanda	32.1	6.7	24.3	-17.6	31.9	18.2	57.2
Sudan	28.8	12.9	15.9	-2.9	81.1	47.0	58.0
Burundi	28.2	8.1	20.1	-12.0	40.3	8.3	20.5
Central African Republic	27.3	10.7	15.2	-4.5	79.6	32.2	40.5
LDCs	**50.7**	**20.3**	**30.0**	**-9.7**	**76.7**	**61.2**	**79.7**
Low-income	54.3	27.0	27.2	-0.3	94.6	101.6	107.3
Low- and middle-income	56.0	28.7	27.2	1.3	103.5	343.9	332.2
High-income OECD	43.0	21.6	21.7	0.5	97.7	5 672.5	5 804.5

Source: UNCTAD secretariat estimates, based on World Bank, *World Development Indicators 2003*, CD-ROM.

Note: Data on exports and imports of goods and services are based on national accounts statistics, except for Equatorial Guinea, the Lao PDR, Liberia, Solomon Islands and Vanuatu, whose data are based on balance-of-payment statistics. The country averages are slightly different from those in chart 13 owing to the use of these data sources.

Afghanistan, Kiribati, Myanmar, Somalia and Tuvalu were not included for lack of data.

a "Openness" is defined by trade as a share of GDP. The LDCs with above average openness are those which have trade as a share of GDP ratio higher than that of low- and middle-income countries.

through the transfer of technology or increased efficiency owing to the pressure of exposure to international trade competition; (e) export-accelerated industrialization, involving a labour re-allocation from agriculture into manufacturing; and (f) relaxation of the balance of payments constraint on sustained economic growth.

The relative importance and the mix of these roles vary between countries. For most LDCs, the primary sector, particularly agriculture, dominates production and employment in the economy, and productive capacities are weakly developed. In this situation, the key role of exports is that they enable the acquisition, through importation, of goods which are necessary for economic growth and poverty reduction, but which are not produced domestically. These include food, manufactured consumer goods, fuel and raw materials, machinery and equipment and means of transport, and intermediate inputs and spare parts.

In the LDCs, exports provide the means through which unexploited natural resources and surplus labour can be translated into the imports that are essential for sustained economic growth.

If there are idle resources in the economy, — a "vent for surplus" consisting of untapped mineral resources, underutilized land or surplus labour — export growth may be achieved without constraining the growth of other domestic sectors. Indeed, exports provide the means through which such unexploited natural resources and surplus labour can be translated into the imports that are essential for sustained economic growth. The income elasticity of demand for imports is likely to be high in the early stages of development. Exports must thus grow sufficiently fast, and in a sufficiently stable way, to meet growing import demand. If not, and in the absence of capital inflows in the form of grants and compensatory financing facilities to cope with temporary shocks to export earnings, the sustainability of economic growth will be threatened by the build-up of an unsustainable external debt.

The import-supply effects of exports are important because a key structural feature of the LDC economies is their high level of import sensitivity.

2. THE IMPORT SENSITIVITY OF LDC ECONOMIES

The import-supply effects of exports are important because a key structural feature of the LDC economies is their high level of import sensitivity (Sachs, 2003). An economy can be described as being highly import-sensitive when import bottlenecks hamper the full utilization of domestic productive capacities, when the import content of investment is high, and when food security also depends on food imports.

The import sensitivity of an economy is related to, but is something different from, the "openness" of an economy, measured by the ratio of trade to GDP. As chart 13 shows, imports constitute on average 30 per cent of GDP, which is the highest proportion of all the country groups. But, import sensitivity is not simply defined by the share of imports in total GDP, but is also related to the structure of the national economy and the composition of imports. The higher the proportion of imports that is essential to the continuation of on-going economic activities and their development, the higher the import sensitivity of the economy.

The higher the proportion of imports that is essential to the continuation of on-going economic activities and their development, the higher the import sensitivity of the economy.

The import sensitivity of LDC economies is clearly illustrated by the experience of many African LDCs in the 1980s when unfavourable movements in the terms of trade, high interest rates, reduced capital inflows and increased debt service obligations interacted with a weak real export performance to create severe import compression. The basic process is well described by Helleiner (1993). Capacity utilization depends heavily on the availability of critically important imports — fuel, other intermediate inputs and spare parts.

When such imports cannot be financed at levels necessary for full utilization of capacity, there is underemployment of labour, capital and resources in the import-dependent sectors. Because these inputs cannot typically be redeployed quickly into other activities, "the entire economy is, in the short- to medium-term, if not longer (particularly where investment activity is also highly import-dependent), also driven to production levels that are well below potential" (ibid.: 124). Once import compression started in the early 1980s, many commercially oriented smallholders began to reduce their marketed output because of the unavailability of such consumer goods as soap, textiles, matches, tea, coffee, sugar, cooking oil, tinned milk, fish, cement, metal roof sheeting, radios and bicycles due to foreign exchange shortages and the inability to utilize domestic manufacturing capacity. The negative effects of such shortages on recorded market output have been extensively studied in Madagascar, Mozambique and the United Republic of Tanzania (Berthelemy and Morrisson, 1989). The partial withdrawal of farmers from the market system reduced export earnings, further reinforcing the foreign exchange shortages and deepening the crisis through a foreign exchange crisis.

Most LDC economies are import-sensitive not simply because of the importance of imports for capacity utilization but also because of the high import content of investment processes.

Most LDC economies are import-sensitive not simply because of the importance of imports for capacity utilization but also because of the high import content of investment processes. This reflects the absence of a domestic capital goods industry and engineering capabilities. The financing of non-inflationary sustained economic growth also depends on an elastic supply of food and other wage goods to meet the needs of the increased demand by additionally employed and/or better-remunerated workers. Food imports can play a role in this. Finally, in some LDCs food security may also be import-sensitive to the extent that imports affect the availability of, and access by households and individuals to, sufficient quantities of food for a nutritious diet.

The sensitivity of food security to imports is an important and complex issue. Hunger is certainly widespread in the LDCs and there are 29 of them where the average per capita calorie supply is below 2,300 calories per day, which is the recommended minimum of the Food and Agriculture Organization of the United Nations and WHO. Furthermore, it is clear that the LDCs are becoming increasingly dependent on food imports (chart 14). During the period 1996–2001 all except seven of the LDCs were net food importers, and for many LDCs food imports are now a significant component of total merchandise imports and exports. If food aid, which is very important for a number of LDCs, is left aside, it is apparent that commercial food imports constituted over 20 per cent of total merchandise exports for 29 LDCs during the period 1996–2001, and over 20 per cent of total merchandise imports in 13 LDCs (table 27). But although this implies that food imports are important for LDCs' balance of payments, the share of food imports in domestic food consumption is low (see last column of table 27). In the Democratic Republic of the Congo, for example, food imports constituted 30 per cent of total merchandise imports and 31 per cent of total merchandise exports during 1996–2001, but only 2 per cent of total food consumption. For almost two thirds of the LDCs food imports are less than 10 per cent of total food consumption. Moreover, in many African LDCs a major part of staple food consumption is based on crops which are only "semi-tradable", such as cassavas, plantains, yams, millet, sorghum and white maize (see UNCTAD, 1998).

This pattern, in which food imports absorb a significant share of total import earnings but at the same time constitute only a minor proportion of total food consumption, may imply that food imports are not actually important for the

CHART 14. FOOD EXPORTS AND IMPORTS OF LDCS AND OTHER DEVELOPING COUNTRIES, 1980–2001

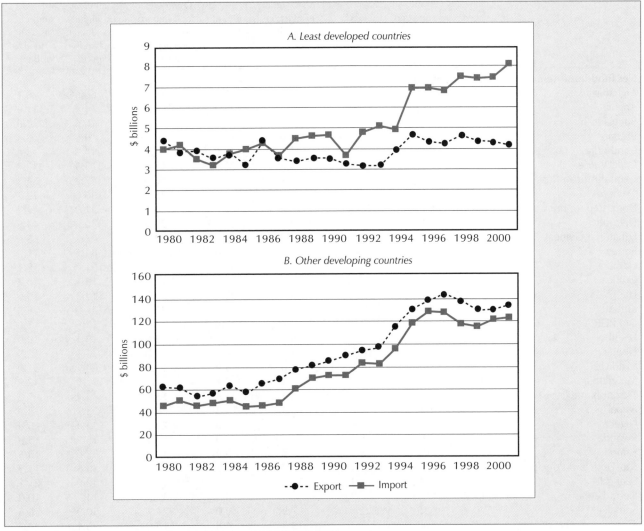

Source: UNCTAD secretariat estimates, based on UN COMTRADE.

food security of the general population but only go to enrich the diets of a small minority. However, it could also be the case that small amounts of food imports are crucial for food security, in spite of their small contribution to total food consumption, because they stabilize food prices at certain times of the year when prices rise. This issue requires further research. But in those LDCs where both investment processes and food security are import-sensitive, there may be a difficult dilemma. This would arise if scarce foreign exchange is serving to alleviate poverty and support food security in the short term, but at the same time, the capacity to import the investment goods which are necessary for sustained economic growth, and also improved food security in the long run (see box 6), is being reduced. This dilemma may be an important policy issue in the field of trade and poverty in some LDCs. It is likely to have important implications for both LDC Governments and the donor community.

Finally, landlocked LDCs have a specific type of import sensitivity which is related to the fact that their international trade is often quite dependent on imported transport and insurance services. There are 11 African landlocked LDCs where such imports are equivalent to over 20 per cent of total exports of goods and services. In this situation, the growth process in those countries is very vulnerable to disruptions in the transit transport system (table 28).

In those LDCs where both investment processes and food security are import-sensitive, there may be a difficult dilemma. This dilemma may be an important policy issue in the field of trade and poverty in some LDCs.

TABLE 27. INDICATORS OF FOOD SECURITY IN LDCs, AVERAGE 1996–2001

	Under-nourished population % of total[a]	Food consumption per capita[b]	Change in food consumption[c]	Agricultural production instability[d]	Food aid as % of total food imports	Commercial food imports as % of total merchandise imports	Commercial food imports as % of total merchandise exports	Food imports as % of food consumption
Net food importers and net agricultural importers								
Afghanistan	70	1 694	..	6.0	30.6	13.4	66.6	6.1
Angola	49	1 878	10.0	4.2	25.3	8.9	4.4	11.4
Bangladesh	32	2 117	4.4	3.1	19.8	12.2	18.6	7.8
Bhutan	..	2 500	..	3.6	28.2	6.4	9.8	3.4
Cambodia	38	1 905	7.6	31.2	20.9	7.5	13.9	3.4
Cape Verde	..	3 227	9.8	13.2	21.3	17.4	373.3	32.7
Central African Rep.	44	1 927	4.6	14.1	5.8	8.6	7.7	2.3
Comoros	..	1 776	-7.6	27.8	14.0	25.8	156.6	12.7
Dem. Rep. of the Congo	75	1 635	-28.7	16.2	9.9	30.2	31.0	2.2
Djibouti	..	2 101	14.6	22.1	15.1	29.3	330.6	43.9
Equatorial Guinea	..	2 500	..	32.8	13.5	22.8	2.2	5.6
Eritrea	61	2 500	..	23.3	33.8	6.9	84.5	11.8
Gambia	27	2 248	-4.8	18.7	32.9	21.9	181.7	38.1
Guinea	28	2 282	15.1	4.1	7.5	12.2	16.1	8.7
Haiti	49	1 984	15.2	3.1	20.7	30.3	112.3	19.6
Kiribati	..	2 896	12.8	15.1	3.1	21.3	127.0	26.5
Lao PDR	22	2 231	8.3	7.4	1.3	4.2	7.6	1.8
Lesotho	25	2 296	2.3	8.9	7.9	9.8	39.1	19.0
Liberia	..	2 148	-10.6	12.7	28.4	8.9	7.1	12.9
Maldives	..	2 548	8.3	3.0	5.9	12.4	64.1	31.0
Mauritania	10	2 716	5.6	3.5	7.2	42.9	37.5	32.9
Mozambique	53	1 904	10.8	8.1	21.8	13.5	44.4	7.2
Nepal	17	2 376	-0.6	4.4	15.3	8.4	23.7	2.7
Niger	34	2 086	3.9	13.2	10.6	22.9	32.4	5.8
Rwanda	41	1 904	1.6	14.0	69.9	8.1	26.9	5.9
Samoa	..	2 500	..	7.3	8.4	12.8	97.0	18.5
Sao Time and Principe	..	2 411	6.5	7.0	14.2	10.8	39.6	14.9
Senegal	24	2 256	0.2	14.5	7.8	20.8	32.9	21.1
Sierra Leone	50	2 001	-2.9	5.3	8.3	35.7	414.7	10.0
Somalia	71	1 635	..	7.9	9.0	24.7	50.9	8.6
Tuvalu	..	2 500	..	13.3	4.8	13.9	346.1	24.7
Yemen	33	2 043	-0.8	5.9	7.0	32.7	28.0	31.2
Zambia	50	1 900	-4.9	10.6	21.1	8.8	6.7	4.5
Net food importers and net agricultural exporters								
Benin	16	2 469	6.7	7.5	6.2	13.7	22.8	5.3
Burkina Faso	17	2 440	8.7	19.7	5.6	14.9	38.6	3.9
Burundi	70	1 639	-13.0	27.5	17.9	6.6	17.2	0.8
Ethiopia	42	2 500	..	14.8	72.0	3.5	8.7	2.0
Madagascar	36	2 038	-1.8	2.3	24.5	9.5	16.6	3.3
Malawi	33	2 126	11.7	9.1	26.4	6.7	7.5	3.6
Togo	25	2 322	6.0	5.4	4.2	9.3	15.8	6.8
Uganda	19	2 306	1.8	3.9	29.0	6.2	16.0	2.9
United Rep. of Tanzania	43	1 936	-8.3	3.4	19.1	13.3	30.9	4.7
Net food exporters and net agricultural exporters								
Chad	34	2 058	23.4	27.0	12.2	7.3	11.5	2.0
Guinea-Bissau	..	2 392	0.5	4.3	43.8	19.6	36.6	11.4
Mali	21	2 324	2.7	6.4	3.0	9.3	13.2	3.7
Myanmar	7	2 799	7.4	5.1	22.6	6.1	11.8	1.9
Solomon Islands	..	2 227	8.8	7.4	3.4	11.3	13.5	14.1
Sudan	25	2 323	5.9	9.2	19.2	12.1	22.4	4.7
Vanuatu	..	2 580	1.9	7.8	14.2	11.3	36.0	13.7
LDCs	**41**	**2 390**	**3.5**	**11.7**	**18.1**	**19.9**	**124.4**	**23.6**

Source: FAO (2003a); and FAO (2003b).

Note: The country classification of net food exporters and net food importers was drawn from FAO trade data on food excluding fish. This classification, according to their agricultural trade and food status, is based on the period 1995–2000.

a Reference period 1999–2001.

b Calories per capita per day.

c Percentage change from 1988–1991 to 1999–2001.

d Measured according to the Agricultural Production Instability Index for the period 1979–2001 and it is defined according to the methodology included in the Explanatory Notes from the Committee for Development Policy's Economic Vulnerability Index (available at http://www.un.org/esa/analysis/devplan/cdp00p21.pdf).

TABLE 28. IMPORTS OF TRANSPORT AND INSURANCE SERVICES AS A PROPORTION OF TOTAL EXPORTS
AND IMPORTS OF GOODS AND SERVICES, 2000[a]

($ millions)

	Imports of transport and insurance (a)	Exports of goods and services (b)	Imports of goods and services (c)	Ratio (%) (a)/(b)	Ratio (%) (a)/(c)
Landlocked LDCs					
Burkina Faso	107.8	237.0	657.6	45.5	16.4
Burundi	19.6	55.2	150.7	35.4	13.0
Central African Rep.	58.7	179.0	244.4	32.8	24.0
Chad	98.5	190.1	411.5	51.8	23.9
Ethiopia	302.3	992.2	1622.1	30.5	18.6
Lao People's Dem.Rep	42.4	506.0	578.3	8.4	7.3
Lesotho	36.2	253.8	770.1	14.3	4.7
Malawi	88.6	437.4	629.1	20.2	14.1
Mali	245.7	644.2	926.9	38.1	26.5
Nepal	119.9	1282.1	1790.1	9.3	6.7
Niger	92.5	336.9	497.8	27.5	18.6
Rwanda	64.8	127.8	423.3	50.7	15.3
Uganda	164.1	663.1	1408.5	24.7	11.7
Zambia	227.5	871.2	1318.0	26.1	17.3
Island LDCs					
Cape Verde	47.6	145.9	325.9	32.6	14.6
Comoros	21.1	49.1	99.3	43.0	21.2
Kiribati	11.0	23.7	44.5	46.4	24.7
Maldives	57.5	457.2	451.7	12.6	12.7
Samoa	5.6	79.9	140.2	6.9	4.0
Sao Tome and Principe	5.4	16.3	36.1	33.3	15.0
Solomon Islands	49.5	226.8	291.7	21.8	17.0
Vanuatu	26.8	157.0	147.1	17.1	18.2
Other LDCs					
Angola	374.4	8188.0	5739.0	4.6	6.5
Bangladesh	1103.8	7214.3	9673.1	15.3	11.4
Benin	141.1	528.4	707.8	26.7	19.9
Cambodia	184.5	1829.6	2267.2	10.1	8.1
Djibouti	50.5	184.9	292.2	27.3	17.3
Eritrea[b]	6.9	97.7	499.7	7.1	1.4
Gambia	36.8	229.0	281.8	16.1	13.1
Guinea	118.3	734.4	871.9	16.1	13.6
Guinea-Bissau	16.9	56.9	88.6	29.7	19.1
Haiti	187.0	192.4	801.7	97.2	23.3
Madagascar	196.0	1187.8	1519.5	16.5	12.9
Mauritania	123.7	424.4	585.3	29.2	21.1
Mozambique	182.9	689.4	1491.8	26.5	12.3
Myanmar	26.8	2139.4	2493.5	1.3	1.1
Senegal	291.7	1276.3	1567.7	22.9	18.6
Sierra Leone	16.8	176.8	248.7	9.5	6.8
Sudan	555.4	1834.1	2013.9	30.3	27.6
Togo	98.7	423.6	602.1	23.3	16.4
United Rep. of Tanzania	223.9	1290.7	2050.0	17.3	10.9

Source: UNCTAD secretariat estimates based on IMF, *Balance of Payments Statistics 2003*.

Note: No data were available for Afghanistan, Bhutan, Democratic Republic of the Congo, Equatorial Guinea, Liberia, Somalia, Tuvalu and Yemen.

a   The data refer to 1991 for Comoros; to 1992 for Rwanda; to 1994 for the Central African Republic, Chad and Kiribati; to 1995 for Dijibouti, Haiti, Mauritania, Myanmar, Nepal, Niger and Sierra Leone; to 1997 for Gambia and Guinea-Bissau; to 1998 for the Lao People's Democratic Republic and Lesotho; to 1999 for Samoa, Senegal and Solomon Islands.

b   Local currency units.

3. THE STRUCTURE OF THE BALANCE-OF-PAYMENTS CONSTRAINT

Increased exports can finance, via foreign exchange, the increased imports which are critical for sustained economic growth and poverty reduction. But increased capital inflows and reduced debt service obligations can also generate the same effects.

Increased exports can finance the increased imports which are critical for sustained economic growth and poverty reduction. But increased capital inflows and reduced debt service obligations can also generate the same effects.

This is important to recognize because a major feature of LDC economies is that they almost all have persistent and large trade deficits. These are mainly financed by aid inflows, but workers' remittances are increasingly important, particularly in a number of LDCs, and FDI inflows are important in some. As chart 15 shows, the trade deficits of the LDCs as a whole were comprised between 5–10 per cent of GDP throughout the 1990s. In the period 1999–2001, the trade deficit was over 10 per cent of GDP in 25 out of 44 LDCs for which data are available, and over 20 per cent of GDP in 11 of them (table 26). For the LDCs as a group, export earnings financed only 77 per cent of imports in those years, and excluding the oil exporters, which tend to have trade surpluses, export earnings financed only 65 per cent of imports. In almost half the LDCs for which data are available, export earnings financed less than two thirds of imports (table 26). Moreover, for LDCs whose major exports are agricultural commodities, export earnings covered a mere 54 per cent of import earnings in 1999–2001.

The role of exports in expanding import capacity and loosening the foreign exchange constraint on economic growth needs to be seen in this context. The fact that exports only finance part of the total import bill and there are persistent trade deficits associated with, and mainly financed by, large aid inflows may lead to two different conclusions. One conclusion, which could be reached at the LDC level, is to say that capital inflows, and particularly aid, can provide a substitute for exports. The other conclusion, which could be reached at the donor country level, is to say that exports can provide a substitute for aid. Both these viewpoints are potentially misleading.

Although the effect of exports and aid on the foreign exchange constraint may seem equivalent, the import-supply effects of aid may not be as growth-enhancing as those of exports.

The first conclusion rests on the view that persistent aid-financed trade deficits are not a problem. This may be true to the extent that aid is provided in grant form on a sustainable basis, and/or concessional loans are used for investment, not consumption, and effectively build productive capacities and generate a sufficient stream of foreign exchange earnings to ensure debt repayments. But, although the effect of exports and aid on the foreign exchange constraint may seem equivalent, particularly when aid takes the form of balance-of-payments support, the import-supply effects of aid may not be as growth-enhancing as those of exports. The reasons for this are the instability of aid (which also applies to commodity exports), the tying of aid to import purchases, the high transaction costs and coordination failures which characterize the aid delivery process, and the difficulty of having genuine national ownership of domestic policies in the context of high levels of aid dependence and unsustainable indebtedness to official creditors. Attempts are being made to deal with these problems through the PRSP approach, with mixed success so far. However, in the end a critical goal of the LDCs must be to reduce aid dependence and to make a progressive transition in which sustained growth is increasingly founded on domestic resource mobilization, the attraction of developmental FDI and the tapping of international financial markets. Export expansion is an essential part of this transition, and a process through which the contribution of domestic resource mobilization to economic growth is enhanced.

CHART 15. NET TRADE IN GOODS AND SERVICES FOR DIFFERENT COUNTRY GROUPS, 1980–2001

(As percentage of GDP)

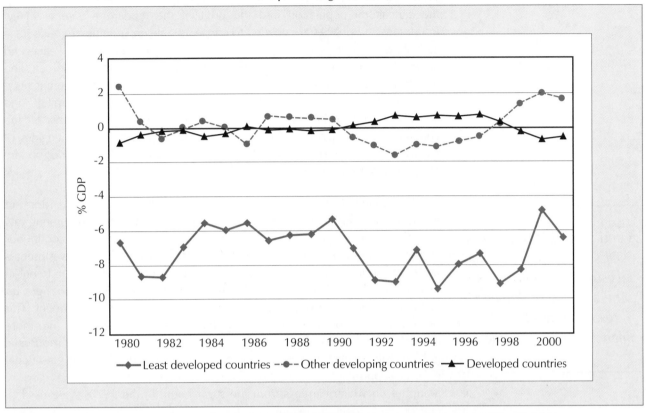

Source: UNCTAD secretariat estimates, based on World Bank, *World Development Indicators 2003*, CD-ROM.

A second conclusion would be to say that exports can provide a substitute for aid. From this perspective export expansion might be seen as an opportunity for donors to reduce their commitments without precipitating an economic crisis, or alternatively as the basis for forgoing a further round of debt relief and even for increasing debt service obligations. This conclusion is as misleading as the earlier one and the approach would be counter-productive. Reduced aid inflows and increased debt service obligations would offset the positive import-supply effects of increased exports. This would risk leaving a country in the same spot despite a major effort to increase its ability to finance its own development. Moreover, if aid inflows are reduced, or debt service obligations increased, when a country achieves an improved export performance, not only would the import-supply effects of exports not materialize, but also there could be negative effects on investment and the government budget. Aid inflows are not only important for balance-of-payments equilibrium, but also play a central role in the accumulation and budgetary processes in LDCs. As will be argued in the next section, the most beneficial effects of export expansion are likely to be achieved if export growth is linked with investment growth. However, these beneficial links between export growth and investment growth will be realized if export growth is accompanied by reductions in aid inflows.

Reduced aid inflows and increased debt service obligations can offset the positive import-supply effects of increased exports. This would risk leaving a country in the same spot despite a major effort to increase its ability to finance its own development.

4. THE INVESTMENT–EXPORT NEXUS

In poor, predominantly agrarian economies like most LDCs, economic growth depends on the development of a range of new capabilities, institutions and services. New agricultural technologies need to be adapted, or developed from scratch, in conformity with the agro-climatic and soil conditions of the country. Schools, universities, hospitals, technical training centres and research and development institutions need to be strengthened or set up. Roads need to be built and extension services need to be established to bring the majority of the agricultural population into the orbit of the modern economy. New institutions and policies are needed to create a stable environment to encourage agricultural producers to adopt the new technologies and inputs. Peace and political stability need to be attained, the rule of law needs to be enforced, and the monopolistic activities of particular interests curtailed. In short, there is need for investment in physical, human, social and institutional capital, and innovation and technological progress adapted to the conditions of the countries. Capital accumulation and technological progress are the engines of growth, and international trade is the fuel for the engine. If the fuel dries up, the engine will not run.

Thus sustained economic growth requires not simply export expansion but also a strong investment–export nexus through which imported equipment, raw material and production inputs are put to good use and lead to continuous improvement of labour productivity in the economy as a whole. If investment is linked to export expansion there can be a virtuous circle in which investment in export activities improves their productivity and leads to greater competitiveness, and export expansion in turn enables greater investment. This process is also associated with the upgrading of the export structure into more dynamic and higher-value-added products. This can occur in a sequential fashion, with foreign exchange earnings and resources derived from traditional exports supporting diversification into new export products. The case of Mauritius, in which earnings from the sugar boom in the 1970s were used to finance investment in manufactures exports in the export-processing zone, exemplifies this virtuous process (Dabee, 2002).

> *A critical problem facing the LDCs in building a strong investment–export nexus is the absence of domestic resources available for financing new investments.*

A critical problem facing the LDCs in building a strong investment–export nexus is the absence of domestic resources available for financing new investments. A telling fact in this regard is that during the period 1995–1999 the average per capita income in the LDCs when measured in terms of current prices and official exchange rates (rather than 1985 PPP dollars) was $0.72 a day and the average per capita consumption was $0.57 a day (see table 25 above). This implies that on average there was only $0.15 a day per person to spend on private capital formation, public investment in infrastructure and the running of vital public services, including health, education, administration, and law and order.

> *It is most likely that establishing a positive investment–export nexus in most LDCs will require an effective partnership between increased trade and increased aid.*

It is against this background that the importance of external finance assumes such significance. Private capital flows can play some role. But it is most likely that establishing a positive investment–export nexus in most LDCs will require an effective partnership between increased trade and increased aid.

D. Export expansion and the inclusiveness of economic growth

Poverty reduction requires sustained economic growth. But sustained economic growth will not be poverty-reducing unless it raises average household consumption substantially through the creation of sufficient productive income-earning opportunities. Achieving this through export expansion alone is difficult in the LDCs. Indeed, there is a great danger that export expansion will not be broad-based but concentrated within an externally oriented enclave with few linkages with the rest of the economy.

1. EXPORT ACTIVITIES AS A SOURCE OF JOBS AND LIVELIHOODS

The danger that export expansion will not be broad-based is rooted in the structure of LDC economies in terms of sectoral composition, types of enterprises and types of employment. Although international trade generally constitutes a large proportion of total GDP, most jobs and livelihoods are not export-oriented in most LDCs. Moreover, the linkages between export-oriented activities and the rest of the economy are not automatic.

It is difficult to get measures of the degree to which the national population is directly employed in export activities. As chart 13 shows, exports only amounted to $113 per worker in LDCs in 1999–2001 compared with $552 per worker in low- and middle-income countries and $8,455 per worker in high-income OECD countries. But these large differences reflect the very low levels of output per worker in the LDCs much more than differences in the export orientation of the workforce.

Although there are some exceptions, agriculture is the main source of livelihood in the LDCs. In 2000, 71 per cent of the population of working age was employed in agriculture in the LDCs as a group, and the proportion engaged in agriculture was more than 50 per cent in all except seven LDCs for which data were available — Cape Verde, Kiribati, Lesotho, Maldives, Samoa, Uganda and Yemen. There are some large-scale capitalist farms (plantations, estates and agribusinesses). However, agricultural production is mainly organized on a household basis with the unit of production and consumption overlapping and part of total household production not entering the market system but being consumed within the household. The larger farming units produce primarily for sale, hire labour and purchase manufactured inputs, and they may also be linked as out-growers to agribusinesses. But smaller farming units, though partly integrated into product and labour markets, tend to be more subsistence-oriented. The subsistence orientation of agricultural production is reinforced by the risks associated with living on a bare minimum to survive and also the weak development of the internal network of marketing, transport and communications.

Both agribusinesses and smallholders are engaged in export production. But, in general, exports constitute only a small fraction of total output. Agricultural exports were equivalent to less than 10 per cent of agricultural value-added in more than half of the LDCs for which data were available (table 29). The ratio of agricultural exports to agricultural value-added is certainly not a perfect measure of the extent to which agricultural livelihoods are export-oriented. But it suggests that the direct involvement of people working in agricultural activities in LDCs in exports is rather limited, with a few notable exceptions, including Guinea-Bissau, Malawi and the West African LDCs which export cotton.

The labour force outside agriculture is engaged in mining, industry and services, and just as in agriculture, the organization of production is characterized by much structural heterogeneity. In general terms, as argued in *The Least Developed Countries Report 2000*, it is possible to identify three types of enterprise (UNCTAD, 2000: 95–97). At one end of the spectrum (stratum A) there are a few large-scale enterprises, either domestically or foreign-owned, which have commercially viable assets, which provide regular full-time jobs for skilled labour, and which are linked with global markets. At the other end of the spectrum (stratum C) there are a mass of micro and small enterprises in which the majority of the unskilled labour is employed in informal ways, including casual wage labour. These enterprises are generally oriented to the domestic market, providing services or producing goods which are affordable for the poor.

Although international trade generally constitutes a large proportion of total GDP, most jobs and livelihoods are not export-oriented in most LDCs. Moreover, the linkages between export-oriented activities and the rest of the economy are not automatic.

71 per cent of the population of working age was employed in agriculture in the LDCs as a group. Agricultural exports were equivalent to less than 10 per cent of agricultural value-added in more than half of the LDCs for which data are available.

TABLE 29. INDICATORS OF IMPORTANCE OF EXPORTS IN TOTAL EMPLOYMENT IN LDCs BY COUNTRY, 1999–2001
(Percentage)

	Rural population as % of total population	Agricultural labour force as % of total labour force	Agricul. exports as % of value added in agriculture	Manufactures value added as % of GDP[a]	Manufacture employment as % of total labour force[b]
Above average "openness"[c]					
Equatorial Guinea	51.9	70.4	7.0	..	..
Maldives	72.4	22.5	..	4.3	7.2
Angola	65.8	71.8	0.5	3.3	0.3
Vanuatu	78.3	80.1	14.0	3.4	1.1
Solomon Islands	80.3	73.1	..	..	2.1
Sao Tome and Principe	53.1	64.4	44.2	4.4	..
Lesotho	72.1	37.9	5.4	12.7	1.8
Gambia	69.3	79.0	10.3	5.0	0.4
Djibouti	16.0	79.0	17.3	2.7	..
Cambodia	83.1	70.1	2.1	5.8	5.7
Samoa	77.9	34.5	14.1	15.4	..
Eritrea	81.2	77.5	1.4	10.5	..
Guinea-Bissau	68.5	82.8	59.3	10.1	..
Mauritania	42.3	52.9	17.3	8.8	0.2
Bhutan	92.9	93.7	9.8	10.4	..
Cape Verde	38.0	23.0	0.4	8.7	..
Togo	66.6	59.7	20.1	9.3	..
Yemen	75.3	36.7	32.6	7.0	0.4
Senegal	52.6	73.7	16.7	17.4	0.8
Malawi	85.3	82.9	77.8	12.9	0.8
Mali	69.8	81.0	23.7	3.8	..
Lao PDR	80.7	76.5	3.7	17.2	..
Liberia	55.1	67.5	..	..	..
Madagascar	70.5	74.2	9.6	12.1	..
Zambia	60.3	50.9	4.8	11.6	1.1
Below average "openness"[c]					
Mozambique	67.9	80.5	5.8	12.1	0.3
Nepal	88.1	93.0	2.6	9.4	4.4
Chad	76.2	75.2	21.9	11.1	..
Guinea	72.5	83.8	4.3	4.2	..
Sierra Leone	63.4	62.1	2.5	4.7	0.6
Comoros	66.8	73.7	6.7	4.0	..
Ethiopia	84.5	82.4	9.6	7.0	0.3
Haiti	64.3	62.2	..	..	..
Benin	57.7	54.0	21.7	8.9	..
Niger	79.4	87.7	9.4	6.6	..
Dem. Rep. of the Congo	..	63.2	1.4	4.5	..
United Rep. of Tanzania	67.8	80.4	13.3	7.4	0.8
Burkina Faso	83.5	92.3	13.7	14.1	0.2
Uganda	85.8	25.0	..	9.8	..
Bangladesh	75.0	55.6	0.9	14.9	5.6
Rwanda	103.5	90.3	5.3	10.0	..
Sudan	63.9	61.0	8.6	9.7	..
Burundi	91.0	90.4	11.8	8.7	0.2
Central African Republic	58.8	72.6	4.5	9.2	0.3
Memo items:					
Afghanistan	78.1	67.0	..		..
Kiribati	61.8	26.5	..	1.1	..
Myanmar	72.3	70.2	..	6.9	5.5
Somalia	72.5	71.1	..	..	..
LDCs	**69.1**	**69.1**	**17.1**	**10.3**	**1.8**
Low- and middle-income	57.8	70.5	9.8	21.3	..

Source: UNCTAD estimates, based on World Bank, *World Development Indicators 2003*, CD-ROM; FAO online data; UNIDO, *Industrial Statistics 2003*, CD-ROM; and Asian Development Bank, *Key Indicators 2003*.

Note: Tuvalu was not included for lack of data.
a 1996–1998 for Cambodia, Kiribati and Maldives.
b The data refer to the following periods: 1991–1993 for Angola, 1990–1991 for Burundi, 1991–1993 for the Central African Republic, 2000 for Bangladesh, Cambodia, Ethiopia, Mauritania, Mozambique and Vanuatu, 1999 for Nepal, 1998 for Lesotho and Burkina Faso, 1996–1998 for Malawi, 1995 for Myanmar, 1995–1997 for Senegal, 1997–1999 for the United Republic of Tanzania, 1994–1996 for Yemen, 1993 for Gambia and Sierra Leone and 1994 for Zambia.
c "Openness" is defined by trade as a share of GDP. The LDCs with above average openness are those which have trade as a share of GDP ratio higher than that of low- and middle-income countries.

In between these two types of enterprises there is a thin stratum of domestically owned enterprises which are medium-sized and may have some degree of involvement in export activities (stratum B). A feature of these activities is that it is difficult to finance their development on commercial terms. They have been called the "missing middle" in LDCs in terms of their enterprise structure (UNCTAD, 2001).

As with agriculture, it is difficult to estimate the numbers of people working in export activities, notably in mining, textile and garment manufacture, and tourism services. But the available data show that manufacturing value-added constituted only 10 per cent of GDP in the LDC group during the period 1999–2001, and even in those LDCs which have diversified into textiles and garments exports, manufacturing value-added is low. In Bangladesh, the Lao People's Democratic Republic, Lesotho and Madagascar it constituted between 12 and 17 per cent of GDP. But in Cambodia and Nepal, manufacturing value-added constituted only 6 per cent and 9 per cent of GDP respectively. It is unlikely that manufacturing employment accounts for a greater proportion of the total labour force. Indeed, UNIDO data, which focus on wage employment in formal jobs, indicate that manufacturing employment constituted in the 1990s less than 2 per cent of total employment in almost all LDCs for which data are available (table 29).

Given the structure of production, enterprise and employment, there is a great likelihood that export expansion will be associated with "enclave-led growth".

2. THE WEAKNESSES OF ENCLAVE-LED GROWTH

Given this structure of production, enterprise and employment, there is no guarantee that export expansion will lead to a form of economic growth which is inclusive. Indeed, there is a great likelihood that export expansion will be associated with "enclave-led growth".[3] This is a form of economic growth which is concentrated in a small part of the economy, both geographically and sectorally. It is exemplified by the pattern of development in the colonial period in African LDCs where a relatively rich commodity-exporting sector, well connected to roads, ports and supported by ancillary services, existed side by side with large undeveloped hinterlands where the majority of the population live. But it can equally occur with expansion of manufactures exports confined to an export-processing zone based on assembly of imported inputs, or tourism enclaves which are supplied through imports, or capital-intensive mines based on FDI.

Enclave-led growth offers a short-term solution to the many binding constraints on economic growth which are characteristic of a low-income trap of underdevelopment and generalized poverty. The lack of investment funds, lack of effective domestic demand and unreliability of domestic suppliers can all be overcome through external sources — using foreign savings to make up for the lack of domestic savings, exports to make up for the lack of domestic demand, and imports to procure inputs of the right international standard. In the event of inelasticity of food supply from domestic agriculture, increased demand by additionally employed and/or better-remunerated workers in the enclave can also be met through increased food imports. But whilst orientation to external markets and suppliers certainly enables economic growth within the enclave — and this will lead to an increasing GDP per capita — economic growth within the enclave can take place together with widespread underemployment and persistent poverty (Mhone, 2001).

Enclave-led growth offers a short-term solution to the many binding constraints on economic growth which are characteristic of a low-income trap of underdevelopment and generalized poverty...

Economic growth solely concentrated in an export-oriented enclave will not be inclusive. Moreover, solely it is also unlikely to be sustainable. In very poor countries, increasing inequalities associated with enclave-led growth are likely to be perceived as illegitimate and may even contribute to civil conflict (see chapter 4).

3. CONDITIONS FOR INCLUSIVE GROWTH

To be inclusive, sustained economic growth must be in a form that increases average household incomes substantially through the creation of sufficient productive income-earning opportunities (jobs and livelihoods). This requires not simply increasing output per capita, but also the achievement of a rate of economic growth and an employment intensity of growth that enable the population of working age to become more and more fully and productively employed. The faster the rate of population growth, the faster the economic growth rate and the greater the employment intensity of growth required to meet this condition.

Export expansion contributes to the achievement of this condition because of the employment created through export activities. These may be more labour-intensive than some import-substitution industries serving the domestic market. However, the total contribution of the tradable sector to employment expansion can be negligible, or even negative, if job creation through export expansion is offset by job loss in tradable sectors serving the domestic market which cannot compete with imports. Many of the stratum B enterprises may be of this type and if they disappear this will exacerbate the problem of the missing middle in the LDC enterprise structure. Moreover, economy-wide expansion of employment depends on growth in the non-tradable sector as well as tradables.[4]

In economies where policy has previously discouraged export production by taxation and other disincentives, there are potential efficiency gains through resource re-allocation away from import-competing activities and non-tradables towards exportables. Such efficiency gains through trade enable greater consumption possibilities for a country for a given labour input. However, getting rid of bias against exports does not mean that import-competing activities and non-tradables can be neglected. Expansion of such income-earning opportunities is a significant component of total employment growth in an inclusive growth process.

Thus although economic growth without export expansion is likely to be unsustainable, economic growth which ignores the domestic market is not likely to be inclusive. Its importance is evident in analyses which estimate the relative importance of different demand-side components of economic growth – the growth of domestic demand, import substitution and export growth. Work by Chenery et al. (1986) on patterns of growth over the period 1950–1983, for example, shows that at the start of the development process the expansion of domestic demand contributed just under 75 per cent of economic growth in both small primary-oriented and small manufactures-oriented countries. In the Republic of Korea (1955–1971) and Taiwan Province of China (1956–1971), usually regarded as the best models of "export-led growth", expansion of domestic demand contributed to 68 per cent and 55 per cent of total economic growth respectively, and the contribution of export expansion was 35 per cent and 43 per cent respectively (Chenery, 1986: table 6.4).

Inclusive growth is also facilitated if export expansion is linked to growth in the rest of the economy, which occurs for example if there are positive synergies between exporting enterprises and local supplies of inputs, providers of services, subcontracting relationships and local purchases of wage goods. It is particularly important that export expansion helps to strengthen domestic linkages and development complementarities between agriculture, where the majority of the population currently earn their livelihoods, and emerging non-agricultural activities.

... But economic growth concentrated in an export-oriented enclave will not be inclusive. Moreover, it is also unlikely to be sustainable.

Although economic growth without export expansion is likely to be unsustainable, economic growth which ignores the domestic market is not likely to be inclusive.

E. Conclusions

The central message of this chapter is that international trade can play a major role in poverty reduction in the LDCs. This is because there is generalized or mass poverty in the LDCs. In these circumstances, poverty reduction requires sustained economic growth, which in turn requires export expansion. Exports are important because the LDCs are import-sensitive economies and face tight foreign exchange constraints. Import bottlenecks hamper the full utilization and efficient development of domestic productive capacities. In some countries food security is also sensitive to the supply of imports.

Through exports it is possible to transform underutilized natural resources and surplus labour into imports which support economic growth. But although export expansion is a necessary condition, export expansion is not in itself a sufficient condition for sustained economic growth. This requires that export expansion be linked to the main engines of economic growth — increased investment and technological progress. Given the limited domestic resources available for financing investment, establishing a strong investment–export nexus is likely to involve increased trade and increased aid.

For economic growth to be poverty-reducing it must be inclusive as well as sustained. This requires a broad-based form of economic growth which substantially increases average household incomes through the creation of sufficient productive income-earning opportunities. This is difficult to achieve in the LDC context because even though LDCs' economies are very open (in the sense of the importance of trade for GDP) most people are not directly engaged in export activities. Indeed, the structure of production, enterprise and employment within LDCs is more likely to lead to enclave-led growth rather than a broad-based pattern of growth.

For economic growth to be poverty-reducing it must be inclusive as well as sustained. This requires a broad-based form of economic growth which substantially increases average household incomes through the creation of sufficient productive income-earning opportunities.

The key conditions which must be fulfilled for export expansion to be part of a process of both sustained and inclusive economic growth are the following:

- Export expansion enables imports of goods and services necessary for the full utilization and efficient development of productive capacities, and sustained economic growth.

- The relaxation of the foreign exchange constraint through increased export earnings is not offset by reduced aid inflows or greater debt service obligations.

- Export expansion reinforces, and is reinforced by, capital accumulation and technological progress in the domestic economy.

- There are developmental linkages between growing export activities and the rest of the economy, and in particular international trade strengthens the development complementarities between agriculture and non-agricultural activities.

- There is an economy-wide expansion of income-earning opportunities, encompassing export and import-competing activities, and non-tradables as well as tradables, which occurs at a rate that exceeds the rate at which the working-age population is growing.

When these conditions are met, export expansion should be poverty-reducing.

Notes

1. The sample includes countries for which data were available and covers low- and lower-middle-income countries with per capita private consumption levels below $2,400 a year (in 1985 PPP dollars). This is the upper limit at which it is possible to make estimates of poverty for the $2-a-day poverty line.
2. Economic growth is also important for food security. For a conceptual framework which relates food security to economic growth, income distribution and the level of food prices, see Timmer (2000). The relationship between income growth and food security is analysed by Haddad et al. (2003).
3. The term 'enclave-led growth' is borrowed from Jones and Marjit (1995), who use it to refer to a more positive process in which the enclave acts to 'discover' human talent in a society.
4. Tradable goods are all domestically produced or domestically consumed goods which are perfect substitutes for internationally traded goods and could potentially enter into international trade. Non-tradables are all domestically produced and domestically consumed goods which have no perfect substitutes among traded goods and that are absorbed only internationally.

References

Bhalla, S. S. (2002). *Imagine There is No Country: Poverty, Inequality and Growth in the Era of Globalization*, Institute for International Economics, Washington DC.

Berthélemy, J. C. and Morrison, C. (1989) *Agricultural Development in Africa and the Supply of Manufactured Goods*, OECD Development Center, Paris.

Chenery, H., Robinson, S., Syrquin, M. (1986). *Industrialization and Growth: A Comparative Study*, Oxford University Press, New York.

Dabee, B. (2002). The role of non-traditional exports in Mauritius. In: Helleiner, G. (ed.), *Non-Traditional Export Promotion in Africa: Experience and Issues*, Palgrave, Hampshire.

Deaton, A. (2004). Measuring poverty in a growing world (or measuring growth in a poor world) (available at http://www.wws.princeton.edu/%7Erpds/downloads/deaton_measuringpoverty_204.pdf).

FAO (2003a). *The State of Food Insecurity in the World*, Rome, Italy (available at ftp://ftp.fao.org/docrep/fao/005/j0083e/j0083e00.pdf).

FAO (2003b). *Food Import Profiles of Least Developed Countries and Net Food Importing Developing Countries*, Rome, Italy.

Haddad, L., Aldermann, H., Appleton, S., Song, L. and Yohannes, Y. (2003). Reducing child malnutrition: how far does income growth take us?, *World Bank Economic Review*, 17:107–131.

Helleiner, G. (1993). Trade, trade policy and economic development in very low-income countries. In: Nissanke, M., Hewitt, A. (eds.), *Economic Crisis in Developing Countries: New Perspectives on Commodities, Trade and Finance: Essays in Honour of Alfred Maizels*, St Martin's Press, London and New York.

Jones, R. W., Marjit, S. (1995). Labour-market aspects of enclaved-led growth, *Canadian Journal of Economics*, 28 (special issue): S76–S93.

Karshenas, M. (2004). Global poverty trends and the millennium goals, Employment Strategy Paper No. 2004/5, International Labour Office, Geneva .

Mhone, G. C. Z. (2001). Enclavity and constrained labour absorptive capacity in Southern African economies, Paper prepared for the UNRISD meeting on "Rethinking Development Economics", 7–8 September 2001, Cape Town, South Africa.

Pyatt, G. (2003). Development and the distribution of living standards: a critique of the evolving database, *Review of Income and Wealth*, 49 (3): 333–358.

Ravallion, M. (2003). Measuring aggregate welfare in developing countries: how well do national accounts and surveys agree, Review of Economics and Statistics, 85 (3): 645–652.

Sachs, I. (2003). From poverty trap to inclusive development in LDCs, background paper prepared for the *Least Developed Countries Report 2004*, Geneva.

Timmer, C. P. (2000). The macro dimensions of food security: economic growth, equitable distribution, and food price stability, *Food Policy*, 25: 283–295.

UNCTAD (1996). *Trade and Development Report, 1996*, United Nations publication, sales no. E.96.II.D.6, Geneva.

UNCTAD (1998). *Trade and Development Report, 1998.* United Nations publication, sales no. E.98.II.D.6, Geneva.

UNCTAD (2000). *The Least Developed Countries 2000 Report*, United Nations publication, sales no. E.00.II.D.21, Geneva.

UNCTAD (2001). Growing micro and small enterprises in LDCs — The "missing middle" in LDCs: Why micro and small enterprises are not growing, UNCTAD/ITE/TEB/5, Geneva.

UNCTAD (2002). *The Least Developed Countries Report 2002 – Escaping the Poverty Trap*, United Nations publication, sales no. E.02.II.D.13, Geneva

UNCTAD (2003). *Trade and Development Report, 2003,* United Nations publication, sales No.E.03.II.D.7, Geneva.

World Bank (2003). *World Development Report*, Washington DC.

How the Trade–Poverty Relationship Works in Practice

Chapter

3

A. Introduction

From the analysis in the previous chapter it is clear that international trade can play a major role in reducing poverty in the LDCs. It is also clear, however, that the links between export expansion and poverty reduction are not automatic, but depend on various domestic and external conditions. This chapter looks at how the trade–poverty relationship works in practice in the LDCs.

The central message of the chapter is that the potential positive role of trade in poverty reduction is not being translated into reality in a large number of LDCs. The major policy challenge in linking international trade to poverty reduction in the LDCs is to bridge the gap between the positive role of trade identified in the previous chapter and the often neutral, and even negative, trade–poverty relationship which, the evidence of this chapter reveals, currently exists in too many LDCs.

The chapter discusses three major areas where international trade may not be working effectively to reduce poverty in the LDCs: trade performance; trade–growth linkages; and the form of economic growth associated with export expansion. Section B discusses the trade performance of the LDCs, indicating in particular the relationship between export structure and export dynamism. The trade performance of many LDCs improved in the 1990s, and section C presents evidence of the frequency with which export expansion during this period was associated with poverty reduction. Sections D and E examine some of the possible missing links between export growth and poverty reduction, focusing firstly on the relationship between trade and the rate of growth, and secondly on the relationship between trade and the form of economic growth. Particular attention is paid in section E to differences amongst the LDCs with regard to the level of income inequality, the balance between domestic demand and export expansion as sources of economic growth, and the intensity of domestic resource mobilization efforts. Section F summarizes the main findings.

The potential positive role of trade in poverty reduction is not being translated into reality in a large number of LDCs.

B. Export structure, trade performance and the international poverty trap

The simplest reason for a breakdown in the trade–poverty relationship is a country's weak trade performance. Differences in export dynamism are closely related to differences in export structure.

1. BASIC FEATURES OF THE EXPORT STRUCTURE OF THE LDCs

The export structure of the LDCs was discussed in detail in *The Least Developed Countries Report 2002.*[1] It is worth recalling here its key features:

Amongst the LDCs, differences in export dynamism are closely related to differences in export structure.

- The total merchandise exports of the LDCs are divided more or less equally between oil exports, non-oil commodity exports and manufactures exports. In the period 1999–2001, oil exports constituted 35 per cent of total merchandise exports, manufactures exports[2] 33 per cent and non-oil primary commodity exports 32 per cent.

- Service exports are a significant component of the total exports of goods and services of LDCs. In 1999–2001, they accounted for 17 per cent of the total.

- On the basis of a classification in the late 1990s, primary commodities are the major source of export earnings in 31 out of the 49 LDCs. Four countries are oil exporters; seven countries are predominantly mineral exporters; and 20 countries are predominantly agricultural exporters. The other 18 LDCs predominantly export either manufactures (mainly textiles and garments) or services (mainly tourism), or some combination of these.[3]

- There is a major difference between African LDCs and Asian LDCs in terms of their diversification into manufactures exports. In 1999–2001, textiles and garments exports constituted 61 per cent of total merchandise exports of Asian LDCs and 2 per cent of total merchandise exports of African LDCs. The main exceptions to the general African trend are Lesotho and Madagascar. Island LDCs generally specialize in services exports. But textiles and garments exports are also important to Cape Verde and Maldives.

The non-oil primary-commodity-exporting LDCs have a low-productivity, low-value-added and weakly competitive commodity sector that is generally concentrated on a narrow range of products serving declining or sluggish international markets.

- Whatever their main exports, the export structure of most LDCs is concentrated on a narrow range of products. For the group as a whole, the three leading export products constituted 76 per cent of total merchandise exports in 1997–1999.

- The non-oil primary-commodity-exporting LDCs have a low-productivity, low-value-added and weakly competitive commodity sector that is generally concentrated on a narrow range of products serving declining or sluggish international markets. In 1997–1999, 84 per cent of total primary commodity exports of this group of countries were unprocessed before export.

- Manufactures exports also tend to be narrowly concentrated on a few low-skill lines of manufacture with competition on the basis of cost, and industries have often been built up on the basis of market access preferences granted by developed countries, including especially the EU and the United States, as well as market access preferences granted by multilateral agreements, namely the Agreement on Textiles and Clothing (commonly known as the Multifibre Arrangement), which will be phased out by 1 January 2005.

2. TRADE PERFORMANCE IN THE 1980s AND 1990s

The trade performance of the LDCs in the 1980s and 1990s has two major faces. On the one hand, there was a great expansion of exports of oil, manufactures and services. As chart 16A shows, the value of manufactures exports increased by more than five times between 1980 and 2001, services exports doubled and oil exports almost quadrupled. On the other hand, however, these successes were offset by stagnation and decline in the value of non-oil commodity exports. By 2001 LDCs' non-oil commodity exports were 15 per cent lower than in 1980 in current value terms. Mineral exports from LDCs declined precipitously over this period, whilst agricultural exports after a recovery between 1986 and 1995 subsequently fell back to a level just over 5 per cent higher than the 1980 value (chart 16B). Components of the weak export performance of commodity-dependent LDCs are discussed in box 7.

The two faces of trade development in the LDCs — stagnation and decline of non-oil commodity exports on the one hand and expansion of exports of manufactures, services and oil on the other hand — would be benign if they were offsetting each other on a country-by-country basis. But in practice, they are not. The main LDC oil exporters are Angola, Equatorial Guinea, Sudan (since 2000) and Yemen; the main LDC manufactures exporters are Bangladesh, Cambodia, Haiti, the Lao People's Democratic Republic, Lesotho, Madagascar, Myanmar and Nepal; and the main services exporters are Cape Verde, Comoros, Djibouti, Gambia, Maldives, Samoa, Tuvalu and Vanuatu. It is these countries that largely drove the more positive export performance of the LDC group in the 1990s. The majority of LDCs — 27 out of 49 — are exporters of non-oil primary commodities. Their export growth rates have been much weaker and also more unstable.

Between 1980 and 2001, there was a great expansion of exports of oil, manufactures and services. However, these successes were offset by stagnation and decline in the value of non-oil commodity exports.

The diverse outcomes can be seen in table 30. An important fact which is evident in the table is that there was a significant improvement in export performance in the LDCs in the 1990s. In real per capita terms, the total exports

CHART 16. TRENDS IN LDCS' EXPORTS, 1980–2001
(Index, 1980 = 100)

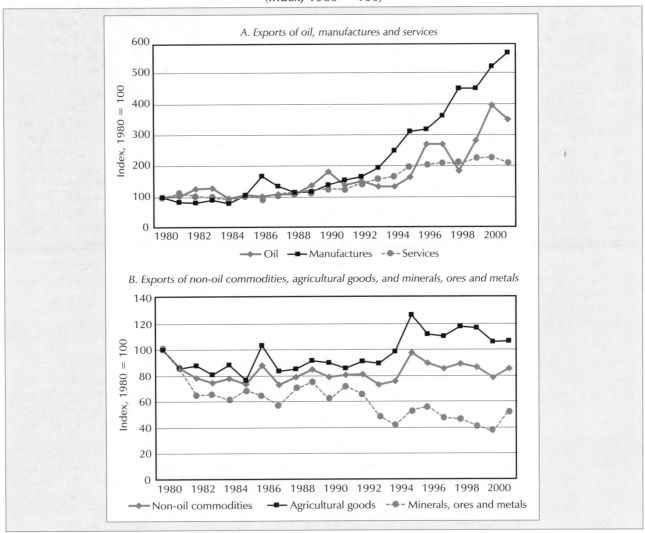

Source: UNCTAD secretariat estimates, based on UN COMTRADE data (merchandise exports) and UNCTAD data (services exports).

Note: Calculations based on data in current dollars.

Box 7. Components of the weak export performance of commodity dependent LDCs

It is possible to have a greater insight into the weak export performance of non-oil commodity-exporting LDCs by identifying some of the factors that directly contribute to it, namely falling commodity prices, a small share of market-dynamic products and lack of competitiveness.

It is difficult to disentangle the influence of these three factors. But falling world commodity prices have had a major adverse effect on the export performance of commodity-exporting LDCs. Between 1980 and 2003, the price of food, including beverages, declined by 73.3 per cent to 26.7 per cent of its 1980 value; the price of agricultural raw materials declined by 60.7 per cent to 39.3 per cent of its 1980 value; and the price of minerals, ores and metals declined by 59.5 per cent to 40.5 per cent of its 1980 value. Declining commodity prices have affected some of the most important commodity exports of least developed countries. In the first half of 2003, the price of coffee was just 17 per cent of its 1980 value, cotton was 33 per cent and copper was 42 per cent.

These falls in commodity prices result in a significant loss of resources.[1] Box table 1 seeks to quantify the direct impact of the commodity price changes on LDC exports by estimating what LDC exports would have been in 2001 if the world prices for selected commodities, for which price data were available, had remained the same as in 1980. The table shows that the LDCs could have earned an additional $1.2 billion through the export of these commodities if their prices had not declined. This is an increase of 12.6 per cent over the 2001 value of these commodities. Coffee-exporting LDCs could have earned an additional $312 million, and cotton-exporting LDCs an additional $386 million. Exports of minerals, ores and metals would have been $715 million higher, that is about 25.1 per cent higher than their 2001 level.

A major reason why commodity-dependent countries find it difficult to achieve high export growth rates is that the growth rate of world exports for these products is slow. This partly reflects falling prices, but also weak import demand. On the basis of ITC estimates, it is apparent that only 12 per cent of the primary commodity exports of the LDCs in 1998 were in market-dynamic products, those in which world import demand was growing faster than average. In contrast, 70 per cent of the manufactures exports of the LDCs were in such products.

However, commodity-exporting LDCs have not only been exporting products for which world export growth rates have been slow, but have also been losing market share in some of their exports. Box table 1 provides some estimates of the direct impact of losses in world market share for specific primary commodities. It should be noted that the losses in market share may not be a matter of uncompetitiveness but rather reflect the fact that within these product groups there may be more market-dynamic or less market-dynamic products. Nevertheless, the patterns are interesting.

If the LDCs' share in world exports of all foods, agricultural raw materials and minerals, ores and metals, which are included in the table, had remained the same in 2001 as in 1980, their non-oil primary commodity exports would have been $14.8 billion instead of $9.3 billion (box table 1). The major losses in export revenue are due to a loss in market share in food exports and mineral exports, which each contribute about half of the total losses in export revenue. There is only a small loss in market share for agricultural raw materials exports. Within these broad commodity groups, there are also successes and failures. Within food exports, the LDCs gained market share in fish, wheat and sugar, but significantly lost market share in cocoa, coffee, fruits, rice, and vegetable oils and oil seeds. Within agricultural raw material exports, they gained market share in raw cotton, wood products, and jute and sisal, but lost market share significantly in tobacco and rubber. Within minerals there were major losses in market share in ore and copper exports, which together account for about 68 per cent of the total losses in market share in the selected commodities. At the same time, however, there were gains in market share in aluminium and gold.

What these data show is that as one disaggregates, the export performance of the non-oil commodity-exporting LDCs has positive aspects. The improved export performance in the 1990s, and the halting of the decline in marginalization of the non-oil commodity-exporting LDCs, reflect the fact that with regard to a number of commodities those countries have started gaining market share. However, their overall export performance is still hampered because their export structure is still focused on products for which growth of world imports is either declining or growing more slowly than average.

Finally, box table 1 provides an estimate of what the value of the LDCs' exports of the selected commodities would have been in 2001 if they had maintained their 1980 share of world exports and also if the level of world prices in 1980 had stayed the same. This simple counter-factual ignores possible increased production and investment which might have occurred if prices had not declined. But it suggests that without loss of market share and the decline in world prices, LDC exports of non-oil primary commodities would have totalled $16.7 billion rather than $9.3 billion. This difference is equivalent to about 3.8 per cent of the GDP of the LDCs in 2001.

---

[1] It is worth recalling in this context that the World Bank (2000) has estimated that the cumulative losses to non-oil-exporting countries in sub-Saharan Africa (excluding South Africa) from adverse terms-of-trade movements over the period 1970–1997 amounted to 119 per cent of the combined GDP of these countries in 1997 and 51 per cent of the cumulative net resource flows to them. That is to say, terms-of-trade losses associated with falls in commodity prices were equivalent to half the value of total capital inflows into those countries over that period.

Box 7 (contd.)

BOX TABLE 1. ESTIMATES OF HYPOTHETICAL EXPORT REVENUE LOSSES OF THE LDCs IN SELECTED COMMODITIES, 1980–2001

Selected commodities and aggregates	Corresponding SITC Rev.2 codes	Actual value of exports in 2001	Scenario 1: If LDC shares in world exports had remained at 1980 levels			Scenario 2: If commodity prices on world markets had remained at 1980 levels			Scenario 3: If LDC shares and commodity prices had remained at 1980 levels		
			Hypothetical value of LDC exports in 2001 value	Export revenue losses[b] (= actual minus hypothetical exports)	% of actual export value	Hypothetical value of LDC exports in 2001 value	Export revenue losses[b] (= actual minus hypothetical exports)	% of actual export value	Hypothetical value of LDC exports in 2001 value	Export revenue losses[b] (= actual minus hypothetical export)	% of actual export value
		$ millions	$ millions	$ millions		$ millions	$ millions		$ millions	$ millions	
Non-oil primary commodities[a]		9 290.2	14 798.5	5 508.3	59.3	10 460.1	1 169.9	12.6	16 683.8	7 393.6	79.6
Foods, beverages, oils		3 290.8	5 347.6	2 056.8	62.5	3 821.0	530.2	16.1	6 370.9	3 080.1	93.6
Beverages		613.0	1 768.5	1 155.5	188.5	911.8	298.8	48.7	2 746.5	2 133.5	348.0
Cocoa and products	072,073	27.7	321.0	293.3	1 060.3	42.9	15.2	55.1	497.8	470.1	1 699.6
Coffee and substitutes	071	443.6	1 208.1	764.5	172.3	755.1	311.5	70.2	2 056.4	1 612.9	363.6
Tea and mate	074	141.8	239.5	97.7	68.9	113.8	-27.9	-19.7	192.3	50.5	35.7
Foods		2 345.6	2 980.7	635.1	27.1	2 455.6	109.9	4.7	2 799.2	453.5	19.3
Bananas and other fruits	057	186.4	808.7	622.3	333.8	82.5	-104.0	-55.8	357.7	171.3	91.9
Beef and other meats	011,012,014	37.1	85.7	48.6	130.9	45.7	8.6	23.3	105.6	68.5	184.6
Fish	034-037	1 562.1	1 289.4	-272.7	-17.5	1 617.1	54.9	3.5	1 334.8	-227.4	-14.6
Maize	044	32.0	61.3	29.3	91.6	38.6	6.6	20.6	73.9	41.9	131.1
Pepper and other vegetables	054	239.0	328.4	89.4	37.4	192.4	-46.6	-19.5	264.4	25.4	10.6
Rice	042	36.8	291.0	254.2	690.1	59.0	22.2	60.2	466.2	429.4	1 165.9
Sugar and products	061,062	228.7	113.2	-115.4	-50.5	388.4	159.7	69.9	192.3	-36.4	-15.9
Wheat	041,046	23.5	3.1	-20.4	-86.7	31.9	8.4	35.7	4.3	-19.2	-81.9
Vegetable oil seeds and oils		332.2	598.3	266.1	80.1	453.6	121.4	36.5	825.3	493.1	148.4
Oilseeds, incl. soybeans	222,223	235.7	339.2	103.5	43.9	315.3	79.5	33.7	453.7	218.0	92.5
Oils, incl. linseed oil	423, 424	96.5	259.1	162.7	168.6	138.3	41.9	43.4	371.6	275.1	285.1
Agricultural raw materials		3 156.6	2 868.0	-288.6	-9.1	3 081.9	-74.7	-2.4	2 846.6	-310.0	-9.8
Textiles		1 291.4	1 086.6	-204.8	-15.9	1 723.5	432.1	33.5	1 442.4	151.0	11.7
Cotton, raw	263	831.5	624.4	-207.0	-24.9	1 217.0	385.6	46.4	914.0	82.5	9.9
Cotton, manufactured	652	97.1	135.5	38.4	39.5	142.2	45.0	46.4	198.4	101.2	104.2
Jute	264	59.4	50.4	-8.9	-15.1	56.3	-3.1	-5.1	47.8	-11.5	-19.4
Sisal and other textiles	651,659	300.8	265.9	-34.8	-11.6	304.6	3.9	1.3	269.4	-31.4	-10.4
Wool	268	2.6	10.3	7.7	289.6	3.3	0.7	24.6	12.8	10.2	385.6
Woods		937.7	557.0	-380.6	-40.6	657.4	-280.3	-29.9	389.6	-548.1	-58.5
Wood, rough	245-248	862.8	508.2	-354.6	-41.1	619.7	-243.1	-28.2	365.0	-497.8	-57.7
Plywood and other manufd. woods	634,635	74.9	48.8	-26.0	-34.8	37.7	-37.2	-49.7	24.6	-50.3	-67.2
Others		927.5	1 224.3	296.8	32.0	701.0	-226.5	-24.4	1 014.6	87.1	9.4
Cattle hides and other hides, manufd.	211	125.6	198.6	73.0	58.1	91.8	-33.8	-26.9	145.1	19.5	15.5
Cattle hides and other hides, raw	611,612	377.8	399.0	21.2	5.6	276.1	-101.7	-26.9	291.6	-86.2	-22.8
Rubber, raw	232,233	36.4	140.7	104.3	286.3	57.4	21.0	57.6	221.7	185.3	508.8
Rubber, manufactured	621,625,628	10.4	24.8	14.4	139.2	16.3	6.0	57.6	39.1	28.7	277.0
Tobacco	121,122	377.4	461.3	83.9	22.2	259.4	-118.0	-31.3	317.1	-60.3	-16.0
Minerals, ores and metals	27,28,68	2 842.8	6 582.9	3 740.1	131.6	3 557.3	714.5	25.1	7 466.3	4 623.5	162.6
Minerals		60.6	116.7	56.1	92.6	62.4	1.8	2.9	120.1	59.5	98.3
Phosphate rock and other minerals	271	60.6	116.7	56.1	92.6	62.4	1.8	2.9	120.1	59.5	98.3
Ores		971.5	2 562.5	1 591.0	163.8	1 058.7	87.2	9.0	2 792.6	1 821.1	187.5
Ores raw (incl. iron, mang., tungst.)	281,282, 287	697.5	1 637.4	939.9	134.7	760.1	62.6	9.0	1 784.3	1 086.9	155.8
Ores, manufactured (incl. iron, mang., tungst.)	67, 689, 699	274.0	925.2	651.2	237.7	298.6	24.6	9.0	1 008.2	734.2	268.0
Metals		990.7	3 784.6	2 793.9	282.0	1 157.6	167.0	16.9	4 366.6	3 375.9	340.8
Aluminium	684	387.7	6.4	-381.3	-98.4	451.6	63.8	16.5	7.4	-380.3	-98.1
Copper	682	601.8	3 576.9	2 975.1	494.4	704.7	102.9	17.1	4 188.5	3 586.7	596.0
Lead	685	0.4	5.7	5.3	1 348.7	0.5	0.1	21.2	6.9	6.5	1 656.3
Nickel	683	0.4	0.5	0.1	24.6	0.5	0.0	9.8	0.6	0.2	36.8
Tin	687	0.2	1.3	1.1	652.4	0.3	0.1	67.1	2.2	2.0	1 157.5
Zinc	686	0.2	193.8	193.6	117330.8	0.1	0.0	-16.9	161.1	160.9	97506.1
Precious metals		820.0	119.1	-701.0	-85.5	1 278.6	458.5	55.9	187.0	-633.0	-77.2
Gold	971	811.0	109.0	-702.0	-86.6	1 263.3	452.3	55.8	169.8	-641.2	-79.1
Silver	681	2.1	3.1	1.0	49.4	3.7	1.6	78.7	5.6	3.5	166.9
Gold, silver ware, etc.	897	6.9	6.9	0.0	0.3	11.5	4.6	67.2	11.6	4.7	67.7

Source: UNCTAD secretariat estimates, based on UN COMTRADE database, and UNCTAD *Commodity Price Bulletin*, various issues.

Note: Commodities included in UNCTAD's *Commodity Price Bulletin* do not always correspond with commodities included in the UN COMTRADE database at the SITC 3-digit level, Revision 2. The classification of commodities in commodity groups is also different in the two databases. The choices made in matching the two databases may have led to both overestimations and underestimations.

UNCTAD's *Commodity Price Bulletin* classifies plywood and sisal as agricultural raw materials, whereas the UN COMTRADE database classifies them as manufactures. Here they were classified as agricultural raw materials. But as plywood (SITC code 634) was classified as an agricultural raw material, other woods manufactures nes (SITC code 635) were classified as an agricultural raw material as well. Other manufactures characterized by their high content of raw materials according to SITC have also been included in the group of raw materials in this exercise.

At the time of this exercise, UNCTAD's *Commodity Price Bulletin* provided commodity price data for the first half of 2003, whereas the UN COMTRADE database provided sufficient trade data only up to 2001. If the price data of 2003 had been applied to the export volume of 2001, the forgone gain associated with price falls in the selected non-oil primary commodities would have been $4.91 billion rather than $1.17 billion.

a　The values of the different aggregates are the sum of the value changes associated with the individual commodities included in the table.

b　A minus sign means that there were export revenue gains rather than export revenue losses.

of goods and services of the LDCs as a group hardly increased during the 1980s — from $15 per capita in 1979–1981 to $16 per capita in 1989–1991. Indeed, real exports per capita were stagnant or declined in the 1980s for 25 of the 43 LDCs for which data are available (i.e. 58 per cent of cases). But in real per capita terms, the total exports of goods and services of the LDC group increased considerably during the 1990s. Between 1989–1991 and 1999–2001, they increased by about a third to $21 per capita. Real exports per capita stagnated or declined in only 8 out of 44 countries in the 1990s (i.e. 18 per cent of cases). Moreover, there were 16 LDCs where real exports per capita more than doubled in that decade (table 30).

Within this more positive picture overall, non-oil commodity-exporting LDCs continue to give cause for concern. Of the six mineral exporters for which data were available for all periods, per capita exports in 1999–2001 were lower in real terms than in 1979–1981 in four countries, and in the other two mineral exporters real exports per capita were lower at the end of the 1990s than at the beginning of the decade. Some of the agricultural exporters had a much improved export performance in the 1990s. But amongst those exporters, real exports per capita at the end of the 1990s were either less than their level in 1979–1981 or about the same value in 6 out of 17 countries in spite of improved performance in the 1990s (table 30).

Another way to describe the export performance of the LDCs is in terms of their share in world exports of goods and services. In 2001, the LDC share in world exports of goods and services was 0.63 per cent. This was 31 per cent lower than their share in 1980. The decline in their share, a process which is often described as the marginalization of the LDCs in global trade, reflects the fact that LDC exports are growing more slowly than world exports.[4] The improved performance in the 1990s is apparent in the fact that from 1980 until 1994 there was a persistent tendency towards increasing marginalization of the LDCs in world trade. But since 1994 the decline in the LDC share in world exports has actually ceased.

Chart 17 shows the shares of different LDC sub-groups in world exports of goods and services between 1980 and 2001. It is apparent that the only sub-groups to reverse the process of marginalization are LDCs diversifying into manufactures exports and, in a less sustained way, services exporters. Since 1990 the share of manufactured goods exporters in world trade has increased from 16 per cent below its 1980 level in 1990 to 58 per cent above that level by the year 2001. The LDCs that export predominantly agricultural commodities also increased their share of world exports of goods and services briefly in the period 1992–1995, but this upward trend subsequently ceased. In 2001, their share of world exports of goods and services was just 56 per cent of its level in 1980. LDC mineral exporters have continued to have a very weak export performance. In 2001, their share in the world export of goods and services was just 16 per cent of what it had been in 1980 (chart 17).

An idea of the economic magnitude of these changes can be gained by making an estimate of what exports of the LDC group as a whole would have been if it had not lost market shares in this way.[5] It can be estimated that export revenues in 2001 would have been $68.5 billion rather than $47.7 billion, that is 44 per cent higher. The difference of $20.8 billion would have increased net ODA disbursements of 2001 by 153 per cent. Most of these foregone earnings were concentrated in the non-oil commodity-exporting LDCs.

Where export performance is weak, import capacity is impaired. Chart 18 shows the export and import trends between 1980 and 2002 in LDCs grouped by their export specialization. This reveals that apart from the oil exporters, all

Had the LDCs' 1980 market shares remained constant, their export revenues in 2001 would have been 44 per cent higher. Most of these foregone earnings were concentrated in the non-oil commodity-exporting LDCs.

Where export performance is weak, import capacity is impaired.

TABLE 30. REAL EXPORTS OF GOODS AND SERVICES IN LDCs, BY COUNTRY,
1979–1981, 1989–1991 AND 1991–2001
(Annual average per capita, constant 1995 $)

	1979–1981	1989–1991	1999–2001
Exporters of primary commodities			
Agricultural exporters			
Afghanistan	14.6	4.4	..
Benin	24.0	38.1	42.2
Bhutan	17.4	50.7	61.2
Burkina Faso	13.4	7.5	10.3
Burundi	5.3	5.7	12.8
Chad	7.4	15.2	10.2
Eritrea	..	..	7.9
Ethiopia	5.9	5.8	6.4
Guinea-Bissau	11.2	8.1	24.3
Kiribati	114.3	74.2	..
Malawi	17.3	14.9	17.3
Mali	11.3	14.3	29.2
Mauritania	77.1	77.1	68.7
Rwanda	10.7	10.5	7.0
Sao Tome and Principe	72.5	26.4	42.2
Solomon Islands	154.6	139.0	178.5
Somalia	9.1	..	..
Togo	40.3	31.8	34.4
Uganda	13.4	5.3	19.2
United Rep. of Tanzania	11.3	6.3	13.5
Mineral exporters			
Central African Republic	18.0	21.1	15.5
Dem. Rep. of the Congo	12.8	23.5	15.8
Guinea	31.8	44.7	37.2
Liberia	92.5	..	..
Niger	24.5	12.5	10.9
Sierra Leone	40.2	31.1	0.2
Zambia	99.9	64.7	75.0
Oil exporters			
Angola	74.4	124.1	181.6
Equatorial Guinea	35.5	48.9	891.7
Sudan	13.9	8.5	16.7
Yemen	31.1	23.1	69.3
Exporters of manufactures and/ or services			
Manufactures exporters			
Bangladesh	3.0	5.9	17.7
Cambodia	..	..	48.9
Haiti	16.6	8.6	21.5
Lao PDR	5.0	11.1	38.6
Lesotho	22.8	25.5	59.1
Madagascar	25.1	18.0	18.4
Myanmar	6.5	4.0	19.3
Nepal	6.1	7.7	19.8
Services exporters			
Cape Verde	15.4	37.2	103.7
Comoros	30.1	30.6	35.3
Djibouti	..	..	53.7
Gambia	47.9	40.4	42.7
Maldives	102.8	233.4	547.3
Samoa	62.5	112.6	198.9
Tuvalu	..	..	..
Vanuatu	264.9	217.0	309.5
Mixed manufactures and services exporters			
Mozambique	8.4	4.8	19.6
Senegal	64.2	58.2	69.3
LDCs	**15.2**	**15.8**	**21.1**

Source: UNCTAD secretariat estimates, based on UNCTAD, *Handbook of Statistics 2003*, for data on goods and services exports in current dollars; and World Bank, *World Development Indicators 2003*, CD-ROM, for deflators of goods and services exports.

Note: No export data were available for Afghanistan, Cambodia, Djibouti, Kiribati, Somalia and Uganda. The export data were deflated by deflators derived from World Bank data on goods and service exports (*World Development Indicators 2003*, CD-ROM). For all countries for which no deflator could be derived, regional deflators were applied. For the Lao People's Democratic Republic, Myanmar, Samoa and the Solomon Islands the deflator for the East Asian/ Pacific region was applied; for Bhutan and Nepal the deflator for the South Asian region was applied, and for Angola, Cape Verde, the Central African Republic, Equatorial Guinea, Guinea, Liberia, Maldives, Sao Tome and Principe, Sudan, the United Republic of Tanzania and Yemen the deflator for sub-Saharan Africa was applied. The deflator for sub-Saharan Africa was also applied to Yemen, although the World Bank classifies Yemen as a member of the Middle East/ North Africa region. But no deflator could be derived for this region. The deflator for least developed countries is the deflator that was derived for the low-income countries group.

CHART 17. TRENDS IN SHARE OF LDC SUB-GROUPS IN WORLD EXPORTS OF GOODS AND SERVICES, 1980–2001

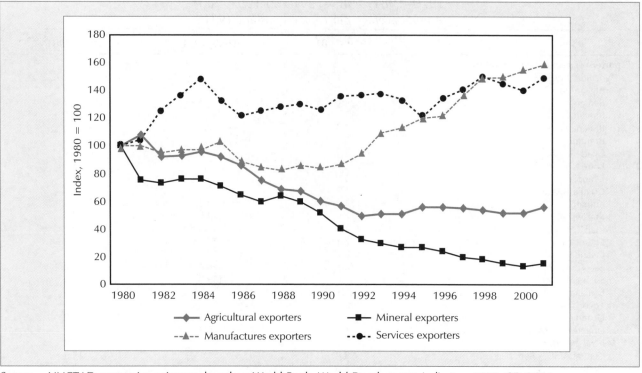

Source: UNCTAD secretariat estimates, based on World Bank, *World Development Indicators 2003*, CD-ROM.

Note: Calculations were based on 16 agricultural exporters, 6 mineral exporters, 5 manufactures exporters and 6 services exporters amongst LDCs for which data were available. For the classification of LDCs by export specialization, see Annex to chapter 1 of Part I.

the LDC groups have persistent high trade deficits. It is also clear that the trends in imports do not exactly follow trends in exports. But over the long term, it is the manufactures exporters, services exporters and oil exporters that have been able to increase their imports most significantly.

Between 1990 and 2002, the current value of the imports of non-oil commodity exporters rose by $2.8 billion, whilst the current value of the imports of manufactures exporters rose by $10 billion (see chart 18). In per capita terms, the contrast is even starker. Imports per capita fell by $11.3 in the non-oil commodity exporters and rose by $31 in the manufactures exporters between 1990 and 2002. Amongst the non-oil commodity exporters, there is also an important difference between the mineral exporters and the agricultural exporters. Between 1990 and 2002, the current value of the imports of mineral exporters fell by $1.5 billion, whilst the current value of the imports of agricultural exporters increased by $4.3 billion. But after a surge in 1993–1996, imports of agricultural exports did not increase much, and in per capita terms actually declined from $72 in 1996 to $65 in 2001.

It is very difficult to reduce poverty in an LDC if exports are not growing, or are growing very slowly, and if import capacity is severely constrained.

3. THE INTERNATIONAL POVERTY TRAP

It is very difficult to reduce poverty in an LDC if exports are not growing, or are growing very slowly, and if import capacity is severely constrained. One may therefore expect the differences in trade performance amongst the LDCs to be associated with differences in the incidence of poverty. Indeed, there is a general association between dependence on primary commodities and the incidence of $1/day poverty in the LDCs.

The evidence presented in *The Least Developed Countries Report 2002* showed that during 1997–1999, 69 per cent of the population of non-oil commodity-exporting LDCs was living on less than a dollar a day, and in

CHART 18. TRENDS IN EXPORTS AND IMPORTS OF GOODS AND SERVICES BY LDC SUB-GROUPS, 1980–2002

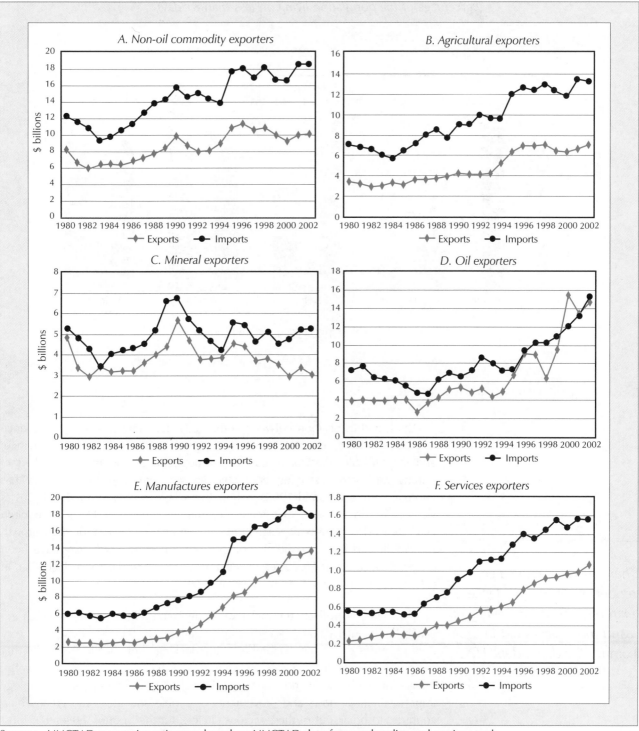

Source: UNCTAD secretariat estimates, based on UNCTAD data for merchandise and services trade.

Note: The calculations are based on 23 non-oil commodity exporters (16 agricultural exporters and 7 mineral exporters), 4 fuel exporters, 7 manufactures exporters and 6 services exporters amongst the LDCs for which data were available.

mineral-exporting LDCs the proportion was over 80 per cent (chart 19). The share of the population living on less than $1/day was lower on average in service-exporting LDCs (43 per cent), whilst in LDCs that have managed to diversify into exporting manufactured goods the incidence of extreme poverty was even lower (25 per cent). There has also been a general tendency for the incidence of extreme poverty to be more persistent in the commodity-dependent LDCs. In the mineral exporters, the incidence of $1/day poverty rose on average from 61 per cent to 82 per cent on average between 1981–1983 and 1997–1999 (chart 19). But there are variations within the sub-groups, particularly in the 1990s.

CHART 19. INCIDENCE OF EXTREME POVERTY IN LDC SUB-GROUPS, 1981–1983, 1987–1989 AND 1997–1999
(Percentage of the population living on less than $1/day)

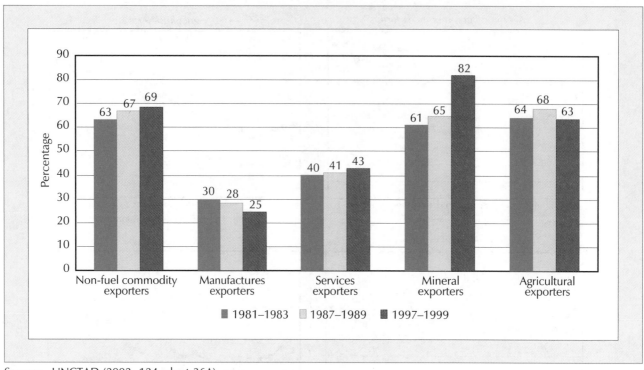

Source: UNCTAD (2002: 124, chart 36A).

There has also been a general tendency for the incidence of extreme poverty to be higher and more persistent in the commodity-dependent LDCs.

The broad association between commodity dependence and the incidence of extreme poverty reflects the impact of export structure on trade performance, and the difficulty that many commodity-dependent economies have had in starting and also sustaining economic growth. Although the situation has improved since the mid-1990s, when the whole record from the 1980s is viewed, it can be seen that many commodity-dependent LDCs have been characterized by economic stagnation or economic regression, or short growth spurts followed by an economic collapse of some sort, which may have been triggered by a natural disaster, a legitimacy crisis leading to civil conflict in extreme cases, or some kind of external shock.

This outcome reflects the fact that many commodity-dependent LDCs are caught in an international poverty trap. As argued in the last chapter, all very poor countries experience a number of interlocking domestic vicious circles that serve to perpetuate a cycle of economic stagnation and mass poverty. Integration with the world economy through trade, investment, technology imports, financial flows and movements of people and ideas can greatly help countries to break out of these vicious circles. But the form of integration must be favourable for this to happen. In the commodity-dependent LDCs, the form of integration is not favourable. Indeed, external trade and financial relations are reinforcing, rather than serving to break, the domestic vicious circles that perpetuate poverty. It is in this sense that the poverty trap can be described as international.

A weak trade performance is an essential ingredient of the international poverty trap. But primary commodity dependence is related to poverty not only through trade, but also through the way in which weak trade performance is related to external indebtedness, and how external indebtedness in turn is related to access to external private capital and aid effectiveness. Associated with slow export growth, and also with large external shocks due to commodity price instability, there has been a build-up of unsustainable external debt in the non-oil commodity exporters. During 1998–2000, before the enhanced HIPC Initiative started to deliver more substantial debt relief, all the primary-commodity-exporting LDCs except Bhutan, Eritrea, Uganda and the Solomon Islands had an external debt burden which according to the international norms of the Initiative was unsustainable.[6] As debts – which are mainly owed to official creditors – have built up, aid disbursements have increasingly been allocated, either implicitly or explicitly, to ensure that official debts are serviced. In this aid/debt service system, the developmental impact of aid has been undermined as the "debt-tail" has been wagging the "aid-dog". But indebtedness has also served as one factor reducing the attractiveness of LDCs to foreign private investors and lenders, thus increasing dependence on official capital inflows.

Poverty reduction in these circumstances requires a concerted effort to escape this international poverty trap (see *The Least Developed Countries Report 2002*). An improved trade performance, as well as increased import capacity, is certainly going to be a necessary condition. But it remains to be seen whether export expansion alone will be sufficient in itself.

C. The frequency of export expansion with poverty reduction

1. THE OVERALL PATTERN IN THE 1990S

Although it is very difficult to reduce poverty in an LDC if exports are not growing and import capacity is severely constrained, this does not mean that the contrary is true — namely, that export growth will reduce poverty. The improved export performance of many LDCs from the late 1980s and in the 1990s provides evidence of whether it actually does. This section examines the frequency with which export expansion in the LDCs has been associated with poverty reduction.

The discussion is based on the charts in the annex to this chapter. These show trends in average private consumption per capita (in 1985 PPP $) and real exports over the past two decades in all LDCs for which data were available. On the basis of the poverty curves in the previous chapter, the trend in average private consumption per capita will be used as a proxy measure of the direction of change in the incidence of $1/day and $2/day poverty (see box 8). This approach does not provide precise quantitative estimates of the incidence and depth of poverty, nor of the number of poor. However, given the close association between average private consumption per capita and the incidence of $1/day and $2/day poverty in countries at the level of development of the LDCs, it enables identification of countries and periods in which export expansion is likely to be associated with a reduction of poverty, with a stagnation of poverty levels, and with a raise of poverty levels. If increases in average private consumption per capita are substantial and sustained over time, it is most likely that the incidence of $1/day and $2/day poverty is decreasing. If average private consumption changes little, it is most likely that the incidence of poverty is not decreasing. If average private consumption per capita is decreasing, it is likely that the incidence of poverty is increasing.

The charts in the annex show that in 19 out of the 32 LDCs for which a sufficiently long data series is available, average private consumption per capita was lower in 2000 than in 1980. This is an indication of the long-term growth

Primary commodity dependence is related to poverty not only through trade, but also through the way in which weak trade performance is related to external indebtedness, and how external indebtedness in turn is related to access to external private capital and aid effectiveness.

Box 8. Trends in average private consumption per capita as a proxy measure for trends in poverty

This chapter and the next two use trends in private consumption per capita (in constant 1985 PPP dollars) as a proxy measure for trends in poverty. This approach is possible in studying poverty trends in an LDC context as there is a close statistical relationship between average private consumption per capita and the incidence of $1/day and $2/day poverty in African and Asian countries with private consumption of less than $2,400 a year (in 1985 PPP dollars) — see previous chapter. Given this relationship, it is possible to use data on average private consumption per capita to analyse general long-term poverty trends but without entering into the statistical controversies about the precise level of poverty in any particular country. With this approach, it has also been possible to make use of the most complete and up-to-date estimates of private consumption in the LDCs from the Penn World Table version 6.1, which were published during the preparation of this Report.

Any proxy measure contains less information than the object which it measures. Because the relationship between average private consumption per capita and poverty is not a straight line (see previous chapter, chart 9), an increase in private consumption per capita can be associated with a greater or lesser fall in the incidence of poverty in different LDCs. This is not captured by the proxy measure.

Also, the statistical relationship between average private consumption per capita and the incidence of poverty is a long-term empirical regularity that is based on a sample of LDCs and other lower-income countries with data from different years. It indicates the typical pattern of the relationship that one would expect to obtain if a country sustained growth in private consumption per capita. But in the short term, it is possible that the precise trend in poverty diverges from the long-term pattern. Such divergences in the short term from the long-term relationship can be observed. In some cases, they indicate that the inequality in consumption expenditure is increasing faster than would be expected if a country followed exactly the long-term trend. However, although this slows down the decrease in the incidence of poverty associated with increasing private consumption, in all the LDCs for which there are survey data and for which trends can be estimated, increasing private consumption per capita was associated with a decreasing incidence of poverty, and vice versa.

A stronger objection to using average private consumption per capita as a proxy measure of poverty is that it contains measurement errors and that it also contains items other than household consumption — notably, consumption by non-profit institutions (Deaton, 2004: 36). Large measurement errors are however contained in household survey means, and the survey averages also exclude items such as imputed rents to homeowners, which are included in national accounts estimates. The reader should be aware of this difference. However, as noted earlier (box 6), this Report is based on the view that national-accounts-consistent poverty estimates are as plausible as household-survey-based estimates, and that private consumption data from national accounts have a role to play.

In the end, analysis of trends in development, trade and poverty in the LDCs is always based on imperfect statistics. The task is to make the best of what is available in order to identify and explain emerging patterns. This is what we seek to do here.

failure discussed in the last section. But in contrast, in almost all the LDCs for which a sufficiently long data series is available — 23 out of 25 countries — exports of goods and services were higher in 2001 than in 1980. Although export instability makes the patterns somewhat complex, there was a more or less dramatic "export take-off" in many of the countries during the past two decades. The dates of export take-off, which are apparent in either an acceleration of export growth or a reversal of export decline, may be roughly identified on the basis of the annex charts:

- Acceleration of a growth in exports — e.g. Bangladesh: 1985 and 1994; Benin: 1996; Burundi: 1996; Cape Verde: 1992; Equatorial Guinea: 1993; Guinea: 1994; Guinea-Bissau: 1993 and 1998; Lesotho: 1990; Madagascar: 1998; Malawi: 1995; Mali: 1988 and 1996; Mauritania: 1997; Mozambique: 1990; Myanmar: 1987 and 1995; Senegal: 1994; Sudan: 1998; Uganda: 1993; Zambia: 1995

- Reversal of a decline in exports — e.g. Benin: 1990; Comoros: 1998; Democratic Republic of the Congo: 1994; Ethiopia: 1992; Madagascar: 1988; Mauritania: 1993; Niger: 1994; Rwanda: 1994; Sao Tome and Principe: 1996; Zambia: 1990.

The cause of the export take-off varies from country to country. In some countries, it is associated with the development of new manufactures or services exports, or the exploitation of mineral or oil resources. In others, it reflects policy reform. However, what is interesting in this context is the frequency with which export expansion is associated with rising average private consumption per capita. The charts show that there is a repeated pattern in which there is a sharp rise in exports that is associated with little change in private consumption per capita or even a decline. These are situations which will be described here as situations of "export expansion without poverty reduction", or, where average private consumption per capita declines substantially, as situations of "immiserizing trade".

Table 31 summarizes the frequency of these different situations in the LDCs for which data are available in the periods 1990–1995 and/or 1995–2000. The observations (one country for each period) are classified into six groups according to whether exports grew or declined over the period and whether private consumption per capita grew by more than 1 per cent per annum, declined by more than 1 per cent per annum, or either grew or declined sluggishly (between +1.0 per cent per annum and –1.0 per cent per annum). From table 31 a number of tendencies are clear:

- Only 15 out of the 66 cases have negative export growth rates.

- Average private consumption per capita is growing by more than 1 per cent per annum in only one out of the 15 cases which have negative export growth rates.

- But out of the 51 cases with positive export growth rates, average private consumption per capita is also growing by more than 1 per cent per annum in 22.

- Out of the 51 cases with positive export growth rates, average private consumption growth per capita is falling by more than 1 per cent per annum in 18.

There is a repeated pattern in which a sharp rise in exports is associated with little change in private consumption per capita or even a decline.

These findings suggest that positive export growth rates are a necessary condition for poverty reduction. But export expansion is no guarantee of poverty reduction. Indeed, situations of export expansion with poverty reduction are less frequent in the LDC context than in situations of export expansion without poverty reduction and situations of immiserizing trade. One third of the cases in the 1990s are situations of immiserizing trade.

A positive aspect of the pattern of change is that there are more cases in which export growth is associated with rising average private consumption per capita in the period 1995–2000 than in the period 1990–1995 (chart 20). Moreover, if one simply divides the countries into those in which average private consumption per capita is rising and those in which it is falling, export expansion is occurring along with rising private consumption per capita in 59 per cent of cases (30 out of 51). However, as chart 20 shows, there is no statistically significant relationship between export growth and growth in average private consumption per capita in either the first half or the second half of the 1990s. Moreover, the evidence of the last chapter indicates that reducing the incidence of $1/day poverty in the LDCs requires sustained and substantial increases in average private consumption per capita. Amongst the 51 cases with positive export growth rates, there are only three countries — Bangladesh, Guinea and Uganda — in which average private consumption growth rates exceeded 1 per cent per annum in both 1990–1995 and 1995–2000.

TABLE 31. CLASSIFICATION OF LDCS ON THE BASIS OF THEIR REAL GROWTH RATES OF PRIVATE CONSUMPTION
PER CAPITA AND OF EXPORTS OF GOODS AND SERVICES, 1990–1995 AND 1995–2000

		Real growth rate of private consumption per capita per annum (1985 PPP $)					
		Over 1%		Between -1% and 1%		Lower than -1%	
Real growth rate of exports of goods and services per annum (%)	Positive	Bangladesh	1990–1995	Benin	1990–1995	Angola	1990–1994
		Eritrea[a]	1992–1995	Cape Verde	1990–1995	Burundi	1990–1995
		Ethiopia	1990–1995	Malawi	1990–1995	Chad	1990–1995
		Guinea	1990–1995	Utd. Rep. of Tanzania	1990–1995	Comoros	1990–1995
		Guinea–Bissau	1990–1995	Burkina Faso	1995–2000	Equatorial Guinea	1990–1995
		Mauritania	1990–1995	Cambodia[a]	1995–2000	Lesotho	1990–1995
		Myanmar[a]	1990–1995	Ethiopia	1995–2000	Madagascar	1990–1995
		Uganda	1990–1995	Mali	1995–2000	Mali	1990–1995
		Yemen[a]	1990–1995	Myanmar[a]	1995–2000	Mozambique	1990–1995
		Zambia	1990–1995	Niger	1995–1999	Vanuatu[a]	1990–1995
		Bangladesh	1995–2000	Zambia	1995–2000	Burundi	1995–2000
		Benin	1995–2000			Dem. Rep. of the Congo	1995–2000
		Cape Verde	1995–2000			Guinea-Bissau	1995–2000
		Equatorial Guinea	1995–2000			Lesotho	1995–2000
		Gambia	1995–2000			Maldives[a]	1995–2000
		Guinea	1995–2000			Sao Tome and Principe	1995–2000
		Madagascar	1995–2000			United Rep. of Tanzania	1995–2000
		Malawi	1995–2000			Yemen[a]	1995–2000
		Mozambique	1995–2000				
		Rwanda	1995–2000				
		Senegal	1995–2000				
		Uganda	1995–2000				
	Negative	Togo	1995–2000	Burkina Faso	1990–1995	Dem. Rep. of the Congo	1990–1995
				Gambia	1990–1995	Niger	1990–1995
				Mauritania	1995–2000	Rwanda	1990–1995
						Sao Tome and Principe	1990–1995
						Senegal	1990–1995
						Sierra Leone	1990–1995
						Togo	1990–1995
						Chad	1995–2000
						Comoros	1995–2000
						Eritrea[a]	1995–2000
						Sierra Leone	1995–2000

Source: UNCTAD secretariat classification based on World Bank, *World Development Indicators 2003*, CD-ROM; and Heston, Summers and Aten (2002).

Note: Countries highlighted in *italics* are those which display sluggish but negative private consumption per capita growth rates.
  a Owing to lack of data, the real growth rate of private consumption per capita was calculated using data in constant local currency units.

2. THE UBIQUITY OF EXPORT EXPANSION WITHOUT POVERTY REDUCTION

Poverty has been increasing in many of the mineral exporters because of a weak trade performance.

Export expansion without poverty reduction and immiserizing trade are found in a wide range of countries regardless of their export structure. One may expect these phenomena to occur in both oil and mineral exporters owing to the possibility of an enclave-based pattern of export expansion and economic growth. In reality, however, poverty has been increasing in many of the mineral exporters because of a weak trade performance. But real export growth rates of over 5 per cent per annum in Niger and Zambia in the period 1995–2000 are associated with very slow increases in average private consumption per capita — less than 1 per cent per annum in each case — and the Democratic Republic of the Congo is a case of immiserizing trade in the same period. Export growth of 11.1 per cent per annum is associated with falling average private consumption per capita of 6.6 per cent per annum. Amongst the oil exporters, Angola and Equatorial Guinea in the first half of the 1990s, and Yemen in the second half of the 1990s, are cases of immiserizing trade. Both Yemen (1990–1995) and Equatorial Guinea (1995–2000) appear to be cases of export expansion with

CHART 20. THE RELATIONSHIP BETWEEN REAL EXPORT GROWTH AND GROWTH IN PRIVATE CONSUMPTION PER CAPITA (IN 1985 PPP $) IN LDCS, 1990–2000

(Average annual growth rate, percentage)

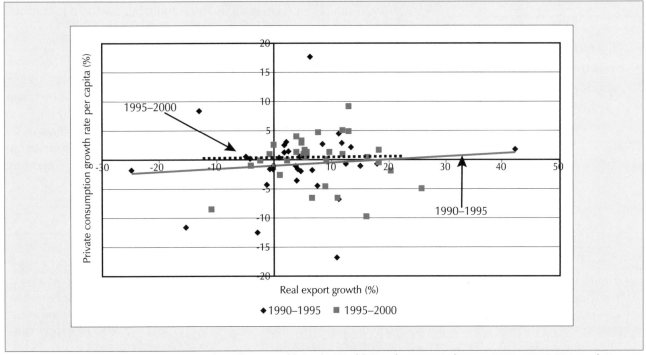

Source: UNCTAD secretariat estimates, based on World Bank, *World Development Indicators 2003,* CD-ROM; and Heston, Summers and Aten (2002).

Notes: The Pearson Product Moment Correlation coefficient between real export growth and growth in private consumption per capita was P = 0.1 for the period 1990–1995 and P = 0.02 for the period 1995–2000. In neither case is the relation statistically significant at the 10 per cent level. Equatorial Guinea and Sierra Leone were excluded from the sample because they were outliers. Export growth rate is based on constant 1995 $.

poverty reduction. But in each case there was a massive increase in oil exports, and consumption growth lagged behind significantly. Guinea's experience seems to be the most favourable amongst the mineral exporters. However, evidence in chapter 5, section F, indicates that the growth of private consumption per capita has been because of a weak link between the capital intensive mining sector and the rest of the economy.

For LDCs exporting agricultural commodities, there is a mixed picture which reflects differences in export performance and also differences in the inclusiveness of the export growth process, which is related to the organization of production (plantations versus smallholders), access by farmers to production inputs (credit, land and labour), trends in productivity and prices, the bargaining power of farmers in relation to traders and processors, and the relationship between export crop expansion and food prices. Amongst the countries which experienced a dramatic surge in exports in the 1990s but very little improvement in the level of private consumption per capita are Ethiopia (1995–2000), Mali (1995–2000) and the United Republic of Tanzania (1990–1995). In those countries, export growth rates in the periods indicated were 9.2 per cent per annum, 11.9 per cent per annum and 17.8 per cent per annum respectively, but at the same time average private consumption per capita stagnated in Ethiopia, only grew by 0.9 per cent per annum in Mali and declined by 0.7 per cent per annum in the United Republic of Tanzania. Burundi is a case of immiserizing trade in both periods, and situations of immiserizing trade are also evident in Chad (1990–1995), Mali (1990–1995), Sao Tome and Principe (1995–2000), Guinea-Bissau (1995–2000) and the United Republic of Tanzania (1995–2000) (see box 9). In three of these cases — Mali, Guinea-Bissau, and

For LDCs exporting agricultural commodities, there is a mixed picture which reflects differences in export performance and also differences in the inclusiveness of the export growth process.

Sao Tome and Principe — export growth rate in the period in question exceeded 5 per cent per annum. Uganda stands out as a positive case of export expansion with sustained poverty reduction. Malawi also had a situation of export growth with poverty reduction in 1995–2000, but the trend towards the end of that period was not so favourable (see annex charts).

It might be expected that manufactures exporters and services exporters would have a more positive trade–poverty relationship than the other country groups. They have had a better export performance than other country groups and the channels through which export expansion feeds through to improved incomes and consumption are likely to be more straightforward than in the mineral and oil economies (where the institutions governing the distribution of rents are critical) and the agricultural economies (where the pass-through of the gains from trade to the farm-gate level may be precarious).

Uganda stands out as a positive case of export expansion with sustained poverty reduction.

BOX 9. THE "MACRO-MICRO PARADOX" IN THE UNITED REPUBLIC OF TANZANIA

Tanzanian economists have described the situation in their country, in which there has been a combination of better macroeconomic performance in the 1990s, particularly from the mid-1990s onwards, but this has not been associated with poverty reduction, as an example of a "macro-micro paradox". In examining possible missing links between macroeconomic growth and poverty reduction at the micro level, Wuyts (2003) highlights five important features of the relationship between trade, growth and poverty in the United Republic of Tanzania.

Firstly, although GDP growth averaged 3–6 per cent per annum between 1991 and 2001, population grew by 2.8 per cent per annum. The resulting average annual growth rate of GDP per capita was only 0.8 per cent per annum. Even with optimistic assumptions about the overall elasticity of poverty reduction with respect to GDP per capita, the resulting effect on poverty reduction would have been modest, given also the slight increase in income inequality over the period in question.

Secondly, the volume of exports increased by nearly 10 per cent per annum for exports of goods and services and by 7.8 per cent for exports of goods during 1987–2001. But adverse terms-of-trade shifts have meant that the purchasing power of exports has grown at a slower rate — 7.2 per cent per annum for goods and services and 4 per cent for goods only. In volume terms, imports of goods and services grew by only 2.4 per cent per annum over the period 1987–2001 and imports of goods increased by only 1.6 per cent per annum. In effect, the terms-of-trade shifts have reduced the pay-off to increased production efforts in terms of expansion of the capacity to import.

Thirdly, for the main cash crop exports, the volume of export growth has been relatively slow, averaging 3.6 per cent per annum over the period 1987–2001. Adverse terms-of-trade shifts mean that the purchasing power of the main cash crop exports actually declined by 1 per cent per annum during the period 1987–2001. This is immensely significant for poverty reduction. It is one key to understanding why there was no significant poverty reduction in rural areas over that period, despite strong export growth. The price index of cash crops in 2001 stood at just 54 per cent of its level in 1994. Falling export prices and falling output have eroded rural incomes.

Fourthly, the rapid export growth in the 1990s was accompanied by a major change in the composition of exports. The share of manufactures exports in total merchandise exports fell from 24 per cent in 1990 to 7 per cent in 2001. Over the same period, there was a shift in the relative importance of agriculture and minerals in merchandise exports. Between 1994 and 2001, the share of the former fell from 65 per cent to 28 per cent, whilst the share of the latter rose from about 17 per cent to 39 per cent. Since the mid-1990s, the share of services, especially tourism, in total exports of goods and services has risen from about 20 per cent to 43–48 per cent of total export earnings.

Fifthly, although mining and tourism have emerged as the new engines of growth in the Tanzanian economy, cash crop production is still a much more important source in people's livelihoods than either mining or tourism. As a consequence, the employment and income effects emanating from the growth sectors are likely not to have been sufficient to offset the depressing effect of falling international agricultural prices on rural incomes.

Wuyts concludes that "successful poverty reduction must come to terms with the question how a country like Tanzania can realistically build upon and dynamically change its comparative advantage in ways that promote productivity and higher standards of living rather than exacting increased efforts for shaky returns." (Wuyts, 2003: 28).

Source: Wuyts, 2003.

Amongst the services exporters, export expansion with poverty reduction is apparent in Cape Verde and the Gambia in the period 1995–2000. But Comoros (1990–1995), Vanuatu (1990–1995) and Maldives (1995–2000) are clear cases of immiserizing trade. Their exports grew by 7.7 per cent per annum, 3.7 per cent per annum and 8.9 per cent per annum respectively. But private consumption per capita declined by 4.5 per cent per annum, 1.1 per cent per annum and 4.6 per cent per annum respectively.

With regard to manufactures exporters, Bangladesh is doing well in terms of both export growth and rising private consumption per capita, but as in Uganda, the rate of growth of consumption lags behind export growth significantly. In Cambodia (1995–2000) export growth of 18.3 per cent per annum is associated with falling private consumption per capita of 0.6 per cent per annum. Lesotho appears to have had a situation of immiserizing trade in both periods — exports expanding by 11.2 per cent per annum and 6.6 per cent per annum in 1990–1995 and 1995–2000, and private consumption per capita falling by 6.8 per cent per annum and 6.5 per cent per annum over the same periods. Madagascar is an interesting case which diversified into manufactures exports in the 1990s. During the first half of the 1990s, it had a situation of immiserizing trade, but in the second half of the 1990s export expansion of 4 per cent per annum was associated with private consumption per capita rising by one per cent per annum.

With regard to manufactures exporters, Bangladesh is doing well in terms of both export growth and rising private consumption per capita, but as in Uganda, the rate of growth of consumption lags behind export growth significantly.

D. The trade–growth relationship

The infrequency of export expansion with poverty reduction in the LDCs may have two causes. First, export growth may not be facilitating sustained economic growth at levels sufficient to lead to substantial poverty reduction. Second, economic growth may not be of an inclusive form that increases average household incomes and consumption. This section looks at the former issue.

1. Exports and economic growth

The relationship between export growth and output growth varies between countries and over time. Chart 21A shows the relationships between export growth and GDP growth in the LDCs and other developing countries in the 1990s. Generally, as one would expect given that exports are a component of GDP in national accounts, there is a positive association between the two variables — the higher the export growth rate, the higher the GDP growth rate. However, the relationship is slightly stronger in the other developing countries than in the LDCs in terms of the closeness of the association between the two variables. It is notable also that the additional GDP growth associated with additional export growth is similar for both the LDCs and the other developing countries. This is apparent in the similar slope of the two trend lines which depict the average relationship. However, at any level of export growth, a given export growth rate is associated with a slightly lower output growth rate in the LDCs than in the other developing countries.

At any level of export growth, a given export growth rate is associated with a slightly lower output growth rate in the LDCs than in the other developing countries.

This is quite significant because a necessary minimum condition for poverty reduction to occur is that the rate of economic growth is fast enough for GDP per capita to increase. Population growth rates tend to be higher in the LDCs, and in these circumstances it is possible that despite the positive relationship between export growth and output growth, export growth may not be generating a sufficiently high output growth rate to ensure increasing GDP per capita.

Chart 21B shows the relationship between export growth and growth of GDP per capita in LDCs and other developing countries in the 1990s. Once again there is generally a positive relationship between the two variables – the higher the export growth rate, the higher the GDP per capita growth rate. Moreover, the relationship is again slightly stronger in the other developing countries than in the LDCs in terms of the association between the two variables and also in the additional GDP per capita growth associated with additional export growth. However, at any level of export growth, a given export growth rate is associated with lower growth of GDP per capita in the LDCs than in other developing countries. For the LDCs, the relationship between export growth and GDP per capita growth is actually such that for a positive export growth rate between 0 and 5 per cent per annum there is a greater probability that export growth will be associated with declining GDP per capita than with increasing GDP per capita.

Amongst the LDCs, positive export growth is associated with declining GDP per capita in about a third of the countries.

It is clear that in almost all cases, whether LDCs or other developing countries, declining exports are associated with declining GDP per capita. But amongst the LDCs, positive export growth is associated with declining GDP per capita in about a third of the countries. This proportion is about three times higher than that of the group of other developing countries. This pattern reflects the fact that a higher proportion of the LDCs have real export growth rates of less than 5 per cent per annum. This is a "zone of ambiguity" where export growth may or may not be associated with output growth rates high enough to increase

CHART 21. THE RELATIONSHIP BETWEEN EXPORT GROWTH AND GDP GROWTH, AND EXPORT GROWTH AND GDP PER CAPITA GROWTH, IN LDCS AND OTHER DEVELOPING COUNTRIES, 1990–2000

(Average annual growth rate, percentage)

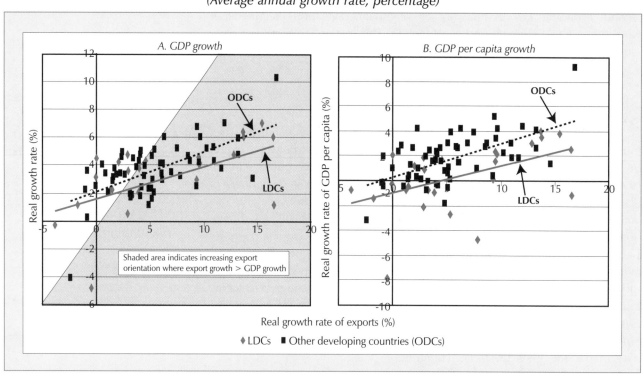

Source: UNCTAD secretariat estimates, based on World Bank, *World Development Indicators 2003,* CD-ROM.

Notes: The Pearson Product Moment Correlation coefficient for the relationship between the real growth rate of exports and real GDP growth is $P = 0.51^*$ for the LDCs and $P = 0.62^*$ for the other developing countries.
The Pearson Product Moment Correlation coefficient for the relationship between the real growth rate of exports and real GDP per capita growth is $P = 0.49^*$ for the LDCs and $P = 0.59^*$ for the ODCs.
* implies 1 per cent significance level.

GDP per capita. But there are also some LDCs with higher export growth rates in which GDP per capita has also been declining.

The relationship between exports and economic growth can also be analysed in terms of changes in the export orientation of the domestic economy (measured by the export/GDP ratio). Chart 21A indicates in which countries real exports were growing faster than real GDP and thus where export orientation was increasing. It is evident that the threshold of real export growth rate of 5 per cent per annum is also important in terms of increasing export orientation. Increasing export orientation was occurring in all the countries, whether least developed countries or other developing countries, with export growth rates above the threshold level. Below that level, there are some countries in which export growth is associated with increasing export orientation and others where it is associated with decreasing export orientation.

It is clear that the LDCs in which GDP per capita growth was fastest also experienced increasing export orientation of their domestic economies. But increasing export orientation was not always associated with increases in GDP per capita. This applies mainly to the LDCs in the "zone of ambiguity", with a positive export growth rates of less than 5 per cent. But the combination of increasing export orientation and stagnant or falling GDP per capita is also apparent in a few other LDCs.

To sum up, there is some support for the proposition that the relationship between export growth and output growth is weaker in the LDCs than in other developing countries. Declining exports are associated with falling GDP per capita in both LDCs and other developing countries, but a higher proportion of the LDCs (almost a third) have positive export growth rates and declining GDP per capita. This reflects three factors. First, the population growth rates of the LDCs are higher. Second, at any given export growth rate, the output growth rate is generally lower in the LDCs than in the other developing countries. Third, a higher proportion of LDCs with positive export growth rates are in the "zone of ambiguity" where export growth rates are below 5 per cent per annum. For such LDCs, there is an equal probability that export growth will be associated with falling GDP per capita or rising GDP per capita.

A basic condition for export growth to translate into output growth is for export growth to be associated with increases in import capacity. But import growth rates lagged behind export growth rates in most LDCs in the 1990s.

2. IMPORTS, INVESTMENT AND ECONOMIC GROWTH

In the previous chapter, it was argued that exports can have an important effect on economic growth in the LDCs through their import-supply effects, and that an important condition for such effects to translate into economic growth was the existence of a dynamic investment–export nexus. It is possible to identify some of the possible missing links in the relationship between exports and economic growth in the LDCs by examining the relationship between export growth and import growth, import growth and investment growth, and investment growth and output growth.

As a major positive impact of exports on growth occurs through their import-supply effects, a basic condition for export growth to translate into output growth is for export growth to be associated with increases in import capacity. The extent to which this has been occurring is evident in chart 22. This shows that import growth rates lagged behind export growth rates in most LDCs in the 1990s. Import growth rates (measured in constant terms) were lower than export growth rates in 24 out of 32 LDCs for which data are available for the period 1990–1995, and in 20 out of 32 LDCs for the period 1995–2001.

CHART 22. THE RELATIONSHIP BETWEEN EXPORT GROWTH AND IMPORT GROWTH IN LDCs, BY COUNTRY, 1990–1995 AND 1995–2001

(Real average annual growth rate, percentage)

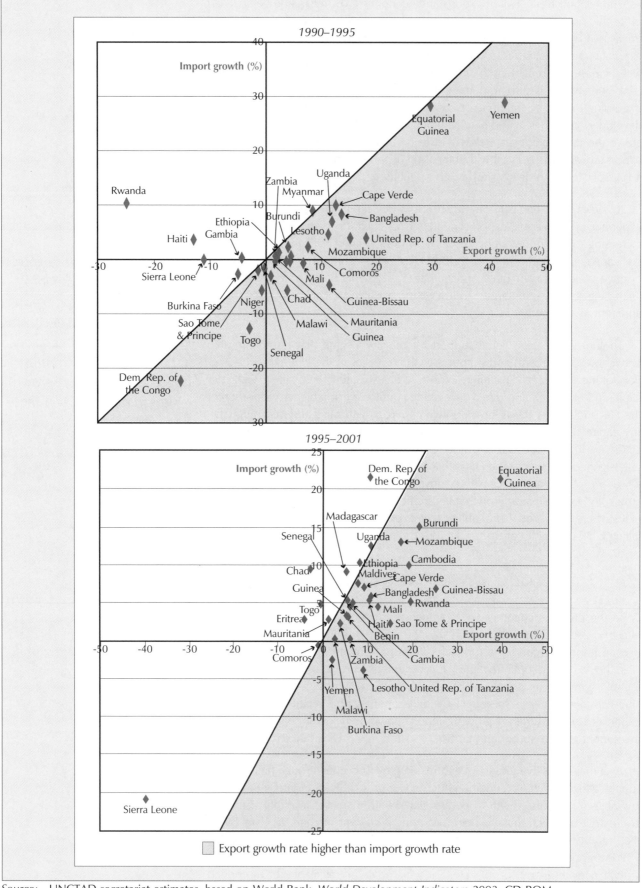

Source: UNCTAD secretariat estimates, based on World Bank, *World Development Indicators 2003,* CD-ROM.

Note: Calculations are based on data in constant local currency.

The precise reasons why improved export growth rates have not been fully reflected in improved import growth rates are unclear. But in some countries, such as Bangladesh, this may be due to declining aid inflows, which have fallen in tandem with rising exports. In other countries it may be related to falling aid coupled with changes in debt service obligations. The situation is complicated here because although the HIPC Initiative has reduced the contractual debt service obligations, many countries were previously accumulating debt repayment arrears to external creditors. Thus in a few cases, the "normalization" of debt service repayments has entailed a decrease in contractual debt service payments but an increase in actual debt service payments. Export growth will not translate into a concomitant increase in import capacity unless debt relief is additional to aid inflows.

Additional import growth is associated with greater increases in investment in the LDCs than in other developing countries.

Given the import sensitivity of LDC economies, import growth may be expected to be strongly associated with investment growth. Chart 23A depicts the relationship between these two variables in LDCs and in other developing countries in the 1990s. There is generally a positive relationship — increases in imports are associated with increases in investment. But the association between import growth and investment growth is closer in the LDCs than in the other developing countries. Moreover, additional import growth is associated with greater increases in investment in the LDCs than in other developing countries. Increases in import capacity can thus be expected to translate into increases in investment in LDCs.

However, whether this will lead to economic growth depends on further conditions. Chart 23B depicts the relationship between investment growth and economic growth in the LDCs and other developing countries in the 1990s. In

CHART 23. THE RELATIONSHIP BETWEEN IMPORT GROWTH, INVESTMENT GROWTH AND GDP GROWTH
IN LDCS AND OTHER DEVELOPING COUNTRIES, 1990–2000
(Average annual growth rate, percentage)

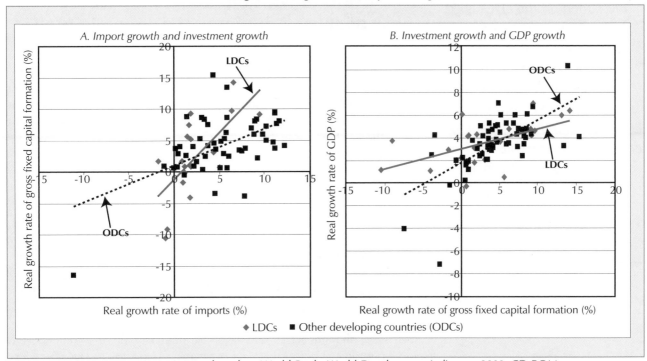

Source: UNCTAD secretariat estimates, based on World Bank, *World Development Indicators 2003,* CD-ROM.

Notes: The Pearson Product Moment Correlation coefficient for the relationship between import growth rates and the real growth rate of gross fixed capital formation is P = 0.67* for the LDCs and P = 0.54* for the ODCs.
The Pearson Product Moment Correlation coefficient for the relationship between the growth rate of gross fixed capital formation and real GDP growth is P = 0.57* for LDCs and P = 0.66* for ODCs.
* implies a 1 per cent significance level.

general, there is a positive relationship — increases in investment are associated with output growth. But in contrast to the import–investment relationship, the association between investment growth and output growth is closer in the other developing countries than in the LDCs. Moreover, additional investment is associated with greater increases in output in the other developing countries than in the LDCs. Increases in investment may thus be expected to have less strong effects on growth in the LDCs than in other developing countries.

...But in contrast to the import–investment relationship, the association between investment growth and output growth is closer in the other developing countries than in the LDCs.

The relationship between investment growth and output growth is a key link in the causal chain through export growth can lead to rates of economic growth high enough to be able to reduce poverty. As analysed in *The Least Developed Countries Report 2000* (part 2, chapter 1), the low efficiency of investment in the LDCs is related to a number of factors, including the low level of investment, the weakness of the domestic entrepreneurial class and the fact that central accumulation and budgetary mechanisms in the LDCs have been dominated by external sources of finance (mainly ODA) rather than by domestic resources. During the period from 1990 to 2001, aid accounted for 50 per cent of total annual capital formation in the LDCs as a group, as compared with 5 per cent in low- and middle-income countries. The importance of aid for capital formation declined in the second half of the 1990s. But by 2001 the median contribution of aid was 62 per cent of total capital formation. In these circumstances, weaknesses in aid delivery, including major coordination problems, lack of national ownership and orientation to national priorities, instability and unpredictability, can all undermine the investment–growth relationship. It is for this reason that improvements in the aid relationship through the PRSP approach, which was initiated at the end of 1999, as well as a successful resolution of the official debt problem, are so important for improving the trade–poverty relationship in the LDCs.

The low efficiency of investment in the LDCs is related to a number of factors, including the low level of investment, the weakness of the domestic entrepreneurial class and the fact that central accumulation and budgetary mechanisms in the LDCs have been dominated by external sources of finance (mainly ODA).

E. Trade expansion, domestic resource mobilization and the form of economic growth

Poverty reduction requires not simply sustained economic growth, but also an inclusive form of economic growth. This section considers three possible factors related to the form of economic growth that may be contributing to trade expansion without poverty reduction and to immiserizing trade. They are the following: the level of income inequality; the demand-side sources of economic growth; and the scale of domestic resource mobilization efforts.

1. LEVEL OF INEQUALITY

One factor affecting the relationship between export growth and growth of private consumption per capita is the level of inequality in a country. One would expect that in high-inequality countries there may be an enclave pattern of growth whereby all the benefits of export expansion are concentrated in the hands of a minority.

Analysis of the impact of the level of inequality on the trade–poverty relationship is difficult because of data constraints. There are 18 LDCs for which there are estimates of income distribution in the 1990s. When these countries are divided into high-inequality, medium-inequality or low-inequality countries, according to whether they are in the top third, middle third or bottom third of developing countries ranked according to their Gini coefficients in the 1990s, it is apparent that there is some evidence that export expansion is less likely to translate into poverty reduction in countries with a high level of inequality. Export growth in the high-inequality LDCs is almost the same as in the low-inequality and intermediate-inequality LDCs, but it is associated with slowly decreasing rather than slowly increasing average private consumption per capita (chart 24).

These patterns need much more research. There are some low-inequality LDCs, such as the United Republic of Tanzania, where export growth is not associated with growth in average private consumption per capita, and some high-inequality LDCs, such as Malawi, where it was so associated in the 1990s. What matters in these cases is not simply the initial level of inequality but also the way in which the level is changing over time with economic growth and export growth.

Export expansion is less likely to translate into poverty reduction in countries with a high level of inequality.

2. BALANCE IN THE DEMAND-SIDE COMPONENTS OF ECONOMIC GROWTH

A second factor that might affect the trade-poverty relationship is the relative importance of different demand-side components of economic growth — domestic demand expansion, export expansion and import substitution. It can be hypothesized that there is a weaker relationship between export expansion and private consumption per capita growth in countries where export expansion predominates as the major demand-side component of economic growth than in countries where there is a more balanced form of economic growth in which export expansion, domestic demand and import substitution all contribute. This hypothesis follows from the fact that there is no logical necessity, from an accounting point of view, for average private consumption per capita to be growing if economic growth is predominantly achieved through export expansion. Domestic demand expansion can be based on increases in

CHART 24. REAL EXPORT GROWTH AND GROWTH OF PRIVATE CONSUMPTION PER CAPITA (IN 1985 PPP $) IN 18 LDCs[a] CLASSIFIED BY LEVEL OF INEQUALITY[b], 1990–2000

(Average annual growth rate, percentage)

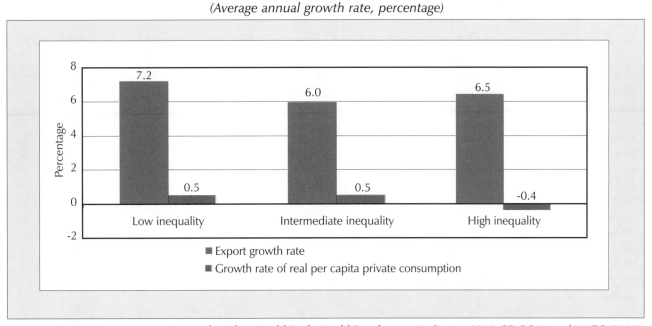

Source: UNCTAD secretariat estimates, based on World Bank, *World Development Indicators 2003,* CD-ROM; and UNDP (2003).

    a   The 18 LDCs for which GINI index, real export (constant 1995 $) and real private consumption (in 1985 PPP $) data are available are: Bangladesh, Burkina Faso, Burundi, Ethiopia, Gambia, Guinea, Guinea-Bissau, Lesotho, Madagascar, Malawi, Mali, Mauritania, Mozambique, Rwanda, Senegal, Uganda, United Republic of Tanzania and Zambia. Sierra Leone was excluded as it was an outlier.

    b   Low inequality refers to countries for which GINI indices are below 42; intermediate inequality refers to countries for which GINI indices are between 42 and 50; and high inequality refers to countries for which GINI indices are above 50.

investment, private consumption or public consumption. Depending on their relative contributions, average private consumption per capita is likely to be rising in countries where domestic demand expansion is making a significant contribution to overall output growth along with export expansion. Given the close relationship between trends in average private consumption per capita and trends in the incidence of poverty, it is likely therefore that in situations where domestic demand expansion is the most important demand-side component of economic growth the incidence of poverty will be falling.

Table 32 shows the results of a simple decomposition of the demand-side component of changes in GDP in the LDCs in the period 1990–1995 and 1995–2000. The basic method is derived from Chenery (1979) and is explained in Morley and Vos (2000). The decomposition has only been applied to countries and periods in which economic growth takes place. It indicates how much of the increase in GDP over each period can be attributed, in a simple accounting sense, to domestic demand expansion, import substitution and export expansion.[7]

TABLE 32. GDP GROWTH DECOMPOSITION ACCORDING TO CONTRIBUTION OF DOMESTIC DEMAND EXPANSION, IMPORT SUBSTITUTION AND EXPORT EXPANSION TO ECONOMIC GROWTH IN SELECTED LDCs, 1990–1995 AND 1995–2000

	GDP change[a] (Constant 1995 $, millions)		Domestic demand (DD) contribution		Import substitution (IS) contribution		Export expansion (EE) contribution		Country classification by type of real GDP growth	
			(As percentage of real GDP change)							
	1990–1995	1995–2000	1990–1995	1995–2000	1990–1995	1995–2000	1990–1995	1995–2000	1990–1995	1995–2000
Bangladesh	7 335.2	10 966.3	89.8	80.5	-12.7	1.1	22.9	18.4	DD1	DD2
Benin	377.1	588.4	72.0	78.1	11.0	7.0	17.0	14.8	DD2	DD2
Burkina Faso	440.3	552.6	79.7	80.9	31.5	13.0	-11.3	6.2	DD2	DD2
Cambodia	-	718.5	-	27.8	-	-26.0	-	98.2	-	EE
Cape Verde	109.9	179.3	108.4	84.0	-33.4	-5.9	25.0	22.0	DD1	DD1
Chad	127.2	237.6	-43.9	77.0	109.3	39.7	34.7	-16.7	IS	DD2
Comoros	8.5	11.2	127.7	45.1	-147.9	78.4	120.2	-23.5	DD1	DD2
Eritrea	-	42.2	-	199.2	-	-80.2	-	-19.0	-	DD2
Ethiopia	645.0	1 584.9	99.7	99.0	3.6	-27.2	-3.3	28.2	DD2	DD1
Gambia	37.7	100.8	138.6	44.6	-8.6	30.0	-30.0	25.4	DD2	DD1
Guinea	616.8	797.0	66.3	70.9	21.6	7.4	12.2	21.7	DD2	DD1
Guinea-Bissau	36.7	-	21.6	-	59.8	-	18.5	-	IS	-
Madagascar	-	654.1	-	111.8	-	-36.5	-	24.7	-	DD1
Malawi	194.9	310.5	15.6	56.0	76.0	26.1	8.4	17.9	IS	DD2
Maldives	-	131.7	-	34.9	-	-22.8	-	87.9	-	EE
Mali	330.2	723.0	40.7	53.3	26.7	11.8	32.6	34.9	DD1	DD1
Mauritania	181.4	250.4	57.1	77.4	16.2	22.6	26.7	0.0	DD1	DD2
Mozambique	344.1	1 070.9	44.6	100.8	19.0	-22.4	36.4	21.6	DD1	DD1
Niger	67.8	-	-129.2	-	229.5	-	-0.3	-	IS	-
Rwanda	-	767.1	-	80.0	-	9.9	-	10.0	-	DD2
Samoa	-	43.8	-	206.8	-	-152.8	-	46.0	-	DD1
Sao Tome and Principe	3.6	5.0	17.0	-50.9	85.2	70.8	-2.1	80.1	IS	EE
Uganda	1 654.0	1 972.1	91.5	102.8	-6.5	-26.4	15.0	23.6	DD2	DD1
Utd. Rep. of Tanzania	447.3	1 163.4	35.9	62.6	-30.9	26.4	95.0	11.0	EE	DD2
Vanuatu	38.1	-	27.1	-	49.7	-	23.2	-	IS	-
Yemen	1 005.2	1 303.1	93.4	27.3	-133.2	59.6	139.8	13.1	EE	DD2
Zambia	-	500.1	-	6.4	-	58.0	-	35.6	-	IS

Source: UNCTAD secretariat estimates, based on World Bank, *World Development Indicators 2003,* CD-ROM; and Heston, Summers and Aten (2002).

Note: A hyphen (-) indicates periods during which either the GDP change was negative or data were not available.
IS, EE and DD countries are countries in which import substitution, export expansion and domestic demand expansion, respectively, are the major demand-side components of economic growth. In DD1 countries, export expansion contributes to over 20 per cent of GDP change and domestic demand remains the major source of GDP change. DD2 countries are the remaining DD countries.
a Difference between end-year and starting-year.

It should be noted that this is a simple accounting procedure that identifies the relative contribution of each of the three components to changes in GDP over the respective periods. It does not imply any causal relations. Nor is it a description of policy. More research is required to get a more detailed view of what is happening through a breakdown at the sectoral level (for which this decomposition is usually applied) and also the identification of the multiplier effects of exports. It is also necessary to stress that the decomposition of demand-side components of economic growth is best complemented with a supply-side growth decomposition. But even though the method is simple, it reveals some interesting results.

First, for most LDCs expansion of domestic demand contributed the most to GDP growth during the 1990s. In the period 1995–2000, it was the major demand-side component of economic growth in 20 out of 24 LDCs for which data are available. For 14 out of the 24 LDCs the expansion of domestic demand contributed over 70 per cent to the total increase of GDP. This figure is in line with Chenery's estimates of the importance of domestic demand for countries in the early stages of development (see previous chapter). The magnitude of the importance of domestic demand implies that LDC Governments would be very unwise to ignore the need for a growing domestic market for economic growth.

For most LDCs expansion of domestic demand contributed the most to GDP growth during the 1990s.

Second, the contribution of import substitution to GDP growth in the LDCs declined in the 1990s. It was the major demand-side component of GDP increase in 1 out of 24 LDCs for which data are available during 1995–2000, as against 6 out of 20 countries in 1990–1995. But more striking is the fact that rather than import substitution, the opposite is occurring in many countries. With rising import-to-GDP ratios, a greater proportion of domestic consumption and investment is being met by imports rather than domestic production. The opposite of import substitution is occurring in 9 out of 24 LDCs. Moreover, in five LDCs — Ethiopia, Madagascar, Mozambique, Samoa and Uganda — the negative demand-side contribution of increasing import penetration was so great that it completely offset the positive demand-side contribution of export expansion as a component of economic growth.

The most favourable trade–poverty relationship seems to be in countries in which expansion of domestic demand contributes most to economic growth and export expansion makes an important complementary contribution.

Third, there is some evidence of increasing export orientation of the LDC economies during the 1990s. This is not apparent in the change in the countries in which export expansion was the major demand-side source of economic growth. This increased from two (United Republic of Tanzania and Yemen) in 1990–1995 to three in 1995–2000 (Cambodia, Maldives, and Sao Tome and Principe). But there were more countries in which the export expansion contribution to economic growth exceeded 20 per cent in the latter period than in the former period.

Is the trade–poverty relationship associated with patterns of economic growth differentiated according to their reliance on domestic demand expansion, export expansion and import substitution? The evidence suggests that it is. As chart 25 shows, the countries in which import substitution is the major demand-side component of economic growth have the lowest export growth rates, and private consumption per capita is also falling. The countries in which export expansion is the major demand-side component of economic growth have the highest export growth rates, but private consumption per capita is falling, and also at the highest rate of decline. On average the best trade–poverty relationship is found in LDCs where domestic demand expansion is the major demand-side component of economic growth. In those countries, exports are not growing as fast as in the countries in which export expansion is the major demand-side component of economic growth. But private consumption per capita is growing.

A closer look at the LDCs in which domestic demand is the major component of economic growth indicates diverse patterns. There is a tendency for private consumption per capita to be declining in countries in which domestic demand is the major component of economic growth, but exports are also declining. In the period 1995–2000 the most favourable trade–poverty relationship seems to be in countries in which expansion of domestic demand contributes most to economic growth and export expansion makes an important complementary contribution. It seems plausible to assume that the trade–poverty relationship is likely to be more favourable when the positive contribution of export growth is not strongly offset by the negative contribution arising because an increasing proportion of domestic consumption and investment is met from imports. But there is no clear evidence of this.

3. DOMESTIC RESOURCE MOBILIZATION EFFORT

A further factor affecting the trade–poverty relationship is the domestic resource mobilization effort associated with export expansion. The paucity of the available data makes this difficult to examine in terms of the conventional indicators of private and public domestic savings. But following the analysis in

CHART 25. REAL EXPORT GROWTH, REAL GDP GROWTH AND GROWTH IN REAL PRIVATE CONSUMPTION PER CAPITA (1985 PPP $) IN LDCs, CLASSIFIED ACCORDING TO DEMAND-SIDE COMPONENTS OF GROWTH, 1990–1995 AND 1995–2000[a]

(Average annual growth rate, percentage)

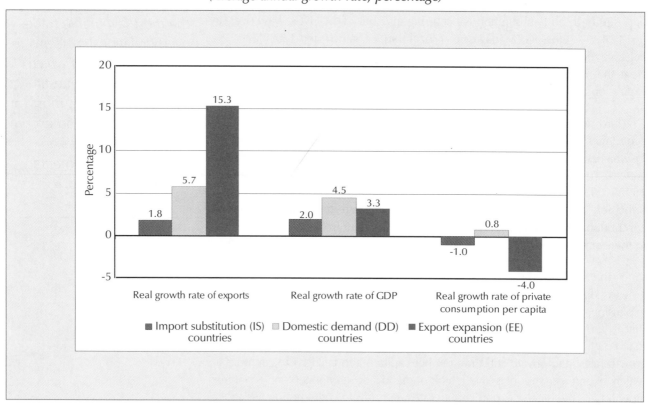

Source: UNCTAD secretariat estimates, based on World Bank, *World Development Indicators 2003,* CD-ROM; and Heston, Summers and Aten (2002).

Notes: Export and GDP data are in constant 1995 $. IS, EE and DD countries are countries in which import substitution, export expansion and domestic demand expansion respectively are the major demand-side contribution to GDP change.

a Based on total number of observations (one country in each period); see previous table.

The Least Developed Countries Report 2000 (part 2, chapter 1), a useful indicator of effort in terms of domestic resource mobilization is the "domestic resources available for finance" (DRAF) as a share of GDP. This section discusses trends in this variable in relation to export expansion.

The amount of "domestic resources available for finance" is calculated as the difference between GDP and private consumption. As a matter of accounting identity, this is equivalent to domestic investment plus government expenditure plus the surplus (or minus the deficit) of exports over imports of goods and services. A rising DRAF-to-GDP ratio indicates an increasing domestic resource mobilization effort. The share of private consumption in GDP is falling and, assuming that the rise is not related to an export surplus (which is equivalent to investment abroad), more domestic resources are being devoted to finance full utilization and development of productive capacities and also government expenditures necessary for the maintenance of an efficient civil service, the enforcement of law and order and the maintenance of stable social relations within civil society, and essential expenditures on health, education, water and sanitation.

An important feature of the LDCs is that in most of them private consumption forms a major share of GDP, and the domestic resources available for financing the full utilization and development of productive capacities, as well as essential government expenditure, are very limited. Based on a sample of 29 LDCs for which data were available private consumption was 81 per cent of GDP during 1990–2000 as against 60 per cent of GDP in other developing countries.[8]

These patterns reflect the fact that in poor economies where a large part of the population survives at near-subsistence levels of consumption, the majority of the inhabitants have to devote most of their resources to maintaining minimal levels of consumption. There is little room for devoting resources to savings and investment. The low DRAF-to-GDP ratios do not reflect a profligate consumption orientation on the part of the population and an unwillingness to save and invest. Rather, they are the result of very low levels of average consumption per capita. In these circumstances, a rising DRAF-to-GDP ratio, indicating an increased domestic resource mobilization effort, may be difficult to achieve. If it occurs, it indicates significant "belt tightening" amongst the population. Moreover, if it occurs in situations where GDP per capita is not growing, average private consumption per capita must inevitably fall.

A further factor affecting the trade–poverty relationship is the domestic resource mobilization effort associated with export expansion.

These relationships are important for understanding why export expansion without poverty reduction and immiserizing trade occur so frequently in the LDCs. Although the DRAF-to-GDP ratios in the LDCs are generally low, they have been increasing in recent years in quite a number of LDCs. These increases are often, though not invariably, related to export expansion.

In terms of achieving sustained economic growth, an increase in the DRAF-to-GDP ratio together with export expansion is positive. It is necessary to further decompose domestic resources available for finance to see exactly what is happening. But doing so is likely to indicate that investment growth is occurring along with export expansion. However, the problem for very poor countries is that "belt tightening" eats into average private consumption per capita. If the trade–growth relationship is weak and export expansion is not translating into growing GDP per capita, an increasing DRAF-to-GDP ratio can be achieved only at the expense of falling levels of private consumption per capita. Moreover, even if GDP per capita is increasing, the increasing DRAF-to-GDP ratio will slow down the rate of growth of private consumption per capita.

Table 33 shows trends in GDP per capita, exports, the DRAF-to-GDP ratio, investment and average private consumption per capita in the LDCs for which data are available for the periods 1990–1995 and 1995–2000. From this table it is apparent that there are two major ways in which the trade–poverty relationship is breaking down. First, export growth is not associated with rising GDP per capita. There are 23 cases where GDP per capita is declining and in 11 of them exports are increasing. In nine of the 11 cases average private consumption per capita is also declining. Second, export growth is associated with rising GDP per capita, but the "belt tightening" associated with domestic resource mobilization implies that average private consumption per capita is falling. There are in fact 34 cases in which GDP per capita is rising, and exports are increasing in 31 of them. But amongst these 31 cases, there are 9 in which private consumption per capita is falling. In 8 of these cases, there is a significant domestic resource mobilization effort in the sense that the DRAF-to-GDP ratio is increasing at more than 1.5 percentage points per annum and the share of private consumption per capita is falling concomitantly.

In the light of these findings, it is worthwhile to return to table 33, which identifies the frequency of situations of export expansion with poverty reduction, export expansion without poverty reduction and immiserizing trade. Once the domestic resource mobilization effort is related to this pattern, it is clear that a large number of the situations of export expansion without poverty reduction and immiserizing trade are related to a domestic resource mobilization effort. Of the 16 cases of immiserizing trade for which data on the DRAF-to-GDP ratio are available, there is evidence of a domestic resource mobilization in 10 of them, and it is strong, in the sense that the DRAF-to-GDP ratio is increasing by over 1.5 percentage points per annum in 8 of them. Of the 8 cases of export expansion without poverty reduction for which data on the DRAF-to-GDP ratio are available, there is evidence of a domestic resource mobilization effort in 5, and it is strong in 3 of them. Thus in almost two thirds of the cases in which export expansion is not likely to be associated with poverty reduction, the breakdown of the trade–poverty relationship is related to a domestic resource mobilization effort.

The coexistence of an increasing domestic resource mobilization effort and export expansion is, as noted earlier, potentially positive from the point of view of sustainable growth. If export expansion is occurring with a rising share of private consumption in GDP and a falling DRAF-to-GDP ratio, the export growth process may fizzle out. But equally in situations where the majority of the population are living at or near subsistence levels of consumption, if private consumption falls as a ratio of GDP this will create hardship. Indeed, such hardship may set a limit to the process of export expansion and also domestic resource mobilization. One example of this is the Gambia in the early 1980s, when a precipitous decline in the share of private consumption in GDP and a concomitant rise in the DRAF-to-GDP ratio were associated with rapid export expansion. But there was also falling private consumption per capita and the process stopped in 1984.

It is not impossible to have increasing exports, a falling share of private consumption in GDP and an increasing DRAF-to-GDP ratio, as well as rising average private consumption per capita, in very poor countries. But it is a matter of concern that out of the 19 cases of export expansion with poverty reduction for which data on the DRAF-to-GDP ratio are available, in only 4 is the domestic resource mobilization effort strong, in the sense that the DRAF-to-GDP ratio is increasing at more than 1.5 percentage points per annum. There were growing exports, increasing domestic resource mobilization (whether strong or weak)

TABLE 33. REAL AVERAGE ANNUAL GROWTH RATES OF EXPORTS, PRIVATE CONSUMPTION PER CAPITA[a], GDP, GDP PER CAPITA AND CHANGE IN DRAF % GDP[b], 1990–1995 AND 1995–2000

| | | Real average annual growth rates of: | | Annual average change in DRAF/GDP ratio (% point) | Real average annual growth rates of: | |
		Exports of goods and services (%)	Private consumption per capita (%)		GDP (%)	GDP per capita (%)
Increasing exports and increasing private consumption per capita						
Equatorial Guinea	1995–2000	46.9	29.0	2.7	36.6	32.9
Rwanda	1995–2000	18.3	1.7	1.9	9.8	3.5
Bangladesh	1990–1995	13.5	2.2	0.6	4.4	2.6
Mozambique	1995–2000	13.0	4.8	2.4	8.7	6.3
Uganda	1995–2000	12.0	5.0	-1.5	6.0	3.0
Mali	1995–2000	11.9	0.9	-0.4	5.6	3.1
Uganda	1990–1995	11.8	2.8	0.1	6.8	3.4
Guinea-Bissau	1990–1995	11.3	4.4	-1.9	2.9	0.2
Bangladesh	1995–2000	9.7	1.3	1.4	5.2	3.4
Ethiopia	1995–2000	9.2	0.0	2.0	4.3	1.7
Cape Verde	1995–2000	7.7	4.7	-3.2	6.6	3.9
Guinea	1995–2000	5.6	1.2	0.6	4.1	1.7
Burkina Faso	1995–2000	5.6	1.0	2.6	4.5	2.0
Benin	1995–2000	5.4	1.6	0.3	5.2	2.4
Zambia	1995–2000	5.2	0.9	0.3	2.2	-0.2
Senegal	1995–2000	4.8	2.9	0.0	5.4	2.5
Gambia	1995–2000	4.8	3.1	0.6	5.0	1.7
Benin	1990–1995	4.4	0.6	0.5	4.2	1.0
Madagascar	1995–2000	4.0	1.2	-0.1	3.9	0.7
Malawi	1995–2000	3.8	3.9	0.2	3.9	1.6
Ethiopia	1990–1995	2.5	1.4	-0.8	3.0	1.3
Mauritania	1990–1995	2.0	3.1	-1.4	3.9	1.1
Guinea	1990–1995	1.8	1.2	-0.1	3.9	1.1
Zambia	1990–1995	1.7	2.4	4.7	-1.1	-3.9
Malawi	1990–1995	0.9	0.4	-1.7	1.6	0.0
Increasing exports and decreasing private consumption per capita						
Equatorial Guinea	1990–1995	29.2	-2.0	1.9	7.0	4.3
Guinea-Bissau	1995–2000	25.9	-4.9	0.9	-2.7	-4.7
Burundi	1995–2000	20.3	-2.0	2.5	-0.3	-2.3
United Rep. of Tanzania	1990–1995	17.8	-0.7	-0.1	1.6	-1.4
Sao Tome and Principe	1995–2000	16.1	-9.8	6.2	2.1	-0.2
Mozambique	1990–1995	14.9	-1.0	2.3	3.2	0.9
Cape Verde	1990–1995	12.5	-0.7	3.0	5.4	3.0
Lesotho	1990–1995	11.2	-6.8	1.9	4.1	1.9
Dem. Rep. of the Congo	1995–2000	11.1	-6.6	-1.7	-3.7	-6.6
Angola	1990–1995	11.0[c]	-11.9	-1.0	-6.7	-9.8
Maldives	1995–2000	8.9	-4.6[d]	2.6	5.5	3.0
Comoros	1990–1995	7.4	-4.5	-0.9	1.1	-1.5
Mali	1990–1995	6.7	-1.8	0.0	2.6	0.0
Lesotho	1995–2000	6.6	-6.5	3.5	2.9	1.2
Madagascar	1990–1995	4.5	-1.9	-0.7	0.1	-2.6
Burundi	1990–1995	4.1	-1.5	-1.3	-2.6	-4.9
United Rep. of Tanzania	1995–2000	2.3	-0.2	1.6	3.9	1.3
Yemen	1995–2000	1.0	-0.5[d]	4.4	5.6	2.6
Decreasing exports and increasing private consumption per capita						
Togo	1995–2000	-0.1	2.6	-1.9	1.9	-1.0
Mauritania	1995–2000	-0.8	0.9	3.9	4.1	0.9
Gambia	1990–1995	-4.1	0.2	-3.0	2.1	-1.5
Burkina Faso	1990–1995	-4.8	0.5	-1.3	4.2	1.8
Decreasing exports and decreasing private consumption per capita						
Senegal	1990–1995	-0.2	-1.6	-0.1	1.3	-1.2
Niger	1990–1995	-0.8	-1.5	-0.4	0.4	-2.9
Sao Tome and Principe	1990–1995	-1.4	-4.3	0.9	1.5	-1.2
Chad	1995–2000	-2.5	-0.3	1.6	3.5	0.7
Togo	1990–1995	-2.9	-12.4	-0.2	-1.0	-3.4
Comoros	1995–2000	-4.1	-1.1	-2.0	1.3	-1.2
Eritrea	1995–2000	-10.9	-8.5[d]	6.2	2.1	-0.6
Sierra Leone	1990–1995	-11.2	-3.8	-9.3	-5.6	-7.9
Dem. Rep. of the Congo	1990–1995	-15.3	-11.5	0.1	-8.0	-11.1
Rwanda	1990–1995	-24.9	-1.7	-4.9	-12.1	-7.2
Sierra Leone	1995–2000	-47.0	-10.5	1.4	-5.1	-7.1

Source: UNCTAD secretariat estimates, based on World Bank, *World Development Indicators 2003,* CD-ROM; and Heston, Summers and Aten (2002).

a   In 1985 PPP $ unless otherwise states.

b   DRAF % GDP refers to the ratio of domestic resources available for financing to GDP, that is (GDP minus household consumption) % GDP. The calculation was based on data in constant local currency units.

c   1990–1994.

d   In constant local currency units.

and increasing private consumption per capita in only two LDCs during both 1990–1995 and 1995–2000 periods — Bangladesh and Benin. This favourable configuration is evident in Uganda in the first period, and in Guinea, Malawi, Mozambique and Rwanda during the second period.

To sum up, it is very difficult to achieve both sustained export expansion and poverty reduction at the same time in very poor countries. A domestic resource mobilization effort can help to sustain export expansion. But it eats into the resources available to finance minimal subsistence levels of consumption. This is very difficult in situations of generalized or mass poverty. If domestic resource mobilization goes too far, the process of export expansion is likely to come to halt as resources have to be diverted back to consumption. If export expansion is strongly associated with increasing GDP per capita, it is possible for growing exports, a falling share of consumption in GDP and increasing average consumption per capita to go hand in hand. But if the trade–growth relationship is weak, as it is in many LDCs, the trade-off between domestic resource mobilization effort and poverty reduction will be particularly sharp. The availability of external resources can play an important role in lessening the trade-off. If these support efficient investment and export development, they can play a major role in promoting a situation in which export expansion without poverty reduction or immiserizing trade is replaced by export expansion with poverty reduction.

> *If the trade–growth relationship is weak, as it is in many LDCs, the trade-off between domestic resource mobilization effort and poverty reduction will be particularly sharp.*

F. Conclusions

This chapter has identified three major areas where international trade is not working effectively to reduce poverty in the LDCs: trade performance, which is weak; trade–growth linkages, which are also weak; and the association of export expansion with a form of economic growth which is not poverty-reducing.

The first and simplest reason why the trade–poverty relationship has broken down is that the trade performance of some LDCs has been inadequate to enable sustained economic growth and poverty reduction. This has been a particular problem in the commodity-dependent LDCs. They have experienced major resource losses owing to falling commodity prices and also loss of market share. The latter phenomenon has been particularly marked for food exports and minerals, ores and metals, but less so for agricultural raw materials. There are some primary commodities in which the LDCs are gaining market share, but they tend not to be market-dynamic products. Weak and unstable export growth has been associated with the build-up of external debts and the creation of an aid/debt service system that has undermined the developmental effectiveness of aid.

Improved trade performance is a necessary condition for escaping this complex poverty trap. But the experience of the 1990s, when trade performance improved in many LDCs, including some of the commodity-dependent LDCs, shows that the relationship between trade and poverty is asymmetrical. Although LDCs with declining exports are almost certain to have a rising incidence of poverty, increasing exports do not necessarily lead to poverty reduction.

Using trends in private consumption per capita as a proxy measure of trends in the incidence of $1/day and $2/day poverty, and focusing on trends in the LDCs in the first and second half of the 1990s, it is apparent that one third of the cases of export expansion can be characterized as immiserizing trade. In these situations, at the same time as export expansion occurs, average private consumption per capita is falling by over 1 per cent per annum. There is evidence of some improvement in the trade–poverty relationship during the decade in the sense that export expansion with rising average private consumption per capita was more common in the period 1995–2000 than in 1990–1995. But there is no statistically significant relationship between export growth and changes in private consumption per capita in either period. Moreover, there are only three LDCs in which export expansion is associated with private consumption per capita rising by over 1 per cent per annum during both periods. Poverty reduction in the LDC context can be expected to occur if there are sustained and substantial increases in average private consumption per capita. But export growth is simply not having such an effect in most of the LDCs.

Against this background, a second reason why the trade–poverty relationship is breaking down is weak trade–growth linkages. For the LDCs, the import-supply effects of exports are an important mechanism through which export growth has a positive impact on output growth. There is indeed a stronger relationship between import growth and investment growth in the LDCs than in other developing countries. This implies the possibility of a strong investment–export nexus through increased exports enabling increased imports, increased imports enabling increased domestic investment, and increased domestic investment leading to higher economic growth. However, in practice, the relationship between export growth and output growth is somewhat weaker in the LDCs than in other developing countries. In the 1990s, at any given export growth rate, output growth was lower in the LDCs than in other developing countries.

Improved trade performance is a necessary condition for escaping this complex poverty trap. But increasing exports do not necessarily lead to poverty reduction.

The evidence suggests that there are two major missing links in the relationship between exports, imports, investment and growth. One is that the growth in import capacity in the 1990s was much slower than export growth. This is likely to reflect decreased aid inflows and changes in contractual debt service obligations. But on top of this, increased investment is not as strongly associated with increased economic growth in the LDCs as in other developing countries. International trade cannot work to reduce poverty in countries where the level and efficiency of investment are not adequate to support sustained economic growth. On the basis of analysis in *The Least Developed Countries Report 2000*, major reasons for the breakdown of the investment–growth relationship are the weakness of the domestic entrepreneurial class, the great dependence of the central budgetary and accumulation processes in the LDCs on aid, and external indebtedness. A basic condition for ensuring a better trade–poverty relationship in the LDCs is the emergence of a domestic entrepreneurial class oriented towards productive activities, more and more effective aid and a durable exit from the debt problem. In the absence of these the emergence of a strong investment–export nexus that would underpin sustained economic growth is unlikely.

High population growth rates also mean that higher export growth rates must be achieved in order to ensure that output growth occurs at a sufficiently fast rate for GDP per capita to increase. Amongst the LDCs, GDP per capita is almost invariably declining in countries where exports are declining, and almost invariably increasing in countries where exports are increasing at more than 5 per cent per annum. But in between, where export growth rates are positive but below the threshold level of 5 per cent per annum, there is a "zone of ambiguity". In this zone, export growth may be associated with rising or declining GDP per capita. Indeed, the relationship between export growth and output growth, and population growth rates in the LDCs, is such that in those countries there is actually a higher probability that export expansion will be associated with falling GDP per capita if real export growth rates are positive but below the 5 per cent threshold level.

The third reason why the trade–poverty relationship is breaking down is that export expansion is not associated with a form of economic growth that is poverty-reducing. Limited data make it difficult to draw general conclusions on the inclusiveness of economic growth. There is some evidence of a tendency for immiserizing trade to occur in high-inequality LDCs. But this issue needs to be pursued further through case studies that include the trade–employment relationship. However, the chapter has two important findings regarding the form of economic growth.

International trade cannot work to reduce poverty in countries where the level and efficiency of investment are not adequate to support sustained economic growth.

First, situations of export expansion with poverty reduction are particularly likely if there is a balanced pattern of economic growth in which domestic demand expansion is the major demand-side component of economic growth, but export expansion also makes a significant contribution to the overall process. In the 1990s the least favourable trade–poverty relationships were found in countries in which import substitution made the major demand-side contribution to economic growth, and also in countries in which export-expansion made the major demand-side contribution.

Second, the trade–poverty relationship is breaking down partly because of domestic resource mobilization efforts associated with export expansion. In two thirds of situations of immiserizing trade and export expansion without poverty reduction in LDCs in the periods 1990–1995 and 1995–2000 there was an increasing domestic resource mobilization effort and a falling share of private consumption in GDP. The domestic resource mobilization effort supporting export expansion is positive from the perspective of growth sustainability to the extent that it is associated with efficient investment. But it is very difficult for such "belt tightening" to occur in very poor countries, where the average consumption of the population as a whole is equivalent to just $1 a day, without a rising incidence of poverty. Moreover, if the "belt tightening" associated with export expansion becomes too much, it may be that the whole growth process cannot be sustained.

The availability of external resources can play a major role in ensuring that export expansion, increased domestic resource mobilization and poverty reduction all occur together.

The trade-off between increased domestic resource mobilization, which can help to strengthen export growth, and reduced poverty is a major dilemma in poor countries. It becomes less acute to the extent that there is not mass poverty and the average private consumption per capita of the majority of the population is not at basic subsistence levels. Moreover, the trade-off between the two desirable goals is loosened if the trade–growth relationship is stronger. But if export growth is associated with slow increases in GDP per capita, as it is in many LDCs, the trade-off is likely to be particularly sharp. The availability of external resources can play a major role in ensuring that export expansion, increased domestic resource mobilization and poverty reduction all occur together.

These findings have important policy implications. However, before discussing what these are, the next chapter completes the analysis of how the trade–poverty relationship works in practice in the LDCs by considering how the relationship is affected by civil conflict.

ANNEX CHART 1. INDICES OF REAL EXPORTS AND REAL PRIVATE CONSUMPTION PER CAPITA IN LDCs, 1980–2001
(Base year 1990 = 100)

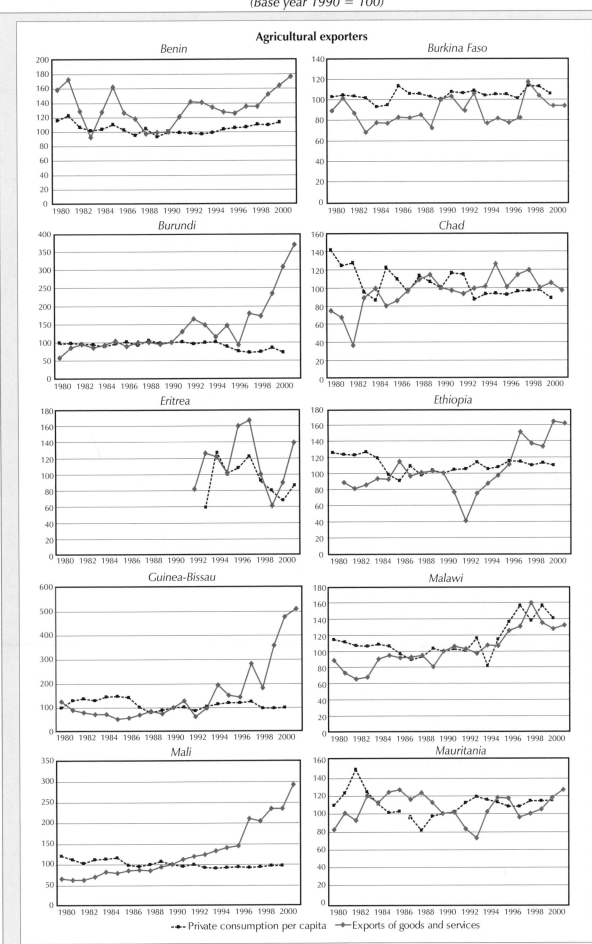

Agricultural exporters

Benin · Burkina Faso · Burundi · Chad · Eritrea · Ethiopia · Guinea-Bissau · Malawi · Mali · Mauritania

- - ■ - - Private consumption per capita ◆ Exports of goods and services

Annex chart 1 (contd.)

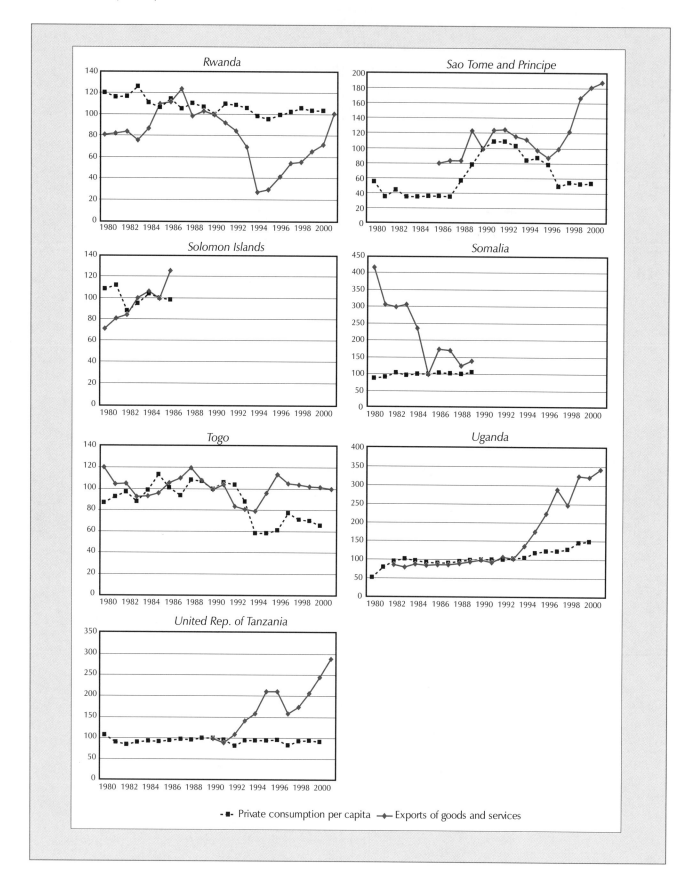

Annex chart 1 (contd.)

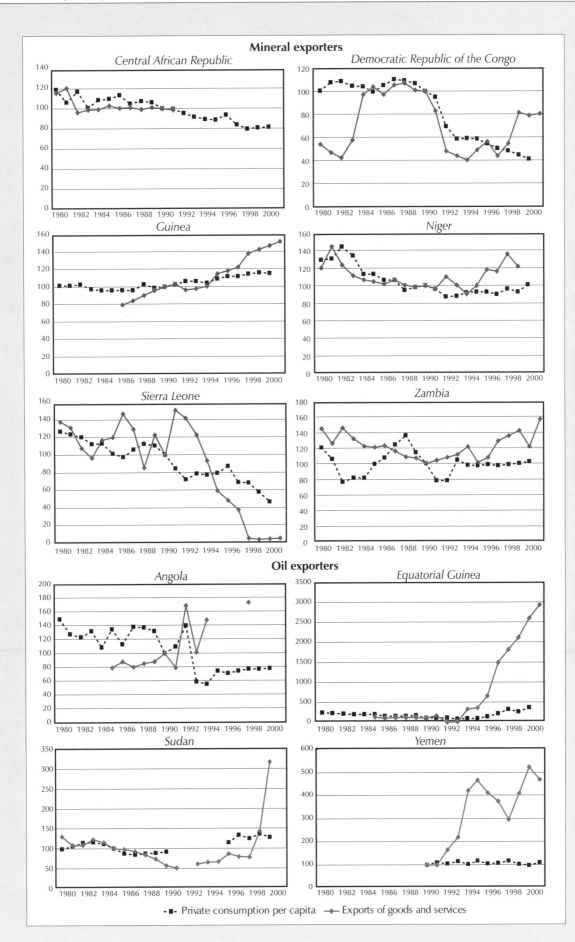

Mineral exporters

Central African Republic · Democratic Republic of the Congo

Guinea · Niger

Sierra Leone · Zambia

Oil exporters

Angola · Equatorial Guinea

Sudan · Yemen

- ■- Private consumption per capita   — ◆— Exports of goods and services

Annex chart 1 (contd.)

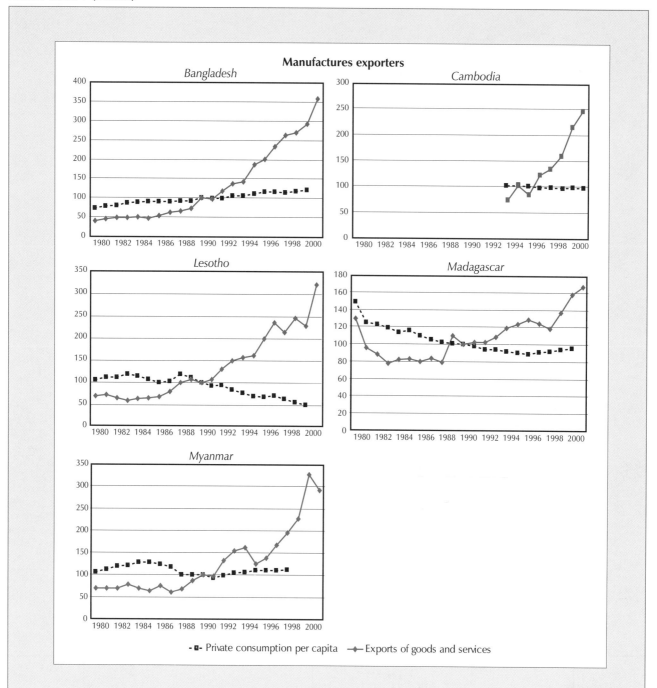

Manufactures exporters

Annex chart 1 (concluded)

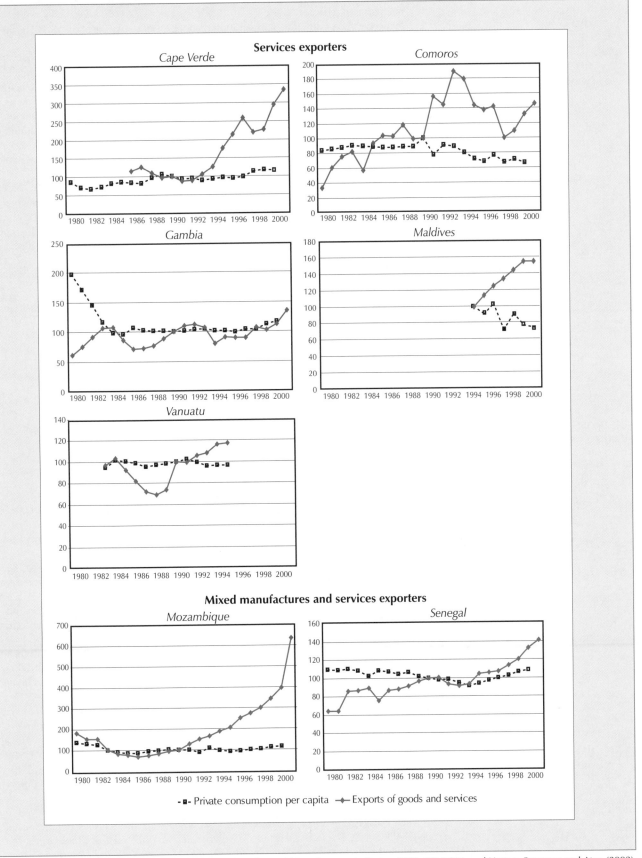

Source: UNCTAD secretariat estimates, based on World Bank, *World Development Indicators 2003*, CD-ROM; and Heston, Summers and Aten (2002).

Notes: The index for real exports of goods and services was calculated on the basis of exports data expressed in constant local currency units. The index for real private consumption per capita is derived from data expressed in 1985 PPP dollars, except for Cambodia, Eritrea, Maldives, Solomon Islands, Somalia and Sudan. For these countries, the index of real private consumption per capita was calculated on the basis of data in constant local currency units since data on private consumption per capita in 1985 PPP dollars were not available.
The base year is 1990 for all LDCs except Cambodia (1995), Eritrea (1995), Maldives (1995), the Solomon Islands (1985), Somalia (1985) and Sudan (1985).
No data are available for Afghanistan, Bhutan, Djibouti, Haiti, the Lao People's Democratic Republic, Liberia, Nepal, Samoa or Tuvalu.

Notes

1. See part two, chapters 3 and 4.
2. In accordance with the Standard International Trade Classification (SITC) system, manufactures are defined by codes 5 to 8, less 68.
3. Throughout this chapter, the LDCs will be classified according to their export specialization at the end of 1990s into: (1) Non-oil commodity exporters including (i) agricultural exporters and (ii) mineral exporters; (2) Oil exporters; and (3) Exporters of manufactures and/or services. The latter has generally experienced, during the last 20 years, a transformation in their exports structure in which the proportion of primary commodities in total exports has declined (relatively or absolutely), and either manufacturing or service activities have become the major export activities.
4. For a review of the trade performance of countries in Sub-Saharan Africa, which highlights similar findings, see Ng and Yeats (2000).
5. Calculations based on World Bank, *World Development Indicators 2003,* CD-ROM. Calculations used exports of goods and services as reported in the balance of payments. The share of the 1999 list of LDC exports in world exports in 1980 (0.91 per cent) was applied to the value of world exports in 2001. The forgone gains are the difference between the actual LDC shares in world exports in 2001 and the hypothetical LDC shares in world exports of that year.
6. By 2003, the only non-oil commodity-exporting LDCs with an unsustainable debt were Bhutan, Eritrea, Kiribati and the Solomon Islands.
7. These three components are identified through the following equation:

$$\left(Y_t - Y_{t-1}\right) = \alpha_{t-1}\left(D_t - D_{t-1}\right) + \left(\alpha_t - \alpha_{t-1}\right)S_t + \alpha_{t-1}\left(X_t - X_{t-1}\right)$$

| GDP increase | Domestic demand contribution | Import substitution contribution | Export effect contribution |

Where:

Y = GDP, D = domestic demand (=Y+M-X), S = total supply (=Y+M), X = total exports of goods and services (fob), M = total imports of goods and services (cif), α = GDP as share of total supply (Y/S), t = final year of period, t-1 = initial year of period. See Morley and Vos (2000).
8. Ratios are calculated on the basis of values in constant 1995 $ and are weighted averages.

References

Bhalla, S.S. (2002). *Imagine There is no Country: Poverty, Inequality, and Growth in the Era of Globalization*, Institute for International Economics, Washington, DC.

Chenery, H.B. (1979). Structural change and development policy, Oxford University Press, Oxford, New York.

David, M. and Herrmann, M. (2002). Recent price changes in primary commodities, 1998-2000: Implications for least developed countries, background report to *The Least Developed Countries Report 2002*, Geneva.

Deaton, A. (2003). Measuring poverty in a growing world (or measuring growth in a poor world) (available at http://www.wws.princeton.edu/%7Erpds/downloads/deaton_measuringpoverty_204.pdf).

Heston, A., Summers, R. and Aten, B. (2002). Penn World Table version 6.1, Center for International Comparison at the University of Pennsylvania (CICUP), October 2002.

Karshenas, M. (2004). Global poverty estimates and the millennium goal: Towards a unified framework, ILO Employment Strategy Papers 2004/5.

Morley, S. and Vos, R. (2000). Export-led economic strategies: Effects on poverty, inequality and growth in Latin America and the Caribbean — research methodology, mimeo.

Ng, F. and Yeats, A. (2000). On the recent trade performance of Sub-Saharan African countries: Cause for hope, or more of the same? World Bank, Working Paper Series 22697, Washington, DC.

Pritchett, L. (2003). Who is not poor? Proposing a higher international standard for poverty, Centre for Global Development, Working Paper 33, Washington, DC.

Ravallion, M. (2003). Measuring aggregate welfare in developing countries: How well do national accounts and surveys agree, *Review of Economics and Statistics*, 85 (3): 645–52.

UNCTAD (2002). *The Least Developed Countries Report 2002: Escaping the Poverty Trap,* United Nations publication, sales no. E.02.II.D.13, New York and Geneva.

UNDP (2003). *Human Development Report 2003*, Oxford University Press, New York and Oxford.

Vos, R., Morley, S., Enrique, G. and Sherman, R. (2004 forthcoming). *Does Trade Liberalization and Export-led Growth Help Reduce Poverty? Success and Failure in Latin America in the 1990s*, Edward Elgar, UK.

World Bank (2000). *Can Africa Claim the 21st Century*, Washington, DC.

Wuyts, M. (2003). Terms of trade, wage goods and the working poor: reflections on economic development and trade integration, based on the Tanzanian experience, background paper to *The Least Developed Countries Report 2004*.

Civil Conflict and the Trade–Poverty Relationship

A. Introduction

This chapter completes the analysis of how the trade–poverty relationship is working in the LDCs by examining some of the interactions between civil conflict, trade and poverty. This is an important issue for the LDCs because many of them experienced civil conflict in the 1970s, 1980s and 1990s, and this has influenced both the incidence of poverty and their trade performance. The chapter begins (section B) with a brief overview of trends in civil conflict in the LDCs and in other developing countries. It then goes on to examine the pattern of conflict, and in particular the association of conflict with low income, economic regression and export specialization (sections C and D). Finally, it discusses the ways in which civil conflict affects trade and poverty within the LDCs. The concluding section summarizes the main findings.

It should be emphasized at the outset that this chapter is not intended to offer a comprehensive analysis of the pattern, causes and consequences of civil conflicts in LDCs. The causes include, but go beyond, economic and trade-related factors, encompassing also social and political issues such as lack of political opportunities; social fragmentation resulting from ethnic, racial, religious or linguistic discrimination (World Bank, 2000: 126); the colonial legacy of a mismatch between territorial boundaries and social allegiances (World Bank, 2000); lack of freedom of all kinds; absence of the rule of law and violations of the fundamental rights of citizens (United Nations, 2001a); inequalities which are closely linked to group identities (Goodhand, 2001); environmental degradation (Homer-Dixon, 1994); and the influence of external economic and political interests (Stewart and Fitzgerald, 2000: Vol.I, chapter 8). The interaction between internal and external factors in both the onset and duration of civil conflicts is a very complex issue. The chapter does not attempt to address this. Rather, it is intended to extend and refine the analysis of the trade–poverty relationship presented in the last chapter.

Many LDCs experienced civil conflict in the 1970s, 1980s and 1990s, and this has influenced both the incidence of poverty and their trade performance.

It should also be stressed that the overview of patterns of civil conflict is based on one international database: the Uppsala/PRIO database on armed conflicts.[1] A major difficulty in conflict research is that different databases have different definitions of what constitutes a conflict and this leads to different views of where and when conflict occurs. There are also different perceptions about the starting and ending dates of a conflict and about the violence threshold that should be used in defining a conflict. The Uppsala/PRIO definition of armed conflict is "a contested incompatibility that concerns government and/or territory where the use of armed force between two parties, of which at least one is the government of a state, results in at least 25 battle-related deaths" (Strand, Wilhelmsen and Gleditsch, 2004: 3). The violence threshold of 25 battle-related deaths is lower than the violence threshold of 1,000 battle-related deaths which a number of other databases use.[2] The widely used Uppsala/PRIO database (see, for example UNDP, 2004) provides information on conflict years and conflict type as well as a classification of conflicts according to their intensity.[3] However, it may not necessarily correspond to national perceptions. Finally, throughout this chapter the term "civil conflict" will be used to refer to internal and internationalized internal armed conflicts which, following Uppsala/PRIO, occur in a country between the

Government of a State and internal opposition groups, possibly with intervention by other States (Strand, Wilhelmsen and Gleditsch, 2004).

B. An overview of trends in civil conflict in LDCs and other developing countries

According to the Uppsala/PRIO conflict database, about 100 countries have experienced at least one armed-conflict event over the last three decades, 87 per cent of which were developing countries,[4] including 36 LDCs. Over 90 per cent of these developing countries have experienced civil conflicts, which suggests that this is the dominant form of armed conflict.

Whereas the number of developing countries experiencing civil conflict (of varying duration and intensity) almost doubled from 18 to 34 between 1970 and 1992, there was a decreasing trend after the end of the Cold War. As shown in chart 26, between 1992 and 2001 the number of countries experiencing civil conflict in other developing countries declined by more than half. In contrast, it did not decline in the LDCs. According to the Uppsala/PRIO database 16 LDCs experienced civil conflicts in 1992. There was a downward trend thereafter until 1995, when the number of LDCs experiencing civil conflict increased once again, reaching the same level in 1998 as in 1992.

Between 1992 and 2001 the number of countries experiencing civil conflict in non-LDC developing countries declined by more than half. In contrast, it did not decline in the LDCs.

Overall, the 1990–2001 period was much more conflict-prone in the LDCs than the 1978–1989 one. The number of LDCs that experienced civil conflict increased from 20 (14 African and 6 Asian) during the period 1978–1989 to 30 (22 African, 7 Asian and 1 in the Caribbean) during the period 1990–2001. As a consequence, more LDCs have been recorded as being conflict-affected than peaceful during the 1990–2001 period.

Data show that during every decade since 1970 the proportion of conflict-affected countries was higher amongst the LDCs than amongst other developing

CHART 26. TRENDS IN CIVIL CONFLICTS IN LDCS AND OTHER DEVELOPING COUNTRIES, 1992–2000

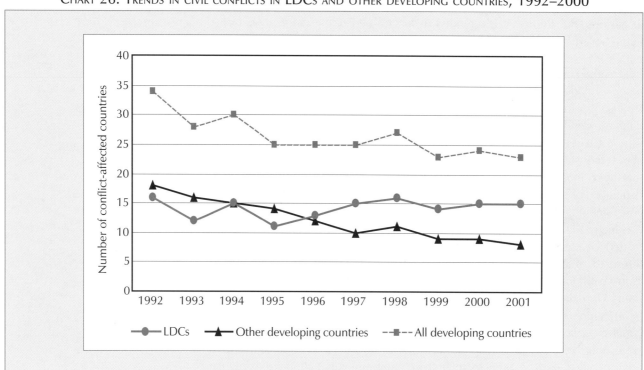

Source: UNCTAD secretariat estimates, based on the Uppsala/PRIO database on armed conflict.

countries. In the 1970s, 36 per cent of the 2002 list of 49 LDCs experienced civil conflicts as compared with less than 25 per cent of other developing countries.[5] But in the 1990–2001 period over 60 per cent of the 2002 list of LDCs experienced civil conflicts as compared with less than 25 per cent of other developing countries. Over 40 per cent of conflict-affected countries were LDCs in the 1970s and 1980s. But this proportion increased to 50 per cent in the period 1990–1995 and to 58 per cent in 1996–2001.

In the period 1970–2001, there were 12 countries (7 African and 5 Asian) from the 2002 list of 49 LDCs that experienced at least 18 consecutive years of civil conflict.[6] It should be noted that one third of them joined the LDC group after decades of civil conflict. Civil conflicts ended in 1992 in two of the 12 countries.[7] But they emerged in other LDCs during the 1990s. Since 1990, a further 8 LDCs (7 African and one Asian) have experienced at least six years of war or civil strife, according to the Uppsala/PRIO database.[8]

There is a common view that Africa is particularly conflict-prone. But the evidence of the Uppsala/PRIO conflict database does not support this view for the LDCs over the three decades since 1970. Until the mid-1990s the incidence of civil conflicts was always higher in Asian LDCs than in African LDCs. However, it declined in Asian LDCs during the 1990s but increased in African LDCs. Between 1990 and 1995, 6 out of 9 Asian LDCs experienced civil conflicts as compared with 16 out of 34 African LDCs. This implies a 67 per cent conflict prevalence rate in Asian LDCs as compared with a 47 per cent prevalence rate in African LDCs. During the period 1996–2001 the prevalence rate fell to 44 per cent in Asian LDCs but increased to 53 per cent in African LDCs. In the late 1990s, Africa, and African LDCs in particular, became the epicentre of civil conflicts in the developing world.

These figures show that the vulnerability of the LDCs to civil conflict is higher than that of other developing countries. Since the mid-1990s LDCs have become the primary locus of civil conflicts in the world. According to the UNDP (2003), more than 3.6 million civilians died during internal conflicts in the 1990s and over 50 per cent of battlefield casualties were children. Out of the total number of civilian deaths, over 1.8 million persons died during civil conflicts in 15 LDCs for which data on battlefield fatalities[9] are available (i.e. about half the total) and over 3.6 million refugees fled those countries. It has been estimated that between 1980 and 2000 no less than a quarter of the total LDC population, that is about 130 million civilians, were affected by conflicts.[10] In the long run, with the destruction of crops, livestock and livelihoods, the spread of diseases such as HIV/AIDS and malaria, and the proliferation of land mines, civilian deaths indirectly caused by civil conflicts may well exceed those directly caused during conflicts (FAO, 2000; UNAIDS, 2003: 1; WHO, 2000: 4).

Over 40 per cent of conflict-affected countries were LDCs in the 1970s and 1980s. But this proportion increased to 50 per cent in the period 1990–1995 and to 58 per cent in 1996–2001.

It has been estimated that between 1980 and 2000 no less than a quarter of the total LDC population, that is about 130 million civilians, were affected by conflicts.

C. Low income and economic regression as economic determinants of civil conflicts

1. Low income per capita

The pattern of civil conflicts indicates that low-income countries are particularly conflict-prone. As a result of both the long duration of old civil conflicts and the emergence of new ones, the proportion of low-income countries that experienced such conflicts increased from 48 per cent in the

1980s to 60 per cent during the period 1990-2001.[11] By comparison, it remained at about 28 per cent for middle-income countries during the same periods. The proportion of low-income countries that experienced civil conflict was more than twice as high as that of middle-income countries during the period 1990–2001 as a whole, and three times higher during the period 1995–2001.

Of the total number of developing countries that experienced civil conflict in the 1980s, 49 per cent were low-income countries. This proportion increased to 56 per cent in the early 1990s and to 73 per cent in the 1995–2001 period.

2. Economic stagnation and regress

Although conflict risk is particularly high in low-income countries, low income level alone is not a sufficient condition for the onset of civil conflict.

It is important to stress that although conflict risk is particularly high in low-income countries, low-income level alone is not a sufficient condition for the onset of civil conflict. This is clear from the fact that 40 per cent of low-income countries experienced civil peace during the period 1990–2001. What appears to be important in the onset of civil conflict is the interaction of low-income level with other adverse conditions. Economic regress or economic stagnation and economic instability are particularly important in this regard. For LDCs that were peaceful in the 1980s but experienced civil conflicts in the 1990–2001 period, their economic performance in the 1980s was systematically either sluggish or negative. A total of 14 LDCs enjoyed civil peace in the 1980s, but experienced civil conflicts of varying intensity and duration during the period 1990–2001.[12] Only two of these countries had per capita growth rates exceeding 2 per cent in the 1980s.[13] All the other LDCs in which civil conflict broke out in the 1990s experienced either negative or sluggish growth rates in the 1980s (see table 34).[14] This suggests that, as Nafziger and Auvinen (2002) have argued, many of the civil conflicts that erupted in the LDCs in the 1990s were reactions to the economic failures of the 1980s. Real GDP growth rates in

TABLE 34. EXPORT SPECIALIZATION AND REAL GDP PER CAPITA GROWTH IN LDCS WHICH HAVE NOT BEEN AFFECTED BY CIVIL CONFLICTS IN THE 1980s BUT WHICH EXPERIENCED AT LEAST ONE CIVIL CONFLICT EPISODE BETWEEN 1990 AND 2001

	Export specialization	Real average annual GDP per capita growth	Standard deviation of real GDP growth[a]
	Late 1990s	*1980s (%)*	*1980s*
Burundi	agriculture	1.6	4.6
Central African Republic	mineral	-1.0	5.7
Dem. Rep. of the Congo	mineral	-1.1	2.2
Djibouti	service	-1.9[b]	1.8[b]
Guinea	mineral	0.5[b]	3.4[b]
Guinea-Bissau	agriculture	1.5	8.8
Haiti	manufactures	0.5	2.9
Lesotho	manufactures	2.0	4.6
Mali	agricultural	-1.9	7.0
Nepal	manufactures	2.3	4.2
Niger	mineral	-3.5	7.2
Rwanda	agriculture	-0.7	3.8
Senegal	manufactures/services	0.3	5.6
Sierra Leone	mineral	-1.6	4.7
Low-income countries	..	4.3	1.0

Source: UNCTAD secretariat estimates, based on World Bank, *World Development Indicators* 2003 CD-ROM, and IMF, *World Economic Outlook* online data.

a In percentage points.
b Calculations, based on IMF, *World Economic Outlook,* online data.

these countries also varied highly from year to year in the 1980s, particularly compared with the group of low-income countries. Thus economic instability may also have played a role in the onset of civil conflict in these countries.

As noted in *The Least Developed Countries Report 1997* "Regress has usually been accompanied by the degeneration of the administrative, coercive and public-service providing capacities of the State, and often, but not always, by internal conflict" (UNCTAD, 1997: 125). Economic stagnation or regression contributed not only to the breakdown of already weak State capacities but also to the de-legitimization of governing elites in a number of countries. As a result, a number of LDCs entered the 1990s with a lower level of income per capita, a smaller fiscal base, a weaker social service delivery system, a lower capacity to maintain law and public order, reduced social cohesion, a reduced institutional capacity and a diminished ability to either manage development policies or to own them. The combination of development failure and State decay contributed to a surge in legitimation crises in a number of LDCs.

The combination of development failure and State decay contributed to a surge in legitimation crises in a number of LDCs.

D. Civil conflicts by type of export specialization

It has been argued that primary commodity dependence (proxied by primary commodity exports as a percentage of GDP) is a major determinant of civil conflicts in low-income countries as such commodities provide opportunities "for extortion, making rebellion feasible and even perhaps attractive" (Collier and Hoeffler, 2001: 16). Available evidence suggests that this argument should be treated with caution, as some primary products may involve a greater risk of greed-motivated conflict than others. Moreover, the pattern of civil conflicts in the LDCs by type of export specialization has changed in the post-Cold War era.

1. Differences between the 1980s and the 1990s

There is an important difference between the 1980s and the 1990s in the pattern of civil conflicts in LDCs. Of the 18 LDCs that were already experiencing civil conflicts in the 1980s, 80 per cent specialized mainly in agricultural exports. On the other hand, of the 14 LDCs experiencing new civil conflict in the 1990s, 4 were agricultural exporters and 5 were mineral exporters, while in 5 of them manufactures and/or services were becoming the major export specialization.[15] As shown in table 34, the GDP per capita performance of all except two of these LDCs (both exporting mainly manufactures) was either sluggish or negative in the 1980s.[16] Judging from these figures, it is apparent that LDCs whose main exports were mineral products, manufactures and/or services, became more prone to civil conflict in the 1990s than in the 1980s.

LDCs whose main exports were mineral products, manufactures and/or services became more prone to civil conflict in the 1990s than in the 1980s.

This shift in the pattern of conflict is related to changes in the underlying dynamics of peace and civil conflict after the end of the Cold War (see for example Luckham et al., 2001). It also reflects the trend towards export diversification in some LDCs. This implies that in the 1990s LDCs which were diversifying out of primary commodity exports into manufactures and/or services also became conflict-prone. Interestingly these include two countries that had a good economic performance in the period before conflict.[17] Their experience suggests that the adoption of an inclusive development strategy is key to reducing conflict risk in poor countries. This applies in situations of economic regress or stagnation as well as in situations of economic growth. As argued by a number of authors, including Nazfiger and Auvinen (2002) and Stewart (2003), vertical inequality (income inequality) and horizontal inequality[18] (inequality associated with group identities) often overlap and result in an increase in the perception of relative deprivation by segments of the population and in increased conflict risk thereafter.

2. CIVIL CONFLICTS IN PRIMARY-COMMODITY-DEPENDENT LDCS

Conflict risk varies amongst the primary-commodity-dependent LDCs. One factor suggested as important is the degree to which some of these countries are subject to commodity price shocks and long-term commodity price declines (Guillaumont et al., 2003; World Bank, 2003). It has also been argued that countries whose exports are highly concentrated in a few primary commodities are particularly vulnerable (Humphreys, 2003). The relationship between declining and unstable commodity prices and poor economic performance is one link between primary commodity dependence and civil conflict. But there is no automatic connection between the outbreak of civil conflict and falling commodity prices in low-income countries experiencing economic regress.[19] More research is required on the link between commodity price shocks and civil conflict.

The relationship between declining and unstable commodity prices and poor economic performance is one link between primary commodity dependence and civil conflict.

Within the group of low-income primary-commodity-dependent LDCs that experienced civil peace in the 1980s and had either sluggish or negative per capita growth rates, it is important to note that the conflict risk was higher in the mineral- dependent LDCs than in the agriculture-dependent ones. Amongst the six mineral- dependent LDCs in this group of countries, only one continued to experience civil peace in the 1990–2001 period.[20] Amongst the nine agriculture-dependent LDCs in this group of countries, more than half continued to enjoy civil peace in the 1990–2001 period. Thus in the group of poorly performing mineral-dependent LDCs that were under peace in the 1980s, 83 per cent experienced civil conflict in the period 1990–2001 as compared to 45 per cent in the group of poorly performing agriculture-dependent ones.[21]

In countries exporting natural resources such as oil, gas and minerals, lack of transparency in management, and of equity — notably across regions — in the distribution of revenues increases the risk of civil conflict.

Some primary commodities entail greater conflict risks than others (Lujala, 2003; Stewart, 2003).[22] Amongst the mineral exporters, the most conflict-prone are the LDCs that produce labour-intensive products and those for which an illicit and lucrative international trade exists. In countries exporting natural resources such as oil, gas and minerals, lack of transparency in management, and of equity — notably across regions — in the distribution of revenues increases the risk of civil conflict (Global Witness, 2004: 73; Herbst, 2001: 5).[23] Good governance of natural resources, both national and international, therefore plays a central role in reducing conflict risk in primary-commodity-dependent countries.[24] Botswana, through equitable and sound management of the revenues generated by its mineral resources[25] coupled with good governance, has not experienced civil conflict.

It is worth noting that within the group of mineral-exporting LDCs that experienced new civil conflicts in the period 1990–2001, all except one were diamond exporters.[26] Moreover, it was only following the recent discovery of alluvial diamonds that a leading bauxite exporter[27] became embroiled in a civil conflict in 2000. In this particular case, it was not the dependence on a capital-intensive mining product such as bauxite that was associated with the eruption of civil conflict, but the country's expanding diamond sector and the presence of neighbouring conflict-affected LDCs.

In the context of civil conflict, diamonds are referred to as "conflict diamonds"; these are "rough diamonds used by rebel movements to finance their military activities including attempts to undermine or overthrow legitimate Governments" (United Nations, 2001b).

The case of alluvial diamonds illustrates most starkly the argument that conflicts can be initiated or prolonged because of personal "greed" and the plundering of national resources for personal benefit. According to Le Billon, Sherman and Hartwell (2002:1), "In some cases, the control over economic activities may be the principal motivation for the initiation or perpetuation of conflict. This is not to say that wars are solely about 'greed'. War frequently becomes an alternative system of profit and power favouring certain groups at the expense of others, occasionally reflecting previous grievances". In recognition of "...the need to address the problem of conflict diamonds fuelling conflicts in a number of countries..." and in acknowledging that "...the problem of conflict diamond is of serious international concern...", the United Nations General Assembly adopted a resolution in December 2000 in support of the Kimberley process (United Nations, 2001b). This consultative process was initiated by African diamond-producing countries earlier that year to develop proposals for a workable international certification scheme aimed at eliminating the presence of "conflict diamonds" and at protecting the legitimate diamond industry. Following a series of meetings attended by key industry representatives, NGOs and governments, the Kimberley Process Certification Scheme was adopted in November 2002.

It is important, however, not to generalize about the role of such opportunistic behaviour in the eruption of civil conflict in all primary-commodity-dependent countries. According to Stewart (2003:21), commodities such as coffee, cotton, tobacco or tea cannot be considered as major sources of finance supporting greed-motivated conflict, and the use of undifferentiated natural exports as a proxy for greed motivation is not appropriate. What is evident is that opportunistic behaviour is much more likely to arise in low-income and poorly performing countries, exploiting a category of products that may generate sufficient revenues to support and even prolong conflict. Such products include particularly alluvial diamonds, timber and narcotic crops.

A particularly troubling feature of the pattern of civil conflict is that certain exports can fuel major civil conflict when illegal resource exploitation becomes one of the main sources of funding for groups involved in perpetuating conflict.[28] In this situation, there can be a cycle of violence in which illicit and illegal natural resource exploitation is linked to arms trafficking, which in turn is linked to conflict.[29]

Whereas export specialization in primary commodities, and particularly in products such as diamonds, oil, timber and narcotic crops, increases the risk of conflict, it usually interacts with a low income level, and poor and unstable economic performance as part of the complex combination of causes which lead to civil conflict.

To conclude, the evidence indicates that in many LDCs that experienced civil conflicts in the 1990s, the negative synergies between low-income level, economic stagnation or regress in the 1980s, economic instability and governance failures were important factors that explained the onset of the crises. Whereas export specialization in primary commodities, and particularly in products such as diamonds, oil, timber and narcotic crops, increases the risk of conflict, it usually interacts with a low-income level, poor and unstable economic performance as part of the complex combination of causes which lead to civil conflict. In countries that export products such as oil, gas and minerals, lack of transparency in the management, and of equity in the distribution, of revenues derived from such natural resources also contribute to exacerbating tensions. The role of grievance in explaining the onset of civil conflict in primary-commodity-dependent countries cannot be ignored. In these countries, and particularly in those exploiting products such as alluvial diamonds, oil, timber and narcotic crops, the emergence of civil conflict most likely reflects a combination of legitimate claims-making ("grievance") by some and opportunistic behaviour for personal advantage ("greed") by others. Transparent and sound economic management of revenues earned from natural resources, strong democratic forms of governance and an inclusive development strategy are necessary for reducing conflict risk in LDCs.

E. Trade and poverty during civil conflict episodes

The effect of civil conflict on trade is a much less researched area than the role of trade as a cause of conflict. However, there is a general assumption that civil conflict has negative impacts on trade. Indeed, the prevalence of conflict in the LDCs has often been cited as a reason for their weak export performance (World Bank, 2003: p.69). This section examines that assumption.

It must be stressed at the outset that there are major problems of data reliability at times of conflict.[30] During civil conflicts there is generally an increase in the share and volume of informal (unrecorded) and illicit exports, as well as an expansion of the domestic informal sector. Despite the data problems, however, some intriguing patterns can be discerned.

The analysis is based on 28 civil conflict episodes for which export, import and GDP data are available for the following periods: the five-year period preceding conflict, the conflict years and conflict intervals. These conflict episodes took place in a total of 19 LDCs, including 15 primary-commodity-dependent LDCs. The conflict episodes are differentiated according to their severity and the previous conflict experience, as these emerge as important variables affecting the change in GDP, exports and imports. Out of the 28 civil conflict episodes, 18 have been classified in the Uppsala/PRIO database as minor conflicts and 10 as intermediate conflicts or wars.[31] Fifteen conflict episodes occurred in LDCs where civil conflicts had not occurred before, and 13 episodes represented recurrence of conflict.[32]

The basic finding of the analysis is that, depending on the level of intensity of the conflict and on the previous conflict experience of the country, civil conflicts do not always result in negative or lower GDP or trade performance. However, the absorption components of the GDP (domestic consumption and investment) are more vulnerable to conflict effects than trade.[33]

Chart 27A shows the real average annual growth rates for exports, imports, absorption and GDP during the 28 conflict episodes for which data are available. Consumption plus investment (absorption) increased slightly, by 0.5 per cent per conflict year, whilst imports grew by almost 3.5 per cent per conflict year and exports grew by 4.6 per cent per conflict year. Absorption was 2.3 percentage points lower during the conflict episodes than during the pre-conflict years. In contrast, export growth was almost 2.2 percentage points higher and import growth almost 3.6 percentage points higher (chart 27B). Within this overall pattern there were of course differences. But export growth was positive during 21 of the 28 conflict episodes, and was actually higher than during the pre-conflict period in 16 conflict episodes.

Whether or not a country has had a previous conflict episode is an important factor affecting trends. The growth rates for GDP, absorption, imports and exports are on average lower in the first conflict episode that a country experiences than in subsequent episodes both in absolute terms and in relation

The emergence of civil conflict most likely reflects a combination of legitimate claims-making by some and opportunistic behaviour for personal advantage by others. Transparent and sound economic management of revenues earned from natural resources, strong democratic forms of governance and an inclusive development strategy are necessary for reducing conflict risk in LDCs.

Depending on the level of intensity of the conflict and on the previous conflict experience of the country, civil conflicts do not always result in negative or lower GDP or trade performance. However, the absorption components of the GDP (domestic consumption and investment) are more vulnerable to conflict effects than trade.

CHART 27. OVERALL TRENDS IN GDP, ABSORPTION, EXPORTS AND IMPORTS DURING CONFLICT EPISODES IN LDCs

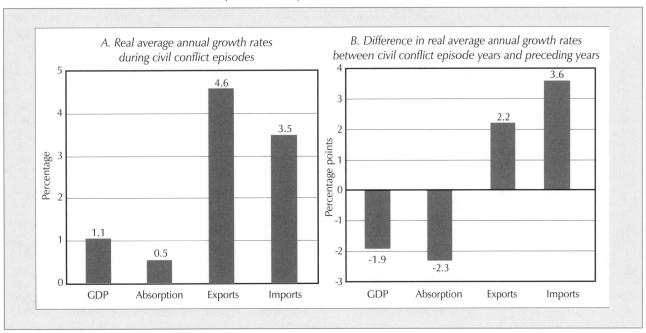

Source: UNCTAD secretariat estimates, based on World Bank, *World Development Indicators 2003* CD-ROM, and the Uppsala/PRIO database on armed conflict.

Note: For sample composition, see note 31. For definition and calculation of absorption, see note 32. Averages are simple averages.

to the period prior to the conflict episode (charts 28A and 28B). This reflects partly the fact that in situations of repeated civil conflicts, some economic agents learn how to cope with conflict, and even to take advantage of it (Fitzgerald, 2001: Introduction, 21). The exploitation of some commodities can even be more profitable during conflict periods, partly because of scarcity (for example, of food and foreign exchange) and partly because the breakdown of the rule of law enables illicit and illegal exploitation of resources.

CHART 28. COMPARATIVE TRENDS IN GDP, ABSORPTION, EXPORTS AND IMPORTS DURING CONFLICT EPISODES IN LDCs: FIRST CONFLICT EPISODES VERSUS EPISODES OF CONFLICT RECURRENCE

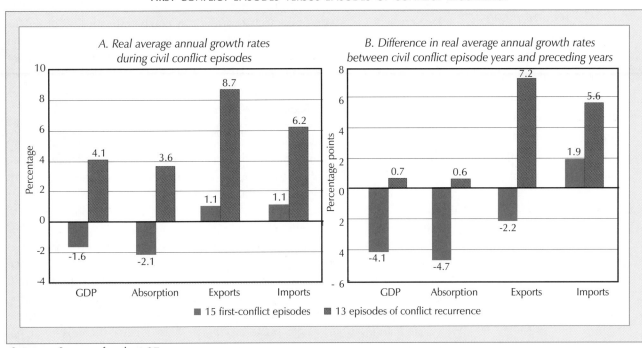

Source: Same as for chart 27.

Note: For sample composition, see note 31. For definition and calculation of absorption, see note 32. Averages are simple averages.

During the 15 first-conflict episodes, the real annual growth rates of GDP and absorption were negative and averaged -1.6 and -2.1 per cent per conflict year respectively. In contrast, the real growth rates of exports and imports were positive, averaging 1.1 per cent per conflict year. These figures highlight the greater vulnerability during civil conflicts of absorption relative to trade. Although positive, the annual growth rate of real exports was on average 2.2 percentage points lower during the conflict years than in the five years preceding the conflict. That of imports was 1.8 per cent higher. This may be explained by the low import growth rate during the pre-conflict period (-0.7 per cent per annum, on average, as compared with 3.2 per cent per annum for exports) and the increase in imports related to emergency assistance.

In the 13 recurring-conflict episodes, it is interesting to note that the real average annual growth rates of GDP, absorption, exports and imports were positive, and even higher during the conflict years than in the period preceding the recurrence of conflict. The dynamism of exports is a particularly troubling feature of these patterns. On average, real exports grew by 8.7 per cent per annum during the conflict years: that is 7.2 percentage points higher than in the period preceding conflict recurrence.[34] Once again, there are variations amongst the countries. But export growth rates were positive in 12 of the 13 episodes of conflict recurrence.

In terms of GDP, a similar pattern of increasing resilience to conflict is evident. Real GDP declined on average by 1.6 per cent per annum during the 15 first-conflict episodes, but during the 13 episodes of conflict recurrence it grew by about 4 per cent per annum. Also, real GDP grew by about a 0.7 percentage point more during the 13 episodes of conflict recurrence than during the pre-conflict-recurrence period. In comparison, the real GDP growth rate was 4 percentage points less during the 15 first-conflict episodes than during the 5 years preceding conflict onset. Real annual GDP growth rates were positive in 10 of the 13 episodes of conflict recurrence and in only 7 of the 15 first-conflict episodes.

The resilience during episodes of conflict recurrence is somewhat lower for absorption, though still apparent. The real growth rate of absorption was positive in 9 of the 13 episodes of conflict recurrence as compared with in 5 of the 15 first conflict episodes. Real absorption increased by 3.6 per cent per annum on average in the 13 episodes of conflict recurrence, that is a 0.6 percentage point more than in the pre-conflict-recurrence period. In comparison, in the 15 first-conflict episodes, real absorption decreased by 2.1 per cent per annum, that is 4.7 percentage points less than in the five years before the onset of conflict.

Data on private consumption per capita (in 1985 PPP dollars) trends are no exception to this pattern of increasing resilience to conflict. On average, private consumption per capita decreased by 1.4 per cent per annum during the total of 28 conflict episodes for which data are available. During the 15 first-conflict episodes, the annual growth rate of real private consumption per capita averaged -4.7 per cent per conflict year and was positive in 2 conflict episodes only. In the 13 episodes of conflict recurrence, real private consumption per capita increased from -0.1 per cent per annum in the pre-conflict-recurrence period to 2.5 per cent per annum during the conflict years and was positive in 9 of the 13 episodes. The increase in private consumption per capita during conflict years does not necessarily imply that poverty decreased during these years. Rather, these results point to the need to analyse the distributional consequences of civil conflicts. According to Stewart and Fitzgerald (2001: Vol.I, Introduction, p. 10), "The analysis of the impact of war needs to differentiate

During the 15 first-conflict episodes, the real annual growth rates of GDP and absorption were negative and averaged -1.6 and -2.1 per cent per conflict year respectively. In contrast, the real growth rates of exports and imports were positive, averaging 1.1 per cent per conflict year.

In the 13 recurring-conflict episodes, the real average annual growth rates of GDP, absorption, exports and imports were positive, and even higher during the conflict years than in the period preceding the recurrence of conflict.

between the effects of conflict on the aggregate supply of goods and services and the impact on the entitlements of vulnerable groups whose basic needs satisfaction is near to survival level...War is a time of dramatic changes, so that a group may lose drastically even while aggregate output is rising...". The distributional consequences of civil conflict implies that export growth in such a context is more likely to be accompanied by an increase in poverty, even when private consumption per capita increases (see charts 29A and 29B). This has important implications for analysis of the trade–poverty relationship.

These results suggest that the country's previous conflict experience is an important factor influencing economic impacts. The greater ability of countries that have been affected by previous conflict to better mitigate the adverse economic effects of their subsequent conflicts and to display positive GDP growth rates thereafter partly reflects the fact that their economic variables started from lower levels as a result of their first conflict episode. But it is also likely to be indicative of the effects of distributional changes associated with conflict, and of the fact that some economic actors increasingly just get on with their business regardless of, and even adjusting or adapting to an environment of repeated conflict. The contribution of each of these factors in explaining the higher resilience of countries to the effect of civil conflicts during subsequent conflict episodes requires further analysis.

In situations of repeated civil conflicts, some economic agents learn how to cope with conflict, and even to take advantage of it.

With regard to the intensity of civil conflicts, the results indicate that minor conflicts have a much less significant impact on GDP and absorption than do intermediate or major conflicts (charts 30A and 30B). This is to be expected in that civil conflicts classified as minor violence tend to be concentrated in remote areas of the country; thus, they do not affect major production and export loci, and allow the economy to continue to display positive growth. But import growth is stronger in non-minor than in minor conflicts. This probably reflects emergency assistance.

CHART 29. COMPARATIVE TRENDS IN PRIVATE CONSUMPTION PER CAPITA AND EXPORTS DURING CONFLICT EPISODES IN LDCs: FIRST-CONFLICT EPISODES VERSUS EPISODES OF CONFLICT RECURRENCE

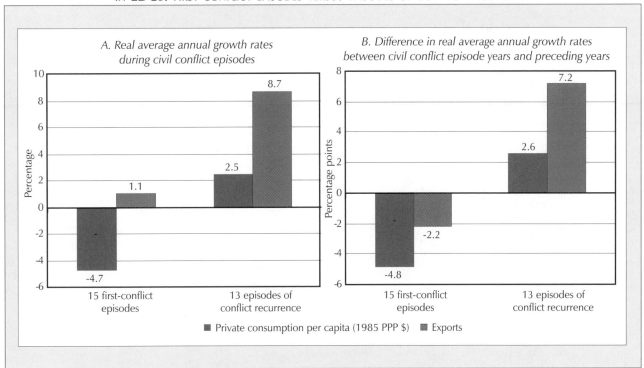

Source: UNCTAD secretariat estimates, based on World Bank, *World Development Indicators 2003,* CD-ROM; Heston, Summers and Aten (2002); and the Uppsala/PRIO database on armed conflict.

Note: For sample composition, see note 31. For definition and calculation of absorption, see note 32. Averages are simple averages.

These results have important implications. First, conflict is clearly a major cause of poverty. This occurs at least in part through its effect on the level and the distribution of income.

Secondly, the general tendency is that exports have, on average, increased during conflict episodes. The dynamism of exports is particularly apparent in countries that have experienced previous conflict episodes. Because the absence of the rule of law during a conflict may enable increased illegal and illicit exports, it is likely that official statistics actually underestimate the increase in exports during civil conflicts.

Thirdly, the tendency for trade to be more resilient to civil conflict than absorption has important implications for the interpretation of the traditional variable used to measure "trade openness" (exports plus imports as a ratio of GDP). This is used as the key indicator of trade integration and also sometimes as a measure of trade liberalization. Furthermore, it is usually assumed that the greater the integration, the more positive it is for the country. The results show that in countries which are prone to conflict it is a poor indicator of either trade policy or beneficial integration into the world economy. Since trade performance tends to be more resilient to civil conflicts than absorption and GDP, the trade/GDP ratio is likely to increase during conflict years. But in this case this measure is not indicative of something that is economically positive. Rather, it reflects economic distress and reduced absorption, which are the direct consequences of civil conflicts (table 35).

Finally, the tendency for trade to expand during civil conflicts also has important implications for the trade–poverty relationship. If the 1990s are taken as a whole, it is apparent that export growth rates are actually higher in conflict-affected LDCs than in those not affected by conflict (chart 31). This difference appears to be counter-intuitive. But it reflects trends in exports during conflict episodes discussed above, and also the fact that the growth rates cover pre-conflict, conflict and post-conflict periods. But whilst export growth rates in the 1990s were higher in the conflict-affected LDCs than in those not affected by

CHART 30. COMPARATIVE TRENDS IN GDP, ABSORPTION, EXPORTS AND IMPORTS:
MINOR CONFLICT EPISODES VERSUS INTERMEDIATE CONFLICTS OR WARS

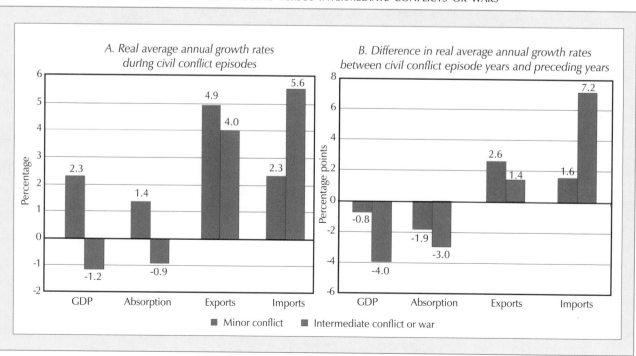

Source: Same as for charts 27.

TABLE 35. HOW OPENNESS, ABSORPTION AND TRADE CHANGED IN CONFLICT EPISODES IN SELECTED LDCs

	"Openness"[a]		Real annual growth rates during conflict years	
	Before conflict	*During conflict*	*Absorption*	*Exports + Imports*
Burundi	37.9	52.0	-2.5	13.2
Democratic Republic of the Congo	35.4	57.0	-1.8	15.5
Guinea-Bissau	25.0	34.8	-15.0	5.4
Rwanda	25.6	34.2	-4.4	5.7

Source: UNCTAD secretariat estimates, based on World Bank, *World Development Indicators 2003* CD-ROM, and the Uppsala/ PRIO database on armed conflict.

a   "Openness" is measured as exports plus imports of goods and services as a percentage of GDP. Calculations are based on data in constant 1995 dollars.

CHART 31. REAL AVERAGE ANNUAL GROWTH RATES OF EXPORTS IN GOODS AND SERVICES AND OF PRIVATE CONSUMPTION PER CAPITA IN CONFLICT-AFFECTED AND NON-CONFLICT-AFFECTED LDCs, 1990–2000

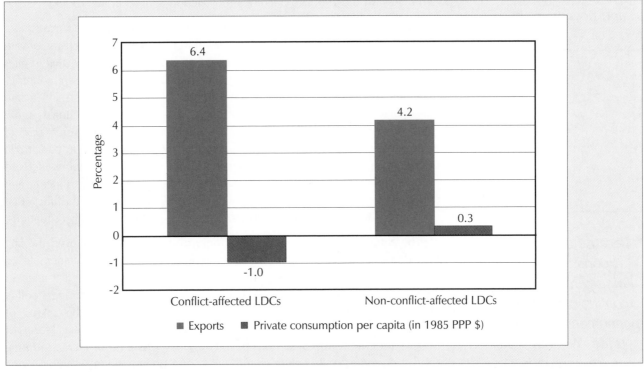

Source: Same as for chart 29.

Note: The sample is based on a group of 26 LDCs for which real exports and private consumption per capita (in 1985 PPP $) data were available for the 1990–2000 period. Of these LDCs, 16 experienced at least one episode of civil conflict in that period and 10 had not experienced civil conflicts for the last two decades. Sierra Leone and Equatorial Guinea are not included in the sample. Averages are simple averages.

conflict, average private consumption per capita was increasing in the latter countries whilst it was decreasing in the former. This implies that in the 1990s poverty was increasing in the conflict-affected countries along with high export growth rates.

F. Conclusions

The main conclusion of this chapter is that civil conflict is an important factor affecting the relationship between trade and poverty in the LDCs. However, the way in which trade, civil conflict and poverty interact is quite complex.

During the 1990–2001 period more LDCs were affected by conflict than unaffected by it. Moreover, since the late 1990s the LDCs became the primary locus of civil conflict in the world. Many factors, both internal and external, and

In the 1990s, export growth rates were actually higher in conflict-affected LDCs than in those not affected by conflict.

encompassing social, political and economic determinants contributed to this situation. But the inter-country pattern of conflict suggests that the interaction of a low income per capita with economic stagnation or regress has played an important role in the onset of civil conflicts in LDCs.

Most of the LDCs that experienced conflict during the Cold War period exported primary commodities, particularly agricultural products. The new civil conflicts of the 1990s occurred in LDCs whose export structure was diversifying into manufactures and/or services, as well as in those that specialized in primary commodities. Nevertheless, it is clear that countries with certain primary commodity exports are particularly conflict-prone. These include oil and gas exporters, as well as those with products that are labour-intensive and for which an illicit and lucrative international trade exists. There was also a particularly strong tendency for mineral exporters that experienced economic stagnation and regress in the 1980s to become embroiled in conflict in the 1990s.

Once civil conflict breaks out, both domestic consumption and investment normally decline. Given the close relationship between average private consumption per capita and the incidence and depth of poverty, this implies that, as one would expect, poverty increases during conflict. In countries experiencing conflict recurrence there tends to be an increase in private consumption per capita during the conflict years. This phenomenon is more likely the result of a change in the distribution of income than a sign of decreasing poverty. Civil conflict does not always result in a bad trade performance. Indeed, more often than not, both exports and imports increase during conflict. There is a particularly strong tendency for exports to increase in countries with a previous experience of conflict, reflecting the fact that economic actors learn how to adjust to or even to profit from conflict situations.

The nature of these trends requires more in-depth study. However, the fact that domestic consumption and investment are much more vulnerable to conflict than exports and imports means that the "openness" of conflict-affected countries, as measured by their trade/GDP ratio, increases during conflict episodes. The extent of this effect may well be underestimated as the collapse of the rule of law gives rise to opportunities to profit from previously illegal forms of trade. Furthermore, because both poverty and exports tend to increase during conflict episodes, civil conflict contributes to the phenomenon of immiserizing trade. Without sustained peace, the trade–poverty relationship is likely to be perverse.

Finally the outbreak and the duration of civil conflicts reflect a combination of legitimate claims-making by some and opportunistic behaviours by others in an environment of deprivation, risk and uncertainty. To prevent more civil conflict in the future, the real challenge at national level is to find ways of promoting inclusive development with sufficient and transparent distribution of domestic resources, including, in particular, those deriving from the primary sector, in a way that is considered equitable for the society in question. This is more likely to be best achieved under a set of concerted actions involving national and international actors from both the private and the public sectors and targeting the improvement or the safeguard of national and international good governance of natural resources.

Civil conflict is an important factor affecting the relationship between trade and poverty in the LDCs.

Because both poverty and exports tend to increase during conflict episodes, civil conflict contributes to the phenomenon of immiserizing trade. Without sustained peace, the trade–poverty relationship is likely to be perverse.

Notes

1. The dataset is a joint project of the Department of Peace and Conflict Studies, Uppsala University, and the Centre for the Study of Civil War at the International Peace Research Institute, Oslo (PRIO).

2. For example, Civil War Termination (CWT), Correlates of War (COW), Doyle and Sambanis and Major Armed Conflicts.

3. Minor armed conflicts are conflicts that resulted in "at least 25 battle-related deaths per year and fewer than 1,000 battle-related deaths during the course of the conflict"; intermediate armed conflicts are conflicts that caused "at least 25 battle-related deaths per year and an accumulated total of at least 1,000 deaths but fewer than 1,000 in any given year"; wars are conflicts that resulted in "at least 1,000 death battle-related deaths per year" (Strand, Wilhelmsen and Gleditsch, 2004: 4).

4. Excluding countries from Central and Eastern Europe.

5. Timor-Leste was not included in this analysis.

6. Afghanistan, Angola, Bangladesh, Cambodia, Chad, Ethiopia, the Lao People's Democratic Republic, Mozambique, Myanmar, Somalia, Sudan and Uganda. The Uppsala/PRIO database reports that the Lao People's Democratic Republic underwent 24 years of civil conflict within the 1970–2001 period. The level of intensity (minor, intermediate or war) was classified as unclear in 18 of these 24 years.

7. These two LDCs are Mozambique and Bangladesh. According to the Uppsala/PRIO database, about two thirds of Mozambique's conflict period was classified as "war" and that of Bangladesh as "minor" armed conflict.

8. Burundi, the Democratic Republic of the Congo, Liberia, Niger, Rwanda, Senegal, Sierra Leone and Nepal.

9. These calculations are based on the International Institute for Strategic Studies' Armed Conflict Database.

10. These calculations are derived from UNDP (2004: Statistical annex).

11. These calculations control for countries shifting from a middle-income level to a low-income level following civil conflict. They are based on a group of 127 developing countries (excluding Central and Eastern Europe) for which GNI per capita data are available, thus allowing for country classification by income level in the 1980s and the 1990s. In the 1980s, low-income countries were countries with a GNI per capita below $410 in 1980. In the 1990s, low-income countries were countries with a GNI per capita below $635 in 1990.

12. Burundi, the Central African Republic, the Democratic Republic of the Congo, Djibouti, Guinea, Guinea-Bissau, Haiti, Lesotho, Mali, Nepal, Niger, Rwanda, Senegal and Sierra Leone.

13. Lesotho, whose civil conflict in 1998 is classified as "minor" in the Uppsala/PRIO database, and Nepal, whose civil conflict broke out in the late 1990s and was still active in 2002.

14. In the Central African Republic and Guinea, civil conflict classified as minor broke out in 2001 and 2000 respectively. Their real GDP per capita growth rates in the 1990s did not exceed 1 per cent.

15. Burundi, Guinea-Bissau, Mali and Rwanda were the agricultural exporters; Guinea, Niger, Sierra Leone, the Central African Republic and the Democratic Republic of the Congo were the mineral exporters; and Djibouti, Haiti, Nepal and Senegal were the manufacturing and/or services exporters.

16. Ten LDCs displayed either negative or sluggish real per capita GDP performance in the 1980s but did not experience civil conflict in the 1980s and 1990s. Those countries are Benin, Equatorial Guinea, Kiribati, Madagascar, Malawi, Samoa, Sao Tome and Principe, the United Republic of Tanzania, Vanuatu and Zambia. No GDP data are available for Tuvalu.

17. In the five years preceding conflict onset, the real GDP per capita growth rate of Lesotho and Nepal averaged 4.4 and 2.8 per cent per annum respectively.

18. It should be noted that lack of data on inequality, and on horizontal inequality in particular, seriously hinders research on the inequality–conflict relationship.

19. For example, Benin had a negative economic performance in the 1980s, but has not experienced civil conflict in the last three decades, although its exports have depended heavily on cotton products, the world price for which decreased sharply during the 1980s. This country's reliance on democratic principles may have contributed to this outcome.

20. The six mineral-dependent LDCs are the Central African Republic, the Democratic Republic of the Congo, Guinea, Niger, Sierra Leone and Zambia. Only Zambia did not experience civil conflict in the 1990s. Liberia, a seventh mineral-dependent LDC, is not on this list because it experienced two conflict episodes, classified as "minor", in the 1980s before the eruption of war in the early 1990s.

21. De Soysa (2001) found that the likelihood of civil conflict was particularly high in countries where non-renewable resources (not total natural resources) are available.

22. Lujala (2003: 3) highlights the need to classify natural resources according to their characteristics and argues that "It is...not sufficient to simply state that natural resources cause and fuel conflicts", as natural resources are not equally lootable.

23. Oil discovery may have contributed to the prolongation and intensification of tensions in Angola, Chad and Sudan.

24. For a more detailed discussion on the need for transparency in revenues and payments from extractive industries see Chapter 6, section C of the Report.

25. Mostly diamonds from kimberlite mines.

26. Niger.

27. Guinea.

28. Collier and Hoeffler (2001: 3-4) have identified three main sources of rebel finance during civil conflict: from primary commodities, foreign governments and diaspora. They have argued that whereas the two first sources of finance are associated with the opportunity thesis, the third one is not.

29. It has been suggested that the mechanism can be quite simple. It has been reported, for example, that in Zaire (just before it became the Democratic Republic of the Congo) rebellion was easy because all that was needed was $10,000 and a satellite phone. The former was enough to hire a small army, whilst with a satellite phone it was possible to start making deals on mineral extraction (Collier, 2002: 9). In cases such as the Democratic Republic of the Congo, resource exploitation has been characterized by intense competition among various political and military actors as they have sought to maintain, and in some instances expand, their control over territory (United Nations, 2003: 14).

30. The example of Sierra Leone is quite striking in this regard. According to official data, exports from Sierra Leone declined by over 95 per cent between 1990, the pre-conflict year, and 2000. But according to Smillie, Gberie and Hazleton (2000: 4), "while the Government of Sierra Leone recorded exports of only 8,500 carats in 1998, the HRD — the Diamond High Council — records imports of 770,000 carats".

31. See note 3 for violence thresholds used to distinguish between minor armed conflict, intermediate armed conflict and war.

32. The group of 15 first-conflict episodes is based on a sample of 15 LDCs for which data were available in the five years preceding conflict onset and during conflict years for the period 1970–2001. These LDCs are: Bangladesh, Burkina Faso, Burundi, Comoros, the Democratic Republic of the Congo, the Gambia, Guinea, Guinea-Bissau, Lesotho, Mali, Niger, Rwanda, Senegal, Sierra Leone and Togo.
The group of 13 episodes of conflict recurrence is based on a sample of 11 LDCs for which data were available during the period before conflict recurrence and during conflict years for the period 1970–2001. These LDCs are: Burundi, Chad, Comoros, the Democratic Republic of the Congo, Ethiopia, Mali, Rwanda, Senegal (2 episodes of conflict recurrence), Sudan (2 episodes of conflict recurrence), Togo and Uganda.

33. Not enough data are available to distinguish the private from the public components of consumption and investments. Absorption (A) has been calculated using data on GDP, exports (XGS) and imports (MGS) of goods and services in real terms (A = GDP – XGS + MGS). Absorption is the sum of (private and public) consumption expenditures and (private and public) investments.

34. Rwanda experienced two war episodes, a first one during the 1990–1994 period and a second one as from 1998. Its exports declined by over 20 per cent during its first conflict episode, but increased by over 16 per cent during the 1998–2001 period. In 2001, the Rwanda's exports volume almost reached its 1989 pre-war level.

References

Collier, P. and Hoeffler, A. (2001). Greed and grievance in civil war, Working Paper No. 2355, World Bank, Washington DC.

Collier, P. (2002). Primary commodity dependence and Africa's future, Working Paper No. 14984, World Bank, Washington DC.

de Soysa, I. (2001). Paradise is a bazaar? Greed, creed, grievance and governance, Discussion Paper No. 2001/42, WIDER University, Helsinki.

FAO (2000). *The State of Food and Agriculture 2000*, Rome, (http://www.fao.org/docrep/X4400E/X4400E00.htm)

Global Witness (2004). *Time for Transparency – Coming Clean on Oil, Mining and Gas Revenues*, (http://www.globalwitness.org/reports/show.php/en.00049.html)

Goodhand, J. (2001). Violent conflict, poverty and chronic poverty, Working Paper No. 6, Chronic Poverty Research Centre, Manchester.

Guillaumont, P. et al.(2003). Dampening the vulnerability to price shocks: a role for aid, Document de travail de la série *Etudes et Documents*, E 2003.25, Centre d'Etudes et de Recherches sur le Développement International, Clermont-Ferrand.

Herbst, J. (2001). The politics of revenue sharing in resource-dependent States, Discussion Paper No. 2001/43, WIDER University, Helsinki.

Homer-Dixon, T. (1994). Environmental scarcities and violent conflict: Evidence from cases?, Peace and Conflict Studies Program, University of Toronto, Toronto, 19(1): 5–40, (http://www.library.utoronto.ca/pcs/evidence/evid1.htm).

Humphreys, M. (2003). Economics and Violent Conflict, Harvard University, Cambridge, MA (http://www.preventconflict.org/portal/economics/Essay.pdf).

Le Billon, P., Sherman, J. and Hartwell, M. (2002). Controlling resource flows to civil wars: a review and analysis of current policies and legal instruments, Background Paper prepared for the conference, *Policies and Practices for Regulating Resource Flows to Armed Conflicts*, organized by the International Peace Academy's Economic Agendas in Civil Wars Project at the Rockfeller Foundation Study and Conference Center, Bellagio, Italy, May 20–24, 2002.

Luckham, R. et al. (2001). Conflict and poverty in sub-Saharan Africa: an assessment of the issues and evidence, Working Paper No.128, Institute of Development Studies, Sussex.

Lujala, P. (2003). Classification of Natural Resources, Department of Economics, Norwegian University of Science and Technology, Trondheim, Norway.

Nazfiger, E.W and Auvinen J. (2002). Economic development, inequality, war and State violence, *World Development*, 30(2): 153–163.

Smillie, I., Gberie, L. and Hazleton, R. (2000). *The Heart of the Matter – Sierra Leone, Diamonds & Human Security*, Partnership Africa Canada Publication, (http://www.pacweb.org/e/pdf/heart%20of%20the%20matter.doc).

Stewart, F. and Fitzgerald, E.V.K. (eds.) (2000). *War and Underdevelopment*, Vol 1, Oxford University Press, Oxford.

Stewart, F. (2003). Global economic influences and policies towards violent self-determination movements: an overview, Queen Elizabeth House Working Paper Series No 98, University of Oxford.

Strand, H., Wilhelmsen, L., and Gleditsch, N.P. (2004). *Armed Conflict Dataset Codebook*, International Peace Research Institute, Oslo.

UNAIDS (2003). HIV/AIDS and conflict, Fact Sheet No 2, August, (http://www.unaids.org/html/pub/Topics/Security/FS2conflict_en_doc.htm)

UNCTAD (1997). *The Least Developed Countries Report 1997*, United Nations publication, sales no. E.97.II.D.6, Geneva.

UNDP (2003). *Human Development Report 2003 – Millennium Development Goals: A Compact Among Nations to End Human Poverty*, Oxford University Press, New York.

UNDP (2004). *Reducing Disaster Risk – A Challenge for Development*, Bureau for Crisis Prevention and Recovery, New York.

United Nations (2001a). Report of the World Conference Against Racism, Racial Discrimination, Xenophobia and Related Intolerance, A/CONF.189/12, Durban, 2001.

United Nations (2001b). Resolution 55/56, General Assembly, 79th plenary meeting, 1 December 2000, A/RES/55/56, New York.

United Nations (2003). Final Report of the Panel of Experts on the Illegal Exploitation of Natural Resources and Other Forms of Wealth of the Democratic Republic of the Congo, 23 October 2003, S/2003/1027.

WHO (2000). Outline Strategy for Malaria Control in Complex Emergencies, Roll Back Malaria Complex Emergencies Network, WHO/CDS/RBM/2000.22, Geneva.

World Bank (2000). *World Development Report 2000/2001– Attacking Poverty*, Oxford University Press, New York.

World Bank (2003). *Breaking the Conflict Trap: Civil War and Development Policy*, World Bank Policy Research Report No. 26671, World Bank and Oxford University Press.

Trade Liberalization and Poverty Reduction in the LDCs

Chapter 5

A. Introduction

The present chapter focuses on the major trade policy — trade liberalization — that LDC Governments have adopted in recent years, and examines whether or not the implementation of this policy is likely to link international trade more effectively to poverty reduction in the LDCs. The chapter is organized into five main sections. Section B describes the extent and depth of trade liberalization in the LDCs, using the IMF's index of trade restrictiveness to measure the degree of openness of their economies. Section C describes the process of liberalization in the LDCs, including its sequencing, timing and speed. Section D discusses trends in poverty during and immediately after trade liberalization in the LDCs. The two subsequent sections examine the extent to which trade liberalization has affected prospects for sustained and substantial poverty reduction discussing: first the issue of the sustainability of economic growth (section E), and then the issue of the inclusiveness of economic growth (section F). The concluding section summarizes the main findings.

B. The depth and extent of trade liberalization

The LDCs have undertaken greater trade liberalization than other developing countries.

The depth and extent of trade liberalization in the LDCs can be gauged using the IMF index of trade restrictiveness, which classifies countries according to their average tariff rate and their extent of use of non-tariff barriers (NTBs). In 2002, on the basis of this evidence, of 46 LDCs for which data were available,

- The average tariff rate of 42 was less than 25 per cent;

- The average tariff rate of 36 was less than 20 per cent;

- The average tariff rate of 23 was less than 15 per cent;

- In 29 LDCs, NTBs were absent or insignificant in the sense that less than 1 per cent of production and trade was subject to NTBs; and

- In 28 LDCs there were no or insignificant NTBs, and average tariff rates were below 25 per cent.

To put these numbers in perspective, it is worth comparing the level of trade restrictiveness in the LDCs with other developing countries, and also with the level of trade restrictiveness in the EU, Japan and the United States, measured by the same index. Chart 32 shows the frequency distribution of the import restrictiveness index in the LDCs and other developing countries in 2002 using the IMF's classification system. From the chart, it is clear that the LDCs have undertaken greater trade liberalization than other developing countries. According to this measure, most of the LDCs have also undertaken deeper trade liberalization than the large industrializing Asian and Latin American economies. The average index for LDCs as a group was 4, which the IMF regards as "open", and it is exactly the same as the average for the EU, Japan and the United States.

CHART 32. TRADE RESTRICTIVENESS FOR LDCs AND OTHER DEVELOPING COUNTRIES, 2002

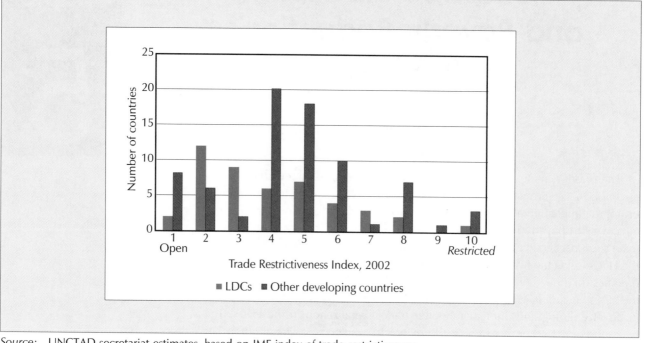

Source: UNCTAD secretariat estimates, based on IMF index of trade restrictiveness.

Note: The index is based on the following classification schemes:

Tariffs	Open	Moderate	Restrictive
Open	1	4	7
Relatively open	2	5	8
Moderate	3	6	9
Relatively restrictive	4	7	10
Restrictive	5	8	10

Tariffs are classified as follows:

Open: average tariff range 0≤t<10 per cent. Relatively open: average tariff range 10≤t<15 per cent. Moderate: average tariff range 15≤t<20 per cent. Relatively restrictive: average tariff range 20≤t<25 per cent. Restrictive: average tariff range 25 per cent or over.

Non-tariff barriers are classified as follows:

Open: NTBs are either absent or minor, and less than 1 per cent of production or trade is subject to NTBs. Moderate: NTBs are significant, covering at least one important sector of the economy but not pervasive, and between 1 per cent and 25 per cent of production or trade is subject to NTBs. Restrictive: many sectors or entire stages of production are covered by NTBs, and more than 25 per cent of production or trade is subject to NTBs.

Data were not available for Afghanistan and Somalia, for LDCs; and for Palau and Tonga, for other developing countries.

There is deeper trade liberalization in the African LDCs than in the Asian ones, and also in the commodity-exporting LDCs than in the manufactures- and/or services-exporting LDCs.

Among the LDCs, there is deeper trade liberalization in the African LDCs than in the Asian ones (chart 33A), and also in the commodity-exporting LDCs than in the manufactures- and/or services-exporting LDCs (chart 33B). This is an intriguing pattern, as, in general, the export performance of the Asian LDCs has been better than that of the African LDCs, usually because of their greater specialization in manufactured exports. However, it would be wrong to think that because the Asian LDCs have more restricted trade regimes, according to the IMF classification, no trade liberalization has occurred there. Bangladesh and the Lao People's Democratic Republic, for example, both undertook extensive trade liberalization in the 1990s. The mean tariff on all products in Bangladesh declined from 114 per cent in 1989 to 22 per cent in 1999 (Khondker and Mujeri, 2002). In 1995, a major tariff liberalization occurred when the Lao People's Democratic Republic's tariff schedule, which had a maximum ad valorem rate of 150 per cent, was replaced by a schedule which had 6 bands, i.e. the number of different tariff rates, and a maximum rate of 40%. (Fane, 2003).

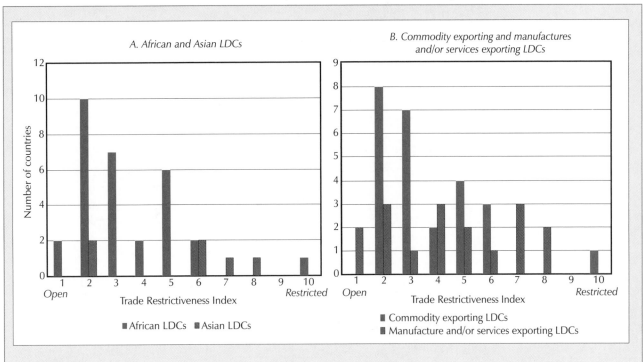

Source: As for chart 32.

Note: Data were not available for Afghanistan and Somalia.

At issue here is how much trade liberalization has been undertaken. The point is not that the Asian LDCs and those exporting manufactures and services have not undertaken trade liberalization. It is that the African LDCs and commodity exporters have undertaken such deep trade liberalization. This point can be underlined by a recent study that proposed establishing Rwanda as an economy-wide free zone following the example of Hong Kong (China) or Singapore. This was regarded as being a practical proposal because Rwanda's trade policy regime was already "not far removed from those of Hong Kong (China) or Singapore" (de Rosa and Roningen, 2002: 31).[1] It is also worth recalling that the famous Sachs-Warner index of openness, which, although widely criticized, has been frequently used to estimate the relationship between openness and economic growth, uses, among others, a tariff rate threshold of 40 per cent as one of the indicators to distinguish "open" from "closed" economies (Sachs and Warner, 1995). According to this criterion, all the LDCs are now "open".

Finally, along with trade liberalization, the LDCs have also introduced more flexible exchange-rate policies, with substantial devaluations[2] of their exchange rates. As shown in chart 34, both the African and Asian LDCs depreciated their currencies to a similar degree between 1980 and 2002, but the time path of change was significantly different. In the 1980s, the average real exchange rate was devalued much more in the Asian LDCs than in the African ones. In the 1990s, the reverse pattern held, with the average real exchange rate being devalued by over 50 per cent in the African LDCs and by 23 per cent in the Asian LDCs during the period 1990–2001. The different time-paths are likely to be related to the build-up of external debt in the African LDCs in the early 1980s and an unwillingness to face the consequences of devaluation in that context. But with the introduction of the IMF-financed programmes under the Structural Adjustment Facility (SAF) and Enhanced Structural Adjustment Facility (ESAF) in the late 1980s, average real exchange rates were sharply devalued. Trade

Both the African and Asian LDCs depreciated their currencies to a similar degree between 1980 and 2002, but their time-path of change was significantly different. The different timing is likely to be related to the build-up of external debt in the African LDCs in the early 1980s and an unwillingness to face the consequences of devaluation in that context.

CHART 34. TRENDS IN REAL EXCHANGE RATES FOR LDCs, 1980–2001
(*Index, 1985 = 100*)

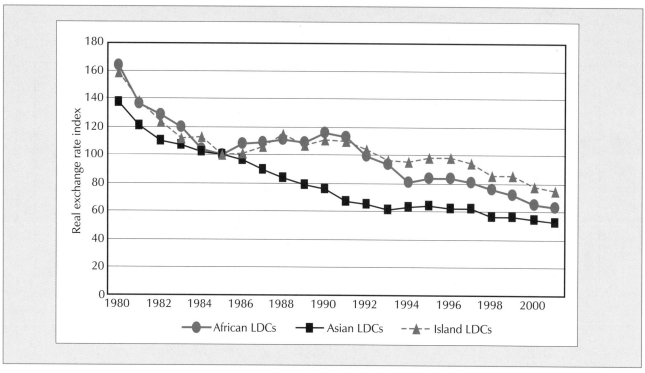

Source: UNCTAD secretariat estimates, based on World Bank, *World Development Indicators 2003*, CD-ROM.

Note: An increase indicates an appreciation while a fall indicates a depreciation.

The country's real exchange rates were calculated as the domestic price index (proxied by the GDP deflator) over the nominal exchange rate multiplied by the US consumer price index.

liberalization and devaluation have also taken place in the context of a general move towards more liberal domestic economic policies through privatization, reduction of the direct role of the State in the economy and domestic financial liberalization.

C. The sequencing, timing and speed of trade liberalization

Trade liberalization has generally taken place in the LDCs as part of the structural adjustment programmes in which most of them have been engaged since the 1980s.

Trade liberalization has generally taken place in the LDCs as part of the structural adjustment programmes in which most of them have been engaged since the 1980s. This has not been part of a negotiated global process of trade liberalization. Rather, it has been associated with IMF and World Bank policy conditionality for aid inflows and debt relief. The promise of economic success through adjustment, together with the marginalization of LDCs in the context of global private capital flows and their dependence on debt relief and aid, explains why the LDCs have gone further than other developing countries in trade liberalization.

1. SEQUENCING OF TRADE LIBERALIZATION

Some trade economists (e.g. Rodrik, 1990; Edwards, 1997) argue that macroeconomic stabilization should come before structural reforms. This is because macroeconomic instability is often one of the most important causes of policy reversal (Edwards, 1992). In practice, however, the stabilization process usually overlaps structural reforms. With regard to the design of trade liberalization, which is part of the process of structural reform, Edwards (1997) has summarized the best sequencing on the basis of experience as follows:

(a) The government should find an alternative source of revenue before the tariff cut is made;

(b) Import licences and prohibitions should be eliminated during the early stages of the liberalization scheme, and tariffs should replace them if necessary;

(c) A real-exchange-rate overvaluation should be avoided and nominal exchange-rate anchors should be introduced at the beginning of the reform; and

(d) A uniform tariff structure should be introduced for efficiency reasons.

From first hand information gathered from the national trade ministries of 16 countries,[3] complemented by international sources on another 11 countries,[4] it was possible to identify a series of common steps that were typically followed by LDCs in their liberalization efforts. These steps conformed somewhat to the sequence recommended by Edwards, as noted above, but there were some divergences which conformed more closely to other views of best practice (see, for example, Michaely, 1986, and Balassa, 1985). Generally, the steps undertaken by the LDCs were:

(a) A macroeconomic reform in the form of exchange-rate reform, necessary to ease constraints on exporters, and currency devaluation;

(b) Abolition of export restrictions, price decontrol and privatization to strengthen the role of the private sector through the elimination of monopolies on foreign trade and through the promulgation of foreign investment laws;

(c) Elimination of quantitative measures and/or convertion of import restrictions into ad valorem tariff rates. The tariff regime was rationalized and simplified through a reduction in the number of tariff bands. Applied rates, on average, were also reduced. Indirect taxes were normally introduced at this stage, or shortly thereafter, to compensate for the lack of tariff revenue accruing to the government;

(d) Introduction of measures to facilitate and support exports; and,

(e) Further liberalization — on a regional basis — while joining free trade areas or customs unions (Borgatti, 2003).

From first-hand information gathered from the national trade ministries of 16 LDCs, complemented by international sources on another 11 LDCs, it was possible to identify a series of common steps that were typically followed by LDCs in their liberalization efforts.

Some policies were undertaken before others. Nepal, Haiti and Cape Verde, for example, undertook export promotion policies years before their tariff reforms were implemented. While tax substitutes were introduced before tariffs were lowered in the majority of LDCs, Guinea, Uganda and Sudan introduced a value added tax (VAT) only when their goods sector was liberalized. In Senegal, a decrease in tariff rates in the mid-1980s was reversed at the end of the decade partly owing to the lack of needed revenues that could replace those obtained from tariffs.[5]

The literature on sequencing often advises the liberalizing countries to undertake gradual trade reform in the presence of an inflationary environment (Edwards, 1992). However, the Gambia, Mozambique and Sudan successfully carried out simultaneous macroeconomic and trade reforms, at a rapid pace and in a highly inflationary environment. The risk of undertaking reforms in such an environment is that the Government might be forced to renege on its pledges and revert to its previous policies.

The end of the liberalization process for LDCs is characterized by widespread participation in regional agreements. The end of the 1990s, in particular, saw a rapid increase in regionalism in the form of free trade areas or customs unions. Regionalism has contributed to widespread uniformity in tariff rates that characterizes the current trade regimes of many LDCs. Members of the West African Economic and Monetary Union (WAEMU), the Common Market for Eastern and Southern Africa (COMESA) and the Caribbean Common Market (CARICOM) have all adopted an external, four-band tariff scheme. Other countries have also adopted uniform rates: the Gambia, Mauritania and Cambodia have a four-band tariff scheme, Uganda a three-band scheme and the United Republic of Tanzania a five-band one.[6] Some Asian LDCs maintain a "cascading" tariff structure with low tariffs levied on investment goods and inputs for industry, while higher tariffs apply to non-essential luxury goods.

Regionalism has contributed to widespread uniformity in tariff rates that characterizes the current trade regimes of many LDCs.

From the information available on the sequencing of capital account liberalization, it seems that LDCs have liberalized their financial and goods sectors simultaneously. In the Gambia, Haiti, Mauritania and Uganda, liberalization of the capital account coincided with liberalization of the goods sector. In Nepal and Togo, interest rates were freed when liberalization of the goods sector was started but not completed. The United Republic of Tanzania eased controls about four years before liberalization of its goods sector. In Zambia, the capital account was first liberalized in 1982, together with the first liberalization of its goods sector. This was followed in 1994 by a policy reversal and a second liberalization of the capital account, which took place two years after the liberalization of the goods sector had started. It is worth noting that in all the countries analysed the liberalization of the capital account never took place after the liberalization of the goods sector (Borgatti, 2003).

In all the countries analysed the liberalization of the capital account took place either before or during the liberalization of the goods sector.

A general feature of the sequencing of trade liberalization in the LDCs is that financial and other support measures to their exporting companies were not introduced either before or during the early stages of trade liberalization. Cape Verde, Haiti and Nepal all introduced export promotion policies before the implementation of tariff reforms. In the case of Cape Verde and Nepal, the export promotion strategy began, respectively, five years and nine years, before their trade liberalization started. In the case of Haiti, it involved the strengthening of trade ties with United States. It is notable that in all these three countries exports of manufactures account for a major part of their merchandise exports.

The liberalization process occurred without any prior preparations to ensure that domestic industries were ready to face exposure to international competition.

Finally, it is evident that the need for actions to nurture the competitiveness of domestic enterprises has become more intense following trade liberalization. The liberalization process occurred without any prior preparations to ensure that before domestic industries were ready to face exposure to international competition.

2. THE TIMING AND SPEED OF TRADE LIBERALIZATION

On the basis of their speed of liberalization, the LDCs can be divided into three groups (table 36):

- Fast liberalizers — countries that liberalized within a five-year period: Benin, Cape Verde, the Gambia, Malawi, Mozambique, Sudan and Zambia;

- Gradual liberalizers — countries that liberalized within 6 to 15 years: Guinea, Haiti, Lesotho, Madagascar, Mali, Mauritania, Nepal, Togo and Uganda; and

TABLE 36. SELECTED LDCs CLASSIFIED ACCORDING TO THE SPEED OF TRADE LIBERALIZATION

Fast	Gradual	Ongoing
Benin (5 years)	Guinea (13 years)	Bangladesh
Cape Verde (5 years)	Haiti (10 years)	Bhutan
Gambia (4 years)	Lesotho (6 years)	Burkina Faso
Malawi (5 years)	Madagascar (8 years)	Burundi
Mozambique (2 years)	Mali (10 years)	Cambodia
Sudan (5 years)	Mauritania (6 years)	Ethiopia
Zambia (4 years)	Nepal (7 years)	Lao People's Dem. Republic
	Togo (9 years)	Maldives
	Uganda (6 years)	Senegal
		Solomon Islands

Source: Borgatti (2003), based on information supplied by national authorities and other international sources.

Note: The figures in brackets refer to the length of the liberalization episodes.

- Current liberalizers — countries that are still undertaking reforms: Bangladesh, Bhutan, Burkina Faso, Burundi, Cambodia, Ethiopia, the Lao People's Democratic Republic, Maldives, Senegal and the Solomon Islands.

The majority of countries for which data were available started to liberalize their economies in the 1980s, and only a few of them are still in the process of completing liberalization. Among the countries that started in the 1990s only Cape Verde, Mauritania and Sudan completed their liberalization process by the end of the decade. Bhutan, Burundi, Maldives and Solomon Islands started to relax their protective measures only in the late 1990s and are still undertaking liberalization.

The majority of countries for which data were available started to liberalize their economies in the 1980s, and only a few of them are still in the process of completing liberalization.

For comparative purposes, some of the LDCs liberalized their economies faster than the countries that are often taken as models for rapidly undertaking liberalizing reforms, notably Chile. Chile liberalized its economy over a five-year period (1974–1979) during a non-optimal economic situation (Meller, 1994). The seven fast liberalizers among the LDCs either liberalized at the same speed or faster than Chile.

Table 37 lists the starting years of the liberalization episodes for 26 countries. The years have been identified through an analysis based primarily on the evolution of tariffs, NTBs and exchange-rate policies. The first column identifies the starting date of the liberalization process in each country analysed, while the second identifies the key episodes of liberalization, at the end of which a country is classified as open. The episodes represent, as objectively as possible, the years when the full spectrum of trade liberalization measures were undertaken by each country.

Some of the LDCs liberalized their economies faster than the countries that are often taken as models for rapidly undertaking liberalizing reforms.

An interesting feature of the timing of trade liberalization in the LDCs is that most of the mineral-exporting LDCs went farthest earliest. In 1997, the first year for which data were available on the IMF trade restrictiveness index, 6 of the 14 LDCs that have an index of 1, 2 or 3 — the most open categories — were mineral exporters, and this included all the mineral-exporting LDCs, except Liberia. This may imply that there was less national concern about the effects of trade liberalization on domestic agriculture and industry in these countries than in the other countries.

The literature on trade liberalization emphasizes the need for a liberalizing country to avoid overvaluations of the exchange rate, used to support high trade

TABLE 37. THE TIMING OF TRADE LIBERALIZATION EPISODES IN LDCs

Countries	Liberalization starting year	Liberalization episodes
Bangladesh	1986	1992–present
Benin	1988	1990–1994
Bhutan	1996	1996–present
Burkina Faso	1991	1992–present
Burundi	2002	2002–present
Cambodia	1994	1994–present
Cape Verde	1987	1997–2001
Ethiopia	1992	1996–present
Gambia	1985	1985–1988
Guinea	1985	1985–1997
Haiti	1986	1987–1996
Lao People's Democratic Republic	1988	1995–present
Lesotho	1984	1994–1999
Madagascar	1988	1988–1996
Malawi	1988	1997–2001
Maldives	1998	1998-present
Mali	1986	1991–2000
Mauritania	1992	1992–1997
Mozambique	1987	1992–1993
Nepal	1986	1986–1992
Senegal	1986	1994–present
Solomon Islands	1997	1998–present
Sudan	1992	1996–2000
Togo	1988	1988–1996
Uganda	1981	1991–1996
United Republic of Tanzania	1984	1990–present
Zambia	1982	1992–1995

Source: Same as for table 37.

barriers. Shatz and Tarr (2000) argue that "protecting" countries are unable to adopt free trade policies if an exchange-rate adjustment does not take place. The evidence for 18 LDCs for which data are available shows that 11 had an undervalued exchange rate during their liberalization episodes, and 5 had a modest overvaluation, in the order of 20 per cent or less. Only Mauritania and Zambia had largely overvalued exchange rates during their liberalization episodes (Borgatti, 2003).

Table 38 shows that, in a sample of 13 LDCs that opened up their economies by 2001 and for which data were available, their real exchange rates appreciated before they started their liberalization process and depreciated thereafter. The only three exceptions to this rule were the Gambia, Togo and Zambia whose real exchange rates depreciated in the five years preceding the start of their liberalization episodes. The reference years for which the real-exchange-rate indices have been constructed are listed in table 39. The extent of the post-liberalization depreciation ranges between some 30 per cent (in Guinea, Togo and Uganda) and 4 per cent (in Mozambique). It is worth noting that Zambia experienced a depreciation of its real exchange rate before it began liberalization, but the initial depreciation was then reversed to an 8-per-cent appreciation in the post-liberalization period, before again depreciating to the level it was at during liberalization.

The literature on trade liberalization emphasizes the need for a liberalizing country to avoid overvaluations of the exchange rate... Out of 18 LDCs, 11 had an undervalued exchange rate during their liberalization episodes.

3. AID AND TRADE LIBERALIZATION

An important feature of the liberalization processes in the LDCs is that they have coincided with large increases in foreign aid to these countries (Borgatti,

TABLE 38. REAL EXCHANGE RATE INDICES[a] DURING, PRE-, AND POST-LIBERALIZATION

Countries	Pre-liberalization	Liberalization episodes	Post-liberalization
Benin	100.3	100	79.2
Cape Verde	119.8	100	..
Gambia	65.9	100	91.7
Guinea[b]	..	100	67.3
Lesotho	120.5	100	75.1
Madagascar	135.1	100	86.3
Malawi	134.1	100	..
Mali	126.0	100	..
Mauritania	132.6	100	70.9
Mozambique	127.6	100	96.5
Togo	93.2	100	65.7
Uganda	155.4	100	69.8
Zambia	80.0	100	108.2

Source: UNCTAD secretariat estimates, based on World Bank, *World Development Indicators 2003, CD-ROM.*

Note: Haiti, Nepal and Sudan were not included for lack of data.

a   The real exchange rate indices were calculated on the basis of the periods defined in table 39, and by taking the average corresponding to the liberalization episodes as 100. The country's real exchange rates were calculated as the domestic price index (proxied by the GDP deflator) over the nominal exchange rate multiplied by the US consumer price index.

b   The period 1986–1997 was taken as the liberalization episode for Guinea for lack of data.

TABLE 39. REFERENCE PERIODS[a] DURING, PRE- AND POST-LIBERALIZATION

Countries	Pre-liberalization	Liberalization episodes	Post-liberalization
Benin	1985–1989	1990–1994	1995–1999
Cape Verde	1992–1996	1997–2001	..
Gambia	1980–1984	1985–1988	1989–1993
Guinea	1980–1984	1985–1997	1998–2001
Haiti	1982–1986	1987–1996	1997–2001
Lesotho	1989–1993	1994–1999	2000–2001
Madagascar	1983–1987	1988–1996	1997–2001
Malawi	1992–1996	1997–2001	..
Mali	1986–1990	1991–2000	..
Mauritania	1987–1991	1992–1997	1998–2001
Mozambique	1987–1991	1992–1993	1994–1998
Nepal	1981–1985	1986–1992	1993–1997
Togo	1983–1987	1988–1996	1997–2001
Uganda	1986–1990	1991–1996	1997–2001
Zambia	1987–1991	1992–1995	1996–2000

Source: Borgatti (2003).

a   The reference periods are the dates used to define liberalization episodes and pre- and post-liberalization periods.

2003). This is associated with the fact that trade liberalization was not undertaken in the context of multilateral negotiations, but rather unilaterally by the countries, usually as part of IMF/World Bank structural adjustment programmes. As shown in UNCTAD's *Least Developed Countries 2000 Report*, there was a major increase in aid per capita in the LDCs undertaking SAF- and ESAF-funded programmes (UNCTAD, 2000: chart 40). The temporal conjunction between increasing aid inflows and trade liberalization reflects the greater financing which countries received upon proper implementation of these structural adjustment programmes. Using a probit econometric model, Borgatti (2003) finds that the probability of international aid flows affecting the timing of trade liberalization in the LDCs is statistically significant, even after accounting for the presence of IMF Structural Adjustment Facilities.

An important feature of the liberalization processes in the LDCs is that they have coincided with large increases in foreign aid to these countries.

D. The short-term impact of trade liberalization on poverty

1. Trade restrictiveness, and trends in private consumption and poverty in the 1990s

The incidence of poverty increased unambiguously in those economies that adopted the most open trade regimes and in those that continued with the most closed trade regimes.

UNCTAD's *Least Developed Countries Report 2002* examined changes in the share of the population living on less than $1/day during the 1990s in a sample of 36 LDCs, classified according to the degree of trade restrictiveness at the end of the 1990s. This was not a comparison of the situation before and after trade liberalization. However, it is reasonable to assume that most countries started the decade with much more restricted trade regimes, and thus the classification groups countries according to how far they liberalized. The results, reproduced in chart 35, show that the incidence of poverty increased unambiguously in those economies that adopted the most open trade regimes and in those that continued with the most closed trade regimes. But in between these extremes there was a tendency for poverty to decline in those countries that had liberalized their trade regimes to a lesser extent, and for poverty to increase in those countries that had liberalized their trade regimes to a greater extent.

An analysis of trends in private consumption per capita using more recent data confirms this conclusion. Focusing on growth rates of exports and private consumption per capita, it is clear that the trade–poverty relationship improved between the first half of the 1990s and the second half of the 1990s in countries which were "open", "moderately open", and "restricted", according to the IMF restrictiveness index for 2000. But the greatest improvement was observed in those which opened up moderately during the decade rather than those which opened up the most (chart 36).

The greatest improvement was observed in those which opened up moderately during the decade rather than those which opened up the most.

As stressed by UNCTAD (2002), it would be wrong to conclude from these trends that trade liberalization is causing poverty. The differences between the groups reflect a range of influences, and, in particular, the fact that although the LDCs exporting manufactures and services have undertaken trade liberalization, they have done so to a lesser extent than the agricultural-commodity-exporting LDCs. It is this factor which explains the apparently anomalous tendency for the most restricted economies to have the highest export growth rates. But from this evidence there is no basis for concluding that trade liberalization, in the short run, reduces poverty or leads to a more virtuous trade–poverty relationship.

2. The diversity of impact

One of the major findings of the increasing body of case-study evidence on the short-term impact of trade liberalization in the LDCs is that there is considerable variability between countries, as well as between social groups and geographical areas. In order to see the patterns of change more clearly, it is useful to distinguish LDCs according to their major export specialization.

(a) Agricultural-commodity-exporting LDCs

The short-term impact of the removal of export taxes and import tariffs on agricultural-commodity-exporting countries is an increase in the prices received by commodity exporters and reduced prices of imported goods. Depending on the production relations in the commodity exporting sector and the nature of intermediation between the producers and the international market, this could have different implications for poverty reduction. For example, if commodity

CHART 35. TRADE LIBERALIZATION AND POVERTY TRENDS IN LDCs DURING THE 1990s

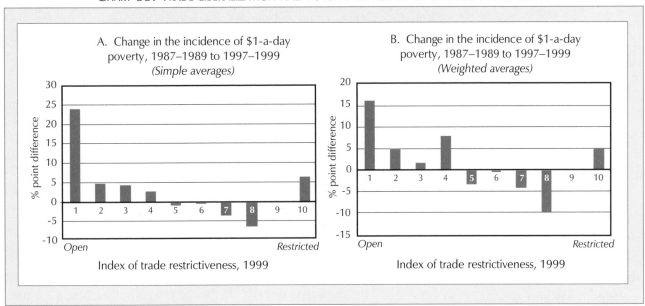

A. Change in the incidence of $1-a-day poverty, 1987–1989 to 1997–1999
(Simple averages)

B. Change in the incidence of $1-a-day poverty, 1987–1989 to 1997–1999
(Weighted averages)

Index of trade restrictiveness, 1999

Index of trade restrictiveness, 1999

Source: UNCTAD (2002: 117, chart 33).

CHART 36. TRADE LIBERALIZATION AND TRENDS IN REAL EXPORTS AND PRIVATE CONSUMPTION PER CAPITA IN LDCs, 1990–1995 AND 1995–2000

(Average annual growth rate, percentage)

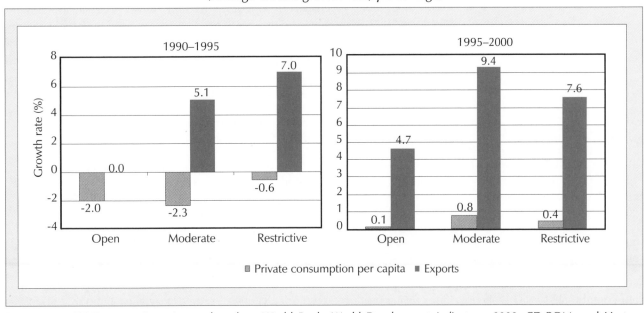

1990–1995

1995–2000

■ Private consumption per capita ■ Exports

Source: UNCTAD secretariat estimates based on World Bank, *World Development Indicators 2003*, CD-ROM; and Heston, Summers and Aten (2002).

Notes: The "open", "moderate" and "restrictive" LDCs are defined according to IMF definitions and the IMF index of trade restrictiveness in 2000. An economy is defined as "open" if it has an index of 1–4; "moderate" if it has an index of 5–6; and "restricted" if it has an index of 7–10. The averages exclude oil exporters and Haiti.

exports are predominantly produced in large plantations, the immediate impact is an increase in the profits of the plantation owners without major short-term implications for poverty reduction in that sector. On the other hand, if export cash crops are produced by medium and small farmers, and if the nature of market intermediation is such that the price increases are passed on to them, then the immediate impact of liberalization will be an increase in income of a broader section of the population engaged in cash crop production. In that case they will doubly benefit, because the prices of imported consumer and producer goods will also fall as a result of trade liberalization. The very small farmers who, along with the landless rural workers are likely to be the poorest of the poor, are most likely to see the benefits from the price increases captured by middlemen and moneylenders, unless specific measures are introduced to provide such farmers with inputs, credit and competitive channels for market access. In fact, if the marketing is monopolized by particular merchants or companies, even the middle and rich farmers will not fully benefit from the price increases. Uganda's experience illustrates some of these tendencies (see box 10).

Many of the poor in the agricultural-commodity-exporting LDCs live in rural areas and are engaged in subsistence-oriented farming of traditional food crops rather than in export activities. This group will not benefit much from a reduction in import prices of wage goods and producer goods following liberalization, as the import content of their expenditures is very low.

Many of the poor in the agricultural-commodity-exporting LDCs live in rural areas and are engaged in subsistence-oriented farming of traditional food crops rather than in export activities. Improved export prices can reach this group if they shift their production mix. But such a production shift is not always possible owing to risk aversion and uncertainty, as well as structural constraints, for example, those related to the gender division of labour. This group also will not benefit much from a reduction in import prices of wage goods and producer goods following liberalization, as the import content of their expenditures is very low. Moreover, if liberalization leads to a substitution of the traditional, home-produced food by cheap, imported food in the expenditure patterns of the more well-to-do sections of society, the traditional-food producers may face declining demand and prices for their produce. In the short run, this may, to some extent, favour the landless poor who are the consumers of such food products.

In Madagascar, there is a strong correlation between changes in the incidence of poverty and remoteness, with those living in the most remote rural areas facing lower prices for the goods they sell, higher prices for the goods they consume, fewer diversification opportunities and lower productivity (Stifel et al., 2003). Thus there has been a tendency towards growing poverty in remote areas. Earlier studies have also suggested that what may be happening in some of the worst areas is that poor households are being squeezed by price changes and price instability and have to increase output in order to sustain their minimal subsistence living standards (Barrett, 1998).

Box 10. Trade Liberalization, Exports and Poverty in Uganda

Data in the Uganda Poverty Status Report 2001 (PMAU, 2002) show that there was substantial reduction in the incidence of poverty, from 56 per cent in 1992 to 35 per cent in 2000, during the period of trade liberalization. Poverty reduction occurred in both the urban and rural areas: in the former, from 29 per cent to 10 per cent, and in the latter, from 60 per cent to 39 per cent (see also Appleton, 1998). In the rural areas, the incidence of poverty amongst cash-crop farmers fell from 63 per cent to 34 per cent. But it fell much less amongst food-crop farmers, from 60 per cent to 46 per cent, actually rising by 3 per cent from 1992-1996, a period which coincides with the trade liberalization episode (Morrissey, O., Rudaheranwa, N., and Moller, L., 2003).

Coffee producers did particularly well during this period of rising coffee prices; there is evidence that, in addition to contributing to higher incomes for existing producers, the price changes spurred a significant supply response by the less well-off, allowing the poor to make better use of their labour (Deininger and Okidi, 2003). On the basis of the household survey of 1999/2000, it may be estimated that 27 per cent of the people in farm households that grow coffee are poor as against 41 per cent of the non-coffee-growing farmers (Booth et al., 2003).

The benefits of agricultural exports do not always reach the poor, as the cases of producers of tobacco, tea and fish illustrate (Morrissey, O., Rudaheranwa, N., and Moller, L. 2003). In Northern Uganda, tobacco-growers who grow tobacco on an annual contractual basis face a market situation in which there is only one buyer, British American Tobacco (BAT) Uganda Ltd., and the farmers are open to exploitation in the grading and pricing of their tobacco. Casual workers on large-scale tea estates are amongst the poorest people in the country. Within the fishing industry on Lake Victoria, fishermen hire boats and sometimes nets from boat owners, with whom they split the catch (often 50/50 but sometimes getting as little as 20 per cent), and then sell to the processors, often at very low prices because of the perishability of the product. There is little upward mobility in the fishing communities, with few fishermen becoming boat-owners. Women generally do not own boats and are excluded from fishing by tradition and cultural norms.

There are also regional differences in the rate of poverty reduction. Although the incidence of poverty has fallen in the country as whole, it has declined little in the northern region, which is affected by conflict (PMAU, 2002).

A particular problem for agricultural-commodity-exporting LDCs is that the widespread adoption of trade liberalization and export-oriented policies has been associated with falling world prices for agricultural commodities. As a consequence, the potential benefits that agricultural producers can gain through higher prices at the national level can be offset by lower prices at the international level. In the worst cases, this will lead to the phenomenon of immiserizing trade (see chapter 3). The Diagnostic and Trade Integration Study (DTIS) for Ethiopia[7] (Integrated Framework, 2003a) gives a graphic picture of the situation of coffee growers and their families. Assuming a household size of 6 or 7 persons, it can be estimated that 7.5 to 8 million people depend on the sector. But as the DTIS notes — without comment and in passing, "the negative margin between farmgate prices and production costs make it clear that production is not currently profitable" (Integrated Framework, 2003a: 49). The DTIS estimates that coffee accounted for 40 per cent of the value of Ethiopian exports in 2001/2002.

The overall short-term impact of trade liberalization in agricultural-commodity-exporting LDCs depends not only on what is happening in rural areas but also in urban centres. Cheaper imports will affect the import-competing industries adversely, which can have a deflationary effect in the urban economy. Factories that cannot compete with cheap imports will close down. Similarly affected could be the processing factories linked to liberalized export cash crops that can no longer compete with foreign competitors. The case of cashew nut processing in Mozambique is a stark example; it is estimated that trade liberalization, in the form of the removal of export quotas and export taxes on raw cashew nuts, led to the loss of approximately 10,000 jobs (Cramer, 1999; McMillan, M., Rodrik, D., Welch, K., 2002). In the absence of social security, the unemployed workers from factories forced to close down add to the numbers of urban poor. The workers who are able to keep their jobs by working in services or industries that manage to survive foreign competition, can benefit from the availability of cheaper imported wage goods. This, however, may not last long. Devaluations of the exchange rate during and after a liberalization episode wipe out the effects of cheap, imported wage goods in real wages. In fact the substantial real-exchange-rate devaluations in the LDCs discussed above, which indicate the change in the prices of non-traded goods to traded goods, imply a substantial real-wage reduction in these countries.[8]

While trade liberalization has often had a negative effect on urban wage employment, as former import-substituting industries or export-processing industries become unable to compete, trade liberalization is often associated with a booming urban informal sector. This is related to the fact that liberalization episodes in the LDCs have usually coincided with large increases in foreign aid to these countries. Such increases, bolstered by exchange-rate devaluations — which increase the domestic currency value of aid-supported expenditures — lead to an economic boom, particularly in the urban areas and in the services sectors. This can have a multiplier effect in the urban informal sector, and can lead to a rise in employment and incomes in that sector. A good example of this pattern is the United Republic of Tanzania during the 1990s (Wuyts, 2001). But this type of boom is not created by trade liberalization; rather, it is an aid-driven boom, which can — and will — be reversed as aid declines in subsequent periods.

(b) Mineral and oil exporting LDCs

The short-term impact of trade liberalization in mineral- and oil-exporting LDCs is complicated because the revenues from mineral exports often directly accrue to the State. Hence the government's direct expenditure and credit

A particular problem for agricultural-commodity-exporting LDCs is that the widespread adoption of trade liberalization and export-oriented policies has been associated with falling world prices for agricultural commodities.

While trade liberalization has often had a negative effect on urban wage employment, as former import-substituting industries or export-processing industries become unable to compete, trade liberalization is often associated with a booming urban informal sector.

policies can overshadow the effect of other policies. Particular complications can arise in the small oil- and mineral-exporting countries facing a commodity boom. Although the exchange rates may be appropriate in relation to their main export, they are likely to be overvalued with respect to other economic sectors. Such countries face extra difficulties in ensuring competitiveness of agricultural and manufacturing exports, at least at their current levels of skills and technological development, since their exchange rates are overvalued in relation to their agricultural and manufacturing sector. This type of overvaluation, however, cannot be remedied by currency devaluations, because such devaluations would lead to even larger mineral export revenues in domestic currency terms and, depending on the fiscal stance of the government, an even bigger inflationary boom. If the government does not use the mineral export revenues for investment and development of the backward agricultural areas, this type of economy will create highly dualistic structures, where the urban areas, and particularly the capital city, will exhibit the latest manifestations of modernity alongside a backward rural sector. Social and political tensions in such societies can become acute as the main source of riches is access to State resources in the form of rents from mineral exports. Trade liberalization under these circumstances will usually exacerbate the duality and socio-political tensions, because under liberalization the modern enclave will be totally cut off from the agricultural sector by importing all its needs from abroad. Zambia's experience exemplifies the short-term impact of trade liberalization on poverty in a mineral economy that has not suffered such problems (see box 11).

> *If the Government does not use mineral export revenues for investment and development of the backward agricultural areas, this type of economy will create highly dualistic structures.*

(c) Manufactures-exporting LDCs

Trade liberalization is taking place more slowly in the manufactures-exporting LDCs. This is particularly so in the large Asian labour surplus LDCs such as Bangladesh, Cambodia and the Lao People's Democratic Republic, which have average trade-restrictiveness indices closer to the other fast-growing Asian manufacturing exporters such as India or Viet Nam. In these cases, trade liberalization will help promote poverty reduction, if it supports the growth rate of industrial employment and the development of dynamic complementarities between agriculture and industry.

> *In the manufactures-exporting LDCs, trade liberalization will help promote poverty reduction if it supports the growth rate of industrial employment and the development of dynamic complementarities between agriculture and industry.*

Employment data for Bangladesh indicate that manufactured exports have played a central role in accelerating the rate of employment growth in the country. This expansion is attributable to market access preferences accorded by the EU, rather than to trade liberalization (see chapter 6). The employment effects of the process of trade liberalization, which began in the 1990s, reflect the balance between the positive effects on employment in manufacturing associated with the impulse that liberalization gives to domestic demand growth and export growth on the one hand, and the negative effects of import penetration. One study shows that with trade liberalization in the 1990s, there was indeed an increase in job losses through import penetration. But at the same time, there was a large increase in employment creation through exports, which far exceeded this negative effect. During the period 1985–1990, 274,194 jobs were created through export growth, and import substitution created a further 8,486 jobs. In 1990–1995, employment creation through export expansion accelerated to the extent of creating 802,205 jobs, while 57,296 jobs were lost through import penetration (table 40; Jenkins and Sen, 2004). Among the LDCs, trade liberalization has occurred relatively slowly in Bangladesh, and this policy has probably ensured that job losses through import penetration were not as high as in African LDCs such as Madagascar and Malawi, discussed later.

BOX 11. TRADE LIBERALIZATION AND POVERTY TRENDS IN ZAMBIA

On the basis of household survey data for 1991, 1996 and 1998, the proportion of the population living in poverty increased dramatically in the period 1991-1996 — a period during and immediately after a rapid and comprehensive trade liberalization. But the situation improved somewhat after 1996, and in 1998 the national incidence of poverty was at around the level it had been in 1991. Using the upper national poverty line, the incidence of poverty increased from 70 to 81 per cent of the population from 1991 to 1996, and then fell back to 72 per cent in 1998.

Within these trends there are significant differences amongst rural and urban areas. In 1991, the incidence of poverty was much higher in rural areas than in urban areas, with 89 per cent living below the upper poverty line in the rural areas and 47 per cent in the urban areas. During the period 1991–1996, in the rural areas the incidence of poverty increased by one percentage point and then fell to 77 per cent by 1998. In contrast, the incidence of poverty rose sharply in urban areas during the period 1991–1996, from 47 per cent to 65 per cent, and then only declined slightly, to 63 per cent, in 1998.

A major factor contributing to increasing poverty in urban areas has been the decline in formal sector employment associated with trade liberalization and economic reform. Since 1991, Zambia has implemented wide-ranging economic reforms. These include stabilization, reforms in agricultural marketing, a large privatization programme, trade policy reforms and reform of the public sector. Zambia's economically active population is estimated to have grown from around 3.2 million in 1991 to over 4.7 million in 1998. While the economically active population grew by 46 per cent, formal sector employment fell by 15 per cent. Most of this is attributable to major restructuring in the mining sector, where the number of workers declined by 39 per cent, from 64,800 in 1991 to 39,434 in 1998. Similarly, in the manufacturing sector formal employment fell by 43 per cent, from 75,400 to 43,320 over the same period. Informal sector employment has been estimated at 2.3 million people in 1993. There was a 15 per cent increase in informal non-agricultural employment between 1995 and 1998.

Within the rural areas, not all the socioeconomic groups have experienced a reduction in the incidence of poverty. Amongst the large-scale farmers, the incidence of poverty fell dramatically from 70 per cent in 1991 to 18 per cent in 1998. Amongst the small-scale farmers, improvements were also apparent, but of a lesser magnitude, with the incidence of poverty falling from 90 per cent to 78 per cent over the period. However, amongst the rural non-agricultural households, the incidence of poverty rose from 70 per cent in 1991 to 80 per cent in 1998. Much of this increase is probably due to the situation of casual agricultural workers rather than that of rural traders and petty service providers. It is notable in this regard that there was a 35 per cent increase in informal agricultural employment in the period 1995 to 1998. Much of this employment growth may be linked to the growing importance of large farms.

Source: McCulloch, N., Baulch, B. and Cherel-Robson, M. (2000).

The experience of the Lao People's Democratic Republic also illustrates generally positive poverty trends associated with trade liberalization (Fane, 2003). Average private consumption per capita rose by between 2.5 and 5.8 per cent between 1992/93 and 1997/98, and the share of the population living below the national poverty line fell from 45 per cent to 38 per cent. Most regions shared in the rising prosperity, but the greatest increases in average private consumption per capita and reductions in poverty occurred in the capital city, Vientiane. At the same time, the incidence of poverty rose in the mountainous and isolated extreme northwest of the country, a region where illegal logging, which had previously been an important source of livelihood, was banned. There was also a significant increase in inequality, with the Gini index for consumption distribution increasing from 29 to 35. The poor gained less than the rest of the population, and the poorest quintile probably lost during the first five years of the reform process (Fane, 2003).

Trade liberalization has occurred relatively slowly in Bangladesh, and this policy has probably ensured that job losses through import penetration were not as high as they were in Madagascar and Malawi.

TABLE 40. MANUFACTURING EMPLOYMENT GROWTH FROM TRADE IN BANGLADESH, 1975–1997

	Domestic demand	Export growth	Import penetration	Productivity growth	Total employment growth	Net employment growth from trade
	a	b	c	d	(a+b+c+d)	(b+c)
1975–1980	3 165	60 362	-25 892	17 512	55 147	34 469
1980–1985	75 254	50 714	-20 699	-48 783	56 486	30 015
1985–1990	276 717	247 194	8 486	27 043	559 440	255 679
1990–1997	435 119	802 205	-57 296	-316 015	864 013	744 909

Source: Jenkins and Sen (2004).

Note: The impact of trade on employment is identified by decomposing the sources of employment change into those due to changes in domestic demand, changes in exports, changes in imports and productivity growth.

3. THE QUESTION OF THE IMPACT OF TRADE LIBERALIZATION

It should be emphasized that all these trends refer to what is happening during and immediately after the trade liberalization process. However, not every development should be attributed to trade liberalization. Many other policy changes were occurring at the same time, and the economies were also affected by exogenous shocks of various kinds. It is particularly difficult to separate the impact of trade liberalization in the LDCs because of the association of trade liberalization episodes with increasing aid. What appears to be a positive effect of trade liberalization might equally be due to the effects of increased aid inflows on a country's balance of payments. Improvements in the export growth rate, for example, are largely related to currency devaluations. This is evident in the export take-off of Bangladesh, Burundi, Cape Verde, Ethiopia, Guinea, Guinea-Bissau, Mali, Mauritania, Mozambique, Senegal and Zambia.

There is great variability in the impact of trade liberalization from country to country and amongst different groups, depending on their factor endowments and expenditure patterns.

The only way to isolate the impact of trade liberalization precisely is to construct a counterfactual of what would have happened without trade liberalization, and to compare this with what would have happened under trade liberalization. This can be done with standard computable general equilibrium models. Some estimates have been made for the LDCs, which show diverse patterns that relate to the country under study and to the nature of the counterfactual that is modelled. Studies which compare the situation with and without tariff barriers indicate that trade liberalization has had a positive effect in Bangladesh (Khondker and Mujeri, 2002), a negative effect in Uganda (Morrissey, 2003), and a mixed effect in Nepal, with the rural population losing and the urban population gaining (Cockburn, 2002). Another approach, which has been used to assess the impact of trade and exchange-rate liberalization in sub-Saharan Africa, focuses on different policy responses to the adverse shocks of the late 1970s and early 1980s. It compares the outcome of a liberalized foreign exchange regime in the face of this shock against de facto foreign exchange rationing as a way to deal with it. On the basis of this comparison, it is concluded that in the Gambia, Madagascar and Niger, trade and exchange-rate liberalization has tended to benefit poor households in both rural and urban areas (Dorosh, P., Sahn, D.E. and Younger, S., 1996; Dorosh and Sahn, 2000).

These country studies show that there is great variability in the impact of trade liberalization from country to country and amongst different groups, depending on their factor endowments and expenditure patterns. Moreover, the conclusions on impact also vary according to the type of counterfactual adopted.

E. Prospects for substantial poverty reduction after trade liberalization: sustainability of economic growth

The deep trade liberalization that has occurred in most LDCs since the mid-1980s has created a new policy environment for development and poverty reduction. The evidence presented above suggests that poverty may increase or decrease during and immediately after trade liberalization. The diverse outcomes are associated in particular with differences in economic structure. An increase in knowledge of the variations between countries could help governments manage the process of trade liberalization in a way that will not hurt the poor in the short run. However, the policy debate now must go beyond such a concern for remedial poverty alleviation. The key issues are:

- What are the prospects of sustained and substantial long-term poverty reduction after trade liberalization?

- How can development and poverty reduction be promoted in a newly liberalized economy?

Substantial poverty reduction in the LDCs depends first of all on the ability to sustain high economic growth rates, and second, on the inclusiveness of the growth process. This section and the next assess whether the prospects for substantial poverty reduction have improved or worsened in the new policy environment, and which factors give cause for optimism and concern in each of these areas. The discussion is based on evidence of what is happening in the LDCs. In spite of diversity of experience and the fact that the liberalized policy environment has not been in place for a very long time, it is still possible to identify some emerging patterns of change.

The deep trade liberalization that has occurred in most LDCs since the mid-1980s has created a new policy environment for development and poverty reduction.

1. ECONOMIC GROWTH, EXPORTS, INVESTMENT AND SAVINGS

The major positive aspect of the post-liberalization economic trends in the LDCs is that rates of economic growth, export growth and investment growth are generally higher than before trade liberalization and the associated economic reforms. This is apparent in table 41, which summarizes pre- and post-liberalization economic trends in a sample of 11 LDCs. These countries have been selected because, according to the IMF criteria and the IMF trade restrictiveness index, they were already considered "open" by 1997. Moreover, from our research on the process of trade liberalization in the LDCs, reported earlier, it is also possible to date the liberalization episodes for these countries and thus compare economic trends before trade liberalization with those in the newly liberalized economy.

The major positive aspect of the post-liberalization economic trends in the LDCs is that rates of economic growth, export growth and investment growth are generally higher than before trade liberalization and the associated economic reforms.

From the table, it is apparent that average annual GDP growth rates were higher in the post-liberalization period than in the pre-liberalization period in 7 out of 10 cases for which data is available. Export growth rates were also higher in 6 out of 9 cases, and the rate of growth of gross fixed capital formation was higher in 5 out of 9 cases. Gross fixed capital formation increased as a percentage of GDP in 9 out of 10 cases. Moreover, export growth rates exceeded the 5 per cent threshold, which was identified in chapter 3 as a key level below which the trade–growth linkages are ambiguous, in 6 out of 9 cases. It is notable that the improvements are found in countries with different economic structures.

TABLE 41. KEY ECONOMIC TRENDS IN SELECTED LDCs IN THE PRE- AND POST-LIBERALIZATION PERIODS

	GDP growth (Annual %)		GDP per capita growth (Annual %)		Export growth (Annual %)		Import growth (Annual %)		Gross fixed capital growth (Annual %)		Gross fixed capital formation as a share of GDP (%)		Gross domestic savings as a share of GDP (%)		Aid per capita growth (Annual %)	
	Pre-liber.	Post-liber.	Pre-liber.	Post-liber.	Pre-liber.	Post-liber.	Pre-liber.	Post-liber.	Pre-liber.	Post-liber.	Pre-liber.	Post-liber.	Pre-liber.	Post-liber.	Pre-liber.	Post-liber.
Benin	0.4	5.1	-2.7	2.3	-11.9	6.8	-9.3	5.0	3.0	8.7	12.5	17.3	-2.3	5.4	21.3	-6.7
Gambia	4.3	3.3	1.2	-0.9	15.6	4.9	-8.8	6.8	-3.1	4.4	21.2	21.6	5.4	8.9	-8.2	-6.1
Guinea	..	3.1	..	0.8	..	3.2	..	3.7	..	5.4	..	20.6	.	17.5	-0.8	-13.9
Haiti	0.3	1.3	-1.6	-0.8	-0.7	5.6	3.7	4.6	-5.0	..	15.8	26.4	5.6	8.7	6.6	-19.9
Madagascar	1.5	4.8	-1.2	1.7	1.2	9.2	-3.7	11.5	..	12.8	9.1	14.6	3.5	7.8	17.8	-21.5
Mauritania	1.7	4.6	-0.7	1.3	-4.7	8.6	-3.5	6.8	-10.3	14.7	22.6	23.4	10.5	10.7	2.4	10.9
Mozambique	4.8	8.8	3.8	6.2	13.7	12.9	1.0	1.0	5.4	12.6	14.7	21.9	-13.2	-1.9	9.8	-6.2
Nepal	3.9	5.3	1.7	2.8	..	..	..	..	..	..	18.1	21.8	10.5	14.2	2.9	-1.8
Togo	3.3	0.2	-0.2	-2.7	4.8	-1.1	11.6	-1.0	17.0	5.7	17.3	16.7	11.1	4.3	2.8	-25.1
Uganda	6.5	5.3	3.3	2.5	3.6	6.1	5.6	15.4	12.0	8.3	10.6	18.2	1.6	6.8	29.7	-1.1
Zambia	0.8	1.5	-2.2	-0.8	-2.9	3.4	-10.8	-1.7	-1.5	9.4	9.6	14.5	12.7	5.1	12.3	3.3

Source: UNCTAD secretariat estimates, based on World Bank, *World Development Indicators 2003,* CD-ROM.

Note: The figures were calculated using data in constant local currency units, except aid per capita which was in current dollars. For the dates of pre- and post-liberalization periods, see table 39.

Three features of the post-liberal growth trends which give cause for concern are: the rates of economic growth given the high population growth rates, the low rates of domestic savings and post-liberalization aid fatigue.

Alongside the positive developments in terms of economic growth, exports and investment, there are three features of the post-liberal growth trends which give cause for concern. First, given the high population growth rates, the rates of economic growth have not been high enough to yield the GDP per capita growth rates necessary to make a major dent in poverty. Only in 6 out of 11 cases have GDP per capita growth rates exceeded 1 per cent per annum. Secondly, although there have been widespread improvements, the rate of domestic savings has remained low: in 8 out of 11 cases, gross domestic savings have been less than 10 per cent of GDP. Thirdly, there is strong evidence of post-liberalization aid fatigue: aid flows have been reduced in the aftermath of a newly liberalized economy. These trends may have been reversed recently (see part one, chapter 1), but in the countries examined here, aid per capita growth rate was lower in the five years following liberalization than in the five years before in 9 out of 11 countries. In 5 of these countries, aid per capita growth rate was more than 20 per cent lower in the post-liberalization than in the pre-liberalization period.

The very low domestic savings rates in the post-liberalization period imply that the sustainability of economic growth remains highly dependent on aid inflows and their effective use to build productive capacities and avoid the build-up of unsustainable external debt. Further research is necessary on the composition of investment to see if the positive growth rates in this area are related to increased investment in equipment or in structures (housing and construction). The limited evidence for African LDCs suggests that trade liberalization was associated with construction booms (Collier and Gunning, 1999).

2. CHANGES IN EXPORT COMPOSITION AND EXPORT CONCENTRATION

Although exports have been growing faster than before, a critical issue for the sustainability of economic growth is whether or not the composition of exports is changing and whether countries are beginning to diversify into more dynamic products. Table 42 shows changes in the revealed comparative advantage (RCA) indices[9] for the 10 major export products of the 11 LDCs pre- and post-

TABLE 42. MAJOR EXPORT PRODUCTS IN WHICH THE LDCs SPECIALIZED[a] IN THE PRE- AND POST-LIBERALIZATION PERIODS, RANKED ACCORDING TO MARKET DYNAMISM[b]

Countries	Pre-liberalization period				Post-liberalization period			
	SITC Rev.2 codes	Products	RCA	Product ranking	SITC Rev.2 codes	Products	RCA	Product ranking
Benin	263	Cotton	133.6	197	263	Cotton	408.9	197
	072	Cocoa	60.5	207	223	Seeds for other fixed oils	33.4	196
	424	Other fixed vegetable oils	39.6	151	222	Seeds for soft fixed oils	21.9	191
	223	Seeds for other fixed oils	12.1	196	057	Fruit, nuts, fresh, dried	7.1	130
	222	Seeds for soft fixed oils	7.3	191	122	Tobacco, manufactured	5.7	52
	423	Fixed vegetable oils, soft	4.1	144	652	Cotton fabrics, woven	4.6	119
	333	Crude petroleum	3.9		042	Rice	2.4	165
	071	Coffee and substitutes	3.4	210	661	Lime, cement and building prdts	1.9	143
	211	Hides skins, exc furs, raw	2.5	190	248	Wood, shaped, rail sleepers	1.6	133
	667	Pearl, prec, semi-prec stones	2.4	87	036	Shell fish fresh, frozen	1.5	83
		Average ranking		175		Average ranking		141
Gambia	423	Fixed vegetable oils, soft	80.7	144	035	Fish salted, dried, smoked	69.7	171
	034	Fish, fresh, chilled, frozen	69.9	76	036	Shell fish fresh, frozen	48.8	83
	222	Seeds for soft fixed oils	64.7	191	014	Meat prepd, prsrvd nes, etc	40.2	135
	035	Fish salted, dried, smoked	30.8	171	289	Prec metal ores, waste nes	34.6	169
	223	Seeds for other fixed oils	23.9	196	423	Fixed vegetable oils, soft	31.5	144
	277	Natural abrasives nes[d]	12.3	184	222	Seeds for soft fixed oils	28.8	191
	667	Pearl, prec, semi-prec stones	8.6	87	034	Fish, fresh, chilled, frozen	25.1	76
	036	Shell fish fresh, frozen	7.3	83	072	Cocoa	18.7	207
	263	Cotton	5.4	197	263	Cotton	11.0	197
	081	Feeding stuff for animals	5.2	163	075	Spices	8.0	160
		Average ranking		149		Average ranking		153
Guinea	287	Base metals ores, conc nes	151.2	181	287	Base metals ores, conc nes	174.6	181
	223	Seeds for other fixed oils	9.7	196	277	Natural abrasives nes	61.0	184
	071	Coffee and substitutes	2.8	210	522	Inorg chem elmnt, oxides, etc	50.8	153
	247	Other wood rough, squared	2.0	186	892	Printed matter	8.3	89
	667	Pearl, prec, semi-prec stones	1.4	87	071	Coffee and substitutes	6.1	210
	072	Cocoa	1.1	207	072	Cocoa	4.3	207
	281	Iron ore and concentrates	0.8	201	047	Other cereal meals, flour	3.8	198
	074	Tea and mate	0.5	187	263	Cotton	3.0	197
	551	Essential oils, perfume, etc	0.5	46	694	Stell, copper nails, nuts, etc	2.3	68
	424	Other fixed vegetable oils	0.4	151	046	Wheat etc, meal or flour	0.8	203
		Average ranking		165		Average ranking		169
Haiti	612	Leather, etc, manufactures	56.1	17	846	Under garments knitted	42.9	7
	223	Seeds for other fixed oils	32.7	196	847	Textile clothing accessoris nes	30.3	40
	846	Under garments knitted	26.2	7	551	Essential oils, perfume, etc	28.3	46
	071	Coffee and substitutes	22.9	210	843	Women's outwear non-knit	21.1	37
	894	Toys, sporting goods, etc	19.1	69	071	Coffee and substitutes	18.1	210
	551	Essential oils, perfume, etc	19.0	46	842	Men's outwear non-knit	14.6	48
	844	Under garments non-knit	15.0	21	845	Outer garments knit nonelastic	12.6	50
	771	Electric power machinery nes	12.2	5	896	Works of art, etc	10.6	156
	772	Switchgear etc, parts nes	10.7	19	848	Headgear, non-textile clothing	8.8	95
	658	Textile articles nes	9.5	57	072	Cocoa	8.4	207
		Average ranking		65		Average ranking		90
Madagascar[c]	075	Spices	427.3	160	075	Spices	261.9	160
	071	Coffee and substitutes	59.6	210	265	Vegetb fibre, exc cotton, jute	94.0	208
	265	Vegetb fibre, exc cotton, jute	30.4	208	941	Zoo animals, pets, etc	80.6	82
	036	Shell fish fresh, frozen	25.5	43	071	Coffee and substitutes	41.1	210
	551	Essential oils, perfume, etc	13.1	46	652	Cotton fabrics, woven	33.9	119
	278	Other crude minerals	11.9	185	036	Shell fish fresh, frozen	30.7	83
	652	Cotton fabrics, woven	7.8	119	654	Other woven textile fabric	24.7	127
	072	Cocoa	5.2	207	278	Other crude minerals	20.1	185
	263	Cotton	4.4	197	058	Fruit prsrvd, preprd	18.0	121
	061	Sugar and honey	4.3	205	551	Essential oils, perfume, etc	17.8	46
		Average ranking		158		Average ranking		134
Mauritania	281	Iron ore and concentrates	189.0	201	281	Iron ore and concentrates	261.9	201
	036	Shell fish fresh, frozen	101.2	83	036	Shell fish fresh, frozen	87.1	83
	034	Fish, fresh, chilled, frozen	20.1	76	034	Fish, fresh, chilled, frozen	73.5	76
	035	Fish salted, dried, smoked	5.0	171	035	Fish salted, dried, smoked	8.6	171
	941	Zoo animals, pets, etc	1.1	82	081	Feeding stuff for animals	3.8	163
	334	Petroleum products, refined	0.9		037	Fish etc prepd, prsrvd nes	2.0	96
	037	Fish etc prepd, prsrvd nes	0.8	96	411	Animal oils and fats	1.3	213
	211	Hides skins, exc furs, raw	0.7	190	211	Hides skins, exc furs, raw	0.9	190
	273	Stone, sand and gravel	0.4	97	291	Crude animal materials nes	0.8	141
	292	Crude vegetb materials nes	0.3	114	334	Petroleum products, refined	0.7	
		Average ranking		123		Average ranking		148

Table 42 (contd.)

Countries	\multicolumn{4}{Pre-liberalization period}	\multicolumn{4}{Post-liberalization period}						
	SITC Rev.2 codes	Products	RCA	Product ranking	SITC Rev.2 codes	Products	RCA	Product ranking
Mozambique	223	Seeds for other fixed oils	69.1	196	223	Seeds for other fixed oils	127.7	196
	036	Shell fish fresh, frozen	67.4	83	036	Shell fish fresh, frozen	121.5	83
	532	Dyes nes, tanning products	26.0	117	263	Cotton	41.8	197
	673	Iron, steel shapes, etc	14.5	173	046	Wheat etc, meal or flour	32.7	203
	263	Cotton	12.6	197	057	Fruit, nuts, fresh, dried	23.6	130
	061	Sugar and honey	12.5	205	061	Sugar and honey	19.4	205
	672	Iron, steel primary forms	11.6	67	035	Fish salted, dried, smoked	13.9	171
	057	Fruit, nuts, fresh, dried	11.5	130	044	Maize (corn), unmilled	13.3	214
	674	Iron, steel univ, plate, sheet	7.7	134	247	Other wood rough, squared	12.8	186
	282	Iron and steel scrap	7.6	126	121	Tobacco, unmanufactd, refuse	11.5	189
		Average ranking		*143*		*Average ranking*		*177*
Nepal	264	Jute, other textile bast fibres	730.1	224	659	Floor coverings, etc	217.2	159
	532	Dyes nes, tanning products	183.3	117	264	Jute, other textile bast fibres	114.4	224
	659	Floor coverings, etc	61.3	159	223	Seeds for other fixed oils	100.6	196
	223	Seeds for other fixed oils	53.2	196	075	Spices	31.3	160
	042	Rice	48.6	165	842	Men's outwear non-knit	19.6	48
	075	Spices	43.6	160	844	Under garments non-knit	14.9	21
	611	Leather	33.9	61	843	Women's outwear non-knit	8.7	37
	658	Textile articles nes	21.8	57	532	Dyes nes, tanning products	8.5	117
	654	Other woven textile fabric	17.8	127	054	Vegtb etc fresh, simply prsrvd	7.7	103
	054	Vegtb etc fresh, simply prsrvd	16.2	103	611	Leather	7.3	61
		Average ranking		*137*		*Average ranking*		*113*
Togo	271	Fertilizers, crude	590.7	221	271	Fertilizers, crude	1024.7	221
	072	Cocoa	55.2	207	263	Cotton	167.0	197
	263	Cotton	40.4	197	661	Lime, cement and building prdts	69.1	143
	223	Seeds for other fixed oils	33.9	196	046	Wheat etc, meal or flour	66.9	203
	661	Lime, cement and building prdts	25.5	143	072	Cocoa	37.9	207
	071	Coffee and substitutes	15.7	210	071	Coffee and substitutes	27.7	210
	277	Natural abrasives nes	14.7	184	223	Seeds for other fixed oils	13.0	196
	941	Zoo animals, pets, etc	13.0	82	693	Wire products, non-electric	7.1	152
	269	Waste of textile fabrics	6.1	80	673	Iron, steel shapes, etc	4.6	173
	046	Wheat etc, meal or flour	3.5	203	247	Other wood rough, squared	4.6	186
		Average ranking		*172*		*Average ranking*		*189*
Uganda	071	Coffee and substitutes	214.8	210	071	Coffee and substitutes	172.4	210
	211	Hides skins, exc furs, raw	23.6	190	074	Tea and mate	113.1	187
	074	Tea and mate	13.8	187	047	Other cereal meals, flour	84.7	198
	291	Crude animal materials nes	7.8	141	121	Tobacco, unmanufactd, refuse	45.0	189
	263	Cotton	7.2	197	291	Crude animal materials nes	34.5	141
	121	Tobacco, unmanufactd, refuse	2.4	189	211	Hides skins, exc furs, raw	30.5	190
	941	Zoo animals, pets, etc	2.0	82	263	Cotton	26.5	197
	222	Seeds for soft fixed oils	2.0	191	034	Fish, fresh, chilled, frozen	25.7	76
	072	Cocoa	1.5	207	35	Electric current	11.0	
	044	Maize (corn), unmilled	1.3	214	269	Waste of textile fabrics	10.3	80
		Average ranking		*＼181*		*Average ranking*		*163*
Zambia	682	Copper	132.8	116	682	Copper	111.8	116
	689	Non-fer base metals nes	79.5	107	689	Non-fer base metals nes	81.2	107
	686	Zinc	11.7	140	269	Waste of textile fabrics	29.4	80
	121	Tobacco, unmanufactd, refuse	6.3	189	263	Cotton	13.1	197
	685	Lead	2.9	204	061	Sugar and honey	10.0	205
	667	Pearl, prec, semi-prec stones	2.1	87	287	Base metals ores, conc nes	9.1	181
	35	Electric current	2.0		351	Electric current	9.0	
	681	Silver, platinum, etc	1.6	180	046	Wheat etc, meal or flour	8.2	203
	263	Cotton	1.5	197	661	Lime, cement and building prdts	7.7	143
	278	Other crude minerals	1.1	185	121	Tobacco, unmanufactd, refuse	6.7	189
		Average ranking		*156*		*Average ranking*		*158*

Source: UNCTAD secretariat estimates, based on UN COMTRADE and UNCTAD, *Handbook of Statistics 2003*; See Butkevicius et al., 2003, for methodology followed for the product ranking.

Note: For reference periods, see table 39.

    a   Specialization is measured by revealed comparative advantage (RCA). For methodology, see text.

    b   Market dynamism is measured by the export value growth of 225 products. The first 29 products have an average annual export value growth higher than 10 per cent, the products ranked between 30 and 153 have an average annual export value growth higher than 5 per cent.

    c   The data for Madagascar do not include exports from the export processing zone.

    d   nes — not elsewhere specified.

liberalization. The table also shows the ranking of these products in a list of 225 dynamic products, from the most dynamic (1) to the least dynamic (225).

From the table, it is apparent that there is a mixed pattern: some countries have reinforced the existing pattern of specialization after trade liberalization, while in other countries the pattern of specialization is somewhat different after their liberalization episode from what it was before. In Benin, Guinea, Mauritania, Mozambique and Togo, the five sectors with the highest RCA index before liberalization experienced an increase in their RCA index after liberalization. Benin, for example, increased its export specialization in cotton four times, while Togo doubled its specialization in exports of crude fertilizers. In contrast, the pattern of specialization has changed in the Gambia, Madagascar and Uganda, though agricultural and mineral products have been predominant among the major products in which they have a revealed comparative advantage. Haiti, Guinea and Togo have increased their specialization in manufactures with the liberalization of their goods sector. Interestingly, in Guinea two of the sectors that revealed the highest RCA are after trade liberalization were in manufacturing (i.e. inorganic chemical elements and printed matter).

Despite these changes, the major conclusion which may be drawn from the table is that these countries began, in the pre-liberalization period, with a very undynamic export structure, and in the post-liberalization period this problem has not been rectified. The average rank of the 10 products in which these countries had the greatest specialization increased in 7 of the 11 countries (implying a move towards a less dynamic export structure). Within the top 10 products, the number of export products with an export growth rate of over 5 per cent (in current US$) over the period 1980–2001 decreased in 8 of the 11 countries.

Table 43 sheds further light on whether export composition is changing in a way that would allow these countries to become less marginalized in the world economy. It shows whether or not these countries were increasing their share of world merchandise trade in the pre- and post-liberalization periods, and identifies the major components behind the trends, namely: (i) the lack of dynamic products in their export composition (estimated by the structural market effect); (ii) the competitiveness of export products (estimated by the market-share effect, which shows whether the country is gaining or losing market share in those products which it exports); and (iii) diversification into more dynamic products (market growth adaptation effect) or into less dynamic products (market stagnation adaptation effect). This is based on the method presented by Laursen (1997, 1998).[10]

The table shows that 7 of the 11 countries were losing market share in the pre-liberalization period and 8 were losing market share in the post-liberalization period. The only countries that were not losing market share in the five years after deep trade liberalization were the Gambia, Haiti and Mozambique. For these countries, the major factor contributing to this situation has been their improved competitiveness in existing exports, rather than diversification. For the 8 LDCs losing market share in the post-liberalization period, the major factors contributing to the situation were the lack of market-dynamic export products and loss of market share in existing export products. Five of the 11 countries had improved their competitiveness in existing markets in the pre-liberalization period, while only four were doing so in the post-liberalization period. Diversification made a very small contribution to the pattern of change in both the pre- and post-liberalization periods in all countries

The revealed comparative advantage for the 10 major export products of 11 LDCs shows that, in the pre-liberalization period, these countries began with a very undynamic export structure, and in the post-liberalization period this problem has not been rectified.

TABLE 43. CONSTANT MARKET SHARE ANALYSIS[a] FOR PRE-LIBERALIZATION AND POST-LIBERALIZATION

	Pre-liberalization[b]						
	Export market share at time t_1 (a) %	Export market share at time t_2 (b) %	Change (b-a) %	Market share effect (c)	Structural market effect (d)	Market growth adaptation (e)	Market stagnation adaptation (f)
Benin	0.079	0.029	-0.05	-0.04	-0.017	-0.0009	0.01
Gambia	0.017	0.027	0.01	0.008	0.003	0.0005	-0.0006
Guinea	0.22	0.27	0.05	0.098	-0.03	0.0002	-0.014
Haiti	0.093	0.31	0.22	0.15	0.016	0.033	-0.0005
Madagascar	0.19	0.15	-0.038	-0.05	0.016	-0.007	0.003
Mauritania	0.16	0.14	-0.02	-0.012	0.001	0.0002	0.001
Mozambique	0.072	0.043	-0.029	-0.028	-0.001	-0.0004	0.002
Nepal	0.039	0.069	0.03	0.023	-0.0006	0.003	-0.0002
Togo	0.11	0.105	-0.005	0.037	-0.021	-0.00013	-0.006
Uganda	0.21	0.08	-0.13	-0.047	-0.11	-0.0004	0.022
Zambia	0.34	0.25	-0.11	-0.13	-0.03	-0.0005	0.012
	Post-liberalization[b]						
	Export market share at time t_1 (a) %	Export market share at time t_2 (b) %	Change (b-a) %	Market share effect (c)	Structural market effect (d)	Market growth adaptation (e)	Market stagnation adaptation (f)
Benin	0.041	0.04	-0.01	0.013	-0.015	-0.0003	-0.0054
Gambia	0.012	0.017	0.005	0.006	-0.0004	0.0003	0.0003
Guinea	0.098	0.092	-0.006	-0.0098	0.0026	-0.0011	-0.0008
Haiti	0.023	0.037	0.014	0.018	-0.0017	0.0014	-0.0017
Madagascar	0.049	0.042	-0.007	-0.0002	-0.0054	-0.0004	-0.0004
Mauritania	0.12	0.075	-0.045	-0.035	-0.006	-0.001	0.002
Mozambique	0.037	0.045	0.008	0.014	-0.0041	0.0001	-0.002
Nepal	0.097	0.074	-0.023	-0.022	-0.01	-0.0001	0.004
Togo	0.05	0.035	-0.015	-0.0044	-0.015	0.00004	0.004
Uganda	0.09	0.07	-0.02	-0.0012	-0.023	0.0005	0.003
Zambia	0.24	0.2	-0.04	-0.01	-0.03	0.00033	0.002

Source: UNCTAD Secretariat estimates, based on UNCTAD, *Handbook of Statistics 2003*.

a For the methodology and definitions of market share effect (c), structural market effect (d), market growth adaptation (e) and market stagnation adaptation (f), see text — the sum of (c), (d), (e) and (f) approximates the difference between (a) and (b). Due to the large quantity of estimated values, the sum of the four effects does not correspond to the change in the export market share for Mauritania, Togo and Zambia.

b For the dates of pre- and post-liberalization periods, see table 39. Within each reference period, the first two (t_1) and last two years (t_2) have been averaged out to smooth the effects of unusual years.

in this sample, except Haiti in the pre-liberalization period. There is slightly more evidence of a tendency in the post-liberalization period for the diversification, albeit small, to involve more dynamic products than static products. But the overall contribution of this positive trend is so small that it does not make a difference to the overall outcome.

A final aspect of the change in export structure is the degree to which it is becoming more or less concentrated. Table 44 shows changes in export concentration in the LDCs between the pre- and post-liberalization periods for the 11 countries using an export concentration indicator — a measure of the share of the top three export products in total merchandise exports — and the number of exports. The table suggests the export concentration has been decreasing and the diversity in the number of products exported increasing in the post-liberalization period. The number of products exported increased in all countries for which data are available, while the export concentration index fell

TABLE 44. EXPORT CONCENTRATION AND NUMBER OF PRODUCTS EXPORTED IN PRE- AND POST-LIBERALIZATION PERIODS

Countries	Export Concentration Index[a]		Share of 3 leading export products in total exports (Percentage)		Number of exported products[b]	
	Pre-liberalization	Post-liberalization	Pre-liberalization	Post-liberalization	Pre-liberalization	Post-liberalization
Benin	*0.48*	0.76	77.5	87.1	21	25
Gambia	*0.44*	0.33	74.0	42.3	..	30
Guinea	*0.92*	0.59	96.1	88.6	..	24
Haiti	*0.20*	0.35	35.5	51.7	..	36
Madagascar	0.45	0.22	74.1	33.8	47	71
Mauritania	*0.62*	*0.53*	*94.6*	*93.8*	20	25
Mozambique	*0.31*	0.40	40.1	60.4	51	62
Nepal	0.25	0.49	30.9	66.0	33	47
Togo	0.51	0.41	72.1	69.4	38	45
Uganda	*0.86*	0.43	96.0	59.6	19	73
Zambia	*0.86*	0.62	91.8	72.4	48	119

Source: UNCTAD secretariat estimates, based on UNCTAD, *Handbook of Statistics 2003*.

Note: For reference periods, see table 4.

a Measured according to the Hirschmann Index normalized to obtain values ranking from 0 to 1 (maximum concentration)

b Number of products exported at the 3-digit SITC, Revision 2.

in 6 of the 11 countries and the share of the three leading products fell in 7 countries. This constitutes a positive trend. But from the market share analysis, it is apparent that the scale of these developments is not sufficient to have had a major positive impact on trends in export market share. Moreover, the average number of products exported by these countries after trade liberalization was 51, which is still very low compared with 129 in other developing countries over the period 1995–2001.

3. IMPACT OF TRADE LIBERALIZATION ON THE BALANCE OF PAYMENTS

Discussions of the impact of trade liberalization within developing countries have generally paid little attention to its effects on the balance of payments. But UNCTAD (1999), as well as some recent research (Santos-Paulino, 2002a; 2002b; Santos-Paulino and Thirlwall, 2004), suggests that this is a significant omission. This is because "while trade liberalization may promote growth from the supply side through a more efficient allocation of resources, it may constrain growth from the demand side unless a balance between imports and exports can be maintained through currency depreciation or deficits can be financed through sustainable capital inflows" (Santos-Paulino and Thirlwall, 2004: 68).

A recent analysis of trends within developing countries as a whole has sought to estimate the impact of trade liberalization on exports, imports and the trade balance, distinguishing between the effects of the removal of export and import duties, and the timing of the whole process of trade liberalization, including the reduction and/or elimination of tariffs, NTBs and administrative restrictions on exports and imports. The following are the main findings for developing countries:

- For one percentage point reduction in export and import duties, a consequent export growth of less than 0.2 per cent has been outweighed by an import growth of between 0.2 and 0.4 per cent.

- Independently from any change in the duty rates, a comparison between the pre- and the post-liberalization regimes shows that exports increased by 2 per cent and imports by 6 per cent.

"While trade liberalization may promote growth from the supply side... it may constrain growth from the demand side unless a balance between imports and exports can be maintained through currency depreciation or deficits can be financed through sustainable capital inflows."

- The income elasticities of demand for imports and exports have been affected almost equally by trade liberalization. However, the price elasticity of demand for imports has increased more than for exports.

- Trade liberalization has worsened the trade balance by over 2 per cent of GDP and the current account by 0.8 per cent of GDP.

- All the regions analysed (Africa, Asia and Latin America) have experienced a deterioration in their trade balance and their current account in the post-liberalization period.

- The positive effect of liberalization on import growth and the negative effect on the trade balance and on the current account are all greater in those countries that started their liberalization from a highly protectionist regime.

- Trade liberalization has had a net positive effect on income growth, but the balance-of-payments consequences may have reduced growth below what might otherwise have been achieved had a balance between exports and imports been maintained (Santos-Paulino and Thirlwall, 2004: 69–70).

The shift to a liberalized trade regime worsens the trade balance both in the LDCs and in developing countries, but less so in the LDCs.

This implies that growth may have been constrained to remain below its productive potential because of the balance-of-payments effects of trade liberalization.

Research on the impact of trade liberalization within LDCs confirms the general pattern identified in developing countries by Santos-Paulino and Thirlwall (2004). The research on the LDCs presents eight basic findings:

- In the LDCs, the effect of a one percentage point reduction in export duties is to raise export growth by 0.19 percentage points, and the effect of a one percentage point reduction in import duties is to raise import growth by 0.12 percentage points (see box 12). These results are of a similar order of magnitude to those obtained in the developing countries.

- In the LDCs, as in the developing countries, the effect of the shift to a newly liberalized trade regime on exports, imports and the balance of trade is greater than the effect of a reduction of export duties and import duties alone.

- The shift to a liberalized trade regime has a much smaller effect on exports in the LDCs than it does in developing countries as a whole. Independently from the change in duty rates, a comparison between the pre- and post-liberalization regimes shows that exports increased by 0.5 per cent in the LDCs compared with 2 per cent in the developing countries.

- The shift to a liberalized trade regime also has a smaller effect on imports in the LDCs than it does in developing countries. Independently of the change in duty rates, a comparison between the pre- and post-liberalization regimes shows that imports increased by 1 per cent in the LDCs compared with 6 per cent in developing countries.

- In the LDCs, as in developing countries, trade liberalization has a significant impact not only on the autonomous growth of imports, but also on their sensitivity to income and price variations.

- The shift to a liberalized trade regime worsens the trade balance both in the LDCs and in developing countries, but less so in the LDCs. Trade liberalization has worsened the trade balance by 1.3 per cent of GDP in the LDCs compared with 2 per cent of GDP in developing countries.

Box 12. Testing for the impact of trade liberalization on export growth, import growth and trade balance

This box summarizes the models used by Santos-Paulino (2003) to test the impact of trade liberalization on export growth, import growth and the trade balance in LDCs, and reports the results obtained.

An export growth equation can be used which relates export growth to the growth of world income and to competitiveness, measured as the price of a country's exports relative to the foreign prices of related goods expressed in a common currency. In estimating the impact of trade liberalization on export growth, this basic model is modified: (i) to reflect the fact that adjustment of export demand to changes in prices or incomes is not instantaneous; (ii) to include two different measures of trade liberalization: export duties (measured as a percentage of total export values) on the one hand, and a dummy variable for the year of significant liberalization on the other; and (iii) variables which capture the sensitivity of exports to price and income changes.

To model the effect of trade liberalization on import growth, the same approach is used. A traditional dynamic import demand function relating imports to relative prices and domestic incomes is estimated. But in addition, an augmented import growth function is estimated, which includes aid as a ratio of GDP. It is expected that import growth is positively related to aid inflows.

To model the effect of trade liberalization on trade balance, a combination of the previous two models is elaborated with trade performance measured as the nominal gap between imports and exports.

Using the GMM[1] estimation technique, the effects of trade liberalization on import and export growth and trade balance was estimated for a group of 17 LDCs from 1970 to 2001. Three separate models were used to capture the individual effects of liberalization on exports, imports and trade balance. The equations and variables used for such an analysis are presented below together with the model's findings, which are discussed in the main text.

The estimated augmented export growth function takes the following form:

$$x_{it} = \beta_1 px_{it} + \beta_2 wy_{it} + \beta_3 x_{it-1} + \beta_4 d_{it} + \beta_5 lib + \beta_6 (px \times lib)_{it} + \beta_7 (wy \times lib)_{it} + \mu_t$$

where:

x_{it} = export growth for country i and time t;

px_{it} = real exchange rate (RER) change;

wy_{it} = world income change;

x_{it-1} = export growth lagged for one period;

d_{it} = rate of export duty;

lib = dummy variable equals 0 before the starting year of the liberalization episodes as per table 37, and 1 thereafter;

$wy \times lib$ and $px \times lib$ are interaction variables;

μ_{it} = error term.

An application of this model gives the following results.

Explanatory variables	Regression results
RER growth	-0.03 (3.33)**
World Income growth	1.72 (5.02)**
Lagged export growth	0.07 (0.92)
Export duties	-0.19 (2.12)*
Liberalization	0.50 (5.15)**
Slope dummy, wy × lib	0.15 (5.05)**
Slope dummy, px × lib	-0.02 (2.94)*
Long-run income elasticity	1.85
Long-run price elasticity	-0.003

Note: Column (ii) of table 2, where figures in parenthesis ( ) are t-ratios and **, * indicate that a coefficient is significant at the 1, 5 significance levels, respectively.

The estimated equation import growth function takes the following form:

$$m_{it} = \alpha_i + \beta_1 pm_{it} + \beta_2 y_{it} + \beta_3 m_{t-1} + \beta_4 d_{it} + \beta_5 lib_{it} + \beta_6 aid_{it} + \beta_7 (pm \times lib)_{it} + \beta_8 (y \times lib)_{it} + \beta_9 (aid \times lib) + \varepsilon_{it}$$

where:

m_{it} = import growth

α_i = are country-specific effects;

pm = the growth in relative prices;

y = the growth of real income;

Box 12 (contd.)

d_{it} = import duties;

lib_{it} = dummy variable that equals 0 before the starting year of the liberalization episodes as per table 37, and 1 thereafter;

aid = the aid variable as a share of GDP;

ε = the error term.

The application of this model gives the following results:

Explanatory variables	Regression results
RER growth	-0.11 (4.82)**
Income growth	1.63 (5.99)**
Lagged import growth	0.13 (1.50)
Import duties	-0.12 (2.09)*
Liberalization	1.87 (5.94)**
Aid growth	0.29 (4.29)**
Slope dummy, y × lib	0.21 (6.05)**
Slope dummy, pm × lib	-0.12 (6.41)**
Slope dummy, aid × lib	0.53 (4.44)**
Long- run income elasticity	1.87
Long-run price elasticity	-0.13

Note: Column (ii) of table 5.

The estimated equation for the trade balance and the current account takes the following form:

$$TB/GDP_{it} \text{ or } CA/GDP_{it} = \beta_1 + \beta_2 (TB \text{ or } CA)_{t-1} + \beta_3 (w)_{it} + \beta_4 (y)_{it} + \beta_5 (p)_{it}$$
$$+ \beta_6 (d_x)_{it} + \beta_7 (d_m)_{it} + \beta_8 (TOT)_{it} + \beta_9 (lib)_{it} + \beta_{10} (y \times lib)_{it} + \beta_{11} (aid)_{it} + \beta_{12} (aid \times lib)_{it} + \varepsilon_{it}$$

where:

w = the growth of world income;

y = the growth of domestic income;

p = the change in RER;

d_x = export duties as share of total exports

d_m = import duties as share of total imports

TOT = the nominal terms of trade;

Lib dummy variable that equals 0 before the starting year of the liberalization episodes as per table 37, and 1 thereafter;

Aid = the ratio of aid to GDP;

Below are the model's results, where the first column gives the results for the trade balance and the second those for the current account:

Explanatory variables	Trade balance
Lagged trade balance	0.97 (5.70)**
World income growth	0.31 (2.73)*
Income growth	-0.2 (2.5)*
RER growth	0.01 (0.22)
Export duties	-0.18 (0.14)
Import duties	0.15 (0.48)
Liberalization	-1.30 (3.21)**
Aid	0.95 (2.23)*
Y * lib	-0.33 (2.91)*
Aid * lib	0.13 (2.72)*
TOT	-0.09 (1.12)

Source: Santos-Paulino (2003).

[1]   For a review of the GMM estimation technique, see Greene (1997).

- In the LDCs, as in the developing countries, the worsening of the trade balance is due not only to the autonomous response of imports to trade liberalization, but also to the fact that trade liberalization has increased the growth rate, which in turn has raised import growth.

- In the LDCs, the autonomous response of imports to liberalization, and the income effect of trade liberalization on imports, have partly been offset by the interaction between aid inflows and trade liberalization. In the post-trade liberalization period there has been a fall in aid, which in turn has reduced import growth and limited the worsening of the trade balance.

These conclusions are important for understanding the impact of trade liberalization on the balance of payments in the LDCs. They suggest that the export response to trade liberalization has been smaller in the LDCs than in other developing countries. This is likely to be related to weaknesses in domestic productive capacities and the incomplete development of the domestic market economy. But at the same time, the import response is also lower in the LDCs. This is related to the fact that the trade liberalization episodes in the LDCs have occurred along with higher aid inflows, and these have tapered off after the economy has liberalized. In contrast, although there is no evidence to support this, it may be hypothesized that in other developing countries trade liberalization has been associated with increased private capital inflows, which magnified the impact of trade liberalization on imports. The overall effect is that in both the LDCs and other developing countries the trade balance has worsened, but more so in other developing countries.

Although the worsening of the trade balance has occurred to a lesser extent in the LDCs than in other developing countries, the fact that the impact of trade liberalization on import growth is higher than its effect on export growth implies that the shift to a liberalized trade regime exacerbates the problem of sustainable financing of the trade deficit, which LDCs always face. The tightening of the balance of payments after trade liberalization in developing countries leads Santos-Paulino and Thirlwall to conclude that "overall, free trade and flexible exchange rate are no guarantee that unemployed domestic resources are easily converted into scarce foreign exchange" (Santos-Paulino and Thirlwall, 2004: 70). The evidence for the developing countries suggests that a similar conclusion can be drawn for the LDCs. Moreover, given the continuing marginalization of the LDCs in the context of private capital flows after economic reforms (see *The Least Developed Countries Report 2002*, chapter 3), the process of trade liberalization has exacerbated aid dependence and, to the extent that aid is not provided in grants and is not building up trade capacity, it has increased the likelihood of another debt crisis in the future.

4. CHANGES IN IMPORT COMPOSITION

The increase in import growth as a result of trade liberalization could have positive effects on the rate and sustainability of growth if increased imports lead to increased investment. But what has been happening in the LDCs after trade liberalization is that there are significant shifts in the composition of exports. Chart 37 shows the emerging pattern. In every case, machinery imports account for a lower share of total merchandise imports after trade liberalization than they did before liberalization. In all cases, consumer-goods imports account for a higher share of total merchandise imports after liberalization than before liberalization. In the majority of cases, food imports are also increasing as a share of total merchandise imports.

The fact that the impact of trade liberalization on import growth is higher than its effect on export growth implies that the shift to a liberalized trade regime exacerbates aid dependence as well as the problem of sustainable financing of the trade deficit, which LDCs always face.

In every case, machinery imports account for a lower share of total merchandise imports after trade liberalization than they did before liberalization. In the majority of cases, food imports are also increasing as a share of total merchandise imports.

CHART 37. IMPORTS OF FOOD AND MACHINERY IN SELECTED LDCS PRE- AND POST-TRADE LIBERALIZATION
(As percentage of total merchandise imports)

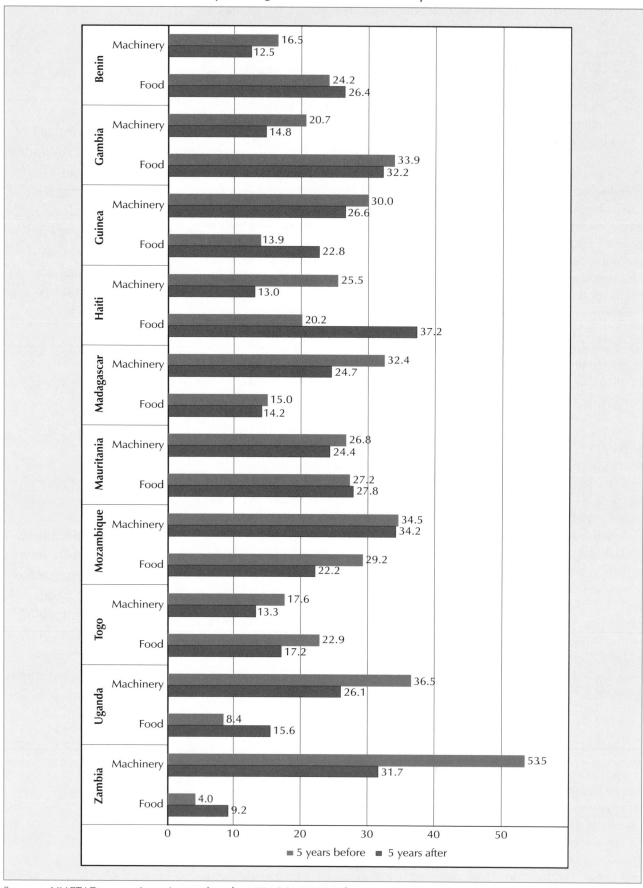

Source: UNCTAD secretariat estimates, based on UN COMTRADE data.
Note: In accordance with SITC, Revision 2, food includes codes 0+1+22+4. Machinery imports, as defined here, include codes
             7-775-781+87+881+884.
             For reference periods, see table 39.

On the basis of these trends, it seems likely that while import growth following trade liberalization may be good for consumption, it is not necessarily good for supporting a sustained increase in the rate of economic growth based on productive investment.

F. Prospects for substantial poverty reduction after trade liberalization: inclusiveness of economic growth

An analysis of the inclusiveness of the economic growth process in the post-liberalization trade regime is much more difficult than an analysis of the sustainability of economic growth. It requires data on changes in inequality and employment, which are simply unavailable at present in the absence of more detailed country studies. However, there are some emerging tendencies that give cause for concern. Drawing in part on findings from the DTIS, three main concerns are discussed here:

(i)   The enclave-led growth in LDCs whose major exports are manufactures, mining or tourism;

(ii) The lack of domestic market integration and limits to agrarian commercialization, which may exacerbate enclave-led growth, but which is also found in agricultural-commodity-exporting LDCs with a low population density; and

(iii) Increasing population pressure and environmental degradation in the agricultural-commodity-exporting LDCs with a high population density, where non-agricultural exports are not being developed quickly enough.

1. ENCLAVE-LED GROWTH

The problem of enclave-led growth is exemplified by two LDCs which have undertaken deep liberalization — Guinea and Madagascar. These two countries are noteworthy because their export performance improved significantly in the 1990s and, in terms of the classification of the trade–poverty relationship on the basis of trends in private consumption per capita (see table 31, chapter 3), both are virtuous cases in which export expansion is associated with an increasing average private consumption per capita of over 1 per cent per annum. Along with rising exports, average private consumption per capita increased by more than 1 per cent per annum during 1990–2000 in Guinea and during 1995–2000 in Madagascar. However, the form of economic growth in both these cases was not broad-based.

The problem of enclave-led growth is exemplified by Guinea and Madagascar, which have undertaken deep liberalization. Both are virtuous cases in which export expansion is associated with an increasing average private consumption per capita. However, the form of economic growth in both these cases was not broad-based.

In Guinea, the export enclave fuelling economic growth is capital-intensive mining focused on bauxite and aluminium. There is an artisanal mining subsector focused on diamonds, in which approximately 100,000 people are employed. This subsector somewhat increases the employment intensity of mining activities. Agriculture is the main source of livelihood for most of the population, employing two thirds of the economically active population, but it contributes just 17 per cent of GDP. According to household survey data, 88 per cent of the poor lived in rural areas in 1994. The overall incidence of poverty for the country as whole was 40 per cent: 7 per cent in the capital city, Conakry, but 53 per cent in the rural areas and 62 per cent in the northern parts of the country (High Guinea).

Since 1986, Guinea has undertaken deep trade liberalization; in the newly liberalized trade regime, exports as a ratio of GDP increased from 19 per cent in 1996 to 28 per cent in 2001. But the DTIS has found that export expansion and open trade has had a "negligible impact" on poverty. It states that "Guinea's current position as a global trading partner, which is highly dependent on mining activities, has not led to genuine poverty reduction. This is primarily due to the fairly capital-intensive nature of the mining sector, its weak ties to the rest of the economy, and to the weakness of the State tax base, which leave little room to use government revenues from the mining sector in poverty reduction programs" (Integrated Framework, 2003b: 8–9). Outside the mining sector import-substitution industries have downsized considerably as "the private sector has not taken over the public enterprises of which a large number have been liquidated" (Integrated Framework, 2003b: 5). Exports of manufactured goods have fallen with the disappearance of public enterprises. Moreover the process of trade liberalization has not led to increased agricultural exports. Rather, the relative importance of agricultural exports has declined under the new liberalized trade regime. Though tourism is expanding, it still plays a minor role in the economy.

> *Whereas Guinea exemplifies the non-inclusive nature of growth in a country with a capital-intensive enclave, Madagascar exemplifies a non-inclusive form of economic growth in a country with a labour-intensive enclave.*

Whereas Guinea exemplifies the non-inclusive nature of growth in a country with a capital-intensive enclave, Madagascar exemplifies a non-inclusive form of economic growth in a country with a labour-intensive enclave. This is particularly important because Madagascar could be seen to offer a successful model in many ways. Trade liberalization has been associated with diversification out of primary commodity exports into fast-growing manufactured exports. The country has been able to attract FDI, which has provided the necessary investment, technology and marketing know-how to break into international markets. At the national level, the whole process has been significantly facilitated through creative institutional innovation, with the establishment of an export processing zone (EPZ). Moreover, at the international level, the process has been accelerated through the provision of preferential access to OECD markets (see next chapter). The share of exports of goods and services in GDP has increased by a third since 1996, and, according to the IMF, the exchange rate reflects the broad fundamentals of the economy (Integrated Framework, 2003c, overview: 11). However, under the post-liberal trade regime, a two-speed pattern of economic growth has emerged, which is likely to leave the majority of the population stuck in extreme poverty.

The three key components of the structure of the economy are: the agricultural sector, which employs 75 per cent of the active population and provides nearly 40 per cent of the GDP; the EPZ, which contributes 2 per cent of GDP, and in 1997 it employed 0.06 per cent of the total economically active population; and domestic industries which account for slightly more than 12 per cent of GDP and provide 150,000 to 200,000 jobs. Most of the poor are located in the rural areas and are employed in agricultural activities. But agricultural growth has been low and volatile, and there is a concern that rice imports will undermine production incentives. With trade liberalization, the decline in agricultural exports of the 1980s has been reversed and there has been diversification into new products. But agricultural exports were lower in 1999 than in 1980, with the rise in non-traditional exports (notably fruits, vegetables, fish and cotton) being insufficient to offset the decline in traditional exports (coffee, spices, sugar and sisal). The most significant growth is fish exports, especially shrimp, but participation of the poor in this activity is through employment in medium- to large-scale operations.

Within the EPZ, the rate of growth of output and employment has been rapid. But in the newly liberalized economy, domestic industries outside the EPZ are "struggling to compete with imports and gradually losing steam"(Integrated Framework, 2003c, Background Reports: 62). In agri-food, beverages and textiles, imports represented only 22 per cent, 12 per cent and 5 per cent of domestic consumption, respectively, in 1996. But over the 1997–1999 period, less than 40 per cent of domestic market growth in these sectors was accounted for by domestic producers; the rest was met by imports. In the paper and printing and leather industries, domestic output fell by 15 per cent and 47 per cent respectively, whereas imports increased strongly by 88 per cent and 159 per cent respectively (ibid: 62–63). The only sectors of Malagasy industry outside the EPZ which grew in the second half of the decade were tobacco and beverages. Thus, "the Malagasy economy is increasingly characterized by segmented growth, the dynamism of the EPZ contrasting with the [anaemia] of the industrial sector outside it" (Integrated Framework, 2003c, overview: viii).

The weak performance of the domestic industrial sector outside the EPZ is important because it is this sector that has the closest linkages with the agricultural economy. The DTIS notes a vicious circle in which industrialists in downstream sectors face high costs of local inputs. Such high costs are attributable to the inability of upstream producers to attain economies of scale because of the small domestic market, and low levels of exports by firms outside the EPZ. High costs of production caused by small-scale production raises the costs of final products. Since final products are expensive, it is difficult to increase their domestic market share or export them, thus reinforcing the suboptimal scale problem. Releasing market forces has strengthened this vicious circle, rather than enabling the development of production complementarities. As the DTIS states, "a pure market solution is unlikely to take place on a sufficient scale to alleviate the problem and may not be enough in itself" (Integrated Framework, 2003c, background reports, 67).

For Madagascar, the projection indicates that an average annual export growth of 13 per cent for garments and 10 per cent for tourism over the period 2000–2009 will result in no change in the incidence of poverty and an increase in the number of poor people by 3.8 million.

The prospects for poverty reduction are not encouraging. The DTIS includes a simulation that assumes growth in garment exports at 20 per cent per annum in the period 2000–2003, and then at 10 per cent per annum during the period 2003–2009; it also assumes growth in tourism at 10 per cent per annum throughout the period. But if agricultural production grows at 1.5 per cent per annum, the same as it did in the 1990s, and domestic industry outside the EPZ grows at 2 per cent per annum, the projection indicates that the proportion of the population living below the poverty line will increase from 71 per cent in 1999 to 72 per cent in 2009. This implies that an average annual export growth of 13 per cent for garments and 10 per cent for tourism over the period 2000–2009 will result in no change in the incidence of poverty and an increase in the number of poor people by 3.8 million.

The key to poverty reduction in Madagascar lies in the agricultural sector. But the DTIS notes that the causes of the steady decline in agriculture "extend beyond trade and price incentives" and "an improvement in trade policies may not be sufficient to restore sustained growth to the agriculture sector" (Integrated Framework, 2003c, overview: 41; Cogneau and Robilliard, 2000). Policy simulations show that liberalization of rice imports is in fact the least effective policy for promoting agriculture (Stifel and Randrianarisoa, 2004).

The cases of Guinea and Madagascar are important, as they are both "successful countries" in terms of export expansion and a slowly rising average private consumption per capita. But the emerging pattern of growth in these newly liberalized economies is not inclusive. It is also possible that because it is not broad-based it will not be sustainable. It is noteworthy in this regard that both these countries have been affected by political instability in the last five years.

Avoiding enclave-led growth requires attention to agricultural development as well as expansion of exports. The experience of Bangladesh offers an example where sustained and substantial poverty reduction has occurred through an increase in rice productivity in rural areas, achieved through a combination of improved seeds, increased fertilizer use and public and private investment in irrigation, and expansion of labour-intensive manufactured exports (Arndt et al., 2002). But even there, international migration and increases in workers' remittances have played a key role in the whole process.

2. LACK OF DOMESTIC MARKET INTEGRATION AND HIGH LEVEL OF SUBSISTENCE PRODUCTION

The competitiveness of domestic markets is adversely affected by the poor physical infrastructure and lack of transport services. High transaction costs in getting produce from farms to markets, as well as the costs and risks of purchasing foodstuffs, have encouraged households to maintain some degree of subsistence production even when they could expect higher returns through specialization in, and sale of, export or food crops.

A second problem regarding the inclusiveness of the growth process arises because of the pursuit of rapid and deep trade liberalization in countries where there is very weak domestic market integration and a high level of subsistence orientation of production in rural areas. This problem is noted in a number of DTISs, including those on Madagascar, Ethiopia and Guinea (see also Tsikata, 2003). The problem can occur along with enclave-led growth of the type discussed above. But it is also likely to occur in agricultural-commodity-exporting LDCs with a low population density.

Countries such as Burkino Faso, Ethiopia, Mali and the United Republic of Tanzania have a low-density road network, and the quality of rural roads is generally poor. Transport services are also expensive under these conditions. A vicious circle can arise in remote areas as high transport costs reduce demand for transport, and low demand for transport increases transport costs. The competitiveness of domestic markets is adversely affected by the poor physical infrastructure and lack of transport services. Thus farmers have few alternatives for selling what they produce or for buying simple consumer goods. With the ending of pan-territorial pricing associated with marketing boards, the terms of trade worsened for farmers in remote areas and private traders often did not replace the public sector in providing production inputs such as fertililizer or seeds.

High transaction costs in getting produce from farms to markets, as well as the costs and risks of purchasing foodstuffs, have encouraged households to maintain some degree of subsistence production even when they could expect higher returns through specialization in, and sale of, export or food crops. According to the Integrated Framework (2003a, vol. 2, annex 12, box 12.2), market failures exist because there has to be a minimum threshold of market development before farmers begin to shift into market-oriented activities since the benefits of these activities depend on how many people within the community are engaged in them. High transaction costs also mean that large segments of rural economies within African LDCs consist of non-tradables such as services, bulky traditional starchy foodstuffs, perishables and locally processed foods. The high proportion of non-tradables implies that there are high multiplier effects from market development and increased integration of these rural communities with the rest of the national economy. But in the absence of such developments, a large part of the rural economy may be demand-constrained in the sense that many people in rural areas can remain unemployed for long periods of time if effective local demand for what they produce does not rise (Delgado, 1992; 1996).

As noted earlier, many of the poor in the agricultural-commodity-exporting LDCs live in rural areas and are engaged in partly subsistence-oriented farming of traditional food crops rather than export activities. The lack of domestic market integration, the high degree of subsistence orientation of rural households and the prevalence of non-tradables imply that large parts of the poorest population tend to be bypassed during the process of trade liberalization and economic reform.

3. RURAL POPULATION PRESSURE, AND ABSENCE OF NON-AGRICULTURAL EMPLOYMENT

The problem of enclave-led growth arises in a situation in which export growth in the non-agricultural sector (manufactures, mining or tourism) is inadequately linked to agricultural development. But there is another, converse type of problem — one in which growth is based on agricultural exports but where non-agricultural employment does not develop rapidly enough to relieve increasing population pressure on land resources. Unlike the first two problems, this is not identified in the DTIS. But it is apparent that it is an emerging problem in agricultural-commodity-exporting LDCs that have a high population density. Examples are Burundi, Malawi and Rwanda.

The lack of domestic market integration, a high degree of subsistence orientation of rural households and the prevalence of non-tradables implies that large parts of the poorest population tend to be bypassed during the process of trade liberalization and economic reform.

Malawi is a particularly good example of the extent to which this problem can be addressed through deep trade liberalization. During the 1970s, economic growth was based on the expansion of agricultural exports – initially tea and tobacco, and then sugar — which were produced on large-scale estates employing wage labour or allowing small farmers to act as sharecroppers. For a time, the growth strategy was highly successful and the country was heralded as a success story because it apparently had avoided "urban bias". There were very high export growth rates and the investment rate also increased strongly. However, the strategy was highly inegalitarian. Smallholders were restricted in the varieties of tobacco they could cultivate and also in the organizations to which they could sell their crops.

Economic reforms began in the early 1980s following an economic crisis. The initial strategy was to increase smallholder production of exportable cash crops through improved price incentives and by liberalizing agricultural markets. However, the implementation of this policy was affected by the Government's concern that this would undermine food self-sufficiency. Dependence on imported food was a particular concern, given the landlocked position of Malawi and consequent high import costs, as well as the dependence of many poor households on purchased food. The restrictions on smallholder participation in most areas of tobacco production remained in place. But in response to the dissent that the highly inegalitarian growth model was fostering, the political leadership encouraged a new wave of smaller estates to be established by entrepreneurial small-scale business people and farmers. According to the Malawi DTIS, the system of production controls on tobacco in the 1970s and 1980s "served as a primary means of allocating opportunities and distributing income and wealth in the country" (Integrated Framework, 2003d: 2).

In 1994, the country held its first democratic elections since 1960. The new Government sought to achieve a more broad-based pattern of growth. One major way it did so was by amending the Special Crops Act to enable a greater participation of smallholders in tobacco exports. By 1996, up to 200,000 smallholders had taken up tobacco cultivation (Integrated Framework, 2003d: 3) and the share of smallholders in the production of Malawi burley tobacco increased from 16 per cent in 1994 to 70 per cent in 2001. The more inclusive growth pattern has contributed to improving the virtuous trade–poverty relationship observed in Malawi in the second half of the 1990s. But in 2001 and 2002 there were increasing problems in terms of declining productivity, falling prices and lower quality.

The more inclusive growth process of the 1990s coincided with the deepening of trade liberalization. But trade liberalization was also associated with de-industrialization. The annual growth of manufacturing value-added fluctuated at around 3.3 per cent between 1987 and 1995, but between 1996 and 1999 it stagnated (Harrigan, 2001). Many firms contracted owing to import competition. Textile production shrank to 44 per cent of its 1990 level by 1996, large firms manufacturing soaps, detergents and oils ceased domestic production, and the poultry industry collapsed (ibid.: 309). Moreover, "the liberalization of imports in the early 1990s virtually wiped out the domestic garment industry owing to large imports of less expensive goods from Asia plus large quantities of second-hand clothes" (Integrated Framework, 2003d, overview: 84). Although formal-sector manufacturing accounted for less than 2 per cent of total employment, the job losses and reduced non-agricultural employment opportunities have created hardships and it has proved difficult to develop manufactured exports for a landlocked country like Malawi. Exports of cotton fabric halved between 1996 and 2000 (ibid.: 85).

> *At present, very few LDCs have restrictive trade regimes. Many have undertaken deep trade liberalization, resulting in a very open trade regime by international standards.*

The World Bank (1997) has noted that in the long-run smallholder agriculture cannot provide rising incomes or employment for 80 per cent of an ever-increasing population in an already densely populated country. Soil fertility is declining and many households live on farms that are too small for them. The critical issue now is how structural transformation, which would allow more people to be employed outside agriculture, could be achieved in this landlocked country after trade liberalization.

G. Conclusions

This chapter has shown that there has been an extensive process of trade liberalization in the LDCs since the late 1980s. At present, very few of them have restrictive trade regimes. In fact many have undertaken deep trade liberalization, in some cases liberalizing faster than Chile did in the 1970s and 1980s resulting in a very open trade regime by international standards. African LDCs have undertaken deeper trade liberalization than Asian LDCs. In the 1980s Asian LDCs depreciated their currencies much more than African LDCs, but in the 1990s the opposite was the case.

> *Until recently, there was no deliberate policy attempt to make trade liberalization work for poverty reduction.*

The liberalization process has been conducted within the framework of IMF and World Bank structural adjustment programmes rather than as part of a multilaterally negotiated reduction of global tariff barriers. Generally the process of trade liberalization has been associated with an increase in aid inflows. The extent and depth of trade liberalization reflects the wide and long-standing involvement of most LDCs with structural adjustment programmes. Using the IMF trade restrictiveness index as a measure of openness, some of the LDCs now have more open trade regimes than other developing countries, and as open as the high-income OECD countries. Until recently, there was no deliberate policy attempt to make trade liberalization work for poverty reduction. But the process of trade liberalization has now created a new environment for development and poverty reduction in the LDCs.

The short-term effects of the process of trade liberalization on poverty vary considerably between countries, with some groups benefiting and others losing. There has been a tendency for the countries that have opened more gradually and less deeply to have a better trade–poverty relationship than those that have opened further and fastest, and better also than those which have been restrictive. These are related as much to export specialization as to trade liberalization, as well as to differences in the speed of trade liberalization in Asian and African LDCs.

The central issue now is whether the new policy environment is likely to facilitate substantial and sustained poverty reduction in the long run. In this regard, there are some positive and some negative elements. For the LDCs which have undertaken deep trade liberalization, comparisons of economic trends before and after trade liberalization indicate that growth rates of GDP, exports and investment are all higher in the post-liberalization economic environment. But given high population growth rates, the rates of economic growth that are being achieved are in many cases not sufficient to yield GDP per capita growth rates that will make a major dent in poverty alleviation. Moreover, there are reasons to believe that sustainability of the positive growth, export and investment trends is still not assured. First, the rate of domestic savings remains very low, and thus the post-liberalization countries remain highly dependent on foreign savings, particularly aid. Secondly, there is evidence of post-liberalization aid fatigue, in the sense that aid inflows tapered off after trade liberalization accelerated. Thirdly, although higher export growth rates have been achieved, the composition of exports is not yet shifting favourably towards greater specialization in dynamic products and increased competitiveness. Certainly, there is a positive trend towards less export concentration, which is associated with the emergence of new export products. But this positive development is as yet so insignificant that it does not affect the overall export performance in terms of reversing the marginalization of these countries in the world economy. The process of trade liberalization in the LDCs has reinforced specialization in commodity exports rather than promoting a shift to manufactured exports. As the next chapter shows, the latter is related more to preferential access in developed-country markets than to trade liberalization in the LDCs themselves.

An analysis of the impact of trade liberalization on the balance of payments in the LDCs shows that the process has increased exports and even more so imports. However, in comparison with developing countries as a whole, the process of trade liberalization has had a smaller effect on exports and imports in the LDCs. In LDCs, the increase in exports is likely to reflect supply responsiveness, but the shift to a more open trading regime is associated with a fall in aid, which in turn has reduced import growth. In the case of developing countries, it may be that higher import growth rates are related to higher private capital inflows in the post-liberalization era. The process of trade liberalization worsens the trade balance in both LDCs and developing countries. The effect is smaller in the LDCs than in developing countries because of the smaller effect of liberalization on import growth. But given the continuing marginalization of LDCs in global private capital flows, the effect on the trade balance implies that the process of trade liberalization has exacerbated aid dependence. Moreover, to the extent that aid is not provided in the form of grants and is not building up trade capacity, it has increased the likelihood of a renewed debt crisis in the future.

The short-term effects of the process of trade liberalization on poverty vary considerably between countries, with some groups benefiting and others losing. There has been a tendency for countries that have opened more gradually and less deeply to have a better trade–poverty relationship.

The process of trade liberalization in the LDCs has reinforced specialization in commodity exports rather than promoting a shift to manufactured exports.

Given the continuing marginalization of LDCs in global private capital flows, the effect on the trade balance implies that the process of trade liberalization has exacerbated aid dependence.

The inclusiveness of the post-liberalization growth process also gives cause for concern. Lack of data implies that there is a need for country studies on changes in inequality and employment within LDCs. However, drawing on information provided by the DTIS, it is clear that enclave-led growth is becoming a problem in some LDCs whose major exports are manufactures mining. With this form of economic growth, there are weak links between the rapidly growing export enclave and the agricultural sector where the majority of the population and the majority of the poor earn their livelihoods. In these circumstances, it is possible to have very high rates of export growth but no change in the incidence of poverty.

Enclave-led growth is becoming a problem in some LDCs whose major exports are manufactures and mining.

A further problem arises, which is diminishing the inclusiveness of the post-liberalization growth process. Deep trade liberalization at the national border has been undertaken in countries with very weak internal transport and communications infrastructure, weak levels of domestic market integration and with a high level of subsistence-oriented production. In these circumstances, many poor people and poor regions are being left out of the growth process, and liberalization alone cannot break the vicious circles that reduce the market involvement of rural households and cause a large proportion of output to be tradable only locally. This is exacerbating the problem of enclave-led growth in countries that export manufactures, mineral and oil; it is also evident in agricultural-commodity-exporting LDCs with a low population density.

In agricultural-commodity-exporting LDCs with a high population density, a different problem is emerging, that of increasing population pressure on land, environmental degradation and impoverishment due to small farm sizes and yields that are too low to support households. The development of non-agricultural employment is necessary to relieve the pressure on land. But in the LDCs for which trends are reported in the DTIS, rapid and deep liberalization has been associated with de-industrialization as import-substituting industries collapse when they are exposed to international competition without any prior preparation, and as the processing of primary products for export is cut back. It has proved difficult for the agricultural-commodity-exporting LDCs with a high population density to sufficiently develop manufactures or services for export as an alternative source of non-agricultural employment, and thus the increasing pressure on land resources continues to intensify.

The policy challenge facing the LDCs and their development partners now is how to promote development and poverty reduction in a very open national economy situated in an asymmetrically liberalized international economy.

The policy challenge facing the LDCs and their development partners now is how to promote development and poverty reduction in a very open national economy situated in an asymmetrically liberalized international economy. At the national level, this requires much more than the adoption of "behind-the-border" measures to ensure that any beneficial effects of trade liberalization are "passed through" to the poor. There is rather a need for innovative thinking about how to promote development and poverty reduction in a newly liberalized economy. Elements of a post-liberalization development strategy that can effectively reduce poverty in countries where extreme poverty is all-pervasive need to be defined. Moreover, it is necessary to address the questions of how aid for trade and the international trade regime can be improved to support development and poverty reduction in such countries. The final two chapters of this Report take up these issues.

There is a need for innovative thinking about how to promote development and poverty reduction in a newly liberalized economy.

Notes

1. According to the IMF trade restrictiveness index, Rwanda has an open trade regime, but it is not quite as open as those of Hong Kong (China) and Singapore.
2. Due to the various exchange-rate regimes adopted by the LDCs, devaluation and depreciation are treated synonymously throughout this chapter.
3. Benin, Burundi, Cape Verde, Ethiopia, the Gambia, Haiti, Madagascar, Mali, Mauritania, Nepal, Senegal, Sudan, Togo, Uganda, the United Republic of Tanzania and Zambia. We would like to thank the national trade Ministries for their helpful support in providing us with the information on changes in their trade policy regimes.
4. Bangladesh, Bhutan, Burkina Faso, Cambodia, Guinea, the Lao People's Democratic Republic, Lesotho, Malawi, Maldives, Mozambique and Solomon Islands.
5. Keen and Ligthart (2002) identify the failure to find alternative sources of revenue as a major reason for trade policy reversal. In the case of Senegal, the change in policy could also have been due to the fact that the country was unable to devalue unilaterally.
6. Rodrik (1992) quantifies uniformity into a maximum of three tariff rates. However, taking into account the characteristics of the LDCs, a tariff scheme with four or five rates may still be referred to as uniform.
7. The Diagnostic Trade Integration Studies are prepared in the context of the Integrated Framework for Trade-Related Technical Assistance (IF, for short).
8. Unless of course there has been a substantial increase in labour productivity in the non-traded goods in these countries, which is highly unlikely.
9. This indicator was calculated as the ratio of two ratios: the ratio of exports for each sector of an economy to that economy's total exports relative to the ratio of world exports for each sector to total world exports. The greater a sector's RCA indicator, the more the economy specializes in that sector with respect to world specialization patterns, thus revealing a stronger comparative advantage in that sector.
10. In mathematical terms, the four components are:

$$\Delta x_j = \sum_i (\Delta x_{ij} y_{ij}^{t-1}) + \sum_i (x_{ij}^{t-1} \Delta y_{ij}) + \sum_i (\Delta x_{ij} \frac{\Delta y_{ij} + |\Delta y_{ij}|}{2}) + \sum_i (\Delta x_{ij} \frac{\Delta y_{ij} - |\Delta y_{ij}|}{2})$$

| Market share Effect | Structural market effect | Market growth adaptation effect | Market stagnation adaptation effect |

where:

$x_j = \sum_i X_{ij} / \sum_i \sum_j X_{ij}$ a country's aggregate share of exports to the total world export

$x_{ij} = X_{ij} / \sum_j X_{ij}$ a country's share of a given sector with respect to its total exports

$y_{ij} = \sum_j X_{ij} / \sum_i \sum_j X_{ij}$ a sector's share of total exports with respect to the total world export

X_{ij} exports by firms located in country j in sector i

References

Appleton, S. (1998). Changes in poverty in Uganda, 1992-1996, Centre for Study of African Economies, Oxford University, mimeo.

Arndt, C., Dorosh, P., Fontana, M., Zohir, S., El-Said, M., and Lungren, C. (2002). Opportunities and challenges in agriculture and garments: a general equilibrium analysis of the Bangladesh economy, Discussion Paper No. 107, International Food Policy Research Institute, Washington, D.C.

Balassa, B. (1985). Exports, policy choices, and economic growth in developing countries after the 1973 oil shock, *Journal of Development Economics*, 18: 23–35.

Barrett C. (1998). Immiserized growth in liberalized agriculture, *World Development*, 26 (5): 743-753.

Booth, D., Kasente, D., Mavrotas, G., Mugambe, G. and Muwonge, A. (2003). Ex ante poverty and social impact analysis: Uganda demonstration exercise, (http://poverty.worldbank.org/files/ 14689_Uganda_Final_PSIA.doc).

Borgatti, L. (2003). Trade policy regimes of the least developed countries, background paper prepared for *The Least Developed Countries Report 2004*, UNCTAD, Geneva.

Butkevicius, A., Kadri, A., Mayer, J. and Pizarro, J. (2003). Dynamic Products in World Exports, *Review of World Economics*, 139(4).

Cockburn, J. (2002). Trade liberalization and poverty in Nepal. A computable general equilibrium micro simulation analysis, Department of CREFA, University of Quebec and Department of CSAE, University of Oxford, Oxford.

Collier, P., and Gunning, J. W. (1999). The microeconomics of African growth, 1950-2000, AERC Collaborative Research Project on *Explaining African Economic Growth, 1950-2000*, (http://www.gdnet.org/pdf/308_Collier-Gunning.pdf).

Cogneau, D. and Robilliard, A. S. (2000). Growth, distribution and poverty in Madagascar: Learning from a microsimulation model in a general equilibrium framework. TMD Discussion Paper No. 61, International Food Policy Research Institute, Washington, D.C.

Cramer, C. (1999). Can Africa industrialise by processing primary commodities? The case of Mozambican cashew nuts, *World Development, 27* (7): 1247–1266.

Deininger, K. and Okidi, J. (2003). Growth and poverty reduction in Uganda: 1999–2000, panel data evidence, *Development Policy Review*, 21(4): 481–509.

Delgado, C. L. (1992). Why domestic food prices matter to growth strategy in semi-open West African economies, *Journal of African Economies* 1(3): 446–71.

Delgado, C. L. (1996). Agricultural transformation: the key to broad-based growth and poverty alleviation in Africa. In: B. Ndulu, N. van de Walle, and Contributors (eds.), *Agenda for Africa's Economic Renewal,* Transaction Publishers, New Brunswick, U.S.A.

De Rosa, D. and Roningen, V. (2002). Rwanda as a free trade zone: an inquiry into the economic impacts, Report prepared for the United States mission to Rwanda of the United States Agency for International Development, ADR Policy Brief No. 11, Virginia, U.S.A.

Dorosh, P. and Sahn, D.E. (2000). A general equilibrium analysis of the effect of macroeconomic adjustment on poverty in Africa, *Journal of Policy Modeling*, 22 (6): 753–776.

Dorosh, P., Sahn, D.E. and Younger, S. (1996). Exchange rate, fiscal and agricultural policies in Africa: does adjustment hurt the poor?, *World Development*, 24 (4): 719–747.

Edwards, S. (1992). The sequencing of structural adjustment and stabilization, Occasional Paper No. 34, International Center for Economic Growth, University of the Pacific, California.

Edwards, S. (1997). Trade liberalisation reforms and the World Bank, *American Economic Review,* papers and proceedings of the 104th annual meeting of the American Economic Association, 87 (2): 43–48.

Fane, G. (2003). Trade liberalisation and poverty reduction in Lao PDR, Economics Division of the Research School of Pacific and Asian Studies, Australian National University, paper prepared for UNU/WIDER Conference on Sharing Global Prosperity, 5-7 September 2003, Helsinki.

Greene, W. (1997). *Econometric Analysis*, Prentice-Hall, New Jersey.

Harrigan, J. (2001). *From Dictatorship to Democracy: Economic Policy in Malawi 1964–2000*, Ashgate Publishing Company, Vermont, U.S.A.

Heston, A., Summers, R., and Aten, B. (2002). Penn World Table version 6.1, Center for International Comparisons, University of Pennsylvania.

Integrated Framework (2003a). Diagnostic Trade Integration Study: Ethiopia, volume 2, annex 8.

Integrated Framework (2003b). Diagnostic Trade Integration Study: Guinea, volume 1, annex 8 and 9.

Integrated Framework (2003c). Diagnostic Trade Integration Study: Madagascar, volume 1, overview and background report.

Integrated Framework (2003d). Diagnostic Trade Integration Study: Malawi, volume 2, annex 8.

Jenkins, R. and Sen, K. (2004). International trade and employment outcomes in the south: four country case-studies, School of Development Studies, University of East Anglia, Norwich, UK.

Keen, M. and Ligthart, J. (2002). Coordinating tariff reduction and domestic tax reform, *Journal of International Economics,* 56(2): 407–425.

Khondker, B. and Mujeri, M. (2002). Poverty implications for trade liberalization in Bangladesh: a general equilibrium approach, Bangladesh Institute of Development Studies, University of Dhaka, Dhaka.

Laursen, K. (1997). The impact of technological opportunity on the dynamics of trade performance, Working Paper No. 96-12, Danish Research Unit for Industrial Dynamics, Denmark.

Laursen, K. (1998). How structural change differs, and why it matters (for economic growth), Working Paper No. 98-25, Danish Research Unit for Industrial Dynamics, Denmark

McCulloch, N., Baulch, B. and Cherel-Robson, M. (2000). Poverty, inequality and growth in Zambia during the 1990s, Institute for Development Studies Discussion Paper No. 67, Brighton, Sussex.

McMillan, M., Rodrik, D., Welch, K. (2002). When economic reform goes wrong: Cashews in Mozambique, mimeo (http://ksghome.harvard.edu/~.drodrik.academic.ksg/).

Meller, P. (1994). The Chilean trade liberalization and export expansion process 1974-90. In: Helleiner, G., ed., *Trade Policy and Industrialization in Turbulent Times*, Routledge, London.

Michaely, M. (1986). The timing and sequencing of a trade liberalisation policy. In: Choksi, S.& Papageorgiu, D. eds., *Economic Liberalisation in Developing Countries,* Basil Backwell Ltd., Oxford.

Morrissey, O., Rudaheranwa, N., and Moller, L. (2003). Trade policies, performance and poverty in Uganda, Uganda Trade and Poverty Project (http://www.odi.org.uk/iedg/projects/utpp_summary.pdf).

PMAU (2002). Uganda poverty status report 2001, PMAU, Ministry of Finance, Planning and Economic Development, Kampala.

Rodrik, D. (1990). How should structural adjustment programs be designed?, *World Development,* 18(7): 933–947.

Rodrik, D. (1992). The limits of trade policy reform in developing countries, *Journal of Economic Perspectives*, 6(1): 87–105.

Sachs, J. and Warner A. (1995). Economic reform and the process of global integration, *Brookings Papers on Economic Activity*, 1–118.

Santos-Paulino, A. (2002a). Trade liberalization and export performance in selected developing countries, *Journal of Development Studies*, 39: 140–164.

Santos-Paulino, A. (2002b). The effect of trade liberalization on import growth in developing countries, *World Development,* 30: 959–974.

Santos-Paulino, A. (2003). Trade liberalization, exports, imports, aid, and the balance of payments in least developed countries, background paper prepared for *The Least Developed Countries Report 2004*, UNCTAD, Geneva.

Santos-Paulino, A. and Thirlwall, A. P. (2004). The impact of trade liberalization on exports, imports and the balance of payments of developing countries, *The Economic Journal*, 114(493): 50-73.

Shatz, H. and Tarr, D.G. (2000). Exchange rate overvaluation and trade protection: lessons from experience, World Bank Working Paper No. 2289, World Bank, Washington, DC.

Stifel, D. and Randrianarisoa, J.-C. (2004). Rice prices, agricultural input subsidies, transactions costs and seasonality: a multi-market model poverty and social impact analysis (PSIA) for Madagascar, Lafayette College, Cornell University, and FOFIFA, U.S.A.

Stifel, D., Minten, B. and Dorosh, P. (2003). Transaction costs and agricultural productivity: implications of isolation for rural poverty in Madagascar, MSSD Discussion Paper No. 56, International Food Policy Research Institute, Washington D.C., U.S.A.

Tsikata, Y. (2003). Making trade work for the poor, High-level Meeting on Trade and Development, Copenhagen, (http://www.um.dk/udenrigspolitik/handel&udvikling/background/ DTIS-paper.pdf)

UNCTAD (1999). *Trade and Development Report 1999. Trade, Finance and Growth*, United Nations publication, sales no. E.99.II.D.1, Geneva.

UNCTAD (2000). *The Least Developed Countries 2000 Report–Aid, Private Capital Flows and External Debt: The Challenge of Financing Development in the LDCs*, United Nations publication, sales no. E.00.II.D.21, Geneva.

UNCTAD (2002). *The Least Developed Countries Report 2002–Escaping the Poverty Trap*, United Nations publication, sales no. E.02.II.D.13, Geneva.

World Bank (1997). Accelerating Malawi's growth: Long-term Prospects and Transitional Problems, Southern Africa Department, Washington, D.C.

Wuyts, M. (2001). Informal economy, wage goods and accumulation under structural adjustment theoretical reflections based on the Tanzanian experience, *Cambridge Journal of Economics*, 25(3): 417–432.

Improving the Trade–Poverty Relationship through the International Trade Regime

Chapter 6

A. Introduction

This chapter and the next one examine how international trade can be made a more effective mechanism for poverty reduction in the LDCs through appropriate international and national policies. The present chapter focuses on the international trade regime, whilst the next one examines how trade can be integrated into national development strategies in a way that supports poverty reduction.

The overall argument is that improving the trade–poverty relationship requires three elements to work together coherently and synergistically — firstly, better national development strategies which integrate trade as a central component; secondly, increased and effective international financial and technical assistance for developing production and trade capacities; and thirdly, a more enabling international trading environment. Improvements in the international trade regime will only be translated into poverty reduction in the LDCs if the latter's Governments formulate and implement appropriate national development strategies, and if donors provide appropriate support for these strategies, including more and better aid for trade. Equally, however, improvements in national development strategies and international assistance will only be translated into poverty reduction in the LDCs if the international trade regime is supportive. All good work done at the national level in improving national development strategies and all good work done in increasing international resource flows and their effective utilization will have a limited impact if the nature of the international trade regime continues significantly to constrain poverty reduction or even promotes immiserization.

All good work done at the national level in improving national development strategies and all good work done in increasing international resource flows and their effective utilization will have a limited impact if the nature of the international trade regime continues significantly to constrain poverty reduction or even promotes immiserization.

The international trade regime is understood here to refer not simply to WTO rules but also multilateral norms, rules and practices which go beyond the WTO legal framework. The most important element in this regard is the working of the international commodity economy, part of which is affected by WTO rules and part of which is not. Another aspect is the nature of agreements on preferential market access between developed countries and LDCs and between developing countries and LDCs, and also the nature of regional trade agreements. It is necessary to define the international trade regime in these broad terms because in practice, as we shall see, many of the key problems facing LDCs in terms of the international trade environment are actually outside the WTO agenda. Limiting the discussion to WTO issues would thus considerably foreclose proper analysis of how it is possible to link international trade to poverty reduction in the LDCs through improvements in the international trade regime.

The basic approach of the chapter is to identify what aspects of the international trade regime are acting as the most serious constraints on poverty reduction in the LDCs, and what concrete measures can be taken to improve that regime in a way in which it can better support poverty reduction in the LDCs. This approach is similar in its conceptual orientation to William Cline's idea of the "poverty intensity of trade" (Cline, 2004). This idea is that the potential impact of the trade of developed countries with developing countries will depend on the extent to which that trade occurs with countries where the poor are to be found and in products that are important to the livelihoods and living standards of the poor. In the present chapter, the analysis is concerned not only with the poverty-reducing impact of the geographical pattern of trade and the poverty-reducing impact of the product composition of trade, but also with the poverty-reducing impact of different types of changes in the international trade regime. Furthermore, in line with the development approach that informs the whole Report, the analysis seeks to bring a dynamic development perspective to the notion of "poverty intensity of trade". What matters is not simply where the poor are located now but where they will be in 15 years' time. Extreme poverty is currently located in rural areas and associated with agricultural livelihoods. But worldwide there is an increasing urbanization of poverty. Moreover, the importance of structural transformation in the development of productive capacities implies that the development of non-agricultural sectors is likely to be as important for poverty reduction as the development of agricultural sectors.

The analysis seeks to bring a dynamic development perspective to the notion of "poverty intensity of trade". What matters is not simply where the poor are located now but where they will be in 15 years' time.

This chapter discusses three distinct aspects of the international trade regime and, focusing mainly on government action, associated types of measures that may be taken to improve it. The first type are "generally applicable measures" in the sense that they concern all countries or at least all developing countries. These include the pursuit of further trade liberalization at the multilateral level, and also such measures to deal with the adverse effects of commodity price instability. The second type are "LDC-specific measures" in the sense that they are specifically targeted to the least developed countries. These measures include market access preferences granted to least developed countries by developed countries and other forms of special and differential treatment which are included within the WTO Agreements. Finally, a third type of measure is "South–South cooperation". Such measures include the market access preferences granted to least developed countries by other developing countries as well as cooperation within regional trade arrangements. Within this framework, the key questions that the chapter seeks to answer are:

- What generally applicable measures are likely to have the most positive impact in linking international trade more effectively to poverty reduction in the LDCs?

- How effective are special international support measures specially targeted at the least developed countries, and how can they be strengthened so that international trade works more effectively for poverty reduction in the LDCs?

- How important is increased South–South cooperation in the field of trade for poverty reduction in the LDCs, and what measures are likely to have the greatest poverty-reducing impact for LDCs and other developing countries?

The chapter is organized into five major sections. Section B examines the potential impact of multilateral trade liberalization on the LDCs, highlighting the importance of developing domestic productive capacities and also the importance of the issue of OECD agricultural support measures for LDCs in the current round of negotiations. Section C focuses on systemic measures beyond trade liberalization which are likely to have a high poverty-reduction intensity within the LDCs. Particular attention is given here to new international commodity policies. Section D summarizes current special international support measures for the LDCs in the field of trade and assesses their effectiveness, whilst section E suggests ways in which they can be improved. Section F highlights the increasing need to complement these measures more effectively through South–South cooperation in the field of trade. The main points of the argument are summarized in the concluding section.

B. The poverty-reducing impact of multilateral trade liberalization

1. MULTILATERAL TRADE LIBERALIZATION AND THE DEVELOPMENT OF PRODUCTIVE CAPACITIES

The potential effects of post-Uruguay Round trade liberalization on developed and developing countries have been assessed using computable general equilibrium (CGE) models in a number of recent studies (for an overview see UNCTAD, 2003a). The models estimate the static gains from multilateral trade liberalization based on the product-specific elasticities of supply and demand which relate output and demand changes to changes in prices associated with the reduction of tariff barriers, and also dynamic gains which incorporate assumptions about induced capital formation and productivity growth following trade liberalization. None of the studies include the least developed countries as a sub-group of developing countries. Moreover, in interpreting the estimated gains it is important to recognize that the models incorporate certain assumptions that diverge from real-world conditions, notably that factors of production are fully utilized and industries are perfectly competitive and there are constant returns to scale and constant elasticities of substitution. However, the studies provide a basis for assessing the possible order of magnitude of the impact of multilateral trade liberalization on the LDCs.

The LDCs cannot be expected to gain much from further multilateral trade liberalization unless improvements are made to their productive capacities to enable them to benefit from any subsequent global growth in trade.

The results of the studies suggest that the LDCs cannot be expected to gain much from further multilateral trade liberalization unless improvements are made to their productive capacities to enable them to benefit from any subsequent global growth in trade. There are two reasons for coming to this conclusion: firstly, the overall magnitude of gains from multilateral trade liberalization; and secondly, the extent to which the LDCs can be expected to share in these gains.

Most recent models suggest that multilateral trade liberalization will increase developing countries' income by approximately 3 to 5 per cent of their GDP (Cline, 2004).[1] The static gains are smaller, ranging from 1 per cent to 2.5 per cent of GDP. The gains are expected to materialize after a period of adjustment and the gains are typically predicted for the years 2010 or 2015.

What these static and dynamic gains imply in terms of poverty reduction depends on assumptions about the relationship between the income gains and poverty. The World Bank (2003) estimates that the dynamic gains from a "realistic" multilateral trade liberalization[2] would be real income gains of $518 billion for the world as a whole and $349 billion for low- and middle-income countries in 2015 in 1997 dollars. Without such trade liberalization the number of people living on less than $1/day in the low- and middle-income countries as a whole would be expected to fall from 1.1 billion in 2000 to 734 million in 2015 and the number of people living on less than $2/day would be expected to fall from 2.7 billion to 2.1 billion over the same period. With such trade liberalization the number of people living in extreme poverty in the low- and middle-income countries would fall by an extra 61 million (8 per cent of the projected 2015 level) by 2015, and the number of people living on less than $2/day would fall by an extra 144 million (7 per cent of the projected 2015 level) by 2015.

How the LDCs would benefit in terms of welfare gains and poverty reduction depends on whether the LDCs are affected in exactly the same way as other developing countries. If one assumes for the moment that they are and that the income gains from multilateral trade liberalization are 5 per cent of GDP (the maximum figure above), this would mean that real income per capita would be 5 per cent higher than it would have been without multilateral trade liberalization. This implies that for a country like Ethiopia, if multilateral trade liberalization had been undertaken in 2000 and the gains had been instantaneous, real per capita income in 2001 would have been $127 rather than $121. In 2000, the population of the LDCs constituted 13 per cent of the total population of low- and middle-income countries. If one assumes that the poverty reduction associated with the income gains is exactly proportional to this share, about 8 million of the extra 61 million people who are lifted out of extreme poverty through multilateral trade liberalization would be inhabitants of the LDCs.[3]

With no changes in policies, the number of the extremely poor living in the LDCs will rise from 334 million in 2000 to 471 million in 2015.

This would clearly be an important achievement. However, what it implies in practice needs to be seen in the context of the fact that the incidence of extreme poverty was not declining in the LDCs in the 1990s and that contrary to the group of low- and middle-income countries the group of least developed countries is predicated to see an increase of poverty, if the trends of the 1990s persist. National-accounts-based poverty estimates and household survey-based poverty estimates give different pictures of the distribution of the extremely poor amongst the LDCs. But both suggest that the incidence of extreme poverty in the LDCs as a group has remained at around 49–50 per cent during the 1990s.[4] Projecting past trends into the future, and applying them to UN population forecasts, it can be estimated that, with no changes in policies, the number of the extremely poor living in the LDCs will rise from 334 million in 2000 to 471 million in 2015.[5] What multilateral trade liberalization would do is to slow down the rate of increase of the number of extremely poor people in the LDCs. To be precise, and assuming that it is 8 million extra people lifted out of extreme poverty in the LDCs through multilateral trade liberalization, the impact of such trade liberalization would be that the number of extremely poor people will increase by 129 million rather than 137 million between 2000 and 2015.

The impact of such trade liberalization would be that the number of extremely poor people will increase by 129 million rather than 137 million between 2000 and 2015.

It may be argued that one should not take the figures derived from a CGE model at face value as they only reflect the assumptions put into the model. However, even studies based on higher dynamic effects and also greater responsiveness of poverty reduction to economic growth than that assumed by the World Bank still produce estimates that suggest that multilateral trade liberalization is not going to make much of a dent in poverty in the LDCs. For example, Cline (2004), using a different model and including stronger dynamic effects and high elasticities of poverty reduction with respect to income gains, found that an extra 650 million people could be lifted out of $2/day poverty by 2015 through global free trade. However, even if more than four times more people are lifted out of poverty than the World Bank estimates imply, as these numbers suggest, the total effect of multilateral trade liberalization on poverty in the LDCs would only be that the number of poor would increase by 105 million instead of by 137 million.

Once again it should be stressed that lifting an extra 32 million people out of poverty over 15 years would certainly be a significant achievement. However, it is likely that these estimates of the impact of multilateral trade liberalization on poverty in the LDCs are optimistic. One basic reason is that, as shown in the previous chapter, many of the LDCs have already undertaken extensive unilateral trade liberalization, and thus the gains from multilateral trade liberalization through further opening of their own markets are likely to be smaller. This is significant as most of the models, including the model used for the World Bank's simulations suggest that the greatest gains from multilateral trade liberalization to developing countries come from liberalization of their own markets. In addition, because preferential market access has been a major international support measure for the LDCs in the past, multilateral trade liberalization will be associated with the erosion of preferences. This issue will be taken up further below. Finally, multilateral trade liberalization will only have the poverty-reducing effects if there is an export supply to the opportunities that result from multilateral trade liberalization. The problem here is that the ability of the LDCs to increase their exports is highly constrained by weak production capacities.

However, it is likely that these estimates of the impact of multilateral trade liberalization on poverty in the LDCs are optimistic.

What the trade ministers of the LDCs themselves repeatedly emphasize as the way to increase the effectiveness of trade as a mechanism for development and poverty reduction is the development of competitive productive capacities (see the annex table to this chapter). This makes sense in that if multilateral trade liberalization boosts global trading opportunities, the LDCs can benefit. But they will only do so if they can sustain their share of world exports of goods and services, and this depends on the development of productive capacities. If they experience a continuing process of marginalization in world trade, increases in global trading opportunities and economic growth will simply pass them by.

If the LDCs had in 2001 maintained the same share of global markets as they had in 1980 their exports of goods and services would have been $20.8 billion more than they actually were.

The importance of this is underlined by the analysis of chapter 3. This showed that if the LDCs had in 2001 maintained the same share of global markets as they had in 1980 their exports of goods and services would have been $20.8 billion more than they actually were. These export losses are due to a range of national and international factors, including changes in the composition of global trade and a decline in commodity prices since 1980. However, their quantitative importance for growth and poverty reduction is evident in that they were equivalent to 11 per cent of the GDP of the LDCs in 2001 alone.

It would be good to think that trade liberalization by itself would induce the development of productive capacities in the LDCs. But the evidence of the previous chapter gives few grounds for optimism in this regard. Rather, it is necessary to focus on developing productive capacities directly if LDCs are to avoid further marginalization (i.e. declining shares) in world trade.

It is necessary to focus on developing productive capacities directly if LDCs are to avoid further marginalization in world trade.

2. THE EFFECTS OF OECD AGRICULTURAL SUPPORT MEASURES ON LDCs

An area of multilateral trade liberalization that is likely to have a strongly positive poverty-reducing impact in the LDCs in the long run is the phasing-out of agricultural support measures in advanced countries in a way that ends the distorting effects of this support on international trade. This issue is vital for the LDCs because agriculture plays such an important role in their economies, contributing 35 per cent of GDP, employing 69 per cent of the total economically active population, and contributing 24 per cent of total exports in 1999–2001.

In the international debate on OECD agricultural support measures most attention has focused on the case of cotton. This is indeed important, as cotton is the product in respect of which the effects of agricultural support measures on poverty have been most clearly identified (see box 13). But in practice, although cotton is a very important export product for a number of LDCs, a relatively small proportion of the total exports of the LDCs are currently adversely affected by OECD agricultural support measures (see discussion below). The key mechanism through which the phasing-out of agricultural support measures can help to reduce poverty in the LDCs is the way in which it will stop low prices and cheap imports undermining the incentives for investment and productivity growth in domestic agriculture.

The key mechanism through which the phasing-out of agricultural support measures can help to reduce poverty in the LDCs is the way in which it will stop low prices and cheap imports undermining the incentives for investment and productivity growth in domestic agriculture.

The effects of the phasing-out of OECD agricultural support measures in the LDCs will, nevertheless, be complex. They depend on what the LDCs produce, export and import now, and also what they potentially can produce, export and import in the future. As shown in part 2, chapter 2, the LDCs have become increasingly dependent on food imports. This implies that in the short run, phasing out will mean higher food prices and also considerable pressure on the balance of payments of many LDCs.[6]

Models which estimate the effects of a phasing-out of OECD agricultural support provide a mixed picture, with Hoekman et al. (2002) indicating welfare gains for the LDCs and Peters (2004) indicating welfare losses.[7] The models are likely to underestimate the benefits of the phasing out of OECD agricultural support to the LDCs for at least three reasons. They assume that factors of production are fully employed. They concentrate on the products that receive agricultural support rather than both those products and potential substitutes for them. Their starting-point is the current pattern of agricultural production and trade, which is itself a product of the agricultural support measures, rather than a

---

Box 13. The impact of cotton subsidies

Cotton subsidies provided by advanced countries have had important negative effects on some least developed countries. The negative effects — which were transmitted through a decline of the cotton price on the world market — were particularly significant for those least developed countries that have the strongest specialization in cotton production. Measured by the total value of cotton exports, Mali is the largest cotton exporter amongst the least developed countries; but measured as share of cotton exports in total exports, Benin, Burkina Faso and Chad are more dependent on cotton exports. In 1999–2001, cotton exports of Benin, Burkina Faso, and Chad accounted for a very larger share of their total merchandise exports (between 60.3 and 77.9 per cent) and a large share of their GDP (between 5.0 and 9.4 per cent).

The cotton subsidies have depressed world cotton prices. On the basis of the assumption that cotton prices per pound in 2001 would have been 12 cents higher if the United States had eliminated cotton subsidies, it has been estimated that Central and Western African countries had forgone foreign exchange earnings of $250 billion (Badine et al., 2002). Similarly, on the basis of the assumption that cotton prices per pound would have been 11 cents higher, an Oxfam study estimates that African producers had forgone foreign exchange earnings of $302 million (Oxfam, 2003). Oxfam estimates forgone foreign exchange earnings for: Benin $33 million, Burkina Faso $28 million, Chad $16 million, the Central African Republic $2 million, Ethiopia $5 million, Guinea $3 million, Madagascar $3 million, Malawi $2 million, Mali $43 million, Mozambique $6 million, Somalia $1 million, Sudan $17 million, Togo lost $16 million, Uganda $5 million, United Republic of Tanzania $21 million and Zambia $8 million.

Simulations exercises show that if full liberalization in the cotton sector takes place, including removal of both trade barriers and production support (along with liberalization in all other commodity sectors), cotton prices would rise above the price that would have prevailed in the absence of reforms. It is estimated that in the next 10 years cotton prices would increase by an average of 12.7 per cent. World cotton trade would increase by 5.8 per cent, while Africa's cotton exports would increase by 12.6 per cent (IMF, 2003a).

pattern of agricultural production and trade that reflects comparative advantage. In the long run, those LDCs that have a comparative advantage in agricultural production should benefit from the phasing-out of agricultural support measures. According to Cline (2004), although many LDCs are net food importers, more than half of them have a comparative advantage in food production.

The phasing-out of agricultural support measures is important for the LDCs because substantial and sustained poverty reduction depends in many of the LDCs on improvements in agricultural productivity and also beneficial complementarities between the agricultural sector and the non-agricultural sector. Without such complementarities, there is likely to be an enclave-based pattern of development. The harmful effects of agricultural support lie precisely in its encouraging this disarticulation in the domestic economy, which then prevents agrarian commercialization and development of national markets. The worst-case scenario for increasing poverty in the LDCs occurs if there is an acceleration of rural–urban migration because it is impossible to find viable livelihoods in rural areas, whilst at the same time few meaningful non-agricultural employment opportunities are developed in the urban centres. The policy combination of extensive trade liberalization undertaken by the LDCs and increasing support measures in the advanced countries has the potential to make this worst-case scenario a reality in some LDCs.

The situation is particularly troublesome as many LDCs have not simply undertaken extensive trade liberalization but have also reduced all kinds of support to their own domestic agriculture sector. This reflects the fact that the pre-structural adjustment agricultural policies tended to tax export crops but also to provide support for food crops. Such support has been radically reduced, one effect of this being the truncation of incipient Green Revolutions in African LDCs. In effect, the effort to remove distortions in the domestic agricultural sector within the LDCs is being subverted by distortions in the domestic agricultural sector in other countries.

In order to illustrate the linkages between OECD agricultural support measures in developed countries and agricultural production and development in the LDCs, it is useful to match the products that are supported by the former with the products that are produced by the latter. This is not a straightforward exercise, since the product classifications that are used in the context of agricultural support measures in the OECD countries are not identical to product classifications used for agricultural production in non-OECD countries. Data related to agricultural support measures and production in OECD countries are provided by the OECD, while the most comprehensive data related to agricultural production in non-OECD countries are provided by the FAO. Moreover, a comprehensive assessment of the potential impact of agricultural support measures in the developed countries on agricultural production in the LDCs should focus not only on products that receive support, but also on products that are their substitutes, in both unprocessed form and processed form (Herrmann, 2003a).

Table 45 provides an overview of all products that currently receive support from OECD countries, regardless of type and level, and are also produced in the LDCs.[8] The table shows the importance of these products in the LDCs in terms of total output and total output per capita. It also shows the output of the LDCs as a share of the output of OECD countries. Beans, beef and veal, cotton, maize, milk, potatoes, rice, sorghum, sugar and wheat, are products that receive support in developed countries and are also of great importance to production in least developed countries. Some of these products received significantly more

Although many LDCs are net food importers, more than half of them have a comparative advantage in food production.

The effort to remove distortions in the domestic agricultural sector within the LDCs is being subverted by distortions in the domestic agricultural sector in other countries.

TABLE 45. PRODUCTS[a] SUPPORTED BY OECD COUNTRIES AND THEIR IMPORTANCE FOR LDCs, 1991–2000

Rank	Average annual output of LDCs				Average annual ouput of LDCs as a share of average annual output of OECD countries			
	In metric tons		In kilogram/capita		%, based on metric tons		%, based on kilogram/capita	
Top 10								
1	Rice	61 155 943	Rice	102.7	Coffeebeans[b]	35 747.4	Coffeebeans[b]	50 713.6
2	Sugar	34 289 431	Sugar	60.8	Rice	255.0	Rice	354.4
3	Maize	15 628 671	Maize	26.1	Beans	64.7	Beans	90.4
4	Milk (cow)	10 267 425	Milk (cow)	17.1	Sorghum	56.3	Sorghum	79.0
5	Sorghum	9 844 374	Sorghum	16.5	Tobacco	27.6	Tobacco	38.7
6	Wheat	6 522 028	Wheat	10.9	Sheepmeat	21.1	Garlic	28.8
7	Potatoes	5 637 666	Potatoes	9.4	Garlic	20.5	Sheepmeat	26.8
8	Cotton	3 248 227	Cotton	5.4	Cotton	18.9	Cotton	26.3
9	Beans	3 134 699	Beans	5.2	Sugar	16.3	Sugar	21.1
10	Beef and veal	2 189 747	Beef and veal	4.3	Onions	13.0	Onions	18.2
Top 20								
11	Eggs	1 376 286	Barley	4.2	Beef and veal	9.2	Beef and veal	13.7
12	Barley	1 222 525	Eggs	2.3	Potatoes	7.1	Potatoes	9.9
13	Onions	1 154 560	Onions	1.9	Wool	6.4	Wool	8.9
14	Tomatoes	1 129 871	Tomatoes	1.9	Maize	5.8	Maize	8.0
15	Poultrymeat	880 889	Poultrymeat	1.5	Eggs	5.3	Eggs	7.3
16	Coffeebeans[b]	802 350	Coffeebeans[b]	1.3	Milk (cow)	4.4	Milk (cow)	6.1
17	Pigmeat	548 852	Rapeseed	1.2	Sunflower	4.3	Tomatoes	5.7
18	Sheepmeat	514 498	Sheepmeat	1.0	Tomatoes	4.1	Sunflower	5.2
19	Grapes	504 773	Pigmeat	0.9	Poultrymeat	3.5	Poultrymeat	4.9
20	Tobacco	332 715	Grapes	0.9	Wheat	3.2	Wheat	4.5
Top 30								
21	Rapeseed	326 920	Sunflower	0.7	Cabbage	2.7	Cabbage	3.8
22	Soyabeans	269 086	Tobacco	0.6	Spinach	2.1	Rapeseed	3.6
23	Sunflower	243 646	Soyabeans	0.5	Rapeseed	2.1	Spinach	2.9
24	Cabbage	223 572	Cabbage	0.4	Pigmeat	2.0	Pigmeat	2.7
25	Garlic	113 516	Garlic	0.2	Pepper, Red	1.8	Pepper, Red	2.5
26	Wool	81 998	Wool	0.1	Barley	1.6	Barley	2.4
27	Oats	53 511	Oats	0.1	Grapes	1.5	Mandarins	1.6
28	Mandarins	50 104	Mandarins	0.1	Mandarins	1.1	Grapes	1.4
29	Pepper, red	46 376	Pepper, red	0.1	Cucumbers	0.8	Cucumbers	1.1
30	Apples	30 810	Apples	0.1	Soyabeans	0.4	Oats	0.5
Remainder								
31	Cucumbers	30 394	Cucumbers	0.1	Oats	0.4	Soyabeans	0.4
32	Spinach	22 817	Spinach	0.0	Apples	0.2	Apples	0.3
33	Pears	4 120	Pears	0.0	Pears	0.1	Pears	0.1
34	Strawberries	0	Strawberries	0.0	Strawberries	0.0	Strawberries	0.0

Source: UNCTAD secretariat estimates, based on OECD PSE/CSE online data, and FAO online data on agricultural production.

Note: The table includes all goods that receive support from OECD countries, regardless of type and level. Support provided for products generally includes, but is not limited to, subsidies.OECD countries provide support to "oilseeds", which include rapeseeds, soyabeans and sunflowers, and support to "other grains", which include barley, oats and sorghum. Here these products are considered on an individual basis.

a Products are ranked by level of average annual output in metric tons.

b Amongst OECD countries, only Mexico provides support for coffee; support is provided in form of consumer support.

support than others. According to OECD estimates, the average producer support per metric ton for the period 1991–2001 was highest for wool, followed by sheep meat, beef and veal, poultry meat, rice, pigmeat, eggs, oilseeds (including rapeseeds, soybean and sunflower), milk, other grains (including barley, oats and sorghum), refined sugar, wheat and maize. The estimated level of aggregate producer support ranged from from $3,020 for wool to $72 for maize per metric tonne.[9]

The least developed countries that can be expected to suffer most from agricultural support measures are those that have the largest specialization in these products, or in substitutes for them. Table 46 shows the top five LDC

TABLE 46. PRODUCTS SUPPORTED BY OECD COUNTRIES, AND TOP FIVE LDC PRODUCERS OF THESE PRODUCTS,[a] BASED ON ANNUAL AVERAGE PRODUCTION IN METRIC TONS, 1991–2000

	Beef and veal	Pigmeat	Poultrymeat	Sheepmeat	Eggs	Milk (cow)	Barley	Maize	Oats	Rice	Sorghum	Wheat	Rapeseed	Soyabeans	Sunflower	Apples	Grapes	Mandarins	Pears	Strawberries	Beans	Cabbage	Cucumbers	Garlic	Onions	Pepper, red	Potatoes	Spinach	Tomatoes	Coffeebeans	Sugar	Cotton	Wool	Tobacco
LDC producers of equivalents[b]																																		
Afghanistan			1			2	2					1			4	1	1		1														2	
Angola																5																		
Bangladesh	4		2		1	3				1		2	1									1	1	2	3		1	1	5		1			3
Benin																											1		4			2		
Bhutan																3											3							
Burkina Faso											2																4					3		
Burundi																					4													
Cambodia		1								4				3																				
Chad																																5		
Dem. Rep. of the Congo		5						5																4	5					3				
Eritrea							5																											
Ethiopia	3		3	3	3	4	1	2	1		3	4	2	5		5	4				3	2								2		3		
Haiti																		3										2						
Lao People's Dem. Rep.																		1																5
Lesotho								2																										
Madagascar	5	3								5						2	4		2		5	3					5			4	4			
Malawi								3														3					3			5				1
Mali										4																						1		
Mozambique															5																			
Myanmar		2	1	2						2			2		1						1			1	1					3				2
Nepal							4	4		3		3															2							
Niger																									2									
Senegal				4																				4			3							
Somalia					4																													
Sudan	1			2	5	1					1	5			3			5					3		5				1	2		4	1	
Uganda		4											1								2			4	4					1				
United Rep. of Tanzania	2				4	5		1			5				2			3			5		5						3	5			5	4
Yemen				5	5		3									4	2	2	3					2	4	5	2		2				4	
Zambia														4					4															
LDC producers of substitutes[b]																																		
Afghanistan						5																												
Angola																															2			
Bangladesh	5	5	5	5		3																										1	1	
Burkina Faso							3	3	3	3	3	3																						
Burundi																5	5	5	5	5														
Central African Republic																														4				
Dem. Rep. of the Congo	3	3	3	3									4	4	4	2	2	2	2	2	1	1	1	1	1	1	1	1	1					
Ethiopia	2	2	2	2			2	2	2	2	2	2									5	5	5	5	5	5	5	5	5	3		5	5	
Madagascar																														5		4	4	
Mali							4	4	4	4	4	4																						
Mozambique													5	5	5						4	4	4	4	4	4	4	4	4					
Myanmar													2	2	2																	3	3	
Nepal	4	4	4	4		4																												
Niger							1	1	1	1	1	1																						
Rwanda																3	3	3	3	3														
Senegal													3	3	3																			
Somalia						1																												
Sudan	1	1	1	1		2							1	1	1																			
Uganda							5	5	5	5	5	5				1	1	1	1	1	3	3	3	3	3	3	3	3	3					
United Rep. of Tanzania																4	4	4	4	4	2	2	2	2	2	2	2	2	2	1		2	2	

Source: UNCTAD secretariat estimates, based on OECD PSE/CSE online data, and FAO online data on agricultural production.

Note: The table includes all goods that receive support from OECD countries, regardless of type and level. Support provided for products generally includes, but is not limited to, subsidies.

a The largest LDC producer for each product is identified by the number "1", while the fifth largest LDC producer for each product is identified by the number "5". In the case of strawberries no significant LDC producers of equivalents have been identified; in the case of oats and rapeseeds there are only two LDC producers of equivalents; in the case of spinach there are only three LDC producers of equivalents; and in the case of pears there are only four LDC producers of equivalents. For all other products there are at least five LDC producers of equivalents. No substitutes have been identified for eggs, coffee and tobacco.

b "Equivalents" are products included in the FAO database on agricultural production that can be directly compared with the products that are supported by OECD countries, whereas "substitutes" are products included in the FAO database on agricultural production that have properties similar to those products that are supported by OECD countries. While the category of "equivalents" includes only goods in their unprocessed form, the category of "substitutes" includes goods in both their unprocessed and processed forms. For a detailed description of the methodology, see Herrmann (2003a).

c Amongst OECD countries, only Mexico provides support for coffee; support is provided in form of consumer support.

producers of the products and also substitutes.[10] The top five producers amongst the least developed countries are ranked by their aggregate output in metric tons, rather than their output in per capita terms. This means that the countries included in the table are LDCs that are likely to derive the greatest benefits in aggregate terms from a phasing-out of support measures, but that relative to their population other LDCs can also expect to gain. The least developed countries that can, for example, be expected to derive the largest absolute gains from a phasing-out of support measures on rice are Bangladesh, Cambodia, Madagascar, Myanmar and Nepal, which are amongst the most important producers of rice, but also Burkina Faso, Ethiopia, Mali, Niger and Uganda, which are important producers of rice substitutes (table 46).

Estimation of the quantitative impact of these OECD agricultural support measures in the LDCs awaits in-country case studies, some of which are currently being undertaken by FAO. However, a rough idea of the possible effects on the LDCs can be gained if one estimates what the LDCs would have gained if their production had been subsidized to the same extent of that in OECD countries. Simply multiplying the average payments per ton of output that OECD producers received during the 1990s by the average production of the different commodities by the LDCs over that period indicates that the LDC producers would have received $11.7 billion per annum during that period.[11] This is on average equivalent to 7 per cent of their GDP over the period. Over half of this amount ($7.9 billion) would be attributable to payments for rice production. But if LDC producers of beef and veal, sugar, sheepmeat, sorghum, maize and wheat were to have received payments at the same rate as OECD producers in the period 1991-2001, they would have received for each of these products $857 million, $741 million, $605 million, $434 million, $382 million and $311 million, respectively.

> *It appears much more reasonable to promote a phasing-out of support that concentrates on a gradual reduction of support to all countries at the same time. However, the process might start by focusing on strategic agricultural goods that are of particular importance to the poorest developing countries.*

It has been proposed that an approach to the phasing-out of subsidies would be to eliminate subsidies on the goods shipped to specific groups of countries. Thus, the French Government has floated the idea of eliminating export subsidies on all goods that are destined for Africa. But while the French proposal is important because it acknowledges the damaging effects of agricultural support measures in developed countries, it is likely to introduce a dual price structure into world markets, with a continuously low food price for non-African countries and a relatively high food price for African countries. It is questionable whether such a structure is to the benefit of African countries, and also whether it could be maintained in reality. This is because African countries may be encouraged to import European agricultural products through third countries rather than from the European Union directly. In order to encourage agricultural production in developing countries effectively it appears much more reasonable to promote a phasing-out of support that concentrates on a gradual reduction of support to all countries at the same time. However, the process might start by focusing on strategic agricultural goods that are of particular importance to the poorest developing countries. If this approach were adopted with the LDCs as the target group, the product ranking identified in table 45 would be of importance. The key strategic products, depending on the method of identification, would include, in alphabetical order, beans, beef and veal, cotton, garlic, maize, milk, onions, potatoes, rice, sheepmeat, sorghum, sugar and wheat. Although coffee is an important product for the LDCs, the OECD support provided to coffee is not of great concern, as the LDC production is large compared to OECD production and as OECD support for coffee is small compared to its support for other products.[12] But given the existence of substitutes as well as equivalent products considered in table 46, such partial elimination of support should be considered a second-best solution to a more comprehensive approach.

Finally, it should be noted that the greatest benefits of the phasing-out of agricultural support will accrue if the phasing-out is linked to increasing international financial and technical assistance to agriculture in the LDCs to promote agricultural productivity growth and commercialization. Given the economic importance that agriculture has to the LDCs, it is a matter of concern that in real terms external assistance to agriculture in the LDCs in the 1990s was half its level in the 1980s. Chart 38 shows that in 2001 fiscal support for farmers in OECD countries — that is, the sum of different payments to OECD producers — was actually seven times the level of total ODA to the LDCs. In 2001 net flows of ODA to LDCs would have been doubled if 14 per cent of the 2001 value of the fiscal support to OECD producers had been redirected in aid to the LDCs. There is thus an opportunity for major poverty reduction benefits through not only phasing out of agricultural support but also increasing international assistance to promote agricultural development in the LDCs.

> *Given the economic importance that agriculture has to the LDCs, it is a matter of concern that in real terms external assistance to agriculture in the LDCs in the 1990s was half its level in the 1980s.*

CHART 38. NET AID DISBURSEMENTS[a] OF OECD COUNTRIES TO LDCS IN COMPARISON WITH SUPPORT[b] OF OECD COUNTRIES TO THEIR AGRICULTURAL SECTORS, 1986–2001
($ billions)

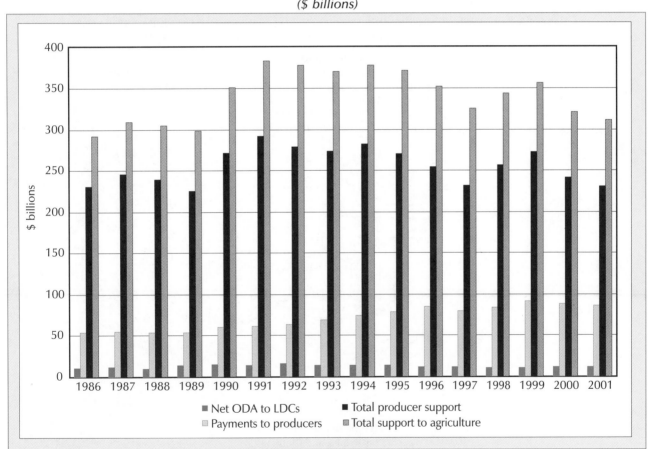

Source: UNCTAD secretariat estimates, based on OECD PSE/CSE online data.

    a   Net official development assistance comprises net disbursements, including imputed multilateral flows.

    b   Data for the year 2001 were provisional at the time of calculation.

C. The importance of generally applicable measures beyond trade liberalization

1. THE RELATIVE IMPORTANCE OF DIFFERENT INTERNATIONAL CONSTRAINTS

A broader view of the generally applicable measures in the field of trade that are likely to have the most positive impact on poverty reduction in the LDCs can be obtained if one asks:

- Which aspects of the international trading regime have the most negative effects on exports and production in the LDCs?

- Which aspects of exports and production are the most important for poverty reduction in the LDCs?

Chart 39 estimates the proportion of exports from the LDCs and other developing countries that are likely to be adversely affected by six different types of international constraints in 1999–2001. The six types of constraints are the following: environment-related trade barriers (including sanitary and phytosanitary standards, and technical product standards);[13] import restrictions

CHART 39. THE SHARE OF MERCHANDISE EXPORTS OF LDCS AND OTHER DEVELOPING COUNTRIES AFFECTED BY SELECTED ADVERSE CONDITIONS, AVERAGE 1999–2001

(Percentage)

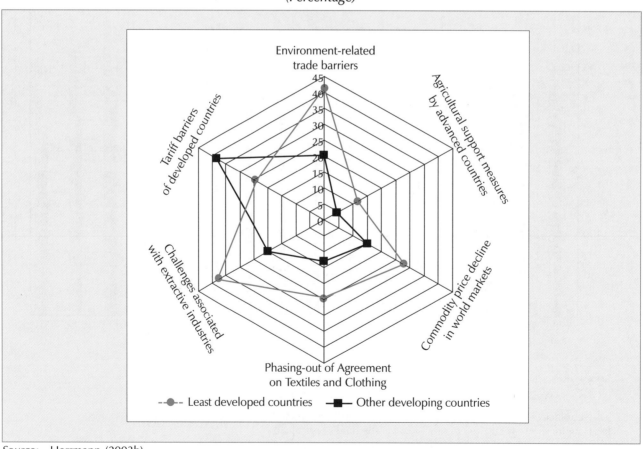

Source: Herrmann (2003b).

Note: Tariff barriers of developed countries are the inverse of the share of goods that benefit from duty-free access to developed countries, which is one measure of progress towards goal 8 of the Millennium Development Goals. The goods admitted duty-free exclude arms and ammunition. Environment-related trade barriers (ETB) are defined in accordance with Fontagné, von Kirchbach and Mimouni (2001). They include sanitary and phytosanitary measures (SPS) and technical barriers to trade (TBT), and are generally motivated by the desire to protect the environment, wildlife, plant health, animal health, human health and human safety.

in developed countries (measured by the proportion of exports that do not enter developed country markets duty-free); the phasing-out of the Agreement on Textiles and Clothing; agricultural support measures in developed countries; declining world commodity prices on world markets; and the special challenges associated with extractive industries (oil, gas and minerals).[14] The last constraint has both national and international aspects, and it is the latter that will be considered here.

From the chart, a number of conclusions can be drawn.

Firstly, the exports of the LDCs as a group are more adversely affected than those of other developing countries by five of out six of these aspects of the international trading system. It is notable that the proportion of LDC exports by value affected by environment-related trade barriers, challenges associated with extractive industries, commodity price falls, agricultural support measures in developed countries and the phasing-out of the Agreement on Textiles and Clothing is more than twice the proportion of exports of other developing countries that are affected. The exception to this general pattern is restrictions on imports into developed country markets. In 1999–2001, the percentage of exports (excluding arms and ammunition) that did not enter duty-free was 38 per cent in other developing countries and 24 per cent in the LDCs.[15] But in the light of new preferential market access initiatives, the five-year average is likely to better reflect the comparative situation.

Secondly, the aspects of the international trading system that adversely affect the highest proportion of LDC exports are commodity-related. The most important constraint for the LDCs as a group is environmental trade barriers, which affected 42 per cent of LDC exports in 1999–2001. This is followed by challenges associated with the development of extractive industries, which affected 38 per cent of LDC exports in the same period, and declining world commodity prices, which affected 28 per cent of LDC exports. Agricultural support measures are a further commodity-related issue. But, as explained above, the adverse effects of agricultural support measures work more through imports undercutting and depressing domestic production than through exports for most of the LDCs (the most important exception being West and Central African cotton producers). With regard to equivalent products, it is estimated that 11 per cent of LDC exports were adversely affected by agricultural support measures in the developed countries. This, and also the estimate for other developing countries, would be higher if substitutes were included and also the effects of agricultural support measures on diversification opportunities.

Thirdly, besides the commodity-related issues the phasing-out of the Agreement on Textiles and Clothing is going to an important problem for the LDCs. Twenty-four per cent of the total exports of the LDCs will be affected by this change in the international trading system. Given the fact that LDC textile and clothing exports have developed on the basis of preferential market access, the pressing problem is how to adapt and be competitive in the emerging new trading environment. Further dimensions of this problem are set out in box 14.

It should be noted finally that chart 39 refers to the LDCs or other developing countries as a group and that within each group there are individual countries that face these constraints to a much greater degree. For the LDCs, the challenges associated with extractive industries are obviously relevant to those that have an export specialization in oil or minerals. The problems associated with the phasing-out of the Agreement on Textiles and Clothing are relevant to the LDCs that have built up export industries in textiles and clothing. Agricultural support measures are important for LDC that export cotton and those that have

The proportion of LDC exports affected by environment-related trade barriers, challenges associated with extractive industries, commodity price falls, agricultural support measures in developed countries and the phasing-out of the Agreement on Textiles and Clothing is more than twice the proportion of exports of other developing countries that are affected.

The most important constraint for the LDCs as a group is environmental trade barriers, which affected 42 per cent of LDC exports in 1999–2001.

Box 14. The phasing-out of the Agreement on Textiles and Clothing

From 1974 until the end of the Uruguay Round, the trade in textiles was governed by the Multifibre Arrangement (MFA), and as of 1995 the trade in textiles has been regulated under the Agreement on Textiles and Clothing (ATC). Although the WTO has aimed for a tariffication of all quantitative restrictions to trade, the ATC continued to allow for quantitative restrictions, namely quotas in specific imports. The trade in textiles and clothing was also characterized by exceptions to the principle of the most favoured nation, which demands that all members in the international trading system treat all other members in the system alike. Under the agreements relegating the trade in textiles, countries were able to treat others in an unequal manner, meaning that they could set different import quotas for textile exports of different countries. But while most countries faced relatively high import barriers of their textile exports, the least developed countries, and countries that are referred to as small suppliers of textile products, benefited from preferential market access in these goods. The relatively high import barriers faced by the majority of countries, on the one side, and the preferential market access enjoyed by the group of least developed countries, on the other, implied considerable preference margin for least developed countries.

It is on this basis that some LDCs have managed to diversify out of commodity exports and develop manufactures exports. As box chart 1 shows, it is the Asian LDCs in particular which have taken advantage of these preferences. Textile exports were equivalent to 61 per cent of the merchandise exports of Asian LDCs, but only 2 per cent of those of African LDCs. During the 1999–2001 period, the textile exports of 14 Asian LDCs accounted for 94.2 per cent of the total textile exports of the 49 LDCs.

The Agreement on Textiles and Clothing entails a 10-year schedule to bring the trade in textiles and clothing under GATT stipulations. In accordance with this schedule, there has been a first group of textile products (at least 16 percent of all relevant products) that has been brought under GATT rules in the period 1995–1997, a second group of textile products (at least 17 per cent of all relevant products) has been brought under GATT rule in the period 1998–2001, a third group of textile products (at least 18 per cent of all relevant products) has been brought under the GATT rule in the period 2002–2004, and a final group of relevant products (all remaining 49 per cent of the relevant products) will need to be brought under GATT rules by 1 January 2005. These changes have gradually eroded the preference margins enjoyed by least developed countries and by 2005 they will have completely eliminated the import quotas and also the preferential margins of these countries.

The overall outcome, however, will also be determined by whether the provision of unilaterally granted market access preferences for LDCs can balance the negative effects of the phasing out of the ATC. It is probable that most non-Asian LDCs will suffer only marginal losses from the phasing out of the textile regime, whereas the group of Asian LDCs may actually experience significant losses. During the past years Bangladesh and Nepal, for instance, have significantly increased their production and export of textiles owning to the provision of market access preferences by developed countries, especially the EU and the United States (Appelbaum, 2003). After the phasing-out of the agreement on textiles and clothing, the Asian LDCs should still benefit from far-reaching market access preferences to the EU as they are eligible for market access preferences granted under the EBA initiative, but they would no longer have the most preferential market access to the United States as they are not eligible for market access preferences granted under AGOA.

At present the United States grants market access to LDCs through three types of market access schemes. Through the African Growth and Opportunity Act, it grants one set of market access preferences to LDCs (and other countries) in sub-Saharan Africa, through the Caribbean Basin Initiative it grants another set of market access preferences to Haiti (and other countries) in the Caribbean, and through its Generalized System of Preferences for Least Developed Countries it grants a third set of market access preferences to all other remaining LDCs, namely those located in Asia. One of the most important differences between the different market access schemes are market access preferences in textiles. The market access for textile and apparel products is relatively good under the first two schemes, but it is much weaker under the third scheme. This means that the Asian LDCs, which are the LDCs with the strongest specialization in textile exports, are confronted by eroding market access preferences for their textile exports, where the market of the United States is concerned.

The overall effect of the phasing-out of the Agreement on Textiles and Clothing on the one side, and the provision of international support measures on the other, depends on how the changes at the different levels interact with each, and how these changes effect other economic variables, such as the flow of investments.

Box 14 (contd.)

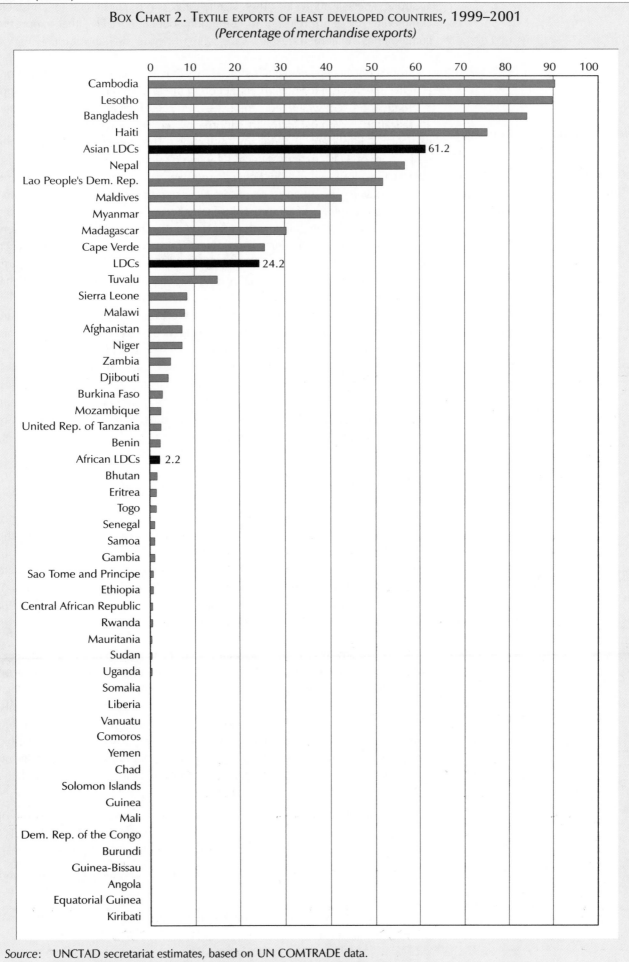

Box Chart 2. Textile exports of least developed countries, 1999–2001
(Percentage of merchandise exports)

Source: UNCTAD secretariat estimates, based on UN COMTRADE data.
Note: Textile exports include codes 65, 82, 83, 84 and 85 in SITC, Revision 2.

a strong specialization in other agricultural goods. Declining or unstable commodity prices are relevant to commodity-dependent LDCs that export the commodities concerned.

From a policy perspective, chart 39 shows that in order to make trade a more effective mechanism for poverty reduction in the LDCs, there is a need to adopt a broad approach which encompasses, but goes beyond, multilateral trade liberalization. Within such an approach, commodity-related issues are particularly important for poverty reduction. This follows partly from the proportion of LDC exports affected by international constraints. But it also reflects the close association between primary commodity dependence and extreme poverty identified in *The Least Developed Countries Report 2002* and discussed in chapter 3 of the present Report. According to our estimates, 79 per cent of the people living on less than $1/day in the LDCs in the late 1990s were living in LDCs whose major exports were primary commodities (UNCTAD, 2002a: 125, table 31). Against this background, generally applicable measures to address constraints on production and exports related to the international commodity economy are likely to have a particularly positive poverty-reducing impact in the LDCs. A particular concern is the LDCs whose major exports are minerals, ores and metals and where the incidence of $1/day poverty rose from 61 per cent to 82 per cent between the early 1980s and the late 1990s. As discussed in chapter 4, this trend is related to civil conflict within the countries. But international measures with regard to the challenge of extractive industries, which are off the radar screen in current analyses of the effects of multilateral trade liberalization (which focus on agriculture and manufactures), are nevertheless likely to be particularly important.

> *International measures with regard to the challenge of extractive industries, which are off the radar screen in current analyses of the effects of multilateral trade liberalization (which focus on agriculture and manufactures), are nevertheless likely to be particularly important.*

2. PRIORITY ELEMENTS OF NEW INTERNATIONAL COMMODITY POLICIES

The failure to tackle the link between extreme poverty and the working of the international commodity economy is the major "sin of omission" in the current international approach to poverty reduction. As President Chirac of France put it, in his address to the Twenty-Second Summit of the Heads of State of Africa and France on 20 February 2003, "There is on the question of commodities a sort of conspiracy of silence. The solutions are not simple…But nothing justifies the present indifference".

> *The failure to tackle the link between extreme poverty and the working of the international commodity economy is the major "sin of omission" in the current international approach to poverty reduction.*

Within the last year there has in fact been some new thinking on the issue. Notable in this regard is the Report of the Meeting of Eminent Persons on Commodity Issues requested by the General Assembly (UNCTAD, 2003c). That report identified a series of practical proposals, including short-term proposals, which involve urgent immediate action in response to severe crises in selected commodity sectors in recent years, medium-term proposals involving feasible reorientation of national and international policies, and long-term proposals on which discussion should be started now. The eminent persons attached the highest priority to the following actions:

- Enhanced equitable and predictable market access for commodities of key importance to developing countries (short-term through WTO negotiations and including the issue of agricultural support measures);

- Addressing issues of oversupply for many commodities (short-term and medium-term);

- Making compensatory finance schemes user-friendly and operational (medium-term);

- Strengthening national capacity and institutions to improve productive capacities and market entry (medium-term);

- Pursuing the possibilities of a new International Diversification Fund, which would focus on diversifying private-sector productive capacity (long-term).

Amongst the priority short-term proposals of particular relevance for the LDCs are action to address the effects of cotton subsidies in developed countries (through their early elimination or measures to mitigate their adverse consequences) and action to help alleviate poverty arising from low coffee prices. The latter is a complex problem, which has no easy solutions (see box 15). Apart from the issue of agricultural support measures in developed countries, which can be addressed through the multilateral negotiations on trade liberalization, the two priority elements of new international commodity policies that are likely to have the most poverty-reducing impact in the LDCs are, first, measures to reduce vulnerability to commodity price shocks, and, second, implementation of greater transparency in reporting of government revenues

---

BOX 15. POSSIBLE RESPONSES TO COMMODITY PRICE DECLINE: THE CASE OF COFFEE

Like other primary agricultural commodities, the world coffee market is characterized by high instability and also, since 1980 there has been a slump in prices. In 2003, world coffee prices were just 17 per cent of their level in 1980. The falling prices have been accompanied and magnified by a major change in the distribution of income between producers and other agents in the coffee value-chain. According to the International Coffee Organization, coffee-producing countries currently earn (exports f.o.b.) just $5.5 billion of the $70 billion value of retail sales, while in the early 1990s they earned some $10–12 billion of the $30-billion value of retail sales (see http://www.ico.org, 25. April 2004).

There are 18 LDCs which export coffee, and for some of these, notably Burundi, the Central African Republic, the Democratic Republic of the Congo, Ethiopia, Lao People's Democratic Republic, Rwanda, Uganda and the United Republic of Tanzania, the crop has been particularly important. But with falling world prices, production prices have fallen so low in many poor countries that large parts of production has become unviable. The Integrated Framework's Diagnostic Trade Integration Study (DTIS) on Ethiopia estimates that coffee contributed 40 per cent of the value of Ethiopian exports in 2001/2002 and that, including dependants, 7.5 million depend on the sector. But "the negative margin between farmgate prices and production costs makes it clear that production is currently not profitable" (Integrate Framework, 2003: 49).

Possible responses to this problem include: upgrading coffee production, supply management to raise coffee prices and diversification.

The opportunity for upgrading is evident in box chart. As well as the major differential between the producer prices and retail price, this shows that LDC coffee producers generally earn less than coffee producers in other developing countries. Producer prices of Arabica coffee in LDCs were on average about 33 per cent of those in other developing countries, and producer prices of Robusta coffee in LDCs were just 55 per cent of those in other developing countries.

These differences between producers reflect tendencies for increasing differentials amongst producers to be occurring at the same time as the gap between retail and producer prices has been widening. The differentials amongst producers reflect: (i) the division between anonymous and non-anonymous sales, mainly for Robusta and hard Arabica; and the emergence of specialty and gourmet coffees, mainly within the mid-Arabica market (Gibbon, 2003). Non-anonymous sales are achieved mainly by large grower-exporters, mostly in large producing countries in Latin America, who are able to consistently supply large volumes, meet quality requirements and provide efficient logistics up to loading of a ship. These exporters can achieve reference prices and obtain medium- and long-term purchasing commitments from traders. By contrast, producers dealing with the anonymous market typically sell smaller volumes of somewhat inferior product through a series of intermediaries. Their production is based on lower inputs and is more weather-dependent, and productivity is lower than that of the large exporters. High premia are also commanded by producers of "specialty coffees", which include shade-grown, organic and fair trade coffees.

LDC could earn higher prices if they could qualify for the non-anonymous commercial and speciality markets. This requires investment and also new institutional arrangements. Participation in the former is unlikely to be possible

Box 15 (contd.)

for groups of smallholders that are not part of much larger organizations. Moreover, there will be a need for an initial investment in land clearing, infrastructure and high-quality public research into improved tree varieties and pest control. Entering speciality markets will require the meeting of certification costs. For example, most of Ethiopia's coffee is actually organically grown and merely needs to be certified to reap a larger premium on international markets. It has been estimated that if there is a Fair Trade Coffee Initiative in which 50 per cent of Ethiopian coffee production qualifies, the income of coffee producers would increase by 25 per cent, and the welfare of the whole poor population would increase by 2 per cent (Integrated Framework, 2003: 15). There is a major role for international assistance to facilitate such upgrading.

The second option, supply management, requires agreement amongst producers. According to Hermann, Burger and Smit (1993), in the year when the provisions of the international coffee agreement were operational prices were raised by 24 to 30 per cent over what otherwise would have been the market-clearing level. A model of the potential impact on LDCs of Brazil, Colombia, Indonesia and Viet Nam (which together constitute 53 per cent of global green coffee export revenues) jointly reducing their exports has shown that a 10 per cent reduction in their exports could result in a 17 per cent increase in the world price and a 21 per cent increase in LDC coffee export revenues (Gabriele and Vanzetti, 2004).

Whether such supply management is now feasible with more open and competitive trading systems is debatable. The uneven distribution of gains would also be a major stumbling block to the formation of such an agreement. But whether such an agreement can be achieved or not, the results show what would happen to global prices of commodities if advanced developing countries were able to move out of primary commodities and increasingly specialize in manufactures. At present the ability of those countries to upgrade their production structures and to increase exports and pursue a stronger specialization is often prevented by relatively high market access barrier by developed countries.

The third option for LDC coffee producers is diversification out of coffee. This is the best long-term option. But both vertical and horizontal export diversification should be part of a national development strategy and will require significant international financial and technical assistance to develop new export sectors (see next chapter). It is in this context that the proposal for a diversification fund is highly relevant.

The scale and challenge can be illustrated by Ethiopia. Its DTIS shows that "there is no single product exported by Ethiopia that has experienced a growing demand in world markets in the late 1990s. All four-digit HS categories have experienced negative growth, even though Ethiopia has been able to perform above average in world markets in a few of these products" (Integrated Framework, 2003: 7). It is from this point that diversification efforts must begin.

BOX CHART 3. PRICE DIFFERENCES BY COFFEE TYPES AND EXPORT MARKETS, 2000–2002

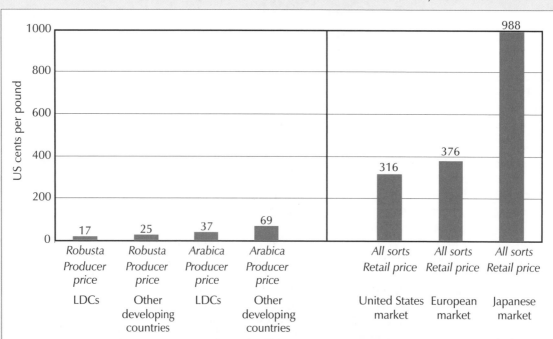

Source: UNCTAD secretariat estimates, based on data provided by the International Coffee Organization
Note: Average prices for different producer countries and consumer countries.

derived from extractive industries (gas, mining and oil industries) and also company payments to governments.

(a) Reducing vulnerability to commodity price shocks

Vulnerability to commodity price shocks affects a large number of those LDCs where the incidence of $1/day poverty is highest. The vulnerability of a country to commodity price shocks reflects the degree of exposure to shocks and also the country's resilience in dealing with them. LDCs are often highly exposed because of the high level of their dependence on one or two commodities. Moreover, they have low resilience because of the limited domestic resources available for dealing with shocks. *The Least Developed Countries Report 2000* found that in 14 out of 24 LDCs for which data were available, the maximum two-year income terms-of-trade loss in the 1990s was over 100 per cent of the domestic resources available above private consumption which is available for financing private investment and government expenditure (UNCTAD, 2000a: 38–39). Relative to the size of such domestic resources available for finance (which was discussed as DRAF in chapter 3), the average LDC economy has, over the last three decades, been exposed to adverse external shocks, with an impact in the worst years of more or less double the developing country average.

The average LDC economy has, over the last three decades, been exposed to adverse external shocks, with an impact in the worst years of more or less double the developing country average.

Such shocks can have a major negative economic impact. The IMF (2003b) has estimated that in developing countries, between 1981 and 2000, negative price shocks on average led to a direct loss of income of 3.5 per cent of GDP. Collier and Dehn (2001) report even higher income losses due to negative price shocks, in the range of 6.8 per cent of GDP. The magnitude of the shock is worth comparing with the prospective benefits from multilateral trade liberalization reported above — which are generally of the order of 3–5 per cent of GDP.

Negative price shocks have a poverty-increasing impact both through their direct effects on producers and through macroeconomic channels (Guillaumont et al., 2003). At the micro level, shocks directly affect incomes and also discourage investment and innovation amongst producers. However, the main impact on poverty is likely to come through macroeconomic channels. A number of studies have now found that negative commodity price shocks significantly depress the economic growth rate of commodity-dependent economies (e.g. Collier and Dehn, 2001; Dehn, 2000). The negative effect on economic growth occurs particularly through the effect of shocks on full utilization of productive capacity, and there is not a similar offsetting positive effect from positive commodity price shocks. Amongst the macroeconomic mechanisms which research has found to be important as transmission channels of price shocks are increasing real exchange rate instability, which leads in particular to poor resource allocation and lower factor productivity, and increasing fiscal instability, which contributes to the build-up of indebtedness and reduces the level of and return on investment (Guillaumont et al., 2003). As noted in chapter 4, there is also some evidence of a link between falling and unstable commodity prices and export revenues and the onset of civil conflict.

Negative price shocks have a poverty-increasing impact both through their direct effects on producers and through macroeconomic channels.

In the past, marketing boards and caisses de stabilisation acted as a buffer between the producer and price shocks. But these have now largely been dismantled. Because of the costs of international buffer stocks, they are not particularly advisable. Two international measures which can help LDCs deal with negative commodity price shocks include the greater use of commodity risk management instruments and the revamping of compensatory financing schemes to offset losses in export earnings associated with negative price shocks.

With regard to the former, the key issue is how to make market-based risk management instruments work in very poor countries. With regard to the latter, an appropriate starting point may be to identify strengths and weaknesses of past compensatory financing mechanisms (such as STABEX and SYSMIN) and to establish a set of criteria for the successful operation of a compensatory financing mechanism that would be responsive to the financing needs of poor commodity-dependent countries (UNCTAD, 2003c).

Finally, there are important opportunities for reducing the adverse impact of negative price shocks on poverty through debt relief mechanisms and aid. As noted in chapter 3, there is a close link between commodity dependence and the build-up of unsustainable external debt in poor countries. Automatic adjustment of debt service in response to price shocks, with the lowering of debt service payments when there is a decrease in tax revenues following world price declines, thus merits serious consideration. There is also a strong case for making aid more counter-cyclical as there is evidence that foreign aid to LDCs has in the past not generally alleviated the effect of short-term external shocks but has rather reinforced the effect of such shocks (UNCTAD, 2000a: 178–182). It may even be possible to envisage automatic grant assistance for poor countries in the event of negative price shocks. The possible modalities of automatic adjustment of debt service to negative price shocks and also automatic grants in the event of such shocks, the latter directly targeted at the LDCs, are elaborated in a preliminary way in Guillaumont et al. (2003).

(b) Transparency in revenue and payments from extractive industries

There is an increasing momentum for a multilateral approach to ensuring greater transparency in payments to Governments by transnational corporations involved in extractive industries (gas, oil and mining) (Global Witness, 2004). This is of vital importance for poverty reduction in oil- and mineral-dependent LDCs, which are becoming the sites of the worst and seemingly most intractable problems of extreme poverty. The relevance of such an approach to LDCs reflects the importance of revenues from extractive industries as the basis for economic growth and development in the mineral- and oil-exporting LDCs, together with the past failure to translate natural resource wealth into development and poverty reduction. There is no doubt that good management of mineral and oil wealth is difficult, particularly in the light of the unusually large size of revenues in relation to national income, price fluctuations in commodity markets and the finite nature of these natural resources (DFID, 2003). Improved transparency through international understandings can be part of a broader approach to improve the governance of oil, gas and mineral resources, which would include measures to ensure improved public financial management at the national level (see next chapter).

Transparency in mineral revenues and payments is required from both Governments and companies. With regard to Governments, this would include any income earned in cash or in kind, including tax receipts, royalties, lease fees, rental payments, bonuses, share of production, dividends and other profit transfers or receipts from asset sales. With regard to companies, this would include payments to host Governments and their agencies, including transfers of funds (in cash or in kind) for the purchase of an asset, or payments of tax dividends, royalties, fee rentals or bonuses (DFID, 2003). At present, companies are not required to report, and do not necessarily report, financial information disaggregated at the country level. Moreover, they may actually be discouraged from doing so because of the existence of confidentiality clauses in contracts with host countries. It is unlikely that unilateral disclosure will work, because

---

There are important opportunities for reducing the adverse impact of negative price shocks on poverty through debt relief mechanisms and aid.

There is an increasing momentum for a multilateral approach to ensuring greater transparency in payments to Governments by transnational corporations involved in extractive industries (gas, oil and mining).

competitors who decide not to make a unilateral disclosure on the part of companies could gain an unfair competitive advantage.

A number of different international mechanisms could be used for increasing companies' transparency, including OECD Guidelines for Multinational Enterprises, the UN Global Compact (as a forum for advocacy), an agreement on international accounting standards in the extractive industry, disclosure rules for securities markets and export credit agency requirements. The Extractives Industry Transparency Initiative (EITI) has indicated that whatever final mechanism is agreed, it is important that there be transparency on the part of Governments as well as companies, and that the key criteria for an effective approach will be the following: collective action (drawing together a critical mass of actors to forge a wide consensus and maximize the acceptability and the application of this initiative); confidentiality (protecting commercial confidentiality and respecting existing contract provisions); comprehensiveness (capturing critical payments and revenues and flows); and comparability (providing easily aggregated data) (DFID, 2003: para. 30).

A voluntary pilot approach is now being implemented through the EITI. There remain many unresolved issues, including:

Transparency in mineral revenues and payments is required from both Governments and companies...A number of different international mechanisms could be used for increasing companies' transparency.

- How will the system be monitored? How will compliance be ensured?

- How will disclosure of information occur (in the "home" country, in the producer country?). How would it be ensured that reporting is harmonized or that there is a minimum set of reporting standards beyond the templates proposed under the EITI?

- Data collection issues. Would there be an aggregation of "country" data to protect commercial confidentiality? Would this negatively affect transparency?

- Technical assistance. How will countries willing to cooperate with the compact finance the costs of implementing it?

- Accounting standards. There is no international agreement for the industry to date in this regard — that is to say, no International Financial Reporting Standard.

The voluntary approach is an important step and will help to provide answers to these questions. It is through the voluntary approach, and also through continued dialogue amongst all stakeholders, that the pros and cons of a compulsory, legally enforceable reporting mechanism, which is being advocated by the "Publish What You Pay" NGO coalition and also in Global Witness (2004), may be assessed.

D. The effectiveness of current international support measures targeted at the LDCs

For the LDCs, the poverty-reducing impact of generally applicable measures in the field of trade will be enhanced if a broad approach, encompassing but not limited to the multilateral trade liberalization agenda, is adopted. But there is also a strong case for complementing generally applicable measures with special international support measures specially targeted at the LDCs.

The need for special international support measures is based on experience that indicates that most LDCs have become increasingly marginalized in international trade and have found it difficult to integrate into the multilateral trading system in a way which supports their development. There is a wide consensus on the need for special international support measures in the area of trade for LDCs because of this. However, from the point of view of poverty reduction, there is also a strong case for focusing special international support measures geographically on the LDCs. This follows from the location of extreme poverty within the global economy. To the extent that a significant proportion of the global population living on less than $1/day live in LDCs, facilitating increased exports and increased ability to develop productive capacities within these countries will make a significant contribution to global poverty reduction.

> *The need for special international support measures is based on experience that indicates that most LDCs have become increasingly marginalized in international trade and have found it difficult to integrate into the multilateral trading system in a way which supports their development.*

Unfortunately, estimates of the global distribution of the extremely poor depend on the methods used to make them. According to the household-survey-based estimates of the World Bank, most of the world's extremely poor live in rural areas outside the least developed countries, particularly in India and China (World Bank, 2003: 106, table 3.1). National-accounts-based poverty estimates suggest a lower number of extremely poor, and according to estimates in *The Least Developed Countries Report 2002*, many least developed countries, particularly in Africa, have a higher incidence of poverty than household-survey-based estimates suggest. As a consequence, the least developed countries are an important locus of extreme poverty in the global economy (UNCTAD, 2002a: 39–100, chapters 1 and 2). It is imperative that increasing efforts be made to reconcile differences in the scale and distribution of poverty in the world economy. Otherwise, the factual basis for geographical targeting, such as international support measures for the LDCs, will be a constant subject of dispute. However, what is important to stress here is that if the trends of the 1990s continue, the problem of extreme poverty in the world will increasingly become an LDC problem, and that by 2015 the majority of the $1/day poor will be located in LDCs, particularly in Africa. The case for international action targeted at the LDCs remains strong, despite disagreements about the current location of the extremely poor, because there is a need to act now to pre-empt this situation and create a better future for the people of the LDCs.

> *The case for international action targeted at the LDCs remains strong, despite disagreements about the current location of the extremely poor, because there is a need to act now to pre-empt this situation and create a better future for the people of the LDCs.*

The international consensus on the need for special international support measures in the field of trade has led to provisions for special and differential treatment that are written into GATT or WTO Agreements. The provisions of special and differential treatment typically provide flexibility in the implementation or application of agreements, and encourage the provision of technical assistance and market access preferences. In some instances, market access preferences are granted through the multilateral agreements directly, but in most instances, they are granted by individual countries or groups of countries.

These measures are exceptions to the most-favoured-nation (MFN) principle, a core principle of the multilateral trading system, which requires all members of the system to treat one another alike. The basis for preferential market access is the Enabling Clause, introduced into the GATT in 1979, and the Waiver System, which is set out in Article IX: 3 of the Agreement Establishing the WTO. These permit countries to grant special treatment to other countries without granting the same treatment to other member States. The Enabling Clause is the legal basis of the Generalized System of Preferences (GSP), under which developed countries grant preferential market access to developing countries, of and the Global System of Trade Preferences (GSTP), under which developing countries grant preferential market access to other developing countries. Going beyond legal provisions explicitly set out in WTO Agreements, actions in favour of developing countries, individually or as a group, may also be taken under "waivers" from the main WTO rules. The General Council Decision on Waivers regarding Preferential Tariff Treatment for Least Developed Countries of 1999 allows developing WTO members to grant preferential tariff treatment to products of LDCs.

Using these two approaches, a number of international support measures have been put in place for the LDCs. However, the effective benefits which they receive through special and differential treatment, including preferential market access, are generally, with a few exceptions, slight.

1. SPECIAL AND DIFFERENTIAL TREATMENT

The provisions for special and differential treatment granted by the various WTO Agreements to different WTO members are complex. Not only do they touch on different aspects of the multilateral trading system, but also they differ in terms of their content, geographical domain of application and time limits. Some are associated with clear rights and obligations, whilst others are mere statements of intent and calls for special assistance. Some apply to all developing countries, whilst others apply only to selected sub-groups of countries. Some are granted for an unlimited duration, while others are restricted in their applicability (WTO, 2000a; Michalopoulos, 2000; Hoekman, Michalopoulos and Winters, 2003).

The provisions for special and differential treatment granted by the various WTO Agreements to different WTO members are complex. Not only do they touch on different aspects of the multilateral trading system, but also they differ in terms of their content, geographical domain of application and time limits.

The different WTO Agreements contain about 124 separate articles or paragraphs containing around 160 provisions for special and differential treatment (WTO, 2000a). An overview[16] of these provisions, their binding nature and defined limits, and their applicability to different country groups, presents the following picture:

- Recommended action: 38 provisions encourage developed WTO members to take into account the special situation of least developed WTO members; 31 encourage different types of financial and/or technical assistance; 21 encourage flexibility in the implementation of agreements; 20 encourage flexibility in the application of agreements; 18 allow for different types of subsidies; 12 encourage the extension of market access preferences; eight encourage favourable treatment in safeguard actions; five allow for different types of import restrictions; one encourages paucity of the principle of full reciprocity; and another one encourages actions to stabilize commodity prices. In addition, there are five other provisions with diverse purposes.

- Binding nature: The majority of the provisions are best-endeavour provisions that do not have a binding nature. These include the 38 provisions that encourage the special consideration of difficulties, the 31 provisions that encourage the provision of technical and/or financial assistance, the 12 provisions that encourage the provision of market access preferences, one provision that encourages action to address commodity price problems, and five other provisions. The provisions that are binding generally include those that grant developing countries more flexibility in the implementation of WTO Agreements and/or flexibility in their application.

- Time limits: Of 124 articles and paragraphs in WTO Agreements that entail special and differential treatment provisions, 19 articles and paragraphs of these agreements have explicitly or implicitly defined time limits, affecting 21 provisions for special and differential treatment. The majority of the provisions of limited duration are related to provisions granting flexibility in the implementation or application of agreements, but several such provisions are related to provisions granting flexibility in trade policies. Of the six articles and paragraphs imposing time limits on the use of trade policies, three impose limits with respect to the use of import restrictions, and the other three impose limits with respect to the use of export subsidies. This in effect means that three out of five provisions that grant flexibility with respect to import restrictions have time limits attached to them, whereas only three out of 18 provisions that grant flexibility with respect to subsidies have an expiration date. Other articles and paragraphs limiting the duration of special and differential treatment provisions relate to provisions that are concerned with special consideration of developing countries and provisions granting market access preferences to least developed countries.

Within this complex field, there are relatively few provisions that are actually targeted at the LDCs. Of the 124 articles and paragraphs extending special and differential treatment, 104 apply to the group of developing countries, which includes all least developed countries, and the remaining 20 apply to different sub-groups of developing countries, which also include many least developed countries. But although most special and differential treatment provisions are also applicable to LDCs, only very few such provisions are specifically targeted at the LDCs. This means that there are only a few provisions that are specifically designed to help this group of developing countries overcome their marginalization in the world economy. In total, there are about 24 articles and paragraphs in the WTO Agreements that extend special and differential treatment explicitly to LDCs. Of these provisions, 15 extend it to both developing countries and least developed countries, six extend it exclusively to the group of least developed countries, two extend it to least developed countries and small suppliers, one extends it to least developed countries and low-income countries, and one extends it to least developed countries and net food-importing countries. A final provision is extended to all developing countries, including least developed countries and net food-importing developing countries.

The majority of the articles and paragraphs that specifically refer to the group of least developed countries, namely 14 out of 24, entail provisions that encourage consideration of the special challenges faced by least developed countries, and a good number of those — 6 out of 14 — do nothing more than encourage special consideration of challenges faced by these countries.

Table 47 summarizes the 24 articles and paragraphs that explicitly refer to the least developed countries, as well as another seven articles and paragraphs that refer to other vulnerable groups of developing countries. These sub-groups of vulnerable countries typically include a large number of least developed countries. This is why the different types of articles and provisions are summarized in one table. The 31 articles and provisions are associated with 42 special and differential treatment provisions. The table shows that there are five provisions that enable the LDCs to use trade policies in the service of productive sector development, one of which is granted by the Agreement on Agriculture, and the other four are granted by the Agreement on Subsidies and Countervailing Duties. The former exempt LDCs from making further commitments on tariff reductions, while the latter allow them to make use of export subsidies. In addition, Article 27.9 and Article 27.10 exempt small suppliers from countervailing duty investigations. Finally, there are eight provisions that extend either flexibility in the implementation or flexibility in the

There are only a few provisions that are specifically designed to help this group of developing countries overcome their marginalization in the world economy.

TABLE 47. OVERVIEW OF SPECIAL AND DIFFERENTIAL TREATMENT (SDT) PROVISIONS GRANTED TO LDCs

Articles/paragraphs of WTO Agreements		Associated provisions of SDT	
	Text	Type	Target country groups
Agreement Establishing the World Trade Organization			
Chapeau	The Parties to this Agreement, Recognizing that their relations in the field of trade and economic endeavour should be conducted with a view to raising standards of living, ensuring full employment and a large and steady growing volume of real income and effective demand, and expanding the production of and trade in goods and services, while allowing for the optimal use of the world's resources in accordance with the objective of sustainable development, seeking both to protect and preserve the environment and to enhance the means for doing so in a manner consistent with their respective needs and concerns at different levels of economic development. — Recognizing further that there is need for positive efforts designed to ensure that developing countries, and especially the least developed among them, secure a share in the growth in international trade commensurate with the needs of their economic development ... agree as follows ... (Agreement Establishing the World Trade Organization, chapeau)	Special consideration	Developing countries LDCs
Market access			
Agreement on Agriculture			
Preamble	Recognition of special and differential treatment; in implementing their commitments on market access, developed country Members to take fully into account the needs and conditions of developing country Members by providing for a greater improvement of opportunities and terms of access for agricultural products of particular interest to those Members, including the fullest liberalization of trade in tropical agricultural products; he possible negative effects of the implementation of the reform programme on least-developed and net-food importing developing countries to be taken into account.	Special consideration / Market access preference	Developing countries LDCs / Net-food-importers
Art. 12.2	Disciplines on export prohibitions and restrictions not applicable, unless the developing country Member is a net-food exporter of the specific foodstuff concerned.	Flexible implementation[a]	Net-food-importers
Art. 15.2 & Schedules	Developing country Members to implement reduction commitments over a period of 10 years (6 years). Least-developed country Members are not required to undertake reduction commitments.	Import restriction	Developing countries LDCs
Art. 16	Developed country Members to take action as provided for within the framework of the Decision on Measures Concerning the Possible Negative Effects of the Reform Programme on Least-Developed and Net-Food Importing Developing Countries. Committee on Agriculture to monitor the follow-up to this Decision.	Special consideration / Aid / Other	LDCs / Net-food-importers
Notification	Certain annual notification requirements in the area of domestic [support] may be set aside, on request, by the Committee on Agriculture. LDCs: Certain notifications only to be submitted every other year.	Flexible appliction	Developing countries LDCs
Agreement on Textiles and Clothing			
Art. 1.2 (& footnote 1)	Members agree to use provisions of Art. 2.18 and Art. 6.6(b) (below) to permit meaningful increases in access possibilities for small suppliers and new entrants.	Special consideration Market access preference	Small suppliers
Art. 1.4	Particular interests of cotton-producing exporting Members should, in consultation with them, be reflected in implementation.	Special consideration	Cotton producing exporters
Art. 2.18	"Meaningful improvements in access" through accelerated increases in growth rates, or through agreed changes with respect to the mix of base levels, growth and flexibility, for Members subject to restrictions on 31 December 1994 and whose restrictions account for less than 1.2 per cent of all restrictions imposed by relevant Members as of 31 December 1991.	Market access preference	Small suppliers
Art. 6.6 (a)	Significantly more favourable treatment to be given to LDCs by Members making use of transitional safeguards.	Safeguard, favourable	LDCs
Art. 6.6 (b)	Members whose export volumes are small in comparison with the total volume of exports of other Members and represent a small percentage of imports of a product into an importing Member shall be accorded differential and more favourable treatment in the fixing of economic terms of Articles 6.8, 6.13 and 6.14, i.e. in fixing levels of export restraint, growth and flexibility (see also Article 1.2).	Special consideration / Market access preference	Small suppliers
General Agreement on Trade in Services			
Art. IV:3	Special priority to be given to LDCs in implementation of Articles IV:1 and 2, and "particular account" to be taken of LDCs' difficulties in accepting negotiated commitments owing to particular development trade and financial needs.	Special consideration	LDCs
GATS Annex on Telecommunications			
Art. 6 (d)	Special consideration to opportunities for LDCs to encourage foreign suppliers to assist in transfer of technology, training and other activities for developing telecoms trade.	Aid	LDCs
Agreement on Sanitary and Phytosanitary Restrictions			
Art. 10.1	In the preparation and application of SPS measures, Members to take into account special needs of developing country and LDC Members.	Special consideration	Developing countries LDCs
Art. 14	May delay for up to 2 years implementation of most provisions of the Agreement relating to measures affecting imports (with the exception of measures not based on relevant or extant international standards). LDCs may delay for up to 5 years implementation of the provisions of the Agreement.	Flexible implementation[a]	Developing countries LDCs
Agreement on Technical Barriers to Trade			
Art. 12.3, 12.7	Members shall, in preparing and applying technical regulations, standards and conformity assessment procedures, take account of the special development, financial and trade needs of developing Members with a view to ensuring that unnecessary obstacles to exports from developing countries are not created. Technical assistance to be provided by Members to that end, taking account of the stage of development of the requesting Members. Particular account to be taken of the least-developed Members in provision of technical assistance.	Special consideration / Aid	Developing countries / LDCs

Table 47 (contd.)

Articles/paragraphs of WTO agreements		Associated provisions of SDT	
Number	Text	Type	Target countries
Auxiliary agreements			
Agreement on Trade-related Aspects of Intellectual Property Rights			
Preamble	Recognition of special interest of LDCs in respect of maximum flexibility in implementation of domestic regulations in order to enable the creation of a sound technological base.	Special consideration	Developing countries
		Flexible implementation[a]	LDCs
Art. 66	LDCs: Delay for up to 10 years for most TRIPS obligations. Possibility of extension following duly motivated request.	Flexible implementation[a]	LDCs
Art. 66.2	Developed country Members to provide incentives to enterprises and institutions in their territories for purpose of encouraging transfer of technology to LDCs.	Aid	LDCs
Agreement on Trade-related Investment Measures			
Preamble	Taking into account trade, development and financial needs of developing countries and especially LDCs.	Special consideration	Developing countries LDCs
Art. 5.2	5 years (2 years) to eliminate TRIMS inconsistent with Agreement. LDCs: 7-year transitional period.	Flexible implementation[a]	Developing countries LDCs
International trade rules			
Agreement on Subsidies and Countervailing Measures			
Art. 27.2 (a)	Developing countries with per capita income below $ 1,000 (and listed in Annex VII) exempted from prohibition on export subsidies. LDCs: Not subject to prohibitions on export subsidies.	Subsidies, various	LDCs Low-income countries
Art. 27.3	Prohibition on subsidies contingent on export performance not applicable for 5 years. LDCs: 8 years.	Subsidies, various	Developing countries
		Flexible implementation[a]	LDCs
Art. 27.5, 27.6	Export subsidies to be phased out within 2 years of attaining "export competitiveness" in any given product; 8-year phase-out for Annex VII Members. "Export competitiveness" is defined as at least 3.25 % of world trade in the "product" (HS Section) for two consecutive calendar years. LDCs: 8 years.	Subsidies, various	Developing countries
		Flexible implementation[a]	LDCs
Art. 27.9, 27.10	Subsidies actionable only if they cause injury or nullify or impair benefits to other Members under GATT 1994. Countervailing duty investigations to be terminated where share of total imports less than 4 per cent and where total import share of developing country Members, each with less than 4 per cent share, does not exceed 9 per cent.	Subsidies, various	Small suppliers
Agreement on Safeguards			
Art. 9.1, footnote 2	Safeguards "shall not be applied" against products originating in developing countries if share of imports is not in excess of 3 per cent, and if developing country Members with less than 3 per cent share do not account collectively for more than 9 per cent of imports.	Safeguard, exemption	Small suppliers
Agreement on Import Licensing			
Art. 3.5(j)	Special consideration to be given to importers importing products from developing countries in allocating non-automatic licences. Consideration to be given to importers' products, especially from least-developed countries.	Aid	Developing countries LDCs
Understanding on Rules and Procedures Governing the Settlement of Disputes			
Art. 21.8	Particular consideration shall be given to the special situation of LDC Members at all stages in the determination of causes of dispute and of dispute settlement.	Special consideration	Developing countries LDCs
Art. 24.1	Members to "exercise due restraint" in raising matters under these procedures involving an LDC Member. If nullification or impairment established, Members to "exercise due restraint" in seeking compensation or authorization to suspend concessions or any other obligation pursuant to these procedures.	Special consideration Safeguard, favorable	LDCs
Art. 24.2	If satisfactory solution not found, Director General or Chairman of Dispute Settlement Board may offer their good offices upon request by LDC to find acceptable solution prior to request for a panel.	Aid	LDCs
Special and differential treatment			
Decision on Waiver			
Art. 1, 2, 3, 4	Considering that the Parties to the World Trade Organization Agreement have recognized the need for positive efforts designed to ensure that developing countries, and especially the least-developed among them, secure a share in the growth in international trade commensurate with the needs of their economic development ..., Members, acting pursuant to the provisions of paragraph 3 of Article IX of the WTO Agreement, decide that: 1. Subject to the terms and conditions set out hereunder, the provisions of paragraph 1 of Article I of the GATT 1994 shall be waived until 30 June 2009, to the extent necessary to allow developing country Members to provide preferential tariff treatment to products of least-developed countries, designated as such by the United Nations, without being required to extend the same tariff rates to like products of any other Member. 2. Developing country Members wishing to take actions pursuant to the provisions of this Waiver shall notify to the Council on Trade in Goods the list of all products of least-developed countries for which preferential tariff treatment is to be provided on a generalized, non-reciprocal and non-discriminatory basis and the preference margins to be accorded. Subsequent modifications to the preferences shall similarly be notified. 3. Any preferential tariff treatment implemented pursuant to this Waiver shall be designed to facilitate and promote the trade of least-developed countries and not to raise barriers or create undue difficulties for the trade of any other Member. Such preferential tariff treatment shall not constitute an impediment to the reduction or elimination of tariffs on a most-favoured-nation basis. 4. In accordance with the provisions of paragraph 4 of Article IX of the WTO Agreement, the General Council shall review annually whether the exceptional circumstances justifying the Waiver still exist and whether the terms and conditions attached to the Waiver have been met.	Special consideration Market access preference[a]	LDCs

Source: UNCTAD secretariat compilation, based on WTO (1999b, 2000a) and WTO website: http://www.wto.org/english/tratop_e/devel_e/anexi_e.doc; http://www.wto.org/english/tratop_e/devel_e/anexii_e.doc (17 December 2003).

Note: All provisions that apply to developing countries in general also apply to least developed countries. If not specified, information provided in parentheses refers to the manner of application of the relevant provisions to developing country WTO members. Low-income countries in the WTO are defined as countries with a GNP per capita of less than $1,000. a Provisions with time limit.

application of an agreement, five provisions that encourage the provision of market access preferences or improvements of market access conditions, and several articles that encourage the provision of technical assistance. But neither the provision of market access nor the provision of assistance is of a binding nature for advanced countries. Interestingly, the Agreement on Trade-Related Aspects of Intellectual Property Rights encourages advanced countries to take measures to promote investments in least developed countries. Such home country measures are very important for the strengthening of productive capacities in least developed countries.

In sum, this survey shows that the vast majority of the special and differential treatment provisions are granted to all developing countries rather than just the least developed countries. Moreover, the majority of the provisions that are granted exclusively to the group of least developed countries are provisions that encourage advanced WTO members to consider the interest of the least developed WTO members, rather than provisions that provide the least developed WTO members with exemptions from WTO rules and regulations in line with their level of development. Many of the provisions are best-endeavour clauses. They are by their nature transitory. Rather than being concerned with the development of productive capacities, they are intended to (a) facilitate the implementation of the WTO Agreements by the LDCs and other developing countries, and (b) to encourage these countries to design and implement trade policies in conformity with WTO Agreements. There is a need for more research on the extent to which special and differential treatment provisions are operational and also on the effective benefits which LDCs derive from them in practice (see, for example, work such as UNCTAD, 2001a).[17] But this initial survey suggests that it is doubtful that current provision are sufficient to enable the LDCs to actively promote their economic development and reduce their international economic marginalization.

2. PREFERENTIAL MARKET ACCESS

(a) The scope of preferential market access

Following the Ministerial Conference of the WTO in Singapore in 1996, and particularly in the context of the Third United Nations Conference on the Least Developed Countries, many developed countries and developing countries have expanded or introduced market access preferences for marginalized developing countries, especially least developed countries. In 2001 the WTO took note of a total of 28 market access initiatives in favour of least developed countries, 19 of which were granted by developing countries or transition economies, and 9 were granted by developed countries, including the Quad countries — Canada, the European Union, Japan and the United States (WTO, 2001a). Table 48 summarizes the current situation with regard to recent market access initiatives of the Quad countries, whilst table 49 summarizes the market access initiatives for non-Quad countries in 2001, the most recent year in which this was systematically surveyed.

Market access preferences enable exporters from the LDCs to pay lower tariffs or even enter markets quota- and duty-free. The potential commercial benefits depend first of all on the preference margin which exporters in the LDCs receive over other exporters. The market access preferences granted to the LDCs are typically more far-reaching than the market access preferences that they grant to other GSP or GSTP beneficiary countries. But there are some developing countries that benefit from even more extensive market access preferences. These are typically countries that are part of a regional trade

The vast majority of the special and differential treatment provisions are granted to all developing countries rather than just the least developed countries.

The market access preferences granted to the LDCs are typically more far-reaching than the market access preferences that they grant to other GSP or GSTP beneficiary countries. But there are some developing countries that benefit from even more extensive market access preferences.

TABLE 48. OVERVIEW OF QUAD MARKET ACCESS INITIATIVES TARGETING LEAST DEVELOPED COUNTRIES, AS AT 2003

Canada

In September 2000, the Canadian Government widened the product coverage of market access preferences granted under the Generalized System of Preferences (GSP) for the benefit of LDCs, and since January 2003 the Government has further expanded the market access preferences for these countries. Unlike the previous market access scheme, the new market access scheme improved market access for textiles and clothing, but continues to exclude sensitive agricultural produce, such as dairy products, eggs and poultry. With these exceptions Canada now provides duty-free access under all tariff items for imports from LDCs. The initiative also changed the rules of origin, introducing an innovative cumulative system that allows inputs from all beneficiary countries.

European Union

The EU originally granted two sets of market access preferences to LDCs. It provided relatively far-reaching market access preferences to the group of African, Caribbean and Pacific (ACP) countries, which includes many LDCs, and provided less far-reaching market access to other developing countries, including non-ACP LDCs. The market access for the former was regulated through the Lomé Conventions and is now being regulated through the Cotonou Agreement, while the market access conditions for the latter have been provided in accordance with other GSP schemes. The existence of different market access schemes meant that the ACP LDCs benefited more from better market access conditions than non-ACP LDCs. In 2001, however, the EU introduced the Everything But Arms (EBA) initiative, which has consolidated and improved the market-access preferences for the group of LDCs as a whole. It grants duty-free and quota-free market access to all types of exports from the LDCs, with the permanent exception of arms and ammunition, and a temporary exception for bananas, rice and sugar. Market access restrictions for the latter goods, however, are going to be phased out between 2006 (bananas) and 2009 (rice and sugar). Because of the different initial market access preferences for LDCs to the markets of the EU, ACP LDCs are likely to derive fewer benefits from the introduction of the EBA initiative than non-ACP LDCs. A prime explanatory variable for this low level of utilization are the EU's rules of origin, although rules of origin have already been simplified, allowing for derogations and promoting regional cumulation.

Japan

The GSP scheme of Japan was recently reviewed, and extended for a new decade (until March 2014). During the 2001/2002 fiscal year, the special treatment granted to LDCs was improved by the addition of a number of tariff lines. All exports from LDCs, under the Japanese scheme, are eligible for duty-free entry and exemption from ceiling restrictions for a list of relevant products. In early 2003, Japan further improved its GSP scheme for the benefit of LDCs. While many industrial goods have already benefited from far-reaching market access preferences under the previous scheme, the new scheme has improved market access preferences primarily for agricultural goods and food items, such as prawns and frozen fish fillets.

United States of America

In contrast to other Quad countries, which today provide the same set of market access preferences to LDCs, the United States provides three distinct sets of market access preferences to these countries. One set of market access preferences is granted through the African Growth and Opportunity Act (AGOA) to LDCs in Africa; another set is granted through the LDC GSP scheme to LDCs in Asia; and a third set is granted through the Caribbean Basin Initiative (CBI) to Haiti, the only LDC in the region. The LDC GSP scheme expired in September 2001 but was reauthorized until December 2006. Unlike the LDC GSP scheme, the other two market access schemes have been significantly revised and expanded in recent years, especially where clothing and apparel are concerned. The LDC GSP scheme, for example, excludes sensitive products such as textiles, work gloves, footwear, handbags, luggage, and watches, while AGOA provides preferential market access for many goods that are typically viewed as sensitive, such as watches, electronic articles, steel articles, footwear, handbags, luggage, flat goods, work gloves, leather wearing apparel, and semi-manufactured and manufactured glass products. The enhancements of AGOA concerned mostly textiles and apparel. Knit to shape products were included, the technical definition for merino wool was revised, the origin of yarn under the Special Rule for designated LDCs was clarified, and "hybrid" apparel articles were made eligible for preferences. Another important difference between the LDC GSP scheme and the AGOA scheme is that the United States reviews the list of products that are eligible for the LDC GSP system on an annual basis, but has decided not to review the list of products that are eligible for AGOA treatment with this frequency. A decrease of the frequency of reviews implies an increase in stability and predictability of market access preferences. In short, the differences between the two schemes imply that Asian LDCs have less favorable market access preferences to the US than African LDCs, and that the Asian LDCs are also subjected to a greater degree of instability of market access preferences than African LDCs. AGOA is therefore also referred to as "super GSP". The difference between the market access schemes has important implication for the export and production in textile and clothing, which also need to be viewed in the context of the phasing-out of the Agreement on Textile and Clothing (see box 2 of this chapter).

Source: UNCTAD secretariat compilation, based on WTO (2001a), UNCTAD (2003e), and EU at http://europa.eu.int/comm/trade/miti/devl/eba.htm (12 March 2003).

arrangement with the preference-granting country or countries that have special free trade arrangements with the preference-granting country.[18] In addition, most market access preferences also contain exceptions. Thus Canada maintains restrictions on dairy products, eggs and poultry; Japan continues to maintain restrictions on selected agricultural goods; the United States maintains restrictions particularly on textiles and apparel; and under the European Union's

TABLE 49. OVERVIEW OF OTHER MARKET ACCESS INITIATIVES TARGETING LDC, AS AT 2001

Argentina/Mercosur

In May 2000, Argentina (on behalf of Mercosur) announced that it provided tariff preferences for LDCs under the Global System of Trade Preferences (GSTP) scheme, and following completion of the ratification process for the offers made in the context of the second round of GSTP negotiations, they would be in a position to enhance their preferences.

Australia

Reported liberal existing market access conditions under the Generalized System of Preferences (GSP) scheme. In May 2000, provided duty- and quota-free access on 93.2 per cent of LDC exports to its market. In terms of tariff rates, nearly 84 per cent of tariff lines were duty-free for LDCs and included preferential rates of duty in products of interest, including agriculture, fish, textiles and clothing. In 1997, 98 per cent of LDC exports entered duty-free. Additional duty-free entry granted to South Pacific Forum island countries under SPARTECA (South Pacific Regional Trade and Economic Cooperation Agreement).

Bulgaria

Continued to grant duty- and quota-free access to its market for a wide range of products from LDCs. In 1997, all LDC exports entered duty-free.

Chile

In May 2000, the Government was in the process of evaluating preferential treatment for products originating in LDCs within its legal requirements. It also announced its intention to consider or finalize initiatives of market access for LDCs at the HLM in 1997.

Czech Republic

In May 2000, imports originating in LDCs through its national GSP scheme enjoyed duty-free treatment.

Egypt

Following the WTO High-Level Meeting on Integrated Initiatives for LDCs' Trade Development held in October 1997 (HLM), Egypt through GSTP in 1998 notified tariff reductions at HS 8-digit level, ranging from 10 per cent to 20 per cent of existing applied duties, for 77 products of export interest to LDCs, and duty-free access provided for about 50 products imported into Egypt. In addition, Egypt bound customs duties, with a 10 per cent reduction for industrial products imported from LDCs.

Hong Kong, China

Stated application of duty- and quota-free access on most-favoured-nation (MFN) basis to imports from all sources, including LDCs.

Hungary

All LDC exports enter duty-free and quota-free under existing GSP. Customs Law, 1996, through legal guarantees strengthened predictability of the preferential market access to LDCs. Liberal application of rules of origin requirements.

Iceland

In May 2000, the Government announced its intention of implementing both tariff-free and quota-free treatment for essentially all products originating in LDCs. An appropriate notification would be submitted at the earliest possible convenience. 0This treatment would apply to products of export interest to LDCs, including textiles.

India

Preferences granted under SAPTA — the Preferential Trading Arrangement (SAPTA) of the South Asian Association for Regional Cooperation (SAARC) — to LDC contracting states. In 1997, India granted tariff concessions on 574 tariff lines exclusively for the LDC members of SAARC, and removed quantitative restrictions on 180 lines exclusively in favor of SAARC LDCs. Further, under the existing GSTP, India provided preferential access to seven LDCs, namely Bangladesh, Benin, Guinea, Haiti, Mozambique, Sudan and the United Republic of Tanzania. Under the Bangkok Agreement, Bangladesh was given preferential access, and Myanmar and Nepal had preferential access to India under bilateral agreements.

Indonesia

Announced intention to consider initiatives to improve market access for LDCs at the HLM in 1997.

Korea, Republic of

In January 2000, the Republic of Korea notified preferential duty-free access on 80 items (HS 6-digit) originating from and of major export interest to LDCs effective from 1 January 2000. In May 2000, it indicated that it would consider further expanding its existing preferential tariff regime for LDCs.

Malaysia

Announced intention to consider initiatives to improve market access for LDCs at the HLM in 1997.

Mauritius

Notified effective September 1998, duty-free access for five tariff lines originating from LDCs. The products comprise certain crustaceans; guavas, mangoes, mangosteens; axes and billhooks; handsaws and files.

Table 49 (contd.)

Morocco

Proposed preferential access for African LDCs at the HLM in 1997.

New Zealand

New Zealand in November 2000, notified its decision to offer duty- and quota-free access to all imports from LDCs effective from 1 July 2001. Prior to this, in 1999, 96.7 per cent of its tariff lines and 99.3 per cent of its imports from LDCs entered duty-free.

Norway

Amendments and improvements to Norway's GSP scheme were notified in 2000-01. It accords duty- and quota-free access to all industrial and agricultural imports from LDCs covered by the GSP programme, with the exception of flour, grains and feeding stuffs; these products are given a preferential margin of 30 percent within indicative tariff ceilings. Rules-of-origin requirements have been revised and progressively simplified. Following harmonization in the application of rules of origin with the EC and Switzerland, from 1 March 1998, bilateral cumulation was permitted and the possibility of future diagonal cumulation of origin was being considered. At the HLM, Norway announced that it had, on an MFN basis, accelerated its Uruguay Round tariff cuts on agricultural products by implementing them from 1 January 1995 instead of 1999. Similarly, it had phased out almost all restrictions on textiles and clothing by 1997–98 instead of 2004.

Poland

Since 1990, Poland has applied preferential treatment for products originating from LDCs and in May 2000, it announced that it was examining autonomous improvements to the existing preferential system with a view to providing duty-free and quota-free market access for essentially all products originating in LDCs, in conformity with national legislation and international agreements.

Singapore

Singapore notified at the HLM duty-free treatment on 107 items (HS 6 digit) of export interest to LDCs in addition to the almost duty-free regime accorded on an MFN basis.

Slovakia

Slovak provided duty-and quota-free access for all imports from LDCs through its GSP. It confirmed in May 2000 that this system would be maintained in the future.

Slovenia

In May 2000, Slovenia announced that it was prepared to provide tariff and quota-free access for essentially all products originating in LDCs, independent of WTO membership, consistent with its domestic requirements and international agreements under its newly established preferential scheme. The Government took this general decision which would be confirmed through decrees.

Switzerland

Switzerland had undertaken a revision of its preferential tariff schedule, and since its entry into force on 1 March 1997, LDCs were able to benefit from zero tariffs for all industrial and most agricultural products. Some 98 per cent of LDC products entered Switzerland duty-free under its notified preferential scheme and improvements thereof. Rules of origin for goods benefiting from preferential access were also simplified. Switzerland harmonized its regulations with the European Union and in the near future materials originating from Switzerland but also from the European Union and Norway would enjoy the right of cumulation treatment. Under the new rules of origin regional economic groupings in developing countries also enjoyed the right of cumulation treatment.

Thailand

At the HLM in 1997, it announced tariff preferences on 74 product groups (at the 6-digit HS level), through which some products would be exempted from import duty and others would be given a margin of preference of 20 per cent from the applied rates. This would be subject to an annual review process.

Turkey

Notified additional preferential tariff rates for imports from LDCs effective from 1 January 1998. These unilateral preferential rates apply to 556 products at the HS 12-digit level. All these products except coffee are granted duty-free access.

Source: UNCTAD secretariat compilation, based on WTO (2001a).

Everything But Arms Initiative (EBA), remaining import restrictions will be phased out between 2006 (bananas) and 2009 (rice and sugar).

(b) The effective benefits of preferential market access

It is still too early to assess the effectiveness of recent preferential market access initiatives for the LDCs. Table 50 shows that the share of Quad countries' imports from LDCs has actually increased slightly since 1999, and that between 2001 and 2002 the imports originating in the LDCs increased by more than the imports originating in other developing countries. While it is possible that the increasing market share of the LDCs in Quad markets may be at least partially attributable to market access preferences granted to the LDCs, it needs to be emphasized that there is not a perfect match between the year in which the exports of least developed countries to the different Quad countries increased and the year in which the Quad countries introduced market access initiatives for least developed countries. The upturn in Canada, where the LDC market share jumped by 35 per cent in 2001, and in Japan, where it jumped by 39 per cent in 2002, suggests that each of these country's initiatives may be having concrete effects. But these seemingly large jumps are from a very low base. The LDC share of imports to Canada and to Japan was 0.18 and 0.44 in 2002, respectively.

It is still too early to assess the effectiveness of recent preferential market access initiatives for the LDCs.

The table shows that unlike the share of LDC exports to Canada and Japan, the share of LDC exports to the EU has not increased much, and LDC exports to the United States have even declined. One reason for the weak increase in market share in the EU is that the Everything But Arms Initiative was associated with only a limited improvement in market access conditions. Research has shown that the greatest benefits to the LDCs from the Initiative are likely to be related to products which are currently excluded, notably sugar (Cernat, Laird and Turrini, 2002). The Initiative has had an immense impact in terms of stimulating discussion of practical and innovative ways to increase market access for LDCs. But the actual commercial value-added to LDC producers, given the exclusion of key products, could only be small, given that, even before the Initiative was introduced, the EU already had a relatively open trade regime for LDCs. Thus, for example, it has been estimated that in 1997, before the Initiatives, only 11 out of 502 items exported to the EU from all LDCs as a group with a value of more than $500,000 were not eligible for duty- and quota-free access (Stevens and Kennan, 2001). Moreover, in contrast to Canada and the United States, where 30 per cent and 15 per cent of LDCs' imports faced tariff peaks of 15 per cent plus in 1999, before the Initiative only 2.8 per cent of LDC imports to the EU faced such tariff peaks (Hoekman, Ng and Olarreaga, 2001). Against this background it is perhaps not surprising that in 2001, only "three one-hundredths of one per cent of total LDC exports to the EU" entered under the EBA (Brenton, 2003: 6).

Unlike the share of LDC exports to Canada and Japan, the share of LDC exports to the EU has not increased much, and LDC exports to the United States have even declined.

TABLE 50. QUAD COUNTRIES' MERCHANDISE IMPORTS FROM LDCS AND OTHER DEVELOPING COUNTRIES, SELECTED YEARS 1982–2002

Importer/ reporter	Exporter/ partner	% of total imports			% change over previous year				
		1982	1992	2002	1998	1999	2000	2001	2002
Canada	Least developed countries	0.1	0.2	0.2	-2.7	-12.5	12.6	35.3	11.3
	Other developing countries	12.4	12.5	17.4	-3.0	-4.5	12.0	2.1	7.4
European Union	Least developed countries	0.8	0.5	0.6	-3.0	-24.2	9.5	14.0	1.9
	Other developing countries	21.2	13.9	16.5	-0.2	4.4	11.5	-1.4	-1.3
Japan	Least developed countries	0.7	0.5	0.4	-4.9	-1.1	-1.1	-3.1	39.2
	Other developing countries	62.4	49.7	59.4	-1.3	1.5	9.3	0.4	1.0
United States	Least developed countries	1.0	0.8	0.8	0.6	-14.8	14.5	7.5	-4.1
	Other developing countries	41.3	40.3	47.2	-4.4	6.2	4.2	-0.5	2.9

Source: UNCTAD secretariat estimates, based on IMF, *Directions of Trade 2003*.

Note: In September 2000 the Canadian Government widened the product coverage of its LDC GSP scheme; in 2001 the EU introduced the EBA; during 2001/2002, the Japanese Government widened the product coverage of its LDC GSP scheme; and in 2000 the United States has introduced the new AGOA initiative to the benefit of selected sub-Saharan African countries. In 2002 the United States further enhanced AGOA, and in 2003 both Canada and Japan further enhanced their LDC GSP schemes.

The African Growth and Opportunity Act (AGOA) has apparently had only a limited impact on the overall share of the LDCs in US imports. But it had positive effects in some African LDCs, notably Lesotho and Madagascar (UNCTAD, 2003e). In 2002, Lesotho's exports to the United States that were covered by AGOA totalled $318 million, representing 99 per cent of that country's total exports to the United States and in the same year Madagascar's exports to the United States that entered under AGOA stipulations were valued at $79.7 million, representing 37 per cent of the country's export to the United States (Office of the US Trade Representative, 2003). In both instances, the increase in merchandise exports to the United States was closely associated with an increase in exports from the textiles and garments sector. The preferential market access granted for textiles and garments exports also triggered significant investments in the textiles and garments industry.

These two countries illustrate the potential positive effects of market access preferences. But they also show that countries must have at least a minimum base of production and supply capabilities to take advantage of such preferences. Improved market access is commercially meaningless if the LDCs cannot produce in the sectors in which they have preferential treatment and if they lack the marketing skills, information and connections to convert market access into market entry. Moreover, unless the new production stimulated by the preferences also strengthens the development of national technological and entrepreneurial capabilities through learning by doing, the sustainability of the development processes may be questionable. In this regard, experience with the Caribbean Basin Initiative has suggested that the fragmented type of industrialization process which follows from the nature of the preferences may slow down the type of technological capacity-building and learning which are necessary for economic sustainability (Mortimore, 1999).

Countries must have at least a minimum base of production and supply capabilities to take advantage of market access preferences.

(c) The problem of underutilization of market access preferences[19]

A particular problem affecting all preferential market access schemes is that utilization of preferences is low. This is apparent in estimates of the utilization rate, defined as the ratio between total imports actually receiving preferences and the total imports eligible for preferences in any given market. Table 51 shows that in 2001 only 68.5 per cent of total imports from LDCs eligible to enter Quad markets at a preferential duty rate actually did so. The rest paid MFN duties. The utilization rate increased by 20 percentage points between 1994 and 2001. But this was mainly based on an increase in the utilization rate of the United States, which was driven by an increase in oil. If oil imports are excluded, the utilization rate in the United States drops from 95.8 per cent to 47 per cent in 2001.

A particular problem affecting all preferential market access schemes is that the utilization of preferences is low.

The low utilization ratios are mainly the result of the insignificant magnitude of the potential commercial benefits; the lack of technical knowledge, human resources and institutional capacity to take advantage of preferential arrangements, which require in-depth knowledge of national tariff systems in various preference-giving countries; and conditions attached to the realization of the potential benefits of the preferences. The effective benefits of market access preferences provided by Quad countries are being significantly limited also by their unpredictability and by non-tariff barriers, notably rules of origin and product standards.

Investors in preference-receiving countries may be hesitant to increase their investments in the Quad countries if preference-granting countries do not make clear commitments with respect to the period during which the market access schemes themselves remain effective, and/or if preference-granting countries do

TABLE 51. EFFECTIVENESS OF MARKET ACCESS PREFERENCES[a] OF QUAD COUNTRIES FOR LDCs
AS MEASURED BY THE IMPORT COVERAGE, THE UTILIZATION RATE AND THE UTILITY RATE, 1994–2001

Country/ country group	Year	Total imports (a)	Dutiable imports (b)	Imports eligible for GSP preferences (c)	Imports receiving GSP preferences (d)	Imports covered by GSP scheme (c)/(b)	Utilization rate of GSP scheme (d)/(c) (%)	Utility rate of GSP scheme (d)/(a)
		($ million)						
Quad	1994	5 347.0	3 917.3	2 071.0	999.0	52.9	48.2	18.7
	1995	6 087.8	4 706.1	2 564.3	1 361.2	54.5	53.1	22.4
	1996	9 956.3	7 451.1	2 985.0	1 517.9	40.1	50.9	15.2
	1997	10 634.1	8 163.4	5 923.1	1 788.2	72.6	30.2	16.8
	1998	9 795.7	7 915.1	5 564.2	2 704.5	70.3	48.6	27.6
	1999	10 486.5	8 950.4	5 869.3	3 487.5	65.6	59.4	33.3
	2000	13 359.2	11 715.5	7 836.0	4 990.2	66.9	63.7	37.4
	2001	12 838.2	11 167.1	7 185.5	4 919.9	64.3	68.5	38.3
Canada	1994	..	..	..	..	..	...	..
	1995	175.9	41.3	6.4	4.1	15.5	64.1	2.3
	1996	336.9	34.5	6.3	2.9	18.3	46.0	0.9
	1997	205.3	47.3	8.6	4.7	18.2	54.7	2.3
	1998	256.0	92.1	9.8	5.8	10.6	59.2	2.3
	1999	154.6	60.7	8.2	4.9	13.5	59.8	3.2
	2000	180.1	75.9	9.9	7.2	13.0	72.7	4.0
	2001	243.2	94.6	11.4	8.0	12.1	70.2	3.3
EU	1994	2 471.2	1 823.4	1 791.7	748.1	98.3	41.8	30.3
	1995	2 814.6	2 277.8	2 246.3	1 077.6	98.6	48.0	38.3
	1996	3 219.0	2 580.3	2 520.1	1 196.8	97.7	47.5	37.2
	1997	3 614.8	2 926.3	2 888.8	770.8	98.7	26.7	21.3
	1998	3 519.4	2 932.1	2 908.0	761.8	99.2	26.2	21.6
	1999	3 562.2	3 100.9	3 075.2	1 035.0	99.2	33.7	29.1
	2000	4 247.1	3 671.7	3 633.6	1 499.5	99.0	41.3	35.3
	2001	4 372.4	3 958.1	3 935.7	1 847.4	99.4	46.9	42.3
Japan	1994	1 120.5	695.5	211.2	200.5	30.4	94.9	17.9
	1995	1 309.8	912.7	241.9	230.1	26.5	95.1	17.6
	1996	1 504.3	939.8	388.9	269.9	41.4	69.4	17.9
	1997	1 204.9	757.3	306.3	222.1	40.4	72.5	18.4
	1998	1 045.4	643.8	364.0	189.9	56.5	52.2	18.2
	1999	989.0	679.6	366.2	231.9	53.9	63.3	23.4
	2000	1 236.5	881.3	615.3	236.0	69.8	38.4	19.1
	2001	1 001.3	398.1	278.3	228.4	69.9	82.1	22.8
USA	1994	1 755.3	1 398.4	68.1	50.4	4.9	74.0	2.9
	1995	1 787.5	1 474.3	69.7	49.4	4.7	70.9	2.8
	1996	4 896.1	3 896.5	69.7	48.3	1.8	69.3	1.0
	1997	5 609.1	4 432.5	2 719.4	790.6	61.4	29.1	14.1
	1998	4 974.9	4 247.1	2 282.4	1 747.0	53.7	76.5	35.1
	1999	5 780.7	5 109.2	2 419.7	2 215.7	47.4	91.6	38.3
	2000	7 695.5	7 086.6	3 577.2	3 247.5	50.5	90.8	42.2
	2001	7 221.3	6 716.3	2 960.1	2 836.1	44.1	95.8	39.3

Source: UNCTAD (2003e).

Note: Values for Quad countries for 1995 exclude Canada; figures are based on member State notifications; figures for Japan are based on fiscal years; figures for the European Union for 1994–1995 exclude Austria, Finland and Sweden.

a Granted through Generalized System of Preferences (GSP).

not make clear commitments with respect to the products and countries that are covered by the market access preferences. While all Quad initiatives make general commitments with respect to products and countries that are covered by those initiatives, all Quad countries also maintain the option to review the list of products and countries that are actually eligible for the initiatives or to introduce ad hoc safeguards. While the list of products is generally reviewed in the light of their economic sensitivity, the list of eligible countries is determined on the basis of non-trade-related concerns.

Rules of origin are rightly regarded as a predominant cause of the under-utilization of trade preferences (e.g. UNCTAD, 2001b, 2003e; Mattoo, Roy and, Subramania, 2002). As preferences are granted unilaterally and non-contractually, preference-giving countries have consistently expressed the view that they ought to be free to decide on the rules of origin, although they have indicated their willingness to hear the views of the beneficiary countries. Preference-giving countries tend to feel that the process of harmonization of rules of origin can be limited to certain practical aspects, such as certification, control, verification, sanctions and mutual cooperation. Even with regard to these aspects, progress has been very limited, as basic requirements and the rationale for rules of origin have remained almost unchanged for nearly 30 years. Implementation difficulties among preference-receiving countries are particularly related to the obligation to devise and operate an accounting system that is conceptually and operationally different from national legal requirements that enterprises are often unable to meet.[20]

Rules of origin are rightly regarded as a predominant cause of the under-utilization of trade preferences.

Overcoming non-tariff barriers to trade and complying with product standards — be they related to technical barriers to trade (TBT) or sanitary and phytosanitary standards (SPS) — constitute a formidable if not more challenging market access problem than tariff barriers. The inability to adhere to strict health or environmental measures (e.g. pesticides residue levels, packaging requirements, eco-labeling) is likely to cause the loss of shares in the market in question, and also, unlike tariff protection, may damage prospects for penetrating other markets (UNCTAD, 2002b, 2002c). LDCs' benefits from preferential market access may therefore be seriously impaired by non-tariff barriers to trade (NTBs). This issue is discussed in more detail in relation to fish exports in box 16.

E. Strengthening international support measures targeted at the LDCs

Priorities for improving international support measures targeted at the LDCs have been a significant issue at the three meetings of trade representatives of LDCs held in 1999, 2001 and 2003.

Priorities for improving international support measures targeted at the LDCs have been a significant issue at the three meetings of trade representatives of LDCs held in Sun City in 1999, Zanzibar in 2001 and Dhaka in 2003 (WTO, 1999a, 2001b, 2003b). The outcomes of these meetings, which are summarized in the annex to this chapter, provide the best basis for what the LDCs themselves see as priorities for improving the current situation with regard to international support measures for the LDCs in the field of trade.

1. STRENGTHENING SPECIAL AND DIFFERENTIAL TREATMENT

At present, the effectiveness of special and differential treatment appears to be undermined by the fact that a good number of special and differential treatment provisions are of a non-binding nature for the member States of the

---

Box 16. Negative effects of environmental barriers on seafood exports

LDCs face significant capacity constraints in meeting stringent technical standards as well as sanitary and phytosanitary measures and environmental requirements. These include a lack of infrastructure, such as internationally accredited and recognized laboratories with advanced testing equipment; poor legislative capacity; limited skills and training; and a lack of engagement in international standard-setting processes that is largely attributable to the small size of these countries' scientific and business communities and to limited government resources. These conditions and measures add to the insecurity and unpredictability of market access in the preference-giving countries and thus to the unattractiveness of the affected country to export-oriented FDI. At present, none of the major initiatives such as AGOA or EBA incorporate capacity building measures to meet standards, which would be critical for enhancing the utilization of the preferences.

The export of fish and seafood – which is amongst the most important exports of the group of least developed countries– is particularly sensitive to alterations in sanitary and phytosanitary standards. The import restrictions and bans imposed by the EU in the 1997-99 period on fishery products exports from Uganda, Mozambique and Tanzania on grounds of cholera and/or fish poisoning from presence of pesticides is illustrative of how exports of LDCs can be affected by these measures. The economic effects of such measures on the affected countries could be devastating. For instance in the case of Uganda the loss from the ban of fish exports in terms of earnings has been estimated at $36.9 million.[1]

Another example for the significant loss that may arise due to import restrictions and bans is provided by Bangladesh's shrimp industry. Shrimps are one of the most important primary commodity exports of Bangladesh, and the shrimp industry is an important employer in the country. A study by the Consumer Unity and Trust Society (CUTS) suggests that about 1.2 million people are directly employed in the shrimp industry and that an additional 11 million people are employed in the fisheries industry. When the European Union banned shrimp imports from Bangladesh between August and December of 1997, the shrimp exports of Bangladesh to the European Union dropped from $65.1 million to zero, but at the same time the shrimp exports of Bangladesh to the other major markets increased by a few million dollars, largely compensating for the loss (see box table 1) (CUTS, 2002).

Box Table 2. Estimated net effects on the shrimp exporting industry of Bangladesh associated with the import ban on shrimp from the European Union in late 1997

($ millions)

Import region	Imports without ban	Imports with ban	Net effects
United States	73.5	102.2	28.7
European Union	65.1	0.0	-65.1
Japan	22.7	26.1	3.4
All others	7.5	25.8	18.3
Total	**168.8**	**154.1**	**-14.7**

Source: Cato and Lima dos Santos (1998), in CUTS (2002).

[1] For further information, see UNCTAD's Trade, Environment and Development website: http://r0.unctad.org/trade_env/index.htm

---

WTO, and by the fact that the right to other such provisions is undermined by the process of accession to the WTO, which requires least developed countries to negotiate all trade rules, including all special and differential treatment provisions, on an individual basis. In order to increase the utility and effectiveness of the different provisions of special and differential treatment, it therefore appears important that the provisions be turned into rights for least developed countries and obligations for other countries, and that they be granted in an automatic manner to all least developed countries that decide to become members of the multilateral trading system. It is also vital that they be well targeted with respect to countries and to problems, and that they be actually associated with corresponding actions — in other words, more than mere statements of intent. Otherwise, they will not be effective and will not achieve their objectives.

At their different meetings, the trade representatives of the LDCs reiterated their request that special and differential treatment provided within the multilateral trading system be better targeted to their needs and related to their level of development. Moreover, at the last meeting they identified a number of major priorities.

Firstly, the Dhaka Declaration emphasizes that WTO members ought to expeditiously implement the guidelines for accession adopted by the General Council of the WTO, and with respect to implementation issues, it emphasized that the WTO members ought to address the issues highlighted in the Ministerial Decision on Implementation-related Issues and Concerns adopted in the context of the WTO's Doha conference. All implementation issues that are not being dealt with in this decision are supposed to become an integral part of the subsequent work programme. Furthermore, the least developed countries requested that they not be forced to make any commitment that is not compatible with their development status.

Secondly, the Dhaka Declaration requested that the LDCs be exempt from the application of safeguards and anti-dumping measures, but it also emphasized that the LDCs should not be subjected to the application of any other contingency measure. In addition, the Dhaka Declaration requested that the LDCs be given the right to use special safeguards and anti-dumping measures so as to prevent severe damage to their domestic economies, especially their agricultural sectors, and to protect themselves against unfair competition from foreign producers, whose international competitiveness is artificially enhanced through various subsidies.

At present, the effectiveness of special and differential treatment appears to be undermined by the fact that a good number of special and differential treatment provisions are of a non-binding nature for the member States of the WTO, and by the fact that the right to other such provisions is undermined by the process of accession to the WTO.

2. STRENGTHENING MARKET ACCESS PREFERENCES

The trade representatives of the LDCs have welcomed recent improvements by Quad countries in market access preferences for least developed countries. But they have requested their development partners to further expand market access preferences and to ensure complete duty-free and quota-free market access. The LDCs also encouraged developed WTO members to increase the stability and predictability of market access preferences by making firm commitments to unrestricted market access for all goods. Complete duty-free and quota-free access implies that the products which are currently excluded from the preferential market access should be included. But in addition to market access for merchandise goods, the least developed countries also urged better market access conditions for services. They requested in particular that the developed countries not restrict market access in areas where the movement of natural persons is concerned (i.e. mode 4 on service trade). Finally, they requested developed countries to eliminate all trade-distorting agricultural support measures that negatively affect their export capacities.

The LDCs also encouraged developed WTO members to increase the stability and predictability of market access preferences by making firm commitments to unrestricted market access for all goods.

Such measures, together with reductions in non-tariff barriers, particularly those related to rules of origin, and also assistance in meeting sanitary and phytosanitary standards, are likely to considerably increase the effective benefits of preferential market access in the short run. But as progress is made towards multilateral trade liberalization, the benefits of preferential market access will slowly be eroded.

In this context, the question of compensation for the loss of preferences has arisen.[21] But there is in fact a larger and more important issue. The provision of market access preferences as an approach to development support was probably the main new theme in the United Nations Programme of Action for the Least Developed Countries for the Decade 2001–2010. As multilateral liberalization occurs, there is not simply erosion of preferences, but also the weakening of the major market-based mechanism through which the LDCs are supported by their development partners. It is important that there be such market-based mechanisms, alongside government-to-government aid and debt relief, for international support for the LDCs. The big and important issue, therefore, is: what might complement and enhance preferential market access as a market-based mechanism to support the LDCs as multilateral trade liberalization occurs?

3. DEVELOPING SUPPLY-SIDE PREFERENCES

A logical shift that can be made is to think not only of market access preferences but also, simultaneously, of what might be called "supply-side preferences". The seed of this idea is apparent in proposals that preferential market access for the LDCs be deepened through measures to enhance the synergies between trade and investment. Thus, as Cline (2004, chapter 2: 29) has put it, "if efforts are to be undertaken to enhance further market access as a means of reducing global poverty, these should be accompanied by measures that help spur direct investment in the countries in question". Similarly, the WTO in its assessment of market access preferences granted to least developed countries has come to the conclusion that "taken together, these results imply that a broad approach is required to assist LDCs improve their export performance. This approach needs to be complemented with efforts to improve supply capacities of LDCs" (WTO, 2002b: 22). Such deepening of market access preferences would improve their efficacy. But as multilateral trade liberalization occurs and as regional trade arrangements expand, market access preferences will inevitably erode. It is important to make the best use of market access preferences while they are available as a policy instrument, but it is equally important to complement market access preferences though other instruments that help the LDCs overcome their marginalization. Supply-side preferences could provide the basis for a new generation of international support measures which would promote trade and development through enhanced supply capabilities in weak countries.

A logical shift that can be made is to think not only of market access preferences but also, simultaneously, of what might be called "supply-side preferences".

The idea of supply-side preferences needs to be further elaborated. But they may be envisaged in three particular areas: technology, FDI and finance. With regard to technology, it is notable that Article 66.2 of the TRIPS urges "Developed country Members to provide incentives to enterprises and institutions in their territories for purpose of encouraging transfer of technology to LDCs". Today, most OECD countries have adopted "home country measures" to promote both technology transfer and foreign direct investment in developing countries. The measures taken by advanced countries to promote technology transfer include advisory services, training and education, promoting the use of specific technology, research and development, and partnerships (table 52). The measures taken to promote FDI include financial support in the form of equity and loans, and the provision of fiscal incentives and insurance. Other forms of assistance concentrate on the dissemination of information about potential investors and support in matchmaking (see table 53). There are also various corporate taxation measures which might be used to encourage FDI. These include reduction of the corporate tax rate to very low levels in specific sectors (i.e. those that are most cost-effective) in such a way as to attract FDI to poor countries (Margalioth, 2003). A more detailed account of different home country measures is to be found in Krut and Moretz (1999).

A number of innovative suggestions have also been made to mitigate risks and encourage FDI in the LDCs. The Ministry of Foreign Affairs of Sweden has commissioned a study looking into different types of risks that discourage investments in LDCs and different types of public and private measures of how these risks can be mitigated (Ministry of Foreign Affairs of Sweden, 2003). Immediate actions in this area suggested by Mistry and Olesen (2003) include:

* Increased funding for multilateral risk insurance agencies in order to partially cover the non-commercial risk in the LDCs;

TABLE 52. EXAMPLES OF MAIN TYPES OF EXISTING HOME COUNTRY MEASURES ENCOURAGING TRANSFER OF TECHNOLOGY

	Partnerships	Promoting the use of specific technology	Provision of expertise		Research and development
			Advisory services	Training and education	
European Union	x	x	x	-	x
Australia	-	-	x	x	-
Austria	-	-	-	-	x
Belgium	x	-	-	x	-
Canada	-	x	x	x	x
Denmark	x	-	x	-	x
Finland	-	x	-	-	-
France	x	-	x	-	x
Germany	-	-	x	-	-
Japan	-	-	x	-	-
Netherlands	-	x	x	-	-
New Zealand	x	-	x	-	-
Norway	x	x	x	x	-
Spain	x	-	x	-	-
Sweden	-	-	x	x	x
Switzerland	-	x	x	-	-
United Kingdom	x	x	-	-	x
United States	x	x	x	x	-

Source: UNCTAD (2000b: 11).

TABLE 53. OUTWARD FDI PROMOTION PROGRAMMES OF SELECTED OECD MEMBER COUNTRIES

	Information and technical assistance					Financial		Fiscal	Insurance
	Information	Match making	Missions	Feasibility studies	Project & start-up	Equity	Loans	Tax sparing	Guarantees
Australia	x	x	x	x	-	-	-	x	-
Austria	x	-	-	-	-	x	x	-	x
Belgium	x	x	-	-	-	x	x	-	x
Canada	x	x	x	x	x	x	-	x	-
Denmark	-	-	-	-	-	x	x	x	x
Finland	x	-	x	x	x	x	x	-	x
France	x	-	-	x	x	x	x	-	-
Germany	x	x	x	x	x	x	x	x	x
Italy	x	x	x	x	x	x	x	-	x
Japan	x	x	x	x	x	x	x	x	x
Netherlands	x	x	x	x	-	x	x	x	x
New Zealand	x	x	-	x	-	x	-	x	-
Norway	x	x	x	x	x	-	x	-	x
Portugal	x	x	x	-	-	-	x	-	-
Spain	x	x	x	-	-	x	x	x	x
Sweden	x	x	-	x	-	x	x	x	-
Switzerland	x	x	x	x	x	x	x	-	x
United Kingdom	-	-	-	-	-	x	x	x	x
United States	x	x	x	x	x	-	x	-	x

Source: UNCTAD (2000b: 9).

- Standard non-commercial risk insurance policies for LDCs;

- Pooling the capacity of non-commercial risk insurers from developed countries in specific public–private partnerships in developing countries. The development of private–public partnerships should be encouraged between developed countries and those developing countries that are becoming a major source of FDI in LDCs (e.g. South Africa in Africa);

- Project-related subsidies to cover non-commercial risks;

- Full or large partial tax credits, and rebates for the equity invested by home country companies in LDCs against their tax liabilities in their home countries.

In elaborating such measures it is important that development-friendly FDI be encouraged. To that end, Te Velde (2002), for instance, has suggested the introduction of a global business linkage fund that is supposed to strengthen linkages between transnational corporations and local small and medium-sized enterprises.

A number of innovative suggestions have also been made to mitigate risks and encourage FDI in the LDCs.

Finally, with regard to finance, a critical problem is to enable both foreign and domestic investors to gain access to concessional loans and with long periods of amortization period credit. The Commonwealth Secretariat is working on a practical proposal in this area (see Hughes and Brewster, 2002).

F. Enhanced South–South cooperation in the field of trade

Enhanced South–South cooperation in the field of trade has an important role to play as a complement to broad system-wide policies and special international support measures for the LDCs in international policies to enhance the effectiveness of trade as a mechanism for poverty reduction. Indeed, there are good reasons to believe that South–South cooperation is becoming increasingly important in policies to link international trade with poverty reduction in the LDCs.

The basic reason why South–South cooperation is becoming increasingly important is that there was a major shift in the geographical direction of the LDCs' trade in the 1990s. On the one hand, the LDCs began to acquire a greater proportion of their total merchandise imports from other developing countries. On the other hand, they began to ship a greater proportion of their total merchandise exports to other developing countries. But this has not been happening in a totally balanced way. As chart 40 shows, the geographical pattern of trade of the LDCs changed little between 1980 and 1989. But between 1989 and 1997 the share of other developing countries in LDC imports rose from 32 per cent to 56 per cent, which is the level at which it was in 2002. Over the same period, the share of LDC exports going to other developing countries rose also, but more slowly, from 15 per cent in 1989 to 34 per cent in 1997, which is also the level at which it was in 2002. As South–South trade has gained in importance, the developed countries have lost importance as a source of the merchandise imports of the LDCs. About 67 per cent of LDC imports originated in developed countries in 1980, but by 2002 the figure was only 39 per cent. But as a destination for LDC exports, developed country markets have retained their importance. Their share of total LDC exports fell only from 69 per cent in 1980 to 62 per cent in 2002, partly because of the decline in LDC exports to former socialist countries.

South–South cooperation is becoming increasingly important in policies to link international trade with poverty reduction in the LDCs.

CHART 40. EXPORTS OF DIFFERENT COUNTRY GROUPS TO DIFFERENT COUNTRY GROUPS, 1980–2002

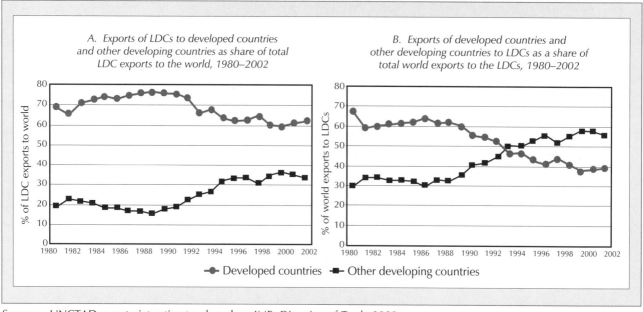

A. Exports of LDCs to developed countries and other developing countries as share of total LDC exports to the world, 1980–2002

B. Exports of developed countries and other developing countries to LDCs as a share of total world exports to the LDCs, 1980–2002

—●— Developed countries   —■— Other developing countries

Source: UNCTAD secretariat estimates, based on IMF, Direction of Trade 2003.

The changes are such that the share of LDCs in the imports of other developing countries was by 2002, despite the progress in the 1990s, 10 per cent less than it was in 1980 (see chart 41). In contrast, the share of other developing countries in the total imports of LDCs was 82 per cent higher in 2002 than in 1980. In relative terms, the LDC share of the imports of other developing countries fell from 0.73 per cent in 1980 to 0.66 per cent in 2002. In absolute terms, the trade balance between LDCs and other developing countries was $15.6 billion in 2002, compared with $5.5 billion in 1990 and $2.2 billion in 1980 in favour of other developing countries.

As table 54 shows, China, Taiwan Province of China, the Republic of Korea, Singapore, South Africa, Thailand, India, Côte d'Ivoire, Indonesia, Malaysia, Kenya and Brazil were all amongst the largest exporters to the LDCs during the period 1999–2001. These economies are also amongst the top importers from LDCs. But in all cases the LDCs export less to the other developing countries than they import from other developing countries.

There was a major shift in the geographical direction of the LDCs' trade in the 1990s.

There is also an interesting difference between African and Asian LDCs in terms of their integration with other developing countries in their respective regions. The share of the exports of African LDCs going to other African countries has remained low since the early 1980s, fluctuating between 7 and 10 per cent of total LDC exports. The share of the exports of Asian LDCs going to developing Asia has been consistently higher. Between 1980–1982 and 2000–2002, it has increased from 38 per cent to 41 per cent of their total merchandise exports. This pattern of trade suggests that the Asian LDCs have been able to link into the growth processes of rapidly growing Asian newly industrializing economies.

The evolving pattern of trade partly reflects the pattern of market access barriers that the LDCs face in other developing countries. The situation is complicated in this regard. Most important developing country trading partners of the LDCs have granted market access preferences to the LDCs (see table 49 above). Moreover, almost all the LDCs, with the exception of Afghanistan, Kiribati, the Solomon Islands, Tuvalu and Vanuatu, are members of some kind of customs union or free trade arrangement (table 55).[22] Through these arrangements, the LDCs receive reciprocal or preferential market access. India,

CHART 41. IMPORTS OF LDCS FROM OTHER DEVELOPING COUNTRIES (ODCS) AND IMPORTS OF OTHER DEVELOPING COUNTRIES FROM LDCS AS SHARE OF THEIR TOTAL IMPORTS RESPECTIVELY,[a] 1980–2002

(Index, 1980 = 100)

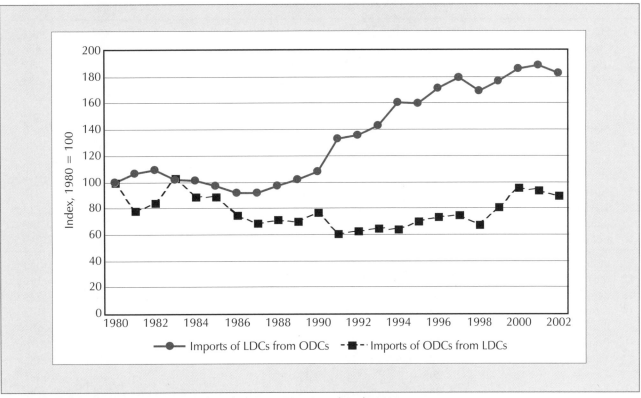

Source: UNCTAD secretariat estimates, based on IMF, *Direction of Trade 2003*.
  a   Imports are merchandise imports.

for example, provides preferential market access for the LDC members of SAARC. However, there is a general tendency for LDCs' exports to face higher tariffs in developing country markets than in developed country markets.

Table 56 summarizes some data on this phenomenon. It is clear that despite the preferences, Brazil, China, India, the Republic of Korea, South Africa and Thailand, which are all important for the LDCs, face higher tariffs there. The increasing imbalance in the trade relations between LDCs and other developing countries is likely to reflect the more extensive process of trade liberalization undertaken in the LDCs in the framework of structural adjustment programmes, which has resulted in significantly improved market access in the LDCs for both developed countries and other developing countries.

Linking into the growth process of more advanced developing countries can offer important trading opportunities for the LDCs. Such linkages can play a key role for LDCs in linking into global growth and serve as a stepping stone for learning how to export. The enhanced development of the LDCs will also increase market opportunities in the more advanced developing countries. There are also opportunities for trade–investment linkages which could also be mutually beneficial. FDI by other developing countries in the LDCs has served as a major mechanism for developing productive capacities and non-traditional exports from the LDCs. Important positive synergies can be achieved as the more advanced developing countries move up the ladder of technological development but seek to continue to derive benefits from simpler products through triangular relationships with LDCs. Finally, landlocked LDCs and their neighboring transit countries both stand to gain from enhanced cooperation in the field of transit transport.

Most important developing country trading partners of the LDCs have granted market access preferences to the LDCs... However, there is a general tendency for LDCs' exports to face higher tariffs in developing country markets than in developed country markets.

TABLE 54. TOP EXPORTERS TO LDCs AND TOP IMPORTERS FROM LDCsᵃ, AVERAGE 1999–2001

	Top exporters to LDCs	Merchandise exports $ millions	Merchandise trade balance $ millions	Top importers from LDCs	Merchandise imports $ millions	Merchandise trade balance $ millions
1	EU	10 956	-407	EU	11 363	-407
2	China, total	4 372	717	United States	8 880	-6 490
	China	3 254	473	China, total	3 656	717
	China, Taiwan Province of	969	316	China	2 781	473
	China, Hong Kong SAR	150	-72	China, Taiwan Province of	653	316
	China, Macao SAR	0	0	China, Hong Kong SAR	222	-72
3	Korea, Republic of	2 662	1 268	China, Macao SAR	0	0
4	United States	2 390	-6 490	Thailand	1 448	428
5	Singapore	2 361	1 732	Korea, Republic of	1 394	1 268
6	South Africa	2 356	2 184	Japan	1 122	1 036
7	Japan	2 158	1 036	India	1 059	730
8	Thailand	1 876	428	Singapore	629	1 732
9	India	1 789	730	Saudi Arabia	323	-4 100
10	Côte d'Ivoire	826	760	Canada	289	-19
11	Indonesia	732	544	Malaysia	264	383
12	Malaysia	647	383	Brazil	212	168
13	Kenya	578	535	Indonesia	188	544
14	Australia	528	385	Ethiopia	184	-102
15	Brazil	380	168	South Africa	171	2 184
16	Pakistan	374	235	Norway	157	74
17	Saudi Arabiaᵇ	282	-41	Australia	143	385
18	Canada	269	-19	Pakistan	140	235
19	Turkey	258	188	Russian Federation	132	98
20	Argentina	248	234	Egypt	120	27
21	Nigeria	236	133	Poland	116	57
22	Zimbabwe	231	184	Nigeria	103	133
23	Norway	230	74	Switzerland and Liechtenstein	98	99
24	Russian Federation	230	98	Ghana	94	42
25	Oman	225	205	Cameroon	90	-1
26	Switzerland and Lichtenstein	197	99	Mexico	80	-59
27	Croatia	178	158	Turkey	70	188
28	Poland	173	57	Côte d'Ivoire	66	760
29	Senegal	153	148	Ukraine	63	3
30	Egypt	147	27	Philippines	58	-26

Source: UNCTAD secretariat estimates, based on UN COMTRADE data for merchandise trade; *UNCTAD Handbook of Statistics 2003.*

a Top exporters to and top importers from LDCs are ranked by value of average annual exports and imports, respectively.
b Export value for Saudi Arabia was based on data for 2001.

Both the LDCs and the more advanced developing countries stand to gain mutually from increased trade and investment linkages between them.

Realizing these positive synergies is difficult in a world in which asymmetries in the global economy make it difficult for the more advanced developing countries to promote development and reduce poverty. Further innovative use of regional trade arrangements can be envisaged. But advances in this area are likely to depend also on a more supportive global environment for more advanced developing countries. Both the LDCs and the more advanced developing countries stand to gain mutually from increased trade and investment linkages between them.

TABLE 55. MEMBERSHIP OF LDCs IN REGIONAL TRADE ARRANGEMENTS, 2002

	Africa										Americas	Asia		Africa /Asia
	Arab Maghreb Union (AMU)	Common Market for Eastern and Southern Africa (COMESA)	Cross Boarder Initiative (CBI)	Economic and Monetary Community of Central Africa (CEMAC)	Economic Community of Central African States (ECCAS)	Economic Community of Western African States (ECOWAS)	Mano River Union (MRU)	Southern African Customs Union (SACU)[a]	Southern African Development Community (SADC)	West African Economic and Monetary Union (WAEMU)	Caribbean Community and Common Market (CARICOM)[a]	Association of South East Asian Nations (ASEAN) Free Trade Area (ASEAN FTA)	South Asian Association for Regional Cooperation (SAARC) Preferential Trading Arrangement (SAPTA)	Arab Free Trade Area (Arab FTA)
Africa														
Angola		X			X				X					
Benin						X				X				
Burkina Faso						X				X				
Burundi		X	X		X									
Cape Verde						X								
Central African Republic				X	X									
Chad				X	X									
Comoros		X	X											
Dem. Rep. of the Congo		X			X				X					
Djibouti		X												
Equatorial Guinea					X									
Eritrea		X												
Ethiopia		X												
Gambia						X								
Guinea						X	X							
Guinea-Bissau						X				X				
Lesotho								X	X					
Liberia						X	X							
Madagascar		X	X											
Malawi		X	X						X					
Mali						X				X				
Mauritania	X					X								
Mozambique									X					
Niger						X				X				
Rwanda		X	X		X									
Sao Tome and Principe					X									
Senegal						X				X				
Sierra Leone						X	X							
Somalia														X
Sudan		X												X
Togo						X				X				
Uganda		X	X											
United Rep. of Tanzania			X						X					
Zambia		X	X						X					
Americas														
Haiti											X			
Asia														
Bangladesh													X	
Bhutan													X	
Cambodia												X		
Lao PDR												X		
Maldives													X	
Myanmar												X		
Nepal													X	
Yemen														X

Source: UNCTAD secretariat compilation, based on WTO (2000b, 2002b, 2003b).

Note: Afghanistan, Kiribati, Samoa, Solomon Islands, Tuvalu and Vanuatu are not members of any customs union or free trade arrangement as classified by the WTO (2002b), but all are members of other regional economic cooperation arrangements. For description, see Herrmann (2004b).

a   CARICOM and SACU are the only customs unions; all other trade arrangments are free trade arrangments.

TABLE 56. APPLIED TARIFF RATES OF IMPORTANT TRADING PARTNERS OF LDCs ON IMPORTS FROM LDCs, 1996–2001

Economy	Year	MFN applied rates				LDC applied rate			
		Simple average	Weighted average	Minimum	Maximum	Simple average	Weighted average	Minimum	Maximum
Top four developed economy trading partners									
Canada	2001	5.7	11.9	0.0	22.5	3.8	11.4	0.0	22.5
European Union	2001	5.9	5.3	0.0	74.9	0.3	0.2	0.0	25.0
Japan	2001	10.3	6.6	0.0	60.0	2.4	1.6	0.0	60.0
United States	2001	5.9	10.9	0.0	350.0	5.6	6.1	0.0	350.0
Other developed economy trading partners									
Australia	2001	7.8	8.3	0.0	25.0	6.7	5.8	0.0	25.0
Norway	1996	14.7	6.1	0.0	249.0	8.2	2.0	0.0	249.0
Switzerland	2001	0.0	0.0	0.0	0.0	0.0	0.0	0.0	0.0
Top four developing economy trading partners									
China	2001	17.4	9.4	0.0	114.0	15.3	9.4	0.0	114.0
Taiwan Province of China	2001	8.5	6.3	0.0	50.0	8.3	6.3	0.0	50.0
China, Hong Kong SAR	1998	0.0	0.0	0.0	0.0	0.0	0.0	0.0	0.0
India	2001	32.9	22.8	0.0	210.0	26.0	18.9	0.0	210.0
Rep. of Korea	1999	8.8	5.3	0.0	50.0	7.9	5.3	0.0	50.0
Thailand	2000	20.9	5.3	0.0	80.0	18.9	5.3	0.0	80.0
Other developing economy trading partners									
Brazil	2001	13.8	5.2	0.0	28.0	13.4	5.2	0.0	28.0
Indonesia	2000	8.7	2.7	0.0	170.0	8.3	2.6	0.0	170.0
Malaysia	1997	3.7	1.1	0.0	352.9	3.7	1.1	0.0	352.9
Singapore	2001	0.0	0.0	0.0	0.0	0.0	0.0	0.0	0.0
South Africa	2001	11.4	9.3	0.0	60.0	10.9	9.3	0.0	60.0

Source: UNCTAD secretariat compilations, based on WTO (2002a).

G. Conclusions

The basic message of the chapter can be summarized as four major points.

Firstly, the LDCs cannot be expected to gain much from the current round of multilateral trade liberalization unless improvements are made in their productive capacities to enable them to benefit from any subsequent global growth in trade. Amongst the issues currently under discussion, the phasing-out of agricultural subsidies in OECD countries is particularly important for the development prospects of the LDCs. Although agricultural support measures may help countries import cheap foods and meet food security needs in the short term, they have a depressing effect on agricultural production in the LDCs, breaking the potential complementarities between agricultural and non-agricultural development that are central to the development process.

There is considerable room for strengthening current international support measures, and practical proposals are available for doing so.

Secondly, and against this background, special international support measures, although they are frequently seen as a second-best option compared with multilateral trade liberalization, still have an important role to play in making international trade a more effective mechanism for poverty reduction in the LDCs. Current special measures, including both market access preferences and other special and differential treatment in favour of the LDCs, have various limitations, which reduce their effectiveness. There is considerable room for strengthening current international support measures, and practical proposals are available for doing so. However, as multilateral trade liberalization deepens, market access preferences for LDCs will gradually erode and the major market-based approach to supporting the LDCs will be undermined. As this happens it is important to consider complementary international support measures for the LDCs. One possible course of action is to introduce new supply-side preferences. Such preferences could encourage FDI and technology transfer to the LDCs, and could also enable domestic investors to gain access to cheaper finance than at present. These could usefully complement and strengthen preferential market access as a market-based approach to supporting LDCs.

Thirdly, there are also a number of systemic international trade measures beyond multilateral trade liberalization, which can play a very important role in making international trade a more effective mechanism for poverty reduction in the LDCs. The major sin of omission in the current international approach to poverty reduction is the failure to tackle the link between commodity dependence and extreme poverty. Any systemic measures in relation to commodities are likely to have a high poverty-reduction intensity in the LDCs. Priority areas include measures to reduce vulnerability to commodity price shocks and initiatives to ensure international transparency in the revenues derived from oil and mineral exploitation. Systemic measures with regard to the mineral economies, which are off the radar screen in current analyses of the effects of multilateral trade liberalization (which focus on agriculture and manufactures), are likely to be particularly important as extreme poverty has been increasing in most mineral-dependent LDCs.

Growth in the more advanced developing countries could play a key role in enabling the LDCs to benefit from global growth rather than face persistent marginalization.

Finally, international trade can be made a more effective mechanism for poverty reduction in the LDCs through increasing South–South cooperation in the field of trade. This has become increasingly important as South–South trade has grown. But there is a danger that LDCs may become marginalized in South–South trade as they are in North–South trade. Measures to reverse the marginalization of LDCs in South–South trade include further use of the Global System of Trade Preferences, the encouragement of regional FDI by more advanced developing countries in the LDCs and of triangular relationships with developed countries, and also special provisions within regional agreements. In the end, a major obstacle to increased South–South cooperation is the difficulties the more advanced developing countries have in the global economy. As these are removed, growth in the more advanced developing countries could play a key role in enabling the LDCs to benefit from global growth rather than face persistent marginalization.

ANNEX TABLE 3. OVERVIEW OF RECOMMENDATIONS OF LDCs MADE WITH RESPECT TO THE MULTILATERAL TRADE AGENDA AT SUN CITY (1999), ZANZIBAR (2001) AND DHAKA (2003)

Recommendations	Sun City, 1999	Zanzibar, 2001	Dhaka, 2003	Special and differential treatment	Preferential market access	Assistance	General
	by Declaration			by Category			
Accession							
WTO members shall expeditiously implement guidelines for accession of LDCs adopted by the General Council			X	X			
WTO members shall automatically recognize the special development status of LDCs, defined by the United Nations	X	X					X
WTO members shall automatically recognize the right of LDCs to special and differential treatment	X	X	X				X
Commitments in accession process shall not exceed what admitted LDCs have committed	X	X	X	X			
Commitments in accession process shall not exceed what is requested in the multilateral trade agreements	X	X	X	X			
Commitments in accession process shall not entail any demands concerning plurilateral agreements	X	X		X			
Accession process should be supported by adequate technical and financial assistance	X	X				X	
Accession process should be facilitated through simpler and clearer procedures	X	X	X	X			
Accession process should be speeded up through fast-track accession option	X	X	X	X			
Market access							
General issues							
Market access to other countries is considered very important			X				X
Least developed countries have undertaken far-reaching liberalization of their trade regimes		X	X				X
International organizations should aim for policy coherence with respect to liberalization demands	X	X	X				X
Agriculture							
Least developed members States should not be requested to make further liberalization commitments in the negotiations	X	X	X	X			
Developed member States should provide duty-free and quota-free market access to all agricultural LDC exports	X	X	X		X		
Support measures by LDCs should be permissible (special and differential treatment, combined w/ subsequent)	X	X		X			
Support measures by developed countries should be eliminated (special and differential treatment, combined w/previous)	X	X	X	X			
Standards: LDCs should be provided with technical and financial assistance to deal with SPS and TBT		X	X			X	
Food security: Member States should establish revolving fund to address food insecurity	X	X	X			X	
Food security: Member States may provide food aid to address food insecurity		X	X			X	
Agricultural development: Member States should provide assistance for agricultural development		X	X			X	
Special safeguards: Least developed member States should be eligible to use special safeguards to protect their agricultural sector			X	X			
Non-agriculture/non-textile							
No restrictions on use of export subsidies	X	X		X			
Exemption from competitiveness thresholds	X	X		X			
Expansion of non-actionable category of subsidies	X	X		X			
Least developed countries should receive financial support to finance their subsidies	X	X		X		X	
Least developed countries shall not be required to make further liberalization commitments in this round of negotiations			X	X[a]			
Preferential market access shall become an integral part of modalities to be established in negotiations			X	X			
Textiles and clothing							
Exemption from anti-dumping duties and safeguard actions	X			X			
Compensation for phasing-out of ATC through extension of market access preferences	X	X		X			
Simplification and harmonization of rules of origin and customs procedures by preference-giving countries		X					X
Services							
LDCs should have flexibility in making commitments with respect to liberalization	X	X	X	X			
LDCs should have flexibility in complying with provisions			X	X			
LDCs should benefit from special and differential treatment regarding subsidies, emergency safeguards and government procurement	X			X			
WTO members, especially developed countries, shall grant full market access for exports of interest to least developed countries			X		X		
Developed country members shall help LDCs with technical and financial resources to develop their competitiveness in services exports	X	X	X			X	
International agencies shall help LDCs through assistance programmes to develop their service sectors and fulfil implementation requirements			X			X	
WTO members should establish disciplining mechanism to deal with anti-competitive practices		X	X				X
LDCs should have the right to provide different treatment to domestic and foreign suppliers		X		X			
LDCs should have the possibility to impose safeguards against foreign suppliers, which are benefiting from trade-distorting subsidies			X	X			
Maritime transport							
Least developed countries require support in negotiations	X					X	
Financial services							
Financial liberalization ought to be coordinated with other macroeconomic policies	X						X
Telecommunication services							
Least developed countries require technical assistance to build human capacities and infrastructure	X					X	
Movement of natural persons							
Least developed countries should not face restrictions of exports under this mode of supply	X	X	X		X		
Preferential market access							
Access to developed markets: Improve stability and predictability through binding commitments on duty- and quota-free access for all products	X	X	X	X			
Access to other developing countries: Encouraged			X		X		
Non-tariff barriers: Improve special and differential treatment with respect to non-tariff measures		X	X	X			
Non-tariff barriers: Provide technical and financial assistance to deal with SPS and TBT		X				X	
Compensation for preference erosion			X	X			
Sanitary, phytosanitary and technical standards							
Help LDCs comply with sanitary, phytosanitary and technical standards	X	X				X	
Sanitary and phytosanitary standards shall not exceed equivalent international standards	X						X
Help LDCs effectively participate in international standard-setting bodies	X	X				X	
Standards shall not be used for protectionist purposes	X						X
Introduction of fast-track dispute settlement body in case of conflicts over SPS and TBT agreements		X		X			
Compensation for standards that are found to be inconsistent with SPS and TBT agreements	X	X		X			
Rules of origin							
In multilateral trading system, rules of origin should be harmonized for all countries	X						X
In multilateral trading system, rules of origin should not impede trade of LDCs	X						X
In preferential trade arrangements, rules of origin should be harmonized and simplified for LDCs	X	X			X		
Auxiliary agreements							
Trade-related intellectual property rights							
Patents: Non-patentability of all life forms	X	X	X				X
Patents: They shall not be granted without prior consent of country of origin	X	X	X				X
Patents: Countries shall be able to develop their own *sui generis* protection regimes	X	X	X				X
Patents: National protection regimes may cover plant varieties, recognized traditional knowledge and farmers' right to use, save and exchange seeds		X	X				X
Patents: National *sui generis* protection regimes may cover folklore	X	X					X
Patents: National protection regimes may cover biological and genetic resources		X	X				X
Patents: All protection regimes shall be consistent with the Convention on Bio-Diversity	X	X	X				X
Patents: All protection regimes shall be consistent with the International Treaty on Plant Genetic Resources for Food and Agriculture			X				X
Patents: TRIPS Agreement shall not endanger food security		X					X
Patents: Geographical indications shall be expanded beyond wines and spirits		X	X				X

Annex Table 3 (contd.)

Recommendations	Sun City, 1999	Zanzibar, 2001	Dhaka, 2003	Special and differential treatment	Preferential market access	Assistance	General
	by Declaration			by Category			
Patents: Geographical indications: LDCs need not provide legal means for enforcement			X	X			
Patents: LDCs should be provided with access to genetic resources		X		X			
Public health: Easy access to essential drugs		X	X	X			
Public health: Automatic compulsory licences for essential drugs	X			X			
Public health: No patentability of essential drugs		X					X
Implementation: Extension of transition periods for TRIPS	X	X	X	X			
Assistance: Member States should fulfil their obligation to provide assistance	X	X	X			X	
Assistance: Relevant agencies should also help LDCs implement the agreement	X					X	
Trade-related investment measures							
Open-ended transition period for agreement for LDCs	X			X			
Complete exemption from agreement for LDCs		X		X			
Singapore issues							
General issues							
Acknowledge start of negotiations after Fifth Minterial Conference in Cancún			X				X
Help LDCs understand implications of Singapore issues for their economies			X			X	
Trade and investment							
LDCs are not demandeurs of a multilateral investment agreements		X					X
Working Group shall highlight whether agreement can help LDCs to attract FDI and improve its quality	X	X	X			X	
Trade and environment							
Trade barriers, LDCs do not want environmental standards to be used for protectionist purposes		X					X
Trade barriers, LDCs want notification system for prohibited goods to increase transparency	X						X
Trade barriers, LDCs ask for enforceable obligation to provide assistance	X					X	
Trade barriers, LDCs encourage positive measures, i.e. capacity-building rather than trade restrictions	X					X	
Trade and competition							
LDCs expect Working Group to highlight implication of competition policy for their economies	X		X			X	
LDCs require help to implement competition law, policies and relevant institutions		X	X			X	
Trade and labour standards							
Labour standards should not be dealt with in the WTO	X						X
Trade and government procurement							
Working Group on issue shall shed light on how agreement would affect LDCs		X	X			X	
International trade rules							
Subsidies and countervailing measures							
Expansion of non-actionable category of subsidies	X	X		X			
Safeguards							
LDCs should not be subjected to any safeguard action	X	X	X	X			
LDCs should be able to impose safeguard actions without compensatory measures	X	X		X			
Anti-dumping							
LDCs should not be subjected to any anti-dumping action	X		X	X			
LDCs should benefit from simplified procedures to initiate anti-dumping actions	X	X	X	X			
Other contingency measures							
LDCs should not be subjected to any other contingency measure			X	X			
Customs valuation							
LDCs should benefit from an extension of the transition periods provided	X	X		X			
LDCs should be able to express reservations concerning minimum values for longer periods		X		X			
Pre-shipment inspections							
Sometimes helpful, but always burdensome							X
Dispute settlement							
Establishment of Legal Advisory Centre for LDCs	X					X	
General implementation issues							
Flexibility: Issues identified in the Decision on Implementation-related Issues and Concerns shall be addressed at Cancun			X	X			
Flexibility: All issues not identified in the Decision on Implementation-related Issues and Concerns shall be addressed on a priority basis			X	X			
Flexibility: Transition periods for implementation of Uruguay Round Agreements shall be extended to a realistic time frame	X			X			
Flexibility: No commitments that are not compatible with the LDCs' development status			X	X			
Simplification of notification requirements for LDCs	X			X			
Trade-related assistance							
General assistance as a right for LDCs and obligation for other member States and key agencies	X					X	
Improvement: Increase of budget of key agencies, including ITC, UNCTAD and WTO	X	X				X	
Improvement: Increase contribution to UNCTAD's Trust Fund in order to increase its support for LDCs		X				X	
Improvement: Welcome the establishment of/ encourage more contributions to WTO's Global Trust Fund to increase its assistance to LDCs			X			X	
Improvement: Special assistance to LDCs to address problems of smallness, remoteness and landlockedness, and economic vulnerability			X			X	
Type: Provide technical assistance to strengthen negotiation capacities	X	X				X	
Type: Provide technical assistance in accession process	X					X	
Type: Provide assistance to strengthen human capacities and ownership of programmes		X	X			X	
Type: Assistance to resolve all implementation-related issues	X	X	X			X	
Type: Assistance to comply with sanitary, phytosanitary and technical standards		X				X	
Type: Assistance to comply with rules of origin	X					X	
Type: Assistance to comply with stipulations of customs valuation and pre-shipment inspections	X					X	
Type: Assistance to build productive capacities		X	X			X	
Type: Assistance to strengthen trade-related infrastructures			X			X	
Type: Assistance to IF: Strengthen the entire framework	X					X	
Type: Assistance to IF: Increase funds available to core agencies		X	X			X	
Type: Assistance to IF: Increase focus on strengthening supply capacities			X			X	
Type: Assistance to IF: Increase focus on strengthening supply capacities			X			X	
Type: Assistance to IF: Strengthen follow-up to Trade Diagnostic Integration studies and move towards concrete projects			X			X	
Type: Assistance to IF: Monitor activities of IF and satisfy LDCs' trade-related capacity-building needs		X				X	
Type: Improve trade facilitation: does not require new rules, just more assistance		X				X	
Type: Improve trade facilitation: requires significant assistance in implementation matters			X			X	
Special and differential treatment		X	X	X			
Should be binding; "best-endeavour provisions" should be changed accordingly	X	X	X	X			
Should better target needs of least developed countries			X	X			
Should help to promote not only trade but also investments							
Sub-totals							
Messages in Sun City Declaration	70[b]			30	3	23	15
Messages in Zanzibar Declaration		76[b]		31	3	25	18
Messages in Dhaka Declaration			68	29	4	22	13

Source: UNCTAD secretariat compilation, based on the three LDC Declarations, which are available at the WTO (1999a, 2001b, 2003a).

a Special and differential treatment is requested only on a temporary basis.

b Both the Sun City Declaration and the Zanzibar Declaration entail a message with two requests, one for special and differential treatment and the other for financial assistance. In these two cases, the number of messages is therefore not equal to the number of implications.

Notes

1. Brown, Deardorff and Stern (2001) derive higher figures, whereas Van Meijl and Van Tongeren (2001) derive lower figures.

2. A realistic trade liberalization is described as one in which industrial countries are assumed to cut agricultural tariffs to no more than 10 percent and a target average of 5 percent, and to reduce tariffs on manufactured goods to no more than 5 percent and a target average of 1 per cent. Developing countries are assumed to implement corresponding ceiling averages of 15 and 10 percent for agriculture and 10 to 5 percent for manufacturing, respectively. There would be complete elimination of export subsidies, specific tariffs and tariff-rate quotas, and antidumping penalties (World Bank, 2003)

3. Other assumptions could be made, for example, that the share of the poverty reduction is proportional to the number of extremely poor people in the LDCs as a share of poor people in the low- and middle-income countries, or the share of LDCs trade in the trade of low- and middle-income countries.

4. This is based on UNCTAD (2002a) and Naschold (2001).

5. This projection assumes that the share of the population living in extreme poverty below $1/day will remain constant at 50 per cent.

6. Proposals for a food financing facility have been put forward to address these adverse effects (UNCTAD, 2003b)

7. The difference in estimations is attributable to differences in methods and policy scenarios. Whereas Hoekman et al. (2002) assume a 50 per cent reduction of domestic support, Peters (2004) assumes a 50 per cent reduction of export subsidies only.

8. These products are those products included in the FAO database on agricultural production that can be considered equivalent to the products that are included in the OECD database on agricultural support.

9. Producer support estimates include support derived from border measures i.e. trade policies. Support through payments to producers is lower. Values for 2001 were provisional at time of calculation. Please note that the level of producer support is only a rough indicator for the level of assistance or the level of protection. A more precise indicator for the former is the nominal assistance coefficient, and a more precise indicator for the latter is the nominal protection coefficient. For definition, see OECD PSE/CSE online database.

10. The table includes substitutes. Substitutes are goods that fall in the same family of products (based on the natural characteristic of the products) and/ or can be used for similar purposes. Safflower seeds, for example, are a direct substitute for rapeseeds because both fall into the category of oilseeds, but palm kernels are considered to be another substitute for rapeseeds, because they can also be used to make margarine. The classification of substitutes used here is a first attempt at systematic classification (Herrmann, 2003a).

11. Fiscal transfers are the sum of direct payments to producers, including payments based on output, on areas planted/animal numbers, historical entitlements, input use, input constraints, overall farming income and miscellaneous reasons. Average OECD support is based on 1991–2001 period, whereas average LDC output is based on 1991–2000 period.

12. According to the OECD, PSE/CSE database, in 2001 Mexico was the only OECD country to provide support for coffee; support was provided in form of consumer support.

13. Environment-related trade barriers include sanitary and phytosanitary measures (SPS) and technical barriers to trade (TBT), and are generally motivated by the desire to protect the environment, wildlife, plant health, animal health, human health and human safety, see Fontagné, von Kirchbach and Mimouni (2001).

14. Special challenges include the challenge to mainstream mineral policy and mineral revenue management into a national development agenda targeting both sustainability and inclusiveness, more precisely: to create sufficient incentives for investors and secure a fair share of mining revenues for public use; to increase transparency and accountability in management of mineral resources and rents; to protect the environment and social and cultural values; to implement an effective mineral tax system and adopt sound fiscal rules; to find means to distribute mineral rents more evenly throughout the economy; to link production enclaves with other economic sectors; and to manage shocks resulting from the instability of mineral revenues and prices.

15. This estimate is based on the database that is being used to monitor the Millennium Development Goals.

16. The overview is based on provisions of special and differential treatment in WTO Agreements of 1994 and the "Decision on Waiver" of 1999. It does not consider provisions entailed in other subsequent Ministerial Declarations and Decisions. It is important to emphasize that although the different agreements, declarations and

decisions are of a binding nature, the provisions of special and differential treatment within them are not necessarily of a binding nature.

17. On the concept of effective benefits see UNCTAD (2001a).

18. For an overview table of different preference schemes granted by the Quad countries, see Hoekman, Ng and Olarreaga (2001: 11, table 3).

19. This section is based on UNCTAD (2003d).

20. In the textiles industry, the concomitance of a peak in imports of fabrics and the low rate of utilization of preferences indicates that manufacturers in the relevant country have forgone tariff preferences because they cannot comply with rules of origin. This has been observed in Bangladesh and Cambodia, which have consistently imported fabrics rather than yarn. Their manufacturing industries are greatly dependent on the sourcing of fabrics from external suppliers, a factor of competitiveness that is generally more important than the use of market access preferences. On this issue, see UNCTAD (2003f).

21. The IMF has sought to quantify the possible effects of erosion of LDC preferential access to Quad markets, which has been published by the WTO (WTO, 2003a). According to this study, it appears that many LDCs do not appear to lose much because they are commodity exporters. The reason is that the MFN tariffs on unprocessed commodities which these countries export is relatively low and thus "there is not a lot of preference to be eroded in the first place" (WTO, 2003a:12). The general picture therefore is that a few LDCs are quite highly dependent on trade preferences for Quad markets, but many derive negligible effective benefits from them.

22. Afghanistan is a member of the Economic Cooperation Organization (ECO); Kiribati, the Solomon Islands, Tuvalu, Vanuatu and Western Samoa are members of the South Pacific Regional Trade and Economic Cooperation Agreement (SPARTECA); and the Solomon Islands and Vanuatu are also members of the Malaysian Spearhead Group (MSG). But none of these regional economic cooperation arrangements has been classified as a free trade area or a customs union by the WTO (2002b).

References

Appelbaum, R. (2003): Assessing the impact of the phasing-out of the Agreement on Textile and Clothing on apparel exports on the least developed and developing countries, mimeo.

Badine, O. et al. (2002). Cotton sector strategies in West and Central Africa, World Bank, Policy Research Working Paper 2867, Washington, DC.

Brenton, P. (2003). Integrating the least developed countries into the world trading system: The current impact of EU preferences under Everything But Arms, World Bank Working Paper 25619, Washington, DC.

Brown, D.K., A.V. Deardorff and R.M. Stern (2001). CGE modelling and analysis of multilateral and regional negotiation options, Research Seminar in International Economics, Discussion Paper No. 468.

CUTS Centre for International Trade, Economics and Environment (2002). Market access implications of SPS and TBT: Bangladesh perspective, Research Report, Jaipur, India.

Cernat, L., Laird, S. and Turrini, A. (2002). The EU's Everything But Arms initiative and the least developed countries, United Nations University, WIDER Discussion Paper No. 2003/47, Helsinki.

Cline, W. (2004): Trade Policy and Global Poverty. Center for Global Development and the Institute for International Economics, Washington, DC.

Collier, P. and Dehn, J. (2001). Aid shocks and growth, World Bank Working Paper 2688, Washington, DC.

Dehn, J. (2000). Commodity price uncertainty and shocks: Implications for economic growth, Center for the Study of African Economies Working Paper Series, No. 120, Oxford University.

Department for International Development (DFID) (2003). The extractive industries transparency initiative, Discussion Paper for International Stakeholders Meeting, 11–12 February 2003.

Fontagné, L., von Kirchbach, F. and Mimouni, M. (2001). A first assessment of environment-related trade barriers, CEPII Document de Travail no. 01–10.

Gabriele, A. and Vanzetti, D. (2004). Long black: Surviving the coffee crisis, background paper prepared for The Least Developed Countries Report 2004.

Global Witness (2004). Time for Transparency: Coming Clean on Oil, Mining and Gas Revenues, London, UK.

Gibbon, P. (2003). Commodities, donors, value-chain analysis and upgrading, background paper prepared for The Least Developed Countries Report 2004, Geneva.

Guillaumont, P. et al. (2003). Dampening the vulnerability to price shocks: A role for aid, background paper for the UNECA Expert Group Meeting on External Debt, Dakar, Senegal, 17–18 November 2003.

Hermann, R., Burger, K. and Smit, H.-P. (1993). *International Commodity Policy: A Quantitative Analysis*, Routledge, London.

Herrmann, M. (2003a). Agricultural support measures of developed countries, and agricultural production in least developed countries: Conceptualization of transmission effects, mimeo.

Herrmann, M. (2003b). Trading under adversity: The marginalization of least developed countries in world trade, mimeo.

Herrmann, M. (2004). Regional trade arrangements and trade flows: How important are they?, mimeo.

Hoekman, B., Michalopoulos, C. and Winters, A. (2003). Special and differential treatment for developing countries: Towards a new approach in the World Trade Organization, World Bank Policy Research Working Paper 3107, Washington, DC.

Hoekman, B. Ng, F. and Olarreaga, M. (2001). Eliminating excessive tariffs on exports of least developed countries, World Bank Policy Research Working Paper 2604, Washington, DC.

Hughes, A. and Brewster, H. (2002). Lowering the threshold: Reducing the costs and risks of private direct investment in least developed, small and vulnerable economies, Commonwealth Secretariat Economic Paper 50, London.

IMF (2003a). Cotton and developing countries: A case study in policy incoherence, Trade Note 10, 10 September 2003.

IMF (2003b). Fund assistance for countries facing exogenous shocks, Washington, DC.

Integrated Framework (2003). Diagnostic Trade Integration Study: Ethiopia.

Krut, R. and Moretz, A. (1999). Home country measures for encouraging sustainable FDI, report prepared for UNCTAD/ CBS Project: Cross-Border Environmental Management in Transnational Corporations.

Margalioth, Y. (2003). Tax competition, foreign direct investments and growth: Using the tax system to promote developing countries, *Virginia Tax Review*, 23: 157.

Mattoo, A, Roy, D. and Subramania, A. (2002). The AGOA and its rules of origin: Generosity Undermined?, World Bank Policy Research Working Paper 2908, Washington, DC.

Michalopoulos, C. (2000). The role of special and differential treatment for developing countries in GATT and the World Trade Organization, World Bank Working Paper 2388, Washington, DC.

Mistry, P. and Olesen, N. (2003). Mitigating risks for foreign investments in LDCs, Development Financing 2000 Project, Stockholm, Norstedts Tryckers AB.

Mortimore, M. (1999). Apparel-based industrialization in the Caribbean Basin: A threadbare garment? *CEPAL Review*, 67, April 1999.

Naschold (2001). Growth, distribution and poverty reduction: LDCs are falling further behind, background paper for *The Least Developed Countries Report 2002*.

Office of the US Trade Representative (2003). Comprehensive report by the President of the United States Congress on US trade and investment policy towards sub-Saharan Africa and implementation of the African Growth and Opportunity Act, the third of Eight Annual Reports, May, Washington DC.

Oxfam (2003). Cultivating poverty: The impact of US cotton subsidies on Africa, Briefing Paper 30, Oxford, UK.

Peters, R. (2004). Roadblock to reform: The persistence of agricultural export subsidies, mimeo.

Stevens, C. and Kennan, J. (2001). The impact of the EU's Everything But Arms Proposal: A report to Oxfam, mimeo, Institute for Development Studies at the University of Sussex, Brighton, UK.

Te Velde, D. W. (2002). Promoting TNC–SME linkages: The case for a global business linkage fund, Note prepared Overseas Development Institute, 5. December 2002.

UNCTAD (2000a). *The Least Developed Countries Report 2000: Aid, Private Capital Flows and External Debt: The Challenge of Financing Development in LDCs,* United Nations publication, sales no. E.00.II.D.21, New York and Geneva.

UNCTAD (2000b). Report of the Expert Meeting on Home Country Measures, held at the Palais des Nations, Geneva, from 8 to 10 November 2000, TD/B/Com.2/27 and TD/B/Com.2/EM.8/3EM.8/2, p. 11, tables 9 and 10.

UNCTAD (2001a). Least developed country status: Effective benefits and the question of graduation, TD/B/49/7, Geneva.

UNCTAD (2001b). Improving market access for least developed countries, UNCTAD/ DITC/ TNCD/ 4, Geneva.

UNCTAD (2002a). *The Least Developed Countries Report 2002: Escaping the Poverty Trap*, United Nations publication, sales no. E. 02.II.D.13, New York and Geneva.

UNCTAD (2002b). Report of the Expert Meeting on environmental requirements and international trade, TD/B/Com.1/EM.19/3, 8 November 2002, Geneva.

UNCTAD (2002c). Trade, environment and development, TD/B/Com.1/52, Geneva.

UNCTAD (2003a). *Back to Basics*, United Nations publication, sales no. E.03.II.D.4, New York and Geneva.

UNCTAD (2003b). Mechanisms for financing imports of basic foodstuffs by net food-importing developing countries and possibilities for improvement, background paper prepared for FAO Roundtable, 2 May 2003.

UNCTAD (2003c). Report of the meeting of Eminent Persons on commodity issues, held at the Palais des Nations, Geneva, 22–23 September 2003, TD/B/50/11, Geneva.

UNCTAD (2003d). Main recent initiatives in favour of least developed countries in the area of preferential market access: Preliminary impact assessment, TD/B/50/5, Geneva.

UNCTAD (2003e). *Investment Policy Review: Lesotho*, United Nations publication, sales no. E.03.II.D.18, Geneva.

UNCTAD (2003f). Trade preferences for LDCs: An early assessment of benefits and possible improvements, UNCTAD/ITCD/TSB/2003/8, New York and Geneva.

Van Meijl, H. and Van Tongeren, F. (2001). Multilateral trade liberalization and developing countries: A North-South perspective on agriculture and processing sectors, paper prepared for the Fourth Annual Conference on Global Economic Analysis, Purdue University, West Lafayette, Ind., 27–29 June

World Bank (2003). *Global Economic Prospects 2004: Realizing the Development Promise of the Doha Agenda*, Washington, DC.

WTO (1999a). The challenge of integrating LDCs into the multilateral trading system, coordinating workshop for senior advisers to ministers of trade in LDC in preparation for the Third WTO Ministerial Conference, Sun City, South Africa, 21–25 June 1999. WT/GC/W/251, 13 July 1999.

WTO (1999b). Guide to the Uruguay Round Agreements, Geneva.

WTO (2000a). Implementation of special and differential treatment provisions in WTO Agreements and Decisions. WT/COMTD/W/77, 25 October 2000.

WTO (2000b). Mapping of regional trade agreements, WT/REG/W/41, 11 October 2000.

WTO (2001a). Market access conditions for least developed countries, Note by the Secretariat: Revision, WT/LDC/SWG/IF/14/Rev.1, 20 April 2001; and Explanatory Notes: Addendum, WT/LDC/SWG/IF/14/Rev.1/Add.1, 25 April 2001.

WTO (2001b). Zanzibar Declaration, meeting of the ministers responsible for trade of the least developed countries, Zanzibar, United Republic of Tanzania, 22–24 July 2001, WT/L/409, 6 August 2001.

WTO (2002a). Basic information on regional trade agreements notified to GATT/WTO and in force, WT/REG/W/44, 7 February 2002.

WTO (2002b). Market access issues related to products of export interest originating from least developed countries, WT/ COMTD/ LDC/ W/ 2, 30 October 2002.

WTO (2003a). *World Trade Report*, Geneva.

WTO (2003b). Dhaka Declaration, meeting of the ministers responsible for trade of the least developed countries, Dhaka, Bangladesh, 31 May – 2 June 2003, WT/L/521, 26 June 2003.

WTO (2003c). Financing of losses from preference erosion: Note on issues raised by developing countries in the Doha Round, Communication from the International Monetary Fund, WT/ TF/ COH/ 14, 14 February 2003.

Improving the Trade–Poverty Relationship through National Development Strategies

A. Introduction

The improvements in the international trade regime discussed in the previous chapter should provide a framework for linking trade more effectively with poverty reduction in the LDCs. However, whether or not the increased opportunity for poverty reduction will be translated into reality depends on whether it is grasped at the national level. The fundamental priority here is that Governments formulate and implement national development strategies that integrate trade within them in a way that effectively promotes sustained development and substantial poverty reduction. This is critical because it is the area where the LDCs themselves potentially have the most leverage to make trade work for poverty reduction.

National development strategies will work best not simply if the international trade regime is enabling but also if increased and effective international financial and technical assistance is provided to the LDCs to help develop their production and trade capacities. The scale of investment needs, the paucity of domestic financial resources and technical know-how, the trade-off between domestic resource mobilization and poverty reduction, and the marginalization of the LDCs in international private capital flows all imply a need for such assistance. Policy incoherence between international assistance and national trade objectives, insufficient and misdirected aid for trade, and the failure to facilitate and nurture national ownership of trade and development policies can all undermine national efforts to grasp opportunities which changes in the international trade regime provide.

Whether or not the increased opportunity for poverty reduction will be translated into reality depends on whether it is grasped at the national level.

This chapter discusses how trade can be integrated into national development strategies in the LDCs, and how these efforts can be supported through international assistance for trade capacity development. For most LDCs, national strategies for poverty reduction are embodied in the Poverty Reduction Strategy Paper (PRSP), and it is intended that international assistance priorities be linked to these documents. The chapter thus begins (section B) by examining how trade issues are currently treated in the PRSPs. The evidence shows that it is a misconception to believe that trade issues are absent from the PRSPs. But there are various weaknesses in the way in which trade is integrated within them. Sections C and D propose an approach to integrate trade more closely into poverty reduction strategies. The essence of this approach is that it involves "two-way mainstreaming" of both trade and development into poverty reduction strategies.[1] Section C focuses on the first part of the approach and the question of integrating development into poverty reduction strategies by anchoring the latter in a broader national development strategy. A critical issue here is the choice of development strategy in the newly liberalized open economy, and a number of "post-liberal" development strategies are outlined in the annex to the chapter. Section D examines the second part of the approach, setting out a methodology for integrating trade into development-oriented poverty reduction strategies and noting the importance of establishing a durable trade policy framework within which this can be applied. Section E discusses policy issues in relation to international assistance for trade capacity development. The concluding section summarizes the major points.

B. Trade in Poverty Reduction Strategy Papers: Recent country experience

1. The evolution of the PRSP approach

In discussing how trade issues are treated in PRSPs, it is important to recognize that the PRSP approach has evolved considerably since it was first introduced at the end of 1999. As discussed in *The Least Developed Countries Report 2000* and *The Least Developed Countries Report 2002*, the first generation of PRSPs essentially sought to integrate pro-poor public expenditure patterns with deeper and broader structural reforms and the macroeconomic policies adopted in earlier structural adjustment programmes. In retrospect, this should not be seen as surprising. The preparation of the PRSP was introduced as a policy conditionality in the context of the Enhanced HIPC Initiative with the aim of ensuring that savings from debt relief were channelled into direct poverty reduction. It is in that context that the emphasis on social-sector expenditure arose. The more recent PRSPs are still linked to policy conditionality for debt relief within the HIPC Initiative, but they have tended to focus much more on the sources of growth and the ways in which it be made more pro-poor.

The more recent PRSPs are still linked to policy conditionality for debt relief within the HIPC Initiative, but they have tended to focus much more on the sources of growth and the ways in which it be made more pro-poor.

Table 57 summarizes the priority actions identified in the Action Matrices of the most recent 13 full PRSPs completed in the LDCs as of March 2002. From the table it is clear that there is diversity, but in a number of the PRSPs a common pattern is emerging in the approach of many of the poverty reduction strategies since mid-2002. This common pattern has four basic pillars:

(i) Ensure strong and sustainable economic growth;

(ii) Develop human resources;

(iii) Improve the living conditions of the poor and vulnerable;

(iv) Ensure good governance.

In addition, the PRSPs generally treat cross-cutting issues such as gender, environment and HIV/AIDS.

Within each of these basic pillars, a number of common concerns also arise. Under pillar one continued emphasis is placed on stabilization, liberalization and privatization, as in the old structural adjustment programmes. But investment in basic infrastructure (transport and communications, energy, and water and sanitation), private sector development, export promotion and the creation of a better investment climate have also emerged as priority concerns in most recent PRSPs. Under pillar two, the priorities are adequate health and education systems and also labour market policies. Under pillar three, social protection, micro-finance and food security are recurrent concerns. Under pillar four, the recurrent objectives are the establishment of efficient, accountable and transparent management of public resources, democratic decision-making, decentralization of basic services to local levels of governance and the prevention of corruption and fraud.

TABLE 57. MAJOR PRIORITY ACTIONS IN RECENT PRSPs OF LDCs

	Benin (Dec. 2002)	Cambodia (Dec. 2002)	Chad (June 2003)	Ethiopia (July 2002)	Gambia (April 2002)	Madagascar (July 2003)	Malawi (April 2002)	Mali (May 2002)	Nepal (May 2003)	Rwanda (June 2002)	Senegal (May 2002)	Yemen (May 2002)	Zambia (March 2002)
1. Ensure strong and sustainable growth	X	X	X	X	X	X	X	X	X	X	X	X	X
Stabilize macroeconomic framework	X	X	X	X	X		X	X	X	X	X	X	X
Pro-poor fiscal policies	X	X	X	X			X	X	X	X	X	X	X
Monetary policy		X	X				X		X	X	X	X	X
Private sector promotion	X	X	X	X	X	X	X	X	X	X	X	X	X
Export promotion		X	X	X		X	X	X	X		X	X	X
Develop basic infrastructure	X	X	X	X	X	X	X	X	X	X	X	X	X
Roads	X	X	X	X	X	X	X	X	X	X	X	X	X
Energy	X	X	X	X	X		X	X	X	X	X	X	X
Water and sanitation	X	X	X	X	X	X	X	X	X	X	X	X	X
2. Development of human resources	X	X	X	X	X	X	X	X	X	X	X	X	X
Adequate health system	X	X	X	X	X	X	X	X	X	X	X	X	X
Adequate education system	X	X	X	X	X	X	X	X	X	X	X	X	X
Adequate labour market policy	X	X	X	X	X	X	X	X	X	X	X		X
3. Improve living conditions of the poor	X	X	X	X	X		X	X	X	X	X	X	X
Social protection	X	X	X		X		X		X	X	X	X	X
Micro-finance schemes	X	X		X	X						X		
Food security	X	X		X			X	X	X				X
4. Good governance	X	X	X	X	X	X	X	X	X	X	X	X	X

Source: UNCTAD secretariat compilation, based on Poverty Reduction Strategy Papers.

The new emphasis on sources of economic growth is a welcome development since it is through sustained economic growth that poverty reduction will take place in LDCs. The nature of the PRSPs still reflects the limitation of national capacities for policy analysis and the consequent need to rely on external expertise. According to senior African policy experts at the third annual meeting of the African learning group of PRSPs, "While the PRSP is an important conceptual shift in development thinking, there is still a lack of symmetry between the objectives and priorities of the PRSP and sectoral plans and strategies. In particular, macroeconomic projections in some PRSPs appear to be too optimistic and inconsistent with country realities. In a number of cases, the growth strategies are not country-specific" (ECA, 2003). The IMF and World Bank similarly point to the problem of "weak links in many PRSPs between overall strategic goals and priority public actions" (IMF/World Bank, 2003: 21). This is particularly evident in relation to the pursuit of strong and sustainable economic growth. Although increased attention is paid to sources of economic growth, "the choices of priority public actions in PRSPs are still not derived from the identified growth sources and risks. In some cases, this is because PRSPs have not adequately identified future sources of growth to guide policy choices. Yet, even where analysis of the sources of growth was undertaken, priority areas are not always linked to the identified obstacles to growth. Thus, proposed public resource allocations are not informed by potential returns on investments in different activities" (ibid.: 20).

The PRSPs are evolving away from the old structural adjustment programmes towards new growth strategies which seek to include the poor. But this transition is still incomplete.

The current situation with regard to the PRSP approach can best be understood as one in which the PRSPs are evolving away from the old structural adjustment programmes towards new growth strategies which seek to include the poor. But this transition is still incomplete. There remain strong concerns about how the ideal of national ownership and policy autonomy can actually be realized in situations where capacities are weak and aid and debt relief dependence are high (see UNCTAD, 2002, for more on the tension between conditionality and ownership).

2. THE TREATMENT OF TRADE ISSUES IN PRSPs

The way in which the PRSPs treat trade issues needs to be understood against this background. There is a general impression that trade is not integrated within the PRSPs. This view underpinned the first evaluation of the Integrated Framework for Trade-Related Technical Assistance in 2000, which recommended that the IF be reoriented to ensure that trade is mainstreamed within PRSPs. This has also been suggested by NGOs, notably Christian Aid, which has argued that trade issues are absent from PRSPs, and particularly the participation process, because the issue of trade reform is "too hot to handle" (Ladd, 2002). The major systematic published analysis of trade in PRSPs, which includes PRSPs up to July 2002, concluded as follows: "...first, the extent and depth of trade coverage in completed PRSPs is limited...Second, the trade content that does exist within PRSPs is rarely underpinned by poverty analysis...Third, within existing PRSPs, some trade policy choices have been considered, but few developing countries go beyond a simple discussion of standard export promotion measures. Supply-side issues which facilitate trade and complement trade policy e.g. infrastructure, marketing, etc. appear to be well-covered in PRSPs and, therefore, require urgent donor attention and resources" (Hewitt and Gillson, 2003: 15–16).

Trade issues have come to occupy a much more central place in the PRSPs. The main problem now is not that trade is not integrated within the PRSPs, but the way in which it is being treated.

Systematic analysis of how trade is treated in the PRSPs of LDCs indicates that there is indeed some validity to the view that trade was not treated in the PRSPs in the past. But with the evolution of the PRSPs towards growth strategies which seek to include the poor, trade issues have come to occupy a much more central place in the PRSPs. The main problem now is not that trade is not integrated within the PRSPs, but the way in which it is being treated.

Trade issues are dealt with in the recent PRSPs of the LDCs in two ways. Firstly, projections of export growth and import growths are part of the macroeconomic framework. These projections occur in all PRSPs and are one of the major quantitative targets in the document. Because of this, trade is already right at the heart of every PRSP. Secondly, the main text of the PRSP includes a wide range of trade objectives and trade policies related to those objectives. In most of the PRSPs prepared by the LDCs there is no separate trade section. But there is no reason to believe that these documents downplay the importance of international trade for both economic growth and poverty reduction.

Chart 42 shows projections of trends of GDP, exports and imports within the macroeconomic frameworks of five LDCs for which it is possible to make comparisons with trends in the recent past. There are four general tendencies in the projections. Firstly, it is expected that GDP growth will be higher than the trend growth rate of the last five years in all cases. Secondly, it is expected that export growth will be higher than the trend growth rate of the last five years in all cases except one, namely Senegal. Thirdly, it is expected that the import intensity of growth will decline in all cases but one. This is contrary to the evidence of what has happened after trade liberalization (see chapter 5). Moreover, in three of the five countries import growth is also projected to grow at a slower rate than GDP.[2] Fourthly, the major part of the increase in GDP is expected to come from export expansion. The only exception, Senegal, is the only country in which an acceleration in the export growth rate is not expected, and it follows that the source of accelerated economic growth is unclear.

These trade objectives in the macroeconomic framework "float freely", having no connection with the more detailed trade objectives and policy measures contained in the main text of the PRSP. There is no analysis of the links

CHART 42. PAST TRENDS AND PROJECTIONS OF GDP, EXPORTS AND IMPORTS IN THE MACROECONOMIC FRAMEWORK OF SELECTED LDCs
($, million)

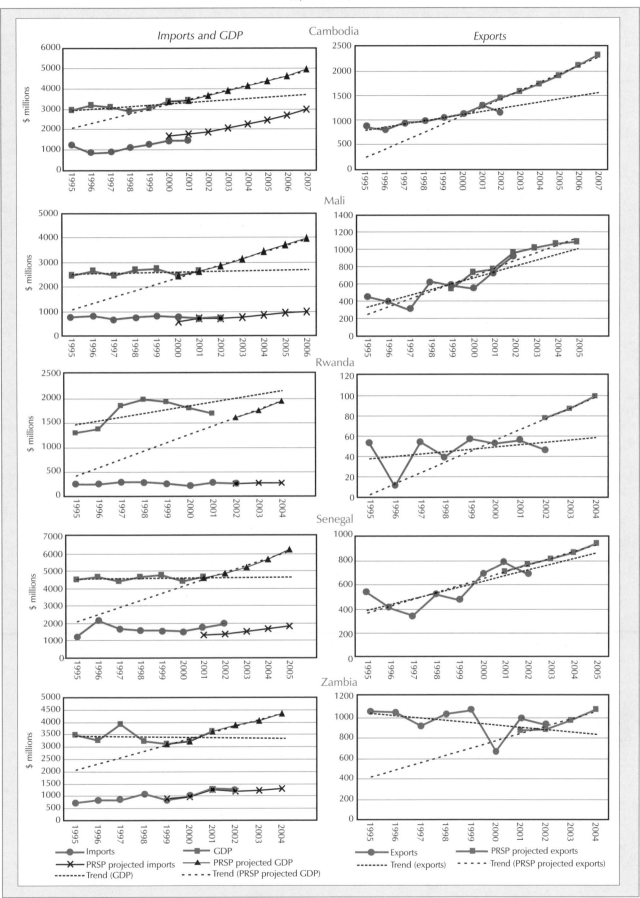

Source: UNCTAD secretariat estimates. The projections are the figures contained in the PRSPs, whilst past trends are based on World Bank, *World Development Indicators 2003*, CD-ROM; and on UN COMTRADE from UNCTAD, *Handbook of Statistics 2003*.

Note: The PRSPs' figures for Mali and Senegal were in local currency and were changed into dollars using the estimated exchange rate included in the PRSP of Mali. The PRSP's GDP figure for Rwanda was also in local currency and was changed into dollars using the exchange rate for 2002 of 511.85, taken from IMF, *International Financial Statistics 2003*, CD-ROM. All data are in current dollars.

between trade and growth. But all the PRSPs include increased openness as an objective. Openness is not always defined in the PRSPs, but it is generally understood as either reduced or more rationalized tariff barriers, or an increased contribution of exports to GDP. The general assumption seems to be that increased openness and/or increased exports will accelerate economic growth. Although it is not often stated, the growth strategy that implicitly underpins these PRSPs is primarily an export-led growth strategy.

Although it is not often stated, the growth strategy that implicitly underpins these PRSPs is primarily an export-led growth strategy.

Table 58 summarizes, as well as possible, the trade policy objectives and policy measures contained in 13 PRSPs as of March 2002. Undertaking such a synopsis entails some qualitative judgements. But it is clear that, as well as openness, increased competitiveness and export diversifications are important objectives in almost all the PRSPs. The development of tourism is seen as important in 12 countries, export-oriented manufacturing in seven countries and high-value-added agricultural products also in seven countries. There is much less consideration of import issues, with no PRSP mentioning better procurement as an objective, one mentioning infant industry protection and five mentioning the need to reduce the import content of domestic consumption. In terms of policy measures, improving infrastructure is seen as the most important issue. Export promotion is identified as a trade policy measure in eight cases, financial incentive schemes for exporters in four cases and the creation of an

TABLE 58. SPECIFIC TRADE POLICY OBJECTIVES AND INSTRUMENTS IN RECENT PRSPs OF LDCs

	Benin	Cambodia	Chad	Ethiopia	Gambia	Malawi	Madagascar	Mali	Nepal	Rwanda	Senegal	Yemen	Zambia
Trade policy objectives													
Openness	x	x	x	x	x	x	x	x	x	x	x	x	x
Export diversification	x	x	x		x		x	x	x	x	x	x	x
Increase competitiveness	x	x	x	x	x	x	x		x		x		x
Development of high-value agricultural products		x		x	x	x	x		x		x		
Development of export-oriented manufacturing activities		x	x	x					x	x		x	x
Trade facilitation	x	x			x	x	x		x		x		x
Tourism development	x	x		x	x	x	x	x	x	x	x	x	x
Reduce import content of domestic consumption to decrease BOP deficit		x		x	x	x					x		
Strengthening production and consumption linkages				x									
Trade policy instruments													
Suitable exchange rate policy				x	x	x	x		x	x		x	
Export promotion policies		x		x	x		x	x			x	x	x
Financial incentive schemes for exporters	x		x					x	x				
Policies aimed at reducing economic weaknesses (e.g. regulatory, geographical and infrastructure)	x	x	x			x	x	x	x		x	x	x
Regionalism	x		x				x				x	x	x
Free economic zones/EPZ		x			x		x					x	x
Cascading tariffs							x						
Infant industry protection		x											
Commercial diplomacy		x											x
Access to developed countries' markets		x					x				x		
Market exports abroad										x			x

Source: UNCTAD secretariat estimates, based on Poverty Reduction Strategy Papers.

export processing zone in five cases. Surprisingly, a suitable exchange rate policy is only mentioned in about half the PRSPs (7). Enhanced regional relationships are important for six countries. However, there is no analysis of demand-side constraints on exports, and only a few of the PRSPs identify commercial diplomacy and access to developed country markets as a means of achieving trade objectives.

An important feature of the way in which the PRSPs treat trade issues is that trade development is closely related to issues of private sector development, the improvement of the investment climate and also the development of productive sectors. Indeed, one reason why it is difficult to isolate the trade objectives and trade policy measures in the PRSPs is that trade is treated in an integrated way with the development of productive capacities and also private sector development. There is an important insight here which should not be lost through an effort to give greater priority to trade per se. The linking of trade to private sector development and the development of production capacities within the PRSPs are an important signal from the LDCs to their development partners on the best way to support trade development in these countries.

One reason why it is difficult to isolate the trade objectives and trade policy measures in the PRSPs is that trade is treated in an integrated way with the development of productive capacities and also private sector development.

Trade objectives and trade measures are, nevertheless, treated in quite a general way. There is no analysis of the impact of past trade policies as a basis for moving forward. There is also little analysis of the links between trade and poverty.

One influence on the content of trade within PRSPs has been the implementation of the Integrated Framework for Trade-Related Technical Assistance (IF). This initiative, which will be discussed in more detail in section E, has led to a much fuller treatment of trade in the Cambodia PRSP. This PRSP differs from almost all the other PRSPs because employment generation is a central focus of the strategy. But this reflects the priority of the Government rather than the influence of the IF. The IF has also led to the inclusion of a more-focused section on trade in the Mauritania PRSP Progress Report. However, in contrast to these cases, the influence of the Diagnostic Trade Integration Study (DTIS) on the Madagascar PRSP appears to be negligible. This may reflect the fact that the DTIS was only finished in June 2003, one month before the completion of the PRSP.

Through the macroeconomic framework, quantified trade targets are at the heart of all the PRSPs.

Finally, it is worth noting that how the PRSP works also depends on the practices of the LDCs' development partners. The PRSPs are intended to work as a nationally owned strategy to which the donors and the international financial institutions gear their operations. But in practice, according to senior African policy makers, "Africa's partners have been very slow in changing adjusting their aid policies to the PRSP approach" (ECA, 2003). Hewitt and Gillson (2003: 9) find that "in a number of cases" PRSPs were consistent with IMF Poverty Reduction and Growth Facility (PRGF) programmes and World Bank Poverty Reduction Support Credit (PRSC) programmes. But 4 of the 10 LDCs in their sample of countries were exceptions. Loan documents did not mention the agricultural-development-led-industrialization strategy of Ethiopia; referred to food import subsidies and adjustment to trade taxes which were not mentioned in the Malawi PRSP; provided much more sectoral discussion of trade policy than the Tanzania PRSP; and included discussion of regional and preferential trade agreements not mentioned in the Uganda PRSP (ibid.: 9–10).

To sum up, although spread widely in the documents, trade is covered in the PRSPs. Through the macroeconomic framework, quantified trade targets are at the heart of all the PRSPs. Moreover, the implicit underlying growth strategy in all of them seems to be export-led growth based on the adoption of an open trade regime. The way in which the PRSPs link the issues of trade development, private sector development and the development of productive sectors has important implications for donor support for trade development. It implies that isolating trade policies as the mechanism of trade development is likely to run counter to the approach which is common in many PRSPs.

The main weakness in the way trade is treated in the PRSPs is the same weakness as that which generally pertains to all policy issues in the PRSP, namely the overall strategic goals are only loosely related to priority public actions. This is particularly evident in the lack of any connection whatsoever between the macroeconomic framework and trade objectives. There is also an imbalance in the PRSPs between the way in which they treat exports and imports, and between demand-side and supply constraints in analysis of trade. The documents do not have a methodology for linking trade with growth and poverty reduction.

C. Mainstreaming development into poverty reduction strategies

The main weakness in the way trade is treated in the PRSPs is the same weakness as that which generally pertains to all policy issues in the PRSP, namely the overall strategic goals are only loosely related to priority public actions.

This section and the next one set out an approach to mainstreaming trade within poverty reduction strategies. The approach is a development approach that is founded on the view that substantial poverty reduction in the LDCs requires sustained economic growth and the development of productive capacities. Its analytical focus is not on the process of adjustment, identifying how poor people are affected during trade liberalization and identifying the complementary policies which need to be in place to alleviate poverty during trade policy reform and to ensure that poor people benefit from this process.[3] Rather, it focuses on identifying trade development objectives that are important for sustained economic growth and long-term development, and the trade policies, including trade liberalization, and non-trade policies, that can facilitate the achievement of those objectives.

This development approach has two steps. Firstly, the poverty reduction strategy is anchored in a national development strategy. Secondly, trade policies are integrated within the development-oriented poverty reduction strategy.

1. THE ELEMENTS OF A DEVELOPMENT-ORIENTED POVERTY REDUCTION STRATEGY

The basic idea of anchoring a poverty reduction strategy in a national development strategy and thus producing a development-oriented approach to poverty reduction strategy is set out in *The Least Developed Countries Report 2002*. The essence of the approach is that priority public actions within the three-year poverty reduction strategies would be derived from an overall long-term national development strategy. The development strategy contains a long-term vision of national development objectives; the strategic elements required to achieve these objectives and their sequencing; and the policy measures and processes required to achieve the objectives. Within a development-oriented approach to poverty reduction strategies, short-term and medium-term issues of macroeconomic stabilization and improvement of the efficiency of resource allocation would not be ignored. But poverty reduction strategies should be anchored in long-term development strategies rather than being dominated by short-term macroeconomic goals of stabilization together with perpetual economic reform aimed at increasing the efficiency of resource allocation. The approach would seek to achieve substantial and sustained poverty reduction through development rather than to ensure that during stabilization and adjustment poverty is alleviated.

From the analysis in this Report, the basic objective of a development-oriented poverty reduction strategy in the LDCs should be to promote rapid and sustained economic growth in a form that will increase average household incomes and consumption substantially. As shown in chapter 2, part two, in situations of mass poverty, doubling average household incomes and consumption should go a long way to reducing the incidence of extreme poverty by half. This can be achieved through a combination of (i) growth-oriented macroeconomic and trade policies which seek to accelerate the rate of capital accumulation in a sustainable way and relax the balance-of-payments constraint; and (ii) sectorally-focused productive development policies which seek to build productive capacities and accelerate learning through meso-level policies (aimed at specific sectors or addressing intersectoral coordination problems) and micro-level policies focused on enterprise development. These policies need to be applied in a way in which the working-age population becomes more and more fully and productively employed. Policies to prevent intra-country marginalization must also be put in place. These should be particularly aimed at increasing the assets of poorer social groups and also the productivity of those assets, including through agricultural reform, SME development and micro-credit. Micro-export projects can also be used to develop export activities in poor communities. An effective and innovative approach to formulate and implement such projects has been elaborated by the International Trade Centre (ITC) (see box 17).

Trade policy is an essential and integral component of the whole set of policies that are together designed to achieve the growth and poverty reduction objectives. The other policies are not complementary to trade policy; rather, all complement one another. Trade policy alone is unlikely to be sufficient to meet even national trade objectives. This requires macroeconomic policies that are appropriate (in terms of the level and stability of exchange rates and also interest rates) and sectorally-focused productive development policies (including enterprise development, research and development, and the building of technology capabilities, physical infrastructure investment, human resource development, and financial policy to ensure that enterprises have access to credit).

2. THE CHOICE OF DEVELOPMENT STRATEGY

Within this general framework it is possible to envisage different development strategies being implemented. The choice of development strategy is a critical issue as it has very important effects on future poverty reduction prospects. Indeed it is this choice, much more than any poverty-oriented projects, that can do most to ensure that the growth process is broad-based and inclusive. As Adelman (1986) has put it with particular clarity, "If one takes the initial distribution of assets and the structure of institutions as given, the major determinant of the course of income inequality and poverty becomes the overall development strategy chosen" (p. 56).

The reasons why the choice of development strategy is so important, Adelman explains, is that "Each strategy is associated with a special configuration of the structure of production and a particular pattern of factor

Poverty reduction strategies should be anchored in long-term development strategies rather than dominated by short-term macroeconomic goals of stabilization together with perpetual economic reform.

Trade policy is an essential and integral component of the whole set of policies that are together designed to achieve the growth and poverty reduction objectives. The other policies are not complementary to trade policy; rather, all complement one another.

"If one takes the initial distribution of assets and the structure of institutions as given, the major determinant of the course of income inequality and poverty becomes the overall development strategy chosen"

BOX 17. MICRO-EXPORT PROJECTS: THE EXPORT-LED POVERTY REDUCTION PROGAMME OF THE INTERNATIONAL TRADE CENTRE (ITC)

In 2002, the International Trade Centre (ITC) launched the Export-Led Poverty Reduction Programme (EPRP). The goal of this programme is to integrate poor communities into international markets. The programme is innovative, with similar potential in the international trade as micro-credit has had in the field of finance.

The EPRP approach rests on two main pillars: (i) the development of the entrepreneurial capacity of the poor with regard to exporting; and (ii) linking that capacity to proven export market opportunities. EPRP projects focus on five sectors based on analysis of demand in regional or international markets and the employment and income-generating potential of these sectors for poor communities. The sectors are:

- Agricultural products (fresh and processed)
- Textiles (fibres and clothing)
- Animal skins leather and leather goods
- Light manufacturing
- Community-based tourism

The viability of proposed projects in the above sectors are assessed via feasibility studies by interested national governments, and together with the ITC, which analyses international market trends, a final project blueprint and action plan is put in place. The feasibility studies address ten key considerations (see box chart 4 below):

1. *Identifying winning products and growth markets.* Projects are selected on the basis of the growth potential of the product in question, and the existence of stable demand for the product. An attempt is made to identify products that can mobilize dormant or under-utilized production capacities by adapting them to the specifications of a clearly identified product-market demand.

2. *Product development, product adaptation, standards and quality.* The product to be exported must be competitive in international markets and meet international quality requirements. The ITC provides technical assistance for this purpose (i.e. assistance at this stage could involve aiding producers in seeking ISO certification, technological support in production and adaptation of the product to the market, or assistance in quality control and packaging). Other examples of assistance are aiding producers with trial orders before a large-scale export order is made to identify and correct any potential problems.

3. *Selecting and organizing poor producers.* The ITC plays a role in ensuring poor producers are organized in some type of network – in cooperatives and other modes – through which they can achieve a sufficient scale to produce, market and distribute their products. In this respect the ITC identifies, trains, and provides funding for local NGOs, whose role would be to build networks/structure the grouping of poor producers, or to ensure increased participation of producers in an existing grouping, in addition to facilitating their training in marketing, production and entrepreneurship. In many countries, groups of export producers have been formed, referred to as "Export Production Villages" (EPVs).

4. *Selecting the right product market for the producer organization.* A key aspect is the ability of the productive organization (poor producers) to sustain production under competitive conditions, as well as its ability to productive organization to meet changing competitive demands. Attention is paid to the strength of the exporter in international markets (see next point).

5. *Linking producers to buyers.* Another crucial element of the EPRP is identifying a "middleman" to link producers and international buyers. This may be an export house, a production house (in the case that products need to be further processed before export) or a producer cooperative, capable of gathering market intelligence and with knowledge of export markets and product requirements. The "export value chain" can take multiple forms, for example, EPVs may export directly or producers may subcontract to other exporters. It is important that there is an equitable relationship between producers and intermediaries/exporters with respect to the sharing of benefits of exporting.

6. *Financing and credit.* Because inaccessibility to credit is one of the major obstacles for small producers to start-up export operations, part of the ITC's role is to find alternative credit sources for EPRP projects, including via formal micro-credit schemes, export-contractors, or other means. The underlying premise is that although government or donor-sponsored funds may be utilized initially, more self-sufficient financing schemes must be set up in the long run to ensure the viability of the project in question.

7. *Human resources.* The development of appropriate managerial skills with a view to making poor producers self-sufficient in the long-run is a key issue addressed via training. The training needs for partners at various levels of the "export value chain" are identified at the outset of the project.

Box 17 (contd.)

8. *Support services*. These are provided by international development organizations, local NGOs, and the private sector. They are necessary to build the capacities of producers and exporters. A needs assessment is done at the outset of the project and adapted throughout the process.

9. *Gender*. Women's participation and their contribution are important considerations in the EPRP.

10. *Environmental considerations*. The production of environmentally friendly products is also considered.

These criteria are not only the "building blocks" of this ITC Programme, but also simultaneously serve to define and guide project benchmarks during the process. For the project to be viable all of the building blocks must be in place. In addition, the entire process is benchmarked, and attention is paid so that it fits the country's national development strategy and priority areas, and that it is complementary to the work of other development partners. Up to the present, the ITC has already launched pilot projects in 11 countries: Afghanistan, Bolivia, Brazil, Cambodia, China, El Salvador, the Islamic Republic of Iran, Kenya, Nepal, South Africa and Viet Nam.

The EPRP is an important initiative due to its potential in enhancing the productive capacities of poor, small-scale producers. The programme also develops networks to share best practice in order to multiply the effects of localized micro-export projects,.

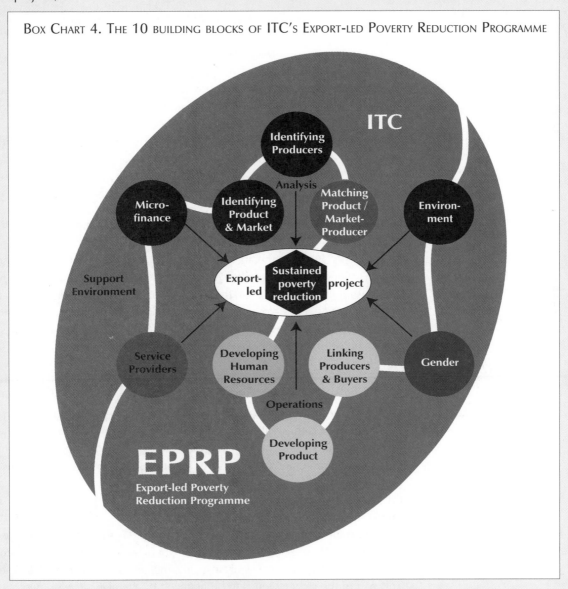

BOX CHART 4. THE 10 BUILDING BLOCKS OF ITC'S EXPORT-LED POVERTY REDUCTION PROGRAMME

Source: ITC (2001a); Raghavendran (2003).

use. It is the development strategy that determines the pre-tax, pre-transfer (i.e. the primary) distribution of income. It governs the speed of absorption of labor into the modern sector, the extent of the income gap that develops between the modern and the traditional sectors, and the degree of income inequality within sectors" (ibid.: 56). She continues: "Once the choice of development strategy has jelled, policies and programs aimed at changing the primary distribution of income can accomplish very little. This is true of both transfer programs and poverty-oriented projects. The size distribution of income tends to be quite stable around the trend established by the basic choice of development strategy. Following any intervention, even one sustained over time, the size distribution of income tends to return to the pre-intervention distribution. Only large, well-designed, complementary packages of anti-poverty policies and programs can change the primary distribution of income somewhat; but, to be effective, they must essentially amount to a gradual change in the overall development strategy" (ibid.: 56).

3. POST-LIBERAL DEVELOPMENT STRATEGIES

Given the importance of the choice of development strategy for poverty reduction, a critical question facing the LDCs at the moment is what development strategies can be adopted in a newly liberalized open economy and what policies can be adopted to implement such strategies.

Given the importance of the choice of development strategy for poverty reduction, a critical question facing the LDCs at the moment is what development strategies can be adopted in a newly liberalized open economy and what policies can be adopted to implement such strategies. There is, in short, a need for clear thinking about post-liberal development strategies.[4] These are development strategies that would be pursued after trade liberalization and that can be implemented in an open-economy trade regime in which incentives are biased in favour neither of exports nor of imports and in which there is no discrimination between agriculture and manufacturing sectors.

Export-led growth is one obvious post-liberal development strategy. It is the growth strategy that, in some form or other, implicitly underpins many of the recent PRSPs. But from the analysis in this Report, it is unlikely that an export-led growth strategy in its pure form will of itself lead to a virtuous trade–poverty relationship in the LDCs. In the context of the LDCs, where most of the population lives at or below income levels which are sufficient to meet only their basic needs, export-led growth is generally synonymous with an exclusionary growth trajectory with benefits concentrated in an enclave.

It is possible that a hybrid strategy combining export-led growth with a basic needs strategy is emerging...

Against this background, it is possible that a hybrid strategy combining export-led growth with a basic needs strategy is emerging. Within this new synthesis, the export-led growth part of the strategy is founded on trade liberalization together with deepening "behind-the-border" measures, such as trade facilitation, to tackle internal rather than border constraints on international trade, and also measures to increase the export supply response to trade liberalization. Increased efforts may also be made to foster linkages so that the effects of export growth reach poorer groups and poorer regions. At the same time, the basic-needs part of the strategy focuses on providing basic social services to the population, and ensuring that there is some minimal safety net to offset the worst adjustment costs of trade liberalization for poor groups and also to provide some protection against any increased post-liberal vulnerabilities. This part of the strategy tends to be financed by the LDC development partners. They are allocating development assistance increasingly to meet social expenditure.

This strategy is certainly likely to result in a more positive trade–poverty relationship than in a pure export-led growth strategy. However, it remains to be seen whether it will be sustainable or inclusive. As limited international assistance becomes absorbed more and more in basic needs provision, it is less available for developing the production sectors and private sector development. The great danger of this strategy is that countries will end up with a deepening debt problem. Increased inclusiveness could be achieved through seeking, at the outset, to change the distribution of assets and the structure of institutions. But in the absence of this, transfer programmes and poverty-oriented projects will be working against the grain of the effects of the development strategy for poverty reduction.

...However, it remains to be seen whether this strategy will be sustainable or inclusive.

Some argue that the deficiencies of an export-led growth strategy are so great that there is a need now for "domestic-demand-led development strategies" (Palley, 2002). This view is particularly associated with the conviction that there is a fallacy of composition in the sense that while an export-led growth strategy might work for one country or a few countries, the simultaneous pursuit of export-led growth by many developing countries will lead to adverse terms-of-trade shifts and "diminishing returns to export-led growth" (Blecker, 2002). This Report has not examined this issue, focusing instead on the question of the inclusiveness of export-led growth in the LDCs. However, the analysis in the Report strongly indicates that export growth is important for the LDCs (see also Felipe, 2003). An appropriate approach to achieve a more virtuous trade–poverty relationship may be an open development strategy which seeks to achieve adequate export growth rather than export-led growth (on this idea, see Vos et al., 2004). In an export-led growth strategy export expansion is the major demand-side component of economic growth. By contrast, in a strategy that seeks adequate export growth, both export expansion and domestic demand expansion are important demand-side components of economic growth. There is thus more balance between domestic demand and export expansion in the process of growth.

There are various possible open development strategies in which export growth is an important component but in which there is more balance between domestic demand and export expansion in the process of economic growth. These include but are not limited to:

There are various possible open development strategies in which export growth is an important component but in which there is more balance between domestic demand and export expansion in the process of economic growth.

- A balanced growth strategy based on agricultural productivity growth and export-accelerated industrialization;

- An agricultural-development-led industrialization (ADLI) strategy – which includes infrastructure investment and technological progress in agriculture together with forward linkages into processing activities – with an export component;

- Development and diversification through management of mineral revenues;

- Development of natural-resource-based production clusters;

- A triadic development strategy which includes the promotion of competitive tradables, employment-intensive non-tradables and labour-saving technological change in subsistence-oriented activities.

The key features of these alternative post-liberal development strategies are set out in the annex to this chapter.

4. POLICIES FOR PROMOTING DEVELOPMENT

Whatever strategy is followed, new types of policies will be required in order to promote development in the new open trading environment. A key insight which must be grasped here is that free trade is not the same as laissez-faire. One of the strongest advocates of the benefits of free trade, Jagdish Bhagwati, has emphasized this point, recognizing the effects of distortions or market failures on the case for free trade. He writes that "free trade could not be declared the necessarily best policy for a small country in the presence of a distortion". But "if the distortion was in domestic markets… a domestic policy, suitably designed and targeted to offsetting that distortion, could be combined with free trade to produce the best outcome" (Bhagwati, 2001: 26–27). It is also notable that the most successful experiences of development and poverty reduction in developing countries, namely those in East Asia, have involved a combination of outward orientation with domestic intervention, the latter seeking to support rather than supplant market mechanisms (see, *inter alia,* Bradford, 1994, and UNCTAD, 1994, 1996).

In implementing post-liberal development strategies, public policies in LDCs should use market-supporting mechanisms aimed at market creation, market development and market acceleration.

In implementing post-liberal development strategies, public policies in LDCs should use market-supporting mechanisms aimed at market creation, market development and market acceleration. These policies should not simply provide the right price incentives, but also create the right institutions and the infrastructure necessary for a modern market economy to function properly. The provision of public goods that address the current gaps and shortages in the productive sectors of LDCs is vital. New investment should also be directed towards increasing the absorption capacity of imported technologies and new techniques of production throughout the economies of the LDCs. Infrastructure investment is a particular priority (see Ali and Pernia 2003; GRIPS Development Forum, 2003). A major effort must be made to develop the domestic enterprise sector that is oriented towards production rather than simply exchange. Particular emphasis must be placed on small and medium-size enterprises, and supporting what has been called the "missing middle" in the LDC enterprise structure (UNCTAD, 2001). New market-oriented approaches to agricultural development need to be devised to fill the vacuum left by the dismantling of old commodity marketing boards.

What is promising here is that there are major advances in thinking about new agricultural policies and industrial policies that are market-supporting. With regard to new agricultural policies, Kydd and Dorward (2002) have suggested that in rural areas of LDCs a key focus should be to address coordination failures which are present when the failure of one's own investment is due to the absence of complementary investments by other players at different stages in the supply chain" (p. 9). This involves encouraging appropriate asset-specific investments through institutional arrangements in which the State is a co-equal, not dominant, partner and a much greater role is given to producers' associations and trade associations (see also Kydd, Dorward and Poulton, 2002). There is also now an expanding body of experience regarding policy successes on which new agricultural policies can build (Gabre-Madhin and Haggblade, 2003). In terms of the new industrial policy, a central focus is on building competitiveness through developing more knowledge- and information-intensive systems of production. There is much experience on how the State can animate and guide private enterprise towards the achievement of development objectives, though these approaches have generally not been applied under a free trade regime (see Amsden, 2001). Following the East Asian approach, priority might be given to rationalization and modernization of specific priority sectors in specific contexts (see Ohno, 2003). The example of the cashew nut

processing industry in Mozambique offers an example of what needs to be done
(see box 18).

BOX 18. IS IT POSSIBLE TO TURNAROUND THE CASHEW NUT PROCESSING INDUSTRY IN MOZAMBIQUE?

The case of the cashew nut processing industry in Mozambique exemplifies the challenge of promoting development in a liberalized trading environment. Following Independence in 1975, the government banned the export
of raw cashew nuts to stimulate domestic processing before export. As part of its economic reforms, the Government lifted the ban on exporting raw cashew nuts in 1991/92 and then gradually reduced export quotas and export taxes (see Cramer, 1999). This, together with the liberalization of cashew marketing, was envisaged as a pro-
poor trade policy which would increase producer prices and allocate resources more efficiently. Producer prices
did indeed rise but the magnitude of the farmers' net gain was very small. Indeed it has been estimated that each
cashew growing household gained $5.29 per year, a sum which was equivalent to four days' wages at the mini-
mum Mozambican wage of $1.65 per day (McMillan et al., 2002). But, the newly privatized processing factories
were unable to compete at the new liberalized prices and many of them went bankrupt soon after the liberalization. In 1997, these factories employed 10,086 workers. But by 2001 none of the highly mechanised factories
were still operational, and the four factories that remain open employed 625 people at full capacity. Factory clo-
sures exacerbated a severe unemployment problem in Mozambique.

Can this situation be turned around? Processing – the conversion of the raw cashew nut into a cleaned kernel – is a
key activity within the cashew industry's value chain. According to Technoserve (2003), the high quality, semi-fin-
ished product can be worth $3,500 per metric ton compared to $400–575 per MT of raw nut. The export of
cashew as raw nuts, rather than as kernels, thus represents a major loss of potential employment and income generating added value. Is it possible to promote and expand the higher-value processing component of the cashew
industry in the new economic environment?

Amongst possible solutions, Technoserve (2003) argues for a sectoral restructuring programme to address the basic
constraint on development of processing activities which is the market-pricing gap. The producers receive prices
for their raw nuts that are too low to justify investments in better care of existing trees and/or planting of new trees.
Yet at the same time, in order to compete with exporters of raw nuts, the prices being paid by existing inefficient
processors are too high for them to make adequate profits and returns on their investments. In this context, Mozambique's entire cashew industry must be restructured if it is to compete successfully in the worldwide cashew
business and regain its former leadership position.

In the last four years there have been some new entrants to cashew processing. These are small and medium-scale
units located in rural areas. The restructuring process, according to Technoserve (2003) should facilitate this trend
focusing on the following issues:

1. Profitability

- Profitability in the cashew industry relies heavily on the quality of the final product (whole and white kernels). This
  requires improving the procurement process by: (i) identifying good quality nut producing areas, (ii) introducing
  grading standards and (iii) providing incentives for good quality nut purchase and production.

- Within the production chain it is important to continuously train the workers in order to achieve higher efficiencies
  and productivity.

2. Producer support

- Processors should identify, and help develop, good smallholder producer associations, and should, on a
  contractual basis, provide them with technical support thus introducing better cultivation practices.

- Wherever possible processors should support development of community nurseries to provide a ready source of
  improved seedlings to growers.

3. Processing

- Technical management of processing activities needs improvement in order to meet benchmarking standards by
  (i) using appropriate processing techniques and machinery to prevent quality loss, (ii) training the workforce to
  ensure competitive capacity, and (iii) gradually introducing international food processing standards. This requires
  greater use of technical experts.

4. Marketing

- To help enlarge and consolidate the Mozambican processors' market share, effort should also go into creating a
  country's brand name for cashew kernels.

Box 18 (contd.)

- The industry should be assisted to introduce second-level processing, thereby adding more value to the product in-country.

5. *Financing*

- Entrepreneurs (processors) need assistance in securing timely financing to avert delays in purchasing. Effort should go into creating an adequate and reliable credit system based on inventory credit / warehouse receipts in order to supply the whole industry at acceptable conditions.

6. *Business plan development*

- Processors need help in developing simple clear business plans. This will help introduce sound financial practices and planning and will enable processors to approach financial institutions to secure adequate and timely financing.

7. *Policy environment*

- The Cashew Business Association should be transformed into an effective forum for solving the problems of private cashew businesses. It should become the opinion leader of the sub-sector, coordinating and making more effective stakeholder influence on the decision- makers.

To succeed in creating an internationally competitive industry, such a sectoral restructuring strategy should be part of a broader development strategy. The international trading environment for cashew nuts is highly imperfect (Cramer 1999), and this may hamper success. But the pressing constraints are within the country. Addressing these will require "a combination of a clear vision, coordination of sector agents, capacity and will to enforce policy change and industry standards, and mechanisms and will to mediate contest and tensions between and within firms " (ibid.: 1262). With such a combination at the sectoral level and also growth-oriented macroeconomic policies, processing cashew nuts could become a key part of an agricultural-development-led industrialization strategy in Mozambique.

Source: Based on Cramer (1999), McMillan et al. (2002) and Technoserve (2003).

D. Mainstreaming trade in development-oriented poverty reduction strategies

1. A METHODOLOGY FOR INTEGRATING TRADE IN DEVELOPMENT-ORIENTED POVERTY REDUCTION STRATEGIES

The sustainability of economic growth will be threatened if export expansion is not sufficient to meet the import demand associated with faster growth. This is particularly important in the LDCs because of the import sensitivity of their economies.

This section sets out a possible methodology for mainstreaming trade policy into a development-oriented poverty reduction strategy or national development strategy. The methodology is based on the view that substantial poverty reduction in the LDCs requires sustained economic growth and that the balance of payments is a major constraint on achieving this. Increased efficient investment, and associated technological change and productivity growth, are the basic source of economic growth. But the sustainability of economic growth will be threatened if export expansion is not sufficient to meet the import demand associated with faster growth. This is particularly important in the LDCs because of the import sensitivity of their economies. Due regard must thus be given to the "foreign exchange productivity of investment" (Hussain, 2001: 95).

The methodology, which is systematized on the basis of a proposal by Hussain (2001), is iterative, as shown in chart 43, but it has ten main steps.

Step one to step four

Firstly, poverty reduction targets are established and an estimate is made of the growth rate required in order to achieve these targets. This estimate requires analysis of the elasticity of poverty reduction with respect to economic growth in the country concerned.

CHART 43. METHODOLOGY FOR MAINSTREAMING TRADE INTO POVERTY REDUCTION STRATEGIES

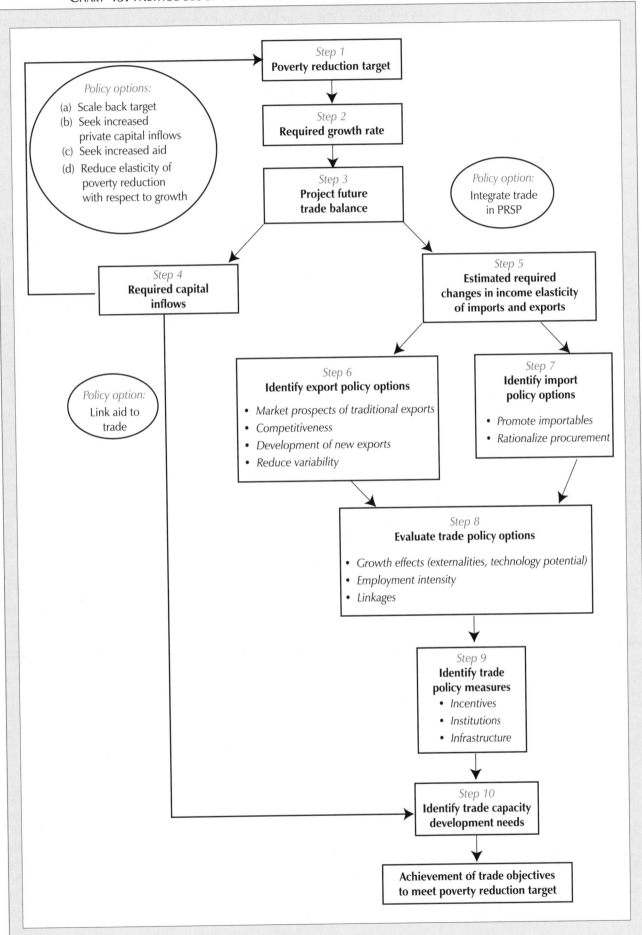

Secondly, projections are made of the capital inflows which are required in order to meet the target poverty-reducing growth rate. These projections should initially assume no change in the key parameters governing export and import growth in the country concerned. Thus import growth should be projected on the basis of past performance in terms of price and income elasticities of demand for imports. Export growth should be projected on the basis of past trends in export volume and terms of trade. If export expansion is not sufficient to meet the import demand associated with the growth rate, capital inflows are required in order to meet the target poverty-reducing growth rate.

Thirdly, the future financing gap is estimated on the basis of the difference between required and expected capital inflows.

Fourthly, policy scenarios are elaborated to address this financing gap. If trade is not integrated into the poverty reduction strategy, there are four basic policy scenarios:

(i) Scale back poverty reduction targets so that they are "realistic" given likely future trends in private capital inflows and international aid;

(ii) Seek to attract more private capital inflows;

(iii) Seek to attract more international aid;

(iv) Reduce the elasticity of poverty reduction with respect to economic growth.

Step five

The policy options can be considerably increased if trade is integrated into the poverty reduction strategy. This is the fifth step in the methodology. Instead of asking "What are the external resources required in order to achieve the poverty-reducing growth target, assuming no change in the trade parameters?", the central question is "What changes in the trade parameters are required in order to achieve the poverty-reducing growth target, assuming no change in the financing gap?"

There are two key parameters that should be the focus of attention: the income elasticity of demand for imports and the income elasticity of demand for exports.

There are two key parameters that should be the focus of attention: the income elasticity of demand for imports and the income elasticity of demand for exports. The smaller the income elasticity of demand for imports, the smaller the increase in imports which is associated with an increase in national income. The higher the income elasticity of demand for a country's exports, the larger the increase in exports as a result of a given percentage increase in world income. The fifth step concentrates on these two parameters, and estimates:

• The income elasticity of demand for imports that would allow the country to grow at the target poverty-reducing growth rate with no change in the financing gap and no change in export parameters;

• The income elasticity of demand for exports that would allow the country to grow at the target poverty-reducing growth rate with no change in the financing gap and no change in the import parameters.

The first estimate indicates the maximum extent to which the import intensity of economic growth needs to decrease in order to ensure sustainable growth. The second estimate thus indicates the maximum extent to which the responsiveness of national exports to growth in global demand must increase in order to ensure sustainable growth.[5]

With this fifth step, trade issues can now be integrated in the poverty reduction strategy. This can be done by focusing on the identification, formulation and implementation of policies that can reduce the income elasticity of demand for imports and increase the income elasticity of demand for exports in a way that supports the sustainability of economic growth at the rate required to meet the growth target. Policies need to address both the import side and the export side of trade development. In the way in which the policy problem has been stated so far, action on either side is equivalent. But in practice, because some capital inflows are debt-creating and because many LDCs have a legacy of unsustainable external debt, it is necessary to ensure that the rate of export growth exceeds the interest rate on external debt. It is necessary that export expansion be sufficient to meet not simply the import demand associated with faster growth but also the servicing of the external debt. If external indebtedness increases too much, the sustainability of the growth process will be seriously compromised as more and more foreign exchange earnings are eaten up in debt service payments and, in response to increasing indebtedness and associated internal domestic policy problems, capital inflows collapse. This implies that particular attention needs to be paid to exports.

It is necessary that export expansion be sufficient to meet not simply the import demand associated with faster growth but also the servicing of the external debt.

Step six to step nine

The sixth step is to identify policy options for increasing the income elasticity of demand for exports. The analysis here can begin with examination of the demand growth prospects characteristics of a country's major traditional exports. Traditional exports may be defined in various ways, but essentially they denote the major products in the export composition of the country in the recent past. For commodity exporters in particular, these are likely to be low.[6] The next questions that arise are:

- To what extent is it possible to increase the income elasticity of demand for exports through improved competitiveness in traditional exports? In this case, the increase in income elasticity of demand requires that the country increase its share of the global market for its traditional products.

- What new products and sectors can be promoted to increase the income elasticity of demand for exports? In this case, such an increase occurs through changing the proportion of dynamic products in the export composition.

- What new markets can be accessed in order to increase the income elasticity of demand for exports? In this case, such an increase occurs through changing the geographical destinations of exports to more dynamic markets.

The overall aim should be not simply to increase the income elasticity of demand for exports but also to decrease the variability of export growth. This may be a further reason for export diversification.

These questions serve to define trade development goals in terms of competitiveness and diversification. Questions of instability of export growth also need to be considered here. The overall aim should be not simply to increase the income elasticity of demand for exports but also to decrease the variability of export growth. This may be a further reason for export diversification.

The seventh step is to identify policy options for reducing the income elasticity of demand for imports in the same way. The analysis may begin here by determining whether there are any opportunities for efficient import substitution given the costs of producing domestically versus the costs of importing. The poverty-reducing effects of export growth are likely to be enhanced if increases in domestic demand are not met wholly by imports and if there is some import substitution. Particularly important are backward linkages effects from export activities in which local suppliers provide inputs of various types to support export production, and also the activities of domestic SMEs in serving the domestic market, particularly the majority of the population, who are poor and live in remoter regions. Promoting the domestic production of importables in a newly liberalized trading environment is likely to be a considerable policy challenge. Thus, alongside the identification of opportunities for efficient import substitution, policy options for better import procurement practice need to be identified. In the context of the untying of aid, the LDCs need to give particular attention to improving government procurement. This is likely to account for at least 13 per cent of GDP in many LDCs (ITC, 1999) and the limited evidence shows that the figure is as high as 30 per cent in one LDC (Odhiambo and Kamau, 2003). Reducing costs of government procurement can thus have a very high economic pay-off. It is also possible to improve the access of SMEs to government procurement in ways which do not compromise efficiency goals (see ITC, 2000). Joint procurement on a subregional basis may also offer economies of scale.

The eighth step is to assess these policy options in terms of their growth and poverty reduction effects. Thus, for example, the identification of promising export products and sectors would start by taking account of comparative advantage (see Schydlowsky, 1984, and Redding, 1999), and also demand growth prospects in world and regional markets (see, for example, Diao et al., 2003). It would also consider the magnitude of the local value-added, externalities associated with these products and their potential for learning. Poverty issues can be integrated into the analysis by examining the employment intensity of specific export activities and also the linkages that they have with the rest of the economy. The analysis may reveal difficult trade-offs in terms of what is most promising in purely economic terms and what is most promising in terms of poverty reduction. An example of this is upgrading. The demand growth prospects are much higher than those of traditional exports, but the ability of this to generate widespread poverty reduction may be limited. The assessment of these options will also relate to the development strategy chosen.

The ninth step is to identify the specific trade policy measures through which the trade objectives can be achieved. There is an increasing body of knowledge on best practices to promote exports in general (ITC, 2001b), and also non-traditional exports in particular (Helleiner, 2003). There is also wide agreement on best practices to reduce import costs through rationalizing supply and procurement (see box 19). The identification of trade policy measures, as well as the identification of policy options, needs to be done in the context of a durable trade policy framework (see below).

Step ten

The tenth step is to identify priority trade-related capacity-building needs that are required in order to achieve the trade objectives and successfully implement the policy. This is a matter not simply of technical assistance but also of financial assistance. At this point the relationship between capital inflows and trade development objectives is seen as a synergetic mutual interrelationship rather than an arithmetic relationship in which increasing capital inflows reduces the need for the achievement of trade objectives, or vice versa. Capital inflows which help to meet trade-related capacity-building needs help to close the financing gap in the short term but can also serve to reduce reliance on capital inflows, and particularly aid inflows, in the future. Both aid and FDI inflows can

Poverty issues can be integrated into the analysis by examining the employment intensity of specific export activities and also the linkages that they have with the rest of the economy. The analysis may reveal difficult trade-offs in terms of what is most promising in purely economic terms and what is most promising in terms of poverty reduction.

Box 19. Best practices to reduce import costs through better procurement

It is possible to reduce import costs through (i) planning and managing supply, (ii) sourcing and managing suppliers, (iii) evaluating offers and contracts, and contract management, and (iv) logistics and inventory management. The best practices in each of these areas are:

1. *Planning and managing supply*

- Reduce excessive variety of imported items (through internal standardisation) – thus allowing for consolidation of suppliers, greater leverage in negotiations with suppliers through larger purchase quantities, consequent reduction in unit logistics and inventory costs.
- Apply international/national standards for imported products/services wherever possible — to ensure quality and avoid waste, allow sourcing under better conditions from a wider range of supply alternatives.
- Use performance-based purchase specifications, to the extent possible.
- Apply value analysis/value engineering techniques to specifications for procurement of high value imported equipment and other goods/services (to obtain better value at reduced cost).
- Improve forecasting of import requirements/demand, to reduce oversupply or stockouts, and avoid waste.
- Reduce lead-time for imported supplies through better management, reducing inventory costs and avoiding waste due to obsolescence resulting from changing market conditions/demand.
- Adopt effective supply strategies for imported goods & services, based on careful assessments of supply risks and costs.
- Consolidate requirements & imports (e.g. through group purchasing or purchasing consortia of SMEs) to achieve economies of scale and improve negotiation leverage with suppliers.

2. *Sourcing/supply markets/managing suppliers*

- Identify and procure from the most competitive sources of supply, breaking away from traditional supply patterns where relevant.
- Understand evolving supply markets, in order to know the best moment to enter the market, avoid supply risks and unforeseen costs, and know how to secure better prices & supply conditions from suppliers, etc.
- Learn to take the best possible advantage of tied aid (wherever this cannot be avoided) by tying oneself to the most competitive source of supply – i.e. first identify the best sources of supply for a requirement, and only then arrange aid financing to procure for it.
- Rationalise the supply base for imported items by consolidating suppliers.
- Carry out careful supplier appraisals, to ensure reliability and lowest total delivered cost.
- Develop long-term supplier partnerships, wherever appropriate.

3. *Evaluating offers, contracting and contract management*

- Evaluate suppliers' offers on the basis of total cost of ownership / life-cycle cost techniques when purchasing high value items such as equipment – rather than considering just the paying price – in order to better understand and reduce total costs.
- Develop effective negotiation skills in order to obtain the best possible supply conditions for imports and develop win-win relationships with suppliers.
- Apply contractual arrangements (e.g. performance-based contracting) that protect the importer against unforeseen costs and risks.
- Implement effective contract management systems to avoid cost overruns, delays and other problems in importing.

4. *Logistics and inventory management*

- Organise import logistics arrangements to minimise risks and optimise costs (e.g. through cargo consolidation, effective assessment of shipping alternatives, reducing shipping lead-times, etc.)
- Optimise inventory levels of imported goods to reduce purchase and holding costs through effective demand management, lead-time reduction, and careful assessment of supply risks and required levels of safety stocks.
- Organise efficient in-country logistics, warehousing and distribution for imported goods.
- Use effective IT systems to monitor, control and expedite the logistics process.

Source: ITC (2004).

play an important role in supporting the development of trade-related capacity building. But the former is particularly important in most LDCs given the marginalization in private capital inflows and also the public goods nature of many trade-related capacity-building needs.

2. The importance of improving the trade policy process

This methodology is a proposal that may be refined. But to work at all, the methodology needs to be used and refined in the context of an effective trade-policy-making process. The priority here, as the OECD/DAC *Guidelines on Strengthening Capacity for Trade Development* stress, must be to establish a durable trade policy framework through which the trade development interests of a country can be identified and ways to realize them are implemented (OECD, 2001).

The trade policy process needs to include institutional capacities to implement the policy, including clear definition of the roles of different actors and also resources allocated to implement recommended actions.

According to these Guidelines, the major elements of a durable trade policy framework are the following:

- A coherent trade strategy that is closely integrated with a country's overall development strategy;

- Effective mechanisms for consultation among the three key stakeholders: government, the enterprise sector and civil society;

- Effective mechanisms for intra-governmental coordination;

- A strategy for enhanced collection, dissemination and analysis of trade-related information;

- Trade policy networks, supported by indigenous research institutions;

- Networks of trade support institutions, such as institutions that offer technical assistance on product quality standards, package design consultants, commercial banks and other financial institutions that offer trade credit, freight forwarders and shippers, training institutions, consulting firms and overseas commercial representatives;

A major problem in many LDCs is that the trade policy process works very poorly.

- Strong linkages amongst private sector organizations involved in trade;

- A commitment to outward-oriented regional strategies.

The trade policy process needs to include institutional capacities to implement the policy, including clear definition of the roles of different actors and also resources allocated to implement recommended actions. A major problem in many LDCs is that the trade policy process works very poorly, with deficiencies including a general lack of resources within trade ministries and trade-related institutions; a lack of capacity to identify policy options and assess their relative merits; a lack of coordination within the Government between the trade ministry and the finance ministry and also amongst the various trade ministry and various sectoral ministries; and weak coordination with stakeholders, particularly the private sector. The methodology outlined here provides a basis for orienting discussions with the trade policy process in terms of identifying a country's trade interests and translating these into policies. But without improvements in the whole trade-policy-making process in line with suggested best practices, the methodology is unlikely to work in terms of either better trade policy formulation or implementation.

E. How donors can support trade capacity development

International assistance can play an important role in supporting the achievement of national trade development objectives. It can do this through assistance for trade capacity development, which is defined here, following Solignac Lecomte (2001: 5), as "technical and financial assistance granted by donor agencies to improve developing countries' capacity to trade internationally". As chart 44 shows, this involves two broad types of activity – support to strengthen trade-policy-making and negotiating capacities, and support to build the export base, the competitiveness of exporters and the efficiency of importers.

International assistance can play an important role in supporting the achievement of national trade development objectives.

CHART 44. NATIONAL DEVELOPMENT STRATEGY AND THE TRADE POLICY PROCESS

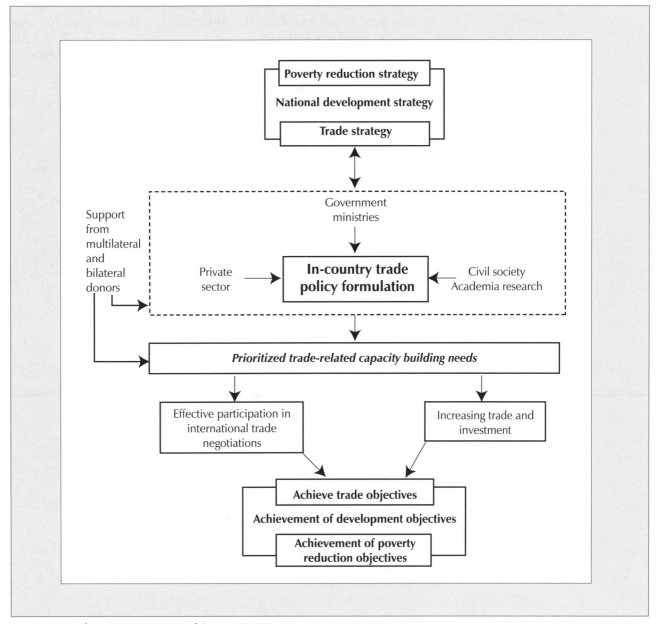

Source: Based on OECD (2001) and Prowse (2002).

This section looks at some general features of international assistance for trade capacity development in the LDCs, including the scale and composition of assistance, some of the risks for donors and recipients which reduce the effectiveness of "aid for trade", the role of the Integrated Framework for Trade-Related Technical Assistance, and the need for increased policy coherence between debt relief and trade capacity development.

Past trends of aid commitments to the LDCs indicate that assistance for trade capacity development has not been a major donor priority.

1. THE SCALE AND COMPOSITION OF DONOR SUPPORT FOR TRADE CAPACITY DEVELOPMENT

Trends in international assistance for trade capacity development can be estimated using data on aid commitments to trade policy and administration and to export promotion within the OECD Creditor Reporting System database (CRS). These data should be treated with care as sector-related aid that might also have supported trade development is not included. However, the OECD/CRS provide the best available information on past trends in aid for trade development in the LDCs. This section relies on this source, and also on the new WTO/OECD database, which has been established to rectify data deficiencies, and which provides a more detailed view of international assistance for trade capacity development in the LDCs 2001 and 2002.[7]

CHART 45. TRENDS IN AID[a] TO THE LDCS FOR TRADE POLICY AND MANAGEMENT AND EXPORT PROMOTION, 1990–2001

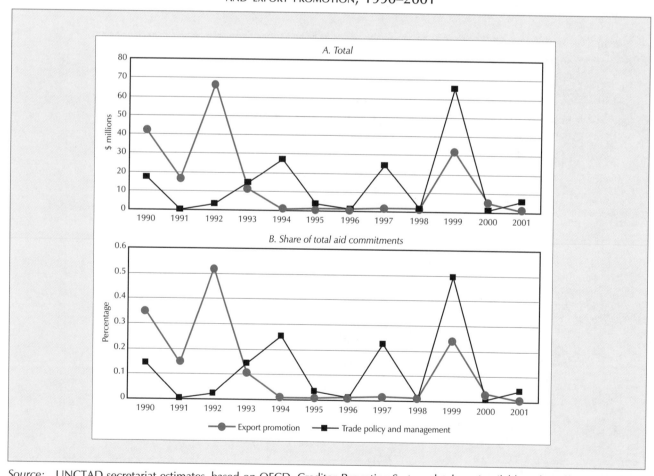

Source: UNCTAD secretariat estimates, based on OECD, Creditor Reporting System database (available at http://www.oecd.org/dataoecd/50/17/5037721.htm).

Note: Aid for export promotion and trade policy and management do not include sector-related aid.
a Both bilateral and multilateral aid are included.

Charts 45A and 45B show the trends in total bilateral and multilateral aid commitments to trade policy and administration and export promotion in the LDCs for the period 1990–2001[8] as recorded in the OECD/CRS. During this period, total bilateral and multilateral aid commitments for trade policy and management to all the LDCs was on average $13.8 million per year, which was equivalent to 0.1 per cent of total aid commitments. In 7 of those 12 years aid commitments for trade policy and administration were less than $6 million for all the LDCs. Regarding export promotion, total bilateral and multilateral aid commitments to the LDCs during the period 1990–1999 were on average $17.5 million per year. The latter data series may be somewhat misleading because the problem of sectoral classification of data is likely to be particularly serious.[9] But overall, the past trends of aid commitments to the LDCs indicate that assistance for trade capacity development has not been a major donor priority.

It is possible to obtain a wider view by looking at aid commitments for trade-related infrastructure. This is also difficult as there is no agreed definition of what this is. Estimates are reproduced in chart 46 based on a working definition of trade-related infrastructure that includes aid for transport and storage (less education and training in transport and storage) plus telecommunications.[10] It is apparent that aid for trade-related infrastructure to the LDCs, defined in this way, has not changed much in current dollars, although there is a slight tendency towards a decline during the decade. However, in real per capita terms, aid for trade-related infrastructure declined by 43 per cent from 1990 to 2001.

This pattern should be seen as part of a general tendency to decrease the proportion of aid to LDCs going to productive development as more goes to social sectors, and also debt relief and emergencies. As aid inflows declined in

It is vital that the upturn in international assistance following the Monterrey Consensus be also associated with a shift in the composition of aid back towards building production capabilities and not simply meeting basic needs and providing social infrastructure.

CHART 46. TRENDS IN AID FOR TRADE-RELATED INFRASTRUCTURE[a] TO LDCS, OTHER LOW-INCOME COUNTRIES (OLIS), LOWER-MIDDLE-INCOME COUNTRIES (LMIC) AND UPPER-MIDDLE-INCOME COUNTRIES (UMIC), 1990–2001

($ millions)

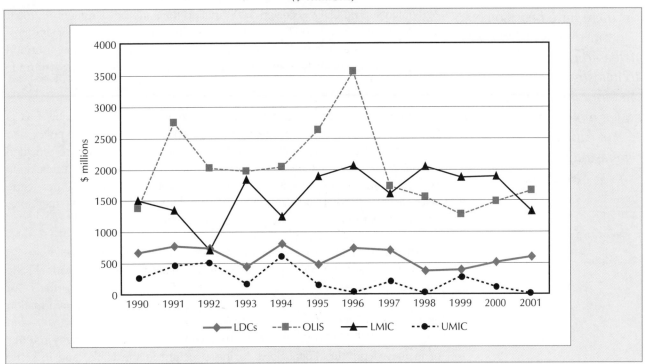

Source: UNCTAD secretariat estimates based on OECD Creditor Reporting System database.

a   For a working definition of aid for trade-related infrastructure, see text.

the 1990s there was also a compositional shift away from economic infrastructure and services (particularly transport, and communications and energy) and production sectors (agriculture, industry, trade and tourism) towards social infrastructure. In the early 1980s, 45 per cent of total bilateral aid commitments by DAC member countries to LDCs went to economic infrastructure, production sectors and multi-sectoral and cross-cutting issues was 45 per cent. But in 2000–2002, this had fallen to 23 per cent. In real terms, external assistance to agriculture in the LDCs in the 1990s was half the level it was in the 1980s (UNCTAD, 2000, 2002). It is vital that the upturn in international assistance following the Monterrey Consensus be also associated with a shift in the composition of aid back towards building production capabilities and not simply meeting basic needs and providing social infrastructure. The monitoring of the scale, composition and effectiveness of aid at the recipient country level remains as pertinent as ever.

According to the WTO/OECD database, aid commitments for trade policy and regulation and for trade development were only 0.5 per cent and 1.5 per cent, respectively, of total aid commitments in 2002.

The recently established OECD/WTO database provides a detailed breakdown of aid for trade-related technical assistance and capacity building in 2001 and 2002. This covers trade policy and regulations, trade development, and infrastructure. The latter includes all aid for transport and storage, communications and energy, and no attempt is made to isolate what constitutes trade-related infrastructure. In 2001 and 2002, infrastructure constituted 77 per cent and 81 per cent respectively of the aid for trade-related technical assistance and capacity building going to the LDCs. In 2002, the LDCs received $1.4 billion in the areas of transport and storage, communications and energy, which accounted for 9 per cent of total donors' commitments to LDCs in that year. Road transport is the most important component of infrastructure aid. But it is striking that very little international assistance goes to improving communications infrastructure in the LDCs (see table 59).

According to the database, the LDCs received $159 million for trade policy and regulations in 2001 and $75 million in 2002. The major priorities in 2001 were for meeting technical barriers to trade (TBT) and sanitary and phytosanitary measures (SPS), and in 2002 it was aid for negotiations on Economic Partnership Agreements). The LDCs received $408 million for trade development in 2001, and $249 million in 2002. The major priorities in 2001 were for business support services and trade finance, and in 2002 they were for business support services and market analysis and development in the agricultural sector for trade development.

There have been some positive signs in terms of increased private capital flows to infrastructure in the LDCs, and in some countries this is now a more important source of capital inflows for infrastructure than official assistance.

This new database indicates that the data on aid commitments in the OECD Creditor Reporting System are likely to underestimate aid for trade policy and administration and export promotion. But even with the fuller picture provided by the WTO/OECD database, aid commitments for trade policy and regulation and for trade development were only 0.5 per cent and 1.5 per cent, respectively, of total aid commitments to LDCs in 2002. It is, therefore, important that more priority be given to these activities.

Increased financial assistance for trade-related infrastructure should also be a priority in the LDCs. A major effort must be made in this regard to meet the quantitative targets in the United Nations Programme of Action for the Least Developed Countries for the Decade 2001–2010. But there is little information on the scale of the needs or costs (see, for example, Fay, 2001, and Fay and Yepes, 2003). Table 60 shows that there have been some positive signs in terms of increased private capital flows to infrastructure in the LDCs, and in some countries this is now a more important source of capital inflows for infrastructure than official assistance. But there are limits to the types of infrastructure

TABLE 59. AID FOR TRADE-RELATED TECHNICAL ASSISTANCE AND CAPACITY BUILDING FOR THE LDCs, 2001 AND 2002

	2001			2002		
	$	Percentage of:		$	Percentage of:	
	Thousands	sub-category total	grand total	Thousands	sub-category total	grand total
Trade policy and regulations	**158 611**	**100.0**	**6.3**	**75 046**	**100.0**	**4.3**
Trade mainstreaming in PRSPs/development plans	11 360	7.2	0.5	3 317	4.4	0.2
Technical barriers to trade (TBT) and sanitary and phytosanitary measures (SPS)	69 599	43.9	2.8	2 206	2.9	0.1
Trade facilitation procedures	51 636	32.6	2.1	10 949	14.6	0.6
Customs valuation	136	0.1	0.0	137	0.2	0.0
Tariff reforms	..	0.0	0.0	49	0.1	0.0
Regional trade agreements (RTAs)	9 682	6.1	0.4	50 350	67.1	2.9
Accession	102	0.1	0.0	472	0.6	0.0
Dispute settlement	4	0.0	0.0	100	0.1	0.0
Trade-related intellectual property rights (TRIPS)	436	0.3	0.0	410	0.5	0.0
Tariff negotiations — non-agricultural market access	108	0.1	0.0	696	0.9	0.0
Rules	111	0.1	0.0	191	0.3	0.0
Training in trade negotiation techniques	1	0.0	0.0	92	0.1	0.0
Trade and environment	482	0.3	0.0	2 068	2.8	0.1
Trade and competition	916	0.6	0.0	510	0.7	0.0
Trade and investment	130	0.1	0.0	300	0.4	0.0
Transparency and government procurement	4	0.0	0.0	198	0.3	0.0
Trade education/training	12 882	8.1	0.5	2 171	2.9	0.1
Trade development	**407 640**	**100.0**	**16.3**	**249 109**	**100.0**	**14.4**
Business support services and institutions	165 857	40.7	6.6	82 407	33.1	4.8
Public–private sector networking	2 032	0.5	0.1	691	0.3	0.0
E-commerce	112	0.0	0.0	1 173	0.5	0.1
Trade finance	134 501	33.0	5.4	39 711	15.9	2.3
Financial policy and administrative management	3 179	0.8	0.1	15 755	6.3	0.9
Formal sector financial intermediaries	117 415	28.8	4.7	18 848	7.6	1.1
Informal/semi-formal financial	13 801	3.4	0.6	4 427	1.8	0.3
Trade promotion strategy and implementation	35 414	8.7	1.4	50 336	20.2	2.9
Agriculture	20 234	5.0	0.8	8 477	3.4	0.5
Fishing	82	0.0	0.0	2 437	1.0	0.1
Industry	14 162	3.5	0.6	22 723	9.1	1.3
Tourism	193	0.0	0.0	15 149	6.1	0.9
Market analysis and development	69 724	17.1	2.8	74 791	30.0	4.3
Agriculture	52 198	12.8	2.1	67 450	27.1	3.9
Fishing	17 257	4.2	0.7	595	0.2	0.0
Industry	238	0.1	0.0	6 192	2.5	0.4
Infrastructure	**1 942 108**	**100.0**	**77.4**	**1 405 020**	**100.0**	**81.3**
Transport and storage	1 096 695	56.5	43.7	610 487	43.5	35.3
Transportation policy and adm. management	87 673	4.5	3.5	110 310	7.9	6.4
Road transport	981 728	50.5	39.1	408 583	29.1	23.6
Water transport	16 074	0.8	0.6	43 632	3.1	2.5
Air transport	2 491	0.1	0.1	42 470	3.0	2.5
Communications	99 681	5.1	4.0	68 058	4.8	3.9
Energy	745 732	38.4	29.7	726 474	51.7	42.0
energy policy and adm. management	262 438	13.5	10.5	158 230	11.3	9.2
electrical transmission	175 523	9.0	7.0	478 176	34.0	27.7
gas distribution	183 000	9.4	7.3	..	0.0	0.0
gas-fired power plants	49 257	2.5	2.0	..	0.0	0.0
hydroelectric power plants	4 226	0.2	0.2	41 013	2.9	2.4
solar energy	30 756	1.6	1.2	2 651	0.2	0.2
Total	**2 508 359**		**100.0**	**1 729 174**		**100.0**

Source: UNCTAD secretariat estimates, based on WTO/OECD database (http://tcbdb.wto.org).

Note: The database has a more detailed classification.

TABLE 60. PRIVATE CAPITAL FLOWS FOR INFRASTRUCTURE AND AID FOR TRADE-RELATED INFRASTRUCTURE
TO LDCS BY COUNTRY, 1990–1994 AND 1998–2002

(Annual average, $ millions)

Countries	Private capital flows	Aid flows	Total	Private capital flows	Aid flows	Total
		1990–1994			*1998–2002*	
Afghanistan	-	..	-	14.0	1.5	15.5
Angola	-	42.7	42.7	15.1	10.1	25.2
Bangladesh	23.2	246.8	270.0	76.0	249.1	325.1
Benin	-	33.6	33.6	18.1	38.6	56.7
Bhutan	-	7.0	7.0	-	7.8	7.8
Burkina Faso	-	29.0	29.0	7.3	26.2	33.5
Burundi	0.1	22.0	22.1	3.1	-	3.1
Cambodia	6.0	21.7	27.8	28.4	38.6	67.0
Cape Verde	-	13.5	13.5	-	7.7	7.7
Central African Republic	-	34.3	34.3	-	16.0	16.0
Chad	-	29.7	29.7	2.6	34.2	36.8
Comoros	-	3.1	3.1	-	0.8	0.8
Dem. Rep. of the Congo	-	35.5	35.5	73.9	1.9	75.8
Djibouti	-	14.6	14.6	10.0	3.9	13.9
Equatorial Guinea	-	2.9	2.9	4.4	0.5	4.9
Eritrea	-	0.9	0.9	8.0	0.5	8.5
Ethiopia	-	75.7	75.7	-	161.5	161.5
Gambia	-	7.2	7.2	1.3	0.1	1.4
Guinea	-	39.1	39.1	1.6	13.3	14.9
Guinea-Bissau	-	8.5	8.5	-	4.4	4.4
Haiti	-	11.2	11.2	3.9	0.5	4.4
Kiribati	0.2	1.1	1.3	-	0.1	0.1
Lao People's Dem. Rep.	-	67.0	67.0	27.3	53.6	80.9
Lesotho	-	4.4	4.4	4.7	9.7	14.4
Liberia	-	0.0	0.0	-	0.0	0.0
Madagascar	1.0	37.5	38.5	4.1	56.1	60.2
Malawi	-	27.0	27.0	6.3	33.4	39.7
Maldives	-	3.0	3.0	-	1.2	1.2
Mali	-	32.7	32.7	8.5	28.8	37.3
Mauritania	-	14.4	14.4	19.9	6.3	26.2
Mozambique	-	136.9	136.9	113.5	107.3	220.9
Myanmar	-	0.4	0.4	-	1.0	1.0
Nepal	-	65.1	65.1	19.7	52.0	71.7
Niger	-	3.3	3.3	-	7.4	7.4
Rwanda	-	33.2	33.2	3.1	0.1	3.2
Sao Tome and Principe	-	2.8	2.8	-	1.2	1.2
Senegal	-	29.0	29.0	49.4	49.6	99.0
Sierra Leone	-	26.7	26.7	4.7	0.5	5.2
Solomon Islands	-	5.2	5.2	2.0	1.9	3.9
Somalia	-	4.6	4.6	0.4	0.6	1.0
Sudan	-	8.2	8.2	-	0.0	0.0
Togo	-	7.2	7.2	1.0	3.3	4.3
Tuvalu	-	0.5	0.5	-	-	-
Uganda	0.9	60.3	61.2	39.1	54.3	93.4
United Rep. of Tanzania	0.4	242.3	242.6	64.0	88.7	152.7
Vanuatu	2.2	2.5	4.7	-	4.7	4.7
Samoa	-	8.1	8.1	-	5.2	5.2
Yemen	5.0	29.8	34.8	68.0	12.1	80.1
Zambia	-	34.6	34.6	10.4	36.2	46.6
LDCs	**39.0**	**1 566.8**	**1 605.8**	**713.8**	**1 232.4**	**1 946.3**

Source: UNCTAD secretariat estimates based on World Bank, PPI database (available at http://rru.worldbank.org/PPI/), and OECD Creditor Reporting System database.

Note: For definition of trade-related infrastructure, see text.

investment in which the profit-oriented private sector is interested and thus the need for increased official assistance to meet the major physical infrastructure development needs in the LDCs remains important.

2. RISKS AND PRIORITIES OF TRADE CAPACITY DEVELOPMENT

Given the major role which trade can play in poverty reduction, there is a strong case for increased assistance for trade capacity development. But analysis of past practice has identified some risks for donors and recipients alike. Solignac Lecomte (2003: 6) identifies the key underlying source of these risks as follows: "As the development objectives of developed countries (as donors) overlap with their commercial interests (as trading powers), they may be prone to decide upon what type of assistance to provide according to their own interests rather than those of recipient countries". On the basis of analysis of the experience of donors and recipients in Africa and the Caribbean he identifies four major risks of trade capacity development:

Mainstreaming trade in aid policies is as important as mainstreaming aid in poverty reduction strategies.

- Negative discrimination. "Donor countries may be reluctant to provide assistance in areas they perceive as being detrimental to their own interests…In the various countries studies, no instance was found of a donor project that promoted trade interests of the recipient country that were diametrically opposed to those of the donor" (p. 17).

- Positive discrimination. "Donors may be tempted to 'positively discriminate' in favour of trade-related assistance which they see as generating benefits for their own economies and firms (e.g. the implementation by developing countries of their commitment under TRIPs) one of the most successful TCD projects in Senegal was the upgrading of fisheries production processes to safety and quality standards imposed by the EU" (p. 17).

- Tied aid. This is falling as a source of risk owing to the implementation of the recommendation that aid to LDCs be untied. But this does not cover technical assistance and "classical aid-tying issues…arise in policy-focused projects involving a high proportion of technical assistance" (p. 17).

- Buy-off in negotiations. "The support granted by donors for enhancing the recipient's negotiating capacity may alter the negotiator's goal and incentives. For any country, effective negotiating capacity means the ability to formulate and defend its own trade interests. Being supported in this by a donor country who happens to be sitting at the same negotiating table (for instance, in the WTO) is a contradiction in terms" (p. 17).

The recommendation that most forms of aid to the LDCs (excluding food aid and technical cooperation) be untied offers an opportunity for a conceptual revolution in which international assistance is not related to the donor's trade development objectives, but rather to the recipient's trade development objectives.

These risks, which are particularly associated with bilateral aid, reduce the efficiency and effectiveness of assistance for trade capacity development from the point of view of the recipient. Another problem that has been identified is the lack of donor coordination. There are also weaknesses in donor capacity. Describing the situation in 2001, Solignac Lecomte states as follows: "Among donors, locally based agencies had very few trade specialists to represent them. Indeed relatively few donors actually engage in trade capacity development projects. If more emphasis were placed on such activities, many agencies would not be in a position to identify and start projects due to inadequate incentives and capacity, especially in the field. Policy-makers in the capitals do not always have access to sufficient trade expertise, whilst the agencies responsible for actually implementing trade policy very rarely have access to such expertise. The tendency of many donors to concentrate on basic needs has reinforced this 'anti-trade bias' " (p. 19).

One implication of this analysis of past practices in trade capacity development is that bilateral aid for trade capacity development might be increasingly channelled through multilateral entities to reduce the risks mentioned above. But in addition to this, it is clear that mainstreaming trade in aid policies is as important as mainstreaming aid in poverty reduction strategies. The recommendation that most forms of aid to the LDCs (excluding food aid and technical cooperation) be untied offers an opportunity for a conceptual revolution in which international assistance is not related to the donor's trade development objectives, but rather to the recipient's trade development objectives.

Trade capacity building should be seen as part of a wider objective of the development of productive sectors and also of private sector development.

Given the weaknesses of the trade policy process in the LDCs, one major priority of trade capacity development should be to foster an efficient trade-policy-making process in which (i) the country's trade interests are clearly identified within an overall development strategy; (ii) these interests are translated into policies and negotiating goals; and (iii) roles and distributed and resources are allocated to implement these policies and to promote these interests (Solignac Lecomte, 2003: 3). The other major priority should be to build up private-sector capacities to export and import efficiently. Poor trade performance is rooted in weak production capacities. Thus trade capacity building should be seen as part of a wider objective of the development of productive sectors and also of private sector development.[11]

3. THE INTEGRATED FRAMEWORK FOR TRADE-RELATED TECHNICAL ASSISTANCE

There are some positive initiatives to improve international assistance for trade capacity development. The OECD/DAC has prepared an excellent manual on best practices in trade capacity building (referred to above), which is relevant to both LDCs and their development partners. The OECD/WTO database has been established to provide greater visibility to the scale and composition of assistance. Various donors have also sought to put greater emphasis on rectifying some of the deficiencies noted above.[12] The Joint Technical Assistance Programme (JITAP) has successfully combined a process-oriented approach that brings together a range of in-country stakeholders and three trade-focused international agencies (ITC, UNCTAD and WTO), with an output approach. But the major initiative through which donors are seeking to improve the efficiency of trade capacity development is the Integrated Framework for Trade-Related Technical Assistance (IF).

The major initiative through which donors are seeking to improve the efficiency of trade capacity development is the Integrated Framework for Trade-Related Technical Assistance.

The IF is an evolving initiative of the LDCs' development partners that was introduced in 1997 as a response to the Uruguay Round Decision on Measures in Favour of Least Developed Countries, which called for "substantial increased technical assistance in the development, strengthening and diversification of their production and export bases including those of services, as well as trade promotion to enable them to maximize the benefits from liberalized access to markets" (GATT secretariat, 1994: 441). There is a more complete discussion in *The Least Developed Countries Report 2002*. In brief, however, the first evaluation, completed in June 2000, identified several weakness of the approach at that time: poor links of the process of trade capacity building with overall development strategies, weak ownership, inadequate coordination and inadequate funding. On this basis, it was decided that a revamped IF should be put in place, whose major aim was to help countries integrate trade within their poverty reduction strategies or development strategies.

CHART 47. INTEGRATED FRAMEWORK PROCESS FLOW CHART

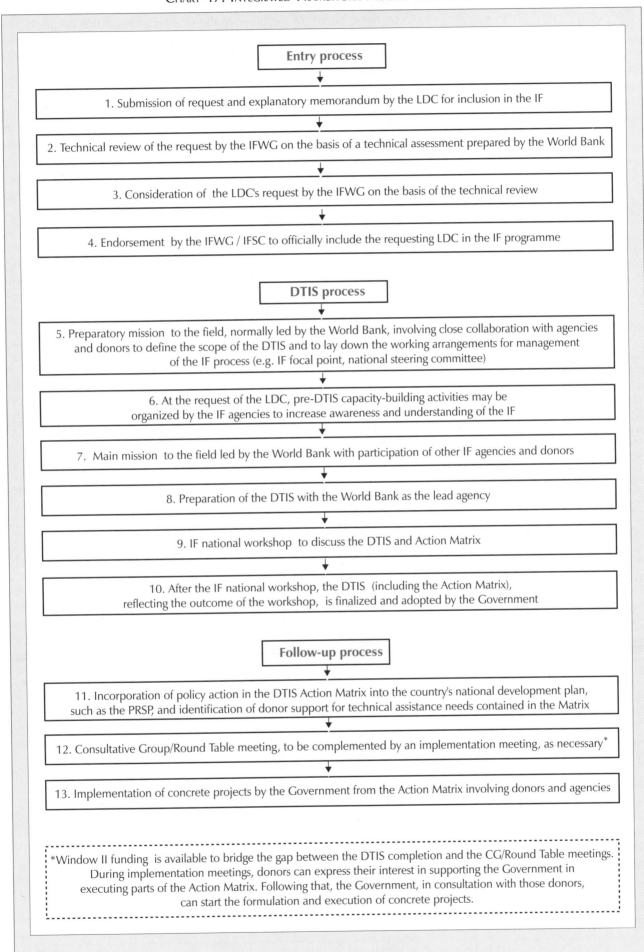

Entry process

1. Submission of request and explanatory memorandum by the LDC for inclusion in the IF

2. Technical review of the request by the IFWG on the basis of a technical assessment prepared by the World Bank

3. Consideration of the LDC's request by the IFWG on the basis of the technical review

4. Endorsement by the IFWG / IFSC to officially include the requesting LDC in the IF programme

DTIS process

5. Preparatory mission to the field, normally led by the World Bank, involving close collaboration with agencies and donors to define the scope of the DTIS and to lay down the working arrangements for management of the IF process (e.g. IF focal point, national steering committee)

6. At the request of the LDC, pre-DTIS capacity-building activities may be organized by the IF agencies to increase awareness and understanding of the IF

7. Main mission to the field led by the World Bank with participation of other IF agencies and donors

8. Preparation of the DTIS with the World Bank as the lead agency

9. IF national workshop to discuss the DTIS and Action Matrix

10. After the IF national workshop, the DTIS (including the Action Matrix), reflecting the outcome of the workshop, is finalized and adopted by the Government

Follow-up process

11. Incorporation of policy action in the DTIS Action Matrix into the country's national development plan, such as the PRSP, and identification of donor support for technical assistance needs contained in the Matrix

12. Consultative Group/Round Table meeting, to be complemented by an implementation meeting, as necessary*

13. Implementation of concrete projects by the Government from the Action Matrix involving donors and agencies

*Window II funding is available to bridge the gap between the DTIS completion and the CG/Round Table meetings. During implementation meetings, donors can express their interest in supporting the Government in executing parts of the Action Matrix. Following that, the Government, in consultation with those donors, can start the formulation and execution of concrete projects.

Participation in the IF involves a number of different steps (chart 47). However, the central building block of the whole process is the completion of the Diagnostic Trade Integration Study (DTIS). This study, whose preparation has generally been led by the World Bank, includes the identification of sectors of export potential, supply-side constraints on trade, human and institutional capacity constraints, measures to be taken to implement and apply international and regional trade agreements, and implications of analysis and recommendations for growth and poverty reduction. It also includes an Action Matrix that identifies the trade-capacity-building priorities. The DTIS is discussed at a national workshop by the Government and stakeholders. After this point, the trade-capacity-building priorities should be integrated into the overall national development strategy (or PRSP). Concrete trade-capacity-building projects then must compete with priority projects in other sectors for donor funding.

To finance the activities of the IF itself, a trust fund has been created with two Windows — Window I finances the DTIS, and Window II serves as an interim

TABLE 61. SUMMARY TABLE OF THE IF ACTION MATRICES AS OF APRIL 2004

Priority actions covered in Action Matrix	Burundi 2003[a]	Cambodia 2001	Ethiopia 2003	Guinea 2003	Lesotho 2003	Madagascar 2003	Malawi 2003	Mauritania 2001	Nepal 2003	Senegal 2002	Yemen 2003
Macroeconomic policy/institutional support for export development	x	x	x	x	x	x	x	x	x	x	x
Elaboration of a full poverty reduction and growth strategy (integration in the PRSP)	x									x	
Implementation of monetary and fiscal reforms	x	x	x	x	x	x	x	x	x	x	x
Debt management	x						x				
Regulatory environment for investment	x		x	x	x	x	x	x	x	x	x
Improve private/public sector dialogue			x	x	x	x	x	x			x
Trade policy	x	x	x	x	x	x	x	x	x	x	x
Strengthening institutional capacity	x	x	x	x	x	x	x	x	x	x	x
WTO accession		x	x				x		x		x
Tariff and duty drawback and tax reforms	x	x	x	x	x	x	x		x	x	x
Trade facilitation	x	x	x	x	x	x	x	x	x	x	x
Customs	x	x	x	x	x	x	x	x	x	x	x
Procedure	x	x	x	x	x	x	x	x	x	x	x
Governance	x	x	x	x	x	x	x	x	x	x	x
Institutional reform	x	x	x	x	x	x	x	x	x	x	x
Transport	x	x	x				x		x	x	x
Improvement of transit transport	x	x	x	x			x	x	x	x	x
Export Promotion/Diversification	x	x	x	x	x	x	x	x	x	x	x
Improvement of supply chain	x	x	x	x	x	x	x	x	x	x	x
Improvement of productivity, quality and standards	x	x	x	x	x	x	x	x	x	x	x
Increase export of non-traditional exports through implementation of a national export promotion strategy	x	x	x	x		x	x	x		x	
Access to credit	x	x	x	x	x	x	x	x	x	x	x
Sectoral priority sectors											
Fisheries		x		x		x		x		x	x
Agriculture		x	x	x		x	x	x	x	x	x
Livestock		x	x			x		x			
Handicrafts				x						x	
Manufacturing			x				x		x	x	
Tea, coffee, tobacco	x	x	x			x	x		x		
Tourism		x	x	x		x	x	x	x	x	
Electricity/water			x		x		x		x		
Telecommunications					x	x	x				x
Cultural industries		x									
Labour services										x	x
Infrastructure				x	x		x	x		x	
Rehabilitation of infrastructure				x	x		x	x		x	
Establish dialogue with commercial users				x			x	x		x	
New ways of financing infrastructure projects				x			x	x		x	
Poverty reduction			x								x
Connect poor households to local, regional and national markets			x								
Market information, studies on access issues and impact assessment of policy reforms			x								x

Source: Integrated Framework, Diagnostic Trade Integration Studies.

     a Year of validation of the Action Matrix.

bridging mechanism for priority capacity-building activities that have been identified in the Action Matrix. As of 31 March 2004, Window I had total pledges amounting to $12.5 million and disbursement amounting to $10.8 million. Window II had total pledges of $8.6 million and total disbursements of $5.5 million.

Table 61 summarizes the activities identified in the Action Matrices of the DTIS of the 11 LDCs that are members of the IF. As of March 2004, one project has benefited from Window II, but a number of projects are under consideration.

The IF is an important initiative. However, despite the revamping, the LDCs themselves have continued to express concerns about what it has delivered. As the Coordinator of the LDC Group in the WTO put it at the ninth meeting of the IF steering committee on 16 May 2003, "the IF has placed a great deal of emphasis on diagnostic activities, rather than on outcomes".

As the DTIS is the building block of the IF it is clear that its content is vital for the overall outcome process of trade mainstreaming. As earlier parts of this Report have shown, there is much useful information in the DTIS. But a major difficulty has been the inability to elaborate a methodology that puts the relationship between trade and poverty at the heart of the DTIS rather than as a separate chapter tacked onto the study. In this chapter, this Report has sought to make a constructive response to this problem by suggesting a methodology for integrating trade into development strategies and poverty reduction strategies. It is also recommended that, in order to ensure that the findings of the DTIS can be taken into account in the design of the PRSP, the timing of the DTIS should be phased to be at least six months in advance of the completion of the PRSP or relevant Progress Report.

In order to ensure that the findings of the DTIS can be taken into account in the design of the PRSP, the timing of the Diagnostic Trade Integration Study should be phased to be at least six months in advance of the completion of the PRSP or relevant Progress Report.

Another key issue regarding the DTIS as an instrument for mainstreaming trade in the PRSP is the effects that it has on country ownership of national policies. All stakeholders recognize that country ownership of the DTIS is critical for successful mainstreaming. There is no better way of securing commitment by the countries in the follow-up to and implementation of the recommendations emerging from the DTIS.

Against this background, special care needs to be taken to ensure that the DTIS is carried out in a way that promotes country ownership. It is clear that although some countries have the capacity to assert ownership, others do not and in these cases this capacity would need to be strengthened. The so-called pre-DTIS activities have an important role to play here. Country ownership can also be facilitated by making the establishment of a durable trade policy framework (as defined in the OECD Guidelines on Strengthening Capacity for Trade Development) the basic criterion to measure whether mainstreaming has taken place. This would ensure that mainstreaming is an ongoing and sustainable process rather than a one-shot outcome.

Developing production and trade capacities of the LDCs will require not only technical assistance but also greatly increased levels of international financial assistance.

4. POLICY COHERENCE BETWEEN DEBT RELIEF AND TRADE CAPACITY DEVELOPMENT

Developing production and trade capacities of the LDCs will require not only technical assistance but also greatly increased levels of international financial assistance. In this regard, it is encouraging that one of the points in the "Spirit of Monterrey" discussion at the Heads of State retreat at the UN International Conference on Financing for Development, held in Monterrey from 18 to 23

March 2002, was "We undertake to assist the world's poorest countries to double the size of their economies within a decade, in order to achieve the MDGs [Millennium Development Goals]". Official capital inflows are likely to contribute the most to this undertaking. However, the potential role of debt relief in trade development should not be ignored. Deeper debt relief can serve to improve the overall investment climate. Moreover, HIPC assistance can provide an additional source of finance for directly building production and trade capacities.

The need for greater policy coherence between debt relief and trade capacity development is all the more pressing because there are 32 LDCs which are HIPCs and, as the representatives of creditor countries agree, "the HIPC Initiative alone will not provide overall debt sustainability for the HIPCs" (World Bank, 2003: 77). The most likely future prospect for many completion point HIPCs, including the LDC-HIPCs, within the next five years is thus likely to be what Edwards (2002) has analysed for the case of Nicaragua, namely "an extremely severe external sector adjustment [which] is likely to require a massive real exchange devaluation [which] in turn will introduce fiscal difficulties in the future" (p. 531).

There is general agreement that debt sustainability depends on economic growth, productive investments and also increasing and stabilizing export earnings through diversified exports. Representatives of the debtor countries themselves argue that the most important risk to achieving the HIPC Initiative objectives is "the need to overcome longstanding vulnerabilities of the HIPC economies" (World Bank, 2003: 75). Dependence on primary commodities, volatile markets and lack of access to key markets are seen as "major impediments to growth and stability in exports", and building resilience to external shocks "remains an important challenge" (ibid.: 75). But because the Initiative has sought not only to enable debt sustainability but also to have a catalytic effect on poverty reduction, HIPC assistance has generally been targeted at social sectors up to now. Thus, for the 13 HIPCs which reached decision point after July 2000 and which had specific numerical targets for how HIPC savings would be allocated, on average 65 per cent of the savings were focused on social sectors, 13 per cent on rural development, 8 per cent on infrastructure, 4 per cent on governance and 2 per cent on structural reforms (World Bank, 2003: 34).

In short, as the evaluation of the HIPC Initiative has concluded, "its design is not consistent with the stated objectives" (World Bank, 2003: 55). In effect, the HIPC Initiative approach has been the channelling of assistance to alleviate the effects of the debt problem, rather than tackling its causes. Certainly, domestic mismanagement played some role in the build-up of the debt. But trade problems are at the heart of the genesis of the debt problem in the case study countries in the World Bank OED Report. As the latter puts it, "Most countries became severely indebted in response to terms of trade shocks and a subsequent decline in revenues, but continued maintenance of overextended public sectors. Their economies were particularly sensitive to export commodity price fluctuations, with adverse weather conditions also playing an important role in the agriculture-dominated economies. The main problem is the high concentration of export earnings in one or a few natural resource or agricultural commodities" (World Bank, 2003: 81).

This Report has established the existence of important indirect links between trade and poverty reduction that work through the development of productive capacities. There is thus no need for development partners to believe that trade

> *The need for greater policy coherence between debt relief and trade capacity development is all the more pressing because there are 32 LDCs which are HIPCs.*

> *There is general agreement that debt sustainability depends on economic growth, productive investments and also increasing and stabilizing export earnings through diversified exports.*

development is too far removed from the cutting edge of direct poverty reduction. To the extent that trade issues are included in the PRSPs in a coherent way that links policy measures to strategic goals, there is a strong case for facilitating the wider use of HIPC assistance for the development of productive sectors and for trade development. This would increase the coherence of the HIPC Initiative itself and could contribute additional and perhaps catalytic resources for trade capacity development. But in the end, if countries are not to be left running faster in the same place as before, highly indebted and very poor, there is a need for re-enhanced debt relief and additional international financial assistance provided in a way that is consistent with the development of productive and trade capacities.

F. Conclusions

The main message of this chapter is that LDC Governments can strengthen the links between international trade and poverty reduction by mainstreaming both trade and development into their poverty reduction strategies. Contrary to common conceptions, trade issues are at the heart of the PRSPs. Export and import growth targets are included in all of them as part of their macroeconomic frameworks, and most also include various trade objectives, such as improved competitiveness and diversification, as well as a range of trade policy instruments, such as infrastructure investment and export promotion. An export-led growth strategy is implicit in many of them. But despite the fact that trade issues are present in the PRSPs, trade objectives and trade instruments are treated in a general way, and there are weak links between strategic goals and priority public actions. This weakness is a general problem with the PRSPs rather than a specific problem of the way in which trade is included in them.

The chapter proposes a methodology for integrating trade into poverty reduction strategies. The methodology focuses on changes in the income elasticity of demand for imports and for exports that are required in order to achieve and sustain growth rates necessary for the poverty reduction target of a country. It also involves analysis of the policy options and instruments to achieve these changes. It is argued that this methodology will only work if there is a durable trade policy framework, including government and the private sector, through which the trade development interests of a country are identified and ways of giving effect to them are implemented. The basic elements of a durable trade policy framework are set out in the OECD/DAC Guidelines on Strengthening Capacity for Trade Development (OECD, 2001).

The links between international trade and poverty reduction can best be strengthened if a poverty reduction strategy is anchored in a national development strategy. The choice of national development strategy is central to future poverty reduction prospects. It governs such key influences on poverty as the rural–urban income gap, the rate of agricultural productivity growth and industrial employment generation.

The evidence of this Report suggests that in an LDC context in which there is generalized poverty and most people live at or below income levels sufficient to meet their basic needs, an export-led growth strategy is not likely to be associated with an inclusive growth process. Against this background, it appears that a hybrid strategy that combines an export-led growth strategy with a basic needs strategy (focused on providing basic social services) is emerging, with the latter leg of the strategy being met through international financial assistance. This

LDC Governments can strengthen the links between international trade and poverty reduction by mainstreaming both trade and development into their poverty reduction strategies.

In an LDC context in which there is generalized poverty and most people live at or below income levels sufficient to meet their basic needs, an export-led growth strategy is not likely to be associated with an inclusive growth process.

approach, which could be called export-led growth with a human face, is certainly going to lead to a more virtuous trade–poverty relationship. But as limited international assistance becomes absorbed more and more in basic needs provision, it is less available for developing the production sectors and for private sector development. The great danger of this strategy is that countries will end up with a deepening debt problem.

There is a need for alternative post-liberal development strategies. These are strategies implemented in an open economy in which incentives are biased in favour neither of exports nor of imports and in which there is no discrimination between agriculture and the manufacturing sectors.

The Report thus argues that there is a need for alternative post-liberal development strategies. These are strategies implemented in an open economy in which incentives are biased in favour neither of exports nor of imports and in which there is no discrimination between agriculture and the manufacturing sectors. Export-led growth and export-led growth with a human face are two such strategies. But it is also possible to elaborate other strategies which seek to achieve adequate export growth rather than export-led growth. The Report identifies five such strategies:

- A balanced growth strategy based on agricultural productivity growth and export-accelerated industrialization;

- An agricultural-development-led industrialization (ADLI) strategy – which includes infrastructure investment and technological progress in agriculture together with forward linkages into processing activities – with an export component;

- Development and diversification through management of mineral revenues;

- Development of natural-resource-based production clusters;

- A triadic development strategy, which includes the promotion of competitive tradables, employment-intensive non-tradables and labour-saving technological change in subsistence-oriented activities.

These are likely to be relevant in different contexts.

Better national development strategies, increased and effective international assistance and a more enabling rather than more constraining international trade environment together can ensure that the major role which international trade could play in poverty reduction in the LDCs becomes a reality.

New types of development policy are required in order to promote development in the new open trading environment. The commitment to an open trade regime does not necessarily imply the need for laissez-faire within a country. Rather, there is a need for a mixed economy in which there is a balance between the State and the market. Governments should use market-supporting mechanisms aimed at market creation, market development and market acceleration. Domestic policies should be used to address coordination failures and to correct distortions in domestic markets, which in situations of underdevelopment are manifold.

It is important that efforts to integrate trade and development into poverty reduction strategies be actively supported through increased and effective international financial and technical assistance to build productive and trade capacities. An important feature of the way in which the PRSPs treat trade issues is that trade development is closely related to the issue of private sector development, improvements in the investment climate and also the development of productive sectors. This is an important signal from the LDCs to their development partners on the best way to treat trade development in those countries.

The evidence shows that aid for trade has not been a major priority in the past and its effectiveness is likely to have been undermined by biases arising from the overlap between the development objectives of developed countries (as donors) and their commercial interests (as trading powers). Mainstreaming trade into aid policies is as important as mainstreaming trade into development strategies.

Finally, it is important to emphasize that although appropriate national development strategies are a sine qua non for making international trade a more effective means of poverty reduction in the LDCs, success will not be assured unless there are supportive international policies as well. The policy configuration that will do most to strengthen the relationship between international trade and poverty reduction is one which has three pillars. The first pillar is better national development strategies that integrate trade issues as a central component. The second is increased and effective international assistance to build productive capacities and trade capacities, and support private sector development. The third pillar is a more enabling rather than more constraining international trade environment. Together these three pillars can ensure that the major role which international trade could play in poverty reduction in the LDCs becomes a reality.

Annex to chapter 7

ALTERNATIVE POST-LIBERAL DEVELOPMENT STRATEGIES

The five strategies outlined here, which are not exhaustive, underline the fact that there are a number of alternative post-liberal development strategies. As defined in the main text, these are strategies that can be implemented in an open trade regime in which incentives are biased in favour neither of exports nor of imports and in which there is no discrimination between agriculture and manufacturing sectors. This Report does not advocate one over the other. It is up to the countries themselves to decide what is most appropriate for them on the basis of their goals and also an evaluation of both demand and supply constraints on what they are doing. This choice may also lead to the view that what is best is export-led growth or export-led growth with a human face.

1. Balanced growth based on agricultural productivity growth and export-accelerated industrialization

This strategy is the most fully elaborated development strategy outlined here. It is applicable to countries which (i) are predominantly agrarian in the sense that, initially, the majority of the labour force is employed in agriculture; (ii) have a small industrial sector alongside agriculture; and (iii) have surplus labour in rural areas owing to a large labour supply in relation to the available land. The strategy seeks to promote development and poverty reduction through a process of industrialization, linked in a balanced way to the development of the rural economy and agriculture. Over time there is a structural transformation in which the proportion of the working population engaged in non-agricultural occupations increases, and the population of working age becomes more and more fully and productively employed. For sustained growth and substantial poverty reduction to occur, various domestic conditions have to be put in place (see Fei and Ranis, 1997). These are as follows:

- Agricultural productivity must rise at a rate sufficient for the production and marketing of enough food to be able to feed the entire population, including the increasing fraction of the population working outside agriculture. This requires continuous technological progress in agriculture, and institutional and organizational changes, including land reform.

- The growth rate of the industrial labour force must be faster than the growth rate of the total labour force. The growth of the industrial labour force depends on the rate of industrial capital accumulation and the employment intensity of industrial investment, which depends on the rate of technological change and the nature of technological choices, particularly whether innovations have a labour-using bias. The effort which is required, in terms of the rate of capital accumulation and the labour-using bias of innovation, to ensure that sufficient industrial employment is created depends on the rate of population growth. The higher the rate of population growth, the greater the effort needed.

- There must be balance in intersectoral labour markets. The number of new employment opportunities created in industry must be in step with the number of persons released from agriculture.

- There must be balance in intersectoral product markets. The domestic intersectoral terms of trade should not shift against agriculture or industry, and must provide sufficient incentives for farmers to purchase consumer goods and modern inputs, as well as a financial surplus for savings and investment, and real urban wages which enable workers to live at a consumption standard which is slightly above that in rural areas (a condition for labour transfer to occur) but not too high to eat into industrial profits and thus slow the industrial accumulation process.

- There must be balance in intersectoral financial markets. Until the economy's centre of gravity moves to the industrial sector and retained profits of industrial enterprises become a key component of domestic savings, the major source of finance for industrial accumulation must come from the agriculture sector. The intersectoral flow of finance out of agriculture, together with retained profits within the industrial sector, must be sufficient to meet the demand for industrial investment but not so great that it undermines agricultural productivity growth.

- The whole process of balanced intersectoral growth must take place at a rate which satisfies a society's impatience to emerge from generalized poverty. As agricultural productivity increases it may be expected that there will be an upward creep in the basic consumption standard and also in rural incomes and wage rates. But if all the agricultural productivity gains are consumed by farm households themselves, the fraction of the population employed outside agriculture cannot rise. Increasing real wages and the labour share similarly eats into industrial profits.

In successful cases, international trade, as well as international capital inflows and technology imports, have facilitated the realization of these domestic conditions. In the early stages agricultural exports enable imports of consumer goods, capital goods and raw materials that are necessary for supporting the development of domestic industrial capacities. After an initial import substitution phase, the development of labour-intensive manufactures exports accelerates the process of structural transformation and increase in the proportion of the labour force productively employed outside agriculture. Later on, exports of labour-intensive manufactures support the development of exports of more skill-intensive and capital-intensive manufactures. International trade supports the employment intensity of the industrial accumulation process because capital goods can be imported and thus the establishment of basic capital goods industries, which tend to be more capital-using than labour-using, can be delayed in the early stages of the development process.

This strategy has been the basis for sustained economic growth and poverty reduction in successful industrializing Asian economies with surplus labour. In these cases, the trade policy has been a mix of import protection and export promotion in the context of very gradual liberalization, and this has been linked to proactive guidance of the process of capital accumulation and technical progress within the domestic economy. Amongst the LDCs, Bangladesh may be seen as a successful application of the balanced growth strategy (see Arndt et al., 2002). In this case, too, trade liberalization has been gradual.

2. A strategy of agricultural-development-led industrialization with primary exports

This strategy is an agriculture-first strategy with the added dimension that agro-industrial development is promoted. The major focus of the strategy is a shift in the sectoral emphasis of public investment towards agriculture (Adelman, 1984). This should be directed to improving primary production technology, rural infrastructure and the marketing system. Improvements in agricultural productivity focused on small- and medium-scale farmers should encourage domestic demand for intermediate and consumer goods produced by domestic industry. Improving the productivity of agriculture and letting farmers share in the fruits of improved productivity build a domestic mass-consumption market. In this situation, industrialization can be agricultural-development-led rather than export-led. But the process of agricultural development can be facilitated through agricultural (and agro-industrial) exports.

This strategy is being pursued by Ethiopia, and is written into its PRSP, but there have been mixed results thus far. Analysis has shown that the agricultural-development-led (ADLI) strategy is not subject to a fallacy-of-composition problem (i.e. it works if one country applies it, but not if all countries apply it) and that its realization would yield benefits for rich countries as well as poor countries (Adelman et al., 1989). The relevance of this strategy to sub-Saharan African has been questioned because of the lack of technologies for sustainable high-productivity food agriculture in fragile tropical ecological environments and the expected low responsiveness of domestic manufacturing industries to the expansion of demand associated with agricultural development (Adelman and Vogel, 1991). However, econometric modelling has demonstrated the superiority of the strategy in Mozambique (Jensen and Tarp, 2004). Bhaduri and Skarstein (2003), though not explicitly working on the topic, also set out some conditions for the successful implementation of an ADLI-type strategy.

3. Development and diversification through management of mineral and oil revenues

This strategy is less well defined than the first two strategies, but there is an increasing body of knowledge on best practices for development in mineral- and oil-based economies. The strategy needs to be adapted to the cycle of mineral exploitation. In the early stages, there is rapid expansion of the mining sector and the key issue is to manage Dutch disease effects – the appreciation of the exchange rate and a weakening of the competitiveness of non-mining tradables in agriculture. In early maturity, there is a slowdown in mining expansion and the encouragement of diversification becomes increasingly important. In late maturity, the mineral sector loses its dynamism as reserves are depleted and other sectors take over as the main sources of economic growth (Auty, 1999).

Throughout the process the central issue is the mechanism for the management of revenues from extractive industries. These revenues should be derived from a taxation system which (i) creates sufficient incentive for investors and (ii) secures a fair share of mining revenues for public use. At the macroeconomic level, the objective is to achieve sound and sustainable management of government expenditure and revenues, including mineral revenues. This requires the adoption of sound fiscal rules, the application of conservative price forecasting and the development of a savings strategy aimed at dealing with temporary revenue fluctuations. Earnings stabilization and sterilization are particularly important in economies whose domestic financial market is too small to absorb excess funds and hence to stem Dutch disease effects (Mayer, 1999).

Diversification can be promoted through using part of resource revenues to improve conditions for establishment of new businesses, for example, through well targeted investment in physical and human infrastructure. Experience from Botswana and Chile seems to show that such efforts yield the best results when the new businesses are linked to the mineral sector in a strategy utilizing the dynamism of natural resource based production clusters (see below). This also means that the regional scope of new activities may be quite narrow, and that broader based diversification has to be supported through building of capacity, particularly human capital.

Separating mineral revenue flows from other revenues makes their management more transparent to policy makers, administrators and the public, can assist in the build-up of pressure to spend incautiously. But a non-renewable natural resources fund should function in support of, not a substitute for, good fiscal management. To be transparent, sound and effective funds must be founded upon three broad principles: (i) a consolidated budget framework whereby the fund is channelled through the general government budget and treasury system; (ii) a liquidity constraint on the government budget, implying that assets accumulated in the fund should not be counterbalanced by new borrowings from other sources; and (iii) limits on domestic investment from the fund in order to maintain the fund's objective of savings strategy (Daniels, 2003).

At regional or local levels, development of mineral projects often leads to demand for special fiscal treatment from the community where the project is located and in extreme circumstances these have led to secession movements or civil war. Such demands are also usually rooted in the perception that the economic benefits from mining projects are unequally distributed and reach only a very small portion of the population, while the rest are exposed to negative effects in terms of rising prices, pressure on public services and social problems arising from an inflow of migrants. Regional or local governments can benefit from special expenditure programmes or revenue instruments. Whereas the former better protect fiscal integrity at the national level, the latter provide local communities with a guaranteed source of funds from which to finance investment in public services. However, since mining projects usually do not start paying taxes until several years into operation, whereas expenditure needs arise much earlier, during construction, revenue sharing systems do not fully solve the problem of distribution of revenues. Overall, the need for a consultative and participatory process is at the heart of the matter

4. A development strategy founded on natural-resource-based production clusters

This strategy seeks to promote the development of incipient natural-resource-based production clusters (Ramos, 1998). These production clusters are sectoral and/or geographical concentrations of enterprises engaged in interlinked activities based on the exploitation and processing of natural resources and the related supporting industries. Analysis of "mature" production clusters in countries which are now developed and also rich in natural resources, such as the Scandinavian countries and Canada, makes it possible to identify a typical process of production cluster formation which includes (i) natural resource extraction with little processing; (ii) greater processing before export and also import substitution of some equipment and inputs (typically under licence to the domestic market); (iii) development, alongside unprocessed and processed natural resource exports, of exports of goods and services originally produced for import substitution purposes, usually in undemanding markets; and (iv) all types of goods exported, including more sophisticated processed goods, inputs and machinery for demanding markets, and design, engineering and consultancy services. This whole process takes a long time, as Ramos illustrates with the case of Finland. The development strategy would seek to accelerate it, following the direction of the natural evolution of market forces (ibid.: 124). In this strategy, particular attention needs to be given to activities that might need more foreign direct investment, the identification of key technologies for the development of the cluster and also infrastructural needs in terms of physical infrastructure, human resources, and scientific and technical knowledge.

This strategy has been proposed as being particularly relevant for countries that are rich in natural resources. The resources can be either agricultural or mineral, and so this strategy could be linked to the last two. It has been advocated as being particularly relevant to Latin America (Ramos, 1998). It is also clear that it has played an important role in the development process in South-East Asia, where the Governments of Malaysia and Thailand followed a dual strategy of promoted exports based natural resources and exports based on abundant low-cost labour (Reinhardt, 2000). The Malaysian approach is likely to be particularly relevant to LDCs.

5. A triadic strategy of employment-led growth

This strategy has been proposed as being particularly relevant for LDCs seeking to escape the poverty trap and promote an inclusive development process (Sachs, 2003). The key to inclusive development is not simply higher rates of economic growth but also the maximization of the employment intensity of growth. Financing non-inflationary sustained growth in LDC-type economies depends on the following: increasing import capacity (through export promotion, import substitution and elimination of non-essential imports); an elastic supply of food and other wage goods to meet the increased demand of additionally employed and/or better remunerated workers (through removing institutional obstacles to agricultural development in particular); and increasing domestic savings (which can come partly as a result of a higher rate of overall growth and partly as a result of an increasing share of savings in GNP).

Within this macroeconomic framework, a triadic strategy should be adopted which addresses tradables, non-tradables and also subsistence activities. High priority should be given to consolidation and expansion of tradable sectors. The more labour-intensive these sectors are, the better it is from the point of view of employment generation. But international competition implies that there may be little margin of freedom in terms of choice of technique, and thus growth within the tradable sectors may have a relatively low employment intensity. Thus the second part of the strategy should be to promote all opportunities for employment-intensive growth in non-tradable sectors. These sectors include infrastructure and housing; basic services (education, health, sanitation, communication, post and public administration); technical services, repair and maintenance, and most transportation services; and also perishable foodstuffs and buly agricultural products. These activities do not face international competition and there are thus much greater possibilities for increasing the employment intensity of growth. There are also opportunities to reduce the savings constraint on investment through exploiting "non-investment sources of growth" (such as better utilization of existing productive capacities and improved maintenance of the existing stock of infrastructure, equipment and buildings) and also non-monetary investment (for example, self-help housing in urban centres and creation of simple rural infrastructure through labour). Finally, the third part of the triadic strategy entails rationalizing and modernizing subsistence activities. This is particularly important in an LDC context not because there is a self-contained subsistence sector, but because a large proportion of the total time available for work is devoted to subsistence activities. Technical innovations in subsistence farming, the supply and storage of water and energy, and cooking, to name but a few subsistence activities, can have an immediate positive impact on personal well-being and also release time to devote to other activities.

Notes

1. The notion of "two-way mainstreaming" was proposed by Lakshmi Puri (2003).
2. The projected GDP growth rates over the period 2002–2004 in Mali, Rwanda and Zambia are 9.9 per cent, 10 per cent and 6 per cent respectively, whilst the projected import growth rates are 8.2 per cent, 2.8 per cent and 4.8 per cent respectively.
3. For a lucid discussion of this approach to mainstreaming trade in PRSPs see McCulloch, Winters and Cirera (2001).
4. The term "post-liberal development strategy" is due to Carter and Barham (1996).
5. Estimates for some African LDCs, based on the growth rates required in order to meet the goal of reducing the incidence of poverty by half by 2015, are given in Hussain (2001).
6. For some estimates for Africa see Ng and Yeats (2002).
7. This database is available at http://tcbdb.wto.org
8. The data for 2002 and 2003, although available, were not taken into account because their provisionality may have altered the evolutionary trends of the series.
9. The series for export promotion from multilateral institutions end in 2000.
10. Within the OECD Creditor Reporting System this is defined by codes 210 and 22020 less 21081.
11. This point is also made in OECD/ECA (2003) which in clarifying the scope of trade capacity building states that: "Comprehensive approaches are required which address *trade policy* constraints together with constraints in *producing and getting products to markets*. Trade capacity building must embrace both the short-term WTO negotiating and implementation agendas with the longer-term supply-side development agenda. Trade capacity building should include also the capacity to influence the agenda setting of international trade rules. And it should not focus solely on compliance with those rules, as market access alone has limited benefits if supply-side issues are not addressed. Finally, the focus should be on imports as well as exports. Increased technology transfers via imports of advanced goods and services is itself a form of capacity building."
12. For a summary of recent initiatives see the WTO/OECD database.

References

Adelman, I. (1984). Beyond export-led growth, *World Development*, 12 (9): 937–949.

Adelman, I. (1986). A poverty-focused approach to development policy, In: *Development Strategies Reconsidered*, ed. by Lewis, J.P, Overseas Development Council, Washington DC.

Adelman, I., Bournieux, J.M. and Waelbroeck, J. (1989). Agricultural development-led industrialization in a global perspective. In: Williamson, J. G. and Panchamukhi, V. R., eds., *The Balance between Industry and Agriculture in Economic Development*, vol. 2, Macmillan Press, London.

Adelman, I. and Vogel, S.J. (1991). The relevance of ADLI for sub-Saharan Africa, *African Development Perspectives Yearbook 1990/1*, II: 258–279.

Ali, I. and Pernia, E.M. (2003). Infrastructure and Poverty Reduction — What is the Connection?, ERD Policy Brief Series No. 13, Economics and Research Department, Asian Development Bank, Manila.

Amsden, A.H. (2001). *The Rise of "the Rest" — Challenges to the West from Late-Industrializing Economies*, Oxford University Press, New York.

Arndt, C., Dorosh, P., Fontana, M., Zohir, S., El-Said, M. and Lungren, C. (2002). Opportunities and challenges in agriculture and garments: A general equilibrium analysis of the Bangladesh economy, Discussion Paper No. 107, International Food Policy Research Institute, Washington DC.

Auty, R. (1999). The transition from rent-driven growth to skill-driven growth: Recent experience of five mineral economies. In: Mayer, J., Chambers, B. and Farooq, A. eds., *Development Policies in Natural Resource Economies*, Edward Elgar, Cheltenham, United Kingdom.

Bhaduri, A. and Skarstein, R. (2003). Notes and comments – Effective demand and the terms of trade in a dual economy: A Kaldorian perspective, *Cambridge Journal of Economics*, 27 (4): 583–595.

Bhagwati, J. (2001). *Free Trade Today*, Princeton University Press, Princeton.

Blecker, R.A. (2002). The diminishing returns to export-led growth, In: Schwenninger, S. and Mead, R.W., eds., *The Bridge to a Global Middle Class*, Council on Foreign Relations, New York.

Bradford, C.I. (1994). From trade-driven growth to growth-driven trade: Reappraising the East Asian development experience, OECD, Paris.

Carter, M.R. and Barham, B.L. (1996). Level playing fields and *laissez faire*: Postliberal development strategy in inegalitarian agrarian economies, *World Development*, 24 (7): 1133–1149.

Cramer, C. (1999). Can Africa industrialise by processing primary commodities? The case of Mozambican cashew nuts", *World Development*, 27 (7): 1247–1266.

Daniels, P. (2003). Mineral revenue management: policy issues for mineral economies in Africa, *Module 3: Mineral Rent and Revenue Management*, UNCTAD/ECA Paper No. ECA/RCID/UNDESA/UNCTAD/020/02, Lusaka, Zambia.

Diao, X., Dorosh, P., Rahman, S.M., Meijer, S., Rosegrant, M., Yanoma, Y. and Li, W. (2003). Market opportunities for African agriculture: An examination of demand-side constraints on agriculture growth, DSGD Discussion Paper No. 1, International Food Policy Research Institute, Washington DC.

Economic Commission for Africa (ECA) (2003). Press release No. 26/2003, Addis Ababa, Ethiopia (http://www.uneca.org/eca_resources/Press_Releases/2003_pressreleases/pressrelease2603.htm).

Edwards, S. (2003). Debt relief and fiscal sustainability. NBER Working Paper No. W8939, National Bureau of Economic Research, Cambridge, Mass.

Fay, M. (2001). Financing the future: infrastructure needs in Latin America, 2000-05, World Bank, Washington DC.

Fay, M. and Yepes, T. (2003). Investing in infrastructure: what is needed from 2000 to 2010?, Policy Research Working Paper No. 3102, World Bank, Washington DC.

Fei, J.C. and Ranis, G. (1997). *Growth and Development from An Evolutionary Perspective*, Blackwell, Oxford.

Felipe, J. (2003). Is export-led growth passé? Implications for developing Asia, ERD Working Paper No. 48, Economics and Research Department, Asian Development Bank, Manila.

Gabre-Madhin, E.Z. and Haggblade, S. (2003). Successes in African agriculture: Results of an expert survey, Conference Paper No. 1, presented at the InWEnt, IFPRI, NEPAD and CTA Conference "Successes in African Agriculture", 1–3 December 2003, Pretoria.

GATT secretariat (1994). The results of the Uruguay Round of Multilateral Trade Negotiations, Geneva.

GRIPS Development Forum (2003). *Linking Economic Growth and Poverty Reduction: Large-Scale Infrastructure in the Context of Vietnam's CPRGS*, National Graduate Institute for Policy Studies, Japan.

Helleiner, G. ed. (2002). *Non-Traditional Export Promotion in Africa: Experience and Issues*, Palgrave, Hampshire.

Hewitt, A. and Gillson, I. (2003). A review of the trade and poverty content in PRSPs and loan-related documents, Report commissioned by Christian Aid, (http://www.odi.org.uk/iedg/Projects/christian_aid_paper.pdf).

Hussain, M.N. (2001). "Exorcising the ghost": An alternate model for measuring the financing gap in developing countries, *Journal of Post Keynesian Economics*, 24 (1): 89–124.

IMF/World Bank (2003). Poverty Reduction Strategy Papers (PRSPS) – Progress in the implementation, 22 September, Washington DC.

International Trade Centre UNCTAD/WTO (ITC) (1999). *Building Value Through Public Procurement: A Focus on Africa*, Geneva.

International Trade Centre UNCTAD/WTO (ITC) (2000). *Improving SME Access to Public Procurement — The Experience of Selected Countries*, Geneva.

International Trade Centre UNCTAD/WTO (ITC) (2001a). *ITC's Export-led Poverty Reduction Programme (EPRP)*, Geneva.

International Trade Centre UNCTAD/WTO (ITC) (2001b). *Converting LDC Export Opportunities into Business: A strategic response*, Geneva.

International Trade Centre UNCTAD/WTO (ITC) (2004). *Purchasing and Supply Chain Management: A Strategic Overview, Coursebook*, Geneva.

Jensen, H.T. and Tarp, F. (2004 forthcoming). On the choice of appropriate development strategy: Insights gained from CGE modelling of the Mozambican economy, *Journal of African Economies*.

Kydd, J., Dorward, A. and Poulton, C. (2002). Institutional dimensions of trade liberalisation and poverty, paper presented at OECD Global Forum on Agriculture, 23–24 May 2002, Paris.

Kydd, J., and Dorward, A. (2002). Locked in & locked out: smallholder farmers and the new economy in low income countries, paper presented at the 13th International Farm Management Congress, 7–12 July 2002, Netherlands.

Ladd, P. (2002). Too hot to handle? The absence of trade policy from PRSPs, Christian Aid, United Kingdom.

Mayer, J. (1999). Conclusions. In: Mayer, J., Chambers, B., Farooq, A. (eds.), *Development Policies in Natural Resources Economies*, Edward Elgar, Cheltenham, United Kingdom.

McCulloch, N., Winters, L.A. and Cirera, X. (2001). *Trade Liberalization and Poverty: A Handbook*, Centre for Economic Policy Research, London (http://cepr.org/pubs/books/P144.asp).

McMillan, M., Rodrik, D., Welch, K. (2002). When economic reform goes wrong: cashews in Mozambique, mimeo, (http://ksghome.harvard.edu/~.drodrik.academic.ksg/).

Ng, F. and Yeats, A. (2002) What can Africa expect from its traditional exports?, Africa Region Working Paper Series No. 26, World Bank, Washington DC.

Odhiambo, W. and Kamau, P. (2003). What measures should be taken to set an effective public procurement system in East Africa?, OECD Development Centre (http://www.eldis.org/static/DOC13878.htm).

OECD (2001). *The DAC Guidelines — Strengthening Trade Capacity for Development*, Paris.

OECD (2002). A summary of discussion at the Mombasa regional workshop on trade capacity building — Experiences in an African context, 26-27 August 2002, Mombasa.

OECD Development Centre (2003). *Public Procurement: Lessons from Kenya, Tanzania and Uganda*, Technical Papers No. 208, DEV/DOC(2003)06, Paris.

Ohno, K. (2003). *East Asian Growth and Japanese Aid Strategy*, National Graduate Institute for Policy Studies, GRIPS Development Forum, Tokyo, Japan.

Palley, T.I. (2002). A new development paradigm: Domestic demand-led growth, why it is needed and how to make it happen, discussion paper presented to the Alternatives to Neoliberalism Conference, 23–24 May 2002, Washington DC.

Prowse, S. (2002). The role of international and national agencies in trade-related capacity building, *The World Economy*, 25 (9).

Puri, L. (2003). Statement at the International Conference on "Trade Growth and Poverty", organised by DFID, European Commission, International Monetary Fund, UNDP, held in London, 8–9 December 2003.

Raghavendran, V. (2003). An Evaluation of the export-led poverty reduction programme of the international trade centre, International Trade Center, Geneva (http://sites.maxwell.syr.edu/intleval/papers/Vimala.htm).

Ramos, J. (1998). A development strategy founded on natural resource-based production clusters, *Cepal Review*, 66: 105–127.

Redding, S. (1999) Dynamic comparative advantage and the welfare effects of trade, *Oxford Economic Papers*, No. 140, 51(1): 15–39.

Reinhardt, N. (2000). Back to basics in Malaysia and Thailand: The role of resource-based exports in their export-led growth, *World Development*, 28 (1): 57–77.

Sachs, I. (2003). From poverty trap to inclusive development in LDCs, background paper prepared for the *Least Developed Countries Report 2004*, Geneva.

Schydlowsky, D.M. (1984). A policymaker's guide to comparative advantage, *World Development*, 12 (4): 439–449.

Solignac Lecomte, H.B. (2001). Building capacity to trade: A road map for development partners — Insights from Africa and the Caribbean, ECDPM Discussion Paper No. 33, Maastricht (http://www.oneworld.org/ecdpm/pubs/dp33_gb.htm).

Solignac Lecomte, H.B. (2003). Building capacity to trade: What are the priorities?, Web Docs No. 11, OECD Development Centre, Paris (http://www.oecd.org/dev/technics).

TechnoServe (2003). Mozambique cashewnut sub-sector, Norwalk, U.S.A., (http://www.technoserve.org/sitemap.html).

UNCTAD (1994). *Trade and Development Report, 1994*, United Nations publication, sales no. E.94.II.D.26, Geneva.

UNCTAD (1996). *Trade and Development Report, 1996*, United Nations publication, sales no. E.96.II.D.6, Geneva.

UNCTAD (2000). *The Least Developed Countries 2000 Report – Aid, Private Capital Flows and External Debt: The Challenge of Financing Development in the LDCs*, United Nations publication, sales no. E.00.II.D.21, Geneva.

UNCTAD (2001). Growing micro and small enterprises in LDCs — The "missing middle" in LDCs: Why micro and small enterprises are not growing, UNCTAD/ITE/TEB/5, Geneva.

UNCTAD (2002). *The Least Developed Countries Report 2002 – Escaping the Poverty Trap*, United Nations publication, sales no. E.02.II.D.13, Geneva.

Vos, R., Morley, S., Enrique, G. and Sherman, R. eds. (2004 forthcoming). *Does Trade Liberalization and Export-led Growth Help Reduce Poverty? Success and Failure in Latin America in the 1990s*, Edward Elgar, United Kingdom.

World Bank (2003). *Debt Relief for the Poorest — An OED Review of the HIPC Initiative*, Work Bank, Washington DC.

Statistical Annex

BASIC DATA ON THE
LEAST DEVELOPED COUNTRIES

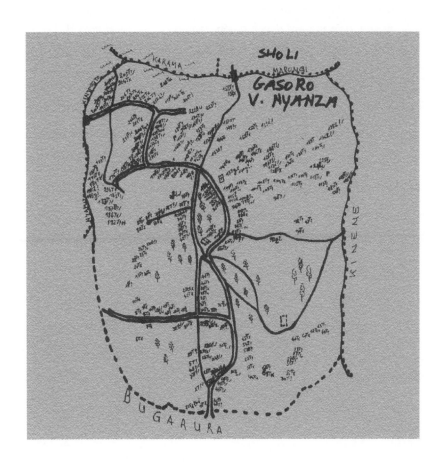

The Statistical Annex has been prepared using the same data sources as recent Least Developed Countries Reports. This is to ensure continuity. Some new indicators have been added. These are related to the Millennium Development ment Goals and the development targets of the Third Programme of Action for the Least Developed Countries for the Decade 2001–2010.

Contents

Explanatory Notes

Definition of country groupings

Least developed countries

The United Nations has designated 50 countries as least developed: Afghanistan, Angola, Bangladesh, Benin, Bhutan, Burkina Faso, Burundi, Cambodia, Cape Verde, the Central African Republic, Chad, the Comoros, the Democratic Republic of the Congo, Djibouti, Equatorial Guinea, Eritrea, Ethiopia, Gambia, Guinea, Guinea-Bissau, Haiti, Kiribati, the Lao People's Democratic Republic, Lesotho, Liberia, Madagascar, Malawi, Maldives, Mali, Mauritania, Mozambique, Myanmar, Nepal, Niger, Rwanda, Samoa, Sao Tome and Principe, Senegal, Sierra Leone, Solomon Islands, Somalia, Sudan, Timor-Leste (as of December 2003), Togo, Tuvalu, Uganda, the United Republic of Tanzania, Vanuatu, Yemen and Zambia.   Except where otherwise indicated, the totals for least developed countries refer to these 49 countries.

Major economic areas

The classification of countries and territories according to main economic areas used in this document has been adopted for purposes of statistical convenience only and follows that in the UNCTAD *Handbook of International Trade and Development Statistics 2003*.[1] Countries and territories are classified according to main economic areas as follows:

Developed market economy countries: Andorra, Australia, Canada, the European Union (Austria, Belgium, Denmark, Finland, France, Germany, Greece, Ireland, Italy, Luxembourg, the Netherlands, Portugal, Spain, Sweden and the United Kingdom), Faeroe Islands, Gibraltar, Iceland, Israel, Japan, Liechtenstein, Malta, Monaco, New Zealand, Norway, Switzerland and the United States.

Countries in Central and Eastern Europe: Albania, Belarus, Bosnia and Herzegovina, Bulgaria, Croatia, Czech Republic, Estonia, Hungary, Latvia, Lithuania, Macedonia, the former Yugoslav Republic of, Poland, the Republic of Moldova, Romania, the Russian Federation, Serbia and Montenegro, Slovakia, Slovenia and Ukraine.

Developing countries and territories: All other countries, territories and areas in Africa, Asia, America, Europe and Oceania not specified above.

Other country groupings

DAC member countries: The countries members of the OECD Development Assistance Committee are Australia, Austria, Belgium, Canada, Denmark, Finland, France, Germany, Greece, Ireland, Italy, Japan, Luxembourg, the Netherlands, New Zealand, Norway, Portugal, Spain, Sweden, Switzerland, the United Kingdom and the United States.

OPEC member countries: The countries members of the Organization of the Petroleum Exporting Countries are Algeria, Indonesia, Iran (Islamic Republic of), Iraq, Kuwait, the Libyan Arab Jamahiriya, Nigeria, Qatar, Saudi Arabia, the United Arab Emirates and Venezuela.

Other notes

Calculation of annual average growth rates. In general, they are defined as the coefficient b in the exponential trend function $y^t = ae^{bt}$ where t stands for time. This method takes all observations in a period into account. Therefore, the resulting growth rates reflect trends that are not unduly influenced by exceptional values.

Population growth rates are calculated as exponential growth rates.

The term "dollars" ($) refers to United States dollars, unless otherwise stated.

Details and percentages in tables do not necessarily add to totals because of rounding.

The following symbols have been used:
   A hyphen (-) indicates that the item is not applicable.
   Two dots (..) indicate that the data are not available or are not separately reported.
   A zero (0) means that the amount is nil or negligible.
   Use of a dash (–) between dates representing years, e.g. 1980–1990, signifies the full period involved, including the initial and final years.

[1]   United Nations Publication, Sales No. E/F.03.II.D.33.

Abbreviations

ACBF	African Capacity Building Foundation
ADF	African Development Fund
AfDB	African Development Bank
AFESD	Arab Fund for Economic and Social Development
AsDB	Asian Development Bank
BADEA	Arab Bank for Economic Development in Africa
BDEAC	Banque de Développement des Etats de l'Afrique Centrale
BITS	Swedish Agency for International Technical and Economic Cooperation
BOAD	West African Development Bank
CCCE	Caisse centrale de coopération économique
CEC	Commission of the European Communities
CIDA	Canadian International Development Agency
DAC	Development Assistance Committee
DANIDA	Danish International Development Agency
DCD	Development Cooperation Department
ECA	Economic Commission for Africa
EDF	European Development Fund
EEC	European Economic Community
ESAF	Enhanced Structural Adjustment Facility
ESCAP	Economic and Social Commission for Asia and the Pacific
EU	European Union
FAC	Fonds d'aide et de coopération
FAO	Food and Agriculture Organization of the United Nations
GDP	gross domestic product
GNI	gross national income
GTZ	German Technical Assistance Corporation
IBRD	International Bank for Reconstruction and Development
IDA	International Development Association
IDB	Inter-American Development Bank
IFAD	International Fund for Agricultural Development
ILO	International Labour Organization
IMF	International Monetary Fund
IRF	International Road Federation
IRU	International Road Transport Union
IsDB	Islamic Development Bank
ITU	International Telecommunication Union
KFAED	Kuwait Fund for Arab Economic Development
KfW	Kreditanstalt für Wiederaufbau
LDC	least developed country
ODA	official development assistance
OECD	Organisation for Economic Co-operation and Development
OECF	Overseas Economic Co-operation Fund
OPEC	Organization of the Petroleum Exporting Countries
PRGF	Poverty Reduction and Growth Facility
SAF	Structural Adjustment Facility
SDC	Swiss Development Corporation
SDR	special drawing rights
SFD	Saudi Fund for Development
SITC	Standard International Trade Classification (Revision I)
UNDP	United Nations Development Programme
UNESCO	United Nations Educational, Scientific and Cultural Organization
UNFPA	United Nations Population Fund
UNHCR	United Nations High Commissioner for Refugees
UNICEF	United Nations Children's Fund
UNTA	United Nations Technical Assistance
USAID	United States Agency for International Development
WFP	World Food Programme
WHO	World Health Organization

1. PER CAPITA GDP AND POPULATION: LEVELS AND GROWTH

Country	Per capita GDP (In 2002 dollars)			Annual average growth rates of per capita real GDP (%)			Population			
							Level (Millions)	Annual average growth rates (%)		
	1980	1990	2002	1980–1990	1990–2000	2000–2002	2002	1980–1990	1990–2000	2000–2002
Afghanistan	..	..	..	..	..	..	22.9	-1.3	4.5	3.5
Angola	987	934	863	0.5	-1.2	6.5	13.2	2.8	2.9	3.2
Bangladesh	220	246	329	1.1	2.4	2.7	143.8	2.6	2.3	2.1
Benin	339	329	410	-0.5	1.7	2.4	6.6	3.0	3.0	2.7
Bhutan	279	466	698	5.4	3.4	4.4	0.9	2.1	3.0	2.8
Burkina Faso	172	182	225	0.8	1.5	2.5	12.6	2.7	2.9	3.0
Burundi	125	143	109	1.2	-3.6	0.7	6.6	3.2	1.0	2.6
Cambodia	..	204	266	1.6	1.8	2.8	13.8	4.1	3.0	2.5
Cape Verde	..	956	1 390	3.8	3.7	1.5	0.5	1.9	2.2	2.1
Central African Republic	338	293	282	-1.0	-0.3	1.4	3.8	2.5	2.4	1.4
Chad	168	216	232	3.4	-0.8	6.5	8.3	2.6	3.1	3.0
Comoros	434	425	343	-0.3	-1.8	-0.4	0.7	3.1	3.0	2.9
Dem. Rep. of the Congo	330	269	111	-1.3	-7.3	-2.1	51.2	2.9	2.6	2.7
Djibouti	..	1 209	861	-6.7	-3.6	-0.4	0.7	5.1	2.3	2.0
Equatorial Guinea	..	973	4 517	-0.8	19.0	-1.9	0.5	5.0	2.6	2.7
Eritrea	..	..	146	..	3.9[a]	5.6	4.0	2.8	1.7	3.7
Ethiopia	..	76	87	-2.1	1.6	3.7	69.0	3.2	3.0	2.5
Gambia	282	281	280	-0.1	-0.3	-0.2	1.4	3.7	3.4	2.9
Guinea	..	328	380	1.7	1.3	2.5	8.4	2.6	2.9	1.5
Guinea-Bissau	151	191	149	1.5	-1.8	-4.8	1.4	2.4	3.0	3.0
Haiti	751	568	437	-2.6	-2.1	-2.6	8.2	2.4	1.5	1.3
Kiribati	513	457	512	-1.4	1.5	0.7	0.1	2.2	1.6	1.5
Lao PDR	..	199	304	1.0	3.9	2.9	5.5	2.6	2.5	2.3
Lesotho	233	295	405	2.5	2.8	3.5	1.8	2.1	1.3	0.4
Liberia	712	194	174	-8.2	0.4	-0.2	3.2	1.4	3.5	4.9
Madagascar	427	341	267	-1.7	-0.9	-6.1	16.9	2.8	2.9	2.9
Malawi	173	141	158	-1.9	2.0	-2.0	11.9	4.6	1.8	2.2
Maldives	..	..	2 000	..	3.8	-0.2	0.3	3.2	3.0	3.0
Mali	255	210	251	-1.6	1.3	2.4	12.6	2.5	2.8	3.0
Mauritania	317	296	350	-0.5	1.5	1.8	2.8	2.3	2.7	3.0
Mozambique	149	135	211	-1.0	3.3	9.8	18.5	0.9	3.0	1.9
Myanmar	..	..	..	..	..	..	48.9	1.8	1.6	1.4
Nepal	137	173	223	2.3	2.5	-0.3	24.6	2.3	2.4	2.3
Niger	298	216	188	-3.2	-1.0	1.3	11.5	3.2	3.5	3.7
Rwanda	232	216	210	-0.9	-1.6	4.4	8.3	3.1	1.3	3.5
Samoa	..	..	1 482	..	3.0	2.7	0.2	0.3	0.8	0.9
Sao Tome and Principe	..	340	321	-0.4	-0.8	0.4	0.2	2.0	2.6	2.5
Senegal	434	444	501	0.2	1.1	1.6	9.9	2.9	2.5	2.4
Sierra Leone	318	277	166	-1.8	-5.6	1.9	4.8	2.4	0.7	3.9
Solomon Islands	561	766	517	3.1	-1.0	-9.7	0.5	3.4	3.2	3.0
Somalia	..	..	..	..	..	..	9.5	0.8	1.9	4.3
Sudan	265	264	410	-0.2	3.0	6.3	32.9	2.5	2.4	2.3
Togo	418	338	288	-1.6	-0.6	0.2	4.8	3.3	2.8	2.6
Tuvalu[b]	..	..	..	..	..	..	0.0	1.6	1.4	1.3
Uganda	..	161	235	-0.6	3.9	2.2	25.0	3.4	3.0	3.2
United Rep. of Tanzania	..	241	259	1.9	0.0	3.6	36.3	3.3	3.0	2.0
Vanuatu	1 113	1 231	1 133	0.5	-0.5	-3.5	0.2	2.4	2.8	2.5
Yemen	..	482	538	..	1.6	-0.5	19.3	3.9	4.2	3.5
Zambia	481	389	344	-2.2	-1.9	2.6	10.7	3.2	2.4	1.3
All LDCs	..	253	281	-0.1	0.9	2.4	699.6	2.6	2.6	2.4
All developing countries	761	901	1 195	1.6	3.1	1.5	5 018.5	2.1	1.7	1.5
Developed market economy countries	18 813	23 832	28 388	2.6	1.7	0.2	871.4	0.6	0.7	0.5
Countries in Central and Eastern Europe	..	3 160	2 781	1.0	-2.1	4.3	335.1	0.7	-5.5	-0.4

Source: UNCTAD, *Handbook of Statistics 2003*; World Bank, *World Development Indicators,* online data.

Note: GDP per capita data are based on World Bank data on GDP and population data are based on United Nations/DESA/Population Division. Data for Ethiopia prior to 1992 include Eritrea. Population data for Bhutan is from national sources.

a 1993–2000.

b Population 10,466 and area 26 km².

2. REAL GDP, TOTAL AND PER CAPITA: ANNUAL AVERAGE GROWTH RATES
(Percentage)

Country	Real GDP							Real GDP per capita						
	1980–1990	1990–2000	2000–2002	1999	2000	2001	2002	1980–1990	1990–2000	2000–2002	1999	2000	2001	2002
Afghanistan	..	..	..	..	..	..	..	..	..	..	..	..	..	..
Angola	3.4	1.6	9.9	3.3	3.0	3.2	17.1	0.5	-1.2	6.5	0.7	0.2	0.1	13.4
Bangladesh	3.7	4.8	4.8	4.9	5.9	5.3	4.4	1.1	2.4	2.7	2.6	3.7	3.1	2.3
Benin	2.5	4.7	5.1	4.7	5.8	5.0	5.3	-0.5	1.7	2.4	2.1	3.1	2.3	2.5
Bhutan	7.6	6.5	7.3	7.0	7.0	7.0	7.7	5.4	3.4	4.4	3.9	3.9	4.0	4.8
Burkina Faso	3.6	4.5	5.6	5.8	2.2	5.6	5.6	0.8	1.5	2.5	2.8	-0.7	2.6	2.5
Burundi	4.4	-2.6	3.4	-1.0	-0.9	3.2	3.6	1.2	-3.6	0.7	-1.9	-2.4	0.9	0.6
Cambodia	5.2	4.9	5.4	5.0	7.7	6.3	4.5	1.6	1.8	2.8	2.3	5.0	3.7	2.0
Cape Verde	5.9	6.0	3.6	8.6	6.8	3.3	4.0	3.8	3.7	1.5	6.3	4.6	1.2	1.9
Central African Republic	1.4	2.0	2.8	3.6	2.3	1.5	4.2	-1.0	-0.3	1.4	1.7	0.6	0.0	2.9
Chad	6.1	2.2	9.7	1.0	0.6	8.5	10.9	3.4	-0.8	6.5	-2.1	-2.4	5.3	7.6
Comoros	2.8	1.1	2.5	1.9	-1.1	1.9	3.0	-0.3	-1.8	-0.4	-1.0	-4.0	-0.9	0.1
Dem. Rep. of the Congo	1.6	-4.9	0.5	-4.4	-7.0	-2.0	3.0	-1.3	-7.3	-2.1	-6.0	-8.9	-4.4	0.2
Djibouti	-0.7	-1.4	1.6	2.2	0.7	1.6	1.6	-6.7	-3.6	-0.4	-1.2	-2.1	-0.6	-0.2
Equatorial Guinea	1.5	22.1	0.8	41.4	16.9	1.3	0.2	-0.8	19.0	-1.9	37.8	13.8	-1.3	-2.4
Eritrea	..	6.1[a]	9.5	0.6	-12.1	9.7	9.2	..	3.9[a]	5.6	-2.7	-15.1	5.9	5.3
Ethiopia	1.1[b]	4.6	6.4	5.2	5.4	7.7	5.0	-2.1[b]	1.6	3.7	2.5	2.7	5.0	2.5
Gambia	3.6	3.1	2.6	6.4	5.6	6.0	-0.6	-0.1	-0.3	-0.2	3.1	2.4	3.0	-3.3
Guinea	4.6	4.3	4.1	3.6	2.3	3.8	4.3	1.7	1.3	2.5	1.8	0.7	2.2	2.8
Guinea-Bissau	4.0	1.2	-2.0	7.8	7.5	0.2	-4.2	1.5	-1.8	-4.8	4.9	4.5	-2.7	-7.0
Haiti	-0.2	-0.6	-1.3	2.2	1.1	-1.7	-0.9	-2.6	-2.1	-2.6	0.8	-0.2	-3.0	-2.2
Kiribati	0.7	3.1	2.2	2.1	-1.7	1.6	2.8	-1.4	1.5	0.7	0.6	-3.2	0.1	1.3
Lao People's Dem. Rep.	3.7	6.5	5.3	7.3	5.8	5.7	5.0	1.0	3.9	2.9	4.8	3.4	3.2	2.6
Lesotho	4.6	4.2	3.9	2.2	3.3	4.0	3.8	2.5	2.8	3.5	1.1	2.4	3.4	3.5
Liberia	-7.0	3.9	4.7	22.9	20.4	5.3	4.2	-8.2	0.4	-0.2	14.5	13.2	0.0	-0.3
Madagascar	1.1	2.0	-3.4	4.7	4.8	6.0	-11.9	-1.7	-0.9	-6.1	1.6	1.7	3.0	-14.4
Malawi	2.5	3.8	0.1	4.0	1.7	-1.5	1.8	-1.9	2.0	-2.0	1.2	-0.8	-3.6	-0.3
Maldives	..	7.0	2.9	7.2	4.8	3.5	2.3	..	3.8	-0.2	4.0	1.7	0.4	-0.7
Mali	0.8	4.1	5.5	6.8	3.7	1.5	9.6	-1.6	1.3	2.4	3.9	0.8	-1.4	6.4
Mauritania	1.8	4.2	4.9	4.1	5.1	4.6	5.1	-0.5	1.5	1.8	1.1	2.1	1.6	2.0
Mozambique	-0.1	6.4	11.8	7.5	1.6	13.8	9.9	-1.0	3.3	9.8	5.4	-0.4	11.7	7.9
Myanmar	..	..	..	..	..	..	..	..	..	..	..	..	..	..
Nepal	4.6	4.9	2.0	4.5	6.1	4.7	-0.6	2.3	2.5	-0.3	2.1	3.7	2.4	-2.8
Niger	-0.1	2.4	5.0	-0.6	-1.4	7.1	3.0	-3.2	-1.0	1.3	-4.0	-4.8	3.3	-0.7
Rwanda	2.2	-0.3	8.0	7.6	6.0	6.7	9.4	-0.9	-1.6	4.4	-2.2	-1.1	2.2	6.6
Samoa	..	3.9	3.7	2.6	6.9	6.2	1.3	..	3.0	2.7	1.7	5.9	5.2	0.3
Sao Tome and Principe	1.8	1.8	3.0	2.5	3.0	3.0	3.0	-0.4	-0.8	0.4	-0.1	0.4	0.4	0.5
Senegal	3.1	3.6	4.1	5.1	5.6	5.7	2.4	0.2	1.1	1.6	2.7	3.1	3.2	0.0
Sierra Leone	0.5	-5.0	5.8	-8.1	3.8	5.4	6.3	-1.8	-5.6	1.9	-10.0	1.0	1.7	2.0
Solomon Islands	6.6	2.2	-7.0	-1.3	-13.4	-10.0	-4.0	3.1	-1.0	-9.7	-4.3	-16.0	-12.6	-6.8
Somalia	..	..	..	..	..	..	..	..	..	..	..	..	..	..
Sudan	2.3	5.4	8.7	6.5	6.1	6.9	10.6	-0.2	3.0	6.3	4.1	3.7	4.5	8.1
Togo	1.7	2.2	2.8	2.4	-1.9	2.7	3.0	-1.6	-0.6	0.2	-1.0	-4.9	0.0	0.5
Tuvalu	..	..	..	..	..	..	..	..	..	..	..	..	..	..
Uganda	2.9	7.0	5.5	7.5	3.5	4.6	6.3	-0.6	3.9	2.2	4.4	0.4	1.4	3.0
United Rep. of Tanzania	5.4	2.9	5.8	3.5	5.2	5.7	5.8	1.9	0.0	3.6	1.2	2.9	3.5	3.7
Vanuatu	3.0	2.3	-1.1	-2.1	2.5	-1.9	-0.3	0.5	-0.5	-3.5	-4.7	-0.1	-4.3	-2.7
Yemen	..	5.8	3.0	3.6	5.1	1.8	4.2	..	1.6	-0.5	0.2	1.6	-1.7	0.6
Zambia	1.0	0.5	4.0	2.2	3.6	4.9	3.0	-2.2	-1.9	2.6	0.2	1.8	3.4	1.8
All LDCs	2.5	3.6	4.9	4.5	4.3	4.9	5.0	-0.1	0.9	2.4	2.0	1.8	2.4	2.5
All developing countries	3.8	4.9	3.0	3.1	5.4	2.6	3.3	1.6	3.1	1.5	1.5	3.8	1.1	1.8
Developed market economy countries	3.2	2.4	0.7	2.8	3.5	0.3	1.1	2.6	1.7	0.2	2.2	2.9	-0.3	0.6
Countries in Central and Eastern Europe	1.6[c]	-2.3	3.9	3.5	6.2	4.2	3.6	1.0[c]	-2.1	4.3	3.9	6.6	4.6	4.1

Source: World Bank, *World Development Indicators,* online data; United Nations/DESA/Population Division.

a 1993–2000. b Data for Ethiopia prior to 1992 include Eritrea.
c Annual average growth rates 1984–1990 for Albania, Bulgaria, Estonia, Hungary, Latvia, Republic of Moldova, Romania, Russian Federation and Slovakia.

3. AGRICULTURAL PRODUCTION, TOTAL AND PER CAPITA: ANNUAL AVERAGE GROWTH RATES

Country	Percentage share of agriculture in:				Annual average growth rates (%) Total agricultural production					Annual average growth rates (%) Per capita agricultural production				
	Total labour force		GDP											
	1990	2002	1990	2002	1990–1992	2000–2002	2000	2001	2002	1990–1992	2000–2002	2000	2001	2002
Afghanistan	70	66	..	..	..	..	..	..	..	..	..	..	..	..
Angola	75	71	18	8	5.9	4.7	12.7	10.5	-0.9	2.4	1.6	9.5	7.3	-3.8
Bangladesh	65	54	29	22	2.0	0.5	6.0	-2.0	3.0	-0.4	-1.6	3.8	-4.0	0.9
Benin	64	52	36	35	5.6	2.0	8.5	-1.5	5.6	2.1	-0.8	5.6	-4.1	2.6
Bhutan	94	94	43	34	0.3	-9.1	-0.7	-0.1	-17.2	-1.2	-11.4	-3.4	-2.6	-19.4
Burkina Faso	92	92	32	38	9.4	14.7	-14.0	27.3	3.3	6.6	11.5	-16.2	23.9	0.4
Burundi	92	90	56	49	2.9	4.4	-6.4	9.6	-0.4	1.0	1.9	-8.0	7.2	-3.2
Cambodia	74	69	56	37	0.9	-3.1	2.3	3.6	-9.4	-2.6	-5.5	-0.4	1.0	-11.6
Cape Verde	31	22	14	11	1.0	0.3	-11.3	-1.0	1.6	-1.1	-1.9	-13.4	-3.3	-0.5
Central African Rep.	80	71	48	55	1.9	0.5	8.7	-2.5	3.5	-0.6	-1.2	6.8	-4.1	1.8
Chad	83	73	29	37	7.7	6.2	-6.3	17.7	-4.2	4.7	2.9	-9.2	14.1	-7.1
Comoros	78	73	39	35	1.0	1.1	2.5	2.0	0.2	-1.9	-1.8	-0.6	-0.9	-2.7
Dem. Rep. of the Congo	68	62	30	56	1.7	-2.0	-2.0	-1.9	-2.2	-2.4	-5.1	-4.7	-4.8	-5.4
Djibouti	82	78	3	4	-12.5	0.1	-0.7	0.1	0.0	-14.5	-1.4	-3.0	-1.7	-1.2
Equatorial Guinea	75	69	62	8	-3.3	-1.0	-1.1	-2.0	0.0	-5.6	-3.7	-4.0	-4.7	-2.7
Eritrea	80[a]	77	31	21	..	-4.0	-12.9	6.3	-13.4	..	-8.1	-16.0	1.9	-17.2
Ethiopia	85[a]	82	49	52	..	2.3	6.0	9.3	-4.2	..	-0.1	3.4	6.6	-6.5
Gambia	82	78	29	40	-5.6	-19.1	10.8	9.0	-40.0	-9.2	-21.1	7.8	6.2	-41.4
Guinea	87	83	24	24	8.2	4.9	1.3	5.4	4.4	4.4	3.4	-0.3	3.8	3.0
Guinea-Bissau	85	82	61	58	0.5	-0.1	4.0	1.6	-1.8	-2.1	-2.4	1.6	-0.6	-4.2
Haiti	68	61	..	..	-1.9	-0.9	6.3	-3.6	1.8	-3.7	-2.5	4.6	-5.1	0.2
Kiribati	30	26	24	21	11.2	1.6	-6.0	1.5	1.6	9.8	0.4	-7.2	0.4	0.4
Lao People's Dem.Rep.	78	76	61	51	0.6	2.9	16.2	4.1	1.7	-2.0	0.5	13.5	1.8	-0.6
Lesotho	41	39	23	18	-5.9	8.3	11.7	-11.3	32.1	-7.9	7.2	10.3	-12.2	30.8
Liberia	72	67	..	..	..	..	..	..	..	..	..	..	..	..
Madagascar	78	73	29	27	0.6	1.8	-1.1	3.9	-0.2	-2.2	-1.1	-3.8	0.8	-3.0
Malawi	87	82	45	39	-6.3	-11.0	13.6	0.5	-21.1	-7.9	-13.0	10.8	-1.8	-22.9
Maldives	33	21	15	11	2.1	0.5	12.0	1.0	0.0	-0.8	-2.5	8.4	-1.9	-3.0
Mali	86	80	46	..	2.5	11.2	-11.5	15.0	7.5	-0.1	8.0	-13.9	11.8	4.4
Mauritania	55	52	30	21	-2.6	-1.5	3.3	-2.1	-0.9	-5.0	-4.4	0.0	-5.0	-3.8
Mozambique	83	81	37	23	-12.2	2.4	-11.2	4.6	0.2	-15.0	0.5	-13.0	2.6	-1.5
Myanmar	73	70	57	57	4.1	4.1	7.9	8.2	0.2	2.3	2.8	6.5	6.8	-1.0
Nepal	94	93	52	39	-2.9	2.3	3.7	3.1	1.5	-5.2	0.0	1.3	0.8	-0.9
Niger	90	87	35	40	6.0	4.4	-7.7	16.5	-6.4	2.6	0.8	-10.9	12.4	-9.7
Rwanda	92	90	33	42	7.2	8.5	21.1	1.1	16.3	14.0	4.8	12.8	-3.3	13.5
Samoa	42	33	..	..	-12.2	1.4	5.1	1.4	1.4	-12.2	1.4	4.5	1.3	1.4
Sao Tome and Principe	71	63	28	20	12.9	1.8	2.1	3.7	-0.1	11.0	0.0	-0.1	2.2	-2.1
Senegal	77	73	20	18	-1.8	-13.0	-1.0	-3.2	-21.8	-4.2	-15.2	-3.4	-5.7	-23.8
Sierra Leone	67	61	32	52	-3.2	5.3	-7.1	9.2	1.5	-3.6	0.7	-9.9	5.0	-3.4
Solomon Islands	77	72	..	..	6.0	1.3	7.3	2.0	0.5	2.6	-2.1	3.7	-1.5	-2.8
Somalia	75	70	65	..	..	..	..	..	..	..	..	..	..	..
Sudan	69	59	43	39	14.7	1.1	1.6	7.9	-5.2	12.1	-1.2	-0.6	5.5	-7.5
Togo	66	59	34	40	-1.2	3.9	-6.0	4.1	3.6	-3.2	1.1	-8.9	1.2	1.0
Tuvalu	33	25	..	..	27.7	-4.7	0.3	-9.2	0.0	27.7	-4.7	0.2	-9.1	0.0
Uganda	85	79	57	31	0.9	3.2	0.2	6.3	0.2	-2.2	0.1	-2.7	3.2	-3.0
United Rep. of Tanzania	84	80	46	45	-1.2	0.6	3.9	1.7	-0.4	-4.6	-1.8	1.5	-0.7	-2.8
Vanuatu	43	35	20	19	-8.3	-6.7	-5.2	-16.9	4.7	-10.9	-9.0	-7.6	-19.0	2.1
Yemen	60	48	24	14	3.1	3.1	5.4	6.7	-0.3	-1.9	-1.0	1.0	2.5	-4.3
Zambia	74	68	21	22	-6.8	0.1	-8.8	-5.6	6.1	-9.4	-2.0	-11.0	-7.6	3.9
All LDCs	76	69	38	33	1.5	1.9	2.2	4.1	-0.4	-1.2	-0.7	-0.4	1.6	-2.9
All developing countries	61	54	15	12	3.4	2.0	2.5	2.1	1.8	1.5	0.4	0.9	0.7	0.2

Source: UNCTAD secretariat calculations based on data from FAO online data; World Bank, *World Development Indicators,* online data.

a   1993.

4. Food production, total and per capita: Annual average growth rates
(Percentage)

Country	Total food production					Per capita food production				
	1990–1992	2000–2002	2000	2001	2002	1990–1992	2000–2002	2000	2001	2002
Afghanistan	..	..	..	..	..	..	..	..	..	..
Angola	6.2	4.9	12.8	10.8	-0.8	2.8	1.8	9.6	7.6	-3.7
Bangladesh	1.9	0.4	5.9	-2.3	3.2	-0.5	-1.7	3.7	-4.4	1.0
Benin	5.2	3.3	5.2	-0.1	6.8	1.7	0.5	2.4	-2.8	3.9
Bhutan	0.3	-9.1	-0.7	-0.1	-17.2	-1.2	-11.5	-3.3	-2.8	-19.5
Burkina Faso	11.7	13.7	-14.8	31.1	-1.5	8.7	10.5	-17.0	27.5	-4.3
Burundi	2.6	4.9	-5.0	10.1	0.0	0.7	2.3	-6.5	7.6	-2.8
Cambodia	0.7	-2.8	2.3	4.3	-9.4	-2.8	-5.2	-0.4	1.6	-11.5
Cape Verde	1.2	0.3	-11.4	-1.0	1.5	-1.0	-1.9	-13.4	-3.3	-0.4
Central African Republic	3.6	0.0	11.4	-2.6	2.7	1.1	-1.7	9.3	-4.4	1.1
Chad	10.2	6.6	-4.5	17.4	-3.2	7.2	3.3	-7.4	13.8	-6.2
Comoros	1.2	1.2	2.7	2.2	0.2	-1.7	-1.7	-0.4	-0.7	-2.8
Dem. Rep. of the Congo	1.9	-1.9	-1.9	-1.7	-2.1	-2.1	-5.0	-4.5	-4.7	-5.3
Djibouti	-12.5	0.1	-0.7	0.1	0.0	-14.5	-1.4	-3.0	-1.7	-1.2
Equatorial Guinea	-2.0	-1.2	-1.3	-2.3	0.0	-4.3	-3.9	-4.1	-5.0	-2.7
Eritrea	..	-4.1	-13.0	6.3	-13.6	..	-8.2	-16.3	1.9	-17.4
Ethiopia	..	2.3	6.1	9.8	-4.6	..	-0.1	3.6	7.2	-7.0
Gambia	-6.2	-19.2	10.8	9.0	-40.1	-9.8	-21.3	7.8	6.3	-41.7
Guinea	8.1	5.3	-0.1	5.8	4.7	4.3	3.9	-1.7	4.2	3.5
Guinea-Bissau	0.9	-0.1	4.0	1.7	-1.9	-1.8	-2.4	1.7	-0.6	-4.2
Haiti	-1.2	-1.0	6.3	-3.5	1.6	-3.0	-2.5	4.6	-5.0	0.0
Kiribati	11.2	1.6	-6.0	1.5	1.6	9.8	0.4	-7.2	0.4	0.4
Lao People's Dem. Rep.	1.2	3.7	14.5	5.2	2.1	-1.4	1.3	11.8	2.8	-0.2
Lesotho	-10.0	9.0	12.1	-12.2	35.2	-12.0	7.8	10.7	-13.2	34.0
Liberia	..	..	..	..	..	..	..	..	..	..
Madagascar	1.2	1.7	-0.5	3.7	-0.3	-1.6	-1.2	-3.3	0.7	-3.0
Malawi	-10.5	-10.7	14.9	3.7	-23.0	-12.1	-12.7	12.1	1.3	-24.7
Maldives	2.1	0.5	12.0	1.0	0.0	-0.8	-2.5	8.4	-1.9	-3.0
Mali	1.4	4.9	-3.5	2.2	7.7	-1.1	2.0	-6.2	-0.6	4.6
Mauritania	-2.6	-1.5	3.3	-2.1	-0.9	-5.0	-4.4	0.0	-5.0	-3.8
Mozambique	-13.1	1.6	-11.4	3.0	0.2	-15.8	-0.3	-13.1	1.2	-1.7
Myanmar	4.0	4.3	7.9	8.4	0.2	2.1	3.0	6.4	7.1	-1.0
Nepal	-2.9	2.3	3.7	3.0	1.5	-5.2	-0.1	1.4	0.6	-0.8
Niger	6.0	5.2	-7.6	17.4	-5.7	2.5	1.5	-10.8	13.3	-9.0
Rwanda	7.5	8.7	22.6	0.2	17.9	14.2	5.0	14.1	-4.0	14.9
Samoa	-12.7	1.5	5.2	1.5	1.5	-12.7	1.4	4.6	1.4	1.5
Sao Tome and Principe	13.1	1.8	2.3	3.7	-0.1	11.2	0.0	0.1	2.2	-2.2
Senegal	-2.3	-13.6	-1.5	-4.1	-22.1	-4.7	-15.7	-4.0	-6.5	-24.0
Sierra Leone	-3.6	5.4	-7.7	9.3	1.6	-4.0	0.8	-10.6	5.0	-3.2
Solomon Islands	6.0	1.3	7.3	2.0	0.6	2.6	-2.1	3.7	-1.5	-2.8
Somalia	..	..	..	..	..	..	..	..	..	..
Sudan	17.3	1.0	1.6	7.6	-5.2	14.7	-1.3	-0.5	5.2	-7.4
Togo	-2.4	0.7	-6.4	0.5	0.9	-4.4	-2.0	-9.3	-2.4	-1.5
Tuvalu	27.7	-4.7	0.3	-9.2	0.0	27.7	-4.7	0.2	-9.1	0.0
Uganda	1.1	2.7	3.4	5.3	0.1	-2.0	-0.4	0.3	2.1	-2.9
United Rep. of Tanzania	-2.5	-0.3	4.2	0.0	-0.5	-5.9	-2.6	1.8	-2.4	-2.8
Vanuatu	-8.3	-6.7	-5.2	-16.9	4.8	-10.9	-9.0	-7.5	-19.0	2.1
Yemen	2.8	2.9	5.3	6.4	-0.3	-2.2	-1.2	1.2	2.1	-4.3
Zambia	-6.6	0.0	-2.5	-6.2	6.5	-9.2	-2.2	-4.7	-8.2	4.3
All LDCs	1.5	1.6	2.6	3.8	-0.4	-1.2	-0.9	0.1	1.2	-2.9
All developing countries	3.5	2.0	2.5	2.0	2.0	1.6	0.4	1.0	0.5	0.4

Source: UNCTAD secretariat calculations, based on data from FAO online data.

5. The manufacturing sector: Annual average growth rates and shares in GDP
(Percentage)

Country	Share in GDP			Annual average growth rates						
	1980	1990	2002	1980–1990	1990–2000	2000–2002	1999	2000	2001	2002
Afghanistan	..	..	..	..	..	..	..	..	..	..
Angola	10[a]	5	4[b]	-11.1[c]	-0.4	10.0[d]	7.1	8.9	10.0	..
Bangladesh	13	13	15	5.2	7.2	6.0	3.2	4.8	6.7	5.4
Benin	8	8	9	5.1	5.8	7.7	4.3	9.0	9.0	6.4
Bhutan	3	8	8	13.0	6.5	6.0	3.7	-6.2	7.3	4.8
Burkina Faso	16	16	15	2.0	5.5	5.4	10.6	7.9	3.3	7.6
Burundi	7	13	9[e]	5.7	-8.0[f]	..	12.3	..	..	..
Cambodia	11[g]	5	6[h]	8.7[i]	8.2[j]	..	..	..	..	..
Cape Verde	8[g]	8	8[b]	8.6[i]	4.8	4.7[d]	4.0	4.5	4.7	..
Central African Republic	7	11	9[l]	5.0	-0.2	4.0	2.0	11.6	4.0	4.0
Chad	11[k]	14	10	..	..	..	..	..	..	..
Comoros	4	4	4	4.9	2.9	1.5	0.0	47.7	1.0	2.0
Dem. Republic of the Congo	14	11	4	..	..	..	..	..	..	..
Djibouti	5[m]	5	3[l]	..	-9.8	..	0.6	1.0	..	..
Equatorial Guinea	..	..	..	..	..	..	..	..	..	..
Eritrea	..	..	11	..	8.5	6.3	1.4	3.5	5.5	7.1
Ethiopia	7[k]	8	7	-0.9	5.5	7.9[d]	2.4	2.1	7.9	..
Gambia	6	7	5	7.8	1.0	6.0	3.0	4.0	6.0	6.0
Guinea	5[m]	5	4[b]	4.0[n]	4.1	5.5[d]	6.5	7.0	5.5	..
Guinea-Bissau	14[o]	8	9	9.2[p]	-2.0	5.9[d]	1.3	2.2	5.9	..
Haiti	..	..	..	..	..	..	..	..	..	..
Kiribati	2	2	1[h]	-0.9[q]	1.8[r]	..	..	..	..	..
Lao People's Dem. Republic	9[m]	10	18[b]	8.9[c]	12.6[j]	..	..	..	..	..
Lesotho	8	6	14[b]	8.5	6.6	7.5	-0.4	4.1	7.0	8.0
Liberia	..	..	..	..	..	..	..	..	..	..
Madagascar	11[a]	11	11	2.1[c]	2.0	-9.0	5.3	5.7	10.7	-25.1
Malawi	14	19	14	3.6	0.4	-1.0	2.1	-2.5	0.5	-2.5
Maldives	..	..	4[h]	9.6[c]	5.9	2.3	8.2	4.4	3.1	1.5
Mali	7	9	4[b]	6.8	3.0	-1.5[d]	-4.0	6.0	-1.5	..
Mauritania	13[a]	10	8	-2.1[c]	-0.5	3.6	12.2	3.3	5.9	1.3
Mozambique	..	10	12	..	17.1[s]	8.2	14.0	11.0	10.3	6.2
Myanmar	10	8	7[l]	..	..	..	14.5	23.0	..	..
Nepal	4	6	9	9.3	8.9	-1.3	5.3	7.2	3.6	-5.9
Niger	4	7	7	-2.7[c]	2.6	3.4	4.5	3.2	3.4	3.3
Rwanda	15	18	10	2.6	-6.0	8.4	-3.4	-4.1	7.8	9.0
Samoa	..	..	..	..	-2.5[s]	13.4[d]	1.3	7.3	13.4	..
Sao Tome and Principe	9[o]	5	4	0.5[p]	1.4	2.8	2.2	2.2	2.7	3.0
Senegal	11	13	18	4.6	4.0	4.7	4.9	4.8	4.7	4.7
Sierra Leone	5	5	5	..	5.0[r]	..	..	..	..	..
Solomon Islands	..	..	..	..	..	..	..	..	..	..
Somalia	5	5	..	..	..	..	..	..	..	..
Sudan	7	..	9	..	..	..	-25.3	9.8	..	..
Togo	8	10	9	1.7	3.3	3.2	-0.9	21.7	5.8	0.7
Tuvalu	..	..	..	..	..	..	..	..	..	..
Uganda	4	6	10	3.7[q]	13.6	3.4	11.7	1.9	2.4	4.4
United Republic of Tanzania	..	9	7	..	2.7	5.7	3.6	4.8	5.0	6.5
Vanuatu	4	6	4[t]	14.9[c]	-4.8[u]	..	..	..	..	..
Yemen	..	9	6	..	4.4	2.5	0.7	6.1	0.9	4.2
Zambia	18	36	11	4.1	0.8	5.0	2.8	3.6	4.2	5.8
All LDCs	11	11	11	..	5.5[f]	..	4.1	..	..	..

Source: UNCTAD secretariat calculations, based on data from the World Bank, *World Development Indicators* online data.

a 1985. b 2001. c 1985–1990. d 2000–2001. e 1999. f 1990–1999. g 1987. h 1998. i 1987–1990. j 1990–1998. k 1983. l 2000. m 1989. n 1988–1990. o 1986. p 1986–1990. q 1982–1990. r 1990–1996. s 1994–2000. t 1996. u 1990–1995.

6. Gross capital formation: Annual average growth rates and shares in GDP

(Percentage)

Country	Share in GDP			Annual average growth rates						
	1980	1990	2002	1980-1990	1990-2000	2000-2002	1999	2000	2001	2002
Afghanistan	..	..	..	..	..	..	..	..	..	..
Angola	18^a	12	29	..	..	..	..	..	..	..
Bangladesh	14	17	24	6.9	9.2	6.5	9.9	7.3	5.8	7.2
Benin	15	14	19	-5.3	5.6	7.7	7.5	7.9	7.5	8.0
Bhutan	31	36	48^b	4.4	9.5^c	..	..	..	..	..
Burkina Faso	17	21	26	8.6	7.2	10.5	12.8	10.3	10.5	10.6
Burundi	14	15	8	6.9	0.4	4.8	1.1	2.9	2.8	6.9
Cambodia	9^d	8	18^b	..	10.5^e	25.5^f	16.7	-10.7	25.5	..
Cape Verde	33^g	23	18	..	0.1	0.7	14.6	-1.4	-4.7	6.3
Central African Republic	7	12	14	..	..	..	..	..	..	..
Chad	3^h	16	55	..	1.6^i	90.9	-26.0	36.0	172.0	34.0
Comoros	33	19	16	-4.2	-4.1	19.6	-17.2	-9.5	7.1	33.5
Dem. Republic of the Congo	10	9	7	-5.1	2.6^j	-4.1	32.7	15.6	-12.1	4.7
Djibouti	..	..	13^k	..	..	..	..	..	..	..
Equatorial Guinea	..	17	92^l	..	44.3	-49.2	20.0	20.0	-64.7	-26.9
Eritrea	..	71	47	..	5.8^j	14.6	17.9	-25.0	9.3	20.2
Ethiopia	13^h	12	20	2.1^m	10.1	22.3	-0.2	-1.2	27.4	17.4
Gambia	27	22	19	0.0	1.7	2.1	-2.8	37.7	3.2	1.0
Guinea	15^g	18	26	3.3^n	2.8	6.2	4.5	5.6	6.0	6.3
Guinea-Bissau	28	30	8	12.9	-10.6	35.1	-31.8	-24.6	86.2	-1.9
Haiti	17	13	31^b	-0.6	3.3	-1.9^f	6.7	1.3	-1.9	..
Kiribati	33	82	..	..	..	..	..	..	..	..
Lao People's Dem. Republic	7^g	..	22^b	..	..	..	..	..	..	..
Lesotho	37	52	36	5.0	0.7	-4.1	-1.4	-15.7	-3.1	-5.1
Liberia	..	..	..	..	..	..	..	..	..	..
Madagascar	15	17	12	4.9	3.4	-8.3	1.4	14.8	22.6	-31.4
Malawi	25	23	9	-2.8	-8.6	-5.3	11.5	-20.4	-10.2	-0.1
Maldives	..	..	22^b	..	7.3^o	6.7^f	9.9	-19.3	6.7	..
Mali	15	23	21	3.6	0.9	6.5	4.5	48.9	-0.4	13.9
Mauritania	26	20	25	6.9	9.2	-3.4	-8.9	57.5	-5.4	-1.4
Mozambique	6	16	46	3.8	13.8	25.6	60.7	-0.2	15.8	36.4
Myanmar	21	13	15^b	..	..	..	13.8	11.3	..	..
Nepal	18	18	24	..	..	..	..	..	..	..
Niger	28	8	13	-7.1	3.8^c	..	-8.8	..	..	..
Rwanda	16	15	19	4.3	1.5	4.1	10.5	-15.1	3.0	5.1
Samoa	..	..	..	..	..	..	..	..	..	..
Sao Tome and Principe	17	16	44	- 0.8	1.6	8.9	4.4	56.6	18.2	0.3
Senegal	12	14	21	5.2	5.0	5.4	-1.7	4.4	4.7	6.2
Sierra Leone	16	10	17	44.9	3.2	5.2	-5.0	3.0	5.0	5.5
Solomon Islands	36	29	..	..	..	..	..	..	..	..
Somalia	42	16	..	..	..	..	..	..	..	..
Sudan	15	..	18^b	..	..	..	9.5	14.9	6.9	..
Togo	28	27	22	2.7	-0.1	5.1	-6.7	3.2	2.5	7.7
Tuvalu	..	..	..	..	..	..	..	..	..	..
Uganda	6	13	22	9.6^p	9.3	3.0	14.1	11.5	2.8	3.2
United Rep. of Tanzania	..	26	17	..	-1.6	5.9	-1.5	7.5	5.8	6.1
Vanuatu	26^q	43	32^r	6.1^p	..	..	..	..	..	..
Yemen	..	15	19	..	8.7	4.4	-10.0	-4.4	0.8	8.2
Zambia	23	17	18	-4.3	5.4	3.5	8.4	14.6	15.9	-7.6
All LDCs	17	16	22	..	8.3^j	7.0^f	7.9	6.1	7.0	..

Source: UNCTAD secretariat calculations, based on data from World Bank, *World Development Indicators,* online data.

a 1985. b 2001. c 1990–1998. d 1988. e 1994–2000. f 2000–2001. g 1986. h 1982. i 1991–2000. j 1993–2000. k 2000. l 1998. m 1981–1990. n 1986–1990. o 1995–2000. p 1983–1990. q 1983. r 1995.

7. INDICATORS ON AREA AND POPULATION

Country	Area				Population				
	Total	% of arable land and land under permanent crops	% of land area covered by forests	Density	Total	Urban	Activity rate[a] %		
	(000 km²)			Pop./km²	(millions)	%	M	F	T
	2001	2000	2002	2002	2002	2000			
Afghanistan	652.1	12.4	2.1	35	22.9	23	88	50	69
Angola	1 246.7	2.6	56.0	11	13.2	36	90	75	83
Bangladesh	144.0	58.9	10.2	999	143.8	26	87	56	78
Benin	112.6	20.1	24.0	58	6.6	44	83	76	79
Bhutan	47.0	3.5	64.2	18	0.9	8	91	60	76
Burkina Faso	274.0	14.6	25.9	46	12.6	17	90	78	84
Burundi	27.8	45.3	3.7	237	6.6	10	94	86	90
Cambodia	181.0	21.0	52.9	76	13.8	18	86	85	86
Cape Verde	4.0	10.2	21.1	113	0.5	65	90	50	68
Central African Republic	623.0	3.2	36.8	6	3.8	42	87	68	77
Chad	1 284.0	2.8	10.1	7	8.3	25	90	70	80
Comoros	2.2	59.2	4.3	334	0.7	35	86	64	75
Dem. Rep. of the Congo	2 344.9	3.4	59.6	22	51.2	31	85	63	74
Djibouti	23.2	..	0.3	30	0.7	84	..	..	..
Equatorial Guinea	28.1	8.2	62.5	17	0.5	51	91	48	69
Eritrea	117.6	4.3	13.5	34	4.0	20	87	77	82
Ethiopia	1 104.3	10.4	4.2	62	69.0	16	86	59	73
Gambia	11.3	22.6	48.1	123	1.4	32	90	70	80
Guinea	245.9	6.2	28.2	34	8.4	28	87	80	84
Guinea-Bissau	36.1	15.2	60.5	40	1.4	33	91	60	75
Haiti	27.8	39.6	3.2	296	8.2	37	82	58	70
Kiribati	0.7	53.4	38.4	119	0.1	39	..	..	..
Lao People's Dem. Republic	236.8	4.0	54.4	23	5.5	20	90	78	84
Lesotho	30.4	11.0	0.5	59	1.8	30	85	50	67
Liberia	111.4	5.4	31.3	29	3.2	46	83	56	70
Madagascar	587.0	6.0	20.2	29	16.9	31	89	71	80
Malawi	118.5	19.8	27.2	100	11.9	16	87	79	83
Maldives	0.3	30.0	3.3	1 037	0.3	29	86	68	77
Mali	1 240.2	3.8	10.8	10	12.6	32	90	74	82
Mauritania	1 025.5	0.5	0.3	3	2.8	61	87	65	76
Mozambique	801.6	5.3	39.0	23	18.5	35	91	83	87
Myanmar	676.6	15.7	52.3	72	48.9	29	90	68	79
Nepal	147.2	21.7	27.3	167	24.6	13	86	58	72
Niger	1 267.0	3.6	1.0	9	11.5	22	93	71	82
Rwanda	26.3	49.4	12.4	314	8.3	6	94	86	90
Samoa	2.8	45.4	37.2	62	0.2	23	..	..	..
Sao Tome and Principe	1.0	55.2	28.3	163	0.2	48	..	..	..
Senegal	196.7	12.7	32.2	50	9.9	49	87	63	75
Sierra Leone	71.7	7.9	14.7	66	4.8	38	85	46	65
Solomon Islands	28.9	2.6	88.8	16	0.5	21	89	82	86
Somalia	637.7	1.7	12.0	15	9.5	29	87	65	76
Sudan	2 505.8	6.6	25.9	13	32.9	38	86	35	61
Togo	56.8	46.3	9.4	85	4.8	35	87	55	71
Tuvalu[b]	0.0	..	0.0	403	0.0	54	..	..	..
Uganda	241.0	29.9	21.0	104	25.0	15	91	81	86
United Republic of Tanzania	883.7	5.2	43.9	41	36.3	34	88	83	86
Vanuatu	12.2	9.8	36.7	17	0.2	23	..	..	..
Yemen	528.0	3.0	0.9	37	19.3	25	84	32	58
Zambia	752.6	7.0	42.0	14	10.7	40	87	67	77
ALL LDCs	20 726.0	6.8	27.6	34	699.6	27	88	66	77
All developing countries	85 027.3	11.5	20.3	59	5 018.5	41	87	60	73

Sources: UNCTAD; *Handbook of Statistics 2003*; FAO, online data and *State of the World's Forest 2003*; ILO, *World Labour Report 2000*; UNDP *Human Development Report 2003*; and UNICEF, *The State of the World's Children 2004*.

a   Economically active population, labour force participation rates calculated as a percentage of those in the labour force at age 15–64 to total population at age 15–64.   b Population 10,466 and area 26 km².

8. INDICATORS ON DEMOGRAPHY

Country	Infant mortality rate (Per 1,000 live births)		Under-5 mortality rate (Per 1,000 live births)		Average life expectancy at birth (Years)						Crude birth rate (Per 1,000 population)		Crude death rate (Per 1,000 population)	
	1990–1995	2000–2005	1990–1995	2000–2005	1990–1995			2000–2005			1990–1995	2000–2005	1990–1995	2000–2005
					M	F	T	M	F	T				
Afghanistan	167	162	292	280	42	42	42	43	43	43	48	47	22	21
Angola	158	140	274	247	38	42	40	39	41	40	52	52	25	24
Bangladesh	90	64	128	87	56	56	56	61	62	61	36	29	11	8
Benin	100	93	169	156	49	53	51	48	53	51	46	42	15	14
Bhutan	75	54	117	80	57	59	58	62	65	63	38	35	11	9
Burkina Faso	110	93	189	160	46	49	48	45	46	46	49	48	18	17
Burundi	132	107	224	188	39	41	40	40	41	41	46	44	23	21
Cambodia	91	73	134	107	54	57	56	55	59	57	41	34	12	10
Cape Verde	44	30	56	36	64	69	66	67	73	70	35	28	8	5
Central African Republic	108	100	186	173	44	50	47	38	41	40	42	38	18	22
Chad	129	115	225	201	43	46	45	44	46	45	49	48	20	20
Comoros	84	67	118	92	55	59	57	59	62	61	39	37	10	8
Dem. Rep. of the Congo	120	120	213	219	42	45	43	41	43	42	49	50	20	21
Djibouti	117	102	202	177	45	49	47	45	47	46	43	40	17	18
Equatorial Guinea	118	101	205	173	46	49	48	48	50	49	43	43	18	17
Eritrea	89	73	132	106	48	52	50	51	54	53	43	40	14	12
Ethiopia	119	100	207	173	45	48	46	45	46	45	47	43	18	18
Gambia	99	81	171	134	49	53	51	53	55	54	41	36	15	13
Guinea	130	102	228	176	44	45	45	49	49	49	44	43	19	16
Guinea-Bissau	140	120	246	210	41	45	43	44	47	45	50	50	22	20
Haiti	79	63	136	112	48	52	50	49	50	50	34	30	15	15
Kiribati	..	..	..	..	52	52	52	..	..	..	..	..	..	..
Lao People's Dem. Republic	104	88	171	141	50	52	51	53	56	54	41	36	16	13
Lesotho	99	92	145	152	52	56	54	32	38	35	35	31	13	26
Liberia	191	147	276	229	38	41	39	41	42	41	50	50	24	22
Madagascar	108	91	178	147	49	51	50	53	55	54	45	42	16	13
Malawi	138	115	221	186	43	47	45	37	38	38	49	45	20	24
Maldives	57	38	76	49	64	62	63	68	67	67	38	36	8	6
Mali	131	119	203	181	47	48	47	48	49	49	50	50	17	16
Mauritania	110	97	181	156	48	51	49	51	54	52	42	42	16	14
Mozambique	137	122	238	215	42	45	43	37	40	38	45	41	21	23
Myanmar	96	83	151	128	53	58	55	55	60	57	30	24	12	11
Nepal	96	71	138	98	55	54	55	60	60	60	37	33	13	10
Niger	144	126	241	210	42	43	43	46	46	46	55	55	22	19
Rwanda	135	112	235	179	23	25	24	39	40	39	44	44	41	22
Samoa	36	26	45	32	63	70	66	67	73	70	32	29	7	5
Sao Tome and Principe	44	32	62	41	64	69	66	67	73	70	35	33	7	6
Senegal	68	61	126	112	48	53	50	51	55	53	41	37	14	12
Sierra Leone	194	177	328	307	33	36	35	33	35	34	50	50	30	29
Solomon Islands	28	21	44	30	64	66	65	68	71	69	38	33	6	5
Somalia	163	118	272	195	39	41	40	46	49	48	52	52	25	18
Sudan	93	77	157	127	52	54	53	54	57	56	38	33	13	12
Togo	88	81	147	136	52	56	54	48	51	50	42	38	13	15
Tuvalu	..	..	..	..	..	..	..	..	..	..	..	..	..	..
Uganda	107	86	187	147	39	44	41	45	47	46	50	51	21	17
United Republic of Tanzania	99	100	157	162	47	51	49	42	44	43	44	39	15	18
Vanuatu	38	29	48	35	64	67	65	67	71	69	36	30	7	5
Yemen	92	71	131	98	55	56	56	59	61	60	49	45	12	9
Zambia	106	105	182	185	42	47	44	33	32	32	46	42	19	28
ALL LDCs	111	97	183	161	47	50	49	49	50	50	42	39	16	15
All developing countries	71	61	103	89	60	63	62	62	65	63	28	24	9	9

Source: United Nations Population Division, *World Population Prospects: 2002 Revision.*

Note: Data refer to medium-variant projections for the period specified.

9. INDICATORS ON HEALTH

Country	Low birth-weight[a] infants (%)	Percentage of women attended childbirth by trained personnel	Percentage of 1-year-old children immunized against:			Estimated number of people living with HIV/AIDS		Adult prevalence rate
			Tuber-culosis	DPT3[b]	Measles	children (0–14 years)	adults and children (0–49 years)	(15–49) years)
	1998–2002[c]	1995–2002[c]		2002			End 2001	End 2001
Afghanistan	..	12	59	47	44	..	..	..
Angola	12	45	82	47	74	37 000	350 000	5.5
Bangladesh	30	12	95	85	77	310	13 000	<0.1
Benin	16	66	94	79	78	12 000	120 000	3.6
Bhutan	15	24	83	86	78	..	<100	<0.1
Burkina Faso	19	31	72	41	46	61 000	440 000	6.5
Burundi	16	25	84	74	75	55 000	390 000	8.3
Cambodia	11	32	63	54	52	12 000	170 000	2.7
Cape Verde	13	89	92	94	85	..	..	..
Central African Republic	14	44	70	40	35	25 000	250 000	12.9
Chad	17[d]	16	67	40	55	18 000	150 000	3.6
Comoros	25	62	90	89	71	..	..	..
Dem. Republic of the Congo	12	61	55	43	45	170 000	1 300 000	4.9
Djibouti	..	..	52	62	62	..	..	..
Equatorial Guinea	13	65	73	33	51	420	5 900	3.4
Eritrea	21[d]	21	91	83	84	4 000	55 000	2.8
Ethiopia	15	6	76	56	52	230 000	2 100 000	6.4
Gambia	17	55	99	90	90	460	8 400	1.6
Guinea	12	35	71	47	54	..	..	..
Guinea-Bissau	22	35	70	50	47	1 500	17 000	2.8
Haiti	21	24	71	43	53	12 000	250 000	6.1
Kiribati	5	85	99	99	88	..	..	..
Lao People's Dem. Republic	14	19	65	55	55	<100	1 400	<0.1
Lesotho	14	60	83	79	70	27 000	360 000	31.0
Liberia	..	51	67	51	57	..	..	..
Madagascar	14	46	73	62	61	1 000	22 000	0.3
Malawi	16	56	78	64	69	65 000	850 000	15.0
Maldives	22	70	98	98	99	..	<100	0.1
Mali	23	41	73	57	33	13 000	110 000	1.7
Mauritania	42	57	98	83	81	..	..	..
Mozambique	14[d]	44	78	60	58	80 000	1 100 000	13.0
Myanmar	15	56	80	77	75	..	..	..
Nepal	21	11	85	72	71	1 500	58 000	0.5
Niger	17	16	47	23	48	..	..	..
Rwanda	9	31	99	88	69	65 000	500 000	8.9
Samoa	4[d]	100	98	96	99	..	..	..
Sao Tome and Principe	..	79	99	92	85	..	..	..
Senegal	18	58	70	60	54	2 900	27 000	0.5
Sierra Leone	..	42	70	50	60	16 000	170 000	7.0
Solomon Islands	13[d]	85	76	71	78	..	..	..
Somalia	..	34	60	40	45	..	43 000	1.0
Sudan	31	86	48	40	49	30 000	450 000	2.6
Togo	15	49	84	64	58	15 000	150 000	6.0
Tuvalu	5	99	99	98	99	..	..	..
Uganda	12	39	96	72	77	110 000	600 000	5.0
United Republic of Tanzania	13	36	88	89	89	170 000	1 500 000	7.8
Vanuatu	6	89	90	54	44	..	..	..
Yemen	32[d]	22	74	69	65	..	9 900	0.1
Zambia	10	43	92	78	85	150 000	1 200 000	21.5
All LDCs	18	31	77	63	63	1 428 000	13 348 000	4.1
All developing countries	17	55	81	73	73	2 928 000	37 476 000	1.4

Source: UNICEF, *The State of the World's Children 2004*; UNAIDS, *Report on the Global HIV/AIDS Epidemic, 2002.*

a   Less than 2,500 grams.
b   Diphtheria, pertussis and tetanus.
c   Data refer to the most recent year available during the period specified in the column heading.
d   Indicates data that refers to years or periods other than those specified in the column heading, differ from the standard definition, or refer to only part of the country.

10. INDICATORS ON NUTRITION AND SANITATION

Country	Total food supply (dairy calories intake per capita)		Population using improved drinking water sources (%) 2000			Population using adequate sanitation facilities (%) 2000		
	1990	2001	Total	Urban	Rural	Total	Urban	Rural
Afghanistan	..	..	13	19	11	12	25	8
Angola	1 748	1 953	38	34	40	44	70	30
Bangladesh	2 082	2 187	97	99	97	48	71	41
Benin	2 308	2 455	63	74	55	23	46	6
Bhutan	..	..	62	86	60	70	65	70
Burkina Faso	2 277	2 485	42	66	37	29	39	27
Burundi	1 879	1 612	78	91	77	88	68	90
Cambodia	1 830	1 967	30	54	26	17	56	10
Cape Verde	3 009	3 308	74	64	89	71	95	32
Central African Republic	1 870	1 949	70	89	57	25	38	16
Chad	1 695	2 245	27	31	26	29	81	13
Comoros	1 897	1 735	96	98	95	98	98	98
Dem. Rep. of the Congo	2 215	1 535	45	89	26	21	54	6
Djibouti	1 864	2 218	100	100	100	91	99	50
Equatorial Guinea	..	..	44	45	42	53	60	46
Eritrea	1 472[b]	1 690	46	63	42	13	66	1
Ethiopia	1 558[b]	2 037	24	81	12	12	33	7
Gambia	2 433	2 300	62	80	53	37	41	35
Guinea	2 000	2 362	48	72	36	58	94	41
Guinea-Bissau	2 423	2 481	56	79	49	56	95	44
Haiti	1 785	2 045	46	49	45	28	50	16
Kiribati	2 591	2 922	48	82	25	48	54	44
Lao People's Dem. Rep.	2 159	2 309	37	61	29	30	67	19
Lesotho	2 242	2 320	78	88	74	49	72	40
Liberia	2 101	1 946	..	..	..	..	..	..
Madagascar	2 139	2 072	47	85	31	42	70	30
Malawi	1 933	2 168	57	95	44	76	96	70
Maldives	2 324	2 587	100	100	100	56	100	41
Mali	2 303	2 376	65	74	61	69	93	58
Mauritania	2 564	2 764	37	34	40	33	44	19
Mozambique	1 825	1 980	57	81	41	43	68	26
Myanmar	2 620	2 822	72	89	66	64	84	57
Nepal	2 494	2 459	88	94	87	28	73	22
Niger	2 151	2 118	59	70	56	20	79	5
Rwanda	1 830	2 086	41	60	40	8	12	8
Samoa	..	..	99	95	100	99	95	100
Sao Tome and Principe	2 386	2 567	..	..	..	..	..	..
Senegal	2 312	2 277	78	92	65	70	94	48
Sierra Leone	1 987	1 913	57	75	46	66	88	53
Solomon Islands	1 946	2 272	71	94	65	34	98	18
Somalia	..	..	..	..	..	..	..	..
Sudan	2 138	2 288	75	86	69	62	87	48
Togo	2 284	2 287	54	85	38	34	69	17
Tuvalu	..	..	100	100	100	100	100	100
Uganda	2 337	2 398	52	80	47	79	93	77
United Rep. of Tanzania	2 133	1 998	68	90	57	90	99	86
Vanuatu	2 492	2 565	88	63	94	100	100	100
Yemen	2 018	2 050	69	74	68	38	89	21
Zambia	1 997	1 885	64	88	48	78	99	64
All LDCs	2 097	2 134	62	82	55	44	71	35
All developing countries[b]	2 516	2 675	78	92	69	52	77	35

Source: FAO, *Food Balance Sheets online data*; WHO/UNICEF, *Water Supply and Sanitation Sector Monitoring Report 1993* and *1996*; WHO, *The International Drinking Water Supply and Sanitation Decade: End of Decade Review* (as at December 1990); Review of National Progress (various issues); and UNICEF, *The State of the World's Children 2004*.

a   Or latest year available.   *b* 1993.

11. INDICATORS ON EDUCATION AND LITERACY

Country	Adult literacy rate						School enrolment ratio								
	(%) 2000			(%) Estimated year 2005			Primary[a] 1997–2001[d]			Secondary[b] 1997–2001[d]			Tertiary[c] 1997–2001[d]		
	M	F	T	M	F	T	M	F	T	M	F	T	M	F	T
Afghanistan	51	21	36	..	..	..	42[e]	15[e]	29[e]	32[e]	11[e]	22[e]	..	..	1
Angola	56	29	42	..	..	..	39	35	37	19	16	18	1	1	1
Bangladesh	49	30	40	52	33	43	88	90	89	45	47	46	8	5	7
Benin	52	24	37	59	28	43	83	57	70	30	14	22	6	1	4
Bhutan	61	34	47	..	..	..	58	47	53	7[e]	2[e]	5[e]	..	..	..
Burkina Faso	34	14	24	39	18	28	42	29	36	12	8	10	..	..	..
Burundi	56	40	48	60	48	54	59	49	54	12	9	10	2	1	1
Cambodia	80	57	68	82	62	71	89	82	85	24	13	19	4	2	3
Cape Verde	84	66	74	87	71	78	100	100	100	75	77	76	..	..	..
Central African Republic	60	35	47	66	43	54	64	45	55	15[e]	6[e]	11[e]	3	1	2
Chad	52	34	43	59	43	51	70	47	58	18	5	11	2	-	1
Comoros	63	49	56	64	50	57	60	52	56	23	18	21	1	1	1
Dem. Rep. of the Congo	73	50	61	78	58	68	33	32	33	24	13	18	1	..	..
Djibouti	76	54	65	80	61	70	37	28	33	23	14	19	1	1	1
Equatorial Guinea	93	74	83	94	80	87	76	68	72	43	19	31	4	2	3
Eritrea	67	45	56	72	50	60	44	38	41	33	24	28	3	-	2
Ethiopia	47	31	39	52	38	45	53	41	47	22	14	18	2	1	2
Gambia	44	30	37	50	35	42	71	66	69	44	31	37	..	..	..
Guinea	55	27	41	..	..	..	52	41	47	20	7	14	..	..	..
Guinea-Bissau	54	24	38	60	30	45	63	45	54	26	14	20	1	-	-
Haiti	52	48	50	57	53	55	78	83	81	21[e]	20[e]	21[e]	..	..	..
Kiribati	..	..	..	..	..	..	..	..	..	..	..	..	..	..	..
Lao People's Dem. Rep.	76	53	65	79	59	69	85	78	81	44	31	38	4	2	3
Lesotho	73	94	83	76	95	86	75	82	78	30	36	33	2	3	3
Liberia	70	37	54	75	43	59	76	65	70	31	20	26	11	3	7
Madagascar	74	60	66	77	64	71	67	68	68	15	14	14	2	2	2
Malawi	75	47	61	77	52	64	97	100	98	40	31	36	..	..	..
Maldives	97	97	97	98	98	98	99	99	99	53	57	55	..	..	..
Mali	36	16	26	40	19	29	51	36	43	20	10	15	..	..	2
Mauritania	51	30	40	53	33	43	66	62	64	22	20	21	6	1	4
Mozambique	60	29	44	66	36	50	59	50	54	14	9	12	1	-	1
Myanmar	89	81	85	90	83	86	83	83	83	40	38	39	8	15	12
Nepal	59	24	42	65	30	47	77	67	72	58	43	51	7	2	5
Niger	24	9	16	27	11	19	36	24	30	8	5	6	2	1	1
Rwanda	74	60	67	78	68	73	97	97	97	14	14	14	2	1	2
Samoa	99	98	99	99	99	99	98	95	97	73	79	75	11	11	11
Sao Tome and Principe	..	..	..	..	..	..	..	..	..	..	..	..	..	..	..
Senegal	47	28	37	52	33	42	66	60	63	21	14	18	4	..	..
Sierra Leone	51	23	36		..	..	68	63	65	29	24	26	3	1	2
Solomon Islands	..	..	..	..	..	..	..	..	..	21[e]	14[e]	17[e]	..	..	..
Somalia	36	14	24	..	..	..	13[e]	7[e]	10[e]	10[e]	6[e]	8[e]	..	..	..
Sudan	69	46	58	73	53	63	54	45	49	31	29	30	7	7	7
Togo	72	43	57	77	50	63	100	82	91	54	24	39	6	1	4
Tuvalu	..	..	..	..	..	..	100	96	98	83	73	78	..	..	..
Uganda	78	57	67	81	63	72	100	100	100	18	12	15	4	2	3
United Rep. of Tanzania	84	67	75	87	73	80	46	48	47	6	5	6	1	..	1
Vanuatu	..	..	..	..	..	..	90	89	89	31	26	28	..	..	..
Yemen	68	25	46	72	33	53	84	49	67	69	25	48	17	5	11
Zambia	85	72	78	88	77	82	66	65	66	26	21	24	3	2	2
All LDCs	62	42	52	65	47	56	67	61	64	30	25	27	..	..	..
All developing countries	81	67	74	83	70	77	84	77	81	59	52	55	..	..	..

Source: UNESCO Institute for Statistics (UIS) estimates and projections, online data, and *World Culture Report 2000*; UNDP, *Human Development Report 2003*; UNICEF, *The State of the World's Children 2004*.

a Net primary school enrolment.
b Gross secondary school enrolment.
c Gross tertiary school enrolment.
d Or latest year available.
e Indicates data that refer to years or periods other than those specified in the column heading, differ from the standard definition or refer to only part of the country.

12. INDICATORS ON COMMUNICATIONS AND MEDIA

Country	Post offices open to the public[a] (Per 100,000 inhabitants)	Circulation of daily newspapers[a]	Television sets[a]	Radio receivers[a]	Telephone mainlines[a]	Cellular subscribers[a]	Internet users[a]
				(Per 1,000 inhabitants)			
	2002	2001	2002	2001	2002	2001	2002
Afghanistan	2	5	14	132	1	..	..
Angola	0	11	52	54	6	6	3
Bangladesh	7	53	59	50	5	4	2
Benin	2	5	12	110	9	19	7
Bhutan	5	..	27	19	28	..	14
Burkina Faso	1	1	79	33	5	6	2
Burundi	0	2	31	152	3	4	1
Cambodia	1	2	8	128	3	17	2
Cape Verde	12	..	101	183	160	72	36
Central African Republic	1	2	6	83	2	3	1
Chad	0	0	1	242	2	3	2
Comoros	4	..	4	141	13	0	4
Democratic Rep. of the Congo	1	3	2	376	0	3	1
Djibouti	2	..	78	84	15	5	7
Equatorial Guinea	6	5	116	428	17	32	4
Eritrea	2	..	50	484	9	0	2
Ethiopia	1	0	6	196	5	..	1
Gambia	1	2	15	394	28	41	18
Guinea	1	..	47	49	3	7	5
Guinea-Bissau	3	5	36	44	9	0	4
Haiti	0	3	6	55	16	11	10
Kiribati	31	..	36	212	51	..	23
Lao People's Democratic Rep.	4	4	52	143	11	5	3
Lesotho	9	8	35	49	13	26	10
Liberia	0	13	25	329	2	0	..
Madagascar	6	5	25	198	4	10	3
Malawi	3	3	4	250	7	5	3
Maldives	68	20	131	129	102	69	53
Mali	1	1	33	54	5	4	2
Mauritania	2	1	99	151	12	43	4
Mozambique	2	3	14	40	5	9	2
Myanmar	3	9	8	70	7	0	1
Nepal	18	12	8	39	14	..	3
Niger	0	0	10	66	2	8	1
Rwanda	0	0	..	102	3	..	3
Samoa	21	..	146	1035	57	..	22
Sao Tome and Principe	6	..	93	272	41	0	73
Senegal	1	5	78	142	22	31	10
Sierra Leone	1	4	13	274	5	5	2
Solomon Islands	31	..	28	141	15	2	5
Somalia	..	1	14	53	10	..	9
Sudan	1	26	386	271	21	3	3
Togo	1	4	123	227	10	26	41
Tuvalu	..	..	484	384	65	..	97
Uganda	1	2	18	127	2	12	4
United Republic of Tanzania	1	4	45	279	5	13	2
Vanuatu	8	..	12	350	33	2	35
Yemen	1	15	308	64	28	8	5
Zambia	2	12	51	160	8	11	5
All LDCs	3	7	50	170[c]	7	6	12
All developing countries[b]	8	40	183	321[c]	143	75	73

Source: UNDP, *Human Development Report 2003*; UNCTAD, *Handbook of Statistics 2003*; UNESCO, *Statistical Yearbook 1999* and *World Culture Report 2000*; Universal Postal Union, *Postal Statistics* online data. World Bank, *World Development Indicators*, online data.

a   Or latest year available.   b Average of countries for which data are available.   c Data refer to 1997.

13. INDICATORS ON TRANSPORT AND TRANSPORT NETWORKS

Country	Road networks[a]			Railways[b]				Civil aviation[c]	
	Total	Paved	Density	Network	Density	Freight	Passenger	Freight	Passenger
	km	%	km/ 1,000 km²	km	km/ 1,000 km²	mill. ton per km	mill. pass. per km	mill. tons. per km.	thousands
Afghanistan	21 000	13.3	32.2	..	..	..	..	7.8[d]	150[d]
Angola	51 429	10.4	41.3	2 523	2.0	1 890	360	51.0	193
Bangladesh	207 486	9.5	1 440.9	2 746	19.1	718	5 348	170.0	1 450
Benin	6 787	20.0	60.3	579	5.1	220	230	7.4	46
Bhutan	3 690	60.7	78.5	..	..	..	..	..	35
Burkina Faso	12 506	16.0	45.6	607	2.2	72	152	7.4	100
Burundi	14 480	7.1	520.2	..	..	..	..	..	12[e]
Cambodia	12 323[d]	16.2[d]	68.1[d]	601	3.3	34	80	..	..
Cape Verde	1 100	78.0	272.7	..	..	..	..	0.4	243
Central African Republic	23 810	2.7	38.2	..	..	..	..	7.4	46
Chad	33 400	0.8	26.0	..	..	..	..	7.4	46
Comoros	880	76.5	393.7	..	..	..	..	..	27[f]
Dem. Rep. of the Congo	157 000	..	67.0	5 088	2.2	1 836	580	..	..
Djibouti	2 890	12.6	124.6	100	4.3	..	..	..	..
Equatorial Guinea	2 880	..	102.7	..	..	..	..	..	21[e]
Eritrea	4 010	21.8	34.1	..	..	..	..	..	..
Ethiopia	31 571[d]	12.0[d]	28.6[d]	781	0.7	103	185	79.0	1028
Gambia	2 700	35.4	239.0	..	..	..	..	..	..
Guinea	30 500	16.5	124.1	940	3.8	660	116	1.4[g]	59[g]
Guinea-Bissau	4 400	10.3	121.8	..	..	..	..	0.1[h]	20[e]
Haiti	4 160	24.3	149.9	100	3.6	..	..	..	..
Kiribati	670	..	922.9	..	..	..	..	0.8[e]	28[e]
Lao People's Dem. Rep.	21 716	13.8	91.7	..	..	..	..	1.6	211
Lesotho	5 940	18.3	195.7	16	0.5	..	..	..	1[g]
Liberia	10 600	6.2	95.2	493	4.4	..	..	..	..
Madagascar	49 827	11.6	84.9	1 030	1.8	93	46	34.0	624
Malawi	28 400	18.5	239.7	789	6.7	48	40	0.8	113
Maldives	..	..	..	..	..	..	..	13.0	311
Mali	15 100	12.1	12.2	642	0.5	4	9	7.4	46
Mauritania	7 660	11.3	7.5	650	0.6	16 623	7	7.4	156
Mozambique	30 400	18.7	37.9	3 150	3.9	1 420	500	6.9	264
Myanmar	28 200	12.2	41.7	2 775	4.1	648	4 675	0.9	398
Nepal	*13 223*	*30.8*	*89.8*	*52*	*0.4*	*..*	*..*	*16.0*	*641*
Niger	10 100	7.9	8.0	..	..	..	..	7.4	46
Rwanda	12 000	8.3	455.6	2 652	100.7	2 140	2 700	..	..
Samoa	790	42.0	279.1	..	..	..	..	2.1	174
Sao Tome and Principe	320	68.1	332.0	..	..	..	..	0.1	35
Senegal	14 576[d]	29.3[d]	74.1[d]	906	4.6	386	179	14.0[g]	6
Sierra Leone	11 330	7.9	157.9	84	1.2	..	..	6.0	14
Solomon Islands	1 360	2.5	47.1	..	..	..	..	1.0	81
Somalia	22 100	11.8	34.7	..	..	..	..	..	..
Sudan	11 900	36.3	4.7	4 756	1.9	1 970	985	33.0	415
Togo	7 520	31.6	132.4	514	9.1	17	132	7.4	46
Tuvalu	8	..	307.7	..	..	..	..	..	..
Uganda	27 000	..	112.0	1 100	4.6	82	315	21.0	41
United Rep. of Tanzania	88 200	4.2	99.8	3 575	4.0	523	935	2.8	171
Vanuatu	1 070	23.9	87.8	..	..	..	..	1.9	98
Yemen	67 000	11.5	126.9	..	..	..	..	32.0	841
Zambia	66 781	18.0	88.7	1 924	2.6	1 625	547	0.5[d]	49

Source: World Bank, *World Development Indicators* online data; IRU, *World Transport Statistics 1996.*

   a   Data refer to 1999.
   b   Data refer to 1996 or latest year available.
   c   Data refer to 2001
   d   2000.
   e   1998.
   f   1996.
   g   1999.
   h   1997.

14. INDICATORS ON ENERGY AND THE ENVIRONMENT

Country	Coal, oil, gas and electricity		Fuelwood, charcoal and bagasse		Installed electricity capacity		Carbon dioxide emissions per capita	
	Consumption per capita in kg. of coal equivalent				kw./1,000 inhabitants		Metric tons	
	1980	2000	1980	1996	1980	2000	1980	2000
Afghanistan	48	23	99	99	25	23	0.1	0.0
Angola	135	174	362	183	85	37	0.8	0.5
Bangladesh	45	114	23	24	11	25	0.1	0.2
Benin	51	116	347	344	4	9	0.1	0.3
Bhutan	9	172	777	262	8	450	0.0	0.5
Burkina Faso	33	43	277	312	6	7	0.1	0.1
Burundi	14	20	252	255	2	7	0.0	0.0
Cambodia	22	20	213	218	6	3	0.0	0.1
Cape Verde	194	155	..	..	21	16	0.4	0.3
Central African Rep.	26	38	358	335	13	12	0.0	0.1
Chad	22	8	206	208	8	4	0.0	0.0
Comoros	48	54	..	..	10	9	0.1	0.1
Dem. Rep. of the Congo	75	37	298	335	64	66	0.1	0.1
Djibouti	326	290	..	..	124	132	1.0	0.6
Equatorial Guinea	124	170	645	383	32	39	0.3	0.4
Eritrea	..	76	..	..	..	46	..	0.1
Ethiopia	21[a]	40	296	285	9	7	0.0	0.1
Gambia	128	93	452	338	17	22	0.2	0.2
Guinea	85	69	246	221	39	24	0.2	0.2
Guinea-Bissau	81	104	177	134	9	15	0.7	0.2
Haiti	56	89	322	288	22	32	0.1	0.2
Kiribati	220	141	..	..	33	24	0.5	0.3
Lao People's Dem. Rep.	30	62	354	308	78	48	0.1	0.1
Lesotho	..	..	..	..	..	..	..	..
Liberia	480	72	709	589	163	113	1.1	0.1
Madagascar	86	57	194	242	11	14	0.2	0.1
Malawi	58	38	288	314	24	17	0.1	0.1
Maldives	129	875	..	..	13	124	0.3	1.8
Mali	27	23	196	191	6	10	0.1	0.1
Mauritania	178	530	1	1	35	43	0.4	1.2
Mozambique	151	76	351	323	156	117	0.3	0.1
Myanmar	65	99	143	149	19	33	0.1	0.2
Nepal	18	70	305	282	5	19	0.0	0.1
Niger	50	46	191	200	6	10	0.1	0.1
Rwanda	28	36	292	232	8	6	0.1	0.1
Samoa	310	405	145	149	84	116	0.6	0.8
Sao Tome and Principe	213	317	..	..	43	40	0.5	0.6
Senegal	214	191	..	..	30	25	0.5	0.4
Sierra Leone	79	48	709	237	29	29	0.2	0.1
Solomon Islands	212	177	..	126	53	27	0.4	0.4
Somalia	108	48[b]	192	315	5	9	0.1	..
Sudan	81	93	282	289	16	24	0.2	0.2
Togo	72	152	66	94	13	8	0.2	0.4
Tuvalu	..	..	..	..	..	..	..	..
Uganda	29	38	235	236	12	11	0.1	0.1
United Rep. of Tanzania	44	58	331	392	14	16	0.1	0.1
Vanuatu	248	193	68	48	85	61	0.5	0.4
Yemen	187	211	45	8	20	45	..	0.5
Zambia	403	159	496	502	301	217	0.6	0.2
All LDCs	66	82	212	210	28	30	0.1	0.2
All developing countries	521	886	125	135	88	221	1.3	1.9

Source: United Nations, Energy Statistics Yearbook 1983 and 2000, and Statistical Yearbook 1985/86. UNDP, Human Development Report 2003, and World Bank, World Development Indicator, online data.

a Includes Eritrea. b 1989.

15. INDICATORS ON THE STATUS OF WOMEN IN LDCs

Country	Education, training and literacy: Female–male gaps[a]				Health, fertility and mortality			Economic activity, employment					Political participation	
	Adult literacy rate	School enrolment ratio[b]			Average age at first marriage (years)	Total fertility rate (births per woman)	Maternal mortality (per 100,000 live births)	Women as a percentage of total:				Female labour force: Agriculture/total	Women in government at ministerial level	Seats in parliaments held by women
		Primary	Secondary	Tertiary				Labour force	Employees	Self-employed	Unpaid family	(%)	(% of total)	
	2001	2000–2001			1997[c]	2002	2000[d]	2002[c]	1998[c]	1998[c]	1998[c]	2002	2000	2003[g]
Afghanistan	..	..	..	..	18	7	1900	36	..	..	..	83	..	..
Angola	..	0.91	..	0.63[f]	18	7	1700	46	..	..	..	83	15	16
Bangladesh	62	1.02	1.05	0.55	17	4	380	42	14	8	74	64	10	2
Benin	46	0.69[f]	0.46[f]	0.24[f]	18	6	850	48	..	64	40	52	11	6
Bhutan	..	..	..	..	..	5	420	40	..	..	..	98	..	9
Burkina Faso	43	0.71	0.65	..	17	7	1000	46	13	16	66	93	9	12
Burundi	74	0.83	..	0.36	22	7	1000	49	13	53	60	97	5	18
Cambodia	72	0.90	0.59	0.38	21	5	450	51	..	..	..	73	7	7
Cape Verde	79	1.01[e]	..	..	25	3	150	39	32	30	54	21	35	11
Central African Republic	60	0.70	..	0.19[f]	19	5	1100	47	10	52	55	78	..	7
Chad	67	0.67	0.31[f]	0.17[f]	17	7	1100	45	..	..	..	84	..	6
Comoros	77	0.87	..	0.73[f]	22	5	480	42	24	25	..	86	..	..
Dem. Rep. of the Congo	70	0.95[e]	0.58[e]	..	20	7	990	43	..	..	..	76	..	..
Djibouti	73	0.77	..	0.70	19	6	730	40	33	28	22	83	5	11
Equatorial Guinea	82	0.89	0.36[e]	0.43[f]	..	6	880	36	..	..	74	89	..	5
Eritrea	67	0.86	0.74	0.15	..	6	630	47	..	..	..	81	12	22
Ethiopia	67	0.77	0.68	0.27	18	6	850	41	26	28	67	79	22	8
Gambia	69	0.93	0.70	..	..	5	540	45	..	..	64	89	31	13
Guinea	..	0.79	0.38[e]	..	16	6	740	47	..	..	60	88	11	19
Guinea-Bissau	45	0.71[f]	..	0.18[f]	18	7	1100	41	..	..	4	95	8	8
Haiti	93	..	..	..	24	4	680	43	44	57	37	49	18	4
Kiribati	..	..	..	..	..	..	..	..	..	..	..	14	..	5
Lao People's Dem. Rep.	71	0.92	0.81	0.59	..	5	650	..	..	..	..	79	10	23
Lesotho	128	1.09	1.54	1.76	21	4	550	37	38	24	39	54	..	12
Liberia	..	..	..	..	19	7	760	40	..	..	..	75	..	8
Madagascar	82	1.01	1.03[e]	0.84	20	6	550	45	..	..	..	82	13	4
Malawi	63	1.07	0.85	0.39[e]	18	6	1800	48	13	57	58	95	12	9
Maldives	100	1.01	1.13[f]	..	19	5	110	44	17	44	29	18	..	6
Mali	45	0.71[e]	..	..	16	7	1200	46	17	15	53	81	33	10
Mauritania	60	0.93	0.78	0.20	19	6	1000	44	15	23	38	63	14	..
Mozambique	49	0.85	0.68	0.79	18	6	1000	48	..	..	82	95	..	30
Myanmar	91	0.99	0.95	1.75	22	3	360	43	..	..	..	73	..	..
Nepal	42	0.87	..	0.27	18	4	740	41	15	36	61	98	15	6
Niger	36	0.67	0.67	0.34	16	8	1600	44	8	17	24	97	10	1
Rwanda	83	1.00[f]	..	0.50	21	6	1400	49	15	33	53	97	13	26
Samoa	99	0.97	1.08	1.05	25	4	130	37	37	9	8	33	8	6
Sao Tome and Principe	..	..	..	..	18	4	..	..	32	26	54	74	..	9
Senegal	60	0.90	..	..	18	5	690	43				81	16	19
Sierra Leone	..	..	0.83	0.40	18	6	2000	37	20	24	72	76	8	15
Solomon Islands	..	..	..	..	21	5	130	46	20	39	..	83	..	0
Somalia	..	..	..	..	20	7	1100	43	..	..	..	82	..	..
Sudan	68	0.83[f]	..	0.92[e]	19	4	590	30	..	..	..	74	5	10
Togo	60	0.82	0.44[e]	0.20[f]	19	5	570	40	15	48	54	61	7	7
Tuvalu	..	..	..	..	..	..	..	..	..	..	..	..	..	0
Uganda	74	0.94	0.72[f]	0.52	18	7	880	48	..	39	74	83	27	25
United Rep. of Tanzania	80	1.04	0.94	0.31	19	5	1500	49	..	..	88	87	..	22
Vanuatu	..	1.10	1.20[e]	0.62[e]	23	4	130	..	..	..	..	37	..	2
Yemen	39	0.58	0.40[e]	0.28[e]	18	7	570	28	8	13	69	75	..	1
Zambia	85	0.99	0.87	0.47	19	6	750	45	16	55	54	75	6	12
All LDCs	70	0.90	..	..	19	5	890	42	..	..	..	78	..	..

Source: UNDP, *Human Development Report 2003;* United Nations, *The World's Women 1970–1990* and *2000: Trends and Statistics; Women's Indicators and Statistics* (Wistat); UNESCO, *Statistical Yearbook* 1999 and *World Culture Report 2000;* UNICEF, *The State of the World's Children 2004;* and FAO, online data.

a Females as percentage of males. b Net primary school enrolment, Net secondary school enrolment, and Tertiary school enrolment is generally calculated as a gross ratio. c Or latest year available. d UNICEF, WHO and UNFPA adjusted from the reported data and estimates for the year 2000. e Data refer to the 1999/2000 school year. f Data refer to the 1998/1999 school year. g Data refer to the lower house only and are as of 1 March 2003.

TABLE 16. LDCs REFUGEES POPULATION BY COUNTRY OR TERRITORY OF ASYLUM OR RESIDENCE, 2002

Country [a]	Refugees population[b]		Asylum-seekers[c]	Returned refugees[d]	Internally displaced[e]	Returned IDPs[f]	Others	Total
	begin year	end year						
Afghanistan[g]	3	3	18	1957958	665156	753344	-	3376479
Angola	12250	12250	928	87544	188728	13272	-	302722
Bangladesh	22173	22025	22	-	-	-	-	22047
Benin	4799	5021	314	-	-	-	-	5335
Bhutan	-	-	-	-	-	-	-	-
Burkina Faso	457	457	377	-	-	-	-	834
Burundi	27896	40533	8777	53287	100000	-	-	202597
Cambodia	50	200	81	-	-	-	-	281
Cape Verde	-	-	-	-	-	-	-	-
Central African Rep.	49239	50725	5348	8	-	-	-	56081
Chad	13199	33455	1034	51	-	-	-	34540
Comoros	-	-	-	-	-	-	-	-
Dem. Rep. of the Congo	362012	332978	397	13489	9000	-	-	355864
Djibouti	23140	21702	462	-	-	-	-	22164
Equatorial Guinea	-	-	-	-	-	-	-	-
Eritrea	2272	3619	5	19676	-	-	100 [h]	23400
Ethiopia	152554	132940	19	213	-	-	-	133172
Gambia	12120	12120	-	-	-	-	-	12120
Guinea	7703	182163	367	-	-	-	-	182530
Guinea-Bissau	178444	7639	40	-	-	-	-	7679
Haiti	-	-	-	-	-	-	-	-
Kiribati	-	-	-	-	-	-	-	-
Lao People's Dem. Rep.	-	-	-	-	-	-	-	-
Lesotho	39	-	-	-	-	-	-	-
Liberia	54766	64956	-	21901	304115	-	-	390972
Madagascar	34	-	-	-	-	-	-	-
Malawi	6200	2166	11068	-	-	-	-	13234
Maldives	-	-	-	-	-	-	-	-
Mali	8412	9095	719	-	-	-	-	9814
Mauritania	365	405	12	-	-	-	29500 [i]	29917
Mozambique	207	207	6983	10	-	-	-	7200
Myanmar	-	-	-	760	-	-	-	760
Nepal	130945	132436	11	-	-	-	-	132447
Niger	83	296	44	-	-	-	-	340
Rwanda	34786	30863	1576	38643	-	-	-	71082
Samoa	-	-	-	-	-	-	-	-
Sao Tome and Principe	-	-	-	-	-	-	-	-
Senegal	20707	20711	1928	15	-	-	-	22654
Sierra Leone	10774	63494	277	75978	-	-	-	139749
Solomon Islands	-	-	-	-	-	-	-	-
Somalia	237	199	215	32050	-	-	-	32464
Sudan	347870	328176	23449	383	-	-	-	352008
Togo	12257	12294	123	-	-	-	-	12417
Tuvalu	-	-	-	-	-	-	-	-
Uganda	199736	217302	544	263	-	-	-	218109
United Rep. of Tanzania	646875	689373	164	9	-	-	-	689546
Vanuatu	-	-	-	-	-	-	-	-
Yemen	69468	82803	2095	670	-	-	-	85568
Zambia	284173	246765	945	-	-	-	-	247710
Total LDCs	2696245	2759371	68342	2302908	1266999	766616	29600	7193836

Source: UNHCR/Governments. Compiled by: UNHCR, Population Data Unit/PGDS.

Notes: The data are generally provided by Governments, based on their own definitions and methods of data collection.
a Country or territory of asylum or residence. b Persons recognized as refugees under the 1951 UN Convention/1967 Protocol, the 1969 OAU Convention, in accordance with the UNHCR Statute, persons granted a humanitarian status and those granted temporary protection. c Persons whose application for asylum or refugee status is pending at any stage in the procedure or who are otherwise registed as a asylum-seekers. d Refugees who have returned to their place of origin during the year. e Persons who are displaced within their country and to whom UNHCR extends protection and/or assistance. f Persons who have returned to their place of origin during the year. g According to the Government, the number of Afghans in the Islamic Rep. of Iran and Pakistan are estimated to be some 2.0 million and 1.8 millions respectively. h Expelled persons from Ethiopia. i Sahrawis (Mauritania)26,000, Mali (3,500).

17. Leading exports of all LDCs in 2000–2001

SITC	Item	Value[a] ($ millions)	As percentage of:		
			LDCs	Developing countries	World
	All commodities	29 240.1	100.00	1.62	0.49
333	Petroleum oils, crude and crude oils obtained from bituminous minerals	8 142.0	27.85	3.22	2.40
842	Outergarments, men's, of textile fabrics	1 636.7	5.60	7.53	4.81
845	Outergarments and other articles, knitted	1 430.2	4.89	5.21	3.33
334	Petroleum products, refined	1 362.8	4.66	1.87	0.89
843	Outergarments, women's, of textile fabrics	1 214.0	4.15	4.38	2.67
844	Undergarments of textile fabrics	1 078.4	3.69	11.36	7.96
667	Pearls, precious and semi-precious stones unworked or worked	1 051.4	3.60	5.77	2.06
846	Undergarments knitted or crocheted	946.0	3.24	5.11	3.07
036	Crustaceans and molluscs, fresh, chilled frozen, salted, in brine or dried	848.6	2.90	7.57	5.14
263	Cotton	805.6	2.76	20.18	10.56
971	Gold, non-monetary	637.5	2.18	8.38	3.10
247	Other wood rough, squared	578.5	1.98	28.92	7.84
034	Fish, fresh, chilled or frozen	555.4	1.90	6.41	2.56
071	Coffee and coffee substitutes	545.0	1.86	7.17	5.15
682	Copper	472.8	1.62	3.79	1.56
287	Ores and Concentrates of base metals, n.e.s	440.8	1.51	4.17	2.25
341	Gas, natural and manufactured	399.9	1.37	1.32	0.49
121	Tobacco, unmanufactured; tobacco refuse	337.1	1.15	10.20	5.80
684	Aluminium	295.1	1.01	3.16	0.62
611	Leather	277.7	0.95	4.01	1.85

Source: UNCTAD secretariat calculations, based on data from the United Nations Statistics Division.

   a   Annual average 2000–2001.

18. Main markets for exports of LDCs: Percentage shares in 2002 (or latest year available)

Country	Developed market economy countries					Countries in Eastern Europe	Developing countries			Other and unallocated
	Total	European Union	Japan	USA and Canada	Others		Total	OPEC	Other	
Afghanistan	26.8	19.8	1.5	4.4	1.0	5.5	66.5	6.9	59.6	1.2
Angola	75.3	27.7	5.0	42.5	0.0	0.0	24.7	0.0	24.7	0.0
Bangladesh	74.6	43.1	1.1	29.3	1.0	0.4	9.0	1.5	7.5	16.0
Benin	27.9	27.5	0.1	0.4	0.0	1.7	70.0	7.1	62.9	0.4
Bhutan	-	-	-	-	-	-	-	-	-	-
Burkina Faso	33.7	26.9	4.9	1.5	0.3	0.5	63.7	2.2	61.5	2.2
Burundi	75.5	41.7	0.7	2.8	30.3	0.6	21.1	0.2	20.9	2.8
Cambodia	89.7	23.6	3.8	61.7	0.6	0.1	10.2	0.0	10.1	0.0
Cape Verde	98.4	90.0	0.0	8.4	0.0	0.0	1.5	0.0	1.5	0.2
Central African Republic	85.4	83.6	0.5	1.2	0.0	1.6	13.0	1.1	11.9	0.0
Chad	64.8	56.7	0.1	8.0	0.0	14.2	20.7	6.2	14.5	0.3
Comoros	85.4	64.5	2.8	17.7	0.4	1.0	13.0	0.4	12.6	0.5
Dem. Republic of the Congo	91.0	75.5	2.0	13.4	0.0	0.1	8.9	0.0	8.9	0.0
Djibouti	3.8	2.5	0.0	1.3	0.0	0.1	96.1	4.4	91.7	0.0
Equatorial Guinea	74.3	34.7	2.5	37.1	0.0	0.0	25.7	0.0	25.7	0.0
Eritrea	-	-	-	-	-	-	-	-	-	-
Ethiopia	53.9	38.6	6.5	5.1	3.7	1.1	42.9	10.2	32.7	2.1
Gambia	73.3	71.9	0.3	1.0	0.0	0.8	25.9	0.2	25.7	0.0
Guinea	78.7	59.8	0.1	16.6	2.2	7.0	14.3	0.0	14.3	0.0
Guinea-Bissau	5.8	5.8	0.0	0.0	0.0	0.0	94.2	0.0	94.2	0.0
Haiti	91.1	4.3	0.1	86.3	0.4	0.0	8.2	0.7	7.5	0.7
Kiribati	64.1	4.3	55.9	3.5	0.4	1.5	34.4	0.0	34.4	0.0
Lao People's Dem. Rep.	28.9	25.4	1.3	1.1	1.2	0.7	48.4	0.7	47.7	21.9
Lesotho	-	-	-	-	-	-	-	-	-	-
Liberia	79.6	73.1	0.0	4.2	2.3	9.0	11.4	0.2	11.2	0.0
Madagascar	86.3	57.1	3.9	24.7	0.5	0.4	10.8	0.7	10.0	2.6
Malawi	61.1	34.4	6.4	17.7	2.6	12.6	19.6	0.0	19.6	6.7
Maldives	69.4	9.9	6.5	52.9	0.0	0.1	30.5	0.1	30.5	0.0
Mali	38.8	35.2	0.3	2.6	0.8	3.7	53.5	2.6	50.9	4.1
Mauritania	74.6	67.4	6.3	0.2	0.7	6.1	17.5	0.4	17.0	1.9
Mozambique	46.1	43.9	1.5	0.7	0.0	0.4	16.4	0.2	16.2	37.2
Myanmar	32.4	13.9	3.7	14.3	0.6	0.3	66.6	1.6	65.0	0.7
Nepal	46.6	15.6	1.1	28.6	1.3	0.3	51.0	0.0	51.0	2.1
Niger	51.7	47.7	2.5	1.2	0.3	0.0	48.1	41.6	6.5	0.2
Rwanda	35.1	32.1	0.0	2.9	0.1	1.5	30.5	0.1	30.4	33.0
Samoa	75.9	2.9	3.1	9.0	60.9	0.6	23.5	11.9	11.6	0.0
Sao Tome and Principe	64.8	51.9	2.0	10.6	0.3	10.7	24.4	0.6	23.8	0.1
Senegal	48.5	46.1	1.3	0.6	0.6	0.3	43.8	0.5	43.3	7.4
Sierra Leone	87.4	81.0	0.8	5.5	0.1	1.3	10.7	0.3	10.4	0.6
Solomon Islands	25.8	1.9	21.7	0.9	1.3	0.3	73.9	0.0	73.9	0.0
Somalia	3.1	2.2	0.0	0.5	0.4	0.0	96.4	51.4	45.0	0.5
Sudan	20.2	10.2	9.8	0.1	0.1	0.5	75.6	7.6	68.0	3.8
Togo	28.1	20.1	0.1	1.2	6.8	2.4	68.8	2.9	66.0	0.7
Tuvalu	87.1	86.1	0.0	0.0	0.9	0.8	12.1	0.0	12.1	0.0
Uganda	75.5	62.7	3.9	4.8	4.1	6.3	17.4	4.0	13.5	0.8
United Republic of Tanzania	53.6	36.5	12.1	3.5	1.6	1.9	44.1	2.1	42.0	0.4
Vanuatu	15.7	4.3	4.7	3.0	3.7	0.0	83.2	22.4	60.8	1.1
Yemen	12.0	2.9	2.2	6.9	0.0	0.0	83.7	5.0	78.7	4.3
Zambia	26.3	15.6	9.0	1.3	0.4	0.4	66.8	0.1	66.7	6.5
All LDCs	63.4	35.7	3.2	20.1	4.4	0.9	31.1	1.8	29.3	4.7
All developing countries	56.9	19.0	8.7	26.6	2.6	1.4	39.6	3.4	36.2	2.0

Source: UNCTAD secretariat calculations, based on data from IMF, Direction of Trade Statistics, CD-ROM.

19. Main sources of imports of LDCs: Percentage shares in 2002 (or latest year available)

Country	Developed market economy countries					Countries in Eastern Europe	Developing countries			Other and un-allocated
	Total	European Union	Japan	USA and Canada	Others		Total	OPEC	Other	
Afghanistan	33.0	13.1	9.6	10.0	0.3	4.8	62.2	1.4	60.8	0.0
Angola	53.3	39.2	1.0	11.1	2.1	1.7	44.9	0.6	44.3	0.0
Bangladesh	25.2	10.2	7.1	3.8	4.0	0.6	61.2	6.6	54.6	13.0
Benin	40.7	35.5	0.6	2.6	1.9	0.3	58.9	2.3	56.6	0.2
Bhutan	-	-	-	-	-	-	-	-	-	-
Burkina Faso	50.1	44.9	1.4	3.5	0.4	0.8	40.9	6.0	34.8	8.2
Burundi	37.7	34.4	1.1	1.7	0.6	0.9	59.8	13.0	46.8	1.5
Cambodia	12.6	6.4	3.9	1.7	0.6	0.1	87.2	0.6	86.7	0.0
Cape Verde	85.7	81.7	0.4	3.4	0.3	0.4	12.5	0.5	12.0	1.3
Central African Republic	54.7	45.9	2.7	5.3	0.8	0.4	21.4	1.4	20.0	23.5
Chad	85.5	51.7	0.2	32.3	1.3	0.8	13.7	6.8	6.9	0.0
Comoros	51.7	47.8	3.3	0.1	0.5	0.1	47.2	9.7	37.5	1.0
Dem. Republic of the Congo	48.9	41.7	1.5	4.2	1.4	0.2	50.7	11.0	39.8	0.2
Djibouti	37.1	24.5	2.3	9.3	0.9	1.7	58.8	21.4	37.4	2.4
Equatorial Guinea	92.3	55.2	0.4	29.6	7.2	0.4	7.2	0.1	7.1	0.0
Eritrea	-	-	-	-	-	-	-	-	-	-
Ethiopia	31.2	22.7	3.2	4.0	1.2	4.1	63.7	30.7	33.0	1.0
Gambia	34.9	30.6	1.3	2.7	0.4	0.4	64.3	3.4	61.0	0.4
Guinea	70.2	57.2	2.0	9.4	1.6	1.2	28.2	2.1	26.1	0.4
Guinea-Bissau	42.3	37.8	1.2	2.4	0.9	0.3	48.9	0.1	48.8	8.6
Haiti	69.3	9.6	2.5	56.3	0.9	0.3	30.4	0.6	29.9	0.0
Kiribati	76.0	31.6	9.4	4.6	30.4	5.4	18.5	0.4	18.1	0.0
Lao People's Dem. Republic	9.3	4.6	2.3	0.6	1.9	1.0	88.0	0.1	87.9	1.7
Lesotho	-	-	-	-	-	-	-	-	-	-
Liberia	50.5	30.3	17.9	0.7	1.6	11.3	38.1	0.1	38.1	0.0
Madagascar	29.1	25.9	1.0	1.6	0.6	0.1	64.4	15.0	49.4	6.4
Malawi	23.7	12.5	2.8	6.3	2.2	0.1	76.2	0.1	76.1	0.0
Maldives	18.3	10.5	1.0	1.8	5.0	0.0	81.4	18.0	63.4	0.3
Mali	30.3	28.3	0.5	1.0	0.6	0.4	61.1	0.9	60.2	8.2
Mauritania	60.7	52.2	3.6	3.4	1.5	5.2	25.3	6.4	18.8	8.8
Mozambique	42.3	21.5	6.0	7.7	7.1	0.0	40.8	1.2	39.6	16.9
Myanmar	8.6	3.1	4.4	0.4	0.7	4.0	87.4	2.7	84.7	0.0
Nepal	16.8	9.9	1.8	2.6	2.5	1.5	78.3	20.6	57.8	3.3
Niger	56.5	44.1	1.3	9.7	1.4	1.4	41.1	9.0	32.1	1.0
Rwanda	35.8	25.3	2.0	4.0	4.5	2.6	39.6	2.4	37.2	22.0
Samoa	59.1	3.2	12.5	4.3	39.2	0.2	40.2	2.7	37.6	0.5
Sao Tome and Principe	90.5	84.8	1.5	3.5	0.7	2.1	7.4	1.1	6.3	0.0
Senegal	58.8	52.8	0.9	3.9	1.2	0.9	38.9	15.2	23.7	1.4
Sierra Leone	71.3	63.1	1.2	6.5	0.4	1.4	24.1	3.4	20.7	3.2
Solomon Islands	43.4	2.2	2.6	2.1	36.6	0.0	54.8	1.1	53.8	1.7
Somalia	11.2	8.6	0.1	1.9	0.5	0.2	76.4	7.8	68.6	12.2
Sudan	39.7	28.8	2.6	2.5	5.7	3.4	54.7	10.3	44.4	2.2
Togo	67.4	60.3	2.8	3.4	0.9	2.0	28.8	2.7	26.1	1.9
Tuvalu	19.2	1.9	12.6	0.0	4.6	67.7	13.1	0.0	13.1	0.0
Uganda	27.6	21.0	3.1	2.8	0.8	0.6	71.6	3.0	68.7	0.1
United Republic of Tanzania	38.6	24.2	4.4	4.9	5.1	0.8	60.4	11.0	49.3	0.3
Vanuatu	60.3	4.1	20.6	0.8	34.8	0.2	37.3	0.3	37.0	2.2
Yemen	38.6	21.3	2.1	12.1	3.1	4.7	54.3	22.1	32.2	2.5
Zambia	18.2	11.1	2.3	4.2	0.7	0.1	80.8	2.1	78.7	0.9
All LDCs	39.0	25.4	4.6	6.3	2.7	2.5	54.6	7.0	47.6	3.9
All developing countries	50.7	19.6	11.1	16.6	3.4	2.2	44.7	6.7	37.9	2.5

Source: UNCTAD secretariat calculations, based on data from IMF, *Direction of Trade Statistics*, CD-ROM.

20. COMPOSITION OF TOTAL FINANCIAL FLOWS TO ALL LDCs
IN CURRENT AND IN CONSTANT DOLLARS
(Net disbursements)

	Millions of current dollars						Millions of 1995 dollars[f]					
	1985	1990	1999	2000	2001	2002	1985	1990	1999	2000	2001	2002
Concessional loans & grants	**9 492**	**16 751**	**12 326**	**12 450**	**13 633**	**17 282**	**8 922**	**13 596**	**12 168**	**12 665**	**13 983**	..
Of which:												
DAC	8 836	16 175	12 175	12 256	13 389	16 548	8 304	13 129	12 019	12 468	13 733	..
Bilateral	5 484	9 888	7 244	7 735	7 602	10 178	5 154	8 026	7 151	7 869	7 797	..
Multilateral[a]	3 351	6 287	4 932	4 521	5 788	6 370	3 150	5 103	4 868	4 599	5 936	..
Grants	6 413	11 842	10 433	10 315	10 617	13 656	6 027	9 612	10 299	10 494	10 889	..
Loans	2 423	4 333	1 743	1 940	2 772	2 893	2 277	3 517	1 720	1 974	2 843	..
Technical assistance	2 221	3 375	2 615	2 706	2 756	3 286	2 088	2 740	2 581	2 753	2 826	..
Other[b]	6 614	12 800	9 561	9 549	10 634	13 262	6 217	10 389	9 438	9 714	10 906	..
OPEC	729	581	130	156	290	751	685	471	129	158	297	..
Bilateral	648	571	107	150	187	653	609	464	106	153	192	..
Multilateral[c]	81	9	23	7	102	98	76	8	23	7	105	..
Grants	434	520	55	78	55	156	408	422	55	79	56	..
Loans	295	60	75	78	235	595	277	49	74	79	241	..
Non-concessional flows	**436**	**745**	**2 432**	**651**	**1 309**	**-2 741**	**410**	**605**	**2 401**	**662**	**1 343**	**..**
Of which:												
DAC	407	806	2 388	630	1 290	-2 708	383	654	2 357	641	1 323	..
Bilateral official	497	692	208	-79	-112	-416	467	561	205	-80	-114	..
Multilateral[a]	248	35	-2	-4	-57	-210	233	28	-2	-4	-59	..
Export credits[d]	-324	-522	209	60	67	-661	-305	-424	206	61	69	..
Direct investment	-64	307	1 904	4	31	-999	-60	249	1879	4	32	..
Other[e]	50	295	70	649	1 360	-422	47	240	69	661	1 395	..
Total financial flows	**9 928**	**17 496**	**14 758**	**13 101**	**14 942**	**14 541**	**9 331**	**14 201**	**14 569**	**13 328**	**15 325**	**..**

Source: UNCTAD secretariat calculations, based on OECD/DAC: *International Development Statistics,* online data.

a   From multilateral agencies mainly financed by DAC member countries.
b   Grants (excluding technical assistance grants) and loans.
c   From multilateral agencies mainly financed by OPEC member countries.
d   Guaranteed private.
e   Bilateral financial flows originating in DAC countries and their capital markets in the form of bond lending and bank lending (either directly or through syndicated "Eurocurrency credits"). Excludes flows that could not be allocated by recipient country.
f   The deflator used is the unit value index of imports 1995 = 100. Data are not yet available for 2002.

21. Distribution of financial flows to LDCs and to all developing countries, by type of flow
(*Percentage*)

	To least developed countries						To all developing countries					
	1985	*1990*	*1999*	*2000*	*2001*	*2002*	*1985*	*1990*	*1999*	*2000*	*2001*	*2002*
Concessional loans & grants	**95.6**	**95.7**	**83.5**	**95.0**	**91.2**	**118.8**	**67.7**	**70.5**	**16.4**	**26.7**	**28.7**	**73.1**
Of which:												
DAC	89.0	92.4	82.5	93.5	89.6	113.8	61.4	62.6	16.1	26.1	27.9	68.8
Bilateral	55.2	56.5	49.1	59.0	50.9	70.0	42.7	45.2	11.1	18.3	18.3	45.0
Multilateral[a]	33.8	35.9	33.4	34.5	38.7	43.8	18.7	17.3	5.0	7.8	9.6	23.8
Grants	64.6	67.7	70.7	78.7	71.1	93.9	40.5	43.7	11.9	20.0	21.7	54.8
Loans	24.4	24.8	11.8	14.8	18.6	19.9	20.9	18.8	4.2	6.1	6.2	14.0
Technical assistance	22.4	19.3	17.7	20.7	18.4	22.6	16.1	15.3	4.6	7.8	8.5	20.8
Other[b]	66.6	73.2	64.8	72.9	71.2	91.2	45.3	47.2	11.5	18.3	19.4	48.0
OPEC	7.3	3.3	0.9	1.2	1.9	5.2	6.6	8.0	0.2	0.4	0.7	4.0
Bilateral	6.5	3.3	0.7	1.1	1.3	4.5	6.3	7.9	0.2	0.4	0.6	3.8
Multilateral[c]	0.8	0.1	0.2	0.1	0.7	0.7	0.3	0.1	0.0	0.0	0.1	0.2
Grants	4.4	3.0	0.4	0.6	0.4	1.1	5.3	7.9	0.1	0.2	0.3	1.8
Loans	3.0	0.3	0.5	0.6	1.6	4.1	1.3	0.1	0.1	0.2	0.4	2.3
Non-concessional flows	**4.4**	**4.3**	**16.5**	**5.0**	**8.8**	**-18.8**	**32.3**	**29.5**	**83.6**	**73.3**	**71.3**	**26.9**
Of which:												
DAC	4.1	4.6	16.2	4.8	8.6	-18.6	32.9	29.1	83.3	72.2	71.3	24.9
Bilateral official	5.0	4.0	1.4	-0.6	-0.7	-2.9	8.3	11.5	6.5	-3.2	-1.2	-0.2
Multilateral[a]	2.5	0.2	0.0	0.0	-0.4	-1.4	20.2	14.9	5.8	6.3	5.8	-10.1
Export credits[d]	-3.3	-3.0	1.4	0.5	0.5	-4.5	3.9	-0.7	1.0	5.5	2.2	-1.6
Direct investment	-0.6	1.8	12.9	0.0	0.2	-6.9	10.5	28.5	50.2	51.9	63.0	91.3
Other[e]	0.5	1.7	0.5	5.0	9.1	-2.9	-9.9	-25.1	19.8	11.7	1.5	-54.6
Total financial flows	**100.0**	**100.0**	**100.0**	**100.0**	**100.0**	**100.0**	**100.0**	**100.0**	**100.0**	**100.0**	**100.0**	**100.0**

For source and note, see table 20.

22. SHARE OF LDCs IN FINANCIAL FLOWS TO ALL DEVELOPING COUNTRIES, BY TYPE OF FLOW
(Percentage)

	1985	1990	1999	2000	2001	2002
Concessional loans & grants	**38.1**	**35.4**	**32.3**	**34.9**	**35.3**	**37.8**
Of which:						
DAC	39.1	38.6	32.4	35.1	35.7	38.5
Bilateral	34.9	32.6	27.8	31.6	30.9	36.2
Multilateral[a]	48.8	54.1	42.5	43.3	44.7	42.9
Grants	43.0	40.4	37.5	38.7	36.4	39.9
Loans	31.5	34.3	17.8	23.6	33.2	33.1
Technical assistance	37.5	32.8	24.4	26.1	24.2	25.3
Other[b]	39.7	40.5	35.5	39.0	40.7	44.2
OPEC	29.9	10.8	34.1	26.8	29.7	29.7
Bilateral	27.9	10.8	30.6	27.5	22.3	27.3
Multilateral[c]	70.2	14.6	72.6	19.7	76.3	72.4
Grants	22.1	9.8	31.2	23.4	13.9	14.1
Loans	62.2	66.4	36.6	31.3	40.6	41.8
Non-concessional flows	**3.7**	**3.8**	**1.2**	**0.7**	**1.4**	**-**
Of which:						
DAC	3.4	4.1	1.2	0.7	1.3	-
Bilateral official	16.2	9.0	1.4	1.9	7.0	-
Multilateral[a]	3.3	0.3	0.0	-	-	3.3
Export credits[d]	-	-	8.9	0.8	2.3	68.1
Direct investment	-	1.6	1.6	0.0	0.0	-
Other[e]	-	-	0.2	4.2	68.8	1.2
Total financial flows	**27.0**	**26.1**	**6.3**	**9.8**	**11.1**	**23.3**

Note: No percentage is shown when either the net flow to all LDCs or the net flow to all developing countries in a particular year is negative.

For other notes and sources, see table 20.

23. Net ODA[a] from individual DAC member countries to LDCs as a group

Donor country[b]	% of GNI					Millions of dollars					% change
	1990	1999	2000	2001	2002	1990	1999	2000	2001	2002	2002/1990
Norway	0.52	0.26	0.27	0.27	0.33	532	455	424	449	625	17.6
Denmark	0.37	0.35	0.34	0.34	0.32	462	549	537	540	547	18.4
Luxembourg	0.08	0.19	0.26	0.25	0.30	10	33	46	47	58	481.4
Netherlands	0.30	0.22	0.21	0.26	0.29	834	632	793	995	1 180	41.4
Sweden	0.35	0.13	0.24	0.21	0.26	775	409	528	458	629	-18.9
Ireland	0.06	0.12	0.14	0.16	0.21	21	92	113	143	210	899.1
Belgium	0.19	0.06	0.09	0.13	0.14	367	177	213	295	353	-3.9
Finland	0.24	0.09	0.09	0.10	0.12	317	105	109	114	154	-51.5
France	0.19	0.05	0.09	0.08	0.11	2 286	1 132	1 141	1 083	1 626	-28.8
Portugal	0.17	0.08	0.11	0.11	0.10	100	124	118	119	120	20.2
Italy	0.13	0.04	0.04	0.04	0.09	1 382	400	388	487	1 045	-24.4
Switzerland	0.14	0.08	0.10	0.10	0.08	325	268	269	257	250	-23.1
Austria	0.07	0.02	0.05	0.06	0.08	61	55	59	106	170	178.6
Germany	0.12	0.05	0.06	0.06	0.07	1 769	1 133	1 207	1 173	1 332	-24.7
United Kingdom	0.09	0.04	0.10	0.12	0.07	834	718	1 406	1 647	1 153	38.2
New Zealand	0.04	0.05	0.06	0.07	0.06	18	32	27	29	30	67.4
Total DAC	**0.09**	**0.05**	**0.05**	**0.05**	**0.06**	**15 153**	**11 103**	**12 169**	**12 019**	**15 137**	**-0.1**
Australia	0.06	0.04	0.06	0.05	0.05	171	172	211	175	192	12.0
Canada	0.13	0.03	0.04	0.03	0.05	740	328	307	231	349	-52.8
Japan	0.06	0.09	0.04	0.04	0.04	1 753	2 619	2 127	1 783	1 813	3.4
Spain	0.00	0.02	0.03	0.03	0.04	194	187	142	193	252	29.7
Greece	-	-	0.02	0.02	0.03	-	4	18	22	37	-
United States	0.04	0.02	0.02	0.02	0.03	2 199	1 479	1 986	1 673	3 012	36.9

Source: UNCTAD secretariat calculations, based on OECD, *Development Co-operation Report*, various issues, and OECD/DAC, *International Development Statistics,* online data.

a   Including imputed flows through multilateral channels.
b   Ranked in descending order of the ODA/GNI ratio in 2002.

24. BILATERAL ODA FROM DAC MEMBER COUNTRIES AND TOTAL FINANCIAL FLOWS FROM MULTILATERAL AGENCIES[a] TO ALL LDCs
(Millions of dollars)

	Net disbursements						Commitments					
	1985	1990	1999	2000	2001	2002	1985	1990	1999	2000	2001	2002
A. Bilateral donors												
Australia	58.2	104.5	90.4	123.3	114.4	135.3	59.1	97.0	161.1	138.9	121.4	101.1
Austria	12.1	60.9	55.1	59.2	56.2	123.0	11.9	132.4	81.3	54.7	60.8	134.6
Belgium	179.2	273.5	130.2	147.6	183.5	249.8	83.5	273.5	136.0	152.7	202.2	257.8
Canada	329.6	391.6	208.8	194.4	195.8	221.7	352.0	354.0	205.5	263.3	203.1	314.7
Denmark	126.0	295.1	412.2	373.4	396.3	370.9	148.6	269.2	359.8	598.4	177.1	370.6
Finland	60.6	194.6	64.8	62.8	67.0	76.4	127.7	129.8	73.7	37.1	98.5	93.5
France	723.9	1 857.1	896.7	845.5	645.3	1 108.7	901.7	1 480.3	1 115.6	891.1	765.3	1 279.9
Germany	584.9	1 160.6	793.6	663.3	599.6	818.2	843.8	1 323.2	939.4	494.3	573.7	947.2
Greece	-	-	0.6	1.8	2.3	9.7	-	-	0.6	1.8	2.3	9.7
Ireland	10.4	13.9	82.4	96.7	121.5	177.9	10.4	13.9	82.4	96.7	121.5	177.9
Italy	420.1	968.8	172.0	240.1	187.2	772.6	530.7	846.0	145.3	269.0	211.3	782.4
Japan	562.9	1 067.2	1 158.8	1 290.1	1 179.9	1 030.7	633.2	1 144.7	1 384.5	1 237.5	1 700.5	1202.0
Luxembourg	-	7.9	29.0	40.0	39.5	50.6	-	-	32.7	39.4	39.5	50.6
Netherlands	256.2	592.8	430.5	559.9	759.3	919.6	251.9	681.7	441.9	607.8	751.4	857.7
New Zealand	7.0	13.3	24.8	22.9	23.9	24.4	12.2	9.7	24.0	22.9	23.9	26.7
Norway	156.8	356.7	333.7	307.3	310.3	444.2	151.1	187.0	413.5	245.6	422.9	465.3
Portugal	-	99.6	120.6	95.1	97.1	80.1	-	-	196.8	240.4	97.1	80.1
Spain	-	96.7	107.2	66.1	77.6	129.4	-	-	107.2	90.9	86.2	137.9
Sweden	200.8	530.2	288.5	335.7	323.3	340.8	210.5	332.4	465.7	292.1	354.3	366.4
Switzerland	87.2	232.1	177.2	165.8	163.2	189.9	137.4	214.9	148.4	203.2	174.2	165.5
United Kingdom	281.6	473.0	628.3	998.9	1 070.5	845.1	232.3	480.0	616.8	1 010.3	1 110.5	874.5
United States	1 427.0	1 098.0	1 038.7	1 045.0	988.2	2 058.8	1 362.4	1 152.2	1 344.1	1 222.2	1 200.8	2 295.7
Total bilateral concessional	5 484.4	9 888.0	7 243.8	7 734.9	7 601.8	10 177.8	6 060.4	9 121.7	8 476.2	8 210.1	8 498.5	10 991.8
B. Multilateral donors												
1. Concessional												
AfDF	173.4	561.3	332.0	206.6	307.2	437.0	344.4	864.4	494.4	398.5	973.3	661.1
AsDB	229.6	448.2	349.4	388.4	271.9	330.6	383.7	536.4	470.3	589.5	422.1	708.5
EC	554.8	1 168.3	1 273.2	996.3	1 472.3	1 697.9	579.0	790.8	2 264.2	2 021.7	1 279.0	1 926.4
IBRD	0.6	-	-	-	-	-	-	-	-	-	-	-
IDA	1 178.9	2 138.0	1 875.6	1 846.4	2 394.5	2 635.8	1 584.4	2 986.0	2 549.0	2 270.4	3 532.4	3 253.6
IDB	10.7	11.7	49.2	26.4	0.3	3.8	24.7	56.0	2.0	1.8	2.0	1.9
IFAD	108.0	120.6	53.5	78.6	88.8	76.7	83.2	72.1	201.2	152.1	158.7	130.0
IMF (SAF/ESAF)	-108.8	297.9	47.1	-33.0	86.0	-56.8	-	-	-	-	-	-
Other:	1 204.1	1 541.1	9 51.6	1 011.2	1 166.5	1 245.5	1 314.9	1 748.3	1 133.4	280.2	318.9	305.7
Of which:												
UNDP	276.2	366.6	263.3	186.8	155.8	152.4	-	-	-	-	-	-
UNFPA	26.4	46.3	64.0	52.4	89.1	104.7	-	-	-	-	-	-
UNHCR	201.8	197.6	104.8	172.1	193.0	250.8	-	-	-	-	-	-
UNICEF	126.6	232.7	160.6	170.6	182.6	167.9	-	-	-	-	-	-
UNTA	62.0	59.0	103.0	113.4	81.3	112.5	-	-	-	-	-	-
WFP	346.3	501.3	206.3	216.6	234.7	241.9	-	-	-	-	-	-
Total	3 351.4	6 287.0	4 931.6	4 520.8	5 787.6	6 370.5	4 314.3	7 053.9	7 114.5	5 714.1	6 686.6	6 987.1
2. Non-concessional												
AfDB	142.9	106.9	-85.9	-100.1	-66.1	-77.3						
AsDB	-0.9	-0.5	18.2	10.2	20.6	24.3						
EC	20.0	-14.0	11.9	46.3	8.3	-1.7						
IBRD	55.0	-82.0	-42.6	-26.3	-17.7	-118.6						
IFC	20.5	18.5	96.3	63.8	-2.5	-36.5						
Other	-	-	-	1.7	-	-						
Total	237.6	28.9	-2.1	-4.3	-57.5	-209.9						
Total concessional (A + B.1)	8 835.8	16 175.0	12 175.3	12 255.7	13 389.3	16 548.2						
Grand total	9 073.4	16 203.8	12 173.2	12 251.4	13 331.9	16 338.4	10 374.7	16 175.7	15 590.7	13 924.3	15 185.1	17 978.9

Source: UNCTAD secretariat calculations, based on OECD/DAC, *International Development Statistics*, online data.

a   Multilateral agencies mainly financed by DAC countries.

25. ODA TO LDCs FROM DAC MEMBER COUNTRIES AND MULTILATERAL AGENCIES MAINLY FINANCED BY THEM: DISTRIBUTION BY DONOR AND SHARES ALLOCATED TO LDCs IN TOTAL ODA FLOWS TO ALL DEVELOPING COUNTRIES

(Percentage)

	Distribution by donor						Share of LDCs in ODA flows to all developing countries					
	1985	1990	1999	2000	2001	2002	1985	1990	1999	2000	2001	2002
Bilateral donors												
Australia	0.7	0.6	0.7	1.0	0.9	0.8	11.9	15.4	15.9	18.5	20.9	22.7
Austria	0.1	0.4	0.5	0.5	0.4	0.7	7.5	157.1	30.8	33.7	21.4	56.3
Belgium	2.0	1.7	1.1	1.2	1.4	1.5	75.6	72.2	51.3	48.1	58.3	59.0
Canada	3.7	2.4	1.7	1.6	1.5	1.3	44.6	39.5	40.1	42.2	43.0	31.9
Denmark	1.4	1.8	3.4	3.0	3.0	2.2	60.6	61.3	54.9	55.5	55.3	54.3
Finland	0.7	1.2	0.5	0.5	0.5	0.5	54.9	53.1	48.0	48.4	50.7	51.6
France	8.2	11.5	7.4	6.9	4.8	6.7	39.1	38.7	27.6	28.9	25.4	31.1
Germany	6.6	7.2	6.5	5.4	4.5	4.9	35.6	29.9	32.5	35.7	28.8	39.6
Greece	-	-	0.0	0.0	0.0	0.1	-	-	4.5	9.5	20.2	41.5
Ireland	0.1	0.1	0.7	0.8	0.9	1.1	92.2	87.3	78.4	81.2	83.3	80.0
Italy	4.8	6.0	1.4	2.0	1.4	4.7	65.0	54.4	64.8	99.3	98.6	91.1
Japan	6.4	6.6	9.5	10.5	8.8	6.2	23.3	17.2	12.8	16.4	19.1	18.6
Luxembourg	-	0.0	0.2	0.3	0.3	0.3	-	60.4	41.1	50.4	51.0	55.2
Netherlands	2.9	3.7	3.5	4.6	5.7	5.6	40.0	37.4	43.5	45.6	45.0	51.6
New Zealand	0.1	0.1	0.2	0.2	0.2	0.1	22.1	22.6	33.8	37.9	38.2	35.4
Norway	1.8	2.2	2.7	2.5	2.3	2.7	58.1	62.2	57.9	57.5	54.3	61.0
Portugal	-	0.6	1.0	0.8	0.7	0.5	-	100.0	63.7	63.1	60.8	48.8
Spain	-	0.6	0.9	0.5	0.6	0.8	-	19.5	19.6	14.3	8.4	18.0
Sweden	2.3	3.3	2.4	2.7	2.4	2.1	50.1	57.8	46.2	46.5	51.3	54.4
Switzerland	1.0	1.4	1.5	1.4	1.2	1.1	51.6	60.1	50.3	49.8	50.4	46.5
United Kingdom	3.2	2.9	5.2	8.2	8.0	5.1	43.4	44.0	40.4	52.4	56.5	40.9
United States	16.2	6.8	8.5	8.5	7.4	12.4	28.2	20.1	29.6	29.6	21.1	31.9
Total	62.1	61.1	59.5	63.1	56.8	61.5	34.9	32.6	27.8	31.6	30.9	36.2
Multilateral donors												
AfDF	2.0	3.5	2.7	1.7	2.3	2.6	83.8	94.4	74.5	71.5	76.1	73.8
AsDF	2.6	2.8	2.9	3.2	2.0	2.0	59.3	41.3	37.3	41.9	33.5	36.5
CEC	6.3	7.2	10.5	8.1	11.0	10.3	59.4	53.0	40.5	37.4	40.4	38.9
IBRD	0.0	-	-	-	-	-	1.9	-	-	-	-	-
IDA	13.3	13.2	15.4	15.1	17.9	15.9	45.4	54.7	43.9	46.2	49.5	50.8
IDB	0.1	0.1	0.4	0.2	0.0	0.0	3.3	10.4	24.2	19.1	0.1	2.7
IFAD	1.2	0.7	0.4	0.6	0.7	0.5	41.8	49.2	45.6	57.1	54.7	54.5
IMF	-1.2	1.8	0.4	-0.3	0.6	-0.3	36.5	92.7	26.7	18.9	101.0	-10.2
UN	12.7	9.5	7.5	7.9	7.6	6.7	48.8	50.3	42.8	43.1	42.6	43.2
Other	0.9	0.1	0.4	0.3	1.1	0.8	60.5	9.2	25.2	19.0	39.8	34.0
Total	37.9	38.9	40.5	36.9	43.2	38.5	48.8	54.1	42.5	43.3	44.7	42.9
Grand total	100.0	100.0	100.0	100.0	100.0	100.0	39.1	38.6	32.4	35.1	35.7	38.5

Source: UNCTAD secretariat calculations, based on OECD/DAC, *International Development Statistics*, online data.

26. TOTAL FINANCIAL FLOWS AND ODA FROM ALL SOURCES TO INDIVIDUAL LDCs
(Net disbursements in millions of dollars)

Country	Total financial flows						Of which: ODA					
	1985	1990	1999	2000	2001	2002	1985	1990	1999	2000	2001	2002
Afghanistan	-6	129	149	162	390	1 285	17	131	143	141	408	1 285
Angola	258	91	1 409	122	854	-337	92	268	388	307	289	421
Bangladesh	1 107	2 167	1 190	1 229	985	895	1 131	2 095	1 215	1 171	1 030	913
Benin	97	243	225	227	291	235	95	268	211	239	274	220
Bhutan	24	50	65	44	60	96	24	47	67	53	61	73
Burkina Faso	190	347	435	344	391	490	195	331	398	336	392	473
Burundi	154	255	64	78	149	186	139	264	74	93	137	172
Cambodia	13	42	281	407	443	207	13	42	277	398	420	487
Cape Verde	71	107	179	119	130	161	70	108	137	94	77	92
Central African Rep.	112	257	159	50	66	54	104	250	118	75	67	60
Chad	179	315	207	-225	201	247	181	314	188	131	187	233
Comoros	51	45	139	-2	16	-105	48	45	21	19	27	32
Dem. Rep. of the Congo	462	1 410	-336	198	288	644	306	897	132	184	263	807
Djibouti	103	192	272	91	71	94	81	194	75	71	58	78
Equatorial Guinea	28	62	9	22	24	-415	17	61	20	21	13	20
Eritrea	0	0	149	184	281	217	0	0	149	176	281	230
Ethiopia	788	988	656	687	1 061	1 093	719	1 016	643	693	1 116	1 307
Gambia	48	108	33	45	46	47	50	99	34	49	54	61
Guinea	108	284	235	332	230	232	115	293	238	153	280	250
Guinea-Bissau	63	135	53	84	59	60	58	129	52	80	59	59
Haiti	142	154	262	176	166	170	150	168	263	208	171	156
Kiribati	12	20	28	18	13	21	12	20	21	18	12	21
Lao People's Dem. Rep.	64	150	304	287	242	265	37	150	295	282	245	278
Lesotho	118	148	18	11	-41	-44	93	142	31	37	56	76
Liberia	-294	519	682	632	1 033	-260	91	114	94	68	39	52
Madagascar	210	430	356	319	372	369	186	398	359	322	366	373
Malawi	118	518	437	431	457	389	113	503	447	446	404	377
Maldives	11	38	32	11	38	52	9	21	31	19	25	27
Mali	377	474	470	385	333	329	376	482	355	360	354	472
Mauritania	224	219	264	211	260	306	207	237	219	212	268	355
Mozambique	330	1 051	1 150	1 147	1 057	1 942	300	1 002	805	877	933	2 058
Myanmar	311	117	150	57	107	78	346	163	81	107	127	121
Nepal	244	429	370	409	475	280	234	426	351	390	394	365
Niger	285	382	189	186	229	194	303	396	187	211	257	298
Rwanda	184	286	376	319	296	360	180	291	373	322	299	356
Samoa	20	54	24	29	43	38	19	48	23	27	43	38
Sao Tome and Principe	12	54	28	36	40	28	13	55	28	35	38	26
Senegal	306	759	657	474	456	541	289	818	535	423	413	449
Sierra Leone	56	64	76	187	343	353	65	61	74	182	345	353
Solomon Islands	22	58	40	55	54	25	21	46	40	68	59	26
Somalia	380	488	120	103	153	197	353	494	115	104	150	194
Sudan	1 117	740	230	320	173	423	1129	822	243	225	185	351
Togo	91	257	-31	60	43	60	111	260	71	70	44	51
Tuvalu	3	5	7	0	10	37	3	5	7	4	10	12
Uganda	220	665	592	805	757	606	180	668	590	819	793	638
United Rep. of Tanzania	556	1 128	904	1 176	1 296	1 011	484	1 173	990	1 022	1 271	1 233
Vanuatu	39	149	72	71	-374	23	22	50	37	46	32	28
Yemen	397	331	771	289	496	759	392	405	458	265	461	584
Zambia	523	583	609	701	382	603	322	480	624	795	349	641
All LDCs	9 928	17 496	14 758	13 101	14 942	14 541	9 492	16 751	12 326	12 450	13 633	17 282
All developing countries	36 815	66 994	233 586	133 697	134 502	62 525	24 941	47 252	38 208	35 673	38 650	45 710
Memo items:												
In current dollars per capita:												
All LDCs	22	39	23	20	22	21	21	37	19	19	20	25
All developing countries	10	16	49	27	27	12	7	12	8	7	8	9
In constant 1995 dollars[a] (million):												
All LDCs	10 563	21 555	14 950	12 878	14 568	..	10 100	20 637	12 486	12 238	13 292	..
All developing countries	39 172	82 537	236 623	131 424	131 140	..	26 537	58 215	38 705	35 066	37 683	..
In constant 1995 dollars[a] per capita:												
All LDCs	23	48	23	19	21	..	22	46	19	18	19	..
All developing countries	11	20	49	27	27	..	7	14	8	7	8	..

Source: UNCTAD secretariat calculations, based on OECD/DAC, *International Development Statistics*, online data; and UNCTAD, *Handbook of Statistics 2003*.

a The deflator used is the unit value indices of imports 1995 = 100. Data are not yet available for 2002.

27. ODA FROM DAC MEMBER COUNTRIES AND MULTILATERAL AGENCIES MAINLY FINANCED BY THEM, TO INDIVIDUAL LDCs

Country[a]	Average: 1990–1992							Average: 2000–2002						
	Per capita ODA $	Total ODA $ mill.	Of which: Technical assistance	Bilateral ODA	Of which: Grants	Multi-lateral ODA	Of which: Grants	Per capita ODA $	Total ODA $ mill.	Of which: Technical assistance	Bilateral ODA	Of which: Grants	Multi-lateral ODA	Of which: Grants
				As percentage of total ODA							As percentage of total ODA			
Mozambique	85.0	1 177.3	11.9	71.5	61.4	28.5	16.8	70.7	1 286.9	14.0	77.8	84.0	22.2	9.4
United Rep. of Tanzania	44.4	1 197.8	18.0	67.5	66.1	32.5	9.8	33.2	1 179.2	13.8	74.2	74.6	25.8	13.4
Bangladesh	16.9	1 889.8	14.1	48.8	49.6	51.2	10.5	7.2	1 017.5	20.9	56.2	65.0	43.8	12.5
Ethiopia	21.2	1 072.9	19.9	44.5	45.1	55.5	43.2	15.1	1 012.9	14.5	40.7	39.8	59.3	18.8
Uganda	36.2	650.0	16.2	40.2	37.4	59.8	19.9	30.8	745.9	19.1	63.9	65.3	36.1	14.1
Afghanistan	10.5	154.7	55.1	70.9	74.7	29.1	30.1	27.2	601.3	14.4	77.4	79.4	22.6	17.8
Zambia	94.8	799.5	16.7	70.5	79.2	29.5	9.7	56.2	593.8	18.2	62.9	64.0	37.1	17.0
Cambodia	11.2	112.7	52.1	51.4	51.4	48.6	48.8	31.7	426.8	27.9	61.3	61.1	38.7	11.7
Senegal	92.0	694.2	25.8	70.3	74.9	29.7	9.6	44.3	426.5	33.1	59.0	66.2	41.0	14.3
Dem.Rep. of the Congo	13.4	521.2	22.0	72.8	66.0	27.2	12.1	8.4	417.4	17.5	47.7	49.5	52.3	32.4
Malawi	55.2	532.8	22.2	39.6	37.4	60.4	35.1	34.4	400.3	24.9	57.5	60.4	42.5	21.3
Burkina Faso	42.1	387.0	30.2	66.9	63.2	33.1	16.6	31.0	379.7	21.3	59.6	60.9	40.4	32.8
Mali	48.1	447.4	25.1	61.9	53.4	38.1	16.9	30.4	373.2	29.9	68.3	71.7	31.7	24.6
Nepal	22.9	437.2	26.3	61.4	49.5	38.6	10.5	15.5	373.0	32.1	69.8	66.6	30.2	12.8
Madagascar	33.0	406.2	20.8	62.2	73.0	37.8	14.3	21.6	354.7	23.8	37.8	42.3	62.2	20.1
Angola	30.7	295.8	20.5	57.9	45.9	42.1	38.4	26.4	337.6	18.1	64.7	61.8	35.3	30.7
Rwanda	51.2	330.1	28.2	60.9	57.9	39.1	21.1	40.6	325.4	20.0	53.6	54.3	46.4	25.2
Sierra Leone	24.4	99.4	27.2	61.0	34.7	39.0	27.8	63.7	292.0	11.5	58.0	56.0	42.0	16.6
Mauritania	102.1	212.5	23.1	52.3	47.6	47.7	21.7	102.5	279.2	12.2	37.1	38.1	62.9	39.1
Yemen	21.4	268.1	36.5	67.0	51.0	33.0	17.6	14.9	277.8	19.7	45.5	48.5	54.5	14.4
Laos	35.8	151.7	24.9	42.8	44.3	57.2	15.7	49.5	267.3	29.1	65.3	64.7	34.7	7.0
Niger	47.5	375.7	30.2	69.3	68.9	30.7	21.2	22.8	254.0	20.0	43.8	49.3	56.2	23.6
Benin	55.9	268.9	20.1	56.6	53.1	43.4	17.8	38.1	243.3	27.2	65.1	68.1	34.9	16.3
Guinea	58.7	372.9	18.5	48.8	39.3	51.2	21.1	27.3	224.9	23.7	50.2	59.8	49.8	31.6
Eritrea	-	-	-	-	-	-	-	57.4	220.9	13.1	58.0	54.6	42.0	14.3
Sudan	28.7	731.1	21.7	44.5	44.6	55.5	36.2	6.2	200.5	17.6	71.5	72.3	28.5	30.6
Chad	45.2	270.8	23.5	57.8	51.3	42.2	17.9	22.5	182.6	17.3	35.3	38.3	64.7	27.5
Haiti	21.3	149.8	38.3	74.2	88.8	25.8	16.8	22.0	178.1	49.3	77.7	78.7	22.3	16.6
Burundi	48.8	278.8	25.1	51.3	47.3	48.7	25.7	20.8	134.0	12.7	44.8	48.2	55.2	44.4
Somalia	57.5	413.6	15.0	71.2	70.7	28.8	23.8	14.2	129.5	17.5	63.6	64.9	36.4	36.3
Myanmar (Burma)	3.7	152.5	22.8	59.4	33.8	40.6	17.7	2.4	115.2	47.6	68.4	69.2	31.6	31.6
Cape Verde	309.3	110.5	29.2	70.9	69.6	29.1	22.6	199.0	88.5	26.0	61.0	54.6	39.0	12.3
Central African Rep.	65.7	198.6	27.3	51.1	49.6	48.9	19.9	17.9	67.3	32.0	69.7	81.6	30.3	29.3
Guinea-Bissau	109.3	114.6	28.4	56.6	52.6	43.4	15.9	47.2	66.4	23.0	49.1	48.8	50.9	42.7
Djibouti	199.8	107.9	40.1	81.3	74.9	18.7	11.2	95.7	65.1	37.1	54.8	57.1	45.2	16.1
Bhutan	89.6	55.4	37.8	55.2	55.2	44.8	34.6	76.6	63.4	30.7	62.6	60.0	37.4	14.2
Lesotho	85.7	136.6	32.0	55.7	50.3	44.3	25.2	32.1	57.6	21.3	46.8	50.2	53.2	29.4
Liberia	61.6	129.6	14.6	32.1	33.3	67.9	59.4	17.2	53.2	32.3	41.6	55.8	58.4	60.7
Togo	64.7	228.5	24.6	60.4	51.8	39.6	17.4	11.2	52.3	47.2	76.3	97.4	23.7	21.9
Gambia	106.4	103.3	24.6	52.4	48.5	47.6	18.8	38.4	51.9	21.5	29.2	31.1	70.8	28.9
Solomon Islands	127.8	42.1	45.9	68.6	66.2	31.4	23.5	112.7	50.7	37.5	43.8	50.1	56.2	55.7
Samoa	316.9	51.1	27.3	54.2	53.9	45.8	15.4	206.1	36.0	51.1	70.6	70.6	29.4	19.9
Vanuatu	308.5	47.4	49.8	77.5	73.7	22.5	11.3	173.2	35.0	57.2	71.3	71.7	28.7	12.7
Sao Tome & Principe	456.4	54.1	19.6	50.0	43.2	50.0	18.6	216.5	33.1	34.4	59.3	54.7	40.7	21.9
Maldives	129.7	28.8	27.2	46.7	46.7	53.3	19.8	82.0	24.6	25.7	56.0	59.1	44.0	13.3
Comoros	96.4	52.3	33.0	53.7	54.1	46.3	31.8	33.1	24.0	37.7	43.5	49.8	56.5	27.0
Equatorial Guinea	164.5	59.6	39.2	64.2	60.5	35.8	21.0	39.5	18.5	40.8	80.9	88.8	19.1	34.3
Kiribati	304.3	22.2	41.3	83.3	83.3	16.7	14.6	199.5	17.0	54.9	85.9	85.9	14.1	7.0
Tuvalu	670.6	6.0	46.9	92.4	92.4	7.6	7.7	813.7	8.4	36.1	86.5	86.5	13.5	9.0
All LDCs	30.9	16 400.6	21.7	58.4	56.0	41.6	19.9	20.6	14 064.4	20.7	60.5	62.9	39.5	19.1
All developing countries	10.8	44 979.3	24.9	70.2	55.2	29.8	14.3	7.8	38 361.1	30.1	66.8	62.6	33.2	15.4

Source: UNCTAD secretariat calculations, based on OECD/DAC, International Development Statistics, online data.

a   Ranked in descending order of total ODA received in 2000–2002.

28. FOREIGN DIRECT INVESTMENT: INFLOW TO AND OUTFLOW FROM LDCS
(Millions of dollars)

Country	FDI inflow						FDI outflow					
	1985	1990	1999	2000	2001	2002	1985	1990	1999	2000	2001	2002
Afghanistan	..	..	6.0	0.2	0.6	0.1	..	..	..	..	..	..
Angola	278.0	-334.5	2 471.4	878.5	2 145.5	1 312.1	..	0.9	-0.4	0.0	-0.1	-0.2
Bangladesh	-6.7	3.2	179.7	280.4	79.1	45.2	-0.3	0.5	0.1	2.0	20.6	4.1
Benin	-0.1	62.4	61.1	59.8	43.8	41.0	..	..	23.3	3.6	2.3	0.0
Bhutan	..	1.6	0.3	-0.1	0.3	0.3	..	..	..	..	..	..
Burkina Faso	-1.4	0.5	13.1	23.2	8.8	8.2	0.0	-0.6	4.5	0.2	0.6	1.2
Burundi	1.6	1.3	0.2	11.7	0.0	0.0	..	0.0	0.8	0.0	0.0	0.0
Cambodia	..	..	230.3	148.5	148.1	53.8	..	..	..	..	..	..
Cape Verde	..	0.3	53.3	33.6	9.0	13.9	..	0.3	0.4	0.0	0.0	0.0
Central African Republic	3.0	0.7	3.1	0.9	5.2	4.3	0.6	3.8	0.0	0.0	0.0	0.0
Chad	53.7	9.4	26.6	114.8	0.0	900.7	0.3	11.5	2.1	0.0	0.0	0.0
Comoros	..	0.4	0.3	0.9	0.0	1.5	..	1.1	..	..	..	..
Dem. Rep.of the Congo	69.2	-14.5	11.3	23.1	0.9	31.9	..	..	..	..	..	..
Djibouti	0.2	0.1	4.2	3.3	3.4	3.5	..	..	..	..	..	..
Equatorial Guinea	2.4	11.1	251.9	107.8	945.0	323.4	..	0.1	1.6	-3.5	4.3	0.0
Eritrea	..	..	83.2	27.9	0.7	21.0	..	..	..	..	..	..
Ethiopia	0.2	12.0	70.0	134.6	19.6	75.0	..	..	-46.0	-1.0	68.9	7.3
Gambia	-0.5	14.1	49.5	43.5	35.5	42.8	..	2.8	4.5	4.7	5.1	4.8
Guinea	1.1	17.9	63.4	9.9	1.6	30.0	..	..	2.9	1.8	1.9	2.2
Guinea-Bissau	1.4	2.0	8.6	0.7	0.7	1.0	..	..	..	0.0	0.0	0.0
Haiti	4.9	8.0	30.0	13.3	4.4	5.7	..	-8.0	-1.0	1.0	0.3	0.1
Kiribati	0.2	0.3	0.5	0.7	0.6	0.5	..	..	..	..	..	..
Lao People's Dem. Rep.	-1.6	6.0	51.6	34.0	23.9	25.4	..	..	0.1	168.0	3.0	57.0
Lesotho	4.5	16.1	32.7	31.5	28.2	24.4	..	..	..	..	..	..
Liberia	-16.2	225.2	256.3	-431.4	-20.1	-65.1	245.0	-3.1	309.6	607.7	-167.0	-50.0
Madagascar	-0.2	22.4	58.4	69.8	92.8	8.3	..	1.3	-0.1	1.0	0.0	0.0
Malawi	0.5	23.3	46.4	-32.5	-20.1	0.0	..	..	3.0	3.2	3.9	3.4
Maldives	1.2	5.6	12.3	13.0	11.7	12.3	..	..	..	..	..	..
Mali	2.9	5.7	51.3	82.6	122.4	102.2	..	0.2	49.9	4.0	17.3	18.7
Mauritania	7.0	6.7	0.9	9.2	-6.5	12.0	..	0.3	..	..	..	..
Mozambique	0.3	9.2	381.7	139.2	255.4	405.9	..	-0.2	0.3	-0.2	0.1	0.1
Myanmar	..	161.2	304.2	208.0	192.0	128.7	..	..	..	..	..	..
Nepal	0.7	5.9	4.4	-0.5	20.9	9.7	..	..	..	..	..	..
Niger	-9.4	40.8	0.3	8.5	22.8	7.9	1.9	0.0	0.2	-0.6	-3.6	0.0
Rwanda	14.6	7.7	1.7	8.1	3.8	2.6	0.0	0.0	0.9	0.8	0.6	0.8
Samoa	0.4	6.6	2.0	-1.5	1.2	1.3	..	..	..	0.9	..	..
Sao Tome and Principe	..	..	0.8	2.2	5.5	1.8	..	..	..	..	..	..
Senegal	-18.9	56.9	136.3	63.1	31.9	93.3	3.1	-9.5	5.8	0.7	-7.0	39.1
Sierra Leone	-31.0	32.4	6.2	4.9	2.9	4.7	0.0	0.1	0.0	0.0	0.0	0.0
Solomon Islands	0.7	10.4	-18.6	1.4	-12.0	-6.6	..	-0.4	..	0.2	..	..
Somalia	-0.7	5.6	-0.8	0.3	0.0	-0.2	..	..	..	..	..	..
Sudan	-3.0	-31.1	370.8	392.2	574.0	681.0	..	..	..	..	..	..
Togo	16.3	22.7	69.7	42.0	63.4	74.7	0.3	4.6	40.9	0.5	-7.2	0.0
Tuvalu	..	..	0.0	0.1	0.0	0.1	..	..	..	..	..	..
Uganda	-4.0	-5.9	222.1	254.4	229.2	274.8	-34.0	-11.7	-8.0	-27.6	-5.2	-13.6
United Rep. of Tanzania	14.5	0.0	516.7	463.4	327.2	240.4	..	..	-0.3	1.0	0.1	0.3
Vanuatu	4.6	13.1	13.4	20.3	18.0	15.0	..	..	..	..	..	..
Yemen	3.2	-130.9	-327.6	6.4	135.5	64.3	0.5	..	..	..	..	..
Zambia	51.5	202.8	162.8	121.7	71.7	197.0	..	..	..	..	..	..
All LDCs	445.2	514.7	5 974.0	3 427.3	5 628.5	5 231.8	217.6	-5.9	395.3	768.3	-61.1	75.3
Developing countries	14 908.8	36 958.5	229 295.2	246 056.6	209 431.2	162 145.1	4 262.9	16 682.9	72 785.6	99 051.7	47 382.0	43 094.5

Source: UNCTAD, FDI/TNC database.

29. EXTERNAL DEBT (AT YEAR END) AND DEBT SERVICE, BY SOURCE OF LENDING
($ millions)

	External debt (at year end)						% of total		Debt service						% of total	
	1985	1990	1999	2000	2001	2002	1985	2002	1985	1990	1999	2000	2001	2002	1985	2002
I. Long-term	**59 048**	**106 263**	**123 861**	**118 623**	**114 046**	**123 394**	**80.2**	**85.1**	**2 203**	**3 061**	**4 091**	**4 334**	**3 794**	**4 052**	**100.0**	**100.0**
Public and publicly guaranteed	58 563	105 411	121 394	116 206	111 717	121 146	79.5	83.6	2 146	2 981	4 044	4 266	3 717	3 984	97.4	98.3
Official creditors	50 749	90 632	111 894	106 787	102 326	111 232	68.9	76.7	1 511	2 228	2 916	2 699	2 443	2 913	68.6	71.9
A. Concessional	38 325	69 415	94 966	91 001	88 580	97 460	52.1	67.2	682	1 243	2 342	2 132	2 077	2 287	31.0	56.4
Of which:																
Bilateral	25 449	39 504	40 761	37 233	34 195	35 415	34.6	24.4	456	756	1 282	1 092	1 126	986	20.7	24.3
Multilateral	12 877	29 911	54 205	53 768	54 384	62 045	17.5	42.8	226	487	1 061	1 040	951	1 301	10.3	32.1
B. Non-concessional	12 424	21 217	16 928	15 786	13 745	13 772	16.9	9.5	828	985	574	568	366	626	37.6	15.5
Private creditors	7 813	14 780	9 500	9 419	9 391	9 913	10.6	6.8	635	753	1 128	1 567	1 274	1 071	28.8	26.4
Bonds	7	10	7	7	7	6	0.0	0.0	1.4	0.6	0	0	0	2	0.1	0.1
Commercial banks	2 913	3 633	5 087	5 438	5 453	5 656	4.0	3.9	283	196	903	1 276	1 084	947	12.8	23.4
Other private	4 893	11 137	4 405	3 974	3 931	4 252	6.6	2.9	351	556	225	291	191	122	16.0	3.0
Private nonguaranteed	486	852	2 467	2 418	2 329	2 249	0.7	1.6	57	81	47	68	77	68	2.6	1.7
II. Short-term	**9 401**	**13 073**	**18 214**	**17 819**	**17 677**	**15 543**	**12.8**	**10.7**	-	-	-	-	-	-	-	-
III. Use of IMF credit	**5 181**	**5 397**	**6 311**	**5 839**	**5 559**	**6 030**	**7.0**	**4.2**	-	-	-	-	-	-	-	-
Total	**73 630**	**124 733**	**148 386**	**142 281**	**137 282**	**144 967**	**100.0**	**100.0**	-	-	-	-	-	-	-	-

Source: UNCTAD secretariat calculations, based on World Bank, *Global Development Finance 2003,* online data; and the World Bank, *World Development Indicators 2003,* online data.

30. TOTAL EXTERNAL DEBT AND DEBT SERVICE PAYMENTS OF INDIVIDUAL LDCs

($ millions)

Country	External debt[a] (at year end)						Debt service[b]					
	1985	*1990*	*1999*	*2000*	*2001*	*2002*	*1985*	*1990*	*1999*	*2000*	*2001*	*2002*
Afghanistan	..	..	..	..	..	..	..	..	..	..	..	..
Angola	0	8 594	10 301	9 410	9 297	10 134	0	283	1 384	1 680	1 448	844
Bangladesh	6 656	12 439	16 570	15 682	15 236	17 037	195	495	605	684	594	624
Benin	854	1 292	1 687	1 602	1 672	1 843	41	33	56	55	37	50
Bhutan	9	84	184	203	265	377	0	5	7	7	6	6
Burkina Faso	513	834	1 579	1 409	1 492	1 580	25	28	56	38	28	42
Burundi	455	907	1 131	1 103	1 070	1 204	21	40	20	14	17	19
Cambodia	7	1 845	2 517	2 634	2 703	2 907	0	29	27	19	6	7
Cape Verde	95	134	327	327	361	414	5	6	20	16	13	21
Central African Rep.	344	699	909	858	822	1066	12	17	12	12	13	0
Chad	217	524	1 141	1 115	1 104	1 281	12	7	27	24	21	24
Comoros	134	187	228	232	243	270	2	1	3	2	2	4
Dem. Rep. of the Congo	6 183	10 259	12 048	11 692	11 519	8 726	300	137	0	0	0	412
Djibouti	144	205	275	262	263	335	4	11	8	11	8	9
Equatorial Guinea	132	241	271	248	239	260	2	1	2	2	2	2
Eritrea	0	0	253	311	414	528	0	0	3	3	6	9
Ethiopia	5 206	8 630	5 544	5 483	5 697	6 523	111	201	144	123	169	96
Gambia	245	369	465	483	487	573	1	30	17	19	13	19
Guinea	1 465	2 476	3 522	3 388	3 254	3 401	61	149	110	132	89	122
Guinea-Bissau	318	692	934	804	668	699	5	6	8	19	23	13
Haiti	749	911	1 182	1 169	1 252	1 248	21	14	34	33	21	15
Kiribati	..	..	..	..	..	..	..	..	..	..	..	..
Lao People's Dem. Rep.	619	1 768	2 527	2 502	2 495	2 665	5	8	29	32	34	35
Lesotho	175	396	682	671	594	637	18	23	49	57	65	63
Liberia	1 243	1 849	2 077	2 032	2 164	2 324	19	2	0	0	0	0
Madagascar	2 530	3 704	4 755	4 701	4 160	4 518	94	155	140	102	62	67
Malawi	1 021	1 558	2 751	2 716	2 604	2 912	76	103	44	46	34	27
Maldives	83	78	219	206	235	270	9	7	17	19	20	21
Mali	1 456	2 468	3 190	2 974	2 911	2 803	34	43	85	67	62	69
Mauritania	1 454	2 113	2 534	2 489	2 296	2 309	76	118	88	67	65	56
Mozambique	2 871	4 650	6 965	7 038	4 449	4 609	57	64	80	76	78	62
Myanmar	3 098	4 695	6 004	5 928	5 670	5 871	185	57	88	75	76	379
Nepal	590	1 640	2 970	2 822	2 693	2 953	13	54	99	93	84	93
Niger	1 195	1 726	1 668	1 686	1 589	1 797	95	71	24	22	27	25
Rwanda	366	712	1 292	1 271	1 283	1 435	14	15	20	21	15	19
Samoa	76	92	192	197	204	234	5	4	5	6	5	5
Sao Tome and Principe	63	150	320	315	313	333	3	2	4	3	4	6
Senegal	2 566	3 736	3 766	3 428	3 482	3 918	103	226	187	180	176	190
Sierra Leone	711	1 197	1 298	1 229	1 295	1 448	15	17	12	19	17	21
Solomon Islands	66	121	165	155	163	180	3	10	11	9	7	6
Somalia	1 639	2 370	2 606	2 562	2 563	2 688	5	7	0	0	0	0
Sudan	8 955	14 762	16 132	15 741	15 414	16 389	89	23	12	7	3	1
Togo	935	1 281	1 521	1 432	1 406	1 581	90	60	31	15	17	1
Tuvalu	..	..	..	..	..	..	..	..	..	..	..	..
Uganda	1 231	2 583	3 492	3 503	3 743	4 100	56	84	89	48	30	57
United Rep. of Tanzania	9 110	6 459	8 066	7 394	6 679	7 244	140	137	180	176	143	133
Vanuatu	16	40	65	69	66	84	1	2	2	2	2	2
Yemen	3 339	6 352	6 194	5 075	5 087	5 290	95	108	122	127	181	139
Zambia	4 499	6 916	5 868	5 731	5 671	5 969	88	173	135	177	75	240
Total LDCs	73 630	124 733	148 386	142 281	137 282	144 967	2 203	3 061	4 091	4 334	3 794	4 052

Source: UNCTAD secretariat calculations, based on information from the World Bank, *Global Development Finance 2003*.

a Figures for total debt cover both long-term and short-term debt as well as the use of IMF credit.

b Figures on debt service cover long-term debt only.

31. DEBT AND DEBT SERVICE RATIOS
(Percentage)

Country	Debt/GDP						Debt service/exports[a]					
	1985	*1990*	*1999*	*2000*	*2001*	*2002*	*1985*	*1990*	*1999*	*2000*	*2001*	*2002*
Afghanistan	..	..	..	..	..	..	..	..	..	..	..	..
Angola	..	84	169	106	98	90	..	8	27	21	22	10
Bangladesh	31	41	36	33	32	36	19	26	9	9	7	7
Benin	82	70	71	71	71	68	13	8	10	11	8	11
Bhutan	5	29	41	42	50	64	..	5	5	5	4	5
Burkina Faso	32	27	56	54	54	51	10	7	..	15	12	18
Burundi	40	80	158	163	155	168	20	43	46	38	48	59
Cambodia	..	166	73	73	73	73	..	..	2	2	1	1
Cape Verde	..	40	56	62	66	67	10	5	9	7	6	8
Central African Republic	40	47	86	90	85	102	14	13	..	..	..	..
Chad	21	30	74	80	66	64	17	4	..	..	..	..
Comoros	117	71	102	113	110	106	9	2	..	..	..	..
Dem. Rep. of the Congo	86	110	255	241	222	153	..	..	..	..	..	..
Djibouti	42	49	51	47	46	56	..	..	..	..	..	..
Equatorial Guinea	166	183	31	18	14	12	..	12	..	..	..	..
Eritrea	..	..	35	49	58	82	..	..	4	3	4	5
Ethiopia	78	100	85	84	88	108	25	39	16	13	18	10
Gambia	109	116	108	115	125	161	10	22	..	..	..	..
Guinea	..	88	102	109	107	106	..	20	16	20	12	14
Guinea-Bissau	221	284	416	373	334	344	52	31	..	..	..	..
Haiti	37	32	29	30	33	36	11	11	..	..	..	..
Kiribati	..	..	..	..	..	..	..	..	..	..	..	..
Lao People's Dem. Rep.	26	204	174	146	142	159	9	9	8	8	9	..
Lesotho	60	64	75	78	77	89	7	4	10	11	12	12
Liberia	133	481	470	375	405	414	9	..	4	1	1	1
Madagascar	89	120	128	121	92	103	42	45	17	10	5	10
Malawi	90	83	152	159	154	153	40	29	13	12	8	8
Maldives	65	36	37	33	38	43	11	5	4	4	5	4
Mali	111	102	124	123	111	83	17	12	13	12	8	7
Mauritania	213	207	265	265	239	238	25	30	..	..	..	..
Mozambique	64	189	175	191	130	128	34	26	16	11	8	6
Myanmar	..	..	..	..	..	..	58	18	5	4	3	..
Nepal	23	45	59	51	49	53	7	16	8	7	7	9
Niger	83	70	83	94	82	83	34	17	..	..	..	..
Rwanda	21	28	67	70	75	83	10	14	26	24	10	15
Samoa	89	82	83	83	84	90	15	6	5	7	..	..
Sao Tome and Principe	120	261	681	678	666	664	29	34	26	25	23	32
Senegal	99	66	79	78	76	78	21	20	14	14	12	13
Sierra Leone	83	184	194	193	173	185	15	10	..	..	..	..
Solomon Islands	41	57	52	53	55	75	5	12	5	7	..	..
Somalia	187	258	..	..	..	..	16	..	..	..	..	..
Sudan	72	112	152	140	127	121	14	9	4	2	2	1
Togo	123	79	107	117	112	114	27	12	9	6	6	3
Tuvalu	..	..	..	..	..	..	..	..	..	..	..	..
Uganda	35	60	59	60	66	71	42	81	14	8	4	7
United Rep. of Tanzania	..	152	93	81	72	77	40	33	18	15	10	9
Vanuatu	13	27	28	30	30	36	1	2	1	1	1	..
Yemen	..	132	83	54	53	53	..	6	5	4	5	3
Zambia	200	210	187	177	156	162	16	15	16	20	11	27
All LDCs	63	81	90	83	78	79	21	16	12	..	..	..

Source: UNCTAD secretariat calculations, based on World Bank, *Global Development Finance 2003*, online data.

Note: Figures for total debt cover both long-term and short-term debt as well as use of IMF credit.

a Exports of goods and services, income and workers' remittances received (workers' remittances include compensation of employees).

32. LDCs' DEBT RESCHEDULINGS WITH OFFICIAL CREDITORS, 1990–2003

Country	Number of debt[a]	Date of meeting	Cut-off date	Consolidation period (months)	Terms	Arrears	Rescheduling of previously rescheduled debt	Goodwill clause	Amounts rescheduled/ consolidated ($ million)
Benin	II	December 1991	31 March 1989	15	London terms	Yes	Yes	Yes	152
	III	June 1993	31 March 1989	29	London terms	Yes	No	Yes	25
	IV[b]	October 1996	31 March 1989	-	Naples terms (67%)[c]	Yes	Yes	No	209
	V	October 2000	31 March 1989	12	Cologne terms	No	Yes	No	5
	VI	April 2003	31 March 1989	-	Cologne terms	Yes	Yes	Yes	65
Burkina Faso	I	March 1991	1 January 1991	15	Toronto terms	Yes	No	Yes	63
	II	May 1993	1 January 1991	32	London terms	Yes	No	No	36
	III[b]	June 1996	1 January 1991	-	Naples terms (67%)[c]	No	Yes	No	64
	IV	October 2000	1 January 1991	12	Cologne terms	No	Yes	Yes	1
Cambodia	III[b]	January 1995[d]	31 December 1985	30	Naples terms (67%)	No	Yes	No	249
Central African Republic	V	June 1990	1 January 1983	12	Toronto terms	No	Yes	No	4
	VI	April 1994	1 January 1983	12	London terms	Yes	Yes	Yes	33
	VII[b]	September 1998	1 January 1983	34	Naples terms (67%)	Yes	Yes	Yes	26
Chad	II[b]	February 1995[d]	30 June 1989	-	Naples terms (67%)	..	..	..	24
	III[b]	June 1996[d]	30 June 1989	32	Cologne terms	..	Yes	No	..
	IV	June 2001	30 June 1989	23	Naples terms	No	Yes	Yes	15
Dem. Rep. of the Congo	X	September 2002	30 June 1983	36	Naples terms	Yes	Yes	Yes	8 980
Djibouti	I	May 2000	31 March 1998	32	Non-concessional	Yes	-	Yes	16
Equatorial Guinea	III	April 1992[d]	..	..	London terms	Yes	Yes	Yes	32
	IV	Febuary 1994[d]	..	..	London terms	Yes	-	Yes	51
Ethiopia	I	December 1992	31 December 1989	37	London terms	Yes	-	Yes	441
	II[b]	January 1997	31 December 1989	34	Naples terms (67%)	Yes	No	Yes	184
	III[b]	April 2001	31 December 1989	37	Naple terms (67%)	Yes	Yes	Yes	430
	IV	April 2002	31 December 1989	29	Cologne terms	No	Yes	Yes	7
Gambia	II	January 2003	1 July 1986	36	Cologne terms	No	Yes	Yes	..
Guinea	III	November 1992	1 January 1986	..	London terms	Yes	Yes	Yes	203
	IV[b]	January 1995	1 January 1986	12	Naples terms (50%)	Yes	Yes	Yes	156
	V[b]	February 1997	1 January 1986	36	Naples terms (50%)	Yes	Yes	Yes	..
	VI	May 2001	1 January 1986	40	Cologne terms	Yes	Yes	Yes	151
Guinea-Bissau	III[b]	February 1995	31 December 1986	36	Naples terms (67%)	Yes	Yes	Yes	195
	IV	January 2001	31 December 1986	37	Cologne terms	No	Yes	Yes	141
Haiti	I[b]	May 1995	1 October 1993	13	Naples terms (67%)	Yes	No	Yes	117
Madagascar	VII	July 1990	1 July 1983	13	Toronto terms	No	Yes	Yes	139
	VIII[b]	March 1997	1 July 1983	35	Naples terms (67%)	Yes	Yes	Yes	1 247
	IX	March 2001	1 July 1983	39	Cologne terms	Yes	Yes	Yes	254
Malawi	IV	January 2001	1 January 1997	37	Cologne terms	Yes	Yes	Yes	..
Mali	III	October 1992	1 January 1988	35	London terms	No	No	No	20
	IV[b]	May 1996	1 January 1988	-	Naples terms (67%)[c]	Yes	Yes	Yes	33
	V	October 2000	1 January 1988	36	Cologne terms	No	Yes	No	4
	VI	March 2003	1 January 1988	-	Cologne terms	No	Yes	No	155
Mauritania	V	January 1993	31 December 1984	24	London terms	Yes	Yes	Yes	218
	VI[b]	June 1995	31 December 1984	36	Naples terms (67%)	No	Yes	No	66
	VII	March 2000	31 December 1984	36	Cologne terms	Yes	Yes	Yes	80
	VIII	July 2002	31 December 1984	-	Cologne terms	Yes	Yes	No	384
Mozambique	IV	June 1990	1 February 1984	30	Toronto terms	Yes	Yes	Yes	719
	V[b]	March 1993	1 February 1984	24	London terms	Yes	Yes	Yes	440
	VI[e]	November 1996	1 February 1984	32	Naples terms (67%)	Yes	Yes	Yes	664
	VII	May 1998	1 February 1984	32	Lyon terms / 90% NPV reduction	yes	yes	yes	1 860
	VIII	November 2001	1 February 1984	-	Cologne terms	No	Yes	No	2 800

Table 32 (cont.)

Country	Number of debt[a]	Date of meeting	Cut-off date	Consolidation period (months)	Terms	Arrears	Rescheduling of previously rescheduled debt	Goodwill clause	Estimated amounts rescheduled ($ million)
Niger	VII	September 1990	1 July 1983	28	Toronto terms	Yes	Yes	Yes	116
	VIII	March 1994	1 July 1983	15	London terms	Yes	Yes	Yes	160
	IX[b]	December 1996	1 July 1983	31	Naples terms (67%)	Yes	Yes	Yes	128
	X	January 2001	1 July 1983	37	Cologne terms	Yes	-	Yes	115
Rwanda	I[b]	July 1998	31 December 1994	35	Naples terms (67%)	Yes	-	Yes	64
	II	March 2002	31 December 1994	17	Cologne terms	No	Yes	Yes	..
Sao Tome & Principe	I[b]	May 2000	1 April 1999	37	Naples terms (67%)	Yes	-	Yes	26
Senegal	VIII	February 1990	1 January 1983	12	Toronto terms	Yes	Yes	Yes	107
	IX	June 1991	1 January 1983	12	Toronto terms	Yes	Yes	No	114
	X	March 1994	1 January 1983	15	London terms	Yes	Yes	Yes	237
	XI[b]	April 1995	1 January 1983	29	Naples terms (67%)	Yes	Yes	Yes	169
	XII[b]	June 1998	..	-	Naples terms (67%)[c]	Yes	Yes	No	428
	XIII	October 2000	1 January 1983	18	Cologne terms	No	Yes	Yes	21
Sierra Leone	V	November 1992	1 July 1983	16	London terms	Yes	Yes	Yes	164
	VI	July 1994	1 July 1983	17	London terms	Yes	Yes	Yes	42
	VII[b]	March 1996	1 July 1983	24	Naples terms (67%)	No	Yes	Yes	39
	VIII[b]	October 2000	1 July 1983	36	Naples terms (67%)	Yes	Yes	No	180
	IX	July 2002	1 July 1983	31	Cologne terms	No	Yes	Yes	3
Togo	VIII	July 1990	1 January 1983	24	Toronto terms	No	Yes	No	88
	IX	June 1992	1 January 1983	24	London terms	No	Yes	Yes	52
	X[b]	February 1995	1 January 1983	33	Naples terms (67%)	No	Yes	Yes	239
Uganda	V	June 1992	1 July 1981	18	London terms	Yes	Yes	Yes	39
	VI[b]	February 1995[d]	1 July 1981	-	Naples terms (67%)[d]	No	Yes	No	110
	VII	April 1998	1 July 1981	-	Lyon terms (80%)[f]	No	Yes	No	110
	VIII	September 2000	1 July 1981	-	Cologne terms[c]	-	-	-	145
United Rep. of Tanzania	III	March 1990	30 June 1986	12	Toronto terms	Yes	Yes	Yes	200
	IV	January 1992	30 June 1986	30	London terms	Yes	Yes	Yes	691
	V[b]	January 1997	30 June 1986	36	Naples terms (67%)	Yes	Yes	Yes	608
	VI	April 2000	30 June 1986	36	Cologne terms	Yes	Yes	Yes	390
	VII	January 2002	30 June 1986	-	Cologne terms			No	1 245
Yemen	I[b]	September 1996	1 January 1993	10	Naples terms (67%)	Yes	..	Yes	113
	II[b]	November 1997	1 January 1993	36	Naples terms (67%)	Yes	No	No	..
	III[b]	June 2001	1 January 1993	-	Naples terms (67%)[c]	-	No	No	420
Zambia	IV	July 1990	1 January 1983	18	Toronto terms	Yes	Yes	Yes	963
	V	July 1992	1 January 1983	33	London terms	Yes	Yes	Yes	917
	VI[b]	February 1996	1 January 1983	36	Naples terms (67%)	Yes	Yes	Yes	566
	VII[b]	April 1999	1 January 1983	36	Naples terms (67%)	Yes	Yes	Yes	1 063
	VIII	September 2002	1 January 1983	27	Cologne terms	No	Yes	Yes	..

Source: Paris Club Agreed Minutes.

a   Roman numerals indicate the number of debt reschedulings for the country since 1976.
b   Naples terms; number in brackets indicates the percentage of reduction applied.
c   Stock reduction.
d   Dates of informal meeting of creditors on the terms to be applied in the bilateral agreements, as creditors did not call for a full Paris Club meeting.
e   Amendment to the November 1996 agreement.
f   Additional stock reduction ("Topping up") on previously rescheduled debt.

33. ARRANGEMENTS IN SUPPORT OF STRUCTURAL ADJUSTMENT IN LDCs (AS OF DECEMBER 2002)

Millions of SDRs (except where otherwise indicated)

Column groups: **IMF arrangements** (Stand-by/Extended Facility; SAF/ESAF/PRGF) — **World Bank loans and credits** (Structural adjustment; Sector and other adjustment)

Country	Stand-by/Extended Facility — Period	Amount	SAF/ESAF/PRGF — Period	Amount	Structural adj. — Date of approval	IDA	African Facility[1]	Co-financing[2]	Sector & other adj. — Date of approval	IDA	African Facility[1]	Co-financing[2]	Purpose
Bangladesh	July 1979 - July 1980	85.0	Feb. 1987 - Feb. 1990	201.3					June 1987	147.8			Industrial policy reform
	Dec. 1980 - Dec. 1983[3]	800.0[4]	Aug. 1990 - Sep. 1993	345[5]					Apr. 1989	137.0		Germany (DM 26m)	Energy sector
	March 1983 - Aug. 1983	68.4							Oct. 1989	1.8[6]			Financial sector
	Dec. 1985 - June 1987	180.0							June 1990	132.7		USAID (18.2)	
									Nov. 1990	2.5[6]			
									Nov. 1991	2.2[6]			
									May 1992	109.3			Public resource management
									Oct. 1992	72.2			Industry
									Dec. 1992	2.5[6]			"
									Feb. 1994	175.0			Jute sector
									May 1994	2.4[6]			"
									Dec. 1994	2.3[6]			"
									Dec. 1995	2.3[7]			"
									Nov. 1996	2.0			"
Benin			June 1989 - June 1992	21.9[7]	May 1989	33.5			Nov. 1993	3.7		DANIDA (4); ACBF (2)	Public expenditure
			Jan. 1993 - May 1996	51.9[5]	June 1991	41.3							Economic management
			Aug. 1996 - Jan. 2000	27.27[7]	March 2001	7.8							
			July 2000 - July 2003	27.07[7]	May 1995	25.8							
Burkina Faso			Mar. 1991 - Mar. 1993	22.1[8]	June 1991	60.0		EC (30); AfDB (20); France (17); Canada (13); Germany (12)	Feb. 1985	13.8		France/CCCE (3.2); Netherlands (2.1); Germany/GTZ (2); France/FAC (1.7);	Fertilizers
			Mar. 1993 - May 1996	53.0[5]	Nov. 1998	11.0			Feb. 1992	49.6		EDF (99); AfDB (60.6); CIDA (29.8); Germany (28.6); West African Development Fund (10.2); BADEA (8.5); CCCE & FAC (7.8); IsDB (5.5); BOAD (3.1); UNDP (0.6);	Transport sector
			June 1996 - Sep. 1999	39.8[5]	Dec. 1999	18.0			June 1992	20.6		France (21);	Agriculture
			Sep. 1999 - Sep. 2002	39.1[7]					Mar. 1994	18.0		EC (20); AfDB (13)	Economic recovery
													Economic management
													Structual adjustment credit III
Burundi	Aug. 1986 - March 1988	21.0	Aug. 1986 - Aug. 1989	29.9	May 1986	13.2	14.3	Japan (11);					
			Nov. 1991 - Nov. 1994	42.7[5]	June 1988	64.9		Switzerland (7.7); Japan (18.1); Germany (6); Saudi Arabia (2.9)					
					June 1992	22.0							
Cambodia			Oct. 1999 - Feb. 2003	84.0[5]					July 1988	11.9	(16.2)		Economic rehabilitation
			Oct. 1999 - Oct. 2002	58.5[7]1					Sep. 1995	25.4			Structural adjustment credit
Cape Verde	Feb. 1998 - May 1999	2.1	Apr. 2002 - Apr. 2005	9.0[7]1					Dec. 1997	21.8			Economic reforms support
	Feb. 1998 - Mar. 2000	2.1											Structural adjustment credit
Central African Republic	Feb. 1980 - Feb. 1981	4.0	June 1987 - May 1990	21.3	Dec. 2001	11.6			July 1987	11.5		Saudi Arabia (2); Japan (6)	Cotton sector
	April 1981 - Dec. 1981	10.4[9]	July 1998 - Jan. 2002	49.4[7]1	Sep. 1986	12.3	14	ADF (25)	Dec. 1999	14.4			Fiscal consolidation credit
	April 1983 - April 1984	18.0[10]			June 1988	28.9							
	July 1984 - July 1985	15.0			June 1990	34.5							
	Sep. 1985 - March 1987	15.0[11]											
	June 1987 - May 1988	8.0											
	Mar. 1994 - Mar. 1995	16.5											

Table 33 (cont.)

Country	IMF arrangements — Stand-by/Extended Facility Period	Amount	SAF/ESAF/PRGF Period	Amount	World Bank — Structural adjustment Date of approval	IDA	African Facility[1]	Co-financing[2]	Sector and other adjustment Date of approval	IDA	African Facility[1]	Co-financing[2]	Purpose
Chad	Mar. 1994 - Mar. 1995	16.5	Oct. 1987 - Oct. 1990	21.4					July 1988	11.9	(16.2)	USAID (23); Germany (22.7): CCCE (13.1); ADF (11.3); BDEAC (10.6); EDF (4.8); OPEC Fund for Int.Dev(4.5); FAC (3.3); UNDP (0.5)	Public finance and cotton sector
									April 1989	45.4			Transport sector
			Sep. 1995 - Apr. 1999	49.6[5]	Feb. 1996	20.2			Mar. 1994	14.4			Economic recovery
					June 1997	18.0							Public sector structural adjustment credit III
			Jan. 2000 - Jan. 2003	48.0[71]	May 1999	22.2							Structural adjustment credit
Comoros			June 1991 - June 1994	3.2	Dec. 2001	31.4			June 1991	6.0	ADF (17); UNDP (1)		Macroeconomic reform and capacity-building
Dem. Republic of the Congo	Aug. 1979 - Feb. 1981	118.0[59]	May 1987 - May 1990	203.7[63]	June 2002	360.4			June 1986	17.6	(60)		Industrial sector
	June 1981 - June 1984[27]	912.0[60]	June 1996 - June 1999	69.5[5]					June 1987	42.2	(94.3)	Japan (15.7)	Agricultural and rural dev.
	Dec. 1983 - March 1985	228.0[61]											Economic recovery
	April 1985 - April 1986	162.0											
	May 1986 - Mar. 1988	214.2[62]											
	May 1987 - May 1988	100.0[64]											
	June 1989 - June 1990	116.4[65]											
Djibouti	April 1996 - June 1997	4.6	Oct. 1999 - Oct. 2002	19.1[71]									
Equatorial Guinea	July 1980 - June 1981	5.5	Dec. 1988 - Dec. 1992	12.9[13]									
	June 1985 - June 1986	9.2[12]	Feb. 1993 - Feb. 1996	12.9[5]									
Ethiopia	May 1981 - June 1982	67.5	Oct. 1992 - Nov. 1995	49.4	June 1993	176.5							
			Oct. 1996 - Oct. 1999	88.5[5]	Jan. 1994	0.3[6]							
			Mar. 2001 - Mar. 2004	100.0[71]	Dec. 1994	0.1[6]							
					June 2001	150.0							Economic rehab. support
					June 2002	96.2							Structural adjustment credit
Gambia	Nov. 1979 - Nov. 1980	1.6	Sep.1986 - Nov. 1988	12.0[16]	Aug. 1986	4.3	9.9	United Kingdom (4.5); ADF (9)					
	Feb. 1982 - Feb. 1983	16.9	Nov. 1988 - Nov. 1991	20.5[5]	June 1989	17.9		ADF (6); Netherlands (2.5)					
	April 1984 - July 1985[15]	12.8[14]	June 1998 - Dec. 2001	20.6[71]									
	Sep.1986 - Oct. 1987	5.1											
Guinea	Dec. 1982 - Nov. 1983	25.0[17]	July 1987 - July 1990	40.5[19]	Feb. 1986	22.9	15.6	France (26.7); Germany (9.4); Japan (27.8); Switzerland (4.8); ADF (12); Japan (11.2)	June 1990	15.4			Education sector
	Feb. 1986 - March 1987	33.0[18]	Nov. 1991 - Dec. 1996	57.9[5]	June 1988	47.0							Public sector
	July 1987 - Aug. 1988	11.6	Jan. 1997 - Jan. 2001	70.8[71]	Dec. 1992	0.1[6]							Structural adjustment credit IV
			May 2001 - May 2004	64.0[71]	Dec. 1997	50.8							
					July 2001	39.3							

Table 33 (cont.)

	IMF arrangements				World Bank loans and credits								
	Stand-by/Extended Facility		SAF/ESAF/PRGF		Structural adjustment				Sector and other adjustment				
						Amount				Amount			
Country	Period	Amount	Period	Amount	Date of approval	IDA	African Facility[1]	Co-financing[2]	Date of approval	IDA	African Facility[1]	Co-financing[2]	Purpose
Guinea-Bissau									Dec.1984	10.1		Switzerland (SwF 4.5 m)	Economic recovery programme[27]
			Oct. 1987 - Oct. 1990	5.3[20]	May 1987	8.0	4	Switzerland (5.2); Saudi Arabia (3.2); ADF (11.3); IFAD (5.3) Netherlands (4.8); USAID (4.5); ADF (12.0)[22]					
			Jan. 1995 - July 1998	11.0[5]	May 1989	18.0							
			Dec. 2000 - Dec. 2003	14.0[71]	May 2000	18.0							
Haiti	Oct. 1978 - Oct. 1981[24]	32.2[23]							Mar.1987	32.8			Economic recovery
	Aug. 1982 - Sep. 1983	34.5											
	Nov. 1983 - Sep. 1985	60.0[25]	Dec.1986 - Dec. 1989	30.9[26]									
	Sep.1989 - Dec.1990	21.0[18]							Dec. 1994	26.8			"
	Mar. 1995 - Mar.1996	20.0	Oct.1996 - Oct. 1999	91.1[5]									
Lao People's Dem. Republic	Aug. 1980 - Aug. 1981	14.0	Sep.1989 - Sep. 1992	20.5	June 1989	30.8							Financial management adj.
			June 1993 - May 1997	35.2[5]	Oct. 1991	30.0							
			Apr. 2001 - Apr. 2004	32.0[71]	Feb. 1996	26.9							
					June 2002	13.5							
Lesotho	Sep.1994 - Sep. 1995	8.4	June 1988 - June 1991	10.6[5]									
	July 1995 - July 1996	7.2	May 1991 - Aug. 1994	18.1[5]									
			Sep.1996 - Sep. 1997	7.2[5]									
			Mar. 2001 - Mar. 2004	25.0[71]									
Madagascar	June 1980 - June 1982	64.5[27]							May 1986	19	(33)	KfW (4); Japan (3); ADF (40); Switzerland (8)	Agricultural sector
	April 1981 - June 1982	76.7[28]							June 1988	90.5			Public sector
	July 1982 - July 1983	51.0[14]	Aug. 1987 - May 1989	46.5[29]									
	April 1984 - Mar. 1985	33.0							Mar.1989	1.1[6]			Public sector
	April 1985 - April 1986	29.5							Oct.1989	0.9[6]			"
	Sep.1986 - Feb. 1988	30.0	May 1989 - May 1992	76.9[5]					Nov.1990	1.2[6]			"
	Sep.1988 - July 1989	13.3[30]							Nov.1991	1[6]			Multisector rehabilitation
									Dec.1992	1[6]			Structural adjustment credit II
			Nov. 1996 - Nov. 1999	81.4[5]	Mar. 1997	48.6							Structural adjustment credit
					Mar. 1997	0.4							
					May 1999	73.5							
			Nov. 1996 - Nov. 2000	24.0[71]	July 2000	15.2							
			Mar. 2001 - Feb. 2004	79.0[71]	Dec. 2000	23.5							
Malawi	Oct. 1979 - Dec. 1981[31]	26.3			June 1981	36.7[33]			April 1983	4.6		IFAD (10.3)	Smallholder fertilizers
	May 1980 - March 1982	49.9[32]			Dec. 1983	51.9	37.3	Germany/KfW (6.4); OECF (22.6); USAID (15)					
	Aug. 1982 - Aug. 1983	22.0[4]	July 1988 - Mar. 1994	67.0[5]	Dec. 1985	28.0			June 1988	50.6		OECF (30); USAID (25); ADF (19.5); EEC (16)	Industrial and trade policy adjustment
	Sep.1983 - Sep. 1986	81.0[34]											
	March 1988 - May 1989	13.0	Oct.1995 - Dec. 1999	51.0[5]	Jan. 1987		8.4	Japan (17.7); United Kingdom (7.5); Germany (5)	Mar. 1989	4.0[6]		USAID (25); United Kingdom (16.5); Netherlands (5); Germany, EEC and Japan (6.1)	Agriculture
									Oct. 1989	3.8[6]			"
									April 1990	52.6			"

Table 33 (cont.)

Country	IMF arrangements — Stand-by/Extended Facility Period	Amount	SAF/ESAF/PRGF Period	Amount	World Bank loans and credits — Structural adjustment Date of approval	IDA	African Facility[1]	Co-financing[2]	Sector and other adjustment Date of approval	IDA	African Facility[1]	Co-financing[2]	Purpose
Malawi (cont.)	Nov. 1994 - June 1995	15.0							Nov. 1991	4.0[6]		AfDB (13.4)	Agriculture
									June 1992	85.4			Entrepreneurship dev. & drought recovery
									Dec. 1992	4.3[6]			"
									Nov. 1994	27.6[6]			"
									Dec. 1994	3.2[6]			
					Nov. 1996	2.4[70]			April 1996	70.3			Fiscal restructuring & deregulation programme
					Dec. 1998	67.2			April 1996	2.9[70]			"
			Dec. 2000 - Dec. 2003	45.0[71]	Dec. 2000	0.4							Fiscal restructuring and and de-regulation program. II
					Dec. 2000	43.1							Program Credit III-IDA reflow
													Program Credit III
Mali	May 1982 - May 1993	30.4							June 1988	29.4		Japan (38.7); Saudi Arabia (5.9); ADF (45)	Public enterprise sector
	Dec. 1983 - May 1985	40.5											
	Nov. 1985 - March 1987	22.9[6]	Aug. 1988 - Aug. 1991	35.6[14]	Dec. 1990	50.3		EC (20); AfDB (18)	June 1990	40.7		FAC/CCCE (50.8); SDC (6.9); Netherlands (5.2); Germany (2.9)	Agricultural sector/investment
	Aug. 1988 - June 1990	12.7											
			Aug. 1992 - April 1996	79.2[5]					Mar. 1994	18.2			Economic recovery
			April 1996 - Aug. 1999	62.0[5]	Dec. 2000	19.6			Jan. 1995	34.3			Education; Economic management
			Aug. 1999 - Aug. 2003	52.0	Dec. 2001	55.0			June 1996	41.6			Economic management; Structural adjustment credit
Mauritania	July 1980 - March 1982[38]	29.7[37]											
	June 1981 - March 1982	25.8											
	April 1985 - April 1986	12.0	Sep. 1986 - May 1989	23.7[39]	June 1987	11.7	21.4	Saudi Arabia (4.8); Germany (2.8)	Feb. 1990	19.4		CCCE (8); Germany (2); WFP (1)	Agricultural sector/investment
	April 1986 - April 1987	12.0	May 1989 - Jan. 1995	50.9[5]					June 1990	30.7		Japan (50); SFD (19.8); KFAED (13.7); AFESD (10.3); Abu Dhabi Fund (6.1); Spain (5); Germany (4)	Public enterprises
	May 1987 - May 1988	10.0											
			Jan. 1995 - July 1998	42.8[5]					Nov. 1990	2.9[6]			Public enterprises
									Nov. 1991	1.9[6]			"
					Feb. 1999	0.1			Dec. 1992	1.6[6]			"
			July 1999 - July 2002	42.5[71]	Nov. 1999	0.1			Jan. 1994	1.0[6]			Public resource management
					May 2000	22.4			Nov. 1996	0.4[6]			"
					Dec. 2000	14.1			Dec. 1997	0.3			Fiscal reform; Fiscal reform
Mozambique			June 1987 - June 1990	42.7					May 1985	45.5	(18.6)	Switzerland (11.2)	Economic rehabilitation programme I
									Aug. 1987	54.5		United Kingdom (17.5); Switzerland (12.8); Germany (10.9); Sweden (9.4); Finland (8.9)	Economic rehabilitation programme II
			June 1990 - Dec. 1995	130.1[5]					May 1989	68.2			Economic rehabilitation programme III
			June 1996 - Aug. 1999	75.6[5]	Feb. 1997	69.1			June 1992	132		Switzerland (6)	Economic recovery
			June 1999 - June 2002	87.2[71]					June 1994	141.7			Economic recovery II
Myanmar	June 1981 - June 1982	27.0											

Table 33 (cont.)

	IMF arrangements				World Bank loans and credits								
	Stand-by/Extended Facility		SAF/ESAF/PRGF		Structural adjustment				Sector and other adjustment				
						Amount				Amount			
Country	Period	Amount	Period	Amount	Date of approval	IDA	African Facility[1]	Co-financing[2]	Date of approval	IDA	African Facility[1]	Co-financing[2]	Purpose
Nepal	Dec. 1985 - April 1987	18.7	Oct. 1987 - Oct. 1990	26.1	Mar. 1987	40.9		KfW (5)					
			Oct. 1992 - Oct. 1995	33.6[5]	June 1989	46.2							
Niger	Oct. 1983 - Dec. 1984	18.0	Nov. 1986 - Nov. 1988	23.6[40]	Feb. 1986	18.3	36.6		June 1987	46.0	15.4		Public enterprises
	Dec. 1984 - Dec. 1985	16.0							Mar. 1994	18.2			Economic recovery
	Dec. 1985 - Dec. 1986	13.5	Dec. 1988 - Dec. 1991	47.2[5]	Mar. 1997	21.6							Public sector
	Dec. 1986 - Dec. 1987	10.1	June 1996 - Aug. 1999	58.0[5]	Oct. 1998	48.0							Public finance reform
	Mar. 1994 - Mar. 1995	18.6	Dec. 2000 - Dec. 2003	59.0[71]	Sep. 2000	26.5							Finance recov. adjustment
					Dec. 2000	9.4							"
					Nov. 2001	54.5							Public expenditure
Rwanda	Oct. 1979 - Oct. 1980	5.0[42]	April 1991 - April 1994	30.7[26]	June 1991	67.5		Switzerland (SwF 10m); Belgium (BF 400m)	Jan. 1995	34.3			Emergency recovery
			June 1998 - Jan. 2002	71.4[71]	Mar. 1999	53.0							Economic recovery
					Dec. 2000	11.8							
Samoa	Aug. 1979 - Aug. 1980	0.7[42]											
	June 1983 - June 1984	3.4											
	July 1984 - July 1985	3.4											
Sao Tome and Principe			June 1989 - June 1992	2.8[43]	June 1987	3.1	2.3	ADF (8.5); ADF(12); IMF (2.6)					Management credit
			Apr. 2000 - Apr. 2003	6.7[71]	June 1990	7.5							
					Nov. 2000	5.8							
Senegal	Oct. 1987 - Oct. 1988	21.3	Nov. 1986	43.0	Feb. 1986	18.3	31.4	7.1	Dec. 1989	35.3			Str.adjustment credit III (supplement)
			Nov. 1986 - Nov. 1988	59.6	May 1987	35.0							Structural credit IV
				144.7	Mar. 1989	4.2							
					Feb. 1990	62.4			Dec. 1995	1.8			Agricultural sector
	Mar. 1994 - Aug. 1994	48.0	Nov. 1988 - June 1992	131.0	May 1990	3.5			Nov. 1996	1.3			Energy sector
			Aug. 1994 - Jan. 1998		Nov. 1990	5.1							Trade reform
			Apr. 1998 - Apr. 2002	107.0[71]	Apr. 1992	3.5							
					May 1998	74.0							
					Sep. 2000	75.7							
Sierra Leone	Nov. 1979 - Nov. 1980	17.0	Nov. 1986 - Nov. 1989	40.5[47]	Oct. 1993	35.9			June 1984	20.3		IFAD (5.4)	Agriculture
	March 1981 - Feb. 1984[45]	186.0[44]			Jan. 1994	0.1[6]			April 1992	31.4			Reconstruction
	Feb. 1984 - Feb. 1985	50.2[46]			Dec. 1994	0.2[6]			April 1992	0.2[6]			Imports
	Nov. 1986 - Nov. 1987	23.2	Mar. 1994 - Mar. 1995	27.0	Dec. 1995	0.2[70]			Dec. 1992	0.2[6]			"
			Mar. 1994 - May 1998	101.9[5]	Nov. 1996	0.1							
					Feb. 2000	21.9							Economic recovery
			Sep. 2001 - Sep. 2004	131.0[71]	Dec. 2000	7.9							Economic recovery
					Dec. 2001	39.4							Economic recovery II
Solomon Islands					June 1999	8.9							Structural adjustment credit
Somalia	Feb. 1980 - Feb. 1981	11.5[48]											
	July 1981 - July 1982	43.1											
	July 1982 - Jan. 1984	60.0											
	Feb. 1985 - Sep.1986	22.1											
	June 1987 - Feb.1989	33.2											
Sudan	May 1979 - May 1982[49]	427.0	June 1987 - June 1990	30.9[26]					June 1989	54.2		ADF (25); BITS (0.5)	Agriculture

	IMF arrangements				World Bank loans and credits								
	Stand-by/Extended Facility		SAF/ESAF/PRGF		Structural adjustment				Sector and other adjustment				
						Amount				Amount			
Country	Period	Amount	Period	Amount	Date of approval	IDA	African Facility[1]	Co-financing[2]	Date of approval	IDA	African Facility[1]	Co-financing[2]	Purpose
Togo	June 1979 - Dec. 1980	15.0[52]			May 1983	36.9							
	Feb. 1981 - Feb. 1983	47.5[53]			May 1985	28.1							
	March 1983 - April 1984	21.4			Aug. 1985		9.7						
	May 1984 - May 1985	19.0			Mar. 1988	33.0		ADF (17.3); Japan (20.8)					
	May 1985 - May 1986	15.4	Mar. 1988 - May 1989	26.9[54]	Mar. 1989	0.1[6]							
	June 1986 - April 1988	23.0	May 1989 - May 1993	46.1[5]	Oct. 1989	0.2[6]							
	Mar. 1988 - April 1989	13.0			Dec. 1990	39.6							
			Sep.1994 - June 1998	65.2[5]					Feb. 1991	10.2			Population and health
									April 1996	32.2			Economic recovery and adjustment
Uganda	Jan. 1980 - Dec. 1980	12.5							Feb. 1983	63.5		Italy/DCD (10)	Agricultural rehabilitation
	June 1981 - June 1982	112.5							May 1984	47.2			Reconstruction
	Aug. 1982 - Aug. 1983	112.5	June 1987 - April 1989	69.7[56]					Sep.1987	50.9	18.8	United Kingdom/ODA (16)	Economic recovery
	Sep.1983 - Sep. 1984	95.0[55]	April 1989 - June 1994	219.2[57]					Mar. 1989	1.3[6]			"
									April 1989	19[6]			"
									Oct. 1989	1.2[6]			"
					Dec. 1991	91.9			Feb. 1990	98.1	(12.8)		
			Sep. 1994 - Nov. 1997	120.5[5]	Dec. 1992	1.0[6]			Nov. 1990	1.5[6]			
					May 1994	57.8			Dec. 1990	69.5			Agriculture
					Dec. 1994	0.4[6]			Nov. 1991	1.2[6]			Economic recovery
			Nov. 1997 - Mar. 2001	100.4[71]	June 1997	90.4			May 1993	72.8			Finance
					Dec. 2000	19.6			Jan. 1994	0.8[6]			
									Mar. 1998	59.2			Education sector Structural adjustment III
United Republic of Tanzania	Sep.1980 - June 1982	179.6[58]	Oct. 1987 - Oct. 1990	74.9					Nov. 1986	41.3	38.2	Germany (17.3); Switzerland (9.2); United Kingdom (7.3); Saudi Arabia (4); ADF (24); United Kingdom (15); Switzerland (14); Netherlands (10)	Multisector rehabilitation
	Aug. 1986 - Feb. 1988	64.2							Jan. 1988	22.5	(26.0)		Multisector rehabilitation
									Dec. 1988	97.6			Industrial rehabilitation and trade adjustment
			July 1991 - July 1994	181.9[5]					Mar. 1989	9.7[6]			Industrial rehabilitation
									Oct. 1989	8.3[6]			Industry and trade adjustment
									Mar. 1990	150.4		Netherlands (40)	Agriculture
			Nov. 1996 - Feb. 2000	181.6[5]	June 1997	93.2[70]			Dec. 1990	11.5[6]		United Kingdom (20)	Agriculture
			Apr. 2000 - Apr. 2003	135.0[71]	Dec. 1997	1.8			Nov. 1991	8.6[6]			"
					Dec. 1999	0.8			Nov. 1991	150.2		United Kingdom (16.8); Switzerland (6.6)	Finance
					June 2000	141.8			Dec. 1992	8.2[6]			Finance
					Jan. 2001	0.6							
					Feb. 2002	0.5			Oct. 2001	119.1			Stru.adjustment credit Stru.adjustment I-IDA Education development Stru.adjustment I-IDA
Yemen	Mar. 1996 - June 1997	132.4			Nov. 1997	58.9			April 1996	53.7			Economic recovery Financial sector Public sec. mgmt. adj. credit
	Oct. 1997 - Oct. 2001	105.9	Oct. 1997 - Oct. 2001	264.8[71]	Mar. 1999	35.8							

Table 33 (cont.)

Country	IMF arrangements				World Bank loans and credits										
	Stand-by/Extended Facility		SAF/ESAF/PRGF		Structural adjustment				Sector and other adjustment					Purpose
						Amount					Amount			
	Period	Amount	Period	Amount	Date of approval	IDA	African Facility[1]	Co-financing[2]	Date of approval	IDA	African Facility[1]	Co-financing[2]		
Zambia	April 1978 - April 1980	250.0			Aug. 1996	62.4			Jan. 1985	24.7	(10)	AfDB (23.4); CIDA (6.8); USAID (5); Switzerland (4.8); Germany (18.8)		Agricultural rehabilitation
	May 1981 - May 1984[24]	800.0[66]			Nov. 1996	5.4			Mar. 1991	149.6				Economic recovery
	April 1983 - April 1984	211.5[67]			Jan. 1999	122.7			Mar. 1991	19.4[6]				"
	July 1984 - April 1986	225[68]			Jan. 1999	2.0			May 1992	7.6[6]				Privatization and industry
	Feb. 1986 - Feb. 1988	229.8[69]			June 2000	105.5			June 1992	146.0				"
					Nov. 2000	1.6			Dec. 1992	15.1[6]				"
					Dec. 2000	23.5			June 1993	72.1				"
					May 2002	5.3			Aug. 1993	7.0[6]				Economic and social adjustment
			Dec. 1995-Dec. 1998	701.7[5]					Jan. 1994	12.1[6]				"
									Mar. 1994	108.9				Economic recovery and investment promotion
									Dec. 1994	9.7[6]				"
			Mar. 1999 - Mar. 2003	254.5[71]					June 1995	19.1				Economic and social adjustment
									July 1995	90.0				Public sector reform and export promotion
									Dec. 1995	8[70]				Fiscal sustainability credit.
									June 1996	16.0				Fiscal sustainability
														Fiscal sustainability
														Fiscal sustainability 5th dim.

Sources: IMF, *Annual Report, 2002* and various issues; *IMF Survey* (various issues); World Bank, *Annual Report, 2002* and various issues; *World Bank News* (various issues).

m = million

1. Special Facility for Sub-Saharan Africa; amounts in parentheses are expressed in millions of dollars.
2. Including special joint financing and bilateral support; amounts are in millions of dollars unless stated otherwise.
3. Extended Facility arrangement, cancelled as of June 1982.
4. SDR 580 m not purchased.
5. ESAF.
6. Supplemental credit.
7. SDR 6.3 m not purchased.
8. SDR 15.8 m not purchased.
9. SDR 2.4 m not purchased.
10. SDR 13.5 m not purchased.
11. SDR 7.5 m not purchased.
12. SDR 3.8 m not purchased.
13. SDR 3.7 m not purchased.
14. SDR 10.2 m not purchased.
15. Cancelled as of April 1985.
16. SDR 3.4 m not purchased.
17. SDR 13.5 m not purchased.
18. SDR 6.0 m not purchased.
19. SDR 11.6 m not purchased.
20. SDR 1.5 m not purchased.
21. Supported by IMF; (SDR 1.88 m purchased in first credit tranche).
22. Additional financing.
23. SDR 21.4 m not purchased.
24. Extended Facility arrangement.
25. SDR 39 m not purchased.
26. SDR 22.1 m not purchased.
27. Cancelled as of April 1981; SDR 54.5 m not purchased.
28. Augmented in June 1981 with SDR 32.3 m; SDR 70 m not purchased at expiration of arrangement.
29. SDR 33.2 m not purchased.
30. Cancelled as of May 1989; SDR 10.5 m not purchased.
31. Cancelled as of May 1980; SDR 20.9 m not purchased.
32. SDR 9.9 m not purchased.
33. IBRD loan.
34. Original amount decreased from SDR 100 m; SDR 24 m not purchased.
35. Extended Facility arrangement; cancelled as of August 1986.
36. SDR 6.6 m not purchased.
37. SDR 20.8 m not purchased.
38. Cancelled as of May 1981.
39. SDR 6.8 m not purchased.
40. SDR 6.7 m not purchased.
41. ESAF; original amount decreased from SDR 50.6 m.
42. Not purchased.
43. SDR 2 m not purchased.
44. Including an increase of SDR 22.3 m in June 1981. SDR 152 m not purchased.
45. Extended Facility arrangement; cancelled as of April 1982.
46. SDR 31.2 m not purchased.
47. SDR 29 m not purchased.
48. SDR 5.5 m not purchased.
49. Extended Facility arrangement; cancelled as of February 1982; SDR 176 m not purchased.
50. SDR 128 m not purchased.
51. SDR 70 m not purchased.
52. SDR 1.75 m not purchased.
53. SDR 40.3 m not purchased.
54. SDR 19.2 m not purchased.
55. SDR 30.0 m not purchased.
56. SDR 19.9 m not purchased.
57. ESAF; original amount increased from SDR 179.3 m.
58. SDR 154.6 m not purchased.
59. SDR 9.0 m not purchased.
60. Cancelled as of June 1982; SDR 737 m not purchased.
61. SDR 30 m not purchased.
62. Cancelled as of April 1987; SDR 166.6 m not purchased.
63. SDR 58.2 m not purchased.
64. SDR 75.5 m not purchased.
65. SDR 41.4 m not purchased.
66. Cancelled as of July 1982; SDR 500 m not purchased.
67. SDR 67.5 m not purchased.
68. Cancelled as of February 1986; SDR 145 m not purchased.
69. Cancelled as of May 1987; SDR 194.8 m not purchased.
70. From IDA reflows.
71. PRGF, Poverty Reduction and Growth Facility Trust, formerly Enhanced Structural Adjustment Facility.

TABLE 34. TIMOR-LESTE: BASIC INDICATORS

	1995/1996	1999	2001
Economic indicators			
GDP (current millions US$)	..	270.1	389.3
GDP per capita (US$)	..	377.6	547.5
Manufacturing, value added (% of GDP)	..	2.8	2.5
Real GDP by sector (as % of total GDP)			
Of which: Agriculture	24.0	25.5	21.3
Manufacturing industry	3.0	3.4	3.5
Construction	23.2	15.7	23.2
Electricity gas and water	0.7	0.9	0.7
Land area, population and labour force			
Land area (sq. km)	14870	14870	14870
Land use, arable land (% land area)	4.7	4.7	4.7
Total populations (thousands)	839.7	779.6	794.3
Annual average population growth rate (%) [a]	2.4	-1.5	0.9
Urban population as % of total	9.5	9.8	..
Labour force participation rate			
of population 15 years and over (%)			
Total	71.8	67.3	56.0
Male	89.6	87.6	76.2
Female	53.4	52.4	35.6
Urban	64.2	63.4	52.1
Rural	72.6	70.4	61.2
Indicators on demography			
Life expecancy at birth, total (years)	53.9	56.0	57.4
Male	52.3	54.2	55.6
Female	55.5	57.7	59.2
Infant mortality rate, total (per 1000 live births)	99.7	86.0	80.1
Male	108.9	94.7	88.4
Female	91.1	77.8	72.3
Under-5 mortality rate, total (per 1000 live births)	183.5	158.8	143.5
Male	196.3	171.6	155.5
Female	171.5	146.7	132.1
Underweight children under-5 (%)	50.6	44.5	..
Indicators on education			
Adult literacy rate, total (as% of age 15 and over)	40.4	40.6	43.0
Urban	79.6	80.4	81.5
Rural	36.2	36.6	37.2
Male	48.6	46.9	43.1
Female	32.0	33.9	42.8
Net school enrolment ratio,total (%)	41.6	45.6	41.2
Male	43.2	48.5	44.9
Female	37.6	42.7	38.4
Gross school enrolment ratio,total (%)	55.5	59.1	56.1
Male	58.1	62.1	58.4
Female	54.2	57.9	55.1
Primary education (net)	71.0	74.2	76.2
Lower secondary education (gross)	60.5	63.9	62.4
Upper secondary education (gross)	36.1	37.2	27.0
Tertiary education (gross)	3.3	5.1	3.9
Housing and living conditions indicators			
Households with own drinking water facilities (as % of total)	14.0	20.4	18.6
Urban	46.5	40.6	35.9
Rural	11.3	18.0	7.6
Housing and living conditions indicators			
Households with own sanitation facilities (as % of total)	45.8	53.6	..
Urban	69.2	77.7	..
Rural	43.8	50.7	..
Indicators on women			
Total fertility rate (per woman)	5.1	3.8	..
Maternal mortality rate (per 100,000 live births)	..	420	..
Birth attended by skilled health staff, total (%)	23.4	30.0	..
Urban	53.9	62.2	..
Rural	20.0	25.4	..

Source: East Timor Human Development Report 2002; World Bank, World Development Indicators 2004 and United Nations Population Division.
  a Annual average growth rate of population are 1990-1995, 1995-1999 and 1999-2001 respectively.

كيفية الحصول على منشورات الامم المتحدة

يمكن الحصول على منشورات الامم المتحدة من المكتبات ودور التوزيع في جميع انحاء العالم · استعلم عنها من المكتبة التي تتعامل معها
أو اكتب الى : الامم المتحدة ،قسم البيع في نيويورك او في جنيف ·

如何购取联合国出版物

联合国出版物在全世界各地的书店和经售处均有发售。请向书店询问或写信到纽约或日内瓦的联合国销售组。

HOW TO OBTAIN UNITED NATIONS PUBLICATIONS

United Nations publications may be obtained from bookstores and distributors throughout the world. Consult your bookstore or write to: United Nations, Sales Section, New York or Geneva.

COMMENT SE PROCURER LES PUBLICATIONS DES NATIONS UNIES

Les publications des Nations Unies sont en vente dans les librairies et les agences dépositaires du monde entier. Informez-vous auprès de votre libraire ou adressez-vous à : Nations Unies, Section des ventes, New York ou Genève.

КАК ПОЛУЧИТЬ ИЗДАНИЯ ОРГАНИЗАЦИИ ОБЪЕДИНЕННЫХ НАЦИИ

Издания Организации Объединенных Наций можно купить в книжных магазинах и агентствах во всех районах мира. Наводите справки об изданиях в вашем книжном магазине или пишите по адресу: Организация Объединенных Наций, Секция по продаже изданий, Нью-Йорк или Женева.

CÓMO CONSEGUIR PUBLICACIONES DE LAS NACIONES UNIDAS

Las publicaciones de las Naciones Unidas están en venta en librerías y casas distribuidoras en todas partes del mundo. Consulte a su librero o diríjase a: Naciones Unidas, Sección de Ventas, Nueva York o Ginebra.

Printed at United Nations, Geneva
GE.04-51027–May 2004–7,785

UNCTAD/LDC/2004

United Nations publication
Sales No. E.04.II.D.27

ISBN 92-1-112581-2
ISSN 0257-7550